Literature and the Bible

This book traces the emergence and development of Literature and the Bible as a field of scholarship, presenting key critical essays alongside more recent criticism that explores new directions. The Western literary tradition has a long and complex relationship with the Jewish and Christian scriptures. Authors draw on the Bible in numerous ways and for different reasons, and there is also the myriad of subconscious ways through which the biblical text enters literary culture. Biblical stories, characters, motifs and references permeate the whole of the literary tradition.

In the last thirty years there has been a growth of critical interest in this relationship. In *Literature and the Bible: A Reader* the editors bring together a selection of the key critical and theoretical materials from this time, providing a comprehensive resource for students and scholars.

Each section contains:

- An introduction from the editors, contextualising the material within and alerting readers to some of the historic debates that feed into the extracts chosen
- A set of previously published extracts of substantial length, offering greater contextualisation and allowing the Reader to be used flexibly
- Lists of further reading, providing readers with a wide variety of other sources and perspectives.

Designed to be used alongside the Bible and selected literary texts, this book is essential reading for anyone studying Literature and the Bible in undergraduate English, Religion and Theology degrees.

Jo Carruthers is Lecturer in the Department of English and Creative Writing at Lancaster University, UK.

Mark Knight is Associate Professor in the Department of English at the University of Toronto, Canada.

Andrew Tate is Senior Lecturer in the Department of English and Creative Writing at Lancaster University, UK.

Routledge Literature Readers

Also available:

The Routledge Queer Studies Reader
World Literature: A Reader
Literature and Globalization
The History of Reading
The Routledge Reader in Caribbean Literature

For further information on this series visit: http://www.routledge.com/books/
series/RLR

Literature and the Bible

A Reader

Edited by

Jo Carruthers, Mark Knight
and Andrew Tate

LONDON AND NEW YORK

First published 2014
by Routledge
2 Park Square, Milton Park, Abingdon, Oxon OX14 4RN

Simultaneously published in the USA and Canada
by Routledge
711 Third Avenue, New York, NY 10017

Routledge is an imprint of the Taylor & Francis Group, an informa business

British Library Cataloguing in Publication Data
A catalogue record for this book is available from the British Library

Library of Congress Cataloging in Publication Data
Literature and the Bible : a reader / edited by Jo Carruthers, Mark
Knight and Andrew Tate.
    pages cm.—(Routledge literature readers)
    Includes bibliographical references and index.
    1. Bible and literature.   2. Bible as literature.   3. Bible—In
literature.   I. Carruthers, Jo editor of compilation.   II. Knight,
Mark, 1972 editor of compilation.   III. Tate, Andrew, 1971 editor
of compilation.
    PN56.B5L58 2013
    809'.93522—dc23

                                                           2013010835

ISBN: 978-0-415-69852-8 (hbk)
ISBN: 978-0-415-69853-5 (pbk)

Typeset in Perpetua
by RefineCatch Limited, Bungay, Suffolk

Contents

Acknowledgements

We are grateful for the helpfulness, enthusiasm and professionalism provided by the staff at Routledge, and also for the expertise of Emma Davis, who helped us navigate the complex world of permissions with good grace. The anonymous readers who read our initial proposal had plenty of insightful things to say, and we have benefitted from their input. Peter Hawkins also offered wise counsel during the early stages of this project, and has remained supportive since. Our colleagues in the English departments at Lancaster and Toronto have been encouraging throughout the project, and we feel privileged to work alongside them. Finally, we would like to thank our family members – Richard, Molly, Elliot, Jo, Samuel and Michaela – for their love and patience. We suspect that they will be more pleased than anyone to finally see this volume in print, even if that doesn't translate into a rush to read it.

Permissions

1a. Erich Auerbach, 'Odysseus' Scar' from *Mimesis: The Representation of Reality in Western Literature*. AUERBACH, ERIC, MIMESIS. © 1953 Princeton University Press, 1981, renewed Princeton University Press, 2003, paperback edition. Reprinted by permission of Princeton University Press.

1b. Yale University Press for permission to reprint Hans W. Frei, 'Introduction' in *The Eclipse of Biblical Narrative* (New Haven: Yale University Press, 1974), 1–16

1c. Indiana University Press for permission to reprint Meir Sternberg, 'Literary Text, Literary Approach: Getting the Questions Straight' in *The Poetics of Biblical Narrative: Ideological Literature and the Drama of Reading* (© 1987 Indiana University Press), pp. 1–34. Reprinted with permission of Indiana University Press.

1d.   Reprinted with permission from 'The Critic as Kabbalist: Harold Bloom and the Heretic Hermeneutic' in *The Slayers of Moses: The Emergence of Rabbinic Interpretation in Modern Literary Theory* by Susan A. Handelman, the State University of New York Press © 1982, State University of New York. All rights reserved.

2a.   Stephen Prickett,'Ways of Reading the Bible: The Problem of the Transparent Text' in *Words and The Word: Language, Poetics and Biblical Interpretation,* pp. 4–12. © Cambridge University Press, 1986, reproduced with permission of Cambridge University Press and the author.

2b.   Eerdmans for permission to reprint David Lyle Jeffrey, 'Scripture upon Scripture' in *People of the Book: Christian Identity and Literary Culture*, copyright © 1996. Wm. B. Eerdmans Publishing Company, Grand Rapids, MI. Reprinted by permission of the publisher; all rights reserved.

2c.   Bloomsbury Academic Publishing for permission to reprint Emmanuel Levinas, 'On the Jewish Reading of Scriptures' in *Beyond the Verse* (London: Athlone Press, 1994) pp. 101–14.

2d.   Yale University Press for permission to reprint Geoffrey H. Hartman, 'The Struggle for the Text' in Geoffrey Hartman and Sanford Budick, eds., *Midrash and Literature* (New Haven: Yale University Press, 1986).

3a.   The Johns Hopkins University Press for permission to reprint Iser, Wolfgang, 'Asymmetry Between Text and Reader' from *The Act of Reading: A Theory of Aesthetic Response*, pp. 163–70. © 1978 The Johns Hopkins University Press. Reprinted with permission of The Johns Hopkins University Press.

3b.   Bloomsbury Academic Publishing for permission to reprint Hans-Georg Gadamer, 'Language and Hermeneutics' in *Truth and Method*, 2nd rev ed., Trans. Joel Weinsheimer and Donald G. Marshall (London: Continuum, 2004), pp. 385–93, 395–98. © Hans-Georg Gadamer, *Truth and Method*, and Continuum, an imprint of Bloomsbury Publishing Plc.

3c.   Yvonne Sherwood, 'Taking Stock: Survivals, Hauntings, Jonah and (Stanley) Fish, and the Christian Colonisation of The Book of Jonah' in *A Biblical Text and its Afterlives: The Survival of Jonah in Western Culture* (Cambridge: Cambridge University Press, 2000), pp. 48–61. © Yvonne Sherwood 2000 published by Cambridge University Press, reproduced with permission. With kind permission of the author.

4a.   'The Task of the Translator' from *Illuminations* by Walter Benjamin. Ed Hannah Arendt (London: Pimlico, 1999), copyright © 1955 by Suhrkamp Verlag, Frankfurt a.M., English translation by Harry Zorn, copyright © 1968 and renewed by Houghton Mifflin Harcourt Publishing Company, reprinted by permission of Houghton Mifflin Harcourt Publishing Company. All rights reserved.
From *Illuminations* by Walter Benjamin
Published by Jonathan Cape
Reprinted by permission of The Random House Group Limited and Suhrkamp Verlag.

4b.   Carcanet for permission to reprint an extract from Gerald Hammond, 'Introduction' in *The Making of the English Bible* (Carcanet Press, 1988).

4c. WWW Norton & Company for permission to reprint Robert Alter, 'To the Reader', in *Genesis: Translation and Commentary* (New York and London: Norton, 1996).

4d. Material reprinted from Jacques Derrida, 'Des Tours de Babel', translated by Joseph F. Graham, in *Difference in Translation*, edited by Joseph F. Graham. Copyright © 1985 by Cornell University Press. Used by permission of the publisher, Cornell University Press.

4e. Narr Francke Attempto Verlag, Tübingen for kind permission to reprint Valentine Cunningham, 'Thou Art Translated: Bible Translating, Heretic Reading and Cultural Transformation', in *REAL: Yearbook of Research in English and American Literature* Vol. 20 Narr Francke Attempto Verlag, Tübingen (2004): 113–26.

5a. From 'Discourse in the Novel' in *The Dialogic Imagination: Four Essays* by M. M. Bakhtin, edited by Michael Holquist, translated by Caryl Emerson and Michael Holquist, © 1981. By permission of the University of Texas Press.

5b. Indiana University Press for permission to reprint Daniel Boyarin, 'Toward a New Theory of Midrash', from *Intertextuality and the Reading of Midrash* (© 1994 Indiana University Press), pp. 1–21. Reprinted with permission of Indiana University Press.

5c. Alicia Ostriker for permission to reprint 'Psalm and Anti-Psalm: A Personal View', *The American Poetry Review*, Jul/Aug 2002; 31, 4; pp. 11–15. Originally published in Alicia Ostriker, *For the Love of God: The Bible as an Open Book,* New Brunswick, NJ: Rutgers University Press, 2007. Reprinted by permission of the author.

5d. Eisenbrauns for permission to reprint David C. Tollerton, 'Reading Job as Theological Disruption for a Post-Holocaust World', *Journal of Theological Interpretation* 3.2 (2009), 197–212.

6a. University of Toronto Press for permission to reprint 'The Double Vision of Language', in *Northrop Frye on Religion: Collected Works of Northrop Frye, Volume 4*, edited by Alvin A. Lee and Jean O'Grady (University of Toronto Press, 2000). The extract was first published in Frye's *The Double Vision* (University of Toronto Press, 1991) and copyright is held by University of Toronto Press. Reprinted by permission of the publisher.

6b. University of Chicago Press and Comité éditorial Fonds Ricoeur for permission to reprint Paul Ricoeur, 'The Nuptial Metaphor' in André LaCocque and Paul Ricoeur, eds., *Thinking Biblically: Exegetical and Hermeneutical Studies* (Chicago: University of Chicago Press, 1998), pp. 265–74.

6c. Indiana University Press for permission to reprint Harold Fisch, Chapter 6 'Song of Solomon: The Allegorical Imperative' (pp. 95–103) in *Poetry with a Purpose: Biblical Poetics and Interpretation* (© 1988, Indiana University Press). Reprinted with permission of Indiana University Press.

7a. Reprinted by permission of the publisher from 'Hoti's Business: Why are Narratives Obscure?' in *The Genesis Of Secrecy* by Frank Kermode, pp. 23–31, 33–34, 39–41, 45–47, 149–52, Cambridge, Mass.: Harvard University Press, Copyright © 1979 by the President and Fellows of Harvard College.

7b. Pearson Education Ltd. for permission to reprint J. Hillis Miller, 'Parable and Performative in the Gospels and in Modern Literature' in *Tropes, Parables and Performatives* (Hertfordshire: Harvester Wheatsheaf, © 1991). Reprinted with permission.

7c. Augsburg Fortress Press for permission to reprint Sallie McFague TeSelle, Chapter 4 'The Parable: The Primary Form' in *Speaking in Parables: A Study in Metaphor and Theology* (Minneapolis: Fortress Press, 1975).

7d. Bloomsbury Publishing Plc. for permission to reprint Susan E. Colón, Chapter 5, '"The Agent of a Superior": Stewardship Parables in *Our Mutual Friend*' in *Victorian Parables* (Continuum, 2011). © Susan Colon, *Victorian Parables* and Continuum, an imprint of Bloomsbury Publishing Plc.

8a. Harvard University Press for permission to reprint Stanley Fish, 'Preface to the Second Edition' in *Surprised by Sin: The Reader in* Paradise Lost, 2nd ed (Cambridge, MA: Harvard University Press, 1997). Stanley Fish, Surprised by Sin, published 1961, reproduced with permission of Palgrave Macmillan.

8b. Cambridge University Press and Regina M. Schwartz for permission to reprint '"And the sea was no more": Chaos vs. Creation' in *Remembering and Repeating: Biblical Creation in Paradise Lost.* © Cambridge University Press, 1988, reproduced with permission.

8c. Ashgate for permission to reprint 'Adam, Eve and the Serpent: Mark Twain' in *The Genesis of Fiction: Modern Novelists as Biblical Interpreters.* Copyright © Terry R. Wright, 2007 Ashgate.

8d. University of Chicago Press and Mieke Bal for permission to reprint Mieke Bal, 'First Memories and Second Thoughts' in *Loving Yusuf: Conceptual Travels from Present to Past* (Chicago: University of Chicago Press, 2008), pp. 1–22.

9a. John Wiley & Sons Inc. for permission to reprint Graham Ward, 'Suffering and Incarnation', in Ward, ed., *The Blackwell Companion to Postmodern Theology* (Oxford: Blackwell, 2001).

9b. University of California Press for permission to reprint Eve Kosofsky Sedgwick, *Epistemology of the Closet* (Berkeley: University of California Press, 1990), pp. 75–82

9c. John Wiley Inc. for permission to reprint Paul S. Fiddes, Chapter 1 'Facing the End' in *The Promised End: Eschatology in Theology and Literature* (Oxford: Blackwell, 2000). Reproduced with permission of Blackwell Publishing Ltd.

9d. Oxford University Press Journals and the author for permission to reprint Jonathan Roberts, 'Wordsworth's Apocalypse' in *Literature and Theology* 20.4 (2006): 361–78. www.oxfordjournals.org

Disclaimer

General Introduction

JO CARRUTHERS, MARK KNIGHT AND ANDREW TATE

'I hear you, sir, in the dark, but I'm a gropin – a gropin – let me catch hold of
   your hand.'
   'Jo, can you say what I say?'
   'I'll say anythink as you say, sir, for I knows it's good.'
'OUR FATHER.'
'Our Father! – yes, that wery good, sir.'
'WHICH ART IN HEAVEN'
'Art in Heaven – is the light a comin, sir?'
'It is close at hand. HALLOWED BE THY NAME!'
'Hallowed by – thy—'
The light is come upon the dark benighted way. Dead!
                    (Charles Dickens, Chapter 47, *Bleak House*, 1852–53)

During a recent experience teaching this scene to undergraduates taking a course in Victorian fiction, one student asked what this religious material was doing in *Bleak House*, a novel that seems to many critics to have little concern with religion. His question is important because it highlights the strangeness of religion for the modern reader. For those unfamiliar with the biblical story, religious allusions may be more jarring than they might have been to earlier readers who were more familiar with the Bible. Early readers would have been unsurprised at finding yet another reference to Scripture in Dickens' work. But questions remain: even if we recognize that the source of the prayer Jo is led in can be traced to Matthew's Gospel and even if we acknowledge that references to Scripture were inevitable in a Victorian literary culture well versed in the biblical tradition, we still have to decide what the allusion is doing and what we might make of it.

The western literary tradition has a long and involved relationship with the Jewish and Christian Scriptures. Biblical stories, characters, motifs and references permeate the whole of literature, as David L. Jeffrey's *A Dictionary of Biblical Tradition in English Literature* (1992) illuminates so clearly. While the presence of the sacred text can be seen most easily in works such as John Milton's *Paradise Lost*, which take direct inspiration from Scripture and explicitly deal with its narrative, literary material with less apparent interest in theological matters can also be heavily indebted to the biblical text. Authors draw on the Bible in all sorts of ways and for different reasons. There are a myriad of subconscious ways through which the biblical text enters literary culture, and different readers across the ages put their own constructions on what textual uses of the Bible might mean. The implications of considering the influence of the Bible on any piece of literature are multiple and complex, even dizzying, and the purpose of this Reader is to provide clarity on the subject of the Bible and literature through reprinting some of the best recent critical work in this area.[1] Although the relationship between the Bible and literature is a mystery to be explored rather than a puzzle to be solved, to borrow Gabriel Marcel's distinction, our hope is that this Reader will help readers (such as the student described at the start of this introduction) think in a more informed way about the relationship between the Bible and literature.[2]

There is a long history of critical writing about the Bible and literature. In putting this Reader together, we have deliberately opted for material from the last three decades rather than trying to provide an older critical lineage. Yet we would do well to remember that the issues discussed by recent critics were also of interest to previous generations, albeit in different ways. One can learn a great deal by going back to the writings on the Bible by mid-twentieth century literary critics such as C. S. Lewis and Helen Gardner, or, earlier still, literary writers who also wrote about the Bible, such as John Milton, Christina Rossetti, and Matthew Arnold. Important though this long history of the Bible's relationship to the literary tradition is, our purpose here is to focus on more recent criticism, which, even in the electronic age, is not always easily located by (or accessible to) those who want to think more critically about the Bible and literature. The selectivity of this volume has been accentuated by our desire to privilege a smaller number of long extracts over a greater number of short pieces. As literary academics, we tend to insist (to ourselves and those we teach) that works are read in their entirety rather than being plundered for juicy quotations. While most of the critical texts under discussion here cannot be reprinted in their fullest form, our hope is that the lengthy extracts provided enable readers of this Reader to appreciate the many layers and perspectives within each of the works reprinted.

We have divided this Reader into nine chapters, grouped within three parts. In Part I, 'The Relationship Between Literature and The Bible', we begin by turning to the work of Erich Auerbach, Hans Frei, Meir Sternberg and Susan Handelman, in Chapter One, as a way of introducing different ways of understanding the relationship between the Bible and literature. The lack of uniformity is important, for rather than following the direction set out by an earlier generation of critics who insisted on the Bible *as* literature, we prefer to think about the relationship between the Bible and literature in more open-ended ways and keep in mind the limitations of the 'literary' as a description. For sure, the biblical texts are full of explicitly literary techniques and can be thought about in terms of their literary function. Yet some biblical texts are less amenable to 'literary' description than others – there are reasons why courses on the Bible *as* literature are more interested in the Song of Songs than I Chronicles, for instance – and it is unhelpful to cut our thought off altogether from the insights of those who insist that the Bible is God's revealed word. The sacred and the literary are not polar opposites. While they are rarely delineated in such stark terms, in practice the description of the Bible as literature has tended to dismiss consideration of Scripture's doctrinal or theological claims. Literature departments, as anyone who has recently spent time in one will know, can be a broad church and the faculty who work there are capable of modes of analysis that fall outside the narrow aesthetic view that typically accompanies talk of the Bible as literature. But there are moments when it is as revealing to think about contrasts and tensions between the Bible and literature as it is to look for points of connection and focus on common concerns. Refusing to treat the Bible solely as another form of literature allows us to appreciate the multiple ways in which different theological and literary communities have understood Scripture, and the material in our opening chapter introduces this interpretative diversity.

Having introduced different ways of thinking about the relationship between the Bible and literature in the first chapter, the book proceeds in the second chapter by investigating different ways of reading, again with a view to opening up the range of critical possibilities available to those who read the biblical text. In the third chapter we turn our attention to the reception history of the biblical text. Reception history focuses on the different ways in which a text has been received and understood over time. In doing so, it destabilizes any sense that the text can only be read in one way and, perhaps more significantly, it reminds us of the temporality of our own reading and foregrounds the bias that all of us bring to our hermeneutical activity. The importance of reception history for our reading of the Bible is made clear through the seminal material we have selected here, from Wolfgang Iser, Hans-Georg Gadamer and Yvonne Sherwood, but as the list of further reading in this section makes clear, there are numerous ways in which reception history shapes our reading of the Bible and there is good reason for the growing critical interest in this area.

Part II of this volume is on 'Literary Reading' and explores three areas that come into view as the literary tradition reads and reimagines the biblical text. Chapter Four considers issues surrounding translation and extends our thought about this beyond the narrower debates in biblical studies regarding translators' fidelity to the original texts. In Chapter Five we turn to the multi-voiced nature of biblical narrative and draw upon one of the major strands of literary theory in the twentieth century. Chapter Six examines the subject of figurative language, particularly metaphor and allegory, an area of thought that is crucial for those who want to grapple with the linguistic reality of the biblical text(s). While the topics of these three chapters do not exhaust or encapsulate all areas of literary inquiry as they pertain to the biblical text, they do provide a helpful series of insights into the rich contribution that the literary tradition makes to our reading of the biblical text.

Our final Part III, 'Theological Interpretation', highlights three representative and prevalent theological themes in the critical tradition: parables, Genesis, and the grouped concerns of salvation, transformation and the Apocalypse. Although our part headings risk perpetuating a classic divide between the literary and the theological, the essays within the second and third parts quickly move to complicate such distinctions. In the chapter on parables, to take just one example, we see a mixture of literary critics and theologians exploring the form and content of parables and recognizing that it makes no sense to look at one without the other. And in the chapter on salvation, transformation and Apocalypse, we see that it is impossible to think adequately about the theological transformations described in the Bible without being sufficiently aware of their literary elements.

This volume is designed so that extracts can be read as and when they are of interest. Neither the book as a whole nor the chapters within it have to be read sequentially: they can be read that way, of course, and we have thought about the narrative trajectory of the volume as a whole, but we have also organized material in such a way that readers can create their own narrative threads between essays. This Reader (like all other readers and anthologies) provides us with a microcosm of the sort of structure that the three of us see in the biblical text, a structure that tells one story and many stories simultaneously and a narrative that encourages counter-voices as it tells its main story. On a more immediate and practical note, we have constructed this Reader in such a way that it does not pre-empt which pieces of literature a student or teacher may be interested in studying. The critical works included here are pertinent to a multiplicity of biblical and literary works, and have much to tell us about the significance of the biblical text(s) on a western literary tradition that remains firmly in its debt.

In the remainder of this Introduction we want to showcase the interpretative richness of the subjects covered in the nine chapters of this Reader by using them to structure a series of reflections on the use of the Bible in the scene in *Bleak House* with which we began. By doing so, we hope to demonstrate that theoretical and theological reflections are enabled through our close reading of literary texts rather than being established in advance and then merely illustrated through works of literature.

I

Trying to isolate precisely how Dickens uses the biblical text to write Jo's closing moments is a fruitless act, for we are confronted with layer upon layer. Jo follows the words of Allan Woodcourt, who is presumably quoting the Lord's Prayer and recounting it as Christians would have done on a regular basis in the nineteenth century. The source of that prayer is the teaching of Jesus, as Matthew records in his Gospel (Matthew 6: 9–13). But it is unclear whether Allan or indeed his author is thinking about Matthew's Gospel specifically, and the sentimental application of the prayer to Jo's dying moment prompts us to remember that the biblical text is being taken up in a particular literary retelling that wants to do more than provide a discrete exegesis of a passage in the New Testament. Yet the specific content of these biblical verses still asserts pressure on Dickens' scene. One contextual reason to insist on the connection to Matthew's Gospel is that the Lord's Prayer is part of a set of teachings by Jesus that we refer to as the 'Sermon on the Mount'. Much of the teaching in that sermon is highly practical and concerned with the social needs of people like Jo. The society in *Bleak House* may need the omniscient narrator to remind its readers that road sweepers like Jo are forgotten too easily, but the Sermon on the Mount begins with Jesus declaring 'Blessed are the poor in spirit, for theirs is the kingdom of heaven' (Matthew 5: 3). Thus, while we may be struck by the pointlessness of Jo uttering a prayer that he does not understand or by the distance between Jo and the religion found elsewhere in the novel, it may be the case that the scene is meant deliberately to draw our attention to the self-serving way in which some religious people in the Victorian era were reading the biblical text.

Whatever the reasons for Dickens relying so heavily on the Lord's Prayer in this particular scene, we are left to think too about the way in which all retellings focus attention on the nature of their relationship with the original. On one reading, Jo's retelling lacks authenticity: he does not know what he says and it may be that his repetition of the Lord's Prayer is an empty utterance. But on another reading, we may ponder how much anyone understands when using human language to talk about God. Furthermore, given that the words of Jesus are a prayer that his followers are taught to repeat, we might conclude that the moment in *Bleak House* where we are prompted to think about what Jo and Allan mean when they repeat the Lord's Prayer is an inevitable manifestation of a phenomenon that the biblical text introduces when Jesus asks those who come after him to repeat his words.

II

Jo dies before he can get to the end of the prayer and it is worth considering where he is cut off. Given the orphan Jo's lack of a surname, we may attach importance to his inability to finish the phrase 'Hallowed be thy name' or note the reversal of hallowing implied by Jo's substitution of the word 'by' for 'be'. In his final moments, perhaps, Jo's lack of agency, in which we even see him struggle to articulate the most basic of prayers, finds recompense in a literary version of the sanctifying work of God: Jo is 'hallowed by' being moved out of the narrative margins and into one of the novel's most memorable scenes. Important though the 'Hallowed be thy name' line is, however, the lines that come after are also conspicuous by their absence. In the biblical text, the prayer proceeds: 'Your kingdom come. Your will be done on earth as it is heaven.' The failure of the novel to get to this point reminds us how far the fictional world of Chancery is from the biblical ideal of the Kingdom as a place where the will of God is manifest on earth as it is in heaven.

The cuts and alterations that *Bleak House* makes to the Lord's Prayer in this particular moment are indicative of the selectivity involved in any act of reading. In reading, words on the page are continually isolated, emphasized, de-emphasized, omitted, changed, forgotten, substituted and translated. Although it is tempting to berate such alterations as bad reading, these alterations are inevitable. For all our hermeneutical efforts, the failure to internalize a text to the extent of understanding it completely is the reason we re-read and discover something new on each occasion. The limitation of our reading is the very quality that makes us reliant on other ways of reading. We have something to learn from the ways that others read, even though we may sometimes disagree with what they conclude.

III

To understand Dickens' use of the Lord's Prayer here, one can simply look up Matthew 6: 9–13 in the King James Version (KJV) in order to think about how Dickens has appropriated this section of Jesus' teaching. But what does this tell us about how the Lord's Prayer signified to Dickens' Victorian readers? What kind of cultural currency had it accrued in the period? Despite its name, the Lord's Prayer is never possessed or contained by Christ and it has taken on many different meanings for those who have uttered it over the years.

The Victorian accent given to the 'Our Father' spoken by the altruistic Doctor Woodcourt and the dying and neglected sweeper boy, Jo, can be intimated from John Ruskin's writings on this verse in which he insists on a shared humanity and care for the whole world: 'that we have such a loving Father, whose mercy is over *all* His works'.[3] In his sermon on Matthew 6.9, given in 1848, F. D. Maurice, the theologian and social reformer, sees these two words as a call to brotherly reconciliation and social being: 'the name Father loses its significance for us individually, when we will not use it as the members of a family'.[4] In seeking to restore an appreciation of the reading community, Maurice's remarks suggest that Victorian readers were increasingly individualistic in their outlook. If this is so then perhaps we should think of Victorians who interpreted the Lord's Prayer as readers caught between a call to community and an individualistic and consequently fractured appropriation of the words that Jesus taught his disciples. And however we think about the Victorian reception of the Bible, we must remember the heterogeneity inherent within the term 'Victorians'. When Jo follows the lead of Allan Woodcourt and repeats the Lord's Prayer, his experience as an orphan presumably shapes his use of the term 'father'. Does Allan's decision to lead him in this act of prayer and acknowledge a heavenly father strike us as an alien and bourgeois imposition, as the Marxist critical tradition has sometimes had us believe, or do Allan's behaviour and words help Jo grasp the warmer family relations championed by Maurice?

Readers bring different assumptions to the text. This is apparent as we distinguish between different generations of readers, for whom the term 'Father' is positive or negative, transcendent or earthly, and as we look outside the Victorian era to those traditions in which the ideal family is conceived differently from its nuclear form and/ or in which the term 'father' is understood with less sentimentality. The assumptions that shape our own encounter with Scripture are always at work as we read other literary accounts of biblical reception. By highlighting the different perspectives interpreters bring, reception history reminds us of the historicity of all reading and the very specific assumptions that all of us bring to the Bible and its literary afterlives.

IV

The Bible is doubly translated here: The KJV's 'Our Father' is from the Greek *Pater hēmōn* but Woodcourt also acts as the translator or interpreter of the prayer, rendering it for Jo to repeat. John Ruskin supported the presentation of a 'simple and comprehensible statement of the Christian Gospel' (p. 8) through the Lord's Prayer 'the first words taught to children all over the Christian world' (p. 9). But we are left to wonder how much the child, Jo, understands here, and whether this is a form of English he can grasp. Equally, if we shift our attention to the one who translates the text for him, we might ask whether Allan does an adequate job of making the words of Scripture comprehensible to the one in his care. For the most part, Allan is one of the few characters with real moral integrity in the novel. Unlike the more doctrinally-motivated characters in the novel, such as Mr Chadband, Allan's religion is generous, simple and demonstrated through deed as much as it is through his words. But this does not mean that Allan's translation of the gospel is necessarily better than that of his fellow characters in *Bleak House*. While many readers will want to think of Allan's religion positively and view his goodness as the ideal embodiment of what religion should be, this reading of the teaching of Jesus is theologically unorthodox in presenting Christ as a good man rather than a divine Saviour. On this reading, we might look to Jo's response to Allan as a sign that the radical grace promised by the Christian Gospel has been lost in translation. As Allan goes through the prayer line-by-line, Jo responds: 'I'll say anythink as you say, sir, for I knows it's good.' Given Jo's plight at this particular moment, it may be that the biblical story should be providing him with something more than a moral exemplar and something more specific than a rhetorical 'anythink'.

While it is possible to pick fault with Allan's translation of the biblical text by pointing to Jo's limited comprehension and/or the questions surrounding Allan's fidelity to the original, it would be wrong to dismiss this act of translation altogether. In contrast to other characters that seek to use Jo for different purposes, Allan is at least with Jo in his hour of need. Perhaps it is uncharitable to claim that Allan's words and deeds convey nothing of the biblical narrative. Allan's translation of the biblical text may be incomplete, but it does convey something profound, and Jo's willingness to take his hand and register the possibility that someone might truly love him is surely in line with the gospel that Dickens privileged.

V

The Lord's Prayer was a cornerstone of the Church of England services of Victorian England and was regularly recited by congregations in a communal act of deference to God. But it could, and indeed was, put to a myriad of other uses. When Guster imagines a larger-than-life secret within the Snagsby household, in Chapter 25 of *Bleak House*, his reference to the Lord's Prayer suggests that its special status, acquired in its weekly church ritualization, has been transformed into a quasi-magical quality: 'there is buried money underneath the cellar, guarded by an old man with a white beard, who cannot get out for seven thousand years because he said the Lord's

Prayer backwards'.[5] The transformation of the Lord's Prayer into a magical pass-word gives the words of Jesus a different meaning than biblical commentators imagine as they read the Gospel of Matthew. But Guster's fearful fancy goes further still, introducing a diabolic dimension through the contemplation of an inverted recitation.

Different uses of the Lord's Prayer in *Bleak House* are a dramatic reminder of the multiplicity of textual voices that sound in all acts of reading. By relying on words that already have a variety of existing meanings before their latest usage, texts are multi-voiced in the sense that meanings emerge that are always more complex than an author can imagine. Appreciating this multivocality is crucial to understanding how the Bible sounds in *Bleak House*, as Janet Larson has made clear in her seminal work on Dickens' uses of the Bible.[6] Larson explores the ways in which Dickens breaks Scripture by relocating phrases and passages in a new context and putting the words of the Bible to his own purposes. But she also shows us how Dickens never has full control over the meaning of the biblical fragments he employs, for these textual fragments acquire multiple meanings over time and resist the singular purposes to which Dickens sometimes puts them. Thus, the Bible that sounds in Dickens' fiction is never uniform or under his complete control. We are further reminded that there is always more than one voice at work in Dickens' text by the narrative structure of *Bleak House*, which switches to and fro between an omniscient, cynical unnamed narrator and the homely figure of Esther. If Esther had been the one to recount the scene in which Allan leads Jo in the Lord's Prayer, we would likely have had a different sense of how the novel reads this part of the biblical tradition.

VI

Our perspective on the way in which *Bleak House* engages with the Bible at the moment of Jo's death is coloured by the figurative tropes of light and darkness that accompany the scene. When Jo gropes in the dark and seeks release in the light, we are taken back to the fog with which the novel so famously begins. The fog never properly lifts throughout the novel, despite Esther's attempts to establish some degree of perspicuity through ignoring the broader mysteries and focussing on a more homely Bleak House in which everything becomes clearer. Given the persistence of a murky, foggy and dark world throughout the events described by the anonymous narrator, we must decide whether the light that waits for Jo in his dying moments offers any sort of resolution.

Yet, as with so much of the language in *Bleak House*, the trope of light at this juncture is overwhelmed by its biblical significances. The New Testament repeatedly reminds us that the Christian tradition views Jesus as the light of the world and we miss an important aspect of *Bleak House* if we move too quickly and see the light that awaits Jo as a secularized resolution to his (and our) general lack of understanding in the novel. Around the time that *Bleak House* was published, Dickens' friend Holman Hunt painted his influential work 'The Light of the World' (1853–54). The use of light in that picture, along with its invocation of the third chapter of Revelation ('Behold I stand at the door and knock . . .', Rev 3: 20), helps describe the religious cultural imaginary through which many early readers of Dickens would have seen a redemptive aspect within Jo's otherwise tragic demise. As George Landow has argued, the Victorians were familiar with a form of Protestant reading that privileged Christ.[7] As such, a life-giving death such as Jo's would have been identified as Christ-like and, consequently, as more meaningful than may be apparent to a modern secular reader.

VII

While parables are complex literary forms that do more than illustrate a simple truth, they bear some resemblance to figurative language in their imaginative capacity to conjoin perspectives. Many writers have commented on the importance of parables to Dickens' work and the use of Lord's Prayer by Woodcourt can be seen as part of an extended reworking of the Good Samaritan story (from Luke 10: 29–37). In contrast to religious figures such as Mr Chadband and those inadequate institutions of the workhouse and hospital that fail Jo at his point of need, Woodcourt picks up the ailing Jo, pays for his food and drink, and finds him lodgings.[8] The parable of the Good Samaritan that Jesus tells is in answer to the question 'who is my neighbour?', from a lawyer concerned to justify himself. If Jesus' answer defies the self-justification of his questioner, perhaps the good actions of Woodcourt are a challenge to self-justification directed towards other characters in the novel and ultimately at Dickens' readers. Rather than seeking payment for his services, Woodcourt pays to help his fellow creature in an act of kindness that confronts the mindset of those in an industrial age who expect to be paid for all that they do.

Dickens' use of a parable at this moment in *Bleak House* can be read in other ways, too. While it is tempting to think of Woodcourt simply as just another good man, his work as a doctor, with its allusion to Jesus as the great physician, raises the salvific stakes of what is meant by his act of kindness towards Jo. And the question, 'who is my neighbour?' means we should cast ourselves as the forgotten and broken Jo, an association that radically contests the bourgeois assumption that we are fundamentally good people with the capacity to save ourselves and others. Or perhaps we need to remember that the result of Woodcourt's intervention proves inadequate and that the only one who can truly tend to Jo's needs is a divine Saviour. While this reading does not undermine the charity that the novel calls for in the immediate aftermath of Jo's dying moments, it might question Dickens' apparent confidence in the power of individual philanthropy to effect the changes needed in the middle of the nineteenth century.

VIII

Explicitly theological readings of novels like *Bleak House* can be uncomfortable to a modern readership that has largely exorcised all memory of the biblical narrative. But they can also cause discomfort for other reasons, including the ethical questions that accompany all theological reflection. Questions regarding human identity and why people act in the way they do are an important part of the stories of origins that we find in the Book of Genesis, and this ethical dimension provides a much more productive way of thinking about creation than contorted comparisons between the opening chapters of the Bible and the findings of modern science. In the comments directly following Jo's death scene, Dickens draws upon questions of ethics and the natural order when the narrator addresses the response of the implied audience to Jo's demise: 'Dead, your Majesty. Dead, my lords and gentlemen. Dead, Right Reverends and Wrong Reverends of every order. Dead, men and women, born with Heavenly compassion in your hearts. And dying thus around us every day.' The readers have been born, he asserts, with compassion. But if this is so, where is their compassion when children are dying daily 'around us'? By setting the readers' heavenly compassion against such uncompromising suffering, the narrator works to undermine certainties of human care as natural and enduring. The term 'heavenly compassion' demands a cosmic level of expectations of care, even if readers have failed to meet such expectations, and the reference to 'Our Father' serves as an additional reminder of fraternal human bonds. Dickens sets his readers in a double bind. If heavenly compassion is not a birthright, why has it not been cultivated? If his readers do assert a divine compassion in human nature, why has it failed? However theologically-minded readers ('Reverends of every order') interpret the proper 'order' of things at the abstract level, the text insists on the ethical imperative of working out practically what it means to live in the world with 'heavenly compassion'.

IX

This scene depicts Jo's end as representative of those 'dying thus around us every day'. High mortality rates and a less clinical attitude to death than the one that governs contemporary western culture were two of the many reasons why Victorian theology and culture had so much to say on the subject of death.[9] The appeal to the Lord's Prayer as a way of responding theologically to this fact of life was not uncommon in the period but Dickens' choice of this prayer is worth reflecting on nevertheless. Why does Woodcourt use this prayer? Is he trying to save Jo's soul in the sense of ensuring that the illiterate orphan articulates the bare minimum considered necessary to secure entry into heaven or is Woodcourt seeking instead to alleviate Jo's suffering? It may be that we are wrong to think in terms of a stark choice between these spiritual and social senses of salvation. The concept of salvation was a rich and complex one in the Victorian period, and Dickens' disquiet about the evangelical emphasis on substitutionary atonement (the idea of a divine Saviour who has to die in our place) did not stop him from finding imaginative energy in this particular theological idea.[10]

According to Larson, Dickens disrupts the sentimental death scene favoured in the Victorian period by making 'Our Father' resonate with social freight at the moment of Jo's death.[11] The injunction to brotherly love is a powerful challenge that disrupts easy sentimental readings of Jo's passing. Earlier in the chapter, Jo is described as 'neither of the beasts nor of humanity', emphasizing the wretchedness of his state, and yet 'Our Father' suggests a fraternity between the boy and the respectable Doctor that challenges any assumptions about Jo's bestial unworthiness. Jo's death constitutes the tragic centre of the novel and Dickens' dramatic and challenging commentary on this death suggests a social apocalypse that demands our response. By couching any thought of Jo's redemption in the way that he does, Dickens' approach opens up the social-political and eschatological dimensions of salvation and restores an element of the biblical story that he felt had been neglected by those religious contemporaries who focussed on one's entry into heaven.

Dickens' opening up of the biblical story of salvation during Jo's final moments encapsulates many of the issues at stake when we think about the Bible and literature. The complexity of the biblical narratives only increases as that story is passed on and reimagined for a new generation. While there are clearly differences between those writers who privilege faithfulness to the original and those who use an episode or quotation from Scripture as inspiration for something quite different, in all cases the relationship between the biblical text and its literary afterlife is rich, layered, uncertain and dynamic. Moreover, it is a relationship that we, as readers, are implicated in. Regardless of whether we read the Bible primarily for religious, political, historical or literary reasons, and regardless of our views on the material we read, we become participants in the narrative. As such, we enter into the territory of literature and the Bible that already has many well-trodden paths and provocative signposts.

Notes

1   Readers are also encouraged to look at some of the recent collections of critical essays on the Bible and literature, such as Rebecca Lemon et al., eds., *The Blackwell Companion to the Bible in English Literature* (Chichester: Wiley-Blackwell, 2009) and Michael Lieb, Emma Mason and Jonathan Roberts, eds., *The Oxford Handbook of the Reception History of the Bible* (Oxford: Oxford University Press, 2011), as well as the many essays published in the journals *Christianity and Literature, Literature and Theology,* and *Religion and Literature.*

2   Gabriel Marcel, *Being and Having,* translated Katherine Farrer (Westminster: Dacre Press, 1949), p. 117.

3   John Ruskin, letter to Mr Malleson, 6th July 1879, in *The Lord's Prayer and the Church, Letters to the Clergy,* 2nd edn (London: Strahan and Co., Ltd., n.d.), p. 11.

4   F. D. Maurice, *The Lord's Prayer: Nine Sermons Preached in the Chapel of Lincoln's Inn, in the months of February, March and April, 1848* (London: John W. Parker, 1849), p. 5.

5   Charles Dickens, *Bleak House,* ed. by Stephen Gill (Oxford: Oxford World's Classics, 2008), p. 375.

6   See Janet L. Larson, *Dickens and the Broken Scripture* (Athens, Georgia: University of Georgia Press, 1985).

7   See George Landow, *Victorian Types, Victorian Shadows: Biblical Typology in Victorian Literature, Art, and Thought* (London: Routledge and Kegan Paul, 1980), Chapter 1.

8   Dennis Walder has argued for the importance of the Good Samaritan story in *Oliver Twist.* See Walder, *Dickens and Religion* (London: George Allen and Unwin, 1981), Chapter Two.

9   See Michael Wheeler, *Death and the Future Life in Victorian Literature and Theology* (Cambridge: Cambridge University Press, 1990).

10   See Jan-Melissa Schramm, *Atonement and Self-Sacrifice in Nineteenth-Century Narrative* (Cambridge: Cambridge University Press, 2012), Chapter 4.

11   Larson, *Dickens and the Broken Scripture*, pp. 26–27.

PART I

The Relationship Between Literature and the Bible

Chapter 1

Introducing the Study of Literature and the Bible

For that, observe, is the real meaning, in its first power, of the word *Bible*.
Not book, merely; but "Bibliotheca," Treasury of Books.

John Ruskin, *The Bible of Amiens* (1880–85)[1]

I cannot help suspecting . . . that those who read the Bible as literature do not
read the Bible.

C. S. Lewis, *The Literary Impact of the Authorized Version* (1950)[2]

In my experience, when you let go of the Bible as explanatory *logos*, you get
it back as depthless myth.

Richard Holloway, *Revelations* (2005)[3]

IT IS SOMETHING OF a paradox that many twenty-first century readers are
quick to acknowledge the complexity of texts in general – novels, films, adverts,
webpages – but hesitant to recognize the intricate character of one of the foundational books in world history. In the late nineteenth century, John Ruskin – who had
been raised in an Evangelical household committed to regular reading of the
Scriptures – reminded his ostensibly Bible-literate audience that the very name given
to their collected sacred writings indicated its rich, diverse identity. For Ruskin, the
Bible was 'the library of Europe' – a work that, in the form given to it by St Jerome
in the fourth century – was 'the "Book of Books"' of which 'all the future art of the
Western nations was to be an hourly enlarging interpretation'.[4] Ruskin's approach
combines aesthetic appreciation – he loved much of the visual and literary art inspired
by different translations – with a theological understanding. In other words, the
'Bible' – as heterogenous, unstable and dynamic as the term has been – can be interpreted as more than one thing. The claim that the Bible should be read 'as literature'
is neither new nor, despite the reservations expressed by C. S. Lewis, is it usually a
controversial one. Yet the literary study of the collected Jewish-Christian Scriptures
is one that inspires radically different approaches and demands constant critical

re-evaluation. Our two keywords are burdened with a range of complex social, artistic and theological associations. The name 'Bible' might prompt thoughts of creation, fall, prophecy, divine law and the world to come but, more prosaically, it has also become short-hand for any authoritative, didactic volume. There are bibles for prospective property developers, social media magnates, football coaches and mountain bikers. 'Literature' is similarly ambiguous: the term can signify both the kinds of work deemed worthy of study at University and unsolicited mail from marketing companies. However, to describe any text as 'literary' is to invoke traditions of aesthetic hierarchy and to distinguish between 'high' and 'low' culture. In what precise sense is the Bible, this 'Treasury of books', literary? Can it be named a 'classic' in the same way as, for example, *The Illiad, Hamlet, Ulysses* or *Beloved* are granted such an epithet? Classic status is a dubious honour indeed: it signifies reverence for a work that is deemed to be of such eternal and unchanging value that the text might appear irrelevant to the contemporary world. Does the Bible belong to an exalted realm that demands reverence rather than comprehension? Is its fate to be unread, gradually forgotten and eventually lost amidst so much venerated cultural detritus?

One alternative is to pick up the book 'with the purpose to read it for the first time as [. . .] any other work'. This was the style of interpretation that Samuel Taylor Coleridge proposed in *Confessions of an Inquiring Spirit* (1840). The Romantic poet identifies, in a strikingly self-aware fashion, the difficulties – and mysterious joy – of reading a book that is both familiar and strange:

> For I neither can, nor dare, throw off a strong and awful prepossession in its favour – certain as I am that a large part of the light and life, in which and by which I see, love, and embrace the truths and the strengths co-organised into a living body of faith and knowledge [. . .] has been directly or indirectly derived to me from this sacred volume, – and unable to determine what I do not owe to its influences.[5]

Innocent readings of any text – let alone the much quoted, re-worked and debated Jewish-Christian Scriptures – are a near impossibility.

These issues remain fundamental to interpretation, especially in an ostensibly post-religious era in which the authority of all texts is continually open to debate. One popular account of the 'rise' of literary studies suggests that it emerged to fill the place vacated by religious belief as a socially cohesive force.[6] Universities challenged churches as places of authority and the Scriptures were rivalled by alternative (and perhaps less morally demanding) poetic voices. The logic of this argument is that 'literature' is a kind of sequel to the Bible, respectful but ready to replace its ageing precursor. Such a view is influential – and easy to accommodate to standard narratives of gradual but inexorable secularization – but it is important not to ignore the complex relationship between popular culture and religious belief. Twenty-first century readers are less likely than Coleridge to be subject to a 'strong and awful prepossession' in favour of the Bible. Yet this set of texts, in its diverse forms and genres, prompts the type of searching questions with which literature students are already very familiar. What kind of reality is evoked by the narrative? Who is writing and for whom? Are all stories equally valid or do some have a special or even unique authority? How do stories challenge or perpetuate our perception of reality? Students of literature are familiar with terms such as 'canon' – the name, perhaps above all others, associated with specious authority and hierarchy.

Literary criticism and biblical exegesis share a simultaneous respect for and audacity towards the written word. The Bible – whether it is regarded as timeless text or storehouse of half-forgotten tall tales – has been vital to the history of popular, democratic narrative traditions. It is a source of argument, imagery and imaginative possibility; a tissue of texts claimed by different groups including religious communities, antiquarians and artists, who are compelled to defend a particular interpretation of this 'Book of Books'.

There was a time in 'Christian' countries when the first 'book' that any reader encountered would have been a translation of the Bible, a book whose stories would influence readings of subsequent 'secular' literature. Today, something of an inversion might well be the case. Many students are likely to have read Jeanette Winterson, for example, before they encounter the King James Version of the Scriptures that inspired this nonconforming, complex novelist. In a lecture on 'The Literary Impact of the Authorized Version' (1950) C. S. Lewis dismissed the claim that a literary approach to the Bible will endure as traditional religious interpretations become untenable and evaporate. This is partly, he suggests, because the Scriptures will not allow themselves to be read for entertainment or pleasant enlightenment:

> Neither Aeschylus nor even Virgil tacitly prefaces his poetry with the formula 'Thus say the gods'. But in most parts of the Bible everything is implicitly or explicitly introduced with 'Thus saith the Lord'. It is [. . .] not merely a sacred book but a book so remorselessly and continuously sacred that it does not invite, it excludes or repels, the merely aesthetic approach.[7]

For more sceptical readers, the Bible – a synthesis of law, prophecy, poetry, narrative and letters – is no longer the property of a believing community. Instead, it is primarily to be studied as a work of historical intrigue or as a kind of spare room of memories, precious images and clarifying, severe language. Richard Holloway, former Anglican Bishop and sometime theological itinerant, observes that 'unbelievers, if they read the Bible at all, are likely to read it as a constellation of myths that continue to express the height and depth of human existence; whereas believers are more likely to try to read it as an information manual, a sort of users' guide to the universe'.[8] Although some 'believers' – a somewhat broad and flexible category – might demur from this kind of nostalgic-sceptic categorization, it is true that many conservative Christians maintain that the Bible is nothing short of the divinely dictated, inerrant word of God. Other people of faith, however, may have a rather more nuanced, complicated view of their holy book, one that neither depends on literal readings of each and every word nor relegates the Bible to the museum of shared memories by treating it as a book that is either enchanting or dangerous, or, more importantly, largely irrelevant to the ways in which we live and think now.

This introductory section includes material by scholars whose work wrestles with some of the defining problems of reading the vexed relationship between the Bible and literature. The first of these extracts is taken from the opening chapter of Erich Auerbach's *Mimesis* (1946), his groundbreaking study of 'the representation of reality in Western literature'. In 'Odysseus' Scar', Auerbach makes a crucial distinction between 'two equally ancient and equally epic texts' of Homer and biblical writing, exemplified by the story of Abraham and Isaac in Genesis 22. Both narratives are, in Auerbach's terms, epic narratives in which a deity – or deities – play an active, speaking role. The biblical narrative is less clearly unified than the carefully refined rhetoric of classical myth; it is also full of ambiguity, fragmentation and gaps of speech and motivation. Biblical narrative differs from Homeric legend in another way: the 'hidden God' of the Jewish scriptures compels readers to acts of interpretation. For Auerbach, as for Lewis, the crucial distinction between these two epic modes is the kind of claims that the writings make about their own status. 'The scripture stories do not, like Homer's, court our favour, they do not flatter us that they may please us and enchant us – they seek to subject us, and if we refuse to be subjected we are rebels'. Homer, in Auerbach's view, represents a rhetorical tradition dedicated to aesthetic pleasure and imaginative escapism. The biblical narrative, in contrast, does not seek 'merely to make us forget our own reality for a few hours, it seeks to overcome our reality: we are to fit our own life into its world'.

Auerbach's striking comparison is quoted by Hans Frei in *The Eclipse of Biblical Narrative* (1974), another pioneering work, the introduction for which is included in full in this section. Frei argues that theology and Christian practice make a grave error when they abandon the concept of the Bible as a narrative with an overall, defining shape: that of the creation, fall and redemption of the world. Frei identifies a tradition of biblical interpretation in which certain theologians, including Augustine, 'envisioned the real world as formed by the sequence told by the biblical stories. That temporal world covered the span of ages from creation to the final consummation to come'. For Frei *figuration* is a vital mode or term which describes the relationship between events in the so-called Old Testament narratives and those in the gospels. Frei proposes a much more complex relationship between history, belief and representation than the dominantly historicizing mode of eighteenth- and nineteenth-century interpretation. Narrative theology emphasizes the importance of an unfolding story – God's story – that should shape the believing community's understanding of the world. The believer is to comprehend his or her life in relation to the grand narrative of biblical redemption rather than vice versa.

'What goals does the biblical narrator set himself?' This is the big question with which Meir Sternberg opens his robust, bracing and dense study of 'ideological literature and the drama of reading', *The Poetics of the Bible* (1987). Sternberg argues that 'our primary business as readers' of biblical narrative 'is to make purposive sense of it, so as to explain the *what's* and the *how's* in terms of the *why's* of communication'. Sternberg proposes a poetics of the Bible that is vigorously critical of many literary readings of Scripture. He argues that 'to offer a poetics of biblical narrative is to claim that biblical narrative is a work of literature' but that this is utterly distinct from describing it as 'artful work' or, for example, 'a work marked by some aesthetic property'. For Sternberg, readers of the Bible need to recuperate a complex and nuanced sense of both intention and context. The 'children of the New Criticism', he suggests, fired by hostility to intentionalist interpretations of writing, often distort good reading practices. 'As interpreters of the Bible,' claims Sternberg, 'our only concern is with "embodied" or "objectified" intention; and that forms a different business altogether [. . .]'. Sternberg emphasizes the role of 'intention' in communication which always relies on an understanding between a 'speaker' and an 'addressee'. This argument is bold in that it suggests that meaning, however complex, resides in text and context and might be encountered by meticulous readers who are asking the right questions.

One of the figures who has continually surprised, challenged and, on occasion, irritated both literary and biblical scholars with distinctive questions and answers is Harold Bloom. The extract from Susan Handelman's *The Slayers of Moses: The Emergence of Rabbinic Interpretation in Modern Literary Theory* (1982) reads Bloom 'through *his* relationship to *his* precursors – that is, through his *own* revisionary ratios'. She locates Bloom alongside such figures as St. Paul, Sigmund Freud and Jacques Derrida in 'the tradition of heretic hermeneutics' and suggests that he 'comes to the critical arena to bring not peace, but a sword, and to expose the power struggle of poetic and critical relations'. 'Heretic hermeneutics' might otherwise be described as modes of interpretation that embody a kind of Promethean challenge to theological convention. Such disputes are, perhaps surprisingly, welcomed by disparate groups: people marginalized by dominant religious ideology who welcome alternatives to the orthodoxy and, indeed, by some conservative believers who are galvanized by the critique represented by new readings.

We might argue that a working knowledge of the Bible and its critical reception will not only enrich understanding of 'secular' literature but that ignorance of 'the Book of Books' is detrimental to an appreciation of why we invest in literature at all. Whether you believe that the Bible is a treasury of tales or ragbag anthology, beautiful lies or divine truth, it's clear that this 'Book of Books' demands reasoning with, re-reading or, indeed, reading for the first time.

Notes

1   The Library Edition of *The Works of Ruskin,* ed. by E.T. Cook and Alexander Wedderburn, 39 vols (London: George Allen, 1903–12), xxxiii, pp. 108–9.
2   C.S. Lewis, *The Literary Impact of The Authorised Version*, the Ethel M. Wood Lecture delivered before the University of London on 20 March 1950 (London: The Athlone Press, 1950), p. 23.
3   Richard Holloway, *Revelations: Personal Responses to the Books of the Bible* (Edinburgh: Canongate), pp. 1–12 (p. 4).
4   Ruskin, pp. 108–10.
5   Samuel Taylor Coleridge, *Confessions of an Inquiring Spirit,* 3rd edn (London: Edward Moxon, 1853), pp. 43–44. For a detailed exploration of the problems that Coleridge identifies see, for example, Stephen Prickett, *Words and the Word: Language, Poetics, and Biblical Interpretation* (Cambridge: Cambridge University Press, 1986), pp. 4–36.

6   See, for example, Terry Eagleton, *Literary Theory: An Introduction* (London: Blackwell, 2008), pp. 20–21.

7   Lewis, p. 25.

8   Holloway, p. 4.

Further reading

Cunningham, Valentine. 'Introduction: The Necessity of Heresy', in *Figures of Heresy: Radical Theology in English and American Writing*, ed. by Andrew Dix and Jonathan Taylor (Brighton: Sussex Academic Press, 2006), pp. 1–18

Dawn, Maggi, *The Writing on the Wall: High Art, Popular Culture and the Bible* (London: Hodder and Stoughton, 2010)

Detweiler, Robert and David Jasper, eds., *Religion and Literature: A Reader* (Louisville: Westminster John Knox Press, 2000)

Jasper, David, *The Study of Literature and Religion* (Macmillan: Houndmills, 1989)

Jasper, David and Stephen Prickett, eds., *The Bible and Literature: A Reader* (Oxford: Blackwell, 1999)

Lemon, Rebecca, Emma Mason, Jonathan Roberts and Christopher Rowland, eds., *The Blackwell Companion to the Bible in English Literature* (Oxford: Blackwell, 2009)

Norton, David, *A History of the Bible as Literature*, 2 vols (Cambridge: Cambridge University Press, 1993)

Sawyer, John F. A., ed., *The Blackwell Companion to the Bible and Culture* (Oxford: Blackwell, 2006)

Wright, T. R., *Theology and Literature* (Oxford: Blackwell, 1988)

Yandell, Keith E., ed., *Faith and Narrative* (Oxford: Oxford University Press, 2001)

(a) Odysseus' Scar

Eric Auerbach

Readers of the *Odyssey* will remember the well-prepared and touching scene in book 19, when Odysseus has at last come home, the scene in which the old housekeeper Euryclea, who had been his nurse, recognizes him by a scar on his thigh. The stranger has won Penelope's good will; at his request she tells the housekeeper to wash his feet, which, in all old stories, is the first duty of hospitality toward a tired traveler. Euryclea busies herself fetching water and mixing cold with hot, meanwhile speaking sadly of her absent master, who is probably of the same age as the guest, and who perhaps, like the guest, is even now wandering somewhere, a stranger; and she remarks how astonishingly like him the guest looks. Meanwhile Odysseus, remembering his scar, moves back out of the light; he knows that, despite his efforts to hide his identity, Euryclea will now recognize him, but he wants at least to keep Penelope in ignorance. No sooner has the old woman touched the scar than, in her joyous surprise, she lets Odysseus' foot drop into the basin; the water spills over, she is about to cry out her joy; Odysseus restrains her with whispered threats and endearments; she recovers herself and conceals her emotion. Penelope, whose attention Athena's foresight had diverted from the incident, has observed nothing.

All this is scrupulously externalized and narrated in leisurely fashion. The two women express their feelings in copious direct discourse. Feelings though they are, with only a slight admixture of the most general considerations upon human destiny, the syntactical connection between part and part is perfectly clear, no contour is blurred. There is also room and time for orderly, perfectly well-articulated, uniformly illuminated descriptions of implements, ministrations, and gestures; even in the dramatic moment of recognition, Homer does not omit to tell the reader that it is with his right hand that Odysseus takes the old woman by the throat to keep her from speaking, at the same time that he draws her closer to him with his left. Clearly outlined, brightly and uniformly illuminated, men and things stand out in a realm where everything is visible; and not less clear—wholly expressed, orderly even in their ardor—are the feelings and thoughts of the persons involved.

In my account of the incident I have so far passed over a whole series of verses which interrupt it in the middle. There are more than seventy of these verses—while to the incident itself some forty are devoted before the interruption and some forty after it. The interruption, which comes just at the point when the housekeeper recognizes the scar—that is, at the moment of crisis—describes the origin of the scar, a hunting accident which occurred in Odysseus' boyhood, at a boar hunt, during the time of his visit to his grandfather Autolycus. This first affords an opportunity to inform the reader about Autolycus, his house, the precise degree of the kinship, his character, and, no less exhaustively than touchingly, his behavior after the birth of his grandson; then follows the visit of Odysseus, now grown to be a youth; the exchange of greetings, the banquet with which he is welcomed, sleep and waking, the early start for the hunt, the tracking of the beast, the struggle, Odysseus' being wounded by the boar's tusk, his recovery, his return to Ithaca, his parents' anxious questions—all is narrated, again with such a complete externalization of all the elements of the story and of their interconnections as to leave nothing in obscurity. Not until then does the narrator return to Penelope's chamber, not until then, the digression having run its course, does Euryclea, who had recognized the scar before the digression began, let Odysseus' foot fall back into the basin.

The first thought of a modern reader—that this is a device to increase suspense—is, if not wholly wrong, at least not the essential explanation of this Homeric procedure. For the element of suspense is very slight in the Homeric poems; nothing in their entire style is calculated to keep the reader or hearer breathless. The digressions are not meant to keep the reader in suspense, but rather to relax the tension. And this frequently occurs, as in the passage before us. The broadly narrated, charming, and subtly fashioned story of the hunt, with all its elegance and self-sufficiency, its wealth of idyllic pictures, seeks to win the reader over wholly to itself as long as he is hearing it, to make him forget what had just taken place during the foot-washing. But an episode that will increase suspense by retarding the action must be so constructed that it will not fill the present entirely, will not put the crisis, whose resolution is being awaited, entirely out of the reader's mind, and thereby destroy the mood of suspense; the crisis and the suspense must continue, must remain vibrant in the background. But Homer—and to this we shall have to return later—knows no background. What he narrates is for the time being the only present, and fills both the stage and the reader's mind completely. So it is with the passage before us. When the young Euryclea (vv. 401ff.) sets the infant Odysseus on his grandfather Autolycus' lap after the banquet, the aged Euryclea, who a few lines earlier had touched the wanderer's foot, has entirely vanished from the stage and from the reader's mind.

[. . .]

The excursus upon the origin of Odysseus' scar is not basically different from the many passages in which a newly introduced character, or even a newly appearing object or implement, though it be in the thick of a battle, is described as to its nature and origin; or in which, upon the appearance of a god, we are told where he last was, what he was doing there, and by what road he reached the scene; indeed, even the Homeric epithets seem to me in the final analysis to be traceable to the same need for an externalization of phenomena in terms perceptible to the senses. Here is the scar, which comes up in the course of the narrative; and Homer's feeling simply will not permit him to see it appear out of the darkness of an unilluminated past; it must be set in full light, and with it a portion of the hero's boyhood—just as, in the *Iliad*, when the first ship is already burning and the Myrmidons finally arm that they may hasten to help, there is still time not only for the wonderful simile of the wolf, not only for the order of the Myrmidon host, but also for a detailed account of the ancestry of several subordinate leaders (16, vv. 155ff.). To be sure, the aesthetic effect thus produced was soon noticed and thereafter consciously sought; but the more original cause must have lain in the basic impulse of the Homeric style: to represent phenomena in a fully externalized form, visible and palpable in all their parts, and completely fixed in their spatial and temporal relations. Nor do psychological processes receive any other treatment: here too nothing must remain hidden and unexpressed. With the utmost fullness, with an orderliness which even passion does not disturb, Homer's personages vent their inmost hearts in speech; what they do not say to others, they speak in their own minds, so that the reader is informed of it.

[. . .]

The genius of the Homeric style becomes even more apparent when it is compared with an equally ancient and equally epic style from a different world of forms. I shall attempt this comparison with the account of the sacrifice of Isaac, a homogeneous narrative produced by the so-called Elohist. The King James version translates the opening as follows (Genesis 22: 1): "And it came to pass after these things, that God did tempt Abraham, and said to him, Abraham! and he said, Behold, here I am." Even this opening startles us when we come to it from Homer. Where are the two speakers? We are not told. The reader, however, knows that they are not normally to be found together in one place on earth, that one of them, God, in order to speak to Abraham, must come from somewhere, must enter the earthly realm from some unknown heights or depths. Whence does he come, whence does he call to Abraham? We are not told. He does not come, like Zeus or Poseidon, from the Aethiopians, where he has been enjoying a sacrificial feast. Nor are we told anything of his reasons for tempting Abraham so terribly. He has not, like Zeus, discussed them in set speeches with other gods gathered in council; nor have the deliberations in his own heart been presented to us; unexpected and mysterious, he enters the scene from some unknown height or depth and calls: Abraham! It will at once be said that this is to be explained by the particular concept of God which the Jews held and which was wholly different from that of the Greeks. True enough—but this constitutes no objection. For how is the Jewish concept of God to be explained? Even their earlier God of the desert was not fixed in form and content, and was alone; his lack of form, his lack of local habitation, his singleness, was in the end not only maintained but developed even further in competition with the comparatively far more manifest gods of the surrounding Near Eastern world. The concept of God held by the Jews is less a cause than a symptom of their manner of comprehending and representing things.

This becomes still clearer if we now turn to the other person in the dialogue, to Abraham. Where is he? We do not know. He says, indeed: Here I am—but the Hebrew word means only something like "behold me," and in any case is not meant to indicate the actual place where Abraham is, but a moral position in respect to God, who has called to him—Here am I awaiting thy command. Where he is actually, whether in Beersheba or elsewhere, whether indoors or in the open air, is not stated; it does not interest the narrator, the reader is not informed; and what Abraham was doing when God called to him is left in the same obscurity. To realize the difference, consider Hermes' visit to Calypso, for example, where command, journey, arrival and reception of the visitor, situation and occupation of the person visited, are set forth in many verses; and even on occasions when gods appear suddenly and briefly, whether to help one of their favorites or to deceive or destroy some mortal whom they hate, their bodily forms, and usually the manner of their coming and going, are given in detail. Here, however, God appears without bodily form (yet he "appears"), coming from some unspecified place—we only hear his voice, and that utters nothing but a name, a name without an adjective, without a descriptive epithet for the person spoken to, such as is the rule in every Homeric address; and of Abraham too nothing is made perceptible except the words in which he answers God: *Hinne-ni*, Behold me here—with which, to be sure, a most touching gesture expressive of obedience and readiness is suggested, but it is left to the reader to visualize it. Moreover the two speakers are not on the same level: if we conceive of Abraham in the foreground, where it might be possible to picture him as prostrate or kneeling or bowing with outspread arms or gazing upward, God is not there too: Abraham's words and gestures are directed toward the depths of the picture or upward, but in any case the undetermined, dark place from which the voice comes to him is not in the foreground.

After this opening, God gives his command, and the story itself begins: everyone knows it; it unrolls with no episodes in a few independent sentences whose syntactical connection is of the most rudimentary sort. In this atmosphere it is unthinkable that an implement, a landscape through which the travelers passed, the serving-men, or the ass, should be described, that their origin or descent or material or appearance or usefulness should be set forth in terms of praise; they do not even admit an adjective: they are serving-men, ass, wood, and knife, and nothing else, without an epithet; they are there to serve the end which God has commanded; what in other respects they were, are, or will be, remains in darkness. A journey is made, because God has designated the place where the sacrifice is to be performed; but we are told nothing about the journey except that it took three days, and even that we are told in a mysterious way: Abraham and his followers rose "early in the morning" and "went unto" the place of which God had told him; on the third day he lifted up his eyes and saw the place from afar. That gesture is the only gesture, is indeed the only occurrence during the whole journey, of which we are told; and though its motivation lies in the fact that the place is elevated, its uniqueness still heightens the impression that the journey took place through a vacuum; it is as if, while he traveled on, Abraham had looked neither to the right nor to the left, had suppressed any sign of life in his followers and himself save only their footfalls.

[. . .]

In the narrative itself, a third chief character appears: Isaac. While God and Abraham, the serving-men, the ass, and the implements are simply named, without mention of any qualities or any other sort of definition, Isaac once receives an appositive; God says, "Take Isaac, thine only son, whom thou lovest." But this is not a characterization of Isaac as a person, apart from his relation to his father and apart from the story; he may be handsome or ugly, intelligent or stupid, tall or short, pleasant or unpleasant—we are not told. Only what we need to know about him as a personage in the action, here and now, is illuminated, so that it may become apparent how terrible Abraham's temptation is, and that God is fully aware of it. By this example of the contrary, we see the significance of the descriptive adjectives and digressions of the Homeric poems; with their indications of the earlier and as it were absolute existence of the persons described, they prevent the reader from concentrating exclusively on a present crisis; even when the most terrible things are occurring, they prevent the establishment of an overwhelming suspense. But here, in the story of Abraham's sacrifice, the overwhelming suspense is present; what Schiller makes the goal of the tragic poet—to rob us of our emotional freedom, to turn our intellectual and spiritual powers (Schiller says "our activity") in one direction, to concentrate them there—is effected in this Biblical narrative, which certainly deserves the epithet epic.

We find the same contrast if we compare the two uses of direct discourse. The personages speak in the Bible story too; but their speech does not serve, as does speech in Homer, to manifest, to externalize thoughts—on the contrary, it serves to indicate thoughts which remain unexpressed. God gives his command in direct discourse, but he leaves his motives and his purpose unexpressed; Abraham, receiving the command, says nothing and does what he has been told to do. The conversation between Abraham and Isaac on the way to the place of sacrifice is only an interruption of the heavy silence and makes it all the more burdensome. The two of them, Isaac carrying the wood and Abraham with fire and a knife, "went together." Hesitantly, Isaac ventures to ask about the ram, and Abraham gives the well-known answer. Then the text repeats: "So they went both of them together." Everything remains unexpressed.

It would be difficult, then, to imagine styles more contrasted than those of these two equally ancient and equally epic texts. On the one hand, externalized, uniformly illuminated phenomena, at a definite time and in a definite place, connected together without lacunae in a perpetual foreground; thoughts and feeling completely expressed; events taking place in leisurely fashion and with very little of suspense.

On the other hand, the extenalization of only so much of the phenomena as is necessary for the purpose of the narrative, all else left in obscurity; the decisive points of the narrative alone are emphasized, what lies between is nonexistent; time and place are undefined and call for interpretation; thoughts and feeling remain unexpressed, are only suggested by the silence and the fragmentary speeches; the whole, permeated with the most unrelieved suspense and directed toward a single goal (and to that extent far more of a unity), remains mysterious and "fraught with background."

I will discuss this term in some detail, lest it be misunderstood. I said above that the Homeric style was "of the foreground" because, despite much going back and forth, it yet causes what is momentarily being narrated to give the impression that it is the only present, pure and without perspective. A consideration of the Elohistic text teaches us that our term is capable of a broader and deeper application. It shows that even the separate personages can be represented as possessing "background"; God is always so represented in the Bible, for he is not comprehensible in his presence, as is Zeus; it is always only "something" of him that appears, he always extends into depths. But even the human beings in the Biblical stories have greater depths of time, fate, and consciousness than do the human beings in Homer; although they are nearly always caught up in an event engaging all their faculties, they are not so entirely immersed in its present that they do not remain continually conscious of what has happened to them earlier and elsewhere; their thoughts and feelings have more layers, are more entangled. Abraham's actions are explained not only by what is happening to him at the moment, nor yet only by his character (as Achilles' actions by his courage and his pride, and Odysseus' by his versatility and foresightedness), but by his previous history; he remembers, he is constantly conscious of, what God has promised him and what God has already accomplished for him—his soul is torn between desperate rebellion and hopeful expectation; his silent obedience is multilayered, has background. Such a problematic psychological situation as this is impossible for any of the Homeric heroes, whose destiny is clearly defined and who wake every morning as if it were the first day of their lives: their emotions, though strong, are simple and find expression instantly.

How fraught with background, in comparison, are characters like Saul and David! How entangled and stratified are such human relations as those between David and Absalom, between David and Joab! Any such "background" quality of the psychological situation as that which the story of Absalom's death and its sequel (II Samuel 18 and 19, by the so-called Jahvist) rather suggests than expresses, is unthinkable in Homer. Here we are confronted not merely with the psychological processes of characters whose depth of background is veritably abysmal, but with a purely geographical background too. For David is absent from the battlefield; but the influence of his will and his feelings continues to operate, they affect even Joab in his rebellion and disregard for the consequences of his actions; in the magnificent scene with the two messengers, both the physical and psychological background is fully manifest, though the latter is never expressed. With this, compare, for example, how Achilles, who sends Patroclus first to scout and then into battle, loses almost all "presentness" so long as he is not physically present. But the most important thing is the "multilayeredness" of the individual character; this is hardly to be met with in Homer, or at most in the form of a conscious hesitation between two possible courses of action; otherwise, in Homer, the complexity of the psychological life is shown only in the succession and alternation of emotions; whereas the Jewish writers are able to express the simultaneous existence of various layers of consciousness and the conflict between them.

The Homeric poems, then, though their intellectual, linguistic, and above all syntactical culture appears to be so much more highly developed, are yet comparatively simple in their picture of human beings; and no less so in their relation to the real life which they describe in general. Delight in physical existence is everything to them, and their highest aim is to make that delight perceptible to us. Between battles and passions, adventures and perils, they show us hunts, banquets, palaces and shepherds' cots, athletic contests and washing days—in order that we may see the heroes in their ordinary life, and seeing them so, may take pleasure in their manner of enjoying their savory present, a present which sends strong roots down into social usages, landscape, and daily life. And thus they bewitch us and ingratiate themselves to us until we live with them in the reality of their lives; so long as we are reading or hearing the poems, it does not matter whether we know that all this is only legend, "make-believe." The oft-repeated reproach that Homer is a liar takes nothing from his effectiveness, he does not need to base his story on historical reality, his reality is powerful enough in itself; it ensnares us, weaving its web around us, and that suffices him. And this "real" world into which we are lured, exists for itself, contains nothing but itself; the Homeric poems conceal nothing, they contain no teaching and no secret second meaning. Homer can be analyzed, as we have essayed to do here, but he cannot be interpreted. Later allegorizing trends have tried their arts of interpretation upon him, but to no avail. He resists any such treatment; the interpretations are forced and foreign, they do not crystallize into a unified doctrine. The general considerations which occasionally occur (in our episode, for example, v. 360: that in misfortune men age quickly) reveal a calm acceptance of the basic facts of human existence, but with no compulsion to brood over them, still less any passionate impulse either to rebel against them or to embrace them in an ecstasy of submission.

It is all very different in the Biblical stories. Their aim is not to bewitch the senses, and if nevertheless they produce lively sensory effects, it is only because the moral, religious, and psychological phenomena which are their sole concern are made concrete in the sensible matter of life. But their religious intent involves an absolute claim to historical truth. The story of Abraham and Isaac is not better established than the story of Odysseus, Penelope, and Euryclea; both are legendary. But the Biblical narrator, the Elohist, had to believe in the objective truth of the story of Abraham's sacrifice—the existence of the sacred ordinances of life rested upon the truth of this and similar stories. He had to believe in it passionately; or else (as many rationalistic interpreters believed and perhaps still believe) he had to be a conscious liar—no harmless liar like Homer, who lied to give pleasure, but a political liar with a definite end in view, lying in the interest of a claim to absolute authority.

To me, the rationalistic interpretation seems psychologically absurd; but even if we take it into consideration, the relation of the Elohist to the truth of his story still remains a far more passionate and definite one than is Homer's relation. The Biblical narrator was obliged to write exactly what his belief in the truth of the tradition (or, from the rationalistic standpoint, his interest in the truth of it) demanded of him—in either case, his freedom in creative or representative imagination was severely limited; his activity was perforce reduced to composing an effective version of the pious tradition. What he produced, then, was not primarily oriented toward "realism" (if he succeeded in being realistic, it was merely a means, not an end); it was oriented toward truth. Woe to the man who did not believe it! One can perfectly well entertain historical doubts on the subject of the Trojan War or of Odysseus' wanderings, and still, when reading Homer, feel precisely the effects he sought to produce; but without believing in Abraham's sacrifice, it is impossible to put the narrative of it to the use for which it was written. Indeed, we must go even further. The Bible's claim to truth is not only far more urgent than Homer's, it is tyrannical—it excludes all other claims. The world of the Scripture stories is not satisfied with claiming to be a historically true reality—it insists that it is the only real world, is destined for autocracy. All other scenes, issues, and ordinances have no right to appear independently of it, and it is promised that all of them, the history of all mankind, will be given their due place within its frame, will be subordinated to it. The Scripture stories do not, like Homer's, court our favor, they do not flatter us that they may please us and enchant us—they seek to subject us, and if we refuse to be subjected we are rebels.

Let no one object that this goes too far, that not the stories, but the religious doctrine, raises the claim to absolute authority; because the stories are not, like Homer's, simply narrated "reality." Doctrine and promise are incarnate in them and inseparable from them; for that very reason they are fraught with "background" and mysterious, containing a second, concealed meaning. In the story of Isaac, it is not only God's intervention at the beginning and the end, but even the factual and psychological elements which come between, that are mysterious, merely touched upon, fraught with background; and therefore they require subtle investigation and interpretation, they demand them. Since so much in the story is dark and incomplete, and since the reader knows that God is a hidden God, his effort to interpret it constantly finds something new to feed upon. Doctrine and the search for enlightenment are inextricably connected with the physical side of the narrative—the latter being more than simple "reality"; indeed they are in constant danger of losing their own reality, as very soon happened when interpretation reached such proportions that the real vanished.

If the text of the Biblical narrative, then, is so greatly in need of interpretation on the basis of its own content, its claim to absolute authority forces it still further in the same direction. Far from seeking, like Homer, merely to make us forget our own reality for a few hours, it seeks to overcome our reality: we are to fit our own life into its world, feel ourselves to be elements in its structure of universal history.

(b) Introduction to *The Eclipse of Biblical Narrative*

Hans W. Frei

Western Christian reading of the Bible in the days before the rise of historical criticism in the eighteenth century was usually strongly realistic, i.e. at once literal and historical, and not only doctrinal or edifying. The words and sentences meant what they said, and because they did so they accurately described real events and real truths that were rightly put only in those terms and no others. Other ways of reading portions of the Bible, for example, in a spiritual or allegorical sense, were permissible, but they must not offend against a literal reading of those parts which seemed most obviously to demand it. Most eminent among them were all those stories which together went into the making of a single storied or historical sequence. Long before a minor modern school of thought made the biblical "history of salvation" a special spiritual and historical sequence for historiographical and theological inquiry, Christian preachers and theological commentators, Augustine the most notable among them, had envisioned the real world as formed by the sequence told by the biblical stories. That temporal world covered the span of ages from creation to the final consummation to come, and included the governance both of man's natural environment and of that secondary environment which we often think of as provided for man by himself and call "history" or "culture."

The preeminence of a literal and historical reading of the most important biblical stories was never wholly lost in western Christendom. It actually received new impetus in the era of the Renaissance and the Reformation when it became the regnant mode of biblical reading. From it, modern biblical interpretation began its quest, in continuity as well as rebellion. Most important were three elements in the traditional realistic interpretation of the biblical stories, which also served as the foci for the rebellion against it.

First, if it seemed clear that a biblical story was to be read literally, it followed automatically that it referred to and described actual historical occurrences. The true historical reference of a story was a direct and natural concomitant of its making literal sense. This is a far cry from taking the fact that a passage or text makes best sense at a literal level as *evidence* that it is a reliable historical report. When commentators turned from the former to the latter interpretive use of literal meaning or used the two confusedly (as happened frequently in the later eighteenth century), it marked a new stage in the history of interpretation—a stage for which deistic convictions, empirical philosophy, and historical criticism form part of the technical intellectual background.

The second element in precritical realistic reading was that if the real historical world described by the several biblical stories is a single world of one temporal sequence, there must in principle be one cumulative story to depict it. Consequently, the several biblical stories narrating sequential segments in time must fit together into one narrative. The interpretive means for joining them was to make earlier biblical stories figures or types of later stories and of their events and patterns of meaning. Without loss to its own literal meaning or specific temporal reference, an earlier story (or occurrence) was a figure of a later one.[1] The customary use of figuration was to show that Old Testament persons, events, and prophecies were fulfilled in the New Testament. It was a way of turning the variety of biblical books into a single, unitary canon, one that embraced in particular the differences between Old and New Testaments.

Far from being in conflict with the literal sense of biblical stories, figuration or typology was a natural extension of literal interpretation. It was literalism at the level of the whole biblical story and thus of the depiction of the whole of historical reality. Figuration was at once a literary and a historical procedure, an interpretation of stories and their meanings by weaving them together into a common narrative referring to a single history and its patterns of meaning.

In the third place, since the world truly rendered by combining biblical narratives into one was indeed the one and only real world, it must in principle embrace the experience of any present age and reader. Not only was it possible for him, it was also his duty to fit himself into that world in which he was in any case a member, and he too did so in part by figural interpretation and in part of course by his mode of life. He was to see his disposition, his actions and passions, the shape of his own life as well as that of his era's events as figures of that storied world.

A story such as that of man's creation and "fall" (Genesis 1–9) made sense in its own right and as part of the larger story into which it was incorporated by Christian interpreters, beginning with St. Paul. But in addition, figuration made sense of the general extra-biblical structure of human experience, and of one's own experience, as well as of general concepts of good and evil drawn from experience. The point is that such experiences, events, concepts were all ranged figurally into the smaller as well as the overarching story. Biblical interpretation became an imperative need, but its direction was that of incorporating extra-biblical thought, experience, and reality into the one real world detailed and made accessible by the biblical story—not the reverse. As Auerbach suggests, in a striking contrast of Homer's *Odyssey* and Old Testament narrative:[2]

> Far from seeking, like Homer, merely to make us forget our own reality for a few hours, it seeks to overcome our reality: we are to fit our own life into its world, feel ourselves to be elements in its structure of universal history . . . Everything else that happens in the world can only be conceived as an element in this sequence; into it everything that is known about the world . . . must be fitted as an ingredient of the divine plan.

In the process of interpretation the story itself, constantly adapted to new situations and ways of thinking, underwent ceaseless revision; but in steadily revised form it still remained the adequate depiction of the common and inclusive world until the coming of modernity. As the eighteenth century went on, this mode of interpretation and the outlook it represented broke down with increasing rapidity. The seeds of disintegration were already there in the seventeenth century, not only among radical thinkers like Spinoza but also among conservatives. Johannes Cocceius in the seventeenth century and Johann Albrecht Bengel in the eighteenth, devout Christians both, signal a subtle transformation made more obvious in retrospect by the Deists' discussions in England and the subsequent rise of historical criticism. Both Cocceius and Bengel, the former using typology far more heavily than the latter, tried to locate the events of their day vis-à-vis the narrative framework of biblical story and history, and to locate by means of biblical sayings the present stage of the actual events we experience and predict future stages as well as the end of actual history. It was hardly an unprecedented preoccupation among Christian writers. But in the fuller context of that particular era it was a sign, though obviously not noticeable to devout minds at the time, of the breakup of the cohesion between the literal meaning of the biblical narratives and their reference to actual events. This kind of prophecy, rather than an anachronism, was the sign of a new cultural development, for its emphasis was on the events, on their likely course and on the hidden signs and references to this "real" world of past and future history, spread through the Bible. The mysterious signs and number schemes to be worked out from biblical verbal configurations represent a kind of proleptic verification of the shape of events not yet come to pass. Ironically— in view of the biblicism of these two men—it was a kind of detachment of the "real" historical world from its biblical description. The real events of history constitute an autonomous temporal framework of their own under God's providential design. Instead of rendering them accessible, the narratives, heretofore indispensable as means of access to the events, now simply verify them, thus affirming their autonomy and the fact that they are in principle accessible through any kind of description that can manage to be accurate either predictively or after the event. It simply happens that, again under God's providence, it is the Bible that contains the accurate descriptions. There is now a logical distinction and a reflective distance between the stories and the "reality" they depict. The depicted biblical world and the real historical world began to be separated at once in thought and in sensibility, no matter whether the depiction was thought to agree with reality (Cocceius and Bengel) or disagree with it (Spinoza).

This logical and reflective distance between narrative and reality increased steadily, naturally enough provoking a host of endeavors to bridge the gap. Not only did an enormous amount of inquiry into the factual truth (or falsity) of the biblical stories develop, but an intense concentration as well on their meaning and religious significance, whether factual or of some other sort. Many of those inquiring into the basic religious meaning of the biblical stories were determined to show that they harmonized with and illuminated extra-biblical experiences and concepts, as well as independent apprehensions of reality, even if many of these same commentators were equally determined that such inquiry must not involve their complete reduction to another framework of fact and meaning.

The point is that the direction of interpretation now became the reverse of earlier days. Do the stories and whatever concepts may be drawn from them describe what we apprehend as the real world? Do they fit a more general framework of meaning than that of a single story? Dr. Conyers Middleton, an English commentator of latitudinarian and skeptical leanings, thought that it didn't matter whether Genesis 1–3 was allegory or fact, since its meaning was the same in either case: "that this world had a beginning and creation from God; and that its principal inhabitant man, was originally formed to a state of happiness and perfection which he lost and forfeited, by following his lusts and passions, in opposition to the will of his Creator."[3] Belief in a creator—the foundation of any and all religion—and the supposition of man's fall—the basis of the need for revealed religion—are the meaning of the story, whether the version of it given in this particular narrative is taken literally or alle- gorically. In other words, whether or not the story is true history, its *meaning* is detachable from the specific story that sets it forth. Middleton was characteristic of many commentators, even some (like Locke) who had no doubt of the historicity of the narrated events: their meaning is nonetheless referable to an external more general context, and the story now has to be interpreted into it, rather than that external pattern of meaning being incorporated—figurally or in some other way—into the story.

If one sign of the breakdown of literal-realistic interpretation of the biblical stories was the reversal in the direction of interpretation that accompanied the distancing between the narratively depicted and the "real" world, the other and related indication was the collapse of figural interpretation. Typology or figuration simply could not cope with this reversal. It had been credible as an extension of literal reading, but once literal and historical reading began to break apart, figural interpretation became discredited both as a literary device and as a historical argument. As a literary or (more basically) logical device, figuration offended against the elementary assumption that a prepositional statement has only one meaning. As a historical argument (i.e. that the Old Testament contained prophecies specifically referring to and fulfilled in Jesus Christ), it strained credulity beyond the breaking point by the suggestion that sayings and events of one day referred predictively to specific persons and events hundreds of years later. Simultaneously of course it faded into oblivion as a means for relating the world of biblical narrative to present experience and to the world of extra-biblical events, experiences, and concepts. Once again, the interpretive demand now became reversed, and figuration found successors in such mirror-image categories of interpretation as allegory and, somewhat later, myth. These and other notions served for the technical classification of biblical stories and also for their meaningful incorporation into an independent sense of a world of experience and of rational interpretation.

As the realistic narrative reading of the biblical stories broke down, literal or verbal and historical meaning were severed and literal and figural interpretation, hitherto naturally affiliated procedures, also came apart. Figural reading had been literalism extended to the whole story or the unitary canon containing it. But now figural sense came to be something like the opposite of literal sense. In the first place, verbal or literal sense was now equated with the single meaning of statements, a logical and grammatical rule prevalent everywhere so that figural reading of the Bible seemed a senseless exception to it. Secondly, the very attempt to read unity out of (or into) the Bible now appeared different from, if not incompatible with, the self-confinement of literal reading to specific texts.

Furthermore, figural reading was no longer a persuasive instrument for unifying the canon. Literal reading came increasingly to mean two things: grammatical and lexical exactness in estimating what the original sense of a text was to its original audience, and the coincidence of the description with how the facts really occurred. Realistic reading came in effect to be identical with the latter; it consisted of matching the written description against the reconstruction of the probable historical sequence to which it referred. Increasingly, historical-critical reading became the heir of the older type of realistic reading. Unlike figural reading, both were not only about history but also about specific historical sequences, so that they were not concerned with the unity of the canon.

Figural reading, to the degree that it had been an extension of literal interpretation in the older kind of realistic, narrative reading, was now bound to look to historical-critical eyes like a rather preposterous historical argument, and it rapidly lost credibility. In the past, one of its chief uses had been as a means for unifying the canon; it had not simply been an awkward historical proof-text. Its breakdown upon being introduced into the arena of historical argument and demonstration was accompanied by a similar failure as an instrument for uniting the Bible. Historical critics were concerned with specific texts and specific historical circumstances. The unity of the Bible across millennia of differing cultural levels and conditions in any case seemed a tenuous, indeed a dubious hypothesis to them. But if it were to be demonstrated, it would have to be done by an argument other than a historical claim to specific miraculous fulfillment of Old Testament sayings and events in the New Testament. In sum, figural reading broke down not only as a means of locating oneself and one's world vis-à-vis the biblical narratives; in addition, it was forced to become a historical-factual argument in favor of the unity of the canon—and a poor one at that. But like its former partner, literal-realistic interpretation, it had to have a successor, for the unity of the Bible was as important to Christian theologians as its reliability.

Realistic, literal reading of the biblical narratives found its closest successor in the historical-critical reconstruction of specific events and texts of the Bible. The question was: How reliable are the texts? Figural reading, concerned as it was with the unity of the Bible, found its closest successor in an enterprise called biblical theology, which sought to establish the unity of religious meaning across the gap of historical and cultural differences. This could be done in a variety of ways. One might try to demonstrate the identity or similarity of the chief religious *concepts* in the whole range of the Bible, or one could try to show that the whole Bible reflects a single, gradually developing and cumulative *history*. This is a history at once of the distinctive or unique events affecting the people of Israel and of the developing and yet unitary as well as unique "Hebrew mind." The distinctiveness of both events and "mind" together constitutes the unity, both natural-historical and divinely guided, of the Bible.

Literal and figural reading of the biblical narratives, once natural allies, not only came apart, but the successors looked with great unease at each other—historical criticism and biblical theology were different enterprises and made for decidedly strained company. Yet each in its own way became crucial for the assertion of the religious and doctrinal authority of the Bible which Protestantism had always maintained. For that authority was bound to be gravely weakened if the Bible was neither reliable nor unitary.

The pages that follow are an investigation of the breakdown of realistic and figural interpretation of the biblical stories, and the reversal in the direction of interpretation. This is not a book about historical criticism of the Bible and its history, even though that procedure became part heir to the older kind of interpretation. Historical criticism will be a pertinent topic at many points, but the question of how to interpret obviously involved more than that topic. To be sure, once that method became standard scholarly practice, the stories were often tested against specific factual occurrence, or identified with a reconstruction of the process by which they originated and of their cultural setting.

But interpretation, and thus hermeneutics—the study of the principles and rules of interpretation and understanding—meant more. Attention continued to be paid to the verbal sense of the stories. In the course of the eighteenth century it came to signify not so much a literary depiction which was literal rather than metaphorical, allegorical, or symbolic, but rather the single meaning of a grammatically and logically sound propositional statement. The basic context for the investigation of verbal meaning often became single words in addition to full statements. In any case, "verbal sense" was philological or "grammatical-historical" (a common technical designation in the later eighteenth century, indicating the lexical in addition to the grammatical study of the words of a text) more than literary.

Beyond the verbal sense of texts was their religious significance, ideational meaning, or subject matter as it was sometimes called to distinguish it from the "merely" verbal sense. Just what that was, and whether it was intrinsic to the text or merely a particular use or application to which a text was put by some readers, became matters of vigorous disagreement. But commentators all agreed that something more than understanding a text's verbal sense was involved in understanding the text. The interpretation of texts and hermeneutics trenched on historical-critical analysis, and some scholars thought that critical reconstruction of the reported events constituted the subject matter of narrative texts. Nevertheless, interpretation, and therefore its theory, also included inquiry into verbal sense and ideational meaning or religious significance, so that despite some confusion about "subject matter" it was not unequivocally or universally reduced to the text's "true" historical occasion or setting.

This book, then, is about one segment of the history of the theory of biblical interpretation rather than the history of biblical criticism, even though one cannot draw a neat or complete distinction between the two enterprises. In particular, its topic is the eighteenth- and early nineteenth-century discussion about the proper rules and principles to guide interpretation of the history-like stories of the Old and New Testaments. It is not a full history of the hermeneutics of biblical narratives during that period but rather a historical study under a thesis and includes preeminently a description and explanation of the ways in which the older realistic and figural approaches to these stories broke down.

To state the thesis: a realistic or history-like (though not necessarily historical) element is a feature, as obvious as it is important, of many of the biblical narratives that went into the making of Christian belief. It is a feature that can be highlighted by the appropriate analytical procedure and by no other, even if it may be difficult to describe the procedure—in contrast to the element itself. It is fascinating that the realistic character of the crucial biblical stories was actually acknowledged and agreed upon by most of the significant eighteenth-century commentators. But since the precritical analytical or interpretive procedure for isolating it had irretrievably broken down in the opinion of most commentators, this specifically realistic characteristic, though acknowledged by all hands to be there, finally came to be ignored, or—even more fascinating—its presence or distinctiveness came to be denied for lack of a "method" to isolate it. And this despite the common agreement that the specific feature was there!

Biblical commentators again and again emphasized the simplicity of style, the life-likeness of depiction, the lack of artificiality or heroic elevation in theme in such stories as the first three chapters of Genesis, the story of Abraham's willingness to

sacrifice Isaac, and the synoptic gospels. In other words, they believed that representation and depiction and what they represented, had a great deal to do with each
other and came very close in these stories. Meaning and narrative shape bear significantly on each other. Even if one was convinced that the history-like or realistic
character of the narratives finally bespoke an illusion, so that their true history either
had to be reconstructed historically or their true sense explained as allegory or myth,
the realistic character was still there. This led to the odd situation described above.
Some commentators explained the realistic feature by claiming that the stories are
reliably or unreliably reported history. Others insisted that they are not, or only
incidentally, history and that their real meaning is unconnected with historical
reporting. In either case, history or else allegory or myth, the *meaning* of the stories
was finally something different from the stories or depictions themselves, despite the
fact that this is contrary to the character of a realistic story.

In the days before empirical philosophy, Deism, and historical criticism, the
realistic feature had naturally been identified with the literal sense which in turn was
automatically identical with reference to historical truth. But once these thought
currents had had their effect, and the "literal sense" of the stories came to be governed
with a heavy hand by, and logically subordinated to, probable and language-neutral
historical veracity, the reverse would have had to be the case: in order to recognize
the realistic narrative feature as a significant element in its own right (viz. as a story's
making literal rather than allegorical or mythical or some other nonliteral sense
regardless of whether the literal sense is also a reliable factual report) one would have
had to distinguish sharply between literal sense and historical reference. And then
one would have had to allow the literal sense to stand as the meaning, even if one
believed that the story does not refer historically. But commentators, especially
those influenced by historical criticism, virtually to a man failed to understand what
they had seen when they had recognized the realistic character of biblical narratives,
because every time they acknowledged it they thought this was identical with
affirming not only the history-likeness but also a degree of historical likelihood of the
stories. Those who wanted to affirm their historical factuality used the realistic character or history-likeness as evidence in favor of this claim, while those who denied
the factuality also finally denied that the history-likeness was a cutting feature—thus
in effect denying that they had seen what they had seen because (once again) they
thought history-likeness identical with at least potentially true history.

In both affirmative and negative cases, the confusion of history-likeness (literal
meaning) and history (ostensive reference), and the hermeneutical reduction of the
former to an aspect of the latter, meant that one lacked the distinctive category and
the appropriate interpretive procedure for understanding what one had actually
recognized: the high significance of the literal, narrative shape of the stories for their
meaning. And so, one might add, it has by and large remained ever since.

It is well to go a little more closely into the realistic and narrative character of
biblical stories and the sort of analytical procedure appropriate to it, in order to bring
into proper relief the extraordinary situation at the end of the eighteenth century.

The synoptic gospels (for example) are partly narrative in character. They may
also be other things, such as *kerygma*, i.e. the proclamatory rather than didactic shape
of the faith of the early Christian community or, to put the matter another way,

written forms of self-committing statements which make sense by evoking similar dispositions on the part of the reader. In addition of course they are documents of their culture and community, with analogues in the structure of the religious and mythological literature of the Near East and of mankind in general, and not, except perhaps incidentally, records reporting some things that may have happened amidst many that undoubtedly did not. All of this is to say that there are many ways of making sense of these stories. But in part they *are* distinctive narratives, a fact agreed upon by most commentators, including many who did not know what to make of it. The distinctiveness is simply indelible and a significant feature the synoptic gospels share with large sections of the Old Testament. We must keep in mind that it was the stories of Genesis and the gospels which provided the main topics for the development of biblical hermeneutics in this period.

By speaking of the narrative shape of these accounts, I suggest that what they are about and how they make sense are functions of the depiction or narrative rendering of the events constituting them—including their being rendered, at least partially, by the device of chronological sequence. The claim, for example, that the gospel story is about Jesus of Nazareth as the Messiah means that it narrates the way his status came to be enacted. There are, of course, other kinds of stories that merely illustrate something we already know; and there are other stories yet that function in such a way as to express or conjure up an insight or an affective state that is beyond any and all depiction so that stories, though inadequate, are best fitted for the purpose because they are evocations, if not invocations, of a common archetypal consciousness or a common faith. In both of these latter cases the particular rendering is not indispensable, though it may be helpful to the point being made. Part of what I want to suggest is that the hermeneutical option espied but not really examined and thus cast aside in the eighteenth and early nineteenth centuries was that many biblical narratives, especially the synoptic gospels, may belong to the first kind, for which their narrative rendering, in effect a cumulative account of the theme, is indispensable.

This is one of the chief characteristics of a narrative that is "realistic." In that term I include more than the indispensability of the narrative shape, including chronological sequence, to the meaning, theme, or subject matter of the story. The term realistic I take also to imply that the narrative depiction is of that peculiar sort in which characters or individual persons, in their internal depth or subjectivity as well as in their capacity as doers and sufferers of actions or events, are firmly and significantly set in the context of the external environment, natural but more particularly social. Realistic narrative is that kind in which subject and social setting belong together, and characters and external circumstances fitly render each other. Neither character nor circumstance separately, nor yet their interaction, is a shadow of something else more real or more significant. Nor is the one more important than the other in the story. "What is character but the determination of incident? What is incident but the illustration of character?" asked Henry James.[4]

In all these respects—inseparability of subject matter from its depiction or cumulative rendering, literal rather than symbolic quality of the human subject and his social context, mutual rendering of character, circumstance, and their interaction—a realistic narrative is like a historical account.[5] This, of course, does not preclude differences between the two kinds of account. For example, it is taken for granted that modern historians will look with a jaundiced eye on appeal to miracle as an explanatory account of events. Historical accounting, by almost universal modern consent, involves that the narrative satisfactorily rendering a sequence believed to have taken place must consist of events, and reasons for their occurrence, whose connections may be rendered without recourse to supernatural agency. By contrast in the biblical stories, of course, nonmiraculous and miraculous accounts and explanations are constantly intermingled. But in accordance with our definition, even the miraculous accounts are realistic or history-like (but not therefore historical and in that sense factually true) if they do not in effect symbolize something else instead of the action portrayed. That is to say, even such miraculous accounts are history-like or realistic if the depicted action is indispensable to the rendering of a particular character, divine or human, or a particular story. (And, in fact, biblical miracles are frequently and strikingly nonsymbolic).

Finally, realistic narrative, if it is really seriously undertaken and not merely a pleasurable or hortatory exercise, is a sort in which in style as well as content in the setting forth of didactic material, and in the depiction of characters and action, the sublime or at least serious effect mingles inextricably with the quality of what is casual, random, ordinary, and everyday.[6] The intercourse and destinies of ordinary and credible individuals rather than stylized or mythical hero figures, flawed or otherwise, are rendered in realistic narratives. Furthermore, they are usually rendered in ordinary language (mixed style, so called by Auerbach as the language shaping together ordinary intercourse and serious effect). Style and account go together; for example, the parabolic mode of Jesus' teaching integrates extraordinary themes with analogies drawn from workaday occurrences; and it does so in pithy, ordinary talk. Action and passion in realistic narrative illustrate the same principle. Believable individuals and their credible destinies are rendered in ordinary language and through concatenations of ordinary events which cumulatively constitute the serious, sublime, and even tragic impact of powerful historical forces. These forces in turn allow the ordinary, "random," lifelike individual persons, who become their bearers in the crucial intersection of character and particular event-laden circumstance, to become recognizable realistic "types," without thereby inducing a loss of their distinctively contingent or random individuality. (Type, unsurprisingly, is a designation of which Marxist literary critics like to make use, though it is a good question whether they do not, in their interpretive procedure, reduce the randomness of the individual completely to his historical typicality. The suspicion, finally warranted or not, is at least in order when one deals with literary interpretations that are governed by extrinsic ideological considerations. Obviously, however, the notion is not confined to them. The resort to human "type" as a necessary device for making literature convincing is shared by men as different as Aristotle and S.T. Coleridge.[7])

Erich Auerbach suggests that the realistic tradition has persisted through the ebb and flow of its own fortunes in Western literature. But he also sees three historical high points in its development: the Bible, Dante's *Divine Comedy*, and the nineteenth-century novel, especially in France. Biblical commentators have generally agreed that this cumulative, realistic, or history-like narrative feature is characteristic of the Bible, though they have obviously had to deny that it pervades the whole Bible or that it is the sole literary feature even of some of the stories that do indeed exhibit it.

Obviously the Psalms, Proverbs, Job, and the Pauline epistles are not realistic narratives. Also, there are highly stylized rather than realistic features in the description of Jesus and in the sequence chain in the Fourth Gospel. They are not even absent from the more nearly realistic synoptic gospels, where the only immediately evident (but obviously important) chronological continuity is the story of the passion, crucifixion, and resurrection of Jesus. But with all of this conceded, there is still general agreement that cumulative realistic narrative of a very serious rather than low, comical, or idyllic sort is characteristic of the Bible, especially if one compares it to other ancient literature of either sacred or profane character.

Explicitly or implicitly, all of this has long been conceded by commentators, including those of the eighteenth and early nineteenth centuries when, coincidentally, there was at least in England a strong resurgence of serious realistic literature and criticism. But in effect, the realistic or history-like quality of biblical narratives, acknowledged by all, instead of being examined for the bearing it had in its own right on meaning and interpretation was immediately transposed into the quite different issue of whether or not the realistic narrative was historical.

This simple transposition and logical confusion between two categories or contexts of meaning and interpretation constitutes a story that has remained unresolved in the history of biblical interpretation ever since. Were we to pursue our theme into the biblical hermeneutics of the twentieth century, I believe we would find that with regard to the recognition of the distinctiveness of realistic biblical narrative and its implications for interpretation, historical criticism, and theology, the story has remained much the same.

Notes

1   Erich Auerbach, *Mimesis* (Princeton: Princeton Univ. Press, 1968), pp. 48f, 73ff, 194ff, 555. See also Auerbach's essay "Figura" in his *Scenes from the Drama of European Literature* (New York: Meridian Books, 1959), pp. 11–76. Auerbach's are the most illuminating analyses available of the figural or typological procedure. (I use the two terms synonymously in this essay.)

2   Auerbach, *Mimesis*, p. 15.

3   "An Essay on the Allegorical and Literal Interpretation of the Creation and Fall of Man," Conyers Middleton, *Miscellaneous Works* (1752), vol. 2, p. 131.

4   "The Art of Fiction," reprinted in Henry James, *The Future of the Novel*, ed. and introd. by Leon Edel (New York: Vintage Books, 1956), pp. 15f.

5   For discussions of the role of narrative in historical accounts and explanations, see Michael Scriven, "Truisms as the Grounds for Historical Explanation," in Patrick Gardiner (ed.), *Theories of History* (Glencoe, Ill.: Free Press, 1959), esp. pp. 470f; Arthur C. Danto, *Analytical Philosophy of History* (Cambridge: Cambridge Univ. Press, 1965), esp. chs. 7, 10, 11; W. B. Gallie, *Philosophy and the Historical Understanding* (2nd ed., New York: Schocken Books, 1968), chs. 1–5; Louis O. Mink, "The Autonomy of Historical Understanding," *History and Theory* 5 (1), 1966, 24–47, esp. 38ff; I have also been helped on this topic by the unpublished Yale Ph.D. dissertation (1968) of Charles L. Lloyd, Jr., "The Role of Narrative Form in Historical and Theological Explanation."

6   Auerbach, *Mimesis*, p. 44.

7   For the importance of "type" in literary realism of Marxist persuasion, see Georg Lukács, *Studies in European Realism* (New York: Grosset and Dunlap, 1964), p. 6. For Marxist

literary analysis as an "extrinsic" approach to literature, see René Wellck and Austin Warren, *Theory of Literature* (New York: Harcourt, Brace and World, 1956), ch. 9.

(c) Literary Text, Literary Approach: Getting the Questions Straight

Meir Sternberg

> The few, by Nature form'd, with Learning fraught, / Born to instruct, as others to be taught, / Must study well the Sacred Page; and see / Which Doctrine, this, or that, does best agree / With the whole *Tenour* of the Work Divine.
>
> John Dryden, "Religio Laici"

What goals does the biblical narrator set himself? What is it that he wants to communicate in this or that story, cycle, book? What kind of text is the Bible, and what roles does it perform in context? These are all variations on a fundamental question that students of the Bible would do well to pose loudly and sharply: the question of the narrative as a functional structure, a means to a communicative end, a transaction between the narrator and the audience on whom he wishes to produce a certain effect by way of certain strategies. Like all social discourse, biblical narrative is oriented to an addressee and regulated by a purpose or a set of purposes involving the addressee. Hence our primary business as readers is to make purposive sense of it, so as to explain the *what's* and the *how's* in terms of the *why's* of communication.

Posing such a question in the clearest terms is a condition for reasonable and systematic inquiry, rather than a panacea or a shortcut to unanimity. The answers to it would doubtless still vary as well as agree, since the reticent narrator gives us no clue about his intentions except in and through his art of narrative. To reconstruct the principles underlying the textual givens, therefore, we must form hypotheses that will relate fact to effect; and these may well differ in interpretive focus and explanatory power. But even the differences, including those not or not immediately resolvable, would then become well-defined, intelligible, and fruitful. That they are not remarkable for being so in the present state of affairs is largely due to the tendency to read biblical texts out of communicative context, with little regard for what they set out to achieve and the exigencies attaching to its achievement. Elements thus get divorced from the very terms of reference that assign to them their role and meaning: parts from wholes, means from ends, forms from functions. Nothing could be less productive and more misleading. Even the listing of so-called forms and devices and configurations—a fashionable practice, this, among aspirants to "literary criticism"—is no substitute for the proper business of reading. Since a sense of coherence entails a sense of purpose, it is not enough to trace a pattern; it must also be validated and justified in terms of communicative design. After all, the very question of whether that pattern exists in the text—whether it has any relevance and any claim to perceptibility—turns on the question of what it does in the text. Unless firmly anchored in the relations between narrator and audience, therefore, formalism degenerates into a new mode of atomism.

What, then, does the biblical narrator want to accomplish, and under what conditions does he operate? To answer this question, both the universal and the distinctive features of his communication must be taken into account. Those features combine, in ways original and often surprising but unmistakable, to reveal a poetics at work. Whatever the nature and origin of the parts—materials, units, forms—the whole governs and interrelates them by well-defined rules of poetic communication.

To many, Poetics and Bible do not easily make a common household even as words. But I have deliberately joined them together, avoiding more harmonious terms like Structure or Shape or Art in order to leave no doubt about my argument. Poetics is the systematic working or study of literature as such. Hence, to offer a poetics of biblical narrative is to claim that biblical narrative is a work of literature. Not just an artful work; not a work marked by some aesthetic property; not a work resorting to so-called literary devices; not a work that the interpreter may choose (or refuse) to consider from a literary viewpoint or, in that unlovely piece of jargon, as literature; but a literary work. The difference is radical. Far from matched by whim or violence, the discipline and the object of inquiry naturally come together. And if this claim made for poetics sounds either tantamount to or more extreme than the alternatives just mentioned, that only shows how liable it is to misunderstanding even from sympathetic quarters—or perhaps, judging by past experience, especially from sympathetic quarters.

[. . .]

My biblical poetics does, I believe, make a reasonably coherent argument along the lines indicated in the opening paragraphs. But were the points at which it opposes various "literary approaches" of a terminological or even conceptual nature only, my quarrel with them would not go much beyond indicating the moot questions. In the circumstances, the great enemy is not disagreement but darkness, shadowboxing, artificial divisions between traditionalists and innovators, with each side more inclined to differ than to ascertain if and where genuine differences lie. This introductory chapter, I hope, will at least get the issues straight and the lines properly drawn.

Kenneth Gros Louis's "Methodological Considerations" introducing a recent anthology to which he has contributed some fine analyses, may serve as a point of departure. Here are the most basic assumptions[1] supposedly shared by "literary critics of the Bible" myself, alas, included:

1. "Approaching the Bible as literature means placing emphasis on the text itself— not on its historical and textual backgrounds, not on the circumstances that brought the text into its present form, not on its religious and cultural foundations." In short, "our approach is essentially ahistorical" (pp. 14–15).
2. "The literary critic assumes unity in the text" (p. 15).
3. "A literary critic begins by being primarily interested in how a work is structured or organized" (p. 17).
4. "Teachers of literature are primarily interested in the literary reality of a text and not its historical reality," literariness being equated here with fictionality: "Is it true, we ask, not in the real world but in the fictional world that has been created by the narrative?" (p. 14).

5. "The literary reality of the Bible can be studied with the methods of literary criticism employed with every other text" (p. 14).

I am sorry to say that, with the possible exception of the second, I do not share any of these tenets, certainly not as they stand and least of all as a package deal. Nor do I see how this quintet adds up to an approach as distinct from a declaration of independence—the less so since almost all its parts would apply to the study of non-literary texts, and none legitimates the literary study of the Bible in terms other than the critic's choice to exercise it. What, if anything, makes the literary critic an overdue arrival rather than an intruder on the biblical scene? But it may be well to sort out these matters in a more orderly fashion. So the three following sections will examine the cruxes that have generated most of the debate between (and within) the various camps; the fourth will then gather up the threads into a more systematic argument for a functional poetics.

Discourse and Source

To the student of theory, the list just cited will have a familiar ring and carry its own note of warning. The literary approaches to the Bible that would uphold those fiats are for the most part children of the New Criticism, inheriting its emphasis on the direct encounter with the text and, less fortunately, its professions of faith. This explains a good deal. The New Criticism, no longer new except in name, arose in the first quarter of this century (and gained a large following in the second) as a reaction against the excesses of historical scholarship. One of its foremost advocates, looking back on the scene of his youth, describes his own sensational contribution "as a kind of banner, or rallying cry, for those literary theorists who would no longer put up with the mishmash of philology, biography, moral admonition, textual exegesis, social history, and sheer burbling that largely made up what was thought of as literary criticism in academic circles."[2] In preaching and practicing close analysis, with particular reference to the language, the New Critics have rendered an invaluable service to the study of literature. But theirs has remained a movement of reaction, iconoclastic, often extravagant, polemical rather than theoretical, speaking in many voices, raising more problems than it would or could handle, and laying itself open to a variety of charges, with self-contradiction at their head. Not much has survived, except the practical and educational effect.

History, it is said, repeats itself. In the face of a situation that duplicates the "mishmash" and bankruptcy of literary scholarship at the beginning of the century, the New Criticism resurged in the biblical arena. The enemy has remained the same, and so have the issues. But the weapons have already proved ineffective beyond shock tactics in the old campaign and cannot achieve much in the new beyond redirecting attention to the text. For good or for ill, such literary approaches express a reaction, an understandable and timely call for a shift of priorities that overreaches itself and falls short of an adequate countertheory. They advocate the methods and rehearse the manifestoes of the New Criticism, but without duly adjusting them to the theoretical revaluations made since or to the conditions of biblical study or even to their own practice as readers (often shrewd readers) of the Bible. As such, their dismissal of historicism makes an ideological rather than a methodological reorientation: polemics may at best clear the ground but not substitute for a scholarly alternative. At times, indeed, the emphasis laid on the classroom and immediate enjoyment, with the occasional hint that neither requires even a knowledge of Hebrew, gives the impression that the object is rather to save the Bible from the hands of the scholars. Which is not such a bad idea, except that there are hands and hands.

Of this antihistorical bias, the notorious problem of intention affords a miniature. Predictably enough, it heads Gros Louis's list of irrelevancies: "We know, as students of literature, that the author's intention, his goals in writing for his contemporary audience, and his religious convictions, play a small role indeed in literary criticism" (p. 16). One wonders who "we" refers to. So far as this is an empirical matter, it can easily be demonstrated that the overwhelming majority of literary critics have ascribed the greatest importance to the author's intention and that the New Critical attacks only set out and indeed managed to refine the appeal to it. Moreover, if this is a matter of theory, then the question of intentionality has little of its usual bearing.

The affirmation of irrelevance alludes, of course, to Wimsatt and Beardsley's classic attack, "The Intentional Fallacy" (1946). In a retrospect already mentioned, the latter co-author describes it as a "designedly subversive and unpleasantly provoking essay" ("Intentions and Interpretations", p. 188). For all its reaction against the mishmash of scholarship, however, the argument is more moderate than its reputation might suggest. The fallacy actually debunked consists in the reliance on external intention, gathered from the author's psychology or biography or "revelations (in journals, for example, or letters or reported conversations) about how and why [he] wrote the poem—to what lady, while sitting on what lawn, or at the death of what friend or brother."[3]

It follows that biblical study can (indeed cannot but) leave on one side the pros and cons of so-called external intention. About this necessity there is even nothing like the aura of heroism that surrounds the rabbinic choice to the same effect. Though committed to the tenet of the divine authorship of Scripture, the ancient sages flatly dismissed the ruling of a heavenly voice that intruded on their deliberations in its authorial capacity:

> Rabbi Joshua rose to his feet and said: "'It is not in heaven' [Deuteronomy 30:12]." What does "not in heaven" mean? Rabbi Jeremiah said: "The Torah has already been given at Mount Sinai, and we pay no heed to any heavenly voice. . . . " Rabbi Nathan met Elijah and asked him: "What did the Holy One, blessed be he, do at that hour?" Elijah answered: "He smiled and said, My sons have defeated me, my sons have defeated me."
>
> (*Baba Metzia* 59b)

In the absence of heavenly voices, the question does not arise at all, since none of the biblical authors has left journals or letters or any other biographical matter outside the writings themselves. The writers of narrative, with the possible exception of latecomers like Ezra and Nehemiah, have not revealed so much of themselves as their names. Had the Bible been the whole stock and store of world literature, Wimsatt and Beardsley would not have penned their—or at least not this—New Critical manifesto.

As interpreters of the Bible, our only concern is with "embodied" or "objectified" intention; and that forms a different business altogether, about which a wide measure of agreement has always existed. In my own view, such intention fulfills a crucial role, for communication presupposes a speaker who resorts to certain linguistic and structural tools in order to produce certain effects on the addressee; the discourse accordingly supplies a network of clues to the speaker's intention. In this respect, the Bible does not vary from any other literary or ordinary message except in the ends and the rules that govern the forms of communication. Minor differences apart, however, this is quite compatible with the original Wimsatt and Beardsley position and a variety of others, including the fairly recent pragmatics or speech-act theory. The more so because "intention" no longer figures as a psychological state consciously or unconsciously translated into words. Rather, it is a shorthand for the structure of meaning and effect supported by the conventions that the text appeals to or devises: for the sense that the language makes in terms of the communicative context as a whole.

With the interpreter removed from the Bible's sociocultural context, intention becomes a matter of historical reconstruction. And to this some would object on grounds familiar to students of literary and biblical hermeneutics alike: for example, that we cannot become people of the past or that to equate meaning with the original author's intention and his audience's comprehension is to impoverish the text. The problems raised and tangled by this influential minority view, itself far from homogeneous, are too complicated for me to go into here.[4] Nor, despite appearances, is a systematic examination really vital, considering the biblical text and its current scholarly ambiance—the New Critical spirit included. With these provisos let me say, quite simply, that the hard antihistorical line in hermeneutics is too condescending and inconsistent (in varying combinations) to make a viable theory.

It is condescending, not to say arrogant, because it still remains to demonstrate that in matters of art (as distinct from their abstract articulation) the child is always wiser than its parent, that wit correlates with modernity, that a culture which produced the Bible (or the *Iliad*) was incapable of going below the surface of its own product or referring it to the worthwhile coordinates of meaning. (The naive assumption turns grotesque when preached by some of the poorest readers that the Bible has known.) Even worse is the equation of author's and audience's meaning. What text the author made and what sense a reader or public made of it are always distinct in principle; and the Bible's practice brilliantly drives home this variance in that it provides, as we shall see, for all levels of reading through a "foolproof" composition.

Nor is this line consistent. The claim that one has the right to fashion and in effect invent the text anew as one pleases would at least enjoy the virtue of unassailability. But nothing short of this will do. From the premise that we cannot become people of the past, it does not follow that we cannot approximate to this state by imagination and training—just as we learn the rules of any other cultural game—still less that we must not or do not make the effort. Indeed, the antihistorical argument never goes all the way, usually balking as early as the hurdle of language. Nobody, to the best of my knowledge, has proposed that we each invent our own biblical Hebrew. But is the language any more or less of a historical datum to be reconstructed than the artistic conventions, the reality-model, the value system? Given their interpenetration, moreover, where does the linguistic component end and the nonlinguistic begin? Or how does one draw the line between the aesthetic shape of cyclical or symmetrical plot and the "religious" belief in God as the shaper of plot? If the whole network of past conventions is empirically unattainable, then dividing the indivisible is even theoretically untenable.

Once the choice turns out to lie between reconstructing the author's intention and licensing the reader's invention, there is no doubt where most of us stand. This does not exclude the literary approaches that seem to profess otherwise or even vacillate in practice. ("*Conscious* art" is one of their favorite phrases.) There remain differences, of course, but regarding emphasis more than substance. And no wonder they should arise, since the practical difficulties of reconstructing the Bible's code, though they hardly amount to a doctrinal objection, are quite troublesome and procedure still requires considerable attention.

"The age of the text makes no difference. It is from the story of David and Bathsheba itself that we infer its poetics, just as we do with *Lolita*, regardless of what its author or the modern theory of literature may say."[5] This generalization has gained some notoriety by being stood on its head. When the first sentence is torn out of context to make a better slogan or target, indeed, it sounds like a call for setting the text free from the prison-house of history. Actually, by an ironic variation on authorial intention, almost the opposite was claimed *and* demonstrated.

The text's autonomy is a long-exploded myth: the text has no meaning, or may assume every kind of meaning, outside those coordinates of discourse that we usually bundle into the term "context." The appropriate coordinates are historical, and the main trouble with the historical approaches to the Bible is their antihistorical performance. Not even the literary critics that they oppose have subjected the biblical text to so many anachronistic (and often bizarre) norms of unity, social conduct, world order, convention, value judgment. This is largely due to the failure to appreciate the striking systematicity of biblical narrative, which enables the interpreter to derive its poetics from its reticent practice, with some aid (but no dictation) from such extratextual clues as have survived. Historical and literary inquiry thus fall into an unhappy symmetry. In their concern with whatever frames or antecedes the text, the historians tend to overlook the chief body of historical evidence that awaits proper interpretation. In their concern with interpretation, the critics tend to overlook the extent to which their goal involves and commits them to the quest for frames and antecedents. It is for a closer interworking of text and context that the rest of this section, and much of this chapter, will argue.

To begin with the "literary" side, I have already noted that language exposes the Achilles' heel of anti-reconstructionism; and the Bible offers the best case in point. Nobody is likely to regard the grammar and semantics of biblical Hebrew as irrelevant to a literary approach. But are they given "in" the text? Surely not, for the Bible presupposes rather than makes explicit its language system, as every message does its code. To determine the meaning of a word, the syntax of an utterance, the possibilities of stylistic variation, the dividing line between idiomaticity and metaphorical force, the interpreter turns to the linguist and/or turns linguist himself, conducting his own analysis of the underlying system. We thus engage in a historical reconstruction that delimits what the writer could have meant against the background of the linguistic knowledge that, even in artful manipulation, he must have taken for granted. Doing so is evidently as far from reducing the text to extrinsic factors—as if it were a storehouse of verbal data—as it is from the making of a new language at will. Nor is it anything like a compromise between the extremes, but simply the normal business of interpretation.

As with linguistic code, so with artistic code. With a biblical metaphor, for instance, the question whether it is stereotyped or newly coined, dead or live, obviously will make an enormous difference to its meaning and effect. But it has quite a similar (and often more easily determinable) bearing on a compositional measure: dialogue, repetition, omission, ring pattern, temporal ordering, narrative stance. Let us take the last of these, which not only bears clear marks of "literariness" but also must be appraised by all readers, because the sense of the information presented depends on the rules and authority of its presentation. For these reasons, as it happens, I was drawn to this issue from the outset and can now retrace some of the inevitable steps in the process of grappling with it.[6]

Given the biblical narrator's access to privileged knowledge—the distant past, private scenes, the thoughts of the dramatis personae, from God down—he must speak from an omniscient position. This establishes authority but not yet originality. Is the stance of omniscience due to tradition or innovation? The formal systematicity of the narrative from Genesis to Kings still leaves this question open, and the critic has no choice except to turn to the literature of the ancient Orient. There he will deduce the conventional nature of the technique from the extant practice of Sumerian, Babylonian, Egyptian, Canaanite storytelling and, with the net cast even wider, Homeric epic too. The end of the road? No, because a structural convention, just like a verbal cliché, may be revitalized by being put to new uses or into new contexts. The most promising place to look for these is the Bible's original world view: unlike all pagan deities, God is truly and exclusively all-knowing. Does this epistemological novelty in the sphere of world order extend to the epistemology and operation of point of view in the narrative? Does the monotheistic article of faith give a new bearing to the inherited rule of omniscience? Is it, for example, that the narrator assumes omniscience because he could not otherwise do justice to an infallible God and impress on the reader, by appropriate suppressions, his own fallibility? Since the Omniscient inspires his prophets, moreover, does the narrator implicitly appeal to the gift of prophecy, so as to speak with redoubled authority as divine historian? And does this storytelling posture link up with another biblical novelty—human usurpation of knowledge right at the beginning of history?

Whatever the answers—and all evidently bristle with significance—they must also reckon with the fact that books like Nehemiah and (partly) Ezra assume the form of eyewitness narrative. Does that mean that the biblical writer, like his modern or for that matter ancient Egyptian counterpart, can choose between two opposed strategies of narration? If so, his choice of persona would in either case take on new import and require explanation by reference to the specific goals and exigencies that determined it in each book. But is it accidental that the instances of limited ("first-person") narration are all very late writings, which find their equivalents only in apocryphal and gospel literature? Is their divergence from the omniscient perspective, then, a measure of artistic choice or of historical change in the Bible's storytelling? Again, the answers can wait. All that needs emphasizing is that for literary analysts to deal responsibly with a compositional issue par excellence they must engage in a poetic valuation of a whole range of so-called extrinsic evidence: from the art of the Oriental tradition through the premises of monotheistic theology to the dating of the biblical canon. Milieu, world view, history of formation—all untouchables prove indispensable to literary study as such.

Notes

1   For the full list see Kenneth R. R. Gros Louis, "Some Methodological Considerations," in *Literary Interpretations of Biblical Narrative II*, ed. Kenneth R. R. Gros Louis with James S. Ackerman (Nashville: Abingdon, 1982) pp. 14–15.

2   Monroe C. Beardsley, "Intentions and Interpretations: A Fallacy Revived" in *The Aesthetic Point of View*, ed. Michael J. Wreen and Donald M. Callen (Ithaca and London: Cornell University Press, 1982) p. 188.

3   W. K. Wimsatt and Monroe C. Beardsley, "The Intentional Fallacy," in *The Verbal Icon* (New York: Noonday, 1958) p. 10.

4   For a vigorous critique see E. D. Hirsch, *The Aims of Interpretation* (Chicago: University of Chicago Press, 1976).

5   Meir Sternberg and Menakhem Perry, "The King Through Ironic Eyes: The Narrator's Devices in the Story of David and Bathsheba and Two Excursuses on the Theory of the Narrative Text," *Hasifrut* 1 (1968): 262–91 (p. 292).

6   The following example draws on a variety of detailed inquiries into the epistemology of biblical narrative: for example, the narrator's knowledge versus the reader's in "The King Through Ironic Eyes" and "Between the Truth and the Whole Truth in Biblical Narrative: The Rendering of Inner Life by Telescoped Inside View and Interior Monologue" (*Hasifrut* 29 [1979] 110–46); knowledge and judgment in "Delicate Balance in the Rape of Dinah: Biblical Narrative and the Rhetoric of the Narrative Text" (*Hasifrut* 4 [1973] 193–231); the rhetoric of divine omniscience and the opposition of God's to man's knowledge in "The Structure of Repetition in Biblical Narrative: Strategies of Informational Redundancy" (*Hasifrut* 25 [1977] esp. 124–28, 134–37).

(d) The Critic as Kabbalist: Harold Bloom and the Heretic Hermeneutic

Susan A. Handelman

> Hebraism and Hellenism—between these two points of influence move our world. At one time it feels more powerfully the attraction of one of them, at another time of the other; and it ought to be, though it never is, evenly and happily balanced between them.
>
> —Matthew Arnold

> He who is willing to work gives birth to his own father.
>
> —Kierkegaard

The wars between Jews and Greeks, so long fought on Mediterranean and European soil, have come, finally, to America.[1] American literary theory, so long under the sway of the New Critics who came to prominence in the 1930s and 1940s, has been radically transformed in the postwar period. The character of the New Critics, led by such figures as John Crowe Ransom, Allen Tate, Robert Penn Warren, and Cleanth Brooks, was predominantly Southern, agrarian, conservative, and Christian. And T. S. Eliot's neo-Catholicism had left its mark on them all. The New Critical Gospel of formalism—that one must pay attention solely to the formal structures of the words on the page—might be summed up in the famous phrase that Wimsatt and Beardsley took from Archibald MacLeish: "A poem should not mean but be."[2]

The New Critics intended to do away with the sloppy excrescences of "meaning" produced by such unhealthy considerations as, in Ransom's terms: "personal regis-trations, which are the declaration of the effect of the art-work upon the critic as reader," "historical studies," "linguistic studies," "moral studies," "any other special studies which deal with some abstract or prose content taken out of the work."[3] Criticism must be "scientific," "precise," "objective," respectful of the autonomy of the work of art. Underlying this vision, of course, is a Hellenistic dream of logic, order, form, and lucidity.

For thinkers like the New Critics, the intellectual movements that have swept through Europe since World War II—existentialism, phenomenology, psycho-analysis, structuralism, deconstructionism—are anathema. Yet while the Yale University English Department harbored the New Critics Warren, Brooks, and Wimsatt, it has also more recently nurtured Harold Bloom, Geoffrey Hartman, Paul de Man, and J. Hillis Miller. And this new generation of Yale scholars has been one of the main conduits through which these recent trends in European literary theory—especially Freud-Lacan-Derrida—have entered the United States. The Yale school has met with much resistance from the American literary heartland, and has been resented as a kind of literary mafia, trying to infiltrate and dominate the plain, honest, objective tradesmen of literary criticism. To the plain folk of criticism, the baroque abstraction of these strange imported European fashions—the attempt to erase the distinction between literary commentary and literature itself, and to subvert the traditional hierarchies of author–text–critic–student—seem arbitrary, irrational, willful, and esoteric.

G. Douglas Atkins points out that the Yale school so threatens and unsettles because its underlying aim is, in his words, to "de-Hellenize" literary criticism.[4] Atkins rightly contends that our contemporary battle of the books is not between ancients and moderns, but between Hebrews and Hellenes. The plainstyle critics, as he calls them, have an implicit faith in logic, reason, and order, i.e., in the classic Hellenistic view of things; the Yale school questions the very possibility of order and unity and turns toward a speculative, visionary, and hermeneutic style. Atkins discerns that the Yale critics' "opposition to Hellenism and the classical logos derives from notions strikingly similar to Hebraic and biblical thought."[5] The Yale critics are by no means unaware of these Hebraic tendencies. Bloom is perhaps their most striking representative. With Bloom, the heretic hermeneutic attains full systematic theoretical self-realization. Bloom focuses his efforts on something we have barely touched upon in the authors studied so far: the will-to-power of interpretation.

Commentary and exegesis are not innocent. Intensively studying Bloom can bring us to a final fuller definition of the heretic hermeneutic, and to uncover the dynamic that links Rabbinic thought to its prodigal sons.

From the Visionary to the Revisionary Company

> Everyone who now reads and writes in the West . . . is still a son or daughter of Homer. As a teacher of literature who prefers the morality of the Hebrew Bible to Homer, indeed who prefers the Bible aesthetically to Homer, I am no happier about this dark truth than you are.[6]

Chances are that the majority of readers whom Bloom so familiarly addresses here do not in fact consider their Homeric heritage a "dark truth." Bloom, however, has openly declared poetic and critical warfare against the Greeks: in the past decade, he has produced a series of books in which his explicit aim has been to "de-idealize" literature and literary criticism. One of Bloom's central axioms is that making and reading poetry is not a highly refined, humanistic endeavor, but a fierce Oedipal struggle, an open warfare conducted between poets and their precursors, as well as readers and their poets: a battlefield in which the combatants are all engaged in trying to create some kind of original space for themselves. The processes of reading and writing well are not, to Bloom, "polite": "Reading is always a defensive process . . . is defensive warfare."[7]

> Strong poets . . . should always be condemned by a humanist morality, for strong poets are necessarily perverse . . . perverse in relation *to the precursor*. . . .
>
> If the imagination's gift comes necessarily from the perversity of the spirit, then the living labyrinth of literature is built upon the ruin of every impulse most generous in us. So we are wrong to have founded a humanism directly upon literature itself, and the phrase "humane letters" is an oxymoron. . . . the strong imagination comes to its painful birth through savagery and misrepresentation.[8]

Reading is a defensive act of battle against a precursor text, a necessary misreading.

For such interpretive battles, Bloom arms himself—not with Aristotle and Plato, classical logic or New Critical formalism; he looks not to the idealizing tendencies of Northrop Frye, nor to the despiritualized theories of structural linguistics, nor the nihilistic aspects of deconstructionism—but to Jewish mysticism, to Kabbalah.

Bloom has written over a dozen books in the past two decades, beginning with studies of the major figures of the romantic era: *Shelley's Mythmaking; The Visionary Company: A Reading of English Romantic Poetry; Blake's Apocalypse; Yeats;* and *The Ringers in the Tower.* But in 1973, Bloom published the first of four theoretical books, which have proposed startling new theories of criticism: *The Anxiety of Influence* (1973); *A Map of Misreading* (1975); *Kabbalah and Criticism* (1975); *Poetry and Repression: Revisionism from Blake to Stevens* (1976); and even a novel—*The Flight to Lucifer: A*

Gnostic Fantasy (1979). Though some might not think it too large a step from Shelley to Gnostic fantasies, Bloom's path from the visionary to the revisionary company has been long and involved.

Perhaps the best place to begin is *The Anxiety of Influence*, in which Bloom first fully articulated his new, radical "manifesto for an antithetical criticism," before he discovered Kabbalah. The key to this work, I think, is Bloom's quotation from Kierkegaard: "He who is willing to work gives birth to his own father."[9] Like Freud and Derrida, Bloom is obsessed with the question of origins.

At the root of Bloom's anxiety in *The Anxiety of Influence* is the despair over not having been self-begotten, at not being one's own father; for the question of birth is ultimately an attempt to overcome death. The primal wound for Bloom is to have been "thrown" into a world not one's own; the primal passion is to reverse one's fall by recreating that world in one's own image, by recreating and rebegetting oneself, thereby becoming one's own father, capturing the power of giving life. Hence the themes of *Anxiety* are belatedness, revisionism, discontinuity, subversion, interpretive reversal—themes that inform all of Bloom's work (and Freud's as well). And hence Bloom considers Milton's Satan "the greatest really Modern or Post-Enlightenment poet in the language. . . . Satan like any strong poet, declines merely to be a latecomer. His way of returning to origins, of making Oedipal trespass, is to become a rival creator to God-as-creator. He embraces Sin as his Muse, and begets upon her the highly original poem of Death, the only poem that God will permit him to write."[10]

In Bloom's vision, poetry is a conflict with God, an attempt at rival divination. The modern poet is heroic because like Satan he refuses the "incarnation of God's son," refuses the creation as ordered by God. Poetic election is a kind of curse, then, because it means belated and ultimately impossible rebellion against one's powerful precursor poet, who functions as God, as it were: a rebellion against culture, history, tradition, all of which exert tremendous influence over the new poet, blocking his own creativity. "The Sphinx, as Emerson saw, is nature and the riddle of our emergence from nature, which is to say that the Sphinx is what psychoanalysts have called the Primal Scene. But what is the Primal Scene for a poet as poet? It is his Poetic Father's coitus with the Muse. There he was begotten? No—there they failed to beget him. He must be self-begotten, he must engender himself upon the Muse his mother. . . . To beget here means to usurp."[11]

The process of this attempted usurpation—Bloom's analysis of the development of the new poet, or *ephebe* as Bloom calls him—becomes the pattern for all acts of reading (and especially the heretic hermeneutic), for essentially what the new poet does in order to clear space for himself is to misread his precursor. Intrapoetic relations are a struggle between fathers and sons, as in the classic Freudian family romance; and the necessary misreadings are at the same time (Freudian) defensive maneuvers of psychic survival. The reader's encounter with the text is no different, in effect, than the new poet's encounters with his predecessor texts, and this encounter is governed by the same Bloomian laws: "The influence relation governs reading as it governs writing, and reading is therefore a miswriting, just as writing is a misreading. As literary history lengthens, all poetry becomes verse-criticism, just as all criticism becomes prose-poetry."[12]

The boundaries, then, between commentary and text dissolve—the ephebe is as much a commentator on previous poems as is the critic. Both in effect are exegetes, grapplers with a Text, which each tries to appropriate for himself in a manner wherein the belated commentary somehow gains power over and appropriates the power of the initial Text, reversing the roles so that, in Wordsworth's famous phrase, "The child is father to the Man." Though Bloom's academic specialty was indeed romantic poetry, finally it is not Wordsworth who guides him along the path to rebirth, but more ancient intimations of immortality—the great revisionist interpretive systems of Gnosticism and Kabbalah: "An implied anguish throughout this book is that Romanticism, for all its glories, may have been a vast visionary tragedy, the self-baffled enterprise not of Prometheus but of blinded Oedipus, who did not know that the Sphinx was his Muse."[13]

The Revisionary Ratios

What, then, are the laws that govern the anxiety of influence, the birth and development of a poet, a reader, a commentary, a text—terms that all become interchangeable in the process? In his first attempt to "map" the process in *Anxiety of Influence*, Bloom proposed six "revisionary ratios."[14] I paraphrase them as follows:

1. *Clinamen (swerve)*. Bloom takes this term from Lucretius, who defines it as the *swerve* of atoms that allows for change in the universe. In the universe of poetry, it is the swerve or movement *away* from the precursor by the new poet: a corrective movement asserting that the precursor has been accurate only up to a point, and that the ephebe will now move in the direction the precursor failed to follow.
2. *Tessera (completion and antithesis)*. This term is taken from the ancient mystery cults, where it denoted a token of recognition. In Bloom's schema, this is a further development of clinamen. Here the new poet "completes" his precursor by retaining the precursor's terms but meaning them in another sense, taking them further.
3. *Kenosis (emptying out)*. The word comes from Paul, for whom it referred to Jesus' emptying himself out of his own godhood, his humbling himself to become human. In this phase, the later poet, so to speak, empties himself of his own imaginary divinity, seeming to cease being a poet. However, this act simultaneously empties the precursor as well, and is subtly another maneuver for power, which Bloom calls a "breaking-device similar to the defense mechanisms our psyches employ against repetition—compulsions; *kenosis* then is a movement towards discontinuity with the precursor."[15]
4. *Daemonization*. This is a Neoplatonic term for the movement which is the new poet's attempt to set up a Sublime counter to that of the precursor. He seeks a power in the parent–poem that in his view does not belong to the precursor, but lies just beyond him.
5. *Askesis*. This term, taken from the practice of pre-Socratic shamans such as Empedocles, denotes a movement of self-purgation towards solitude, in which

the later poet yields up part of himself in order to separate himself from others, including the precursor. But in so doing, he simultaneously effects an *askesis*, a truncation of the precursor's poem.

6.   *Apophrades* (the Athenian unlucky days when the dead returned to inhabit their former homes). In this final state, the later poet returns from his solipsism to open his poem to the precursor, but in a new way—out of strength rather than weakness—and the effect is such that the later poet appears to have written the earlier poet's work.

At first glance, these terms might appear confusing and difficult. Bloom has continually revised them in his subsequent three books, refining his concepts but nevertheless keeping their basic structure. In *A Map of Misreading* he elaborates the insight, barely touched upon in *The Anxiety of Influence*, that "the Revisionary Ratios have the same function in intrapoetic relations that defense mechanisms have in our psychic life."[16] He matches the Freudian schema of defense mechanisms to each of his revisionary ratios: reaction formation to clinamen; reversal and turning against the self to tessera; undoing to isolation, regression to kenosis, repression to daemonization; sublimation to askesis; and introjection and projection to apophrades.[17] Bloom then adds a third set of parallels, matching each revisionary ratio and psychic defense with the classical rhetorical tropes. Clinamen, for example, corresponds to the trope of irony, tessera to synecdoche, kenosis to metonymy, daemonization to hyperbole, and askesis to metaphor.

After writing *The Anxiety of Influence*, Bloom came across the work of Gershom Scholem, the famed scholar of Jewish mysticism. Bloom claims that he then realized he had been working on a Kabbalistic model all along, and proceeds in *A Map of Misreading* and *Kabbalah and Criticism* to further complicate his already baroque schema by matching up the revisionary ratios, psychic defenses, and tropes with a fourth parallel series: terminology from the kabbalistic theory of creation. But we are getting ahead of ourselves.

It is not yet necessary to examine Bloom's overt advocacy of Jewish mysticism as an interpretive paradigm to perceive his Rabbinic tendencies; they seem to me already evident in *The Anxiety of Influence*. Bloom is unusual only in being more acutely aware of and unembarrassed about his dependence on and exploitation of theological models than others. Part of the way I want to read Bloom is through *his* relationship to *his* precursors—that is, through his *own* revisionary ratios. He, along with Paul, with Freud, with Derrida, belongs to the tradition of heretic hermeneutics I began to define in the previous chapter. The kinds of displacements and discontinuities, the need to slay Moses and give the New Law, to rewrite origins and usurp the father, to make the son one with the father—above all through acts of revisionary interpretation—ties all these figures together. The heretic hermeneutic as a complex of identification and displacement is I think, ultimately what Bloom maps in his misreadings.

That Bloom locates this subversive revisionary impulse in Kabbalah and Gnosticism, instead of within Rabbinic tradition, itself is a misreading we will later have to investigate; for, in essence, the Rabbinic tradition contains within it, even in the legalistic writings, the mechanism for its own interpretive reversals, a mechanism clearly at work, for example, in the famous Talmudic passage about R. Eliezer's dispute with the sages. In that passage, the majority of Rabbis force God to say, "My sons have defeated me, my sons have defeated me." In fact, one of the keys to understanding what some perceive as the bewildering excesses and fantastic nature of Rabbinic thought—especially in its midrashic form—is precisely the concept of revisionism. And it is Bloom who has given us our most profound insight into revisionist philosophy and psychology.

The Revisionary Warfare of Christian Exegesis

Indeed, Bloom's revisionary ratios may also be the most accurate guide to the interpretive warfare between Jews and Christians which we traced earlier. The movements of clinamen and tessera correspond to the Christian striving to correct and complete Hebrew Scripture. The New Testament declares emphatically that it is *new* and the Hebrew Scriptures now *old;* that is, though chronologically prior, they are no longer complete, authoritative, primary. The birth and figure of Jesus constitutes a decisive *swerve* that serves to complete the precursor text. As Bloom writes, tessera is the "later poet's attempt to persuade himself and us that the precursor's Word would be worn out if not redeemed as a newly fulfilled and enlarged Word of the ephebe."[18] Jesus comes, the Gospel of Matthew assures us, not to destroy but *to fulfill* the law (Matt. 5:17). The incarnation of the poet in Bloom's schema corresponds to the incarnation of the new Christian god. Clinamen and tessera depend on an act of "poetic misprision" (a necessary misreading and misinterpretation of the precursor text). And so, the apostle Paul tells us, the Greeks and Jews know not whereof they speak, no longer possess the true meaning, the correct interpretation. With Jesus only is the veil rent, and the true sense of the Bible now made manifest; without Jesus, all is yet darkness. To the Jews, of course, this is all extreme misreading of the text.

Kenosis and daemonization work to repress the memory of the dead.[19] The very term *kenosis* is taken from Paul to describe Jesus' *emptying out* his divinity to become human, an action which simultaneously empties the "Old" Testament of its divinity. Its words are now superseded by the centrality of the Incarnational Event. This act also isolates the ephebe and undoes the father-precursor. In Bloom's succinct formula, echoing Freud: "Where the precursor was, there shall ephebe be, but by the discontinuous mode of emptying the predecessor of *his* divinity, while appearing to empty himself of his own."[20]

Further following Bloom's schema, the New Testament sets up its own "counter-sublime" to the Hebrew vision as part of the attempt to repress its precursor; the New Testament constructs an entirely new image of the divine and relation of divinity to the world. But complete repression of the precursor is never possible, according to Bloom. Using Freud's insight that tradition is "equivalent to repressed material in the mental life of the individual," Bloom claims that daemonization allows the ephebe to "augment repression, by absorbing the precursor more thoroughly into tradition than his own courageous individuality should allow him to be absorbed."[21] In parallel fashion, the Old Testament is not discarded, but absorbed, and seen as a foreshadowing of the New Gospel.

The next movement, of askesis, or purgation, involves a kind of struggle for sublimation, and an ensuing solipsism. Askesis is the "contest proper, the match-to-the-death with the dead." (Though Bloom, in his own revisionary reading of his precursor Freud, asserts that poetic sublimation is not—as Freud would have it—the sublimation of the *sexual* instincts, but of the *aggressive* instincts.) With energy turned on himself, the new poet wrestles with his precursors to attain a new solitude and independence. Using Freud's insight from *The Ego and the Id* that sublimation is related to identification with the object, but a distorted identification which can even transform into the opposite, Bloom sees poetic sublimation as a kind of "self-curtailment which seeks transformation at the expense of narrowing the creative circumference of precursor and ephebe alike."[22] This movement involves a certain sacrifice and estrangement from the precursor and all other selves in its harsh egocentric expression of the new poetic will.

But finally comes apophrades, the return of the dead, the reincorporation of the precursor. For strong precursors can never be entirely repressed, nor do they completely die, but maintain a power over their successors, returning to haunt them. This final revisionary ratio accomplishes a last inversion by which the former becomes later, and the later earlier. The tyranny of time is reversed: "The triumph of having so stationed the precursor in one's own works, that particular passages in *his* work seem not to be presages of one's own advent, but rather to be indebted to one's own achievement, and even (necessarily) to be lessened by one's greater splendor. The mighty dead return, but they return in our colors, and speaking our voices." The ephebe fulfills "his precursor's prophecies by fundamentally re-creating those prophecies in his own unmistakeable idiom."[23] Similarly, in the Christian revision of the Hebrew Scriptures, the "Old" Testament remains, but now speaking the Christian message, its glory lessened.

The interpretive tradition of *figura*, which became so important for New Testament writers and the Church Fathers, is obviously relevant here. The central idea is that the figures of the Old Testament somehow foreshadow, predict, and are fulfilled in the New Gospel. Bloom is well aware of this tradition of Scriptural interpretation and its influence on secular literature. He is, however, quite critical of it and argues against its use and advocacy by Auerbach, Tertullian, and the Christian interpreters.

> The basic principle of poetic misprision is: No later poet can be *the fulfillment of any earlier poet*. He can be the reversal of the precursor, or the deformation of the precursor, but whatever he is, to revise is not to fulfill. Unlike *figura*, poetic misprision must be seen as the troping or erroring it is. But so, of course, contra Auerbach and Tertullian is *figura*, and it is surely time to see *that figura* was always a revisionary mode, and so a lie against time. The Old Testament is far too strong, as poetry, to be fulfilled by its revisionary descendent, the self-proclaimed New Testament. "New" means "Early" here and "Old" means "Late" and precisely what the New Testament lacks in relation to the Old is a transumptive stance, which is why the New Testament is a weak poem.
>
> We may wonder whether the idea of figura was ever more than a pious self-deception.[24]

The idea of figura is piously self-deceiving because in defining the connection between two terms, texts, poets, or Scriptures, it postulates a harmless and idealized relation, wherein the second term is the canonical, fulfilling truth; the first term merely signifies itself and foreshadows the second. Figura pretends that this relation is free of anxiety, power-play, misreading, will and counterwill, the agonies of history, and the anxieties of creation.

> The New Testament purports to "fulfill" the Old. Blake came, he sometimes thought, to "correct" Milton. Eduard Bernstein, founder of the modern science of "revisionism," anticipated many after him supposedly seeking to fulfill and correct Marx, a double quest since undertaken with respect to Freud by Jung and many heresiarchs after him. All revisionists, however irreligious, are anagogists, though frequently shallow in their anagogy. Spiritual uplift too frequently is exposed as the drive towards power over the precursors, a drive fixed in its origins and wholly arbitrary.[25]

Bloom's intense hostility towards the idea of fulfillment is perhaps a reflection of the Jewish mentality of exile, which we also noted in Freud and Derrida. There is truth, somehow, only in deferment, mediation, interpretation, yearning, agon—but there can be no fulfillment: the Messiah has not come. At the same time, Bloom as revisionist must, by his own terms, also be an anagogist; with whom is his struggle for power—what original father, precursor text?

Bloom comes to the critical arena to bring not peace, but a sword, and to expose the power struggle of poetic and critical relations and the illusion of fulfilling idealizations:

> Poets no more fulfill one another than the New Testament fulfills the Old. It is this carry-over from the tradition of figural interpretation of Scripture to secular literature that has allowed a curious over-spiritualization of texts canonized by poetic traditions. Since poets also idealize themselves, and their relations to other poets, there is already an excessive self-regard in poetic and critical tradition. Modern theories of mutually benign relations between tradition and individual talent, including those of T. S. Eliot and Northrop Frye, have added their idealizations, so that it becomes an enormous labor to clear away all of this noble obfuscation.[26]

Bloom's intent is to again de-idealize the conventional view of literature and criticism. Eliot and Frye are Bloom's obvious targets here, and Bloom places them in an essentially Christian tradition of Scriptural interpretation.

Notes

1   Matthew Arnold, *Culture and Anarchy*, ed. J. Dover Wilson, (1869; reprint ed., Cambridge: Cambridge Univ. Press, 1960), p. 130.

2   "Ars Poetica" by Archibald MacLeish, quoted in W. K. Wimsatt and Monroe C. Beardsley, "The Intentional Fallacy," 1954; reprinted in *20th Century Literary Criticism*, ed. David Lodge (London: Longman's, 1972), p. 335.

3   John Crowe Ransom, "Criticism, Inc.," *The World's Body* (1938; reprint ed., Baton Rouge: Louisiana State Univ. Press, 1968), reprinted in Lodge, *20th Century Literary Criticism*, pp. 235–36.

4   G. Douglas Atkins, "Dehellenizing Literary Criticism," *College English* 41 (1980): 769.

5   Ibid., 769–70, 776.

6   Harold Bloom, *A Map of Misreading* (New York: Oxford Univ. Press, 1975), p. 33.

7   Harold Bloom, *Kabbalah and Criticism* (New York: Seabury Press, 1975), p. 104.

8   Harold Bloom, *The Anxiety of Influence* (New York: Oxford Univ. Press, 1973), pp. 85–86.

9   Bloom, *Anxiety*, p. 56.

10   Bloom, *Map*, p. 37.

11   Bloom, *Anxiety*, p. 37.

12   Bloom, *Map*, p. 3.

13   Bloom, *Anxiety*, p. 10.

14   Ibid., pp. 14–15.

15   Ibid., p. 14.

16   Ibid., p. 88.

17   *Map*, p. 84.

18   *Anxiety*, p. 67.

19   Ibid., p. 122.

20   Ibid., p. 91.

21   Ibid., p. 109.

22   Ibid., pp. 122, 119.

23   Ibid., pp. 141, 152.

24   Bloom, *Poetry and Repression* (New Haven: Yale Univ. Press, 1976), pp. 88–89.

25   *Map*, p. 83.

26   *Poetry*, p. 95.

Chapter 2

Ways of Reading

INTERPRETATIONS OF THE BIBLICAL text vary considerably. Those who read literally, or at least those who seek to make a literal level of meaning primary, are likely to come to very different conclusions than writers who seek broader inspiration in the images that appear throughout Scripture. The readings of the fundamentalists so often associated with interpretative literalism are very different than the readings provided by the Romantic poet William Blake, for example, who hones in on Scripture's imaginative resources and treats its extensive use of symbolism as a call to explore the theological imagination further. But it would be wrong to think that our mode of reading is a straightforward choice between the literal and the figurative. Religious believers can read figuratively (when interpreting references to Jesus as the Lamb of God or the Lion of Judah, to take just two obvious examples) and non-religious writers can be literal in their reading (as in the literal sense of being born again pursued in Angela Carter's *The Passion of New Eve* (1977)). Furthermore, there are many other ways of reading, from the legalistic to the playful, from the mythological to a modern historical-critical method focussed on factual reconstruction, and from readings that emphasize textual unity to those that are more interested in fractures or fissures.

Faced with a multiplicity of ways of reading, it can seem impossible to determine whether the biblical text shapes our reading or whether our ways of reading are prior to our study of Scripture. Both claims are true at some level and the formal work of hermeneutics or 'the science of interpretation' emerged in the eighteenth century (through thinkers such as Friedrich Schleiermacher) in an effort to think this question through more systematically. Hans-Georg Gadamer's contribution to hermeneutics in the middle of the twentieth century was to think of interpretation as a dynamic act rather than one with clearly defined and mutually agreed starting points. But the notion of interpretation as dynamic rather than fixed does not entail relativism, and the question of why we read in the way that we do remains crucial for understanding some of the different ways in which scholars have thought about the relationship between literature and the Bible. In the 1970s and 1980s a number of literary scholars encouraged us to think about the Bible as literature. Critics such as Robert Alter sought to read the Bible as they would any other literary text, with an emphasis on the formal particularities of language and narrative.[1] Whilst such readings were productive, reading the Bible as literature sometimes relied on too narrow an understanding of what literary reading should involve. As such, the ways of reading pursued were alien to many biblical scholars and sometimes hostile to other approaches to the Bible, such as devotional reading or the use of Scripture in systematic theology. The limitations of reading the Bible as literature were also evident in the choice of Scriptural texts: it was easy to praise the poetic power of the Hebrew language when it came to discussing Genesis and the Psalms but it was altogether harder to see the literary value of the list of names that dominates texts such as I Chronicles.[2]

Although reading the Bible as literature is restrictive in some ways, English Literature is a wide-ranging discipline and its interpretative methods are more diverse than the modes of reading that were so influential a few decades back might have suggested. In this chapter we consider four powerful and provocative examples. The first is an extract from Stephen Prickett's *Words and the Word: Language, Poetics and Biblical Interpretation* (1986), Prickett's influential reading of the Bible is shaped by his understanding of eighteenth- and nineteenth-century European literature, culture and philosophy. He starts his opening chapter on 'Ways of Reading the Bible' by taking issue with the presumption of those who approach the Bible as a transparent text that transcends the culture in which it is understood. Prickett questions the stated goal of the translators of the Good News Bible, 'to understand correctly the meaning of the original' and points instead to the cultural presuppositions of all readers and translators, presuppositions that shape meaning by presuming Divine Revelation to be simple or complex, focussed on the People of God or addressed to all. To illustrate his point, Prickett considers the ambiguity of the passage in I Kings 19: 8–12, where Elijah encounters the voice of God. Stripped of contextual details, the passage describes 'Elijah's long-delayed meeting with God' as 'a revelation so ambiguous as to resist any modern attempt to reduce it to a direct simple statement.' As Prickett goes on to observe: 'Herein lies the translator's problem.'

Although parts of the Christian community of readers have privileged the clarity of the biblical message, other parts of that community have been more willing to embrace Scripture's capacity to mean different things at different times. This is one of the ideas to emerge in David Lyle Jeffrey's argument in *People of the Book: Christian Identity and Literary Culture* (1996) for the importance of the Church as a reader of the biblical text. In the extract included here, Jeffrey turns his attention to a practice of reading known as typology. One of the ways in which early Christian readers sought to rethink the texts of their Jewish heritage in the light of Christ was through the Apostle Paul's understanding of 'God's actions in the shaping of Israel's history' as *typoi*, instances that prefigure God's future work. On this reading, Jeffrey explains, Paul described Adam as 'the prototype of all fallen humanity . . . the *typos*, the "figure" or "type of the one who was to come"'. Typological reading was extremely popular among Christian readers for many centuries and it has attracted criticism for the narrowness of an interpretative vision that tends to read everything in terms of Christ. Typology has also been accused of a disregard for the writings of a pre-Christian past, in which Christ is not seen as the focal point of human history. Yet Jeffrey's account of the rationale behind typological interpretation suggests that this way of reading is more aware than one might think of the passing of time. Indeed, typology enables new readings: aware that particular historical meanings pass away, it seeks to revitalize meaning in the light of subsequent events.

Although Christian typological reading is more sophisticated than some critics have implied, it is not without its difficulties. One problem is the way in which it situates its own practice of 'reading in quest of the spirit', to quote Jeffrey, as a freer alternative to an allegedly legalistic (Jewish) reading that is chained to the letter of the law. Our next extract, by Emmanuel Levinas in *Beyond the Verse* (1994), shows this common Christian characterization of Jewish thought to be misplaced: the Jewish tradition's concern with the letter of the law has been much more fertile than Christian detractors have acknowledged. Levinas reveals this by turning to a Jewish way of reading known as Midrash, in which close attention to the minute details of the text opens up discussion among a community of interpreters. For Levinas, midrashic reading shows us how 'the statement commented upon exceeds what it originally wants to say': discussion of the smallest of textual details creates a communal space in which different viewpoints can be considered and through which the text can be rethought endlessly. Each act of vigilant attention to the original text can be seen as part of the 'inimitable' and vital nature of Jewish commentary on the Law rather than an act of close-minded legalism.

Equally insistent on the indeterminate proliferation of historic Jewish reading is Geoffrey Hartman, whose interest in the historic practice of Midrash intersects with his own experiences of the theoretical developments in literary criticism during the second half of the twentieth century. The extract from Hartman included here, 'The Struggle for the Text', was originally included in an influential collection of essays on *Midrash and Literature* that Hartman edited with Sanford Budick in 1986. In a characteristically rich, thoughtful and layered essay, Hartman turns to the account of Jacob wrestling with an angel in Genesis 32 as the starting point for his discussion. Describing the midrashic commentaries on this biblical passage as a reminder to 'secular literary studies of the richness and subtlety of those strange rabbinic conversations', Hartman not only explores the connection between Jacob's wrestling and our own struggles to lay hold of textual meaning but also thinks through the tensions and proximity between sacred and secular reading, between the reading of the Rabbis and the approach of modern literary theorists who typically do not see themselves as writing within a religious realm. Although Hartman's essay does much to illuminate our interpretative struggle for the meaning of the biblical text, it eschews neat solutions, concluding: 'The accreted, promissory narrative we call Scripture is composed of tokens that demand the continuous and precarious intervention of successive generations of interpreters, who must keep the words as well as the faith.'

Notes

1   See, for example, Alter's *The Art of Biblical Narrative* (New York: Basic Books, 1981), *The Art of Biblical Poetry* (New York: Basic Books, 1985) and, as joint editor with Frank Kermode, *The Literary Guide to the Bible* (Cambridge, MA: Harvard University Press, 1987).

2   For a wonderful 'literary' reading of I Chronicles, see Salena Godden's response to this biblical text in *Sixty-Six Books: 21st-Century Writers Speak to the King James*

Bible (London: Oberon Books, 2011). By refusing to limit themselves to a narrow sense of the literary, Godden and the other writers who respond to the biblical texts in this collection find more imaginative space for their work than those who operate strictly within the parameters of an approach to the Bible *as* literature.

Further Reading

Cunningham, Valentine, *Reading After Theory* (Oxford: Wiley-Blackwell, 2002)

Gadamer, Hans Georg, *Truth and Method* (London: Continuum, 2004)

Jasper, David, *A Short Introduction to Hermeneutics* (Westminster: John Knox Press, 2004)

Knight, Mark, *An Introduction to Religion and Literature* (London: Continuum, 2009)

Loughlin, Gerard, *Telling God's Story: Bible, Church and Narrative Theology* (Cambridge: Cambridge University Press, 1996)

Moore, Stephen D. and Yvonne Sherwood, *The Invention of the Biblical Scholar: A Critical Manifesto* (Minneapolis, Fortress Press, 2011)

Schwartz, Regina, ed., *The Book and the Text: The Bible and Literary Theory* (Oxford: Basil Blackwell, 1990)

Watson, Francis, *Text, Church and Truth: Redefining Biblical Theology* (Edinburgh: T. & T. Clark, 1998)

Wood, Ralph, *Literature and Theology* (Nashville: Abingdon Press, 2008)

Wright, T. R. *Theology and Literature* (Oxford: Basil Blackwell, 1988)

(a) Ways of Reading the Bible: The Problem of the Transparent Text

Stephen Prickett

> *Belinda:*   Ay, but you know we must return good for evil.
> *Lady Brute:* That may be a mistake in the translation.
>
> (Vanbrugh, *The Provok'd Wife*, 1697, I.i.)

We start with two quotations – both about the Bible. First Coleridge:

> I take up this work with the purpose to read it for the first time as I should any other work, – as far at least as I can or dare. For I neither can, nor dare, throw off a strong and awful prepossession in its favour – certain as I am that a large part of the light and life, in which and by which I see, love, and embrace the truths and the strengths co-organised into a living body of faith and knowledge . . . has been directly or indirectly derived to me from this sacred volume, – and unable to determine what I do not owe to its influences.[1]

Our second quotation is from a far more respectable source in its own time than was Coleridge's *Confessions of an Inquiring Spirit* in 1849: the Preface to the *Good News Bible* of 1976:

> The primary concern of the translators has been to provide a faithful translation of the Hebrew, Aramaic, and Greek texts. Their first task was to understand correctly the meaning of the original . . . the translators' next task was to express that meaning in a manner and form easily understood by the readers . . . Every effort has been made to use language that is natural, clear, simple, and unambiguous.

Now an observer from another culture – let us say, the man on the Peking omnibus – might be forgiven for assuming that the tone of breezy confidence exuded by the translators of the *Good News* in 1976 came from their having understood and resolved the problem that concerned Coleridge. Where he found himself hesitant, tentative, and uncertain, they, carried forward by the progress of scholarship in the intervening 150 years, could be knowledgeable and precise. The fruits of the modern sciences of archeology, anthropology, and linguistics, together with a more sophisticated notion of history than the early nineteenth century, had, he might suppose, at last given an authoritative biblical text. Yet, of course, our baffled Peking everyman would once again have been deceived by the inscrutable Occident.

The thrust of Coleridge's *Confessions* becomes clearer if we recall that the work was originally entitled 'Letters on the Inspiration of the Scriptures', and that it was his nephew and editor Henry Nelson Coleridge who substituted the personal and subjective title of the published version. Coleridge's hesitancy was in the face of a particular and very complex dilemma: that of cultural relativity in perhaps its most extreme form. His difficulty lay not merely in the enormous problems inherent in translation from one cultural world to another, separated by at least two thousand years, but also in the fact that this cultural relationship was apparently asymmetric. He was uncomfortably aware how many of his basic cultural assumptions might be derived from the Bible in ways that, by definition, were inaccessible to impartial investigation. He had come to consciousness within a society which, while it was clearly very different from anything to be found in the Old or New Testaments, had taken many of its most basic presuppositions from them. The very system of criteria by which he might try to read the Bible as he would 'any other work' was already enmeshed by an almost unravellable tangle of likeness and unlikeness extending from the simplest equivalents down to the most complex unconscious premises. The dual metaphors of the passage, organically connected by a striking Coleridgean ellipsis: 'The light . . . by which I see', the 'life by which I . . . love', suggest the scope of his problem. 'Light' and 'life' are not objects of consciousness or perception, they are their *conditions*. We do not 'see' light, we see other things by it; we are not 'conscious' of life; it is the ground of consciousness – a ground peculiarly resistant to analysis by autopsy – as Wordsworth had succinctly put it, 'we murder to dissect'.

In short, Coleridge perceives the problem of cultural relativity in terms as much existential as analytic: the totality of a cultural world is one that can only be experienced as a participator, from the inside. 'In the Bible,' he admits a few pages later in the *Confessions*, 'there is more that *finds* me than in all other books put together'.[2] There is, and can be, no impartial observer. Hence his final inability to 'determine' what he did 'not owe to its influences' is not so much a disarming admission of failure, perhaps to be solved in due course by the advance of scholarship, as a staking-out of the limits of human enquiry.

By contrast, the translators of the Bible Society's *Good News Bible* appear to be afflicted by no such inhibiting doubts. Their appointed task 'to understand correctly the meaning of the original', though undoubtedly difficult in places, is in their estimation by no means impossible – given the aids of the various sciences hypothesized by our mythical observer, and given also, they would probably feel, the aid of the Holy Spirit, which had providentially ensured that the Bible *was* fully translatable into all languages: a process that could only enhance rather than diminish our understanding of the treasures encoded in the original Hebrew and Greek. Such confidence is, it would seem, rooted in a belief in the text itself as an objective entity over and above any debilitating niceties of cultural relativity and academic debate. Hence their commitment to conveying the 'correct meaning' of the original in 'language that is natural, clear, simple, and unambiguous'. As a gloss on this approach a member of the Bible Society has described the *Good News Bible* as being for 'the unsophisticated' or 'average reader' who 'is likely to be grateful rather than offended at being delivered from theological subtleties', arguing that since God 'stooped to the level of human language to communicate with his people' it was the translators' task to set forth the 'truth of the biblical revelation in language that is as clear and simple as possible'.[3] The *text* has a 'meaning' that is finally independent of our cultural presuppositions.

Yet Coleridge's problem has a way of persisting. Take for example, a well-known story from the Elijah cycle. I quote from the *Authorized Version* of 1611:

> And he arose, and did eat and drink and went in the strength of that meat forty days and forty nights unto Horeb the mount of God. And he came thither unto a cave, and lodged there; and, behold, the word of the Lord came to him, and he said unto him, What doest thou here, Elijah? And he said, I have been very jealous for the Lord, the God of hosts; for the children of Israel have forsaken thy covenant, thrown down thine altars, and slain thy prophets with the sword: and I, even I only, am left; and they seek my life, to take it away. And he said, Go forth, and stand upon the mount before the Lord. And, behold, the Lord passed by, and a great and strong wind rent the mountains, and brake in pieces the rocks before the Lord; but the Lord was not in the wind: and after the wind an earthquake; and after the earthquake a fire; but the Lord was not in the fire: and after the fire a still small voice.
>
> I Kings xix, 8–12

This is such a well-known story that it is easy to miss how enigmatic and puzzling it becomes once we start looking beyond the bare and stark biblical narrative. We are simply not given any answers to the 'obvious' circumstantial and naturalistic questions. What, for instance, *was* this 'fire'? Was it some kind of electrical storm, or was it a bush fire? Was it connected with the earthquake? What did it burn? Similarly, what was this 'voice'? What is the status of this third-person narrative, anyway? Since Elijah was alone, do we conclude that this is his own account? There is no answer to these and a host of related questions. Stripped of what Erich Auerbach calls 'fore-ground' detail[4] the story concentrates exclusively on its central theme: that of Elijah's encounter with God.[5] And it is here that we begin to suspect this bare account of extreme complexity. Elijah's long-delayed meeting with God turns out to be not at all what we are told he had expected. Instead, his original assumptions are discon-firmed by a revelation so ambiguous as to resist any modern attempt to reduce it to a direct simple statement. Herein lies the translator's problem.

Translation, especially from one period of time to another, is not just a matter of finding the nearest equivalents for words or syntactic structures. In addition it involves altering the fine network of unconscious or half-conscious presuppositions that underlie the actual words or phrases, and which differentiate so characteristically the climate of thought and feeling of one age from that of another. Thus according to G. B. Caird, the biblical translator always 'runs the double risk either of modernising or of archaising: to modernise is to ignore the culture gap of many centuries and to read the Bible as though it were contemporary literature; and to archaise is to exag-gerate the culture gap and to ignore the similarities between the biblical world and our own'.[6] Caird's dilemma, we may suppose, is one common to many modern translators – and our story from the Elijah cycle is apparently a case in point.

What the prophet hears after the earthquake, the wind, and the fire may be liter-ally translated from the Hebrew into English as 'a voice of thin silence'.[7] As we have seen, the King James *Authorized Version* of 1611 renders this curious oxymoron into English as the well-known 'still small voice'. Bearing in mind that in Elizabethan English 'small' could still mean 'thin' (as in Wyatt's 'her arms long and small' or the Shakespearean 'small beer') this is a remarkably accurate translation. In so far as it is obscure and ambiguous, it is an obscurity and ambiguity that is at least faithful to the original. Something very odd had apparently happened to Elijah.

The modern English translations, however, seem to be quite unanimous in *rejecting* any ambiguity or oddity perceived in the original. In the *Good News Bible* what Elijah hears is no more than 'the soft whisper of a voice'. The *New English Bible* hope-fully tries reducing the 'voice' to a metaphor, translating it as 'a low murmuring sound', while the Catholic *Jerusalem Bible* outdoes the nascent naturalism of its Protestant rivals by eliminating all suggestion of speech with its 'sound of a gentle breeze' – which is a fair translation of the Vulgate's '*Et post ignem sibilis aurae tenuis*' ('and after the fire, a thin whistling sound of the air'). *Aura* refers literally to motion of the air – either wind or breath according to context. For an age with a typological cast of mind, the associations of the 'breeze' with the Holy Spirit would have been irresistible. The Hebrew word for 'wind' in this passage corresponds to the Greek word for 'spirit' in the Septuagint and the New Testament[8] and so what Elijah hears is made conveniently to prefigure its antitype of the Holy Spirit in the Gospels and the rushing wind of Pentecost. Yet such a chain of associative thinking, almost second-nature until the early nineteenth century, is lost in the modern context. It is interesting to speculate, therefore, why both the translators of the *New English Bible* and the Bible Society, supposedly unhampered by the mistranslation of the Latin tradition, should have been almost as eager as their Catholic peers to produce an implicitly naturalistic reading rather than follow the mysteriously suggestive Hebrew – an impressively accurate translation of which already existed in English.

Part of the answer clearly lies in the cultural milieu of the new translations. A noticeable feature of modern English that increasingly separates it from the critical sensibility of its past is an intolerance of ambiguity. We have come to expect that narrative will convey its own frame of reference so that we know, almost at once, for instance, whether we are reading what purports to be 'fact' or 'fiction' and adjust our mental sets accordingly. Writers who mix their genres are apt to leave us uneasy. Explanations may only operate at one level of our experience. We need to know whether Elijah's theophany was visionary or miraculous – whether the 'voice' is to be understood as 'internal', an event presumed to be *within* Elijah's own mind, or 'external', producing a phenomenon in nature to be detected by the presence of a witness. These distinctions between 'outer' and 'inner', or 'natural' and 'supernatural', are not, of course, biblical categories and the *Authorized Version*'s 'still small voice' should prevent us from applying them to Elijah's mysterious experience. Yet the *New English Bible* offers us no choice: we are given the 'low murmuring sound' as an apparently *natural* if not immediately identifiable phenomenon. There is nothing peculiar or odd about low murmuring sounds, after all. They are as 'natural' as earthquakes, winds, and fires, if somewhat less noisy. If any ambiguity remains, it is only whether that 'murmuring' is a metaphor (as in 'murmuring breeze') or a literal voice – an altogether arbitrary ambiguity which, as we have seen, is quite foreign to the original. (So *that's* what the sound was: it was just a gentle breeze: no problems with miracles now; no theophany either!) After these, the *Good News Bible* seems positively pietistic in suggesting that what Elijah heard might, after all, have been speech, but its 'soft whisper' is as naturalistic as the other two, and to the secular ear has a conspiratorial or even sexy flavour. Not one of these three major modern translations manages to suggest an inherent peculiarity about the event that might indicate a quite *new* kind of experience. Indeed, it is precisely that oddity or paradox in the original text that the modern translators, themselves responding to the unstated assumptions of the scientific revolution, found either untranslatable, or, more probably, unacceptable. Since our distinctions between 'inner' and 'outer' are un-biblical categories (so the argument appears to run) we can only be 'modern' by treating the whole story at one level: it must be made *either* miraculous *or* natural. The modern mind cannot have an event that does not fit snugly into one of the two categories. Yet such rationalism would seem to strike right at the heart of the original story. Though no record survives of the seventeenth-century translators' attitude to this particular passage, we know from the notes of John Bois, who was both a translator and a member of the final revision committee for part of the New Testament, that he and his committee were careful in general to preserve textual ambiguity. Of the word 'praise', which might refer either to Jesus or the church members, in I Peter i, 7, he comments, 'We have not thought that the indefinite sense ought to be defined.'[9] In this, the King James translators may well have had an eye on the rival Catholic translators of the English *Rheims* and *Douai* Bibles (New and Old Testaments respectively) who had attacked the Protestants for mollifying hard places, whereas they themselves, they claimed, 'religiously keep them word for word, and point for point, for fear of missing or restraining the sense of the holy Ghost to our phantasie . . .'[10] Protestant and Catholic translators alike in the seventeenth century were under no doubt that oddities in the Hebrew or Greek texts were there for a divinely ordained purpose.[11] In contrast, Professor Kenneth Grayston, one of the translators of the *New English Bible*, has described their brief in terms very similar to those set forth by the *Good News* panel:

> We have conceived our task to be that of understanding the original as precisely as we could (using all available aids) and then saying again in our native idiom what we believed the author to be saying in his.

'And so,' he continues, 'in equivocal passages, the translators had to come off the fence and say "we think it means this". In ambiguous passages they had to write out the meaning plainly, and in obscure passages, to refrain from reproducing nonsense in translation.'[12] Interestingly, the possibility that something original and altogether new in human experience might be emerging into words in this (or similar) 'ambiguous' passages is not one that Grayston is altogether blind to. Rather, he firmly shuts his eyes to it. That the language of 'Spenser, Sidney, Hooker, Marlowe and Shakespeare' was a richer denser thing than his own he freely admits – but the poetic density of the *Authorized Version* is attributable not to a greater richness of *content*, but to an altogether different and apparently separable thing he calls 'style':

> The *New English Bible* does not compete with the *Authorized Version*, certainly not in language and style: this is not a period of great writers equal to Spenser, Sidney, Hooker, Marlowe and Shakespeare. Modern English, it seems to me, is slack instead of taut, verbose and not concise, infested with this month's cliché, no longer the language of a proud and energetic English people, but an international means of communication. And 'means of communication' gives the game away: it seems to me a repository for the bad habits of foreigners speaking English. This is how we must speak if people are to listen and grasp what we say.[13]

This belief that religious experience, and the historic record of mankind's deepest questionings and insights, can only be adequately described today in the slack, verbose and cliché-ridden language of international communication would be disconcerting if it were not – by Grayston's own admission – so evidently self-defeating. How far it is possible, in the words of the *Good News Bible's* Preface, 'to use language that is natural, clear, simple, and unambiguous', when the Bible is *not about* things that are natural, clear, simple, and unambiguous? or for the linguistically-enfeebled modern theologians struggling on the *New English Bible* to 'write out the meaning plainly' of what to the taut and concise translators of the seventeenth century was essentially ambiguous and obscure? The answer – in so far as Grayston seems to perceive that this question exists – appears to be 'that the *Authorized Version* was a translation made by men who knew far less than we know'[14]: in short, a matter of the textual and archeological progress correctly supposed by our mythical but puzzled observer on the Peking omnibus. Yet in this instance Grayston's hermeneutical confidence hardly satisfies.

What is quite clear is that the paradoxical 'voice of thin silence', which is the true manifestation of Yahweh, does not belong to the same associative 'set' as earthquakes and the rest. Ancient Hebrew, we are told, had no word for (and therefore no concept of) 'nature': the normal progression of the seasons were seen as being as much the result of God's direct action as the whirlwind that whisked Elijah to heaven.[15] As a result there was no concept of 'the miraculous' either. The relationship between man and his environment was fundamentally different.[16] Yet it is nevertheless clear that there is an essential discontinuity between the old cyclical world of nature-mysticism or 'primal participation' (as expressed in the cult of Baal) and the world of meaningful change, and therefore of History, into which Yahweh was perceived as bringing his people.[17] Let us concentrate on this ambiguous discontinuity for a moment.

The account of Elijah's experiences on Horeb is given a very specific and apparently historical setting. After the rout and slaughter of the prophets of Baal, Jezebel the Queen has threatened his life, and Elijah, believing himself to be the sole survivor of the faithful, has fled to Horeb. The full force of the dramatic disconfirmation that follows depends on our recognizing that Horeb is traditionally associated with Sinai, the 'mountain of the Lord', where Moses himself had encountered God before the burning bush. Elijah had come to Horeb with certain expectations precisely because of that sense of history that was already, in Israel, distinctively the mark of men of God. Before the assembled prophets of Baal he had already vindicated Yahweh in pyrotechnics – proving once again the power of the God who had traditionally manifested himself by fire.[18] Now he had come to receive the divine revelation for which he believed he had been preparing himself. What followed was the more unexpected. Paradoxically, his notion of Yahweh was disconfirmed by a greater display of natural violence than any yet. But Yahweh is *not* a fire God. His presence, when at last it is revealed, is experienced as something mysteriously apart from the world of natural phenomena that had been in such spectacular convulsions. Elijah's own categories are overthrown. What comes is a simple question: 'What doest thou here, Elijah?' He had come expecting one thing and found another – entirely different. To begin with, his own report of the situation turns out to be untrue: there are, apparently, yet seven thousand in Israel who have not bowed the knee to Baal.[19] Elijah is told to return and organize what amounts to two separate *coups d'état*. Hazael is to be made king of Syria, and Jehu King of Israel. History is yet again to be shaped by revelation, just as long before, Moses had been sent back from Horeb by God to lead his people out of Egypt. Finally – and ominously – Elijah is ordered to appoint his own successor.

At every level the ambiguous discontinuity persists. Any attempt at 'explaining' the contrast between the fire and the 'voice of thin silence' is in danger of losing that sense of an immediate but unstated connection between the two that is emphasized even by the very act of dissociation. Yahweh is not a fire God – nor one of winds and earthquakes – yet from whom, if not from him, did these things come? Moreover, what about those modern categories in which, it is true, we are culturally conditioned to think? Are we to interpret Elijah's experience as a 'miracle' (which would, for instance, link it even more closely with the parallel story of Moses and the burning bush (Exodus iii, 1–17), associated with the same place) or are we to understand it as a 'vision' (in the same category, perhaps, as Isaiah's vision of the Lord in the Temple when he, too, is purged by fire (Isaiah vi))? Can we, instead, dispense with the supernatural altogether, as the modern translators unanimously seem to believe, and interpret it as soft whispers in the night, or the wind on the heath? The Hebrew holds us poised at every level between two different kinds of event that cannot, and *must* not, be told in any other way without destroying the meaning – just as Kierkegaard discovered in *Fear and Trembling* that the story of Abraham and Isaac could not be 'interpreted' and re-told. The whole effect of Elijah's mysterious experience seems to be to deny, *and* simultaneously affirm, certain connections. Thus Yahweh *is*, and *is not*, a God of natural phenomena (a paradox more familiar under the theological terms 'immanence' and 'transcendence'); revelation is both 'miraculous' and 'natural'; God is concerned with both the individual and the shaping of history. The story seems to insist that at each level these two modes are both completely discontinuous and yet inseparable.

Notes

1   S. T. Coleridge, *Confessions of an Inquiring Spirit*, 2nd edn, 1849, p.9.
2   Coleridge, *Confessions*, p, 13.
3   Letter to the Editor of *Theology*, May 1978.
4   Erich Auerbach, *Mimesis*, Princeton University Press, 1953, Ch. 1, pp. 3ff.
5   That the story is self-evidently 'mythological' in this restricted literary sense of carrying a particular weight of meaning, does not, of course, imply anything about its historical factuality. The Tangshan earthquake of July 1976, the year of Mao's death, in China, for instance, was preceded by a display of natural phenomena almost identical to those described here, and, according to a witness, Dr Jocelyn Chey, was followed by an absolutely unearthly stillness without any sound of living creature or movement of the elements.
6   G. B. Caird, *The Language and Imagery of the Bible*, Duckworth, 1980, p. 2.
7   I am grateful to Professor Sten Stenson for this translation. See also Aharon Wiener: 'The Hebrew words "*kol dammanah dakkah*" are usually taken to mean "gentle breeze" or "quiet voice", occasionally also "shrill whistling". They are accordingly interpreted either as a spiritualisation of Elijah's image of God, as a lesser theophany, in which the Divine is hardly perceptible, or as an expression of the demonic aspect of God. However the literal translation of the text, "small voice of silence", expresses as a *coincidentia oppositorum* the *mysterium tremendum et fascinons* of Elijah's theophany.' 'The Talmud', he adds, 'regards the "*kol dammanah dakkah*" as "soundless stillness".' (*The Prophet Elijah in the Development of Judaism*, Routledge, 1978, p. 14.)
8   Alan Richardson (ed.), *A Theological Word Book of the Bible*, S.C.M. Press, 1950, pp. 234 ff.
9   Ward Allen (ed.), *Translating for King James*, Allen Lane, The Penguin Press, 1970, p. 89.
10   A. W. Pollard, *Records of the English Bible*, Oxford University Press, 1911, p. 308. The Catholic translators of the period were no less tolerant of ambiguity and fully prepared to cite the Greek as well as the Vulgate. I Peter ii, 2, they rendered by 'As infants even now borne, reasonable, milke without guile desire ye', commenting, 'We do so place *reasonable*, of purpose, that it may be indifferent both to infants going before, as in our Latin text: or to milke that followeth after, as in other Latin copies and in the Greeke . . .' (Ward Allen, *Translating for King James* ibid.)
11   The fifteenth-century German translator, Nicholas von Wyle, had been even more uncompromising, insisting that even errors should be faithfully transcribed. See George Steiner, *After Babel: Aspects of Language and Translation*, Oxford University Press, 1976, p. 262.
12   Kenneth Grayston, 'Confessions of a Biblical Translator', *New Universities Quarterly*, vol. 33, no. 3, Summer 1979, p. 288.
13   Ibid., p. 287.
14   Ibid., p. 286.
15   See H. Wheeler Robinson, *Inspiration and Revelation in the Old Testament*, Oxford University Press, 1962, p. 34.

16   The most stimulating discussion of this changing relationship for me is to be found in Owen Barfield's *Saving the Appearances*, New York, Harcourt Brace, 1957, culminating in a discussion of this passage on p. 114. Whether Israel's withdrawal from primal participation in the natural world was fundamentally similar to that of the evolution of other societies, or, as Barfield convincingly argues, fundamentally different, is not important to my argument at this point, though, of course, it does have a very profound influence on how we interpret the Elijah story.

17   See, for instance, Claus Westermann, 'The Interpretation of the Old Testament', tr. Dietrich Ritschl, *Essays on Old Testament Hermeneutics*, ed. Westermann, (English tr. ed. J. L. Mays, Richmond, Va., John Knox Press, 1966), p. 44; or Martin Buber, *The Prophetic Faith*, N.Y., Harper Torchbooks, 1960, p. 46.

18   Illustrating how this is one of a group of polemical stories against Baal-worship, Leah Bronner writes: 'Ugaritic sources indicate that Baal was not only the god of rain, vegetation, and fertility, but also controlled fire and lightning.' The great drought (I Kings, xvii–xviii) was thus one attack on Baal's efficacy; so also were 'the various Biblical passages where Elijah enlisted the aid of fire to prove that God rules over all these forces, aimed to undermine a popular belief that Baal had dominion over this element'. (*The Stories of Elijah and Elisha*, Leiden, E. J. Brill, 1968, pp. 55 and 62.) See also, Wiener, *The Prophet Elijah*, p. 7.

19   A point that appealed greatly to Augustine. See *De Civitate Dei*, xvii. 22; *Enn. II in Ps., c. 5; En. II in Ps. 30*, s. 2, c. 7.

(b) Scripture upon Scripture

David Lyle Jeffrey

> *Secret things belong to the Lord our God, but the revealed things belong to us and to our children forever, to observe all the words of this law.*
>
> DEUTERONOMY 29:29

> *These things happened to them to serve as an example, and they were written down to instruct us, on whom the ends of the ages have come.*
>
> 1 CORINTHIANS 10:11

Christian identity, it may fairly be said, is still derivatively Jewish. As such, it is inextricably bound up with book culture. The formative elements in Judaism are well known: the giving of the Law to Moses at Sinai, God's repeated commandments to Moses his *nabi'* and to successive generations of prophets to speak or write (Deut. 1:1–5; Isa. 8:1ff.; Ezek. 2:9–3:4; Amos 7:14–15; cf. Rev. 1:10–11, etc.) and the subsequent creation of book-inscribed rather than exclusively oral traditions of law, history, and poetry. Even by themselves these features have been sufficient to guarantee the central authority of the Book in Jewish cultural identity.

When the prophets were sent to call Israel back to repentance and faithfulness, they did so by repeated reference to the authority of the Scriptures. In the annals of the four evangelists Jesus does the same, even intensifying the relationship of righteousness to "right reading" of Scripture. He does this by proposing a way of reading Scripture that surpasses the merely literal observance of the text with an insistence upon "fulfillment" of the Scripture, real conformity to the spirit or intent of the text, an ultimate holiness of thought as well as deed before God and the world. In the four evangelists, but especially in the prologue to John's Gospel, Jesus himself is the perfected fulfillment of all that the law and the prophets have spoken, the promised full expression of God's divine Authorial intent for the world, the Word from the Beginning now made flesh in his Incarnation — effectively the Living Book of God. All written Scripture, past and present, the evangelists suggest, testifies to him.

Paul in his letters and the early church generally echo and advance this dramatic escalation of the place of "the Book" in Christian identity to the point where in the minds of some outsiders it can finally seem, as it did to Muhammed, that Christians had become, perhaps most self-consciously, the "People of the Book."[1]

[. . .]

Saint Paul

For later writers of the New Testament and the whole of subsequent Christendom the gospel which told of Christ's coming was not, like much of what the prophets told their hearers, to such a striking degree "bad news." Rather, the call of Jesus to repentance, so like that of the prophets in many respects, was joined by virtue of the resurrection to an unprecedented emphasis on the *teudah*, the optative word of comfort. For Christians therefore — those to whom Paul could write "If Christ be not resurrected . . . then is your faith in vain" (1 Cor. 15:12–14) — Christ's coming permitted a new order of hope: the Gospel accounts, like the many verbal accounts which ran around the Mediterranean world, were truly to their hearers "good news" (Gk. *euangelion;* Lat. *evangelium*).

Not that this "good news" was unthreatening to established patterns of religious thinking. At its very least, what we might call the "literary theory of Jesus" involved a radical proposal for re-reading the entire Hebrew Scriptures. In this reading, which effectively does become the theory or hermeneutic of St. Paul and the early church, the whole of the Hebrew Scriptures suddenly becomes a *prolepsis*, a text preliminary to another text, dependent for closure and full meaning upon that which is now to come. At one level of imaginative integration — the prophetic anticipation of the messianic Son of David and Israel's final redemption — it might be argued that this re-reading had been inscribed from the beginning in Scripture's text. However, another heuristic reading of Scripture could be racked with frustration and offense. Plainly, by Jesus' death upon the cross, his resurrection, and his ascension, the long anticipated "last days" were seen by his followers as having now only begun, with hope for final closure projected into an indefinite future. At the very least, this dimmed the hope that in Jesus there was for their present oppression any political or social "solution" available.

Yet there is more: for those within the Jewish community who came to see Jesus as the promised Messiah, that the Scriptures could now be seen as the historic and textual preparation for the final and perfect work of God in history made of the Hebrew Scriptures the literary record of their "Old Covenant," or "Old Testament" as it came to be called. For the followers of Jesus — unlike most of their fellow Jews — this designation was not pejorative, for they saw the Old Testament, on the authority of

Jesus, as necessarily foundational to the "New Testament in his blood" (Matt. 26:28; Mark 14:24; Luke 22:20; 1 Cor. 11:25). Jesus' own reading of the "Old Testament" thus became the pivot upon which all subsequent Christian reading of the Bible would turn: it provided a single coherent scheme for understanding history and the text, with himself as the focus. As R. T. France observes:

> Such a use of the Old Testament was not only original; it was revolutionary. It was such that a Jew who did not accept it must violently oppose it. It is not surprising that a community founded on this teaching soon found itself irreconcilably divided from those Jews who still looked forward to a Messiah.[2]

New Testament writers after the evangelists — Paul, John, Peter, James, Jude, and the unknown author of the Epistle to the Hebrews — exhibit no significant dependence upon contemporary Jewish ways of reading the Old Testament. They are rather — and emphatically — dependent upon the literary theory of Jesus.[3] This remains true for the early church and, with modifications, for the Western church generally.[4]

The basis of this "literary theory of Jesus" is what has come to be called *typology*, from Paul's original use of the Greek word *typos* "as a term for the prefiguring of the future in prior history."[5] Paul's novel employment of the word seems to derive from its normative use in referring to a "blow" by a hammer or molding instrument; *typos* could signify a struck image such as is produced by the imprint of a mold or seal — the obverse, so to speak, being the finished coinage for which the mold was designed.[6] For Paul, God's actions in the shaping of Israel's history are such *typoi*, the molds or seals from which the life of Jesus and of the church is pressed out in the fabric of the world: in his first letter to the Corinthians Paul writes,

> I do not want you to be unaware, brothers and sisters, that our ancestors were all under the cloud, and all passed through the sea, and all were baptized into Moses in the cloud and in the sea, and all ate the same spiritual food, and all drank the same spiritual drink. For they drank from the spiritual rock that followed them, and the rock was Christ.
>
> (1 Cor. 10:1–4)

Paul goes on to say that "these things occurred as examples for us" (v. 6), and as such *typoi* "they were written down to instruct us, on whom the ends of the ages have come" (v. 11).

This notion of the *typos* as example is further reaching than the English translation here suggests. In Romans Paul will describe Adam, the prototype of all fallen humanity, as the *typos*, the "figure" or "type of the one who was to come" (5:14) — that is, Christ. Christ is the obverse of Adam, so to speak:

> For since death came through a human being, the resurrection of the dead has also come through a human being; for as all die in Adam, so all will be made alive in Christ.
>
> (1 Cor. 15:21–22)

The resurrection of Jesus reverses the imprint of death (v. 26), and "in Christ," bearing now his "image" rather than the image of fallen humanity, the Christian has a hope which transcends that mortal stamp: "Just as we have borne the image of the man of dust, we will also bear the image of the man of heaven" (v. 49).

Most of these "hammer-blows" or drop-molds which leave their redoubtable impression upon the New Testament text derive, as Jean Daniélou among others has shown,[7] from the book of Exodus. Exodus is the narrative concerned with Israel's liberation from bondage, exile, and pilgrimage toward the Promised Land, and the role in that narrative of "law" and "promise" is reciprocal. When members of the community at Corinth read Paul's words about Christ being "our passover," they would be unable to miss the connections: the crucifixion of Jesus is not only "like" the slaying of the sacrificial lamb in Egypt, a substitutionary atonement which protects the "chosen" from the wrath of God; they are led to see the slain paschal lamb as but the "sign" or "type" whose fulfillment is the finally redemptive messianic coinage for the whole world. Analogy becomes the relation of type and antitype, mold and coin, old and new:

> Your boasting is not a good thing. Do you not know that a little yeast leavens the whole batch of dough? Clean out the old yeast so that you may be a new batch, as you really are unleavened. For our paschal lamb, Christ, has been sacrificed. Therefore, let us celebrate the festival, not with the old yeast, the yeast of malice and evil, but with the unleavened bread of sincerity and truth.
>
> (1 Cor. 5:6–8)

This typological reading leads to a revision of the central notion of the *berith*, the covenant itself. Whereas in the Old Testament it was unmistakably the assurance of God's election of his chosen people Israel, the descendents of Abraham, Isaac and Jacob, now the covenant promise is seen — because of Jesus' reading of the Old Testament in reference to himself — as having not only the messianic hope as its context but the person of the promised Christ as its ultimate recipient or, as in a "last will and testament," its intended beneficiary: "Now the promises were made to Abraham and to his offspring; it does not say 'And to offsprings' as of many, but it says 'And to your offspring', who is Christ" (Gal. 3:16). By this revolutionary redirection of the text of the old covenant so that its final intention is seen to be not the many but the One, or as envisioning not the whole narrative of God's unfolding authorship in history but its metonym in his Word fulfilled in Jesus, the whole fabric of Old Testament narrative becomes open to a charged or layered potential in interpretation: semeity opens to polysemeity, albeit in an order of focus which centers all the more intensively upon Jesus. When patristic and medieval commentators make Isaac a type of Christ, they are thinking not only about the almost sacrifice and the substitionary lamb on Mt. Moriah, they are thinking about God's astonishing covenant promise to barren Sarah and to aged Abraham, and to "his seed after him," Christ.[8]

The basic pattern in all of the "reading" of the old Testament by Jesus, then, is that afforded by what Paul came to call the *typoi*, typology. Paul's own ready extension of this typological impulse takes on, however, a somewhat expansive form. In his epistle to the Galatians just quoted he moves on from the *typos* of the promise to

Abraham to discuss the two offspring of Abraham. The first of these was the natural son whom, as a result of Sarah's despair and his own impatience, he had by Sarah's Egyptian handmaiden Hagar. To Abraham's own mind (Gen. 17:18), Ishmael was God's promised heir, and he was surprised as well as overjoyed when the promised covenantal or "spiritual" son, Isaac, was conceived and born to Sarah. Ultimately Hagar and her son were, at Sarah's request, sent away, and in the first Old Testament record of a covenant promise of the deity to a woman, Hagar is promised, that Ishmael will be the father of many nations — most of whom, ironically enough for Jewish readers of the Genesis text, were understood to be their now not very friendly neighbors (Gen. 21:17–18; cf. 16:10–13).

When Paul "reads" this story for his friends in Galatia (4:21) he describes these things not as *typoi* but as *allegoria*, an allegory.[9] Here his reading clearly follows the typological impulse, but the reach of the analogy is both wider than the usual singular focus on Christ, and in respect of the Old Testament — here Torah — subversive of the normative expectation one might have even of a moralized reading of the passage:

> Tell me, you who desire to be subject to the law, will you not listen to the law? For it is written that Abraham had two sons, one by a slave woman and the other by a free woman. One, the child of the slave, was born according to the flesh; the other, the child of the free woman, was born through the promise. Now this is an allegory: these women are two covenants. One woman, in fact, is Hagar from Mount Sinai, bearing children for slavery. Now Hagar is Mount Sinai in Arabia and corresponds to the present Jerusalem, for she is in slavery with her children. But the other woman corresponds to the Jerusalem above; she is free, and she is our mother. For it is written,
>
> > "Rejoice you childless one, you who bear no children,
> > burst into song and shout, you who endure no birth pangs;
> > for the children of the desolate woman are more numerous
> > than the children of the one who is married."
>
> Now you, my friends, are children of the promise, like Isaac. But just as at that time the child who was born according to the flesh persecuted the child who was born according to the Spirit, so it is now also.
>
> (Gal. 4:21–29)

Two things are notable here. First, in what for the Jewish Christians to whom Paul was writing must have been a shocking novelty, the Law is associated by the apostle not with Isaac, the son of the covenant promise, but with the father of the Arab nations. Paul's explanatory analogy extends to link the Law with carnality and the "natural son" who is a "slave"; it therefore connects the spiritual son, born in "freedom," with the state of grace, the enriched existence of those who by believing in the One who has fulfilled the Law now live according to his spirit in perfect freedom (4:31–5:1, 13–14). Second, the redirection of the usual typological flow (which depends upon the historical fulfillment of the Law and the prophets in Jesus) effects a subversion of the sacrosanct place of Torah (the Law) as the singular source of type; implicitly, Jesus himself is now the spiritual Isaac, the freeborn son according to the promise, and the Christians to whom Paul writes are *his* heirs, even as he was Abraham's in the previous chapter (3:16). This subtle shift from normative typology to what Paul calls here allegory is, in effect, the exchanging of one hammer for another, or of the original seal for its imprint. The typos imprint is now the seal, the mold, for some subsequent kinds of reading. When Paul wants to talk about the life of the Christian in the church, he invites his readers to see that life as molded according to the stamp of Christ, *imitatio Christi* not the stamp of the Law either in its functional sense of legal proscription or even in its broader sense as the pattern of patriarchal history:

> There is therefore now no condemnation for those who are in Christ Jesus. For the law of the Spirit of life in Christ Jesus has set you free from the law of sin and of death. For God has done what the law, weakened by the flesh, could not do: by sending his own Son in the likeness of sinful flesh, and to deal with sin, he condemned sin in the flesh, so that the just requirement of the law might be fulfilled in us, who walk not according to the flesh but according to the Spirit. For those who live according to the flesh set their minds on the things of the flesh, but those who live according to the Spirit set their minds on the things of the Spirit. To set the mind on the flesh is death, but to set the mind on the Spirit is life and peace.
>
> (Rom. 8:1–6)

Here we see, of course, that the "law" which the Christian ought to eschew is the "law of sin and death" (v. 2) — not the Law or Torah which Christ came to fulfill. For Paul the "law of sin and death" nonetheless problematizes our relationship to Torah. The scriptural Law proves to be, by virtue of mere human flesh, too "weak" (v. 3) to bring about its own purpose ("that the just requirement of the Law might be fulfilled in us") — that is, in mere human flesh the Law could not come to fulfillment because human nature is too much subject to the lower law of our fallen nature, the "law of sin and death." Christ, however, in our place has actually *fulfilled* already the scriptural Law, bodied forth at last its Word in total obedience, freeing us to live no longer tyrannized by the law of our flesh (fallen nature) or by the impossibility of our mortal and fallen nature ever fulfilling the written Law of God.

By living in his "Spirit" we experience life anew as though it were now for us stamped out in his image. Ironically again, only the mind which turns away from the flesh and its "law of sin and death" can ever hope to "submit to God's law" (v. 7) as it is found in Torah, and "imitate" in this way the life of Christ. This "imitation" or mimesis, as submission to God's gift to us of a perfect fulfillment of the law in Jesus, is the highest order of freedom, in that by it we are "conformed to the image of his Son" (v. 29), the fullest revelation of our human potential. This submission (bearing Christ's image) is for a Christian the New Law, or the Law renewed in Christ, what St. James calls elsewhere "the perfect law of liberty," because what is done is done not through fear or constraint but through love, the love that imitates the beloved.[10]

"In Christ," Paul says to the Romans, we are no longer living "in a spirit of slavery" (v. 15) but in the spirit of those who have, by "adoption," been made full legal members of the covenant and accordingly joint heirs of its promise made to

Abraham. Here too, Paul's Gentile readers can find their place in the text. The narrative of the old covenant is not their genetic lineage, the promise to Abraham not their family promise. Yet even though they are not in any racial sense "heirs" (Jesus was above all the "heir" of the *berith* for Paul), by understanding that Isaac is a type of Jesus and that the promise made to Abraham that all the world (not just Jews) would be blessed in him has been extended to the Gentiles through Jesus (Gen. 12:3), the Gentile believers in Jesus also suddenly have access to God as Father.

> For [God] says to Moses,
> "I will have mercy on whom I have mercy,
> and I will have compassion on whom I have compassion."
> So it depends not on human will or exertion, but on God who shows mercy.
> (Rom. 8:15–16)

Typology focuses the light of Scripture forward from the Old Testament onto Christ; allegory typically refracts the intensified light back upon the Scriptures from the prospect of the experience or life of the church. If *typology* in the early church continues to be, as it was in the Gospels, the interpretation of the scriptural text in terms of the life of a Person — the person of Jesus of Nazareth — *allegory*, much as it is elsewhere in the hellenized world, becomes in this light the interpretation of one text in terms of another text. In Paul specifically nonetheless, allegorical interpretation is still a function of the modeling of life upon a text. Now, however, the life is his own and that of all Christian believers, and the "text" is not only the Old Testament but also the life of Jesus. The "Suffering Servant" of Isaiah (53), a prophetic poem seen by the early church as fulfilled and made historically concrete in the New Testament life of Jesus (Rom. 10:15–16; Acts 8:32–35; 1 Peter 2:22–25; cf. Matt. 8:17; John 12:38), is by the Christian's "life in the Spirit" also rendered *imitatio Christi*, a full pattern for authentic life for those who follow Jesus at any time. This application or "imitation" opens the door to a view of history (whether personal or general) in which one can read concrete events as though they were written down in a book, and ordinary books as though they could best be understood in reference to "the Book," the Scriptures Old and New. Pivotal for Christian allegory is thus a schema which, unlike typology, is not extensively developed in the Bible itself. Here the New Testament is unambiguously the central text, and the Word made flesh in Jesus has become as the message to humanity to which all of the Old Testament was merely proleptic, while that which comes after the New Testament is necessarily a kind of exposition.

On such a view the New Testament becomes a generative or foundational text, much as the Old Testament had been, and capable of replacing it in relation to subsequent Christian writing. In this way, pretty much all Christian literature until well after the Middle Ages was regarded as "'literary' application of the New Testament to life."[11] Accordingly, the literary theory of early Christian culture itself becomes an imprint, a mirror image as well as an elaboration of the literary theory of Jesus, and that literary theory becomes in turn a fundamental source of identity in the Christian community. When Paul writes his second letter to the Corinthian community he says to them:

Surely we do not need, as some do, letters of recommendation to you or from you, do we? You yourselves are our letter, written on our hearts, to be known and read by all; and you show that you are a letter of Christ, prepared by us, written not with ink but with the Spirit of the living God, not on tablets of stone but on tablets of human hearts. Such is the confidence that we have through Christ toward God. Not that we are competent of ourselves to claim anything as coming from us; our competence is from God, who has made us competent to be ministers of a new covenant, not of letter but of spirit; for the letter kills, but the Spirit gives life.

(2 Cor. 3:1–6)

Reading in quest of the spirit rather than the letter privileges the trope; it also suggests that the letter, the sign, is the impermanent and fragile element, whereas the Spirit, that to which the sign points, is enduring — indeed will last forever (Matt. 24:35). The Christian view of language and its implied principles of literary theory are hardly then, *pace* Bloom and Derrida, bound to the mere semeity of texts. Human words are creatures of the moment, even as are the bodies of those who speak the words; fleetingly they are present and then they pass away. For Paul the writer, this very human fragility teaches us the fundamental virtue of God's Word, its enduring and hence extraordinary power. In a metaphor which for our own time unavoidably calls up images of Bedouin shepherds peering at long lost scrolls wrapped up in clay jars in the caves of Q'mran, Paul writes:

But we have this treasure in clay jars, so that it may be made clear that this extraordinary power belongs to God and does not come from us. We are afflicted in every way, but not crushed; perplexed, but not driven to despair; persecuted, but not forsaken; struck down, but not destroyed; always carrying in the body the death of Jesus, so that the life of Jesus may also be made visible in our bodies. For while we live, we are always being given up to death for Jesus' sake, so that the life of Jesus may be made visible in our mortal flesh.

(2 Cor. 4:7–11)

The scroll in the jar is a worthy treasure, because it conveys through its words the Word of God. For Paul and the early church, however, the better text is the life of Jesus, and the only time this text can be "read" and handed on is when, through death to the obtrusive self, the imprint of Jesus becomes legible in the "mortal flesh" the "earthen vessel" (KJV), of an ordinary life. Ironically, the most necessary "text" is thus the most vulnerable; yet *imitatio Christi* becomes hereafter the only mode of authentic "reading" for Christian People of the Book.

Notes

1   In Orthodox Judaism, it should be noted, the term has particular association with the old European pratice of *Lernen*, lifelong dedication to study and spiritual meditation upon

biblical texts, mystical tracts, and especially Talmud. This tradition, and its continuance in American Jewish Orthodoxy, is the subject of a book by Samuel C. Heilman, *People of the Book: Drama Fellowship and Religion* (Chicago: University of Chicago Press, 1983).

2   *Jesus and the Old Testament* (London: Tyndale Press, 1971), 224. A useful further study is A. T. Hanson's *Jesus Christ in the Old Testament* (London: SPCK, 1965).

3   France echoes Goppelt: "The school in which the writers of the early church learned to use the Old Testament was that of Jesus" (225).

4   See E. E. Ellis, *Prophecy and Hermeneutic in Early Christianity* (Grand Rapids: Eerdmans, 1978).

5   Goppelt, *Typos*, 4–5.

6   Ibid., 5, n. 14.

7   Jean Daniélou, *From Shadow to Reality: Studies in the Biblical Typology of the Fathers*, trans. W. Hibberd (Westminster, Md.: Newman, 1961), Cf. Michael Walzer's *Exodus and Revolution* (New York Basic Books, 1985) which argues for the character of Exodus as a historic template for revolutionary politics — precisely the application which Jesus and the writers of the New Testament rejected. Walzer's reading is, however, very instructive for Jewish history, especially in respect of messianism (including Marx), and it is a key to the difference between Walzer's subject and New Testament typology on this point that he can say of the Jewish tradition: "It is the prophet Moses, not David the king, who hovers in the background of this messianic vision and suggests the nature of the deeds to come" (137).

8   See, e.g., Augustine, *Sermone* 130.3; *De Consensu Evangelistarum* 25.39; also J. Daniélou, "La typologie d'Isaac dans le Christianisme primitif," *Biblia* 28 (1947): 363–93.

9   The Antiochine fathers, committed to typology and the literal sense and resistant to the allegorical methods of the Alexandrian school, are echoed in the opinion of some modern scholars who incline to the view that Gal. 4:22–27 is still technically not allegory. This view has, however, been rejected by the majority of modern scholars, who find the passage to embody a truly allegorical method — one of two such New Testament passages to do so, the other being I Cor. 9:9ff. See here the useful summary and discussion of Richard Longenecker, *Biblical Exegesis in the Apostolic Period* (Grand Rapids: Eerdmans, 1975). See also E. E. Ellis, *Paul's Use of the Old Testament* (Edinburgh: Oliver and Boyd, 1956), and R. P. C. Hanson, *Allegory and Event* (London: SPCK, 1959). It is interesting that St. Jerome translates Paul's Greek directly as "sunt per allegoriam dicta" and, by contrast, is discriminating about *typos*. When it refers to persons or events of the historical past Jerome has *figura* (e.g., 1 Cor. 10:6); where *typos* clearly means a prefiguration of Christ (e.g., 5:14), Jerome translates *forma*, and where the model is more impersonal (as with respect to the plan of the tabernacle in Hebrews 8:5) he uses *exemplar* (cf. Vulg. Titus 2:7; 1 Tim. 4:12).

10 James 1:25; 2:12; cf. John 13:34–35; 2 Cor. 3:17; Gal. 5:1. The "law of liberty" is opposed to what Paul calls "the law of sin and death."

11 The apt phrase is John Freccero's, in "Dante's Medusa: Allegory and Autobiography," in *By Things Seen: Reference and Recognition in Medieval Thought*, ed. D. L. Jeffrey (Ottawa: University of Ottawa Press, 1979).

(c) On the Jewish Reading of Scriptures

Emmanuel Levinas

It is not a question here of drawing up an inventory of the figures of Jewish hermeneutics of the Bible. This would require a vast amount of research, taking into account the diversity of epochs and tendencies. It would also mean determining the credibility of the interpreters measured less by any consensus than by the intelligence of each person and his familiarity with tradition. R. Ishmael's often-quoted 'Thirteen figures of the interpretation of the Torah', or the famous four levels of reading: *peshat* (plain meaning), *remez* (allusive meaning), *derash* (solicited meaning), *sod* (secret meaning), whose vocalized acronym gives the word *pardes* (orchard), call in their turn for exegesis, and constitute only aspects of rabbinism in its relation to the text. Only the modern formulation of this relation, which has yet to be done, might put an end to the improper teachings where traditional sources are quoted as if, beneath the Hebrew letters that conceal them, they all derived from the same depth.

Our more modest intention is to illustrate, by examples, certain ways of reading. We shall do this by presenting a Talmudic extract which produces, in the form of arguments, the exegesis of biblical verses. Nevertheless, in doing this we shall find ourselves being led to some propositions of a more general character, for the chosen extract, in its final section, concerns precisely the scope of exegesis. Exegesis of the exegesis, a privileged text, even if it does not exclude different insights into the same subject. This is in keeping with the characteristic pluralism of rabbinical thought, which paradoxically aspires to be compatible with the unity of the Revelation: the multiple stances of the scholars would constitute its very life, all of them being the 'words of the living God'.

The Talmudic passage that we shall comment upon will also introduce us in particular to the meaning that, for Jewish religious consciousness, commentary of the Scriptures can take on as the path towards transcendence. It is, perhaps, essential to the actual creation of this notion.

But a Talmudic text that comments on verses requires an interpretation in its turn. What it intends to do is not immediately apparent in terms which, for an inexperienced reader, may seem unusual, and which in fact allow for several levels and dimensions. Hence a third stage in the final section of our commentary: an interpretation of the Talmudic exegesis of the exegesis. This reading of the Talmud would not be possible for us without recourse to a modern language – in other words, without touching on the problems of today. Admittedly, it too is not the only possible reading, but it has the value of a testimony. It testifies to at least one of the ways in which contemporary Jews understand traditional Jewish hermeneutics, and above all to the way in which they understand it when they ask it for food for thought and teachings on the content.

1 Preliminary Remarks

The text we shall comment upon is taken from one of the last pages of the Tractate Makkoth in the Babylonian Talmud. This short Tractate of about fifty pages deals with judicial punishments of which one, in reference to Deuteronomy 25: 2–3, is flogging (*makkoth* = blows). The passage dealing with the exegesis of page 23b has as its immediate context a theologico-legal discussion: is it possible, through the penalty of flogging, inflicted by a human tribunal, to make atonement for the punishment known as being 'cut off from among their people', decided, according to the Talmud, by the 'celestial tribunal'? Being 'cut off from among their people', the most serious theological punishment, means being excluded from the 'world to come', which designates the eschatological order in its ultimate terms, whereas the 'Messianic epoch', still belonging to History, constitutes a penultimate stage of the 'end of times'. How can a human decision – in the case of flogging atoning for being 'cut off' – intervene in a domain which exceeds man? How can it be guaranteed to be in keeping with the divine will? These questions imply transcendence and a relation which passes through this absolute distance. They touch on the problem of the possibility of such a relation, which also arises in the exegesis examining divine thought.

Before tackling the text, it would be useful to make some general remarks which, for a reader coming from outside, are called for by the particular or outdated nature of being flogged or cut off. This whole evocation of 'blows', of the transgression and guilt it presupposes, may wound our liberal souls; just as the reference to a 'celestial tribunal' may go against our modern minds by the dated or questionable 'vision of the world' which it implies.

But in order to move towards a meaning which is retained despite an apparently antiquated language, it is necessary first of all to accept patiently – as one accepts the conventions of a fable or a stage setting – the particulars of the text in their specific universe. It is necessary to wait for them to set themselves in motion and free themselves from the anachronisms and local colour on which the curtain rises. In no way must this 'exotic' or 'outmoded' language stop thought by its picturesque elements, or by the immediate meaning of the things and deeds it names. This will change. Often from apparently incongruous or insignificant questions. Without fading before their concepts, things denoted in a concrete fashion are yet enriched with meanings by the multiplicity of their concrete aspects. This is what we call the paradigmatic modality of Talmudic reflection: notions remain constantly in contact with the examples or refer back to them, whereas they should have been content as springboards to rise to the level of generalization, or they clarify the thought which scrutinizes by the secret light of hidden or isolated worlds from which it bursts forth; and simultaneously this world inserted or lost in signs is illuminated by the thought which comes to it from outside or from the other end of the canon, revealing its possibilities which were awaiting the exegesis, immobilized, in some way, in the letters.

2 The Tribunal And The Love Of One's Neighbour

Let us come back now to the principal points of a discussion on flogging, being 'cut off from among their people', and the punishments of the human and celestial tribunal. Let us accept these figures of speech and the legal formal nature of the words.

According to R. Hananiah b. Gamaliel, those who are guilty of certain transgressions that the Law of the Pentateuch punishes by cutting them off obtain remission from this damnation if they submit to the flogging imposed by the earthly tribunal. The human tribunal would thus have to be aware of sins which expel human beings from the human (the decision of God's tribunal would measure the seriousness of the sin), and would thereby have to repair the irreparable. Can the tribunal do as much as celestial compassion or mercy? Is mercy shown at the tribunal? Reference is made by R. Hananiah to Deuteronomy 25:3: 'Forty stripes may be given him, but not more; lest, if one should go on to beat him with more stripes than these, your brother be degraded in your sight.' The word 'brother' would be essential here. It is a matter of punishing without degrading: would the tribunal and justice have the secret of the extreme measure of a difference which is a differential? In any case, R. Hananiah breaks with the dark mythological fatality whose eventuality would indicate a religious tyranny, in order to proclaim that no sin exists in relation to Heaven which cannot be expiated among men and in the light of day. The tribunal would thus also be the place where the divine regenerative will is revealed. Admittedly, there is violence. But it is an act without a spirit of violence, contempt or hatred. A fraternal act, without passion. It proceeds from a responsibility for others. To be the guardian of others, contrary to the vision of the world according to Cain, defines fraternity. For the tribunal which reasons and weighs up, the love of one's neighbour would be possible. Justice dispensed by the just becomes compassion – not in uncontrollable indulgence, but through a judgement. God speaks with a compassion that is born in the severity of the tribunal. Excessiveness? It certainly is. But pure indulgence, free forgiveness, is always at the expense of someone innocent who does not receive it. The judge is allowed such indulgence only if he personally assumes the costs.[1] But it is proper for the earthly judge, for man, for the brother of the guilty party, to restore to human fraternity those who have been excluded. To be responsible to the point of being answerable for the other's freedom. This heteronomy among the conditions of autonomy in human fraternity is acutely thought in Judaism with the category of divine paternity as its point of departure.[2] Divine justice arrays itself in fraternity by revealing itself in a human tribunal.

R. Hananiah b. Gamaliel's second argument is an 'a fortiori'. If the transgression of certain interdicts 'cuts off a human being from his people', then all the more reason for his carrying out the Law to return him to them. Now, to suffer the flogging decided on by the tribunal is to obey the Law to which a guilty person is subject. But why 'all the more reason'?[3] Because divine compassion is still more certain than its severity. A theme that is present throughout rabbinical thought, and to which R. Hananiah implicitly refers. Is it not written (Exodus 34: 7):

> [The Lord keeps] steadfast love for thousands [of generations], forgiving iniquity and transgression and sin, but who will by no means clear the guilty, visiting the iniquity of the fathers upon the children and the children's children, to the third and the fourth generation . . .?

And the Rabbis gloss 'thousands' as at least two thousand! For at least two thousand generations steadfast love granted to merit is handed down; for four generations iniquity cries out for justice: compassion is thus five hundred times greater than divine severity. Behind this arithmetic of mercy there is moral optimism: the triumph of evil has one time only; nothing is ever lost from the triumph won over evil or from good.

From this point onwards, R. Simeon intervenes with the merit attached to the obedience to the interdicts. An intervention which, above and beyond the theological meaning of the terms, defines a certain conception of human life: 'One who desists from transgressing is granted reward like one who performs a precept'. The constraint imposed on the spontaneity of life, such as is provided for in the negative command-ments of Leviticus 18 (whose sexual interdicts appear as the privileged example of negative commandments), is asserted by R. Simeon as the guarantee of 'rewards'. The negative commandment is the constraint *par excellence*, restraining the tendencies where life is lived in its spontaneity as an 'outgoing force', and in particular the blind abundance of sexual desire. It would be the promise of rewards, if we are to believe R. Simeon. Certainly one can expect from this promise what simple and unques-tioning faith expects: longevity, eternal life or earthly happiness – just as one can denounce its spirit of repression which abuses that faith. But as a reward for a life accepting limitations, one can also understand the nature of this very life: the limita-tion of the wild vitality of life, through which this life wakes from its somnambulant spontaneity, sobers up from its nature and interrupts its centripetal movements, in order to be opened up to what is other than self. A life in which Judaism is recog-nized, limiting through the Law this wild, animal vitality, accepting this restriction as the best share – that is, as a 'reward'.[4] The plenitude of a sense of responsibility and justice is preferred to life intoxicated with its own essence, to the invasion of the unharnessed appetite of desire and domination where nothing, not even other people, can stand in its way.

R. Simeon b. Rabbi deduces the reward reserved for those who do not transgress the interdicts from the promise made in Deuteronomy 12: 23–25 to the person who refrains from eating blood: if the abstinence consonant with a natural loathing is rewarded, how much more so is the resistance against what is desirable! Perhaps the horror of blood here has a meaning which is not only of a gastronomic nature. Resistance to sexual excesses and to the taste for plunder is, *a fortiori*, worthy of merit. And yet this is the 'true life', if we follow the literary writers of the great Metropoles! All this accounting of merits and rewards has a wider meaning. Life as it is lived, natural life, begins, perhaps, in naivety, in tendencies and tastes which are still in keeping with a code of ethics; but if it is allowed to run its course unhindered, it ends in loveless debauchery and plunder established as a social condition, and in exploitation. The human begins when this apparently innocent but virtually murderous vitality is brought under control by interdicts. Does not authentic civili-zation, however it may be marked by biological failures or political defeats, consist in holding back the breath of naive life and remaining fully awake in this way, 'for generations and generations to come, to the end of all generations'?[5]

We can now understand R. Hananiah b, 'Akashia's thought which closes the *Mishnah*: 'The Holy One, blessed be He, desired to make Israel worthy, therefore gave he them the law (to study) and many commandments (to do)'; and '[the Lord made] the law great and glorious' (Isaiah 42: 21). This is certainly not to create arti-ficial merits or to put up hurdles deliberately. It is for the greatness of justice and for his glory that commandments are necessary against a life lived as an 'outgoing force'. Even in cases – such as the horror that may be felt in eating or shedding blood – where nature seems to protect us from evil! There is no natural tendency that is healthy enough not to be able to be inverted. Holiness is necessary for the healthiness of the healthy.[6]

But the greatness of justice evoked by R. Hananiah b. 'Akashia, which is conditioned by a life obeying the many commandments, is also the glory of the tribunal and the judges. To make the law glorious! Only the judges who themselves practise the many commandments can form the glorious council to which God's will aspires. The judge is not just a legal expert of laws; he obeys the Law he administers, and he is trained by this obedience; the study of the Law is itself the essential form of this obedience.[7] Such a situation is necessary in order for earthly punishment to reduce celestial punishment; for it to be rightfully thought, with the Psalmist, that 'God has taken his place in the divine council', and that 'in the midst of the gods [judges] he holds judgement' (Psalms 82: 1). It is necessary in order simply to justify man's judgement passed on man and the punishment inflicted by one on the other – that is to say, the responsibility of one person for the other. This is the strange ontological structure presupposed by this responsibility whereby one person assumes the destiny and the very existence of another, and is answerable for this other in a way, however, that is not characteristic of him. It is a responsibility that precedes freedom, which would mean precisely belonging to God, a unique belonging which, anterior to freedom, does not destroy freedom and thereby defines, if one may say so, the meaning of the exceptional word: God. God appearing *through* a council of the just, itself called divine; God as the actual possibility of such a council. And, conversely, a council of the just which is not only the ultimate source of his judgement: a different will wills within it, the judge's judgement is inspired and exceeds or overflows human spontaneity. This is what our text will say further on. Justice cannot be reduced to the order it institutes or restores, nor to a system whose rationality commands, without difference, men and gods, revealing itself in human legislation like the structures of space in the theorems of geometricians, a justice that a Montesquieu calls the 'logos of Jupiter', recuperating religion within this metaphor, but effacing precisely transcendence. In the justice of the Rabbis, difference retains its meaning. Ethics is not simply the corollary of the religious but is, of itself, the element in which religious transcendence receives its original meaning.

3 Transcendence And Exegesis

In the Talmudic extract we are commenting upon, the text relating to transcendence comes immediately after the one that discusses the powers a human tribunal would have in order to modify the decisions of Heaven in some way, and to be certain of agreeing with the absolute Tribunal. Here are the terms in which the problem is put: 'Said R. Joseph: Who has gone up (to Heaven) and come (back with this information)?'

The answer is supplied by another scholar, Abaye, in the name of a Tanna master, R. Joshua b. Levi:

> 'Three things were enacted by the (mundane) Tribunal below, and the Celestial Tribunal on high have given assent to their action'; (we might also exclaim,) who has gone up (to Heaven) and come (back with this information)? Only, we (obtain these points by) interpreting certain texts; and, in this instance too, we so interpret the texts.

R. Joshua. b. Levi would thus entrust to the interpretation of texts, what the Rabbis call *Midrash* (exposition of meaning), the ability to force open the secret of transcendence.

Here are the three 'things' which are said to have been instituted by the earthly tribunals whose exegesis would prove to have the assent of the celestial will. First of all, the established custom, under the magistracy of Mordecai and Esther, of the liturgical reading of the 'Scroll of Esther' on the Feast of Purim. It would find its justification in a biblical verse (Esther 9: 27): 'They confirmed, and the Jews took upon them and their seed [The Jews acknowledged and accepted]'. Why two almost synonymous verbs in this verse? Because confirmation [acknowledgement] and taking upon themselves [acceptance] were two distinct acts: acceptance below, acknowledgement in Heaven.

Then the authorization of saluting another person with the Divine Name: in Ruth 2: 4, Boaz (whom the Rabbis class among the judges) greets the reapers: The Lord be with you!'; and in Judges 6:12 the angel says to Gideon: 'The Lord bless thee, thou mighty man of valour'.

Finally, the prescription of bringing the tithe (due to the Levites) to the Temple-chamber, established as a custom by Ezra according to Nehemiah 10: 39. It is confirmed by the prophet Malachi (3: 10): 'Bring ye the whole tithe unto the store house that there may be food in My house, and try Me herewith, saith the Lord of Hosts, if I will not open you the windows of heaven and pour you out a blessing, until there be no enough'. And the Talmud adds: 'What means: "until there be no enough"? Said Rami b. Rab: (It means), until your lips weary of saying "Enough, enough"!'

Do not such 'proofs' imply the inspired origin of the whole biblical canon? Does it not present the notions of height and transcendence as established, and the very idea of God as clear and distinct?

Unless R. Joseph's question, in its apparent naivety, is an extremely audacious one, questioning the mythological meaning of transcendence and the revelation it seems to acknowledge. Unless, in questioning the idea of someone 'going up to Heaven', he goes so far as to concern the great man called upon in Exodus 24: 12: 'Come up to me on the mountain, and wait there; and I will give you the tables of stone, with the law and the commandment'. A calling upon whose reality in fact would be vouched for, ultimately, only by a text which itself already belongs to the statement of the truth which it ought to be able to establish: *petitio principii* which would hint at the whole of historical criticism today. But does not Abaye's reply indicate that he already understands his interlocutor on this higher level? Instead of establishing exegesis on some dogmatism of traditional metaphysics adopted as a truism, does not Abaye's reply consist in basing a new meaning for transcendence, and the old vocabulary, on the structure of the Book of books inasmuch as it allows for exegesis, and on its privileged status of containing more than it contains – in other words, of being, in this sense exactly, inspired?

The reading processes that we have just seen at work suggest, first, that the statement commented upon exceeds what it originally wants to say; that what it is capable of saying goes beyond what it wants to say; that it contains more than it contains; that perhaps an inexhaustible surplus of meaning remains locked in the syntactic structures of the sentence, in its word-groups, its actual words, phonemes and letters, in all this materiality of the saying which is potentially signifying all the time. Exegesis would come to free, in these signs, a bewitched significance that smoulders beneath the characters or coils up in all this literature of letters.[8]

Rabbinical hermeneutics is rashly considered as neglecting the spirit whereas the aim of the signified by the signifier is not the only way to signify; whereas what is signified in the signifier, according to its other modes, answers only to the mind that solicits it and thereby belongs to the process of signification; and whereas interpretation essentially involves this act of soliciting without which what is not said, inherent in the texture of the statement, would be extinguished beneath the weight of the texts, and sink into the letters. An act of soliciting which issues from people whose eyes and ears are vigilant and who are mindful of the whole body of writing from which the extract comes, and equally attuned to life: the city, the street, other men. An act of soliciting which issues from people in their uniqueness, each person capable of extracting from the signs meanings which each time are inimitable. An act of soliciting issuing from people who would also belong to the process of the signification of what has meaning. This does not amount to identifying exegesis with the impressions and subjective reflections left by the word once it has been understood, nor to including them gratuitously in the 'outside' of meaning. It does, however, amount to understanding the very plurality of people as an unavoidable moment of the signification of meaning, and as in some way justified by the destiny of the inspired word, so that the infinite richness of what it does not say can be said or that the meaning of what it does say can be 'renewed', to use the technical expression of the Rabbis. As the people of the Book, for whom the demanding reading of the Scriptures belongs to the highest liturgy, would not Israel also be the people of continued revelation?

But in the light of this, the language that is capable of containing more than it contains would be the natural element of inspiration, despite or before its reduction to the instrument of the transmission of thoughts and information (if it can ever be entirely reduced to this). One may wonder whether man, an animal endowed with speech, is not, above all, an animal capable of inspiration, a prophetic animal. One may wonder whether the book, as a book, before becoming a document, is not the modality by which what is said lays itself open to exegesis, calls for it; and where meaning, immobilized in the characters, already tears the texture in which it is held. In propositions which are not yet – or which are already no longer – verses, and which are often verse or simply literature, another voice rings out among us, a second sonorous voice that drowns out or tears the first one. The infinite life of texts living through the life of the men who hear them; a primordial exegesis of the texts which are then called national literature and on to which the hermeneutics of universities and schools is grafted. Above and beyond the immediate meaning of what is said in these texts, the act of saying is inspired. The fact that meaning comes through the book testifies to its biblical essence. The comparison between the inspiration conferred on the Bible and the inspiration towards which the interpretation of literary texts tends is not intended to compromise the dignity of the Scriptures. On the contrary, it asserts the dignity of 'national literatures'. Yet how is it that a book is instituted as the Book of books? Why does a book become Bible? How is the divine origin of the Word indicated? How is it signed in Scripture? And does not this signature, which is more important for people living today than 'the thunderings and the lightnings' of Sinai, betray simple faith?

Inspiration: another meaning which breaks through from beneath the immediate meaning of what is meant to be said, another meaning which beckons to a way of hearing that listens beyond what is heard, beckons to extreme consciousness, a consciousness that has been awoken. This other voice resonating in the first takes control of the message as a result of this resonance coming from behind the first. In its purity of message, it is not just a certain form of saying; it organizes its content. The message as message awakens listening to what is indisputably intelligible, to the meaning of meanings, to the face of the other man.[9] Awakening is precisely this proximity of others.[10] The message as message in its method of awakening is the modality, the actual 'how' of the ethical code that disturbs the established order of being, unrepentantly leading its style of being.[11] With its referent as reading, as the book – yet no less wondrous for all that – do we not have here the original figure of the beyond freed from the mythology of ulterior worlds?[12]

That *ethics* is not determined in its elevation by the pure height of the starry sky; that all height takes on its transcendent meaning only through ethics and the message incessantly breaking (hermeneutically) the texture of the Book *par excellence:* these, undoubtedly, will constitute the teaching to be drawn – one of the teachings to be drawn – from the passage we are commenting upon.

Curiously, the biblical text first cited by R. Joshua b. Levi in consideration of the agreement between the earthly tribunal and the celestial tribunal is taken from the book of Esther from which, it might be said, God has gone so far as to withdraw his name, the word by which he is named. Yet in this book the message emerges from between the events recounted according to their 'natural' motivation, the necessities and the casting of lots. That these events, instituted as liturgy by Mordecai and Esther, could have been understood as belonging to holy History is the 'miraculous' surplus of their place in the divine plan. There arises the historical order of the facts (their established order), and consciences are awoken at the highest ethical moment in which Esther disturbs royal etiquette and consents to her ruin in order to save other men. The order upset by this awakening is paralleled by the king's insomnia. Does not a Midrash from the Tractate Megillah compare the insomnia of Ahasuerus to the very insomnia of God? As if, in the impossibility of sleeping, the ontological rest of being were to be torn and entirely sobered up. Is not the relation to transcendence this extreme consciousness?

No less remarkable is the second text in which the epiphany of God is invoked in the human face. The face of the other, irreducible difference, bursting into all that gives itself to me, all that is understood by me and belongs to my world; an appearance in the world which un-makes and dis-orders the world, worries me and keeps me awake. That is what is perceived by bringing together Ruth 2: 4 and Judges 6: 12. A transcendence both in the text in which exegesis finds more than the written seems to say, and in the ethical content, the message, which is thus revealed.

The third moment – in which the gift of the tithe is transformed by being brought to the Temple – would signify the transformation of the very act of giving into an absolutely free act of generosity where the person giving, not knowing the beneficiary, does not hear the expression of the latter's personal gratitude.[13] Is that not one of the meanings, the figure, as it were, of the cult itself? What 'strong minds' would be tempted to mock as duties towards an 'empty heaven' is enigmatically the absolute opening of the soul: the opening of dis-interestedness, of sacrifice without reward, of discourse without answer or echo, which 'confidence in God' and prayer must have the strength to reach. The opening of self to the infinite that no confirmation can equal, and that is proven only by its very excessiveness. That would be the abundance for which lips cannot be enough, drying out through saying 'enough', of which Rami b. Rab speaks in his strange hermeneutic of Malachi 3:10. A beyond the discourse. This is probably what this sudden transformation is: in the dis-interested generosity of the act of giving, receiving becomes infinite, the opening on to the infinite.

4 The Ambiguity

In our reading of the Talmudic passage, inspiration and the exegesis that discovers it, we have discerned the spirituality of the spirit and the actual figure of transcendence. Have we been right to do so? Have we been right to recognize in the ethical code on the level of the tribunal, understood as a council of the just, the actual place in which the spirit blows and the Other penetrates the Same? Will a person today not resist such readings by reducing the transcendence of inspiration, exegesis and the moral message to man's interiority, to his creativity or his subconscious? Is not ethics basically autonomous? In order to dispute such modern-day resistance, would it not have been necessary to interpret as inspiration the reasons of reasoning reason in which philosophy, in its logic, recognizes the reign of Identity which nothing that is *other* could disrupt or guide?

Now this is precisely what the final section of the Talmudic extract that concerns us wishes to suggest R. Eleazar intervenes to confirm in his own way the general argument of Makkoth 23b on the possible agreement between earthly courts of law and celestial justice. He refers to Genesis 38:26, where Judah, the son of Jacob, recognizes the injustice of the accusation he had brought against his daughter-in-law Tamar (this 'is said to have taken place', according to our text, at the Tribunal of Shem, Noah's son, who was still alive). R. Eleazar refers to I Samuel 12: 3–5, where all of Israel testifies at the Tribunal of Samuel to the disinterestedness of the judge Samuel; and he refers to I Kings 3: 27, where King Solomon, in his own Tribunal, recognizes the mother among the two women arguing over a child. Confession of the guilty party, testimony of the people, sentence of the king: to each of these human speeches (unquestionably human in the verses quoted), R. Eleazar – in the name of a supremely audacious exegesis, but probably also in the name of a daring thought – lifts out, under various pretexts, the ends of verses which he attributes to the echo of a heavenly voice. Will the holy spirit thus have been present at men's tribunals?

One interlocutor, Raba, questions such extravagance: there is no need to have voices intervening in discourses where reason is sufficient. But it is R. Eleazar's lesson that the Talmudic text retains. It retains it without discussion, in the name of tradition. Inspiration is thus said to be in the exercise of reason itself! The logos would already be prophetic! Through the uncertainties and presumptions of reasoning thought, the light of evidence would come as if under the trauma of the Revelation. A message would be declared in all evidence.

This is true, but it should be emphasized that despite tradition, the redactors of the Talmudic text recorded the opinion that was rejected: Raba's scepticism. It is still written down. As if an ambiguity had to remain in the conclusions of the lofty debate that has just taken place according to the style of the Talmud, with remarks that are apparently without relief and made 'without appearing to be made'.

Would not the man of today recognize in this ambiguity the alternating movements of his own thought?

To say that the ideas on transcendence and the very idea of transcendence come to us through the interpretation of writings is, admittedly, not to express a subversive opinion. Yet it is less dogmatic to people today. It suggests on the one hand that language, at the hour of its ethical truth – that is, of its full significance – is inspired, that it can therefore say more than it says, and that prophecy is thus not an act of genius, but the spirituality of the spirit expressing itself, the ability of human speech to extend beyond the primary intentions that carry it. This is perhaps possession by God, through which the idea of God comes to us. But this language offered to transcendence is also the object of philology; thus the transcendence that is expressed through it would be just an illusion, the prestige of influences to be demystified by History. Let us prefer, then, the genesis of every text to its exegesis, the certainties of given signs to the hazards of mysterious messages, the combinations of the shadows in the Cave to the uncertain calls from outside! This is also a science, at times an admirable one, to destroy false prophecies.

Alternative or alternation. And even an alternation of alternations before the letters of Scripture. These letters, for those who respect them as for those who mock them, may still support the dogmatic principles of a God, a power stronger than others, who interrupts – like a monstrous force or a heroic person – the necessities of nature. Then, through a science that they nurture with their presence as relics, these letters strike their readers, one and all, and rescue them from the level of asserted or denied mythologies. But in this start that readers receive there is a new alternation of movements: they go from the traumatic experience of the unknown and strange meaning to the grammar which, already operating on another level, restores order, coherence and chronology. And then there is a movement back: from history and philology to the understanding of meaning coming from behind the literature of letters and anachronisms, an understanding that again affects and awakes, forcing us out of the bed of the preformed and customary ideas that protect and reassure.

An alternation which, admittedly, testifies to the hesitation of our little faith, but from which also stems the transcendence that does not impose itself with denials through its actual coming and which, in inspired Scripture, awaits a hermeneutic – in other words, reveals itself only in dissimulation.

Notes

1 'In rendering legal judgment, [the judge] used to acquit the guiltless and condemn the guilty; but when he saw that the condemned man was poor, he helped him out of his own

purse [to pay the required sum], thus executing judgment and charity . . .' Tractate Sanhedrin 6b. [*Translator's note:* Levinas indicates that he is quoting from the translation into French by the Great Rabbi Salzer.]

2   It is against the paganism of the notion of the 'Oedipus complex' that it is necessary to think forcefully about apparently purely edifying verses such as that in Deuteronomy 8: 5: 'Know then in your heart that, as a man disciplines his son, the Lord your God disciplines you'. Paternity here signifies a constituent category of what has meaning, not of its alienation. On this point, at least, psychoanalysis testifies to the profound crisis of monotheism in contemporary sensibility, a crisis that cannot be reduced to the refusal of a few dogmatic propositions. It conceals the ultimate secret of anti-Semitism. Amado Lévy-Valensi has insisted throughout her work on the essentially pagan character of the myth of Oedipus.

3   [*Translator's note:* The Soncino edition of the Babylonian Talmud renders the *a fortiori* argument as 'how much more should one . . .']

4   Curiously, in the final paragraphs of the pages we are studying in the Tractate Makkoth, the distant noise of unsuppressed and triumphant life, the noise of Rome, is heard. 'Long ago, as Rabban Gamaliel, R. Eleazar b. 'Azariah, R. Joshua and R. Akiba were walking on the road, they heard the noise of the crowds at Rome (on travelling) from Puteoli, a hundred and twenty miles away. They all fell a-weeping, but R. Akiba seemed merry. Said they to him: Wherefore are you merry? Said he to them: Wherefore are you weeping? Said they: These heathens who bow down to images and burn incense to idols live in safety and ease, whereas our Temple, the "Footstool" of our God, is burnt down by fire, and should we then not weep? He replied: Therefore, am I merry. If they that offend Him fare thus, how much better shall fare they that do obey Him!' How much more shall we one day be rewarded or how much better do we who are just fare already, despite our misfortunes? When we are walking on the road and are tired, whether or not we are Rabban Gamaliel, R. Eleazar b. 'Azariah and R. Joshua, the greatest of the great, the sounds of Rome may for a moment cause us to question, in our minds and in our nerves, the soundness of the just life. R. Akiba alone is able to be merry: despite the failures, he is certain of receiving the best share. He is certain of it not through painful empirical experience, but through an *a fortiori* reasoning that is not here the guarantee of a promise, but of a value.

5   These are the words with which R. Simeon b. Rabbi closes his intervention in the Talmudic text we are commenting upon: 'One who refrains therefrom [shall] acquire merit for himself and for generations and generations to come, to the end of all generations!'

6   On the subject of the interdicts, it would be interesting to quote the lines which figure in what follows in our text of pages 23a and 23b of the Tractate Makkoth: 'R. Simlai when preaching said: Six hundred and thirteen precepts were communicated to Moses, three hundred and sixty-five negative precepts, corresponding to the number of solar days (in the year), and two hundred and forty-eight positive precepts, corresponding to the number of the members of man's body. Said R. Hamnuna: What is the (authentic) text for this? It is, *Moses commanded us torah, an inheritance of the congregation of Jacob* (Deuteronomy 33: 4), "*torah*" being in letter-value, equal to six hundred and eleven, "*I am*" and "*Thou shalt have no (other Gods)*" (not being reckoned, because) we heard from the mouth of the Might (Divine)'. [*Translator's note:* The ending of Levinas's translation differs substantially from that given here: 'If one adds to this the first two commandments of the Decalogue pronounced at Sinai and which we heard from the very mouth of the Lord, that makes six hundred and thirteen'.] A bizarre sort of accounting! In actual fact, it gives at least three lessons:

(a)   Every day lived under the sun is potential depravity and thus requires a new interdict, a new vigilance which yesterday's cannot guarantee.

(b)   The life of every organ of the human body, of every tendency (the accuracy or arbitrariness of the anatomy or physiology counting two hundred and forty-eight matters little, since the number of 'positive' precepts divulges the secret of this figure), is the source of possible life. A force that is not justified in itself. It must be dedicated to the most high, to serving.

(c)   The code containing the six hundred and thirteen precepts is not met by the number given by the breakdown of the numerical value of the letters making up the word Torah. It is not a system justified uniquely by its coherence. It institutes the order of life only because its transcendent source is personally asserted in it as word. True life is inspired.

7   Cf. *Quatre lectures talmudiques* [*Four Talmudic Readings*].

8   The word of the 'rabbinical scholars', the word setting out or commenting on the Torah, can be compared to the 'glowing coals', to use a phrase from the Pirqe Aboth in the *Tractate of Principles* of the Babylonian Talmud. A remarkable Talmudist, a disciple of the Gaon of Vilna (one of the last great masters of rabbinical Judaism, on the eve of the nineteenth century, the Jewish age 'of Enlightenment'), Rabbi Hayyim Volozhiner, interpreted this remark approximately as follows: the coals light up by being blown on, the glow of the flame that thus comes alive depends on the interpreter's length of breath.

9   The Book *par excellence* of what has meaning. And this is without yet highlighting the testimony given to this book by a people who have existed for thousands of years, or the interpenetration of their history and of this book, even if such communication between history and book is essential to genuine scriptures.

10   Cf. my study 'De la conscience à la veille', *Bijdragen*, 3–4 (1974), 235–49.

11   Ethics – appearing as the prophetic – is not a 'region', a layer or an ornament of being. It is, of itself, actual dis-interestedness, which is possible only under a traumatic experience whereby 'presence', in its imperturbable equality of presence, is disturbed by 'the other'. Disturbed, awoken, transcended.

12   In the texts invoked, indeed, determined situations and beings – equal to themselves, being held in definitions and boundaries that integrate them into an order and bring them to rest in the world – are passed through by a breath that arouses and stirs their drowsiness or their identity as beings and things, tearing them from their order without alienating them, tearing them from their contour like the characters in Dufy's paintings. The miracle of beings presenting themselves in their being and awakening to new awakenings, deeper and more sober. It cannot be denied that as a disturbing of order, as a tearing of Same by Other, it is the miracle, the structuring – or de-structuring – of inspiration and its transcendence. If purely thaumaturgical miracles seem spiritually suspect to us and acceptable as simple figures of the Epiphany, it is not because they alter the order but because they do not alter it enough, because they are not miraculous enough, because the Other awakening the Same is not yet other enough through them.

13   On the importance attached to this modality of the gift, cf. Baba-Bathra 10b.

(d) The Struggle for the Text

Geoffrey H. Hartman

> "O which one? Is it each one?"
>
> G. M. Hopkins

The question I have put to myself is: how is this text, the Hebrew Bible, different from all other texts? Is there a basis to the distinction between fiction and scripture? Can we discriminate the two kinds by rhetorical or textual qualities, rather than by external criteria that remain mysterious? To call the Bible a sacred text is to set it apart, to constitute it as such for the reader, but as Auerbach[1] and others have argued there is something in the text that prompts us toward this, not in order to keep the text's message hidden or enclosed, but on the contrary to make us enter its originative space: the unsaid as well as the said, the unmarked as well as the marked terrain, where the going is complex from both a scholarly and a spiritual point of view. What complicates the critic's situation is also, of course, that we cannot even begin to move into that territory without certain assumptions: for example, that despite the antiquity of the Bible or our removal in time from it, it has not become estranged beyond repair, or that it was not totally other to begin with (that, divinely inspired or not, it speaks, as the rabbis said, in the language of men), or that it was faithfully transmitted, or that, however accidented it may be, however diversified from book to book as well as within each book, there is something like a unitary perspective, if only as a horizon. Moreover, I cannot claim to possess enough global knowledge of texts that function as Scripture within other cultures to be sure that the qualities of the Hebrew Bible make it unique. My question as to its special character makes sense primarily within a tradition whose poetics have been Hellenic rather than Hebraic, so that the Bible, however influential, has never been entirely naturalized and even today remains a resident alien, at once familiar and unfamiliar.

Jacob's struggle with the angel, in Genesis 32, has become an inexhaustible source for parables and analogies in the Western tradition; in that sense it is not at all strange but rather a familiar guest in the literary and popular mind. The words are all known, and there are very few of them. One of the most uncanny stories in the Bible, it is also one of the sparest, even more so in Hebrew than in English. The core narrative consists of six verses and seventy words in all: to these are added an epilogue in which Jacob names the place of encounter, Peniel, and supplies the etymology "for I have seen God face to face," while the narrator appends what scholars call an etiological frame, which links this event to a dietary taboo.

The economy of presentation is closer to the Classical than to the Shakespearean stage: in the spotlight a man and another man, wrestling, then exchanging three sets of words. But the context remains unlit. Why does the fight begin? We are not told. Its outcome is as mysterious as its onset, though decisive for at least one of the protagonists. On the fringes, of course, are the people in the patriarchal narratives, reduced for this exceptional moment to extras: Esau and the Edomites, Laban and his retainers, the family and flock of Jacob. The Classical stage, after its stychomythia, often relieves and broadens its perspective by the great odes of the chorus. But here, where we might expect a breach in the narrative style, where a song-like elaboration might occur modeled on Genesis 27, Isaac's blessing of Jacob and then of Esau— episodes that anticipate the famous copia of blessings Jacob and Moses bequeath before their death on the B'nei Israel—here the style remains so laconic that one could suspect a decision to truncate, to allow the present moment a minimal telling. Wit, at this juncture, is not the wit of words: there is no rush of rhetoric, no verbal testing as so often in Shakespeare, where the characters parry and thrust and wound by overflowing puns. Wit is a matter of bearing up under, standing under, a directive called the Covenant or Promise or Blessing. It is no accident that the story turns on the manifestation of a name and a blessing: these charged vocatives have ominous as well as nominative value and are to be won rather than willfully seized or expended.

The words, then, stacked so close, with their roots still showing, are, as Auerbach says, *deutungsbedürftig*: demanding interpretation. Their meaning is a sediment that needs settling, almost like the wandering patriarchs themselves. I shall come back to this point; let me stress for the moment that the presence of a redactor, fusing cult legends centered on person and place, is more than an erudite hypothesis. The redactional process, provable or not, is descriptive of a style in which every sentence is a jealously guarded deposit, as if language had to have authority, whatever uncertainties encompassed the reported event or act of naming it. In that sense Jacob's struggle continues within the interpretive communities that receive this story as Scripture. In its determinate indeterminacy, in its authoritative and inscriptive spareness, one is reminded of Herman Melville's impression of Judea: "Stones of Judea. We read a good deal about stones in Scripture. Monuments and memorials are set up of stones; men are stoned to death; the figurative seed falls in stony places. . . . Judea is one accumulation of stones."[2]

Here is, in the King James version, what I call the core story, framed by Gen. 32:1–22 and 33:

> And Jacob was left alone; and there wrestled a man with him until the breaking of the day. And when he saw that he prevailed not against him, he touched the hollow of his thigh; and the hollow of Jacob's thigh was strained, as he wrestled with him. And he said, Let me go, for the day breaketh. And he said, I will not let thee go, except thou bless me. And he said unto him, What is thy name? And he said, Jacob. And he said, Thy name shall be called no more Jacob, but Israel: for thou hast striven with God and with men, and hast prevailed. And Jacob asked him, and said, Tell me, I pray thee, thy name. And he said, Wherefore is it that thou dost ask after my name? And he blessed him there. And Jacob called the name of the place Peniel: for I have seen God face to face, and my life is preserved.

Nothing readies us for this event. Jacob is journeying to Canaan; he reaches Maḥanaim and makes preparations for meeting Esau. Suddenly, at night, this man (*ish*) appears. Was it a dream, perhaps? Maimonides thought so. Jacob, who had a vision at Beth-el, now has a vision at Peni-el. He is always, in his semitic state, in his wanderings, met by angels or divine messengers. Yet there is a difference. The meeting is not only sudden, like a vision or dream—this time what happens can be called a vision only by analogy, because the text is so terse, and says "man" not "angel," and no word about dreaming. Emily Dickinson expresses our feeling when she concludes a poem inspired by the episode,

> And the bewildered Gymnast
> Found he had worsted God.[3]

Such bewilderment is not lessened by the placement of the story, as chapter 32 becomes chapter 33. It is a combat not necessary to the sequence of events. We could omit it and still have a continuous narrative—indeed, a more continuous one.

Remember the circumstances in which Jacob finds himself. He is afraid of Esau and wants to appease him. He settles down for the night in the camp (v. 14) and sends before him an avant-garde of propitiatory gifts: "two hundred she goats and twenty he goats, two hundred ewes and twenty rams, thirty milch camels," and so forth. A few lines further on we read again: "So these gifts passed over before him; and he himself lodged that night in the camp." Then, as if he were woken by a dream or unsure that enough gifts had been sent before, the text informs us, "he rose up that night, and took his two wives and two handmaidens, and eleven children, and passed over the ford of the Jabbok. He took them, and sent them over the stream, and sent over that which he had" (v. 23). From that somewhat tautological statement, which sounds to me like an attempted coda, we go to the laconic struggle with the "man." But in terms of the narrative we could cross easily to chapter 33, assuming the night has gone by, "Jacob lifted up his eyes, and looked, and behold, Esau came, and with him four hundred men."

Now everything is sequential, logical: this is how Jacob's camp meets that of Esau, and Jacob's cunning preparations work out. The brothers reconcile. Chapter 33, in fact, does not refer to Jacob as Israel but still as Jacob: the struggle by night is clearly an episode that has inserted itself into a funny-fearful story illustrating Jacob's resourcefulness.

So the struggle with the angel is not only a stark, mysterious event, but unnecessary in terms of the unfolding narrative. This narrative exhibits Jacob's character, or his conduct, which is prudent though not exactly courageous. In his wish to appease and flatter Esau, Jacob is almost blasphemous. In words that strangely echo "for I have seen God face to face and my life is preserved," Jacob says to his brother, "If I have found favor in your sight, receive my gift, for indeed I have seen your face as one sees the face of God."

Jacob is not an admirable person, patriarch though he may be. (Gunkel, in *The Legends of Genesis*, laconically entitles one section, "The Patriarchs not Saints."[4]) But it is not entirely Jacob's fault, for this is the story of two camps, Maḥanaim (Gen. 32:2–3), two nations, Edom and Israel, from the start—from the very womb of Rebeccah in which Jacob and Esau struggle. There too is a wrestling, and Jacob's name comes from that neonatal fight. "His hand had hold of Esau's heel (*akev*), and they called him Jacob (*Yaakov*)." You will also recall his tricking Esau out of his birthright and blessing; and his behavior with Laban. "*Vayignov Yaakov Lavan* . . . (31:20). Jacob is a ganev, though I won't claim Laban was much better; Jacob, I am sorry to say, is what he is called in the Bible: a heel.

Let me continue to put together what is well-known. The mysterious episode of Jacob's contest is actually what gives him his chance to prove himself. He has struggled with men and prevailed—but at some cost to his father, his brother, and *our* moral sense. No redactorial revision, no appeal to his fated role in a providential drama, can remove the suspicion that he is cunning rather than noble—in short, a trickster. It is true that Abraham and Isaac too can use deceit and subterfuge, but they are less called upon to do so. Did Abraham try to pass off a ram for his child? That is not what the Bible says. Yet about Jacob it is candid; and Jacob too, of course, will be deceived by his children when they break his heart by showing him Joseph's technicolor coat dipped in goat's blood.

How does Jacob prove himself during that night-contest? Think first of the irony of his situation: he prepares to meet the wrath of Esau; he puts his property and even his family in front of him, and whom does he meet, and when? "And Jacob was left alone." As Speiser says, "The carefully calculated never comes off."[5] There is nothing between Jacob and the wrestler, that antagonist from nowhere. Then it turns out the man is not a man, but God himself. Even if he is an angel and not God, no other patriarch, no other Biblical character except for Moses has so direct and dangerous an encounter with a divine agent.

Genesis Rabbah makes a startling suggestion when it quotes R. Berekiah. "There is none like God (Deut. 32:26); yet who is like God? Jeshurun, which means Israel the Patriarch. Just as it is written of God, And the Lord alone shall be exalted (Isaiah 2:11), so of Jacob too: And Jacob was left alone (Genesis 32:25)."[6] This is more than eulogy, for the allusion that identifies Jacob and Jeshurun is underwritten by the opening proof-text of the midrash: "There is none like unto God, O Jeshurun." The word *alone* acquires two senses: *only* Jacob, among all men, is noble or straight enough to be compared to God; but also, more radically, the *loneliness* of the human Jacob in this encounter can remind us of the *aloneness* of God. Jacob wrestles with God as God wrestles with Himself.

Through this unmediated encounter, everything shady in Jacob is removed: the blessing he stole he now receives by right; and his name, tainted by his birth and subsequent behavior, is cleared. No longer will he be called Jacob, that is, Heel or Usurper, but Israel, the God-fighter—quite a title, even if the redactor draws back and shows some cunning of his own, claiming it means "You have striven with God [Midrash: Angels] *and with men*." "As with men" would seem more exact, if it is an anaphoric reference to Jacob's trouble with Laban and Esau. Or should we take "You have striven with God [*elohim*] and with men" as a hendyadis, intending "you have striven with godlike men," or "with a godlike man"? The narrator's gloss tries to settle the meaning of *Yisrael*, but only complicates it. In the recent Torah Commentary issued by the Union of the American Hebrew Congregations, modern scholarship develops, without alluding to it, Rabbi Berekiah's midrash. "Jeshurun," another name for Israel the Patriarch, "means noblest and best": the rabbis suspect the name is rooted in the word for "upright" (*yashar*). So Yisrael, we learn from this newest Commentary, is probably derived from *yashar-el*, the one whom God makes straight, as opposed to *yaakov-el*, the one whom God makes to limp.[7] Moreover, it has been suggested, the stems *akov* (heel) and *avek* (wrestle) may chime like anagrams. It hardly matters: the eponymic privilege passes to Jacob, whatever the title means. The name change denotes a character change, or the inner sense of Jacob's previous life breaking through. *Anokhi imkha*, God had said to him in the Beth-el or house of God vision (Gen. 28:15); there "I am with you" sounded comforting, but here the testing and dangerous side of it is disclosed, as a divinely inflicted bruise replaces a flaw of character.

"It is no sin to limp," Freud writes at the end of *Beyond the Pleasure Principle*.[8] He knows his démarche in this treatise has not been as straightforward, not as logical or scientific as he might wish; and I can only repeat Freud's genial self-defense. For you may wonder what is literary about my reflections so far. Am I not constructing a homily or midrash, and so competing with the Rabbinic sages instead of separating out a literary field with its own distinctive boundary?

While midrash must be viewed as a type of discourse with its own rules and historical development, and while we cannot assume that its only function was exegetical, little is more important today than to remind secular literary studies of the richness and subtlety of those strange rabbinic conversations which have been disdained for so long in favor of more objective and systematized modes of reading. Moreover, for any text to remain alive requires the attention and supplementation of commentary. But this sets up a paradox involving the relation of source-text to the concept *literature*. If we accept von Rad's view that the lateness and literariness of the Yahwist (the supposed author-redactor of the combat story) go hand in hand, and that "becoming literature meant in a sense an end for this [Biblical] material, which until then had already had a varied history behind it,"[9] then the proper task of midrashic or non-midrashic exegesis is to keep the Bible from becoming literature. Becoming literature might mean a material still capable of development turning into a closed corpus, a once-living but now fossilized deposit. The only virtue I can claim for the literary study of the Bible is, therefore, that while it can hardly be more imaginative than the masters of old, *it can dare to go wrong*. Let me try.

I return to our brief story. I have suggested its extraordinary summation of Jacob's character, its conversion of a cunning person, a sort of Jewish Odysseus, into a consecrated patriarch, touching and touched by God. Yet there are disturbing currents in the episode, which the Rabbis picked up but did not always pursue explicitly. Berekiah's remarks on "Jacob was left alone" show what the Rabbis could do. For the contemporary reader one perplexing feature is the sudden appearance of that "man." Another is the fact that he wishes to leave before sunrise. Finally, there is the unusual theme of wrestling with and overcoming divinity.

Maimonides, as I reported, thought it must have been a prophetic dream of Jacob's.[10] Rashi, abbreviating various commentators, suggests that the mysterious man was indeed an angel, but of a special sort—Esau's guardian angel. The encounter has a divine but also an unkosher aspect: this may be Esau's protector waylaying Jacob. In this case the surprise would be that Jacob encounters not the flesh-and-blood Esau, for whom he has so carefully prepared, but his demonic double. Being a ghost or demon, moreover, would explain why the man must get away before sunrise, although Rashi will not say more about this peculiarity than that the angel leaves to praise at break of day.

Gunkel too senses something strange in a story seemingly unable to make up its mind about the natural-supernatural character of this episode. "Jacob was really a Titan, and consequently we can scarcely avoid seeing a faded out myth."[11] Now Jacob himself, as well as his opponent, is more than human. In Genesis Rabbah we find, to our surprise, that the conversation turns mainly on the nature of angels: whether or not "The Holy One, blessed be He" creates a new company of angels every day, who utter a song before Him and then depart (i.e., cease to exist).[12] (This is a thought, by the way, which still haunted Walter Benjamin's imagination, as Scholem has shown.) Do we need this additional distraction, however beautiful, especially since it introduces yet another uncertainty? If, indeed, the angels are new each morning and do not last the rest of the day, what sort of being is this phantom of the night? Rabbi Helbo has an answer. "It was Michael or Gabriel, who are celestial princes; all others are exchanged, but they are not exchanged." In sum, the man may be divine and not divine; he may be a demon and not a demon; while Jacob may be a man or a transformed Titan, a usurper or a heroic challenger who wrests the blessing from God even as he had wrested it, by sleight of hand, from his father.

So far everything I have said merely emphasizes the betwixt-and-between status of Jacob: he is a wanderer; he dwells in the space of Maḥanaim, the double camp on this and the other side of the river; the outcome between him and his brother is not assured; and the combat itself, climaxing in the key phrase "you have striven with elo-him and with men," keeps the nature of the opponent undecidable. On what side of the stream Jacob was, what the name of a person is or what it means, whether Peni'el or Penu'el is the right spelling, and whether Jabbok is or is not a metathesis of Ya'akov cannot be determined like a clearly marked border.

The same questionable border affects the filiation, in this episode, of folktale and Scripture. Gunkel sees in the combat a faded myth; we may also recall legends in which an evil spirit waylays, through jealousy or malice, a person chosen to be superior to the realm of such spirits. The rabbi's learned discussion about the praising, ephemerid angels may not be a digression after all, but rather a tacit acknowledgment that there is not always peace in the high heavens; that even up there beings exist who are jealous of man, who accuse him the more they praise God. For there is no praise without slander; and the angel who attacks Jacob may be the Satan who accuses Job. It is, fundamentally, Jacob's good name that is in question. What is man, that thou (God) shouldst magnify him? It is just as well the angels last only as long as sunrise, for this guarantees our safety: the dawn which means a return of life to us, of the soul to the body, means they cannot carry our night-thoughts before God's throne. They praise Him, then cease to exist.

Nothing said so far, I want to emphasize again, is strictly literary, except for the question of how much legend or folktale Scripture has displaced. But the type or structure of displacement, which will interest Roland Barthes, for example, has not been explored. What interests me are the fault lines of a text, the evidence of a narrative sedimentation that has not entirely settled, and the tension that results between producing one authoritative account and respecting traditions characterized by a certain heterogeneity. In Scripture, despite doubled stories and inconsistencies, there is a sometimes laconic, sometimes wordy, but always imperious unity. In Jacob's combat that unifying tension reaches a peculiar pitch. Listen once more to the following sentence:

> And when he saw that he prevailed not against him, he touched the hollow of his thigh, and the hollow of Jacob's thigh was strained, as he wrestled with him. And he said, Let me go . . .

There is something twisted here, because while it is Jacob who is wounded, it is his antagonist who immediately pleads for release. This fact is sometimes explained by saying that Jacob triumphed despite the wound inflicted on him. But suppose that the text has passed over or modified a difficulty in the received versions. That difficulty would be, as I see it, that it was Jacob who touched the man's thigh and wounded him, but that it seemed impossible—to the narrator—for a divine being to be physically, literally hurt. One tradition or solution, therefore, might be to represent Jacob's antagonist as a "man." Yet the story has little point unless it bestows on Jacob the title *Yisrael*, and its connotation of a consecrating contact with divinity. It is possible, moreover, that the tradition was handed down in ambiguous form and made more believable or homogeneous by a redactorial process which, however, was careful to leave some traces. To understand the process, all we have to do is omit one word, the name *Ya'akov* from verse 26. The first "he" could then be Jacob rather than the angel: "And when he saw that he prevailed not against him, he touched the hollow of his thigh, and the hollow of his thigh was strained, as he wrestled with him." It could be Jacob who touched his opponent's thigh and by that blow—a low blow—assured victory for himself. This could be consistent with the Jacob we know, the trickster who gains the blessing by deceit.

It is the privilege of a literary interpreter to revive this uncomfortable perspective, though not in order to slander Jacob. Rather, once again, to reveal the *maḥanaim* situation, the doubleness and duplicity out of which Jacob must always emerge. Or simply to respect the hendyadic, even polyphonic nature of all texts, as they strive for a single, authoritative point of view. There are interesting asymmetries and superfluities in so economical a story—the entire story itself, in fact, introduces something baffling on the level of narrative that cannot be smoothed over or harmonized without further redactional or interpretive moves. Without producing incoherence these baffles raise questions that are at once textual and interpretive. A stronger way of putting it is that the mode of existence of the text and the mode of representation (mimesis) have fused beyond alteration—though not, of course, beyond analysis.

Imagine a section of Genesis beginning, "Call me Israel." However deep, struggling, or myriad-minded the ensuing narrative, we would know ourselves in the presence of fiction, not Scripture. The same holds, of course, for texts more scrabbled than the Bible, texts like Joyce's *Finnegans Wake*. "Shem is as short for Shemus as Jem is joky for Jacob." The problem we face, strangely enough, it not that we cannot define Scripture but that having gradually redefined fiction in the light of Scripture we now find it hard to distinguish between them. We see both within a global definition of what textuality is; and the same merging occurs as we recover a knowledge of midrash, so that literary criticism and midrashic modes begin to blend into each other. It is no accident that recent theories of intertextuality have devalued the principle of unity as it lodges with some organic or magical mastery attributed to the author of the work. The authority of the author, as that of the Biblical redactor or redactors, comes from the way the intertextual situation is handled; and in this authors are close to being redactors, even if they do not acknowledge it. Any text, however seemingly autonomous, is also what Coleridge said truth is: a ventriloquist. Through this text other texts speak. Eliot, when he characterized poetry as a "medium" that digested the most disparate experiences, raised the same issue of the unstable unity of art, or the tensions within it. The New Criticism explored these tensions as the source of aesthetic value and identified them with such formal properties as paradox, irony, ambiguity and the use of complex or multiple plots. The newer criticism, however, is less concerned with unity and more with the uniformity that comes through too anxious an emphasis on unity. It uses intertextuality as a "technique of suspicion" directed against both the romantic myth of originality and the classicist myth of normative language behavior.

The awareness that all writing is a fusion of heterogeneous stories or types of discourse—that it is layered or even macaronic while seeking the appearance of unity—has been fostered by some of the most important scholarship of recent times. Although there are anthropologists and historians of religion who still aim to find the dominant myth of a particular culture (that of the "High God," for example), many others dispute that there is a myth *an sich* rather than a corpus of stories interacting with a commentary-process that continually modifies, updates and syncretizes what is at hand. Levi-Strauss, while maintaining the concept of a "myth of reference" as the hypothetically stable, synoptic focus of stories called myths, and while trying to extract from them a logic common to all minds, savage or sophisticated, also describes the bricolage that repairs or revises the always faltering mythic narrative. Mikhail Bakhtin discloses a "heteroglossia" within novels that seem spoken or coordinated by a single authorial presence. Clifford Geertz and Jonathan Smith train our eyes like good literary exegetes to appreciate the thick tricky texture of native informants as well as distant fables. This more complex understanding came initially through the Higher Criticism of the Bible, which analyzed a unified, authorless narrative into its redacted and blended strands. With the Higher Criticism we are back, of course, to German scholarship of the nineteenth century, which introduced a sort of geologically structured sense of time into the development of Scripture.

I would like to assert that Scripture can be distinguished from fiction by its frictionality: not only its respect for friction, which exists also in literary texts, but its capacity to leave traces, which incite and even demand interpretation of what it has incorporated. Yet the contemporary theories I have described, which derive partly from Biblical scholarship, make such a distinction more difficult. There may be more cryptomnesia in fiction than in the Bible. But if there is a major difference, it bears on the fact that the respect which shapes variant stories into a narrative does not—in Scripture—reflect only the aesthetic problem of blending them into a unified whole. It recalls, or should recall, the authority of traditions handed down, each with its truth claim—a respect which makes every word, and not only the characters, "schwer von ihrem Gewordensein," to quote Auerbach: heavy with the fullness of having had to be formed.

Let me conclude by exemplifying this problem of definition in the work of Roland Barthes, whose essay "The Struggle with the Angel" on Genesis 32 is, except for Auerbach's chapter in *Mimesis*, the best modern commentary on a Biblical episode. Barthes is not interested in what makes this text Scripture rather than fiction. After Propp and Levi-Strauss he might dispute such a distinction. In his *Morphology of the Folktale* Propp established the structure of that form by analyzing out a finite number of "functions" or type-episodes which every folktale combines.[13] To describe Jacob's combat Barthes cites numbers 15 through 19, including the perilous *passage* from place to place; *combat* between villain and hero; *branding or marking* the hero or bestowing on him a special gift; *victory* of the hero; and so forth. Associated episodes such as the difficult crossing of a ford guarded by a hostile spirit also identify Jacob's struggle as having the same structure as a folktale. But this resemblance is not what holds Barthes's attention, and doubtless he could have analyzed a Homeric sequence in the same structuralist fashion. "What interests me most in this famous passage," he writes, "is not the 'folkloristic' model but the abrasive frictions, the breaks, the discontinuities of readability, the juxtaposition of narrative entities which to some extent run free from an explicit logical articulation. One is dealing here (this at least is for me the savour of reading) with a sort of *metonymic montage*: the themes (Crossing, Struggling, Naming, Alimentary Rite) are *combined*, not 'developed.'" Barthes ends by claiming that this "asyndetic character" or "metonymic logic" of the narrative expresses the unconscious and he asks for a reading that would lead to the text's "symbolic explosion," its "dissemination, not its truth," so that we would not reduce it to a signified, whether "historical, economic, folkloristic or kerygmatic," but would manage "to hold *its significance* fully open."[14]

Barthes's powerful application of Propp places the folkloric context beyond doubt. Yet one peculiarity of his account must be mentioned. How can he talk of the "asyndetic character of the narrative" when its most obvious syntactical feature is parataxis or syndeton: the linking of every verse segment by the conjunction *va* (and)? Only the last verse differs by substituting a coda-like *al ken* (therefore) and *ki* (because), which are simply heightened conjunctives.

Barthes cannot reply that he is referring to structural juxtapositions, for he has said specifically he is commenting on the "savour of the reading" not the "structural exploitation." In truth, this proclitic and ubiquitous *va* is like the rarer enclitic *yah* or *el*, signifying God. Barthes cannot value this initial sign tacked onto so much and pointing to a teleological direction, even if God remains hidden most of the time. Von Rad, a theologian, is nearer the mark when he observes that "the divine promise is like a sign before and over all these individual narratives, and within this bracket, so to speak, there is much good and evil."[15]

Barthes, then, is too obviously "deconstructing" a text normally identified as belonging to Scripture and ideological in its orientation. He does not see that the teleolological impulse participates in the concatenative power of storyteller or redactor, in that motivating *va*, and in the will to shape by combining. The process of composition here is not exclusively unifying or agglomerative: divergencies are not always resolved. This produces a textual quality which is peculiar enough to be given a separate name, despite structural similarities with saga, folklore, or stories stuck together by what scholars call "contamination."

When Barthes, therefore, asks us to hold the significance of this Bible story "fully open," by stressing an asyndetic and metonymic logic that unsettles the signified and enables the story's "dissemination, not its truth," he leaves out, even structurally, what Auerbach in his *akedah* interpretation stresses so effectively. The truth claim of the Bible, Auerbach says, is so imperious that reality in its sensuous or charming aspect is not dwelt upon; and the spotlight effect, which isolates major persons or happenings, is due to the same anagogical demand that excludes all other places and concerns. Bible stories do not flatter or fascinate like Homer's; they do not give us something artfully rendered; they force readers to become interpreters and to find the presence of what is absent in the fraught background, the densely layered (Auerbach uses the marvelous word *geschichtet*) narrative.

By comparing two passages, the *akedah* from the Bible and a recognition scene from the nineteenth book of the *Odyssey*—passages that do not have the slightest thematic relation—and by refusing to disqualify one in the light of the other or to find the same basic structure in them, Auerbach maintains a gap between Scripture and fiction, if only in the form of Hebraic versus Hellenic. It is possible to object that this gap narrows because of the New Testament, or because of the Hellenic phase Hebrew learning goes through. It is also possible to plead that the Hellenizing did not really change the Hebraic tradition in the long run. What remains important is that one mind brings together radically divergent modes of representation under the sign of difference. This would not have been possible if both stories did not belong, at some level, to the same culture. This culture is, or was, a reading culture: the curator not only of widely divergent types of literature but also of informed modes of interpretation that encourage a perspectival empathy. Yet by the time Auerbach wrote, a nationalism that had fostered the development of the vernaculars in the Renaissance, and made *Mimesis* possible by reflecting the depth and concreteness of historical life, was imposing a doctrinaire canon and tyrannical unity of expression. As an expatriate victim of German National Socialism, Auerbach was himself a *maḥanaim* figure, though he did not seek a truer homeland, like Abraham, nor did he venture, like Odysseus, to return to his old place, in the hope it would still know him.

The question of the relation of place to destiny or spiritual strength is given extraordinary resonance by the story of the patriarchs and here by Jacob's combat. I am reminded of Booker T. Washington's remark about another people emerging from slavery. "They must change their names. They must leave the Old Plantation." In the Hebrew Bible this imperative is related to literature from the beginning: these narratives of exodus (starting with the command to Abraham, *lekh lekha*, or "get out"), these episodes fixing place names or proper names by paranomasia to a partic- ular theophany, continue to demand an exegete despite various etiological frames intending to make those names less opaque. Each storied reasoning upon names recharges the name: semantic opaqueness is not removed, it is simply surrounded by the possibility that there was an original meaning or a specific and authoritative act of designation. Where did that authority, that performative strength come from? Does *nomen* become *numen*, except through the story inspired by it? Can spirit and place ever coincide except through the extended naming fiction enables?

The universality of Jacob's combat with the angel lies, finally, in that struggle for a text—for a supreme fiction or authoritative account stripped of inessentials, of all diversions, of everything we might describe as arbitrary, parochial, even aesthetic. It centers on a sparse and doubtful set of words, handed on by an editorial process which in its conflations or accommodations could seem to be the very antithesis of the unmediated encounter it describes. Nicknames like Yaakov or Yisrael, place names like Peni'el, and other agnominations accumulate as a sacred or a silly burden: they are, we sense, a stock of vocatives (ex-vocatives, perhaps) which the redactors cannot let go but count and recount, sorting gods and goats into something more than a list, a proprietary catalogue, a hoard of names. The accreted, promissory narrative we call Scripture is composed of tokens that demand the continuous and precarious intervention of successive generations of interpreters, who must keep the words as well as the faith.

Notes

1   Erich Auerbach, *Mimesis: The Representation of Reality in Western Literature*, trans. Willard R. Trask (New York: Doubleday, 1957).

2   Herman Melville, *Journal of a Visit to Europe and the Levant, October* 11, 1856—*May* 6, 1857, ed. Howard C. Horsford (Princeton: Princeton University Press, 1955).

3   Emily Dickinson, "A little east of Jordan," in *Complete Poems*, ed. Thomas H. Johnson (Boston: Little Brown, 1960), no. 59.

4   Hermann Gunkel, *The Legends of Genesis: The Biblical Saga und History*, trans. William Herbert Carruth (New York: Schocken Books, 1970), pp. 113–16.

5   *The Anchor Bible: Genesis*, ed. and trans. Ephraim Avigdor Speiser (Garden City, N.Y.: Doubleday, 1964–83), p. 256.

6   *Genesis Rabbah*, vol. 1 of *Midrash Rabbah*, ed. Harry Freedman and Maurice Simon (London: Soncino Press, 1961), p. 710. Cf. the remarkable "we do not know who was victorious," p. 712. Berekiah's remarks do more than ennoble Jacob. They make Jacob and his story also reveal something about God: an attribute, or *His* "character." God, after all, is the ultimate author of Scripture and midrash holds up the mirror to that textual image in order to search out and catch what is knowable about Him.

7   *The Torah: A Modern Commentary*, ed. W. G. Plaut, B. J. Bamberger and W. Hallo, Union of American Hebrew Congregations (New York, 1981).

8   Sigmund Freud, *Beyond the Pleasure Principle*, in *The Standard Edition of the Complete Psychological Works of Sigmund Freud*, trans. James Strachey (London: Hogarth Press, 1955), vol. 18, p. 64.

9   Gerhard von Rad, *Genesis: A Commentary*, rev. ed. (Philadelphia, 1972), p.18.

10   Moses ben Maimon (Maimonides), *The Guide of the Perplexed*, 2d ed., trans. Michael Friedlander (New York: Dover Publications, 1956), pt. 2, chap. 43 (in some editions chap. 42).

11   Gunkel, *Legends of Genesis*, p. 120.

12   *Genesis Rabbah*, p. 710.

13   Vladimir I. Propp, *Morphology of the Folktale*, rev. ed., trans. Laurence Scott, ed. Louis A. Wagner (Austin: University of Texas Press, 1968).

14   Roland Barthes, "The Struggle with the Angel," in *Image Music Text*, trans. Stephen Heath (London: Fontana Collins, 1977), pp. 125–41.

15   Von Rad, *Genesis: A Commentary*, p. 268. Von Rad also describes eloquently the stratified nature of this text. He writes: "In this narrative more than in any other of the ancient patriarchal traditions something of the long process of formation to which this material was subjected in history becomes clear. . . . There are scarcely examples in Western literature of this kind of narrative, which combines such spaciousness in content with such stability in form. Many generations have worked on them, as in the case of an old house; much of the content has been adjusted in the course of time, much has again been dropped, but most has remained. . . . Here is a passage where a much older form of our saga is revealed. . . . one might think at first, in view of the hopelessness of the fight, that Jacob has won the upper hand over his antagonist (by a trick of fighting?). This interpretation would best suit the continuation, in v. 26, where the antagonist asks Jacob to let him go and then also the later statement that Jacob had prevailed (v. 28b). This monstrous conception, however, that Jacob nearly defeated the heavenly being, is now concealed by the clear text of v. 25b and v. 32b" (pp. 320–21).

Chapter 3

Reception History

ALTHOUGH THERE IS A long history of writers, scholars and theologians acknowledging and attending to the role of the reader, the recent interest in the way that texts are received is rooted in the concerns of several twentieth-century literary theorists. Following Roland Barthes' famous critique of the idea that textual meaning was located in the author's intention, other theorists debated whether a stable meaning could be found elsewhere.[1] One of the most notorious contributions to this discussion was Stanley Fish's *Is There a Text in This Class: The Authority of Interpretative Communities* (1980), which argued that textual meaning was constructed by readers, or rather 'interpretive communities', and was not inherent to a text: 'Interpretation is not the art of construing but the art of constructing.'[2] While Fish's polemical style of writing made his work an obvious rallying point for those who wished to draw attention to the role of the reader, there were other centres for thinking along these lines, particularly Hans-Georg Gadamer's work on philosophical hermeneutics, and the use of social scientific methods by Wolfgang Iser and his colleagues at the University of Constance in Germany to analyse the historic reception of texts.

Recent scholarly interest in the ways that texts have been understood and thought about by people in different periods has tended to be less polemical than Fish's approach and more concerned with recovering the historical and material details of reception. But it is worth remembering that this effort is still caught up in broader philosophical debates about literary meaning and the practice of hermeneutics. In contrast to those who think that reading the Bible requires the application of a historical-critical method, focussed on understanding the historicity of the text's initial production and on reconstructing the ways in which the earliest audience might have received and understood the biblical texts, others insist that the long history of a text's reception helps us appreciate the interpretive fertility of the biblical texts and to recognize the historicity of our interpretive standpoint. Whereas advocates of the historical-critical method tend to see literary rewritings of the Bible as a historical curiosity, an illustration of existing theological ideas, or a site for doctrinal deviation, those who embrace reception history are likely to see literary rewritings of the Bible as a reminder of the different ways in which the Bible can be read over time and also a point of commentary on why we read in the ways we do.

Before we get to the three extracts chosen for this section, it is worth high-lighting two recent projects on the reception history of the Bible. The first is the *Oxford Handbook of the Reception History of the Bible* (2011), edited by Michael Lieb, Emma Mason and Jonathan Roberts. Containing over 40 essays by a wide range of contributors, this book on reception history favours diversity over a more uniform sense of what sort of material such a volume should include. While this approach makes for very different approaches, it also alerts us to the complexity and instability of the concept of reception history, an important point given reception history's concern with the time-bound prejudice of all reading. A similar sense of the multiplicity of perspectives opened up by a focus on reception history is evident in the *Blackwell Bible Commentary Series* that examines the different books of the Bible through reception history (in the arts, culture, history and theology). Readers of the present volume who are interested in exploring the subject of reception history further are encouraged to look at this series more closely.

Turning to the material included here, the first extract, from Iser's *The Act of Reading: A Theory of Aesthetic Response* (1978), locates the contribution of the reader to the meaning of a text within a very specific framework. Drawing on social psychology and psychoanalytical thought, Iser understands the reader as one who fills in textual gaps. Iser's account acknowledges the contribution of the reader to questions of textual meaning but he makes the reader subservient to a guiding partner (the text). One of the reasons Iser steers away from an understanding of interpretation that grants text and reader more mutual roles is his view that texts are fixed partners, unable to adapt to the reader in the way that a living person might interact with his or her interlocutor. When someone reads, he or she is the only one able to alter their projects as they experience a perspective other than their own. As Iser puts it, the reader 'is drawn into the events and made to supply what is meant from what is not said'. But the meaning of the text for Iser is inaugurated by the text and the gaps that the reader fills in are 'on terms set by the text'. This unequal relationship is one that Iser describes as asymmetric.

Gadamer's thoughts about reception in *Truth and Method* (1960) are arguably more ambitious than those of his countryman. In some respects, the comparison between the two thinkers is unfair: Gadamer's work explores the shape, content and nature of hermeneutics across the human sciences and he is concerned with the philosophy underlying all acts of interpretation rather than the narrower act of reading considered by Iser. But while we should be cautious about comparisons with Iser, the greater ambition of Gadamer's work is significant for what he has to say about the specific act of reading, which he describes in terms of an interpretative conversation. For Gadamer, the conversation is genuinely open ended and not controlled by either of its participants. Gadamer uses the concept of conversation to think about hermeneutics as an event, a moment in time where text and reader interact. He is aware, of course, that texts cannot answer back in the way that a human interlocutor might, but he argues that the concept of conversation remains useful because the meaning of a text changes as it is received over time: 'in being changed back by understanding, the subject matter of which the text speaks itself finds expression. It is like a real conversation in that the common subject matter is what binds the two partners, the text and the interpreter, to each other.' For Gadamer, the common subject matter is meaning, understood as a series of historic events rather than a transcendent entity that exists outside of each act of reading.

If all interpretation can be understood as a conversation, then the extract by Yvonne Sherwood, taken from *A Biblical Text and Its Afterlives: The Survival of Jonah in Western Culture* (2000), is evidence of how many twists and turns that conversation can and does take over time. Combining the work of reception history with the theoretical insights of an array of thinkers such as Jacques Derrida, Michael Foucault, Stephen Greenblatt and Stanley Fish, Sherwood reads the biblical story of Jonah playfully but also with a sharp eye to important theological, political and social concerns. She is especially interested in the readings of the Christian tradition, which have had very different things to say about Jonah and the whale over the years: 'I can think of no better prooftext for a Fishy foregrounding of the role of the reader than a text that, between the Christian period and critical biblical studies, manages to rotate in meaning through *one-hundred-and-eighty degrees*.' But Sherwood is also attentive to the readings of this story by a modern academic readership that can be equally oblivious to its own bias. Through an entertaining and thoughtful tour of Jonah's reception, Sherwood interrogates 'voices from the past' but also most 'recent voices' surrounding this biblical text, voices which, she insists, 'speak with a suspiciously strong European accent'. Against those who presume that their modern reading is somehow free from prejudice, Sherwood insists that all reading of the biblical text reflects historical, cultural and geographic bias.

Notes

1   See Roland Barthes, 'The Death of the Author', in *Image, Music, Text* (London: Fontana Press, 1977), pp. 142–48.
2   Stanley Fish, *Is There a Text in This Class? The Authority of Interpretative Communities* (Cambridge, MA: Harvard University Press, 1980), p. 327.

Further reading

Bockmuehl, Markus, *Seeing the Word: Refocussing New Testament Study* (Grand Rapids, MI: Baker Academic, 2006)
Fish, Stanley, *Is There a Text In This Class? The Authority of Interpretive Communities* (Cambridge, MA: Harvard University Press, 1980)
Holub, Robert C., *Crossing Borders: Reception Theory, Poststructuralism, Deconstruction* (Madison: The University of Wisconsin Press, 1992)
Jauss, Hans Robert, *Towards an Aesthetics of Reception*, trans. Timothy Bahti (Brighton: Harvester University Press, 1982)
Jeffrey, David Lyle, ed., *A Dictionary of Biblical Tradition in English Literature* (Grand Rapids, MI: Eerdmans, 1992)
Knight, Mark, '*Wirkungsgeschichte*, Reception History, Reception Theory', *Journal for the Study of the New Testament*, 33.2 (2010), 137–46.
Lieb, Michael, Emma Mason and Jonathan Roberts, eds., *The Oxford Handbook of the Reception History of the Bible* (Oxford: Oxford University Press, 2011)
Luz, Ulrich, *Matthew 1–7: A Commentary*, trans. Wilhelm C. Linss (Edinburgh: T & T Clark, 1990)

Parris, David Paul, *Reception Theory and Biblical Hermeneutics* (Eugene, OR: Pickwick Publications, 2009)

Rowland, Christopher, 'Re-imagining Biblical Exegesis', in Mark Knight and Louise Lee, eds., *Religion, Literature and the Imagination: Sacred Words* (London: Continuum, 2009), pp. 140–49.

(a) Asymmetry Between Text and Reader

Wolfgang Iser

Conditions of Interaction

In our discussion so far, we have concentrated mainly on the two partners in the communication process, namely, the text and the reader. It is time now to take a closer look at the conditions that give rise to and govern this communication. Reading is an activity that is guided by the text; this must be processed by the reader, who is then, in turn, affected by what he has processed. It is difficult to describe this interaction, not least because the literary critic has very little to go on in the way of guidelines, and, of course, the two partners are far easier to analyze than is the event that takes place between them. However, there are discernible conditions that govern interaction generally, and some of these will certainly apply to the special reader–text relationship. The differences and similarities may become clear if we examine the types of interaction that have emerged from social psychology and psychoanalytical research into structures of communication.

The theory of interaction, as advanced by Edward E. Jones and Harold B. Gerard in *Foundations of Social Psychology*, begins by categorizing the different types of contingency that are to be found in, or arise out of, all human interactions. We need not concern ourselves too closely with these types (i.e., pseudocontingency, asymmetrical, reactive, and mutual contingency); what is important for us is the *fact* that unpredictability is both a constitutive and differentiating element in this process of interaction.

1. We have pseudocontingency when both partners know each other's 'behavioral plan' so well that the replies and their consequences can be accurately predicted; in this case, the conduct of the partners resembles a well-rehearsed scene, and through such ritualization the contingency disappears.

2. Asymmetrical contingency occurs when Partner A gives up trying to implement his own behavioral plan and without resistance follows that of Partner B. He adapts himself to and is absorbed by the behavioral strategy of B.

3. Reactive contingency occurs when the respective behavioral plans of the partners are continually overshadowed by their momentary reactions to what has just been said or done. Here contingency becomes dominant and blocks all attempts by the partners to bring their own plans into play.

4. Mutual contingency involves orienting one's reactions in accordance with one's behavioral plan *and* with the momentary reactions of the partner. This can have two possible consequences: "The interaction might be a triumph of social creativity in which each is enriched by the other, or it might be a spiraling debacle of increasingly mutual hostility from which neither benefits. Whatever the content of the

interaction's course, there is implied a mixture of dual resistance and mutual change that distinguishes mutual contingency from other classes of interaction."[1]

Contingency as a constituent of interaction, arises out of the interaction itself, for the partner's respective behavioral plans are separately conceived, and so it is their unpredictable effect on each other that brings about the tactical and strategical interpretations and adjustments. As a result of the interaction, the behavioral plans are subjected to various tests, and these, in turn, show up deficiencies which themselves are contingent in so far as they reveal limitations in the plans that might not otherwise have been revealed. Such deficiencies generally tend to be productive, because they can bring about new strategies of behavior, as well as modifications in the behavioral plan. It is at this point that contingency is transformed into one or another of the different types of interaction. Herein lies its productive ambivalence: it arises out of interaction and, at the same time, stimulates interaction. The more it is reduced, the more ritualized becomes the interplay between partners; and the more it is increased, the less consistent will be the sequence of reactions, culminating in an extreme case, with the annihilation of the whole structure of interaction.

Similar conclusions may be drawn from psychoanalytical research into communication, as carried out by R. D. Laing, H. Phillipson, and A. R. Lee, whose findings provide insights that can be utilized in assessing text–reader interaction. In *Interpersonal Perception*, Laing writes: "My field of experience is, however, filled not only by my direct view of myself (ego) and of the other (alter), but of what we shall call *meta*perspectives—*my view* of the *other's* . . . view of me. I may not actually be able to see myself as others see me, but I am constantly supposing them to be seeing me in particular ways, and I am constantly acting in the light of the actual or supposed attitudes, opinions, needs, and so on the other has in respect of me."[2]

Now the views that others have of me cannot be called 'pure' perception; they are the results of interpretation. And this need for interpretation arises from the structure of interpersonal experience. We have experience of one another in so far as we know one another's conduct; but we have no experience of how others experience us. In another book, *The Politics of Experience*, Laing writes: ". . . *your experience of me is invisible to me and my experience of you is invisible to you*. I cannot experience your experience. You cannot experience my experience. We are both invisible men. All men are invisible to one another. Experience is man's invisibility to man."[3] It is this invisibility that forms the basis of interpersonal relations—a basis which Laing calls a "no-thing."[4] "That which is really 'between' cannot be named by any things that come between. The between is itself no-thing."[5] In all our interpersonal relationships we build upon this "no-thing," for we react as if we knew how our partners experienced us; we continually form views of their views and then act as if our views of their views were realities. Contact, therefore, depends upon our continually filling in a central gap in our experience.

Using this observation as their starting-point, Laing, Phillipson, and Lee study the products of this 'filling-in' process, assessing and drawing distinctions between the factors of pure perception, projected phantasies, and interpretation.[6] Although the details of their study need not concern us here, it is interesting to note that, according to their findings, interpersonal relationships begin to assume pathological traits to the degree in which individual partners fill the gap with projected phantasies. However, it must be borne in mind that the multiplicity of human relations would be impossible if their basis were already fixed; the dyadic and dynamic interaction comes about only *because* we are unable to experience how we experience one another, which in turn proves to be a propellant to interaction. Out of this fact arises the basic need for interpretation, which regulates the whole process of interaction. As we cannot perceive without preconception, each percept, in turn, only makes sense to us if it is processed, for pure perception is quite impossible. Hence dyadic interaction is not given by nature, but arises out of an interpretative activity, which will contain a view of others and, unavoidably, also an image of ourselves.

Now the fact that we cannot experience the way others experience us does not by any means denote an ontological boundary; it only arises out of the dyadic interaction itself. If there *is* a boundary, it can only be in the sense that the limitations shown up by the interaction give rise to continual attempts to transcend them, i.e., to cross the boundary. Thus the dyadic interaction produces the negativity of experience (we cannot experience how others experience us), and this, in turn, stimulates us into closing the resultant gap by way of interpretation, at the same time putting us in a position to reject our own interpretative gestalten and so remain open to further experience.

An obvious and major difference between reading and all forms of social interaction is the fact that with reading there is no *face-to-face situation*.[7] A text cannot adapt itself to each reader with whom it comes in contact. The partners in dyadic interaction can ask each other questions in order to ascertain how far their views have controlled contingency, or their images have bridged the gap of inexperienceability of one another's experiences. The reader, however, can never learn from the text how accurate or inaccurate are his views of it. Furthermore, dyadic interaction serves specific purposes, so that the interaction always has a regulative context, which often serves as a *tertium comparationis*. There is no such frame of reference governing the text–reader relationship; on the contrary, the codes which might regulate this interaction are fragmented in the text and must first be reassembled or, in most cases, restructured before any frame of reference *can* be established. Here, then, in conditions and intention, we find two basic differences between the text–reader relationship and the dyadic interaction between social partners.

Now it is the very lack of ascertainability and defined intention that brings about the text–reader interaction, and here there is a vital link with dyadic interaction. Social communication, as we have seen, arises out of contingency (behavioral plans do not coincide, and people cannot experience how others experience them), not out of the common situation or out of the conventions that join both partners together. The situation and conventions regulate the manner in which gaps are filled, but the gaps in turn arise out of contingency and inexperienceability and, consequently, function as a basic inducement to communication. Similarly, it is the gaps, the fundamental asymmetry between text and reader, that give rise to communication in the reading process; the lack of a common situation and a common frame of reference corresponds to the contingency and the "no-thing" which bring about the interaction between persons. Asymmetry, contingency, the "no-thing"—these are all different forms of an indeterminate, constitutive blank which underlies all processes of interaction. As has already been pointed out, this blank is not a given, ontological fact, but is formed and modified by the imbalance inherent in dyadic interactions, as well as in that between text and reader. Balance can only be attained if the gaps are filled, and so the constitutive blank is continually bombarded with projections. The interaction fails if the mutual projections of the social partners do not change, or if the reader's projections superimpose themselves unimpeded upon the text. Failure, then, means filling the blank exclusively with one's own projections. Now as the blank gives rise to the reader's projections, but the text itself cannot change, it follows that a successful relationship between text and reader can only come about through changes in the reader's projections.

Thus the text provokes continually changing views in the reader, and it is through these that the asymmetry begins to give way to the common ground of a situation. But through the complexity of the textual structure, it is difficult for this situation to be definitively formulated by the reader's projections: on the contrary, it is continually reformulated as the projections themselves are readjusted by their successors. And in this process of continual correction there arises a frame of reference for the situation—a definite, though not a definitive, shape. It is only through readjustment of his own projections that the reader can experience something previously not within his experience, and this something—as we saw in a preceding chapter— ranges from a detached objectification of what he is entangled in, to an experience of himself that would otherwise be precluded by his entanglement in the pragmatic world around him. With dyadic interaction, the imbalance is removed by the establishment of pragmatic connections resulting in an action, which is why the preconditions are always clearly defined in relation to situations and common frames of reference. The imbalance between text and reader, however, is undefined, and it is this very indeterminacy that increases the variety of communication possible.

If these possibilities are to be fulfilled, and if communication between text and reader is to be successful, clearly, the reader's activity must be controlled in some way by the text. The control cannot be as specific as in a *face-to-face situation*, equally it cannot be as determinate as a social code, which regulates social interaction. However, the guiding devices operative in the reading process have to initiate communication, the success of which is indicated by the constitution of a meaning, which cannot be equated with existing frames of reference, as its own specific quality manifests itself in questioning existing meanings and in altering existing experiences. Nor can the control be understood as a tangible entity occurring independently of the process of communication. Although exercised *by* the text, it is not *in* the text. This is well illustrated by a comment Virginia Woolf made on the novels of Jane Austen:

> Jane Austen is thus a mistress of much deeper emotion than appears upon the surface. She stimulates us to supply what is not there. What she offers is, apparently, a trifle, yet is composed of something that expands in the reader's mind and endows with the most enduring form of life scenes which are outwardly trivial. Always the stress is laid upon character. . . . The turns and twists of the dialogue keep us on the tenterhooks of suspense. Our attention is half upon the present moment, half upon the future. . . . Here, indeed, in this unfinished and in the main inferior story, are all the elements of Jane Austen's greatness.[8]

What is missing from the apparently trivial scenes, the gaps arising out of the dialogue—this is what stimulates the reader into filling the blanks with projections. He is drawn into the events and made to supply what is meant from what is not said. What *is* said only appears to take on significance as a reference to what is not said; it is the implications and not the statements that give shape and weight to the meaning. But as the unsaid comes to life in the reader's imagination, so the said "expands" to take on greater significance than might have been supposed: even trivial scenes can seem surprisingly profound. The "enduring form of life" which Virginia Woolf speaks of is not manifested on the printed page; it is a product arising out of the interaction between text and reader. Communication in literature, then, is a process set in motion and regulated not by a given code but by a mutually restrictive and magnifying interaction between the explicit and the implicit, between revelation and concealment. What is concealed spurs the reader into action, but this action is also controlled by what is revealed; the explicit in its turn is transformed when the implicit has been brought to light.

Virginia Woolf's observations have their basis in the specific nature of language, which Merleau-Ponty has described as follows:

> The lack of a sign can itself be a sign; expression does not consist in the fact that there is an element of language to fit every element of meaning, but in the fact that language influences language—an influence that suddenly shifts in the direction of the meaning of the language. Speaking does not mean substituting a word for every thought: if we did that, nothing would ever be said, and we would not have the feeling of living in language; we would remain in silence, because the sign would at once be obliterated by a meaning. . . . If language gives up stating the thing itself, it irrevocably gives expression to that thing. . . . Language is meaningful when, instead of copying the thought, it allows itself to be broken up and then reconstituted by the thought.[9]

The text is a whole system of such processes, and so, clearly, there must be a place within this system for the person who is to perform the reconstituting. This place is marked by the gaps in the text—it consists in the blanks which the reader is to fill in. They cannot, of course, be filled in by the system itself, and so it follows that they can only be filled in by another system. Whenever the reader bridges the gaps, communication begins. The gaps function as a kind of pivot on which the whole text–reader relationship revolves. Hence the structured blanks of the text stimulate the process of ideation to be performed by the reader on terms set by the text. There is, however, another place in the system where text and reader converge, and that is marked by the various types of negation that arise in the course of the reading. Blanks and negations both control the process of communication in their own different ways: the blanks leave open the connections between perspectives in the text, and so spur the reader into coordinating these perspectives—in other words, they induce the reader to perform basic operations *within* the text. The various types of negation invoke familiar or determinate elements only to cancel them out. What is canceled, however, remains in view, and thus brings about modifications in the reader's attitude toward what is familiar or determinate—in other words, he is guided to adopt a position *in relation* to the text.

To sum up, then, the asymmetry between text and reader stimulates a constitutive activity on the part of the reader; this is given a specific structure by the blanks and the negations arising out of the text, and this structure controls the process of interaction.

Notes

1   Edward E. Jones and Harold B. Gerard, *Foundations of Social Psychology* (New York, 1967), pp. 505–12 (quotation 512).
2   R. D. Laing, H. Phillipson, A. R. Lee, *Interpersonal Perception: A Theory and a Method of Research* (New York, 1966), p. 4.
3   R. D. Laing, *The Politics of Experience.* (Harmondsworth, 1968), p. 16.
4   Ibid., p. 34.
5   Ibid., in this context there is a relevant observation made by Umberto Eco, *Einführung in the Semiotik* (UTB 105), transl. by Jürgen Trabant (Munich, 1972), p. 410, "at the root of every possible communication there is no code, but only the absence of all codes."
6   See Laing, Phillipson, Lee, *Interpersonal Perception*, pp. 18f.
7   See also E. Goffman, *Interaction Ritual: Essays on Face-to-Face Behavior* (New York, 1967).
8   Virginia Woolf, *The Common Reader. First Series* (London, 1957), p. 174. In this context, it is well worth considering Virginia Woolf's comments on the composition of her own fictional characters. She remarks in her diary: "I'm thinking furiously about Reading and Writing. I have no time to describe my plans. I should say a good deal about *The Hours* and my discovery: how I dig out beautiful caves behind my characters: I think that gives exactly what I want; humanity, humour, depth. The idea is that the caves shall connect and each comes to daylight at the present moment." *A Writer's Diary. Being Extracts from the Diary of Virginia Woolf*, Leonard Woolf, ed. (London, 1953), p. 60. The suggestive effect of the "beautiful caves" is continued in her work through that which she leaves out. On this subject, T. S. Eliot once observed: "Her observation, which operates in a continuous way, implies a vast and sustained work of organization. She does not illumine with sudden bright flashes but diffuses a soft and placid light. Instead of looking for the primitive, she looks rather for the civilized, the highly civilized, where nevertheless something is found to be *left out*. And this something is deliberately left out, by what could be called a moral effort of the will. And, being left out, this something is, in a sense, in a melancholy sense, present." "T. S. Eliot, 'places' Virginia Woolf for French Readers," in *Virginia Woolf, The Critical Heritage*, Robin Majumdar and Allen McLaurin, eds. (London, 1975), p. 192.
9   Maurice Merleau-Ponty, *Das Auge und der Geist. Philosophische Essays*, transl. by Hans Werner Arndt (Reinbek, 1967), pp. 73f.

(b) Language and Hermeneutics

Hans-Georg Gadamer

Language As The Medium Of Hermeneutic Experience

We say that we "conduct" a conversation, but the more genuine a conversation is, the less its conduct lies within the will of either partner. Thus a genuine conversation is never the one that we wanted to conduct. Rather, it is generally more correct to say that we fall into conversation, or even that we become involved in it. The way one word follows another, with the conversation taking its own twists and reaching its own conclusion, may well be conducted in some way, but the partners conversing are far less the leaders of it than the led. No one knows in advance what will "come out" of a conversation. Understanding or its failure is like an event that happens to us. Thus we can say that something was a good conversation or that it was ill fated. All this shows that a conversation has a spirit of its own, and that the language in which it is conducted bears its own truth within it—i.e., that it allows something to "emerge" which henceforth exists.

In our analysis of romantic hermeneutics we have already seen that understanding is not based on transposing oneself into another person, on one person's immediate participation with another. To understand what a person says is, as we saw, to come to an understanding about the subject matter, not to get inside another person and relive his experiences (Erlebnisse). We emphasized that the experience (Erfahrung) of meaning that takes place in understanding always includes application. Now we are to note *that this whole process is verbal*. It is not for nothing that the special problematic of understanding and the attempt to master it as an art—the concern of hermeneutics—belongs traditionally to the sphere of grammar and rhetoric. Language is the medium in which substantive understanding and agreement take place between two people.

In situations where coming to an understanding is disrupted or impeded, we first become conscious of the conditions of all understanding. Thus the verbal process whereby a conversation in two different languages is made possible through translation is especially informative. Here the translator must translate the meaning to be understood into the context in which the other speaker lives. This does not, of course, mean that he is at liberty to falsify the meaning of what the other person says. Rather, the meaning must be preserved, but since it must be understood within a new language world, it must establish its validity within it in a new way. Thus every translation is at the same time an interpretation. We can even say that the translation is the culmination of the interpretation that the translator has made of the words given him.

The example of translation, then, makes us aware that language as the medium of understanding must be consciously created by an explicit mediation. This kind of explicit process is undoubtedly not the norm in a conversation. Nor is translation the norm in the way we approach a foreign language. Rather, having to rely on translation is tantamount to two people giving up their independent authority. Where a translation is necessary, the gap between the spirit of the original words and that of their reproduction must be taken into account. It is a gap that can never be completely closed. But in these cases understanding does not really take place between the partners of the conversation, but between the interpreters, who can really have an encounter in a common world of understanding. (It is well known that nothing is more difficult than a dialogue in two different languages in which one person speaks one and the other person the other, each understanding the other's language but not speaking it. As if impelled by a higher force, one of the languages always tries to establish itself over the other as the medium of understanding.)

Where there is understanding, there is not translation but speech. To understand a foreign language means that we do not need to translate it into our own.

When we really master a language, then no translation is necessary—in fact, any translation seems impossible. Understanding how to speak is not yet of itself real understanding and does not involve an interpretive process; it is an accomplishment of life. For you understand a language by living in it—a statement that is true, as we know, not only of living but dead languages as well. Thus the hermeneutical problem concerns not the correct mastery of language but coming to a proper understanding about the subject matter, which takes place in the medium of language. Every language can be learned so perfectly that using it no longer means translating from or into one's native tongue, but thinking in the foreign language. Mastering the language is a necessary precondition for coming to an understanding in a conversation. Every conversation obviously presupposes that the two speakers speak the same language. Only when two people can make themselves understood through language by talking together can the problem of understanding and agreement even be raised. Having to depend on an interpreter's translation is an extreme case that doubles the hermeneutical process, namely the conversation: there is one conversation between the interpreter and the other, and a second between the interpreter and oneself.

Conversation is a process of coming to an understanding. Thus it belongs to every true conversation that each person opens himself to the other, truly accepts his point of view as valid and transposes himself into the other to such an extent that he understands not the particular individual but what he says. What is to be grasped is the substantive rightness of his opinion, so that we can be at one with each other on the subject. Thus we do not relate the other's opinion to him but to our own opinions and views. Where a person is concerned with the other as individuality—e.g., in a therapeutic conversation or the interrogation of a man accused of a crime—this is not really a situation in which two people are trying to come to an understanding.[1]

Everything we have said characterizing the situation of two people coming to an understanding in conversation has a genuine application to hermeneutics, which is concerned with *understanding texts*. Let us again start by considering the extreme case of translation from a foreign language. Here no one can doubt that the translation of a text, however much the translator may have dwelt with and empathized with his author, cannot be simply a re-awakening of the original process in the writer's mind; rather, it is necessarily a re-creation of the text guided by the way the translator understands what it says. No one can doubt that what we are dealing with here is interpretation, and not simply reproduction. A new light falls on the text from the other language and for the reader of it. The requirement that a translation be faithful cannot remove the fundamental gulf between the two languages. However faithful we try to be, we have to make difficult decisions. In our translation if we want to emphasize a feature of the original that is important to us, then we can do so only by playing down or entirely suppressing other features. But this is precisely the activity that we call interpretation. Translation, like all interpretation is a highlighting. A translator must understand that highlighting is part of his task. Obviously he must not leave open whatever is not clear to him. He must show his colors. Yet there are borderline cases in the original (and for the "original reader") where something is in fact unclear. But precisely these hermeneutical borderline cases show the straits in which the translator constantly finds himself. Here he must resign himself. He must state clearly how he understands. But since he is always in the position of not really

being able to express all the dimensions of his text, he must make a constant renunciation. Every translation that takes its task seriously is at once clearer and flatter than
the original. Even if it is a masterly re-creation, it must lack some of the overtones
that vibrate in the original. (In rare cases of masterly re-creation the loss can be made
good or even mean a gain—think, for example, of how Baudelaire's *Les fleurs du mal*
seems to acquire an odd new vigor in Stefan George's version.)

The translator is often painfully aware of his inevitable distance from the original. His dealing with the text is like the effort to come to an understanding in conversation. But translating is like an especially laborious process of understanding, in
which one views the distance between one's own opinion and its contrary as ultimately unbridgeable. And, as in conversation, when there are such unbridgeable
differences, a compromise can sometimes be achieved in the to and fro of dialogue,
so in the to and fro of weighing and balancing possibilities, the translator will seek the
best solution—a solution that can never be more than a compromise. As one tries in
conversation to transpose oneself into the other person in order to understand his
point of view, so also does the translator try to transpose himself completely into his
author. But doing so does not automatically mean that understanding is achieved in a
conversation, nor for the translator does such transposition mean success in
re-creating the meaning. The structures are clearly analogous. Reaching an understanding in conversation presupposes that both partners are ready for it and are trying
to recognize the full value of what is alien and opposed to them. If this happens mutually, and each of the partners, while simultaneously holding on to his own arguments,
weighs the counterarguments, it is finally possible to achieve—in an imperceptible
but not arbitrary reciprocal translation of the other's position (we call this an
exchange of views)—a common diction and a common dictum. Similarly, the translator must preserve the character of his own language, the language into which he is
translating, while still recognizing the value of the alien, even antagonistic character
of the text and its expression. Perhaps, however, this description of the translator's
activity is too truncated. Even in these extreme situations where it is necessary to
translate from one language into another, the subject matter can scarcely be separated from the language. Only that translator can truly re-create who brings into
language the subject matter that the text points to; but this means finding a language
that is not only his but is also proportionate to the original.[2] The situation of the
translator and that of the interpreter are fundamentally the same.

In bridging the gulf between languages, the translator clearly exemplifies the
reciprocal relationship that exists between interpreter and text, and that corresponds
to the reciprocity involved in reaching an understanding in conversation. For every
translator is an interpreter. The fact that a foreign language is being translated means
that this is simply an extreme case of hermeneutical difficulty—i.e., of alienness and
its conquest. In fact all the "objects" with which traditional hermeneutics is concerned
are alien in the same unequivocally defined sense. The translator's task of re-creation
differs only in degree, not in kind, from the general hermeneutical task that any text
presents.

This is not to say, of course, that the hermeneutic situation in regard to texts is
exactly the same as that between two people in conversation. Texts are "enduringly
fixed expressions of life"[3] that are to be understood; and that means that one partner

in the hermeneutical conversation, the text, speaks only through the other partner, the interpreter. Only through him are the written marks changed back into meaning. Nevertheless, in being changed back by understanding, the subject matter of which the text speaks itself finds expression. It is like a real conversation in that the common subject matter is what binds the two partners, the text and the interpreter, to each other. When a translator interprets a conversation, he can make mutual under-standing possible only if he participates in the subject under discussion; so also in relation to a text it is indispensable that the interpreter participate in its meaning.

Thus it is perfectly legitimate to speak of a *hermeneutical conversation*. But from this it follows that hermeneutical conversation, like real conversation, finds a common language, and that finding a common language is not, any more than in real conversation, preparing a tool for the purpose of reaching understanding but, rather, coincides with the very act of understanding and reaching agreement. Even between the partners of this "conversation" a communication like that between two people takes place that is more than mere accommodation. The text brings a subject matter into language, but that it does so is ultimately the achievement of the interpreter. Both have a share in it.

Hence the meaning of a text is not to be compared with an immovably and obsti-nately fixed point of view that suggests only one question to the person trying to understand it, namely how the other person could have arrived at such an absurd opinion. In this sense understanding is certainly not concerned with "understanding historically"—i.e., reconstructing the way the text came into being. Rather, one intends to *understand the text itself*. But this means that the interpreter's own thoughts too have gone into re-awakening the text's meaning. In this the interpreter's own horizon is decisive, yet not as a personal standpoint that he maintains or enforces, but more as an opinion and a possibility that one brings into play and puts at risk, and that helps one truly to make one's own what the text says. I have described this above as a "fusion of horizons." We can now see that this is what takes place in conversation, in which something is expressed that is not only mine or my author's, but common.

We are indebted to German romanticism for disclosing the systematic signifi-cance of the verbal nature of conversation for all understanding. It has taught us that understanding and interpretation are ultimately the same thing. As we have seen, this insight elevates the idea of interpretation from the merely occasional and pedagogical significance it had in the eighteenth century to a systematic position, as indicated by the key importance that the problem of language has acquired in philosophical inquiry.

Since the romantic period we can no longer hold the view that, in the absence of immediate understanding, interpretive ideas are drawn, as needed, out of a linguistic storeroom where they are lying ready. *Rather, language is the universal medium in which understanding occurs. Understanding occurs in interpreting.* This statement does not mean that there is no special problem of expression. The difference between the language of a text and the language of the interpreter, or the gulf that separates the translator from the original, is not merely a secondary question. On the contrary, the fact is that the problems of verbal expression are themselves problems of understanding. All understanding is interpretation, and all interpretation takes place in the medium of a language that allows the object to come into words and yet is at the same time the interpreter's own language.

Thus the hermeneutical phenomenon proves to be a special case of the general relationship between thinking and speaking, whose enigmatic intimacy conceals the role of language in thought. Like conversation, interpretation is a circle closed by the dialectic of question and answer. It is a genuine historical life comportment achieved through the medium of language, and we can call it a conversation with respect to the interpretation of texts as well. The linguisticality of understanding is *the concretion of historically effected consciousness*.

The essential relation between language and understanding is seen primarily in the fact that the essence of tradition is to exist in the medium of language, so that the preferred *object* of interpretation is a verbal one.

(a) Language as determination of the hermeneutic object

The fact that tradition is essentially verbal in character has consequences for hermeneutics. The understanding of verbal tradition retains special priority over all other tradition. Linguistic tradition may have less perceptual immediacy than monuments of plastic art. Its lack of immediacy, however, is not a defect; rather, this apparent lack, the abstract alienness of all "texts," uniquely expresses the fact that everything in language belongs to the process of understanding. Linguistic tradition is tradition in the proper sense of the word—i.e., something handed down. It is not just something left over, to be investigated and interpreted as a remnant of the past. What has come down to us by way of verbal tradition is not left over but given to us, told us— whether through direct retelling, in which myth, legend, and custom have their life, or through written tradition, whose signs are, as it were, immediately clear to every reader who can read them.

The full hermeneutical significance of the fact that tradition is essentially verbal becomes clear in the case of a *written* tradition. The detachability of language from speaking derives from the fact that it can be written. In the form of writing, all tradition is contemporaneous with each present time. Moreover, it involves a unique co-existence of past and present, insofar as present consciousness has the possibility of a free access to everything handed down in writing. No longer dependent on retelling, which mediates past knowledge with the present, understanding consciousness acquires—through its immediate access to literary tradition—a genuine opportunity to change and widen its horizon, and thus enrich its world by a whole new and deeper dimension. The appropriation of literary tradition even surpasses the experience connected with the adventure of traveling and being immersed in the world of a foreign language. At every moment the reader who studies a foreign language and literature retains the possibility of free movement back to himself, and thus is at once both here and there.

A written tradition is not a fragment of a past world, but has already raised itself beyond this into the sphere of the meaning that it expresses. The ideality of the word is what raises everything linguistic beyond the finitude and transience that characterize other remnants of past existence. It is not this document, as a piece of the past, that is the bearer of tradition but the continuity of memory. Through it tradition becomes part of our own world, and thus what it communicates can be stated immediately. Where we have a written tradition, we are not just told a particular thing; a past humanity itself becomes present to us in its general relation to the world. That is why our understanding remains curiously unsure and fragmentary when we have no written tradition of a culture but only dumb monuments, and we do not call this information about the past "history." Texts, on the other hand, always express a whole. Meaningless strokes that seem strange and incomprehensible prove suddenly intelligible in every detail when they can be interpreted as writing—so much so that even the arbitrariness of a corrupt text can be corrected if the context as a whole is understood.

Thus written texts present the real hermeneutical task. Writing is self-alienation. Overcoming it, reading the text, is thus the highest task of understanding. Even the pure signs of an inscription can be seen properly and articulated correctly only if the text can be transformed back into language. As we have said, however, this transformation always establishes a relationship to what is meant, to the subject matter being discussed. Here the process of understanding moves entirely in a sphere of meaning mediated by the verbal tradition. Thus in the case of an inscription the hermeneutical task starts only after it has been deciphered (presumably correctly). Only in an extended sense do non-literary monuments present a hermeneutical task, for they cannot be understood of themselves. What they mean is a question of their interpretation, not of deciphering and understanding the wording of a text.

In writing, language gains its true ideality, for in encountering a written tradition understanding consciousness acquires its full sovereignty. Its being does not depend on anything. Thus reading consciousness is in potential possession of its history. It is not for nothing that with the emergence of a literary culture the idea of "philology," "love of speech," was transferred entirely to the all-embracing art of reading, losing its original connection with the cultivation of speech and argument. A reading consciousness is necessarily a historical consciousness and communicates freely with historical tradition. Thus it is historically legitimate to say with Hegel that history begins with the emergence of a will to hand things down, "to make memory last."[4] Writing is no mere accident or mere supplement that qualitatively changes nothing in the course of oral tradition. Certainly, there can be a will to make things continue, a will to permanence, without writing. But only a written tradition can detach itself from the mere continuance of the vestiges of past life, remnants from which one human being can by inference piece out another's existence.

The tradition of inscriptions has never shared in the free form of tradition that we call literature, since it depends on the existence of the remains, whether of stone or whatever material. But it is true of everything that has come down to us by being written down that here a will to permanence has created the unique forms of continuance that we call literature. It does not present us with only a stock of memorials and signs. Rather, literature has acquired its own contemporaneity with every present. To understand it does not mean primarily to reason one's way back into the past, but to have a present involvement in what is said. It is not really a relationship between persons, between the reader and the author (who is perhaps quite unknown), but about sharing in what the text shares with us. The meaning of what is said is, when we understand it, quite independent of whether the traditionary text gives us a picture of the author and of whether or not we want to interpret it as a historical source.

Let us here recall that the task of hermeneutics was first and foremost the understanding of texts. Schleiermacher was the first to downplay the importance of writing for the hermeneutical problem because he saw that the problem of understanding was raised—and perhaps in its fullest form—by oral utterance too. We have outlined above[5] how the psychological dimension he gave hermeneutics concealed its historical dimension. In actual fact, writing is central to the hermeneutical phenomenon insofar as its detachment both from the writer or author and from a specifically addressed recipient or reader gives it a life of its own. What is fixed in writing has raised itself into a public sphere of meaning in which everyone who can read has an equal share.

[. . .]

All writing claims it can be awakened into spoken language, and this claim to autonomy of meaning goes so far that even an authentic reading—e.g., a poet's reading of his poem—becomes questionable when we are listening to something other than what our understanding should really be directed toward. Because the important thing is communicating the text's true meaning, interpreting it is already subject to the norm of the subject matter. This is the requirement that the Platonic dialectic makes when it tries to bring out the logos as such and in doing so often leaves behind the actual partner in the conversation. In fact, the particular weakness of writing, its greater helplessness as compared to speech, has another side to it, in that it demonstrates with redoubled clarity the dialectical task of understanding. As in conversation, understanding here too must try to strengthen the meaning of what is said. What is stated in the text must be detached from all contingent factors and grasped in its full ideality, in which alone it has validity. Thus, precisely because it entirely detaches the sense of what is said from the person saying it, the written word makes the understanding reader the arbiter of its claim to truth. The reader experiences what is addressed to him and what he understands in all its validity. What he understands is always more than an unfamiliar opinion: it is always possible truth. This is what emerges from detaching what is spoken from the speaker and from the permanence that writing bestows. This is the deeper hermeneutical reason for the fact, mentioned above,[6] that it does not occur to people who are not used to reading that what is written down could be wrong, since to them anything written seems like a self-authenticating document.

Everything written is, in fact, the paradigmatic object of hermeneutics. What we found in the extreme case of a foreign language and in the problems of translation is confirmed here by the autonomy of reading: understanding is not a psychic transposition. The horizon of understanding cannot be limited either by what the writer originally had in mind or by the horizon of the person to whom the text was originally addressed.

It sounds at first like a sensible hermeneutical rule—and is generally recognized as such—that nothing should be put into a text that the writer or the reader could not have intended. But this rule can be applied only in extreme cases. For texts do not ask to be understood as a living expression of the subjectivity of their writers. This, then, cannot define the limits of a text's meaning. However, it is not only limiting a text's meaning to the "actual" thoughts of the *author* that is questionable. Even if one tries to determine the meaning of a text objectively by regarding it as a contemporary document and in relation to its original *reader*, as was Schleiermacher's basic procedure, one does not get beyond an accidental delimitation. The idea of the contemporary addressee can claim only a restricted critical validity. For what is contemporaneity? Listeners of the day before yesterday as well as of the day after tomorrow are always among those to whom one speaks as a contemporary. Where are we to draw the line that excludes a reader from being addressed? What are contemporaries and what is a text's claim to truth in the face of this multifarious mixture of past and future? The idea of the original reader is full of unexamined idealization.

Furthermore, our conception of the nature of literary tradition contains a fundamental objection to the hermeneutical legitimacy of the idea of the original reader. We saw that literature is defined by the will to hand on. But a person who copies and passes on is doing it for his own contemporaries. Thus the reference to the original reader, like that to the meaning of the author, seems to offer only a very crude historico-hermeneutical criterion that cannot really limit the horizon of a text's meaning. What is fixed in writing has detached itself from the contingency of its origin and its author and made itself free for new relationships. Normative concepts such as the author's meaning or the original reader's understanding in fact represent only an empty space that is filled from time to time in understanding.

(b) Language as determination of the hermeneutic act

This brings us to the second aspect of the relationship between language and understanding. Not only is the special object of understanding, namely tradition, of a verbal nature; understanding itself has a fundamental connection with language. We started from the proposition that understanding is already interpretation because it creates the hermeneutical horizon within which the meaning of a text comes into force. But in order to be able to express a text's meaning and subject matter, we must translate it into our own language. However, this involves relating it to the whole complex of possible meanings in which we linguistically move. We have already investigated the logical structure of this in relation to the special place of the *question* as a hermeneutical phenomenon. In now considering the verbal nature of all understanding, we are expressing from another angle what we already saw in considering the dialectic of question and answer.

Here we are emphasizing a dimension that is generally ignored by the dominant conception that the historical sciences have of themselves. For the historian usually chooses concepts to describe the historical particularity of his objects without expressly reflecting on their origin and justification. He simply follows his interest in the material and takes no account of the fact that the descriptive concepts he chooses can be highly detrimental to his proper purpose if they assimilate what is historically different to what is familiar and thus, despite all impartiality, subordinate the alien being of the object to his own preconceptions. Thus, despite his scientific method, he behaves just like everyone else—as a child of his time who is unquestioningly dominated by the concepts and prejudices of his own age.[7]

Insofar as the historian does not admit this naivete to himself, he fails to reach the level of reflection that the subject matter demands. But his naivete becomes truly abysmal when he starts to become aware of the problems it raises and so demands that in understanding history one must leave one's own concepts aside and think only in the concepts of the epoch one is trying to understand.[8] This demand, which sounds like a logical implementation of historical consciousness is, as will be clear to every thoughtful reader, a naive illusion. The naivete of this claim does not consist in the fact that it goes unfulfilled because the interpreter does not sufficiently attain the ideal of leaving himself aside. This would still mean that it was a legitimate ideal, and one should strive to reach it as far as possible. But what the legitimate demand of the historical consciousness—to understand a period in terms of its own concepts—really means is something quite different. The call to leave aside the concepts of the present does not mean a naive transposition into the past. It is, rather, an essentially relative demand that has meaning only in relation to one's own concepts. Historical consciousness fails to understand its own nature if, in order to understand, it seeks to exclude what alone makes understanding possible. *To think historically* means, in fact, *to perform the transposition that the concepts of the past undergo* when we try to think in them. To think historically always involves mediating between those ideas and one's own thinking. To try to escape from one's own concepts in interpretation is not only impossible but manifestly absurd. To interpret means precisely to bring one's own preconceptions into play so that the text's meaning can really be made to speak for us.

In our analysis of the hermeneutical process we saw that to acquire a horizon of interpretation requires a fusion of horizons. This is now confirmed by the verbal aspect of interpretation. The text is made to speak through interpretation. But no text and no book speaks if it does not speak a language that reaches the other person. Thus interpretation must find the right language if it really wants to make the text speak. There cannot, therefore, be any single interpretation that is correct "in itself," precisely because every interpretation is concerned with the text itself. The historical life of a tradition depends on being constantly assimilated and interpreted. An interpretation that was correct in itself would be a foolish ideal that mistook the nature of tradition. Every interpretation has to adapt itself to the hermeneutical situation to which it belongs.

Notes

1   If one transposes oneself into the position of another with the intent of understanding not the truth of what he is saying, but him, the questions asked in such a conversation are marked by the inauthenticity described above (pp. 355f.).

2   We have here the problem of "alienation," on which Schadewaldt has important things to say in the appendix to his translation of the *Odyssey* (RoRoRo-Klassiker, 1958), p.324.

3   Droysen. *Historik.* ed. Hübner (1937), p.63.

4   Hegel, *Die Vernunft in der Geschichte*, ed. Lasson, p.145.

5   Pp. 185ff. and 295ff. above.

6   Cf. pp. 273f.

7   Cf. p.354 above, in particular the quotation from Friedrich Schlegel.

8   Cf. my note on H. Rose's *Klassik als Denkform des Abendlandes*, in *Gnomon*, (1940), pp. 433f.

[*GW*, V. 353–56]. I now see that the methodological introduction to "Platos dialektische Ethik" (1931) [*GW*, V, 6–14] implicitly makes the same criticism.

(c) Taking Stock: Survivals, Hauntings, Jonah and (Stanley) Fish, and the Christian Colonisation of the Book of Jonah

Yvonne Sherwood

(a) Jonah and (Stanley) Fish, or how the figure of Jonah rotates through one-hundred-and-eighty degrees

Like the author of the book of Jonah, I can't resist a pun, and so can't resist playing with the famous double act 'Jonah and the Fish', substituting Jonah's aquatic, scaly companion with the iconic figurehead of 'reader-response', the president of the so-called *Reader's Liberation Movement*.[1] In one sense the move is a tired one: the Fish now floats belly-up on the surface of the postmodern aquarium displaced by bigger, brighter, more exotic specimens – and many biblical scholars, visitors to the wild postmodern fairground, have already brought home a (gold)Fish as one of the tamest souvenirs. And yet, since Jonah criticism seems to suggest that the discipline's self-assurance about its own objectivity still stands largely unassailed, one more theoretical volley (using the bulky polemic of relativism and subjectivity, rather than a more subtly honed tool) is perhaps not entirely out of place.

Certainly the aesthetics are hard to resist, for Jonah criticism provides a beautiful set of prooftexts for Fish. Even the most epistemologically assured reader, moving through the historically kaleidoscoped readings catalogued in this chapter, must experience something of a sense of interpretative vertigo or sea-sickness. And were I to remove the arbitrary barriers that separate the readings into four neat chunks, they would all look at each other in bemusement and then start arguing vociferously. From their places in sections 2 and 3 respectively, Luther and Calvin are already busy shouting abusive names like 'wanton sophist' and 'cavillator' back at the Church Fathers cowering in section 1, and taking them to task for their cotton-wool apologetics. Similarly, the Enlightenment biblical scholars, though by instinct more restrained and polite, would feel a professional compulsion to shout down Chrysostom's equation between a nationalistic, doubting Christ and a nationalistic, doubting Jonah, since this would do fatal damage to the contrast between Christian universalism and Jewish nationalism, on which their argument depends. The cacophony that results makes it extremely difficult to continue to subscribe to the reading myth of the ever-rich text, that, like the fabulous porridge pot of fairytale, or the magic jars of meal and cruses of oil that last forever in the books of Kings (see 1 Kings 17.8–16; 2 Kings 4.2–7), manages to generate more and more substance, ever new readings. Even the most credulous of readers must begin to suspect that if all these readings are somehow *in* the text, in essence, then the 48-verse book of Jonah must be an immensely rich concentrate. Even side by side, safely cordoned off from one another, the different readings compliantly foreground textual plasticity. For, depending on your vantage point, your politics, and your churchmanship, the expulsion from the fish can mean both the resurrection and the purgation of the rebellious Jonasses, and the Ninevites can be superlative gentiles or a sign of clownish Catholics.

Frankly, I can think of no better prooftext for a Fishy foregrounding of the role of the reader than a text that, between the early Christian period and critical biblical studies, manages to rotate in meaning *through one-hundred-and-eighty degrees*. For Jonah, as shape-shifter and riven signifier, completely at odds with himself, functions as both a Christ-figure and, if not exactly the antichrist, as the Jew as the antithesis of a benevolent Christianity. Whereas the Church Fathers (busy scribbling anti-Gnostic tracts such as Tertullian's *Against Marcion*) see Jonah as a type and sign of Christ, a neo-Marcionite tendency in post-Enlightenment criticism leads scholars to read Jonah as the absolute antithesis of the Christ figure. The neat geometry of the turn (from Jonah-Christ to Jonah-Jew) mirrors, in a perfect diagrammatic arc, the logical and symmetrical theoretical turn from the foregrounding of text, to reader. Fascinatingly the only common rubric that makes all these readings 'Christian' is that the text must have *some* relationship to Christ and the New Testament – the rules about how that relationship is to be worked out are entirely fluid. In early readings the book achieves Christian relevance by acting out familiar New Testament scenes in (what seem to the modern eye) lumpish and rather hammed up allegories; in Enlightenment readings it must defend its own status by becoming an outpost of proto-Christian *concepts* in a retrogressive Old Testament. Seismic shifts in Jonah's personality and signification reflect Christianity's own shifts in identity in relation to the Old Testament and the figure of the Jew. And it seems that 'Christianity' – defining itself, in different contexts, as anti-Gnostic, neo-Gnostic, and taking on different significations in response to different cultural pressures/conversations – is itself an entity whose voices and manifestations are legion. In the context of the book of Jonah 'Christianity' defines its dominant meaning, variously, as the internalisation of discipline in the storm-tossed soul; as social discipline (submitting to one's 'apoynted vocacyon'); as a natural (reasonable) religion consonant with Enlightenment/scientific values; or as the supersession of the exhausted religion of the Jews. Each reading selects a singularly illustrative narrative moment which it then abstracts, magnifies to billboard proportions and plasters a lesson over, as it were in red paint. For the Church Fathers the key moment is the expulsion/resurrection and the message ALL MEANING CULMINATES IN CHRIST; for the Enlightenment critics the revealing moment is Jonah fuming over a repentant Nineveh and the lesson is REJECT ANACHRONISM; SUSPECT THE JEW. For Calvin, the key moment is the lancing of Jonah's ego in the fish-belly hospital and the attendant lesson is SUBMIT TO GOD; for Hooper the iconic image is the storm-tossed ship of state and the lesson – DON'T ROCK THE BOAT.

Despite popular condensations of 'what Stanley Fish says' (or said) there is nothing monolithic about a book like *Is There a Text in This Class?*, and reading it again, alongside these re-performances of Jonah, sparks off all kinds of provocative associations.[2] Fish's study of the gushy, euphoric homiletics of Lancelot Andrewes resonates with my reading of the Fathers – in both texts Christ releases the writer into a free associative freedom, so that all roads lead to Christ and 'every but is an and, every however an also, and every transition is nothing more than the opportunity to take a breath'.[3] This gallery of readings amply demonstrates the capacity of readers to hammer all howevers into alsos and to subordinate recalcitrant textual elements to a monologic reading of the text. Similarly, Fish's discussion of 'significant absences', and their infinite potential for generating vast exegetical capital,[4] resonates with Luther's reading of the *qiqayon* and the way in which the unmentioned fruit is converted to significant fruitlessness, which in turn is converted to an allegorical condemnation of the Jews. If readers, as Fish reminds us, provide not only the meaning of a text, but its illocutionary force and the tone in which it is to be read, this nicely glosses our readers' predilection for supplying a sense of the book's tone and the book's Author. Calvin's Jonah is to be performed in a trembling contrite voice, the Jonah of modern biblical criticism speaks in the authoritative, rational tones of the *Aufklärer*, Hooper's Jonah rants and threatens – all readings come with an implied tone and stage directions, as well as with a pre-packaged message.

Yet reader-response theory is a roughly hewn tool for exploring the intricate relations between text and society. It tends to replace (at least by implication) an autonomous Author with an autonomous Reader and to imply a relatively free, unencumbered reading subject, who is constrained only by her membership of an 'interpretative community'. Interpretative communities sound rather vague and sinister to me these days, rather like Masonic clubs. In the world of Biblical Studies they are often reductively interpreted as religious communities so that readings can be simply and mechanistically dismissed as manifestations of the reader's Protestantism, agnosticism, Jewishness, atheism, and so on.[5] Since it is a fair assumption that Pusey, Eichhorn, Augustine, Calvin, Luther, *et al.* are all Christian, to point to the Christ-centredness of their readings is not to say very much. But what invites analysis is the radically different shapes the 'Word' takes as it shapes itself, and accommodates itself, to different intellectual and social environments.

Hovering in the background of this study, but not yet explicitly visible, are some assumptions gleaned from Cultural Studies and particularly New Historicism. The New Historicisms (and here I am using the term quite generally) dissolve the autonomy of both the writing and the speaking subject, proclaiming that the 'freely self-creating and world-creating Individual of so-called bourgeois humanism is – at least in theory – now defunct'.[6] The New Historicism is a response to (and in a sense an inversion of) New Criticism in which texts are not seen as self-contained objects of value, hermetically sealed off from the world, but as 'part of human life, society and historical realities of power, authority and resistance'.[7] Similarly the writing or interpreting subject is seen (after Foucault) as one who is subject to the influence of external forces, and authors/interpreters become 'cultural artefact[s]'[8] rather than creators *ex nihilo* who bequeath the text to the world. In a move that can be applied as much to the way that we interpret and package texts as to how we write them, New Historicism confronts the myth that 'whole cultures possess their shared emotions, stories and dreams only because a professional caste invented them and parcelled them out'[9] and breaks down the perceived wall between 'literary symbolism and symbolic structures operative elsewhere'.[10] It dissolves the neat demarcations between present and past, and problematises the ideal of a butter-wouldn't-melt-in-your-mouth objectivism by demystifying history as 'not merely a chronicle of the past, but . . . a pragmatic weapon for explaining the present and controlling the future'.[11] From a defamiliarising New Historicist perspective, histories are stories that we tell ourselves about ourselves, stories that define us 'in relation to hostile others (despised and feared Indians, Jews, Blacks) and disciplinary power (the King, Religion, Masculinity)', stories that strategically select documents and data and interpret and plot them as 'Romance, Comedy, Tragedy, and Satire'.[12] And the act of emplotment is never innocent: by placing events which have no inherent structure into a coherent narrative, the historian gives it an ideological and moral structure, (promoting, for example, 'Anarchism, Conservatism, Radicalism or Liberalism').[13]

Though rubbing culture's nose in the mud of politics (as Edward Said puts it) can be a messy business,[14] the process is a vital one for writers in Biblical Studies. For, more than any other Western cultural artefact, the Bible is perceived as occupying a transcendent zone, and as speaking an eternal message directed to 'the unchanging transhistorical core of the human'.[15] In discussions of 'the Bible' and 'Power', the Bible is habitually assumed to be the ally of social institutions and social hierarchies, dispensing power downwards, as it were from on high. Little attention has been given, to date, to the way in which the Bible and biblical texts are themselves caught in a network of power relations, reforming themselves under the impact of what Stephen Greenblatt would (loosely) term 'social anxiety and social desire'.

Certainly the influences that spill into the readings catalogued here are far more extensive than those that could be summarised in the views, biographies, and religious dispositions of 'Eichhorn', 'Michaelis', 'Hooper', 'Pusey' as discrete authorial entities (the *Dictionary of National Biography* is of limited use here). In the 1550s (a period of perceived social instability and doubts about the ability of the Protestant Bible to replace the Church as agent of control) the book of Jonah becomes an idealised picture of dissident forces being pitched overboard and turbulent social storms calmed, aided by a strict and uncompromising Protestant Word. In Germany in the 1780s the book first learns to speak in the sweet tones of reason, to internalise *die Judenfrage* and to expel the retrogressive ghetto-Jew. In 1860 a fish's body is covered with mathematical calculations and inscribed with the zoological idiom of the *Origin of Species*. These readings suggest a curious textual-social chemistry bubbling away: a complex chain reaction that cannot be explained by individual quirks, or anti-Semitic 'interpretative communities'. For there is something very apt and canny about the way in which the text mutates, chameleon-like, into a rod of discipline, an anti-Jewish tract, and a biblicised biology. Ever-expansive, ever committed to survival, the Word absorbs social anxieties (about social discipline, a retrogressive Old Testament, a Bible superseded by science), processes and answers them and gives back to society an ideal view of itself (all dissidents purged; a rational Bible; a scientifically plausible, naturalised text). Thus the edges of 'The Bible' dissolve, the text itself becomes a subjected entity, drawing new lifeblood from different social contexts, forever reshaping, reforming itself.

This picture of the evolutionary biblical text, the text that reanimates itself by grafting itself onto different ideological contexts, has the potential to undermine a different, more familiar story of 'biblical evolution'. For a common story told in Biblical Studies circles is the story of the Old Testament's gradual theological progress from primitive religion, embarrassing anthropomorphisms, polytheistic slips, towards ethical monotheism and universalism. These New-Testament-like sentiments reach their healthy evolutionary climax in Jonah, Ruth and Deutero-Isaiah, but are contrasted with a mutant, retrogressive strain, a falling off into the 'dark age' of narrow xenophobic post-exilic Judaism.[16] But the healthy, and indeed the dominant theological DNA strain finds its way into the New Testament, where it flourishes and becomes characteristically 'Christian'.

A New Historicist story of the evolutionary Bible may shake our faith in this other story of evolution. For if our histories, even our theological histories, are stories that we tell ourselves about ourselves, stories that define us 'in relation to hostile others (despised and feared Indians, Jews, Blacks)', then we must begin to suspect an evolutionary scheme that sees the Jewish as an aberration, and climaxes in the Christian. When the Jewish question is enacted at the heart of a biblical text, then we may suspect that our biblical history, and its attendant theologies, have become 'a pragmatic weapon for explaining the present and controlling the future'.[17] In the strain to hear voices from the past, we may be listening in not on Ancient Judaean ghosts, but on more recent voices – voices that speak with a suspiciously strong European accent.

It is to the question of the haunting of the present, and indeed the control of the future, that I now want to turn.

(b) How the traces of the dead make themselves heard in the voices of the living: the haunting of twentieth-century Jonah criticism

According to Stephen Greenblatt, 'The dead conspire to leave textual traces of themselves, and those textual traces make themselves heard in the voices of the living.'[18] In Jonah commentary the spectres of the past are particularly vocal, like screeching poltergeists or wailing banshees. Of the four readings toured in this chapter, one ('Jonah the Jew') dominates, and one ('Jonah as a disciplinary tract') survives. Two ('Jonah and the *cani cacharis*' and the early Christian reading of the Jonah-Christ) have clearly slipped off the page altogether.

First, an obituary to the two dead (or at least missing, presumed dead) readings. A tour of twentieth-century commentary proves conclusively that the Jonah-Christ figure has been killed off by his evil twin Jonah the Jew, and that the dissection of the body of the *cani cacharis/Menschen Fresser*, though the most recent reading, is (perhaps for that reason) the most noticeably out of fashion. If, as Greenblatt puts it, a certain 'minimal adaptability' is the key to survival[19] and readings linger on the basis of the survival of the fittest, a Darwinian reading has (appropriately) been ousted by a Darwinian mechanism of selection. Pusey's quasi-scientific ruminations on the species of the fish and the size of its teeth now seem to us childish 'old salt's tales'[20] – they cannot survive the changes in 'cultural value' and the body of the *cani cacharis* enters the twentieth century 'dead on arrival'. (These days, rather than trying to map the fish's bigness onto some naturally calibrated scale, critics tend to stress the fish's littleness, its minnow-like insignificance. The fish is but a textual red-herring[21] a 'one-verse wonder',[22] the sojourn in the fish's belly is a 'mere intermezzo':[23] the fish may indeed not be a verifiable species, but then again it is not *really* important, and only has a minor swim-on bit part.)

And yet, with the pointed exception of the fish, the tendency to graft the biblical text onto the 'natural' (that is, the scientifically and archaeologically verifiable) world still persists. As if in testimony to its survival, a recent article in the journal *Zeitschrift für die Alttestamentliche Wissenschaft* goes to great lengths (thirteen pages to be exact) to trace the Hebrew and botanical roots of Jonah's *qiqayon*. Just as Pusey, one hundred years before him, attempted to assess the prophet-swallowing potential of the *cani cacharis*, so Bernard Robinson, writing in 1985, attempts to compare the prophet-shading potential of the *ricinus communis*/the gourd/the ivy/the vine/the *Palma Christi* entwining the tendrils of biology and etymology to discuss the ricinus's 'erect stem and palmate leaves', and its capacity to grow (depending on which authority you read) to 'four metres or more', 'ten feet high', or 'between three and twelve feet'.[24] And as Robinson sits in one corner of the scholarly laboratory, carefully doing chlorophyll tests on the leaves of the biblical text, musing over Zohary's *Plants of the Bible*, and reasoning that 'the withering of the plant because of the attack of the worm suggests a plant with a supple stem',[25] other scholars submit the claim that Nineveh was three days' walk across to various feasibility and time-and-motion studies. Taking a tape-measure or trundle-wheel around Nineveh's city limits, they aim to assess whether this is a reference to Nineveh's circumference or diameter. Scrawling his calculations across the whiteboard, Leslie Allen works out (in a very Pusey-like calculation) that, if 'an inscription of Sennacherib mentions that the circumference of [Nineveh] was 9,300 cubits, less than 3 miles' and then Sennacherib added '12,515 cubits', and if archaeological surveys 'suggest a circumference of 7 and a half miles', but 'the oblong area had on its widest axis a diameter of 3 miles'[26] – then regrettably we are still far short of the required fifty-mile diameter (assuming that a prophet walks at normal walking speed). The text can be proved not by division (the body size of a shark divided by eleven) but by a simple addition, in which the sum of the evidence must come to approximately fifty miles. Finding that all his calculating, digging and rummaging in archives thus far have only given him three, Allen finds the rest by trigonometry, or at least by the ingenious use of triangles, reasoning that maybe Nineveh means 'Nineveh' in the broadest sense and the area we are dealing with is actually an 'administrative triangle stretching from Khorsabad in the north to Nineveh and Nimrud in the east'.[27]

Thus, even while Pusey's carefully catalogued fish takes its last gasp on the beach of the twentieth century, the cult of the tape-measure, the mathematical scribblings, and the botany/biology cross-referencing survives. The textual body is submitted to classification, taxonomy, calculation, and so transformed into an object for *serious* study; exaggeration is quantified, the gap of incredulity measured, and so made manageable (Nineveh is precisely 47 miles too big; the *qiqayon* is improbable by about a couple of feet and a couple of days). Awed by the master-lexis of science, the biblical text still feels the embarrassment of its own childishness, its own wide-eyed innocence. The 'big plant' becomes a *ricinus communis*, and the big three-days'-walk-across city becomes a mappable 'administrative triangle stretching from Khorsabad in the north to Nineveh and Nimrud in the east', and thus (big fish notwithstanding), we reach scientific *terra firma* – the reassuringly real world of academic precision.

So to the living readings. For if the Jonah-Christ equation and the story of Jonah and the *cani cacharis* are certifiably dead, the concept of Jonah as a disciplinary tract – a supremely strong reading – flexes its muscles and brandishes a cane. For many twentieth-century 'disciples' as for Calvin, Jonah is emphatically a book about learning to keep one's passions within due limits and about 'hold[ing] our [rebellious] thoughts captive'.[28] As Calvin describes how Jonah is 'tamed and subdued by so heavy a chastisement',[29] so E. M. Good celebrates the way in which Yhwh 'takes the ego out of Jonah' and makes him into an 'underling',[30] and H. W. Wolff smiles at the story of a 'dismally mulish prophet' and how 'God handles him'.[31] Yet, though criticism still quivers with a sense of God capable of ego-extraction and (rough?) handling, Wolff's and Good's descriptions are less violent, less knuckle-dusting than Calvin's. And, instead of taking Jonah to prison, to hospital, or to the torture chamber, these critics take Jonah to another ostensibly moderate, humane, and regimented disciplinary site (and another Foucauldian chapter) – the schoolhouse – (in fact Wolff specifically refers to Jonah as a hardhearted *pupil*).[32] Like the remedial disciples in the Gospel of Mark, Jonah becomes the foil for the text's education programme: he is, as William Tyndale so wonderfully put it, 'but yet a young scholar, weak and rude'.[33] The disciplining of Jonah the errant prophet is coupled with the discipline of Jonah the misfit text: as pedagogy masquerading as story, narrative pared down to a point – the text-as-blackboard clearly 'demonstrates an important truth',[34] serves a utilitarian purpose, and so earns its place in the canon.

As the bell sounds and the book of Jonah separates out into a classroom, the text, the critic, Jonah, and the readers all take up their clearly demarcated places. Jonah, the unruly hard-hearted and hard-headed pupil, shuffles in and sits between Wolff and Good, for in the properly structured classroom things should be so arranged that 'an unruly and frivolous pupil should be placed between two who are well behaved and serious, a libertine either alone or between two pious pupils'.[35] The critics variously position themselves as exemplary children, monitors, prefects, and assistant teachers (deputies of the ultimate instructor, God himself).[36] And the book of Jonah obligingly proffers itself as a teaching text, a catechism, a 'means of correct training'. The old Peake's commentary frames the text – in chalked Edwardian copperplate – with captions such as 'Jonah vainly attempts to Evade the Mission to which God Appoints Him' (Jonah 1) and Jonah's Intolerance Rebuked and God's Mercy Vindicated' (Jonah 4),[37] while the *Good News Bible*, simplifying the book for a more junior class, uses the didactic captions 'Jonah disobeys the Lord' (Jonah 1) and 'Jonah obeys the Lord' (Jonah 3). Jack Sasson expounds the book as the story of the student Jonah's graduation from 'obstinacy' to 'submission', and Stuart (in his own words) helpfully 'boils down' the text to the essential warning 'Don't be like Jonah' (so resolutely distilling all the meaty and comic juices off, and reducing the text to its bare pedagogic bones).[38] The book contains all the classic components of an ideal Victorian teaching text:[39] the naughty strong-willed child who resists authority and is subjected to horrors, and a plot in which submission is coerced, indeed ensured, by a highly efficient system of snares, traps and swallowings. It reminds me of the parodic teaching-texts of Hilaire Belloc, in which children eat string, tell lies, run away, and die in ghastly ways, and learn, as their heads are detached from their bodies and roll off down the hill, that they should 'always keep a hold of nurse for fear of finding something worse' (is the lesson of Jonah, then, 'always keep a hold of God, for fear of encountering a worse "monster"'?). In my Disneyed and Sunday-schooled young brain, Jonah the rebellious prophet became entangled with Pinocchio the rebellious puppet, and the mixing (which was probably based on no more than Jonah's whale and Pinocchio's 'Monstro') proved to be intuitive. For both are on a moral quest to become a real boy (or a real prophet); both are lamentably wooden-headed, errant pupils who run away to Tarshish/Pleasure Island; but both inhabit a storyworld where the progress from naughtiness to obedience is absolutely ensured, where noses grow if you tell lies, and where whales and winds and consciences will retrieve you and deposit you on the pre-prescribed plot-line at the first sign that you are beginning to branch out into your own little subplot.[40]

Notes

1   The idea of the revolt of the reader and the Reader's Liberation Movement comes from Terry Eagleton's spoof on reader-response in T. Eagleton, 'The Revolt of the Reader', *New Literary History* 13 (1982), pp. 439–52. This is also not the first time that Jonah has been paired with Stanley Fish: A. K. M. Adam has very effectively beaten me to it in 'The Sign of Jonah: A Fish-Eye View'.

2   When I first read *Is There a Text?* I was a callow undergraduate in an English Literature department, and I read it as a cuphoric manifesto for 'reader-response'. Revisiting it, from a different disciplinary address in a department of Theology and Religion, it now seems to be a book that is very much about Christianity. Fish spends fifteen pages dissecting a sermon of Lancelot Andrewes and discusses, among other things, how Christ emerges in Samson Agonistes, and how divine providence asserts itself in the interpretative framework of the baseball player Pat Kelly. The fact that I had never noticed before how religion-saturated *Is There a Text?* is, seems to triumphantly confirm the Fishy thesis that 'what anyone sees is not independent of his (or in this case her) verbal and mental categories (and disciplinary preoccupations) but is in fact a product of them' (S. Fish, *Is There a Text in This Class?: The Authority of Interpretive Communities* (Cambridge, Mass.: Harvard University Press, 1980), p. 271).

3   Fish, *Is There a Text?* pp. 181–96 (193). The study of Andrewes is called 'Structuralist Homiletics', in a play on Jonathan Culler's 'Structuralist Poetics'. Provocatively Fish is making an equation between the anti-humanism of structuralism, in which the subject is eliminated in favour of discursive systems which 'speak it', and the belief that the Christian subject is not a maker of meaning, but is 'found', and 'spoken' by Christ.

4   The context is a discussion of the interpretative history of Milton's 'Samson Agonistes', in which critics have claimed that 'Samson Agonistes is about Christ because he is nowhere mentioned' (*Is There a Text?*, pp. 272–4).

5   Actually, this is probably only a return to the 'interpretative community's' religious roots. For, according to Samuel Weber, Fish's phrase comes from Josiah Royce's *Problem of Christianity*, where it is used in reference to the Christian interpretative community that shaped the Christian story under the authority of the figure of Jesus. See S. Weber, 'Introduction to Demarcating the Disciplines', in *Glyph Textual Studies* 1 (Minneapolis: University of Minnesota Press, 1986), p. xi, cited in V. Cunningham, *In the Reading Gaol: Postmodernity, Texts and History* (Oxford: Blackwell, 1994), p. 405, n. 14.

6   L. A. Montrose, 'Professing the Renaissance: The Poetics and Politics of Culture', in H. Aram Veeser (ed.), *The New Historicism* (London: Routledge, 1989), pp. 15–36 (21).

7   J. N. Cox and L. J. Reynolds, *New Historical Literary Study: Essays on Reproducing Texts, Representing History* (Princeton: Princeton University Press, 1993), p. 1.

8 S. Greenblatt, *Renaissance Self-Fashioning: From More to Shakespeare* (Chicago and London: University of Chicago Press, 1980), p. 3 (citing C. Geertz, *The Interpretation of Cultures: Selected Essays* (London: Fontana, 1973)).

9 Greenblatt, *Shakespearean Negotiations*, p. 4.

10 Greenblatt, *Renaissance Self-Fashioning*, p. 3.

11 H. Aram Veeser, *The New Historicism Reader* (London: Routledge, 1984), p. 11.

12 Veeser, *The New Historicism*, p. xiii.

13 H. White, *Metahistory: The Historical Imagination in Nineteenth Century Europe* (London: Johns Hopkins Press, 1973), p. x.

14 E. W. Said, *Orientalism: Western Conceptions of the Orient* (Harmondsworth: Penguin, 1995; 1st edn 1978), p. 13. Because Said makes it clear that ideological/postcolonial criticism is not about introducing a sense of context, so much as politicising and contaminating the sense of context which has long surrounded and shrouded textual studies, his comments are worth quoting in full. He writes: 'Most humanistic scholars are, I think, perfectly happy with the notion that texts exist in contexts, that there is such a thing as intertextuality, that the pressures of conventions, predecessors and rhetorical styles limit what Walter Benjamin once called the "overtaxing of the productive person in the name of creativity" in which the poet is believed on his own and out of his pure mind, to have brought forth his work. Yet there is a reluctance to allow that political, institutional, and ideological constraints act in the same manner on the individual author. A humanist will believe it to be an interesting fact to any interpreter of Balzac that he was influenced in the *Comédie Humaine* by the conflict between Geoffroy Saint-Hilaire and Cuvier, but the same sort of pressure on Balzac of deeply reactionary monarchism is felt in some way to demean his literary "genius" and therefore to be less worth serious study. Similarly . . . philosophers will conduct their discussions of Locke, Hume, and empiricism without ever taking into account that there is an explicit connection in these classic writers between their "philosophic" doctrines and racial theory, justifications of slavery, or arguments for colonial exploitation.'

15 J. Hawthorn, *Cunning Passages: New Historicism, Cultural Materialism and Marxism in the Contemporary Literary Debate* (London: Arnold, 1996), p. 71.

16 This evolutionary scheme, and the idea of the falling-off of post-exilic Judaism can be traced back to Julius Wellhausen and his predecessors; although, as John Barton has argued, issues of anti-Semitism in Wellhausen may not be as clear-cut as they would appear (see J. Barton, 'Wellhausen's *Prolegomena to the History of Israel*: Influences and Effects', in D. Smith-Christopher (ed.), *Text and Experience: Towards a Cultural Exegesis of the Bible* (Sheffield: Sheffield Academic Press, 1995), pp. 316–29). The legacy is clearly inscribed in many contemporary introductory texts: Anderson, for example, includes a section on 'The Weaknesses of Judaism', in his discussion of the post-exilic era, and argues that 'Devotion to the Torah easily lapsed into legalism . . . We have only to read the New Testament to become aware of this weakness within Judaism . . . Preoccupation with Torah seemed to stifle the spirit of prophecy' (B. W. Anderson, *Understanding the Old Testament* (Englewood Cliffs, N.J.: Prentice-Hall, 1986), p. 538). On the way in which Ruth becomes a 'universalist' companion-piece to Jonah, see, for example, G. A. F. Knight, *Ruth and Jonah: Introduction and Commentary* (London: SCM, 1960). Though the anti-Judaism tends to be less focused and overt, it still remains the shadow-side of a celebration of universalism, and Flanders, Crapp, and Smith, for example, see Ruth as an indictment of the exclusivity of the Jews: 'In this light the particularism of the Jews is shown to be shallow and selfish and a stance that should be surrendered to a more hospitable attitude toward those gentiles who desired to share blessings from Yahweh' (H. Jackson Flanders, *et al., People of the Covenant: An Introduction to the Old Testament* (New York: The Ranald Press, 1973), p. 470). (I am grateful to Julia O'Brien for pointing out these examples in her article 'On Saying "No" to a Prophet', in J. Capel Anderson and J. L. Staley (eds.), *Taking It Personally: Autobiographical Biblical Criticism* (Semeia 72; Atlanta: Scholar's Press, 1995), pp. 111–21 (119).)

17 Veeser, *The New Historicism Reader*, p. 11.

18   Greenblatt, *Shakespearean Negotiations*, p. 1.

19   *Ibid.*, p. 7.

20   E. Bickerman, *Four Strange Books of the Bible: Jonah, Daniel, Qoheleth, Esther* (New York: Schoken Books, 1967), p. 3.

21   R. P. Carroll, 'Jonah as a Book of Ritual Responses', in K. Schunck and M. Augustin (eds.), '*Lassel uns Brilcken bauen . . .*': *Collected Communications to the Fifteenth Congress of the International Organization far the Study of the Old Testament, Cambridge, 1995* (Frankfurt: Peter Lang, 1998), pp. 261–68 (268).

22   G. Campbell Morgan, *The Minor Propheis* (1960), p. 69, cited in L. C. Allen, *Joel, Obadiah, Jonah and Micah* (London: Hodder and Stoughton, 1976), p. 192.

23   Koch, *The Prophets*, II, p. 182.

24   B. P. Robinson, 'Jonah's Qiqayon Plant', *Zeitschrift für die alttestamentliche Wissenschaft.* 97 (1985), pp. 390–403 (399). The worm that nibbles the plant has also come in for some degree of scrutiny, though with less emphasis on scientific precision; Jack Sasson observes how translators have variously regarded the worm as 'larva', 'maggot', 'weevil', 'beetle' or 'centipede' (see J. Sasson, *Jonah* (The Anchor Bible; New York: Doubleday, 1990), p. 301).

25   Robinson, 'Jonah's Qiqayon Plant', p. 402.

26   L. C. Allen, *Joel, Obadiah, Jonah and Micah*, pp. 221–22.

27   *Ibid.*, pp. 221–22.

28   Calvin, *Commentaries*, p. 128.

29   *Ibid.*, p. 128.

30   E. M. Good, 'Jonah: The Absurdity of God', in *Irony in the Old Testament* (London: SPCK, 1965), pp. 39–55 (47).

31   H. W. Welff, *Obadiah and Jonah* (trans. M. Kohl; Hermencia; Minneapolis: Augsburg, 1988), p. 176.

32   *Ibid.*, p. 183.

33   From Tyndale's prologue to his translation of Jonah in D. Daniell (ed.), *Tyndale's Old Testament: Being the Pentateuch of 1530, Joshua to 2 Chronicles of 1537 and Jonah* (New Haven: Yale University Press, 1992), p. 631.

34   L. C. Allen, *Joel, Obadiah, Jonah and Micah*, p. 177.

35   Foucault, *Discipline and Punish*, p. 147, citing Jean Baptiste de la Salle's *Conduite des ecoles chrétiennes*.

36   This seems to be another instance of commentators zealously reinforcing what they perceive to be the ideology of the text (and in the process making a text that is arguably more stringent than the 'original'). In an earlier study, *The Prostitute and the Prophet*, I explored how commentators, like faithful henchmen, carry out the threats issued against the uncooperative woman in the text (Y. M. Sherwood, *The Prostitute and the Prophet: Hosea's Marriage in Literary-theoretical Perspective* (Sheffield: Sheffield Academic Press, 1996), p. 261). In this study, it seems that commentators are faithful assistant teachers, reinforcing what they see as the text's stern education programme.

37   A. S. Peake, 'Jonah', in *Peake's Commentary on the Bible* (London: Nelson and Sons, 1919), pp. 556–8.

38   D. Stuart, *Hosea–Jonah* (Word; Waco, Texas: Word Books, 1987), p. 434.

39   For a fascinating discussion of the evolution of children's Bible stories, including the use of the Bible to reinforce parental discipline, see R. B. Bottigheimer, *The Bible for Children: From the Age of Gutenberg to the Present* (New Haven: Yale University Press, 1996). Bottigheimer's fascinating study explores some unlikely children's stories including Noah's drunkenness, the sacrifice of Isaac, Jael and Sisera and the rape and murder of the Levite's 'wife', but says nothing, unfortunately, about the various mutations and manipulations of the book of Jonah.

40   The moral design of Pinocchio is very much a Disney addition. In Disney, Gepetto prays for a son, whereas in Collodi, he simply makes him; in Disney, the Blue Fairy puts the boy-puppet on a conscious quest to become a real boy, by learning to be 'brave, truthful and

unselfish', whereas in Collodi, Pinocchio simply blunders about, has adventures, and discovers what he might become. The difference between the two versions provides a striking analogy with Jonah, suggesting the tantalising question, if we could shake ourselves loose of the Disneyfying, moralising layer of scholarship, and Jonah's conscious education programme, what kind of story would Jonah then become?

Literary Reading

Chapter 4

Translation

The best way to crack a word half open in order to let the thought or thoughts it shelters be revealed (for, I forgot to point this out, it happens frequently that a single word gives shelter to a whole range of thoughts, born of couplings about which we know very little and which do not necessarily resemble each other very much) is to try and translate a word. Translation, as everyone knows, is similar to an exercise in cartography.

Marc Augé, *Oblivion* (2004)[1]

... though to recount almighty works
What words or tongue of seraph can suffice,
Or heart of man suffice to comprehend?

John Milton, *Paradise Lost* (1667)[2]

ALTHOUGH THE BIBLICAL CANON is a collection of books written largely in Hebrew and Greek, the novels, poems and plays of English literature engage with a very English Bible. Considered by many to be an icon of literary English, the King James Version of the Bible is strangely both a translated text – inherently foreign – but also one very much at home in the English language. As such, the translatedness of the Bible is often something overlooked and easy to ignore. Yet the translation of the Bible into English was what David Daniell calls 'a true revolution in the history of the West' that turned around the English language, its literatures and even British politics.[3] In the sixteenth and seventeenth centuries, people largely learnt to read from the new English Bible translations, provoking the prominence of private reading (rather than group discussion) as well as vastly higher literacy levels. Its influence expanded well beyond a narrow religious sphere. Christopher Hill comments upon 'its use for political and other purposes, and its unforeseen effects on literature, political theory, social relations, agriculture and colonization, among other matters'.[4] The Bible in its first English incarnations was a radical text, defying the *De Heretico Comburendo*, an act of 1401 that banned the owning or reading of Scripture in English by penalty of being burnt alive. We owe to those early translators many of our common idioms, such as 'by the skin of his teeth'

(Job 19) or 'the salt of the earth' (Matthew 5). As Gerald Hammond explains, the syntactical phrasing of English was metamorphosed to reflect Hebrew in its 'variations in word order, its use of verbal redundancies, and its readiness to hang verbless clauses on the end of poetic statements'.[5] From its very beginnings, translation of the Bible was undertaken in order to bring the Scriptures into the access of everyday people – even for the ploughboy in the field, as Wycliffe famously asserted.[6] Since the Reformation, the intention of translators has overwhelmingly been to render this foreign text into something understandable. The extracts in this section explore the implications and difficulties of the translation of sacred Scripture into the vernacular.

The two quotations that open this section express an optimistic and pessimistic approach to translation. The first articulates the meaning-making experienced in translation. Translation as cartography, Augé claims (originally in French, rendered here through its English translation), enables one to 'crack open' a word. The act of mapping a word's meaning is invasive, anatomical and revelatory – it identifies connotations that we are usually unaware of in the everyday use of words. Translation, for Augé, is exploratory and bureaucratic, the delineation of a previously unknown and uncharted territory. The words of Raphael quoted from *Paradise Lost* point, instead, to the way in which translation is something inescapably compromised. Inadequacy must be a condition of the translation, Raphael argues, because of the ineptitude of humanity to comprehend the divine:

> . . . acts of God, more swift
> Than time or motion, but to human ears
> Cannot without process of speech be told,
> So told as earthly notion can receive.
>
> (VII. 176–79)

Brought into the human domain, acts of God are circumscribed by the clunky process of speech and the limitations of human cognition. Translation comes into being, then, precisely because of a limitation and is unable to capture and deliver meaning.

Yet both quotations also contain the force of their opposite pole: both admit success and failure. (Auge's word has so much meaning 'about which we know very little' that it is, surely, unmappable; Raphael's reservations about translation are undermined by his own successful communication of 'acts of God' to earthly humanity in Adam.) It is this gulf between the text to be translated and the host language that Friedrich Schleiermacher discusses in his essay *On the Different Methods of Translating* (1813) when he poses the quandary: 'Either the translator leaves the author in peace as much as possible and moves the reader towards him; or he leaves the reader in peace as much as possible and moves the writer towards him'. Schleiermacher, like many after him, privileged the former, what is now called 'foreignization' (as opposed to 'domestication') in recent translation theory.[7] It is this gulf that concerns the writers included in this section on translation.

Walter Benjamin's hugely influential essay on translation asserts the importance of maintaining foreignness in translation. Benjamin objects to the idea that its purpose is to transmit information to a reader unfamiliar with the original language (what he calls 'the sterile equation of two dead languages'). Instead, good translations are organically linked to the original and are part of its afterlife. The translation of artworks 'marks their stage as continued life', 'life' suggesting growth in translation, or to use Benjamin's metaphor, its 'flowering'. Benjamin looks to what he calls the 'pure language', which owes its meaning to Jewish *kabbalah*. In this strand of Jewish mysticism, the vessels carrying divine light are shattered at creation and it is through retrieving these fragments, or divine sparks, that divine unity can be restored. Translation acts to gather linguistic fragments to partake in an act of *tiqqun* or reparation: the original and the translations are both mere elements, fragments, of a 'greater language': to translate is to start to map a totality of all languages that exists beyond and as a result of individual languages. The most influential element of Benjamin's difficult text is that picked up by the other writers represented in this section: the carrying over, in translation, of the foreign into the host language. The foreign affects word order and syntax in a way that paraphrasing can never do in its subjugation of the unfamiliar into vernacular idioms and metaphors. The foreign must work upon and create something new in the host language. Translation is inherently creative, therefore, for Benjamin.

Both Gerald Hammond's (1982) and Robert Alter's (1996) essays provide a glimpse of the literary complexities of the Hebrew Bible or 'Old Testament': what it is, how it works, and what has been carried over into English translation. For Hammond this is a literary question and he contends that the AV has benefited from the early Renaissance translators' imitation of Hebrew syntax and word order. Hammond argues that 'the life of anything written lies in its words and syntax', that the way something is expressed is constituent of what is expressed. To echo the word choice and order from the Hebrew into the English is to recognize the literary wealth and beauty of the Hebrew, thereby enriching the English translation. Whilst for Benjamin the interlinear version of the Bible – which offers the original languages against the vernacular, word by word, so that the correspondence between original and translation can be identified – is 'the prototype or ideal of all translation', for Hammond the KJV is also such a prototype because it follows Hebrew word order and idioms faithfully. He claims that such word-for-word translation successfully communicates 'the Hebrew way of thought', its 'ponderousness of expression' as found in the AV's poetic phrase 'the bread of affliction'. As a result, 'the most literal rendering is often the most powerful'. For Hammond, the problem with modern translations is the assumption that 'a modern Bible should aim not to tax its readers' linguistic or interpretative abilities one bit', what Alter calls the 'the heresy of explanation'. This concept is expanded on by Alter in the extract here, taken from the introduction to his English translation of the book of Genesis. Alter attempts to outline what it is that characterizes the Hebrew literature of Genesis: it 'loves to set ambiguities of word choice and image against one another in an endless interplay that resists neat resolution', a deliberate embracing of ambiguity that he sets against the philologist's desire for clarity. Translations that aim for clarity only 'reduce, simplify, and denature the Bible'. The ideal, as Benjamin outlines, is not transparency, but to remind of the 'strangeness of the Hebrew original'. Alter defends the use of parataxis (clauses linked by 'and') in English translations of the Hebrew as 'artfully effective', drawing attention to its use in various contemporary English writers. He highlights the sonic qualities of the 'mesmerizing' repetition of 'and' on which the biblical text's poeticism depends. For Alter, as for Hammond, the complexities of biblical translation are not a problem but lend to its beauty.

In his discussions of the Tower of Babel narrative, Derrida turns to the simultaneous necessity and impossibility of translation. This tower is built, according to the Genesis story, when a single language existed. God disrupts the building of the tower and confuses communication into multiple languages. God frustrates the people's building, Derrida suggests in this extract, because they wanted to make a name for themselves, creating both a unity of place and unity of language to provide security. He quotes from Chouraqui's word-for-word, literal (Derrida cites Cicero's term, *verbum pro verbo*) translation that states:

> he proclaims his name: Bavel, Confusion,
> for there YHWH confounds the lip of all the earth.

Derrida enlarges on the theologies of translation in his analysis of this story to assert that God '*at the same time* imposes and forbids translation'. At Babel, translation became necessary for the first time. Pure equivalency between languages – a shared understanding – became impossible; yet the division of languages created a need to work towards shared understanding. There can never be a pure rendering of a foreign other but instead something untranslatable always persists. Derrida comments on Benjamin's essay asserting as among its central arguments that 'neither reception, nor communication, nor representation' are the work of the translation: translation is not for the receiver, nor does it transmit information, and it is 'neither an image or a copy'. The overriding thrust of this extract is that 'it is difficult to translate and so to understand', but that even God, in the giving of his name, Babel, nonetheless demands a translation (of 'confusion'). 'He has not finished pleading for the translation of his name even though he forbids it.' Desire is not dissipated but rather fed by impossibility.

The claim articulated by Benjamin – that the best translation carries with it something foreign and transformative – is the focus of Valentine Cunningham's article that considers the English Bible as an exemplar of translation's work of what he calls 'cultural metamorphosis'. Translation produces a change that is aligned with heresy – the English Bible being the result of heretical translators. Thus, translation and heresy are brought together through their common ground of 'transgressivity' and 'translation is inevitably a species of heretic re-reading'. Cunningham's claims are wide-reaching: from the cascading transformations of translated text to the 'wholesale conversion, transformation, metamorphosis, of Crusoe and his island and his world' and beyond that, the transformation of English literature through the emergence of the novel form in Crusoe's image. The legacy of Bible translation – Cunningham includes various political revolutions and the 'modern sense of the self' – is modern culture as we know it.

Notes

1   Marc Augé, *Oblivion*, trans by Marjolijn de Jager, foreword by James E. Young, (London, Minneapolis: University of Minnesota Press, 2004), p. 9.
2   John Milton, *Paradise Lost*, ed. by Alastair Fowler, 2nd edn (London and New York: Longman, 2007), VII. 112–14.

3   David Daniell, *The Bible in English: Its History and Influence* (New Haven and London: Yale University Press, 2003), p. xix.

4   Christopher Hill, *The English Bible and the Seventeenth-Century Revolution* (London: Penguin, 1994), p. 4.

5   Gerald Hammond, *The Making of the English Bible* (Manchester: Carcanet, 1982), p. 20.

6   Relayed in John Foxe, *Acts and Monuments* (1570), VIII, p. 1264.

7   See Lawrence Venuti, *The Translator's Invisibility: A History of Translation* (London: Routledge, 1995), Chapter 1 'Invisibility'.

Further Reading

Daniell, David, *The Bible in English: Its History and Influence* (New Haven and London: Yale University Press, 2003)

— (ed.), *Tyndale's New Testament (1534)* (New Haven and London: Yale University Press, 1995)

Greenslade, S. L., ed., *The Cambridge History of the Bible: Volume 3, The West from the Reformation to the Present Day* (Cambridge: Cambridge University Press, 1963)

Hammond, Gerald, 'English Translations of the Bible' in *A Literary Guide to the Bible*, ed. by Robert Alter and Frank Kermode (London: HarperCollins, 1987), pp. 647–66

— *The Making of the English Bible* (Manchester: Carcanet, 1982)

Hill, Christopher, *The English Bible and the Seventeenth Century Revolution* (London: Penguin, 1994)

Lefevre, André, ed., *Translation/History/Culture: A Sourcebook* (London and New York: Routledge, 1992)

Metzger, Bruce M., *The Bible in Translation: Ancient and English Versions* (Grand Rapids, MI: Baker Academic, 2001)

Venuti, Lawrence, *The Translation Studies Reader*, 3rd edn (Oxford: Routledge, 2000)

Ward, Allen, *Translating for the King James: Notes Made by a Translator of King James's Bible* (Nashville, Tennessee, 1969)

(a) The Task of the Translator: An Introduction to the Translation of Baudelaire's *Tableaux Parisiens*

Walter Benjamin

In the appreciation of a work of art or an art form, consideration of the receiver never proves fruitful. Not only is any reference to a certain public or its representatives misleading, but even the concept of an 'ideal' receiver is detrimental in the theoretical consideration of art, since all it posits is the existence and nature of man as such. Art, in the same way, posits man's physical and spiritual existence, but in none of its works is it concerned with his response. No poem is intended for the reader, no picture for the beholder, no symphony for the listener.

Is a translation meant for readers who do not understand the original? This would seem to explain adequately the divergence of their standing in the realm of art.

Moreover, it seems to be the only conceivable reason for saying 'the same thing' repeatedly. For what does a literary work 'say'? What does it communicate? It 'tells' very little to those who understand it. Its essential quality is not statement or the imparting of information. Yet any translation which intends to perform a transmitting function cannot transmit anything but information – hence, something inessential. This is the hallmark of bad translations. But do we not generally regard as the essential substance of a literary work what it contains in addition to information – as even a poor translator will admit – the unfathomable, the mysterious, the 'poetic,' something that a translator can reproduce only if he is also a poet? This, actually, is the cause of another characteristic of inferior translation, which consequently we may define as the inaccurate transmission of an inessential content. This will be true whenever a translation undertakes to serve the reader. However, if it were intended for the reader, the same would have to apply to the original. If the original does not exist for the reader's sake, how could the translation be understood on the basis of this premise?

Translation is a mode. To comprehend it as mode one must go back to the original, for that contains the law governing the translation: its translatability. The question of whether a work is translatable has a dual meaning. Either: Will an adequate translator ever be found among the totality of its readers? Or, more pertinently: Does its nature lend itself to translation and, therefore, in view of the significance of the mode, call for it? In principle, the first question can be decided only contingently; the second, however, apodictically. Only superficial thinking will deny the independent meaning of the latter and declare both questions to be of equal significance . . . It should be pointed out that certain correlative concepts retain their meaning, and possibly their foremost significance, if they are referred exclusively to man. One might, for example, speak of an unforgettable life or moment even if all men had forgotten it. If the nature of such a life or moment required that it be unforgotten, that predicate would not imply a falsehood but merely a claim not fulfilled by men, and probably also a reference to a realm in which it *is* fulfilled: God's remembrance. Analogously, the translatability of linguistic creations ought to be considered even if men should prove unable to translate them. Given a strict concept of translation, would they not really be translatable to some degree? The question as to whether the translation of certain linguistic creations is called for ought to be posed in this sense. For this thought is valid here: If translation is a mode, translatability must be an essential feature of certain works.

Translatability is an essential quality of certain works, which is not to say that it is essential that they be translated; it means rather that a specific significance inherent in the original manifests itself in its translatability. It is plausible that no translation, however good it may be, can have any significance as regards the original. Yet, by virtue of its translatability the original is closely connected with the translation; in fact, this connection is all the closer since it is no longer of importance to the original. We may call this connection a natural one, or, more specifically, a vital connection. Just as the manifestations of life are intimately connected with the phenomenon of life without being of importance to it, a translation issues from the original – not so much from its life as from its afterlife. For a translation comes later than the original, and since the important works of world literature never find their chosen translators at the time of their origin, their translation marks their stage of continued life. The idea of life and afterlife in works of art should be regarded with an entirely unmetaphorical objectivity. Even in times of narrowly prejudiced thought there was an inkling that life was not limited to organic corporeality. But it cannot be a matter of extending its dominion under the feeble sceptre of the soul, as Fechner tried to do, or, conversely, of basing its definition on the even less conclusive factors of animality, such as sensation, which characterize life only occasionally. The concept of life is given its due only if everything that has a history of its own, and is not merely the setting for history, is credited with life. In the final analysis, the range of life must be determined by history rather than by nature, least of all by such tenuous factors as sensation and soul. The philosopher's task consists in comprehending all of natural life through the more encompassing life of history. And indeed, is not the continued life of works of art far easier to recognize than the continual life of animal species? The history of the great works of art tells us about their antecedents, their realization in the age of the artist, their potentially eternal afterlife in succeeding generations. Where this last manifests itself, it is called fame. Translations that are more than transmissions of subject matter come into being when in the course of its survival a work has reached the age of its fame. Contrary, therefore, to the claims of bad translators, such translations do not so much serve the work as owe their existence to it. The life of the originals attains in them to its ever-renewed latest and most abundant flowering.

Being a special and high form of life, this flowering is governed by a special, high purposiveness. The relationship between life and purposefulness, seemingly obvious yet almost beyond the grasp of the intellect, reveals itself only if the ultimate purpose toward which all single functions tend is sought not in its own sphere but in a higher one. All purposeful manifestations of life, including their very purposiveness, in the final analysis have their end not in life, but in the expression of its nature, in the representation of its significance. Translation thus ultimately serves the purpose of expressing the central reciprocal relationship between languages. It cannot possibly reveal or establish this hidden relationship itself; but it can represent it by realizing it in embryonic or intensive form. This representation of hidden significance through an embryonic attempt at making it visible is of so singular a nature that it is rarely met with in the sphere of nonlinguistic life. This, in its analogies and symbols, can draw on other ways of suggesting meaning than intensive – that is, anticipative, intimating – realization. As for the posited central kinship of languages, it is marked by a distinctive convergence. Languages are not strangers to one another, but are, a priori and apart from all historical relationships, interrelated in what they want to express.

With this attempt at an explication our study appears to rejoin, after futile detours, the traditional theory of translation. If the kinship of languages is to be demonstrated by translations, how else can this be done but by conveying the form and meaning of the original as accurately as possible? To be sure, that theory would be hard put to define the nature of this accuracy and therefore could shed no light on what is important in a translation. Actually, however, the kinship of languages is brought out by a translation far more profoundly and clearly than in the superficial and indefinable similarity of two works of literature. To grasp the genuine relationship between an original and a translation requires an investigation analogous to the argumentation by which a critique of cognition would have to prove the impossibility of an image theory. There it is a matter of showing that in cognition there could be no objectivity, not even a claim to it, if it dealt with images of reality; here it can be demonstrated that no translation would be possible if in its ultimate essence it strove for likeness to the original. For in its afterlife – which could not be called that if it were not a transformation and a renewal of something living – the original undergoes a change. Even words with fixed meaning can undergo a maturing process. The obvious tendency of a writer's literary style may in time wither away, only to give rise to immanent tendencies in the literary creation. What sounded fresh once may sound hackneyed later; what was once current may someday sound quaint. To seek the essence of such changes, as well as the equally constant changes in meaning, in the subjectivity of posterity rather than in the very life of language and its works, would mean – even allowing for the crudest psychologism – to confuse the root cause of a thing with its essence. More pertinently, it would mean denying, by an impotence of thought, one of the most powerful and fruitful historical processes. And even if one tried to turn an author's last stroke of the pen into the *coup de grâce* of his work, this still would not save that dead theory of translation. For just as the tenor and the significance of the great works of literature undergo a complete transformation over the centuries, the mother tongue of the translator is transformed as well. While a poet's words endure in his own language, even the greatest translation is destined to become part of the growth of its own language and eventually to be absorbed by its renewal. Translation is so far removed from being the sterile equation of two dead languages that of all literary forms it is the one charged with the special mission of watching over the maturing process of the original language and the birth pangs of its own.

If the kinship of languages manifests itself in translations, this is not accomplished through a vague alikeness between adaptation and original. It stands to reason that kinship does not necessarily involve likeness. The concept of kinship as used here is in accord with its more restricted common usage: in both cases, it cannot be defined adequately by identity of origin, although in defining the more restricted usage the concept of origin remains indispensable. Wherein resides the relatedness of two languages, apart from historical considerations? Certainly not in the similarity between works of literature or words. Rather, all suprahistorical kinship of languages rests in the intention underlying each language as a whole – an intention, however, which no single language can attain by itself but which is realized only by the totality of their intentions supplementing each other: pure language. While all individual elements of foreign languages – words, sentences, structure – are mutually exclusive, these languages supplement one another in their intentions. Without distinguishing the intended object from the mode of intention, no firm grasp of this basic law of a philosophy of language can be achieved. The words *Brot* and *pain* 'intend' the same object, but the modes of this intention are not the same. It is owing to these modes that the word *Brot* means something different to a German than the word *pain* to a Frenchman, that these words are not interchangeable for them, that, in fact, they strive to exclude each other. As to the intended object, however, the two words mean the very same thing. While the modes of intention in these two words are in conflict, intention and object of intention complement each of the two languages from which they are derived; there the object is complementary to the intention. In the individual, unsupplemented languages, meaning is never found in relative independence, as in individual words or sentences; rather, it is in a constant state of flux – until it is able to emerge as pure language from the harmony of all the various modes of intention. Until then, it remains hidden in the languages. If, however, these languages continue to grow in this manner until the end of their time, it is translation which catches fire on the eternal life of the works and the perpetual renewal of language. Translation keeps putting the hallowed growth of languages to the test: How far removed is their hidden meaning from revelation, how close can it be brought by the knowledge of this remoteness?

[. . .]

The task of the translator consists in finding that intended effect [*Intention*] upon the language into which he is translating which produces in it the echo of the original. This is a feature of translation which basically differentiates it from the poet's work, because the effort of the latter is never directed at the language as such, at its totality, but solely and immediately at specific linguistic contextual aspects. Unlike a work of literature, translation does not find itself in the center of the language forest but on the outside facing the wooded ridge; it calls into it without entering, aiming at that single spot where the echo is able to give, in its own language, the reverberation of the work in the alien one. Not only does the aim of translation differ from that of a literary work – it intends language as a whole, taking an individual work in an alien language as a point of departure – but it is a different effort altogether. The intention of the poet is spontaneous, primary, graphic; that of the translator is derivative, ultimate, ideational. For the great motif of integrating many tongues into one true language is at work. This language is one in which the independent sentences, works of literature, critical judgments, will never communicate – for they remain dependent on translation; but in it the languages themselves, supplemented and reconciled in their mode of signification, harmonize. If there is such a thing as a language of truth, the tensionless and even silent depository of the ultimate truth which all thought strives for, then this language of truth is – the true language. And this very language, whose divination and description is the only perfection a philosopher can hope for, is concealed in concentrated fashion in translations. There is no muse of philosophy, nor is there one of translation. But despite the claims of sentimental artists, these two are not banausic. For there is a philosophical genius that is characterized by a yearning for that language which manifests itself in translations. '*Les langues imparfaites en cela que plusieurs, manque la suprême: penser étant écrire sans accessoires, ni chuchotement mais tacite encore l'immortelle parole, la diversité, sur terre, des idiomes empêche personne de proférer les mots qui, sinon se trouveraient, par une frappe unique, elle-même matériellement la vérité.*'* If what Mallarmé evokes here is fully fathomable to a philosopher, translation, with its rudiments of such a language, is midway between poetry and doctrine. Its products are less sharply defined, but it leaves no less of a mark on history.

If the task of the translator is viewed in this light, the roads toward a solution seem to be all the more obscure and impenetrable. Indeed, the problem of ripening the seed of pure language in a translation seems to be insoluble, determinable in no solution. For is not the ground cut from under such a solution if the reproduction of the sense ceases to be decisive? Viewed negatively, this is actually the meaning of all the foregoing. The traditional concepts in any discussion of translations are fidelity and license – the freedom of faithful reproduction and, in its service, fidelity to the word. These ideas seem to be no longer serviceable to a theory that looks for other things in a translation than reproduction of meaning. To be sure, traditional usage makes these terms appear as if in constant conflict with each other. What can fidelity really do for the rendering of meaning? Fidelity in the translation of individual words can almost never fully reproduce the meaning they have in the original. For sense in its poetic significance is not limited to meaning, but derives from the connotations conveyed by the word chosen to express it. We say of words that they have emotional connotations. A literal rendering of the syntax completely demolishes the theory of reproduction of meaning and is a direct threat to comprehensibility. The nineteenth century considered Hölderlin's translations of Sophocles as monstrous examples of such literalness. Finally, it is self-evident how greatly fidelity in reproducing the form impedes the rendering of the sense. Thus no case for literalness can be based on a desire to retain the meaning. Meaning is served far better – and literature and language far worse – by the unrestrained licence of bad translators. Of necessity, therefore, the demand for literalness, whose justification is obvious, whose legitimate ground is quite obscure, must be understood in a more meaningful context. Fragments of a vessel which are to be glued together must match one another in the smallest details, although they need not be like one another. In the same way a translation, instead of resembling the meaning of the original, must lovingly and in detail incorporate the original's mode of signification, thus making both the original and the translation recognizable as fragments of a greater language, just as fragments are part of a vessel. For this very reason translation must in large measure refrain from wanting to communicate something, from rendering the sense, and in this the original is important to it only insofar as it has already relieved the translator and his translation of the effort of assembling and expressing what is to be conveyed. In the realm of translation, too, the words εν αρχη ην ο λογος [in the beginning was the word] apply. On the other hand, as regards the meaning, the language of a translation can – in fact, must – let itself go, so that it gives voice to the *intentio* of the original not as reproduction but as harmony, as a supplement to the language in which it expresses itself, as its own kind of *intentio*. Therefore it is not the highest praise of a translation, particularly in the age of its origin, to say that it reads as if it had originally been written in that language. Rather, the significance of fidelity as ensured by literalness is that the work reflects the great longing for linguistic complementation. A real translation is transparent; it does not cover the original, does not block its light, but allows the pure language, as though reinforced by its own medium, to shine upon the original all the more fully. This may be achieved, above all, by a literal rendering of the syntax which proves words rather than sentences to be the primary element of the translator. For if the sentence is the wall before the language of the original, literalness is the arcade.

Fidelity and freedom in translation have traditionally been regarded as conflicting tendencies. This deeper interpretation of the one apparently does not serve to reconcile the two; in fact, it seems to deny the other all justification. For what is meant by freedom but that the rendering of the sense is no longer to be regarded as all-important? Only if the sense of a linguistic creation may be equated with the information it conveys does some ultimate, decisive element remain beyond all communication – quite close and yet infinitely remote, concealed or distinguishable, fragmented or powerful. In all language and linguistic creations there remains in addition to what can be conveyed something that cannot be communicated; depending on the context in which it appears, it is something that symbolizes or something symbolized. It is the former only in the finite products of language, the latter in the evolving of the languages themselves. And that which seeks to represent, to produce itself in the evolving of languages, is that very nucleus of pure language. Though concealed and fragmentary, it is an active force in life as the symbolized thing itself, where as it inhabits linguistic creations only in symbolized form. While that ultimate essence, pure language, in the various tongues is tied only to linguistic elements and their changes, in linguistic creations it is weighted with a heavy, alien meaning. To relieve it of this, to turn the symbolizing into the symbolized, to regain pure language fully formed in the linguistic flux, is the tremendous and only capacity of translation. In this pure language – which no longer means or expresses anything but is, as expressionless and creative Word, that which is meant in all languages – all information, all sense, and all intention finally encounter a stratum in which they are destined to be extinguished. This very stratum furnishes a new and higher justification for free translation; this justification does not derive from the sense of what is to be conveyed, for the emancipation from this sense is the task of fidelity. Rather, for the sake of pure language, a free translation bases the test on its own language. It is the task of the translator to release in his own language that pure language which is under the spell of another, to liberate the language imprisoned in a work in his re-creation of that work. For the sake of pure language he breaks through decayed barriers of his own language. Luther, Voss. Hölderlin, and George have extended the boundaries of the German language. – And what of the sense in its importance for the relationship between translation and original? A simile may help here. Just as a tangent touches a circle lightly and at but one point, with this touch rather than with the point setting the law according to which it is to continue on its straight path to infinity, a translation touches the original lightly and only at the infinitely small point of the sense, thereupon pursuing its own course according to the laws of fidelity in the freedom of linguistic flux. Without explicitly naming or substantiating it, Rudolf Pannwitz has characterized the true significance of this freedom. His observations are contained in *Die Krisis der europäischen Kultur* and rank with Goethe's Notes to the *Westöstlicher Divan* as the best comment on the theory of translation that has been published in Germany. Pannwitz writes: 'Our translations, even the best ones, proceed from a wrong premise. They want to turn Hindi, Greek, English into German instead of turning German into Hindi, Greek, English. Our translators have a far greater reverence for the usage of their own language than for the spirit of the foreign works. . . . The basic error of the translator is that he preserves the state in which his own language happens to be instead of allowing his language to be powerfully affected by the foreign tongue. Particularly when translating from a language very remote from his own he must go back to the primal elements of language itself and penetrate to the point where work, image, and tone converge. He must expand and deepen his language by means of the foreign language. It is not generally realized to what extent this is possible, to what extent any language can be transformed, how language differs from language almost the way dialect differs from dialect; however, this last is true only if one takes language seriously enough, not if one takes it lightly.'

The extent to which a translation manages to be in keeping with the nature of this mode is determined objectively by the translatability of the original. The lower the quality and distinction of its language, the larger the extent to which it is information, the less fertile a field it is for translation, until the utter preponderance of content, far from being the lever for a translation of distinctive mode, renders it impossible. The higher the level of a work, the more does it remain translatable even if its meaning is touched upon only fleetingly. This, of course, applies to originals only. Translations, on the other hand, prove to be untranslatable not because of any inherent difficulty, but because of the looseness with which meaning attaches to them. Confirmation of this as well as of every other important aspect is supplied by Hölderlin's translations, particularly those of the two tragedies by Sophocles. In them the harmony of the languages is so profound that sense is touched by language only the way an aeolian harp is touched by the wind. Hölderlin's translations are prototypes of their kind; they are to even the most perfect renderings of their texts as a prototype is to a model. This can be demonstrated by comparing Hölderlin's and Rudolf Borchardt's translations of Pindar's Third Pythian Ode. For this very reason Hölderlin's translations in particular are subject to the enormous danger inherent in all translations; the gates of a language thus expanded and modified may slam shut and enclose the translator with silence. Hölderlin's translations from Sophocles were his last work; in them meaning plunges from abyss to abyss until it threatens to become lost in the bottomless depths of language. There is, however, a stop. It is vouchsafed to Holy Writ alone, in which meaning has ceased to be the watershed for the flow of language and the flow of revelation. Where a text is identical with truth or dogma, where it is supposed to be 'the true language' in all its literalness and without the mediation of meaning, this text is unconditionally translatable. In such case translations are called for only because of the plurality of languages. Just as, in the original, language and revelation are one without any tension, so the translation must be one with the original in the form of the interlinear version, in which literalness and freedom are united. For to some degree all great texts contain their potential translation between the lines; this is true to the highest degree of sacred writings. The interlinear version of the Scriptures is the prototype or ideal of all translation.

Note

*   'The imperfection of languages consists in their plurality, the supreme one is lacking: thinking is writing without accessories or even whispering, the immortal word still remains silent; the diversity of idioms on earth prevents everybody from uttering the words which otherwise, at one single stroke, would materialize as truth.'

(b) Introduction to *The Making of the English Bible*

Gerald Hammond

The Authorized Version and the New English Bible

> . . . wee haue not tyed our selues to an vniformitie of phrasing, or to an identitie of words, as some peraduenture would wish we had done, because they obserue, that some

learned men some where, haue beene as exact as they could that way. . . . But, that we should express the same notion in the same particular word: as for example, if we translate the *Hebrew* or *Greeke* word once by *Purpose*, neuer to call it *Intent*: if one where *Iourneying*, neuer *Traveiling*; if one where *Thinke, neuer Suppose*; if one where *Paine*, neuer *Ache;* if one where *Ioy*, neuer Gladnesse, &c. Thus to minse the matter, wee thought to sauour more of curiositie then wisedome, and that rather it would breed scorne in the Atheist, then bring profite to the godly Reader. For is the kingdome of God become words or syllables?

from the Preface to the Authorized Version

Nearly four hundred years on 'yes' is, ironically, the answer which the advocate of the Authorized Version must make to this question. 'Yes' because there has been so great a shift in our attitude to translating the Bible. The whole range of Renaissance approaches, from Puritan pedantry to Catholic dogmatism, stands in one camp utterly opposed to what the modern translator attempts—and at the basis of the opposition is the way we regard, if not words and syllables, then words and syntax.

The opening words of the Song of Songs, in Hebrew, are *yishaqeni minshiqot pihu*, literally (with one hyphenated unit corresponding to one Hebrew word): 'let-him-kiss-me with-kisses-of his-mouth'. Miles Coverdale, who had no first hand knowledge of the Hebrew, had translated them like this in his 1535 Bible: 'O that thy mouth would give me a kiss'. This is attractive enough as the beginning of the love song, but it is grammatically and semantically misleading. In the Hebrew the speaker is not addressing a person but talking about him and she asks for a number of kisses, not one. By 1611 the English rendering had become completely literal: 'Let him kiss me with the kisses of his mouth.' The trouble with this, for the modern English translator, is that it presents logical and linguistic weaknesses. To kiss with a kiss is tautologous: even more so is to kiss with a kiss of the mouth. These are not weaknesses in the original Hebrew any more than are any language's idioms, but the modern translator believes in translating not word for word but idiom for idiom—hence the New English Bible's modern idiomatic equivalent: 'that he may smother me with kisses'. Now the rebarbatively alien tautologies have been replaced by an immediately acceptable modern phrase. But in rejecting the alien and introducing the familiar the modern version has ceased to be a translation. Set against even the unscholarly Coverdale's version it has lost everything which makes the Hebrew so erotically powerful. 'The mouth' may appear tautologous, but it is not—both Coverdale and the Authorized Version had embedded in their renderings the implication that the kissing will be of the frankest and most mutual kind, mouth to mouth. In the New English Bible there is no mutuality: smothering with kisses presents only one-sided abundance.

There is a more general point to be made here: that to translate meaning while ignoring the way that meaning has been articulated is not translation at all but merely replacement—murdering the original instead of recreating it. It is partly a matter of the creative inferiority of the modern translators: normally they are scholars and exegetes whose instincts are to replace the dangerous ambiguities of poetry with the safer specificities of prose. They do not see that the life of anything written lies in its words and syntax. While the Renaissance Bible translator saw half of his task as reshaping English so that it could adapt itself to Hebraic idiom the modern translator wants to make no demands on the language he translates into.

This is something which goes far beyond Bible translation. Walter Benjamin's introduction to a translation of Baudelaire's *Tableaux Parisiens*, called 'The Task of the Translator', addresses just this point. He builds his thesis on the argument that the form of expression is, in large part, the nature of what is expressed. For the translator not to betray this fact he must above all give 'a literal rendering of the syntax' thereby proving 'words rather than sentences to be the primary element of the translator'; and he quotes Rudolf Pannwitz's argument that 'the basic error of the translator is that he preserves the state in which his own language happens to be instead of allowing his language to be powerfully affected by the foreign tongue'. Benjamin's conclusion is, intriguingly, that 'the interlinear version of the Scriptures is the prototype or ideal of all translation'.[1] Now the Authorized Version is close enough to its original for it not to ask great efforts from us to turn it into such a prototype—its word order is for many verses at a time the word order of the original and it translates the great majority of Hebrew idioms literally. But what survives as Hebraic in the New English Bible is, more often than not, only the translators' occasional remembrances of the Authorized Version.

Sometimes, when they are the result of scholarly emendation, the modern translation's changes are understandable, if still regrettable. [. . .]

But too often the change seems to come from either a resentment at the poetic possibilities of Old Testament Hebrew or a feeling that modern readers are idiots incapable of any kind of imaginative interpretative response. How else can we understand what happens to 1 Samuel 25:37? This verse describes Nabal's awakening after a night of drunkenness to be told by his wife Abigail how she had saved him from David's wrath. This is from the Authorized Version:

> But it came to pass in the morning, when the wine was gone out of Nabal, and his wife had told him these things, that his heart died within him, and he became as a stone.

Here the most expressive phrase is 'his heart died within him'—a literal translation of the Hebrew, it carries into English the simultaneously physical and spiritual effects of what Nabal hears. Why do the modern translators abandon this and render it, as the New English Bible does, 'and he had a seizure and lay there like a stone'? If the answer is that today's readers would not understand the literal meaning of the original, then today's readers must have extraordinarily limited interpretative capacities. If the answer is that the Hebrew really means 'had a seizure', but in a primitive culture the only way to express such medical details was figuratively, then why not treat 'lay there like a stone' the same and translate it as 'lay paralysed'?

There are many such examples. In 1 Kings 22:27 the king orders Micaiah to be thrown into prison. The Authorized Version renders it:

> Put this *fellow* in the prison, and feed him with bread of affliction and with water of affliction, until I come in peace.[2]

The expressive Hebrew phrases here are *lechem lachats* and *mayyim lachats*. *Lachats* is a noun derived from a verb meaning 'to squeeze, press, oppress', so that 'bread of oppression' and 'water of oppression' are, as we might expect, literal renderings. Any reader will grasp that the phrases mean a prison diet of bread and water, but it is the ponderousness of expression which makes the king's sentence so forbidding. All the effect disappears, though, when the New English Bible spells out the meaning:

> 'Lock this fellow up', he said, 'and give him prison diet of bread and water until I come home in safety.'

What is lost in the modern translation is the Hebrew way of thought, and without this there can be no successful translation. There is, I suppose, room for disagreement here. The New English Bible translators would presumably argue that the Authorized Version's rendering of Ecclesiastes 11:1 was, although literal, misleading:

> Cast thy bread upon the waters: for thou shalt find it after many days.

Their case would be that in English the Hebrew idiom sounded too much like wilful waste when, in fact, it represented good economic practice—hence their export or die rendering:

> Send your grain across the seas, and in time you will get a return.

But more typical is the kind of small but revealing change made to Job 21:26. Here Job has just described two types of men: one dies 'in his full strength, being wholly at ease and quiet', the other dies in 'the bitterness of his soul'. But really there is no distinction between them:

> They shall lie down alike in the dust, and the worms shall cover them.

Those were the Authorized Version's words. The New English Bible also emphasizes their identity—more so than the Authorized Version because it renders the Hebrew word *yachad* (AV 'alike') as 'side by side':

> Side by side they are laid in earth
> and worms are the shroud of both.

It is not 'side by side', nor 'shroud' (the Hebrew has *təchaseh*, 'will cover') which interests me so much as the transformation of the active verb into the passive: 'they shall lie down' becomes 'they are laid'. Of course the New English Bible is logically right. Corpses do not go and lay themselves down, but poetically it has missed the point which the Authorized Version's literal rendering had made—that the sudden will to die is as much the province of the vigorous and confident as it is of the weak and embittered.

This is the first paragraph of the New English Bible's rendering of Ezekiel 33:

THESE WERE THE WORDS OF THE LORD TO ME: Man, say to
your fellow-countrymen, When I set armies in motion against a land, its
people choose one of themselves to be a watchman. When he sees the
enemy approaching and blows his trumpet to warn the people, then if
anyone does not heed the warning and is overtaken by the enemy, he is
responsible for his own fate. He is responsible because, when he heard
the alarm, he paid no heed to it; if he had heeded it, he would have
escaped. But if the watchman does not blow his trumpet or warn
the people when he sees the enemy approaching, then any man who is
killed is caught with all his sins upon him; but I will hold the watchman
answerable for his death.

This covers only six verses, but in those six verses there are numerous important
deviations from the original Hebrew, so that what in the Authorized Version is a
powerful prophetic warning becomes, here, something more like a civil defence
handout. These are some of them: 'man' and 'fellow-countrymen' in verse 2 the
Authorized Version renders literally as 'son of man' and 'the children of thy people'.
The New English Bible is doubtless right in its assumption of what the Hebrew idioms
mean, but in the case of 'man' it could hardly be said to have found a modern idiomatic equivalent—'you' would fit the bill much better. But more important is the
loss of the mentality behind the Hebrew idioms where 'son' and 'child' embody both
kinship and dependence.

Later in the same verse 'when I set armies in motion against' is the translators'
strange idea of a modern idiomatic equivalent for a Hebrew which the Authorized
Version translates literally as 'when I bring the sword upon the land'. The sword is
the key image of the passage. The Authorized Version follows the Hebrew in
repeating it in verse 3, 'if when he seeth the sword come'; in verse 4, 'if the sword
come, and take him away'; and in verse 6, 'if the sword come, and take away any
person from among them'. All of these are demetaphorized to 'enemy' by the New
English Bible: 'the enemy approaching' in verses 3 and 6, and 'overtaken by the
enemy' in verse 4. In verse 4, too, there is a syntactic simplification of the Hebrew.
The New English Bible says, simply, 'if anyone does not heed the warning', but the
Hebrew makes a distinction between the two actions, first hearing and then not
heeding—as in the Authorized Version's 'then whosoever heareth . . . and taketh
not warning . . .' Its syntax may not be as concise as the New English Bible's, but
there is no virtue in making prophetic utterance concise.

The New English Bible ends the verse with a characteristic replacement of idiom:
compare its 'he is responsible for his own fate' with the Authorized Version's literal
'his blood shall be upon his own head'. It is not just that the original idiom does not
need to be replaced but that the New English Bible has completely lost the linking of
'sword' and 'blood' in this verse and the next.

In verse 5 the New English Bible rearranges the syntax so that the impression
given is of a defensive, self-justifying God:

He is responsible because, when he heard the alarm, he paid no heed
to it.

But the Hebrew is more assertive and aggressive, as is the Authorized Version's rendering which follows the Hebrew word order:

> He heard the sound of the trumpet, and took not warning: his blood shall
> be upon him.

Verse 6, too, shows the modern translators' mistrust of Hebrew syntax. Their rendering presents simple and characterless cause and effect:

> But if the watchman does not blow his trumpet or warn the people when
> he sees the enemy approaching, then any man who is killed is caught with
> all his sins upon him.

The Hebrew, though, is more interesting than this because it recreates the whole narrative so far, of a watchman who sees, fails to warn, and the massacre which follows. The Authorized Version again keeps to the Hebrew word order and gets much closer to this effect:

> But if the watchman see the sword come, and blow not the trumpet, and
> the people be not warned; if the sword come, and take *any* person from
> among them, he is taken away in his iniquity.

One might add, too, that the New English Bible's 'with all his sins upon him' seems to be one Hebraism which it has retained, even at the risk of employing an archaism. But this is not so. The Hebrew has only the one word, translated accurately by the Authorized Version's 'in his iniquity'. What do we make of translators who impose that kind of archaism where it does not exist in the original but who, in the next verse, replace the graphic (and literal) 'his blood will I require' with 'I will hold . . . answerable for his death'?

Not straitening the Holy Ghost was the expression used by the Rheims translators and it applies well to the whole English tradition culminating in the Authorized Version. Those translators—Tyndale, Coverdale, the Geneva and Rheims translators—cultivated ambiguity and evocative vagueness. Their modern successors invariably move towards one fixed and unreverberative meaning. Take two examples from early in Genesis. In 2:24 Adam follows his identification of woman with a statement about the overriding importance of marriage. In the words of the New English Bible he says:

> That is why a man leaves his father and mother and is united to his wife
> and the two become one flesh.

'Is united' implies that the Hebrew verb in question here is connected with the word *'achad*, 'one'—but it actually translates *dābaq*, a verb whose primary sense is 'to cling' or 'to stick'. It is, for example, the verb used in Deuteronomy 13:18, where God orders that not one thing of the city of Belial will stick to the Israelites' hands after they have burnt it down; and in Lamentations 4:4 God's curse is that the tongue

of the sucking child will stick to the roof of its mouth because of thirst. Adam, therefore, is saying something stronger than that man and woman will unite—by using
that verb the New English Bible limits the becoming one flesh to the act of sexual
intercourse—he is describing a clinging and sticking together, hence the Authorized
Version's rendering:

> Therefore shall a man leave his father and his mother, and shall cleave
> unto his wife: and they shall be one flesh.

'Cleave' is a powerfully evocative verb. It carries all of the abstract sense of the two
making one, but it insists too upon a concrete joining. Woman has just been created
by a cleaving—in the word's other sense—of a rib from Adam's body. The circle is
completed in this verse when the body is made whole again. The New English Bible's
'united' makes the 'one flesh' at the end the figurative consequence of the sexual
union; but the Authorized Version's 'cleave' carries images of clinging, clutching,
and separation from the rest of humanity.

There is a further point of importance in connection with 'cleave' and
this is consistency of translation. In the other two examples I gave of the
Hebrew word's occurrence the Authorized Version also uses 'cleave': in
Deuteronomy, 'and there shall cleave nought of the cursed thing to thine hand',
and in Lamentations, 'the tongue of the sucking child cleaveth to the roof of
its mouth'. No reader of the New English Bible could begin to guess that in these
three instances the same Hebrew word was used: in Deuteronomy it is translated
as 'found in thy possession', and in Lamentations it is, unexpectedly, 'cleaves to its
palate'.

Part of my complaint is, I suppose, the old puritan hankering to be able
to compare text with text and make the comparisons stick—the kind of thing
the Authorized Version preface warns against. But, crucially, in examples like
this it is the Authorized Version which stands for consistency. There are, for
example, four more places where the Old Testament uses the image of the tongue
sticking to the roof of the mouth or the jaws. The Authorized Version translates them
like this:

> The nobles held their peace, and their tongue cleaved to the roof of their
> mouth (Job 29:10).
> If I do not remember thee, let my tongue cleave to the roof of my mouth
> (Ps. 137:6).
> And I will make thy tongue cleave to the roof of thy mouth, that thou
> shalt be dumb (Ezek. 3:26).
> My strength is dried up like a potsherd, and my tongue cleaveth to my
> jaws (Ps. 22:15).

The New English Bible's renderings of these four are, respectively: 'every man held
his tongue'; 'let my tongue cling to the roof of my mouth'; 'I will fasten your tongue
to the roof of your mouth'; 'my tongue sticks to my jaw'. Worse than such inconsist-
ency is its corollary. Once the translator allows himself to pick and choose among

English equivalents, then he will almost always choose too specific a word, so that expressiveness is sacrificed to an unnecessary precision. Compare these further renderings of *dābaq* in the two versions:

2 Samuel 23:10, describing one of David's mighty men, the model for Bunyan's Valiant-for-Truth:

> *A V:*   He arose, and smote the Philistines until his hand was weary, and
>   his hand clave unto the sword.
> *NEB:*   . . . his hand stuck fast to his sword

Here 'stuck fast' is too gluey—perhaps the translators are thinking of the stickiness of blood. 'Clave' gives the hand more of its own identity, and the sword becomes a prop to support it in its tiredness. Psalm 44:26:

> *A V:*   For our soul is bowed down to the dust: our belly cleaveth unto
>   the earth.
> *NEB:*   For we sink down to the dust and lie prone on the earth.

Having decided to ignore the Hebrew word *nepesh*, 'soul', in the first half of the verse, the New English Bible becomes highly specific in the second—'prone', of course, not 'supine'. Entirely lost is the grand poetic contrast of a soul bowed down and a belly cleaving, i.e. a soul forced to act against its will and a belly all too ready to embrace the earth.

Genesis 34:3, Jacob's daughter Dinah is raped by Shechem. This verse describes Shechem's feelings immediately after the rape:

> *A V:*   And his soul clave unto Dinah . . . and he loved the damsel.
> *NEB:*   But he remained true to Dinah . . . he loved the girl.

'Remained true' is exactly the wrong phrase since it implies fidelity and honour: the point of the story is that Shechem's lust is not fulfilled by one act of rape. He keeps possession of Dinah until he and his men are massacred. The Authorized Version's image of his soul cleaving to her—the Hebrew again has *nepesh* as the subject of the verb—conveys much better the intensity of Shechem's feelings which led him to do such a mad act.

By rewriting the original and reinterpreting it in the terms of modern idiom the New English Bible misses crucial ambiguities and contrasts which Renaissance English Bibles had retained. My second example from Genesis 4:1 illustrates this: it is Eve's reaction to the birth of her first son, Cain. Here the New English Bible has her saying, 'With the help of the Lord I have brought a man into being.' But the Hebrew is more direct. It uses the verb *qāneh*, and the sense of this is not to bring into being, but to acquire—even, to buy, for nouns like *miqneh*, 'cattle', and *miqnāh*, 'purchase' are derived from it. Cain is a possession acquired with the aid of, or, and the Hebrew will allow this, from the Lord—as in the Authorized Version's rendering: 'I have gotten a man from the Lord.' And 'gotten' is a brilliant translation of Tyndale's (showing, incidentally, the value of first thoughts: in his 1534 version he changed it to 'obtained') which the Authorized Version did well to keep. It unites acquiring something with begetting it.

Eve's reaction to Abel's birth is not described, but after Abel's death she has a third son, Seth, and at his birth she uses a significantly different form of words from those she used at the birth of Cain. It would be difficult, though, to see what kind of contrast there was if we had to depend on the New English Bible. It has Eve saying:

> God has granted me another son in place of Abel.

The Authorized Version is more literal:

> God . . . hath appointed me another seed instead of Abel.

In the New English Bible the contrasts are between bringing into being and being granted, and between 'man' and 'son'. In the Authorized Version they are between 'getting' and 'being appointed', and between 'man' and 'seed'—a more effective revelation of what Abel's murder has taught her about the ownership of children and about death and continuity.

The modern translator's scholarly desire to be specific will inevitably make the Bible's most poetic passages prosaic. In Genesis 6:13 God's resounding warning to Noah, in the words of the Authorized Version, 'the end of all flesh is come before me', becomes in the New English Bible, 'the loathsomeness of all mankind has become plain to me'. Three pieces of scholarship have helped turn God from an awesome figure into a bureaucrat. The Hebrew word $q\bar{e}ts$, a common word meaning 'end' and one which often has eschatological implications, is clearly not specific enough—hence 'loathsomeness', which is based, one guesses, on a conjectured emendation. Then the word $b\bar{a}s\bar{a}r$, normally used in the Bible to mean 'flesh', is narrowed down to mankind—but why this should be I find difficult to understand, since the flood destroyed all creatures as well as man. And, finally, the Hebrew $b\bar{a}$ $\partial p\bar{a}nai$, 'has-come before-me', has lost the Hebraic vagueness which the Authorized Version had retained, and has been made plain for the modern reader to understand.

The verb $m\bar{a}taq$ means, essentially, 'to be sweet'. It occurs three times in Job, and twice the New English Bible gives it its essential meaning: in 21:33 'the dust of the earth is sweet to him', and in 20:12 'though evil taste sweet in his mouth'. But its most evocative use is in 24:20, and because it is so evocative, the modern scholars choose to emend it—hence the huge difference between the New English Bible's 'the worm sucks him dry' and the Authorized Version's 'the worm shall feed sweetly on him'.

One of the lessons which the Renaissance translators taught, but which the modern translators do not care to learn, is that the most literal rendering is often the most powerful. Take the Hebrew construct form, its chief way of expressing genitival or adjectival relationships. So natural and simple is it to use a *noun*+ '*of* +*noun* form to render it into English—largely because it preserves the Hebrew word order—that it is difficult to understand why the modern translators avoid it, unless it be from fear of the ambiguities it encourages. In Psalm 127:2 the man who works without the Lord's help is described as one who, in the words of the

Authorized Version, is 'to sit up late, to eat the bread of sorrows'. In the New English Bible he is addressed as one who will 'go late to rest, toiling for the bread you eat'.

[. . .]

The basic distinction between the Renaissance and the modern translators is one of fidelity to their original. Partly the loss of faith in the Hebrew and Greek as the definitive word of God has led to the translators' loss of contact with it, but more responsibility lies in the belief that a modern Bible should aim not to tax its readers' linguistic or interpretative abilities one bit. If this aim is to be achieved then it seems clear that a new Bible will have to be produced for every generation—each one probably moving us further away from the original text, now that the initial break has been made. In the New English Bible's title 'new' is the operative word. The contrast with the Authorized Version could scarcely be greater, for almost every one of the examples of the Authorized Version's renderings which I have cited in this Introduction can be traced back to Tyndale, Coverdale, or the Geneva Bible. And the translators, in their preface, took pride in their inheritance:

> . . . we never thought from the beginning that we should need to make a new translation, nor yet to make of a bad one a good one . . . but to make a good one better, or out of many good ones one principal good one.

The New English Bible had no such base to build on, no certainty about the text it translated from, and no faith in its readers' abilities. It has, in effect, unmade a Bible which took ninety years to make, and which held the imaginations and emotions of its readers for three hundred and fifty years.

[. . .]

Notes

1   *Illuminations*, ed. Hannah Arendt, transl. Harry Zohn (London 1973), pp. 69-82.
2   The italics here, and elsewhere, are the translator's device to signal a word not found in the original.

Acknowledgments

The author wishes to thank Ward Allen and Vanderbilt University Press for permission to reprint Mr. Allen's translation and transcription of the notes of Jones Bois, as given in his *Translating for King James*.

Extracts from the Authorized King James Version of the Bible, which is Crown Copyright, are reproduced by permission; and from the New English Bible, 2nd edition © 1970, by permission of the Oxford, and the Cambridge, University Presses.

(c) To the Reader

Robert Alter

I. The Bible in English and the Heresy of Explanation

[. . .] For the philologist, the great goal is the achievement of clarity. It is scarcely necessary to say that in all sorts of important, but also delimited, ways clarity is indispensable in a translator's wrestling with the original text. The simplest case, but a pervasive one, consists of getting a handle on the meaning of particular terms. It is truly helpful, for example, to know that biblical *naḥal*[1] most commonly indicates not any sort of brook, creek, or stream but the kind of freshet, called a *wadi* in both Arabic and modern Hebrew, that floods a dry desert gulch during the rainy months and vanishes in the heat of the summer. Suddenly, Job's "my brothers have betrayed like a *naḥal*" (6:14) becomes a striking poetic image, where before it might have been a minor puzzlement. But philological clarity in literary texts can quickly turn into too much of a good thing. Literature in general, and the narrative prose of the Hebrew Bible in particular, cultivates certain profound and haunting enigmas, delights in leaving its audiences guessing about motives and connections, and, above all, loves to set ambiguities of word choice and image against one another in an endless interplay that resists neat resolution. In polar contrast, the impulse of the philologist is—here a barbarous term nicely catches the tenor of the activity—"to disambiguate" the terms of the text. The general result when applied to translation is to reduce, simplify, and denature the Bible. These unfortunate consequences are all the more pronounced when the philologist, however acutely trained in that discipline, has an underdeveloped sense of literary diction, rhythm, and the uses of figurative language; and that, alas, is often the case in an era in which literary culture is not widely disseminated even among the technically educated.

   The unacknowledged heresy underlying most modern English versions of the Bible is the use of translation as a vehicle for *explaining* the Bible instead of representing it in another language, and in the most egregious instances this amounts to explaining away the Bible. This impulse may be attributed not only to a rather reduced sense of the philological enterprise but also to a feeling that the Bible, because of its canonical status, has to be made accessible—indeed, transparent—to all. (The one signal exception to all these generalizations is Everett Fox's 1995 American version of the Torah. Emulating the model of the German translation by Martin Buber and Franz Rosenzweig [begun in 1925, completed in 1961], which flaunts Hebrew etymologies, preserves nearly all repetitions of Hebrew terms, and invents German words, Fox goes to the opposite extreme: his English has the great virtue of reminding us verse after verse of the strangeness of the Hebrew original, but it does so at the cost of often being not quite English and consequently of becoming a text for study rather than a fluently readable version that conveys the stylistic poise and power of the Hebrew.) Modern translators, in their zeal to uncover the meanings of the biblical text for the instruction of a modern readership, frequently lose sight of how the text intimates its meanings—the distinctive, artfully deployed features of ancient Hebrew prose and poetry that are the instruments for the articulation of all meaning, message, insight, and vision.

One of the most salient characteristics of biblical Hebrew is its extraordinary concreteness, manifested especially in a fondness for images rooted in the human body. The general predisposition of modern translators is to convert most of this concrete language into more abstract terms that have the purported advantage of clarity but turn the pungency of the original into stale paraphrase. A good deal of this concrete biblical language based on the body is what a linguist would call lexicalized metaphor—imagery, here taken from body parts and bodily functions, that is made to stand for some general concept as a fixed item in the vocabulary of the language (as "eye" in English can be used to mean "perceptiveness" or "connoisseur's understanding"). Dead metaphors, however, are the one persuasive instance of the resurrection of the dead—for at least the ghosts of the old concrete meanings float over the supposedly abstract acceptations of the terms, and this is something the philologically driven translators do not appear to understand. "Many modern versions," Gerald Hammond tartly observes, "eschew anything which smacks of imagery or metaphor—based on the curious assumption, I guess, that modern English is an image-free language." The price paid for this avoidance of the metaphorical will become evident by considering two characteristic and recurrent Hebrew terms and the role they play in representing the world in the biblical story.

[. . .]

There are, alas, more pervasive ways than the choice of terms in which nearly all the modern English versions commit the heresy of explanation. The most global of these is the prevalent modern strategy of repackaging biblical syntax for an audience whose reading experience is assumed to be limited to *Time, Newsweek,* and the *New York Times* or the *Times* of London. Now, it is often asserted, with seemingly self-evident justice, that the fundamental difference between biblical syntax and modern English syntax is between a system in which parallel clauses linked by "and" predominate (what linguists call "parataxis") and one in which the use of subordinate clauses and complex sentences predominates (what linguists call "hypotaxis"). Modern English has a broad array of modal and temporal discriminations in its system of verbs and a whole armament of subordinate conjunctions to stipulate different relations among clauses. Biblical Hebrew, on the other hand, has only two aspects[2] (they are probably not tenses in our sense) of verbs, together with one indication of a jussive mode—when a verb is used to express a desire or exhortation to perform the action in question—and a modest number of subordinate conjunctions. Although there are certainly instances of significant syntactic subordination, the characteristic biblical syntax is additive, working with parallel clauses linked by "and"—which in the Hebrew is not even a separate word but rather a particle, *waw*[3] (it means "hook"), that is prefixed to the first word of the clause.

The assumption of most modern translators has been that this sort of syntax will be either unintelligible or at least alienating to modern readers, and so should be entirely rearranged as modern English. There are two basic problems with this procedure. First, it ignores the fact that parataxis is the essential literary vehicle of biblical narrative: it is the way the ancient Hebrew writers saw the world, linked events in it, artfully ordered it, and narrated it, and one gets a very different world if their syntax is jettisoned. Second, rejection of biblical parataxis presupposes a very simplistic notion of what constitutes modern literary English. The implicit model seems to be, as I have suggested, the popular press, as well as perhaps high-school textbooks, bureaucratic directives, and ordinary conversation. But serious writers almost never accept such leveling limitation to a bland norm of popular usage. If one thinks of the great English stylists among twentieth-century novelists—writers like Joyce, Nabokov, Faulkner, and Virginia Woolf—there is not one among them whose use of language, including the deployment of syntax, even vaguely resembles the workaday simplicity and patly consistent orderliness that recent translators of the Bible have posited as the norm of modern English. It is also well to keep in mind that literary style, like many other aspects of literature, is constantly self-recapitulative, invoicing recollections of its near and distant literary antecedents, so that modernists like Joyce and Faulkner sometimes echo biblical language and cadences, and a mannered stylist like Hemingway, in making "and" his most prominent connective, surely has the King James Version of the Bible in mind. And in any event, the broad history of both Semitic and European languages and literatures evinces a strong differentiation in most periods between everyday language and the language of literature.

The assumption of biblical philologists that parallel syntax is alien to modern literary English is belied by the persistent presence of highly wrought paratactic prose even at the end of the twentieth century. A variety of self-conscious English stylists in the modern era, from Gertrude Stein to Cormac McCarthy, have exhibited a fondness for chains of parallel utterances linked by "and" in which the basic sentence-type is the same structurally as that used again and again in biblical prose. What such a style makes manifest in a narrative is a series of more or less discrete events, or micro-events, in a chain, not unlike the biblical names of begetters and begotten that are strung one after another in the chains of the genealogical lists. The biblical writers generally chose not to order these events in ramified networks of causal, conceptual, or temporal subordination, not because hypotaxis was an unavailable option, as the opening verses of the second Creation story (2:4–5) clearly demonstrate. The continuing appeal, moreover, for writers in our own age of this syntax dominated by "and," which highlights the discrete event, suggests that parallel syntax may still be a perfectly viable way to represent in English the studied parallelism of verbs and clauses of ancient Hebrew narrative.

Since a literary style is composed of very small elements as well as larger structural features, an English translator must confront the pesky question of whether the ubiquitous Hebrew particle that means "and" should be represented at all in translation. This is obviously not a problem when the *waw* simply connects two nouns—as in "the heavens and the earth"—but what of its constant use at the beginning of sentences and clauses prefixed to verbs? The argument against translating it in these cases is that the primary function of the *waw* appended to a verb is not to signify "and" but to indicate that the Hebrew prefix conjugation, which otherwise is used for actions yet to be completed, is reporting past events (hence its designation in the terminology of classical Hebrew grammar as "the *waw* of conversion"). It is far from clear, as modern Bible scholars tend to assume, that the fulfillment of one linguistic function by a particle of speech automatically excludes any others; on the contrary, it is entirely likely that for the ancient audience the *waw* appended to the verb both converted its temporal aspect and continued to signify "and." But, semantics aside, the general practice of modern English translators of suppressing the "and" when it is attached to a verb has the effect of changing the tempo, rhythm, and construction of events in biblical narrative. Let me illustrate by quoting a narrative sequence from Genesis 24 first in my own version, which reproduces every "and" and every element of parataxis, and then in the version of the Revised English Bible. The Revised English Bible is in general one of the most compulsive repackagers of biblical language, though in this instance the reordering of the Hebrew is relatively minor. Its rendering of these sentences is roughly interchangeable with any of the other modern versions—the Jerusalem Bible, the New Jewish Publication Society, Speiser—one might choose. I begin in the middle of verse 16, where Rebekah becomes the subject of a series of actions:

> . . . and she came down to the spring and filled her jug and came back up. And the servant ran toward her and said, "Pray, let me sip a bit of water from your jug." And she said, "Drink, my lord," and she hurried and tipped down her jug on one hand and let him drink. And she let him drink his fill and said, "For your camels, too, I shall draw water until they drink their fill." And she hurried and emptied her jug into the trough, and she ran again to the well to draw water and drew water for all his camels.

And this is how the Revised English Bible, in keeping with the prevailing assumptions of most recent translations, renders these verses in what is presumed to be sensible modern English:

> She went down to the spring, filled her jar, and came up again. Abraham's servant hurried to meet her and said, "Will you give me a little water from your jar?" "Please drink, sir," she answered, and at once lowered her jar on her hand to let him drink. When she had finished giving him a drink, she said, "I shall draw water also for your camels until they have had enough." She quickly emptied her jar into the water trough, and then hurrying again to the well she drew water and watered all the camels.

There is, as one would expect, some modification of biblical parataxis, though it is not so extreme here as elsewhere in the Revised English Bible: "And she let him drink his fill" is converted into an introductory adverbial clause, "When she had finished giving him a drink" (actually in consonance with the otherwise paratactic King James Version): "and she hurried" is compressed into "quickly"; "and she ran again" becomes the participial "hurrying again." (Moves of this sort, it should be said, push translation to the verge of paraphrase—recasting and interpreting the original instead of representing it.) The most striking divergence between these two versions is that mine has fifteen "and's," corresponding precisely to fifteen occurrences of the particle *waw* in the Hebrew, whereas the Revised English Bible manages with just five. What difference does this make? To begin with, it should be observed that the *waw*, whatever is claimed about its linguistic function, is by no means an inaudible element in the phonetics of the Hebrew text: we must keep constantly in mind that these narratives were composed to be *heard*, not merely to be decoded by a reader's eye. The reiterated "and," then, plays an important role in creating the rhythm of the story, in phonetically punctuating the forward-driving movement of the prose. The elimination of the "and" in the Revised English Bible and in all its modern cousins produces—certainly to my ear—an abrupt, awkward effect in the sound pattern of the language, or to put it more strictly, a kind of narrative arrhythmia.

More is at stake here than pleasing sounds, for the heroine of the repeated actions is in fact subtly but significantly reduced in all the rhythmically deficient versions. She of course performs roughly the same acts in the different versions—politely offering water to the stranger, lowering her jug so that he can drink, rapidly going back and forth to the spring to bring water for the camels. But in the compressions, syntactical reorderings, and stop-and-start movements of the modernizing version, the encounter at the well and Rebekah's actions are made to seem rather matter-of-fact, however exemplary her impulse of hospitality. This tends to obscure what the Hebrew highlights, which is that she is doing something quite extraordinary. Rebekah at the well presents one of the rare biblical instances of the performance of an act of "Homeric" heroism. The servant begins by asking modestly to "sip a bit of water," as though all he wanted were to wet his lips. But we need to remember, as the ancient audience surely did, that a camel after a long desert journey can drink as much as twenty-five gallons of water, and there are ten camels here whom Rebekah offers to water "until they drink their fill." The chain of verbs tightly linked by all the "and's" does an admirable job in conveying this sense of the young woman's hurling herself with prodigious speed into the sequence of required actions. Even her dialogue is scarcely a pause in the narrative momentum, but is integrated syntactically and rhythmically into the chain: "And she said, 'Drink, my lord,' and she hurried and tipped down her jug. . . . And she hurried and emptied her jug into the trough, and she ran again to the well to draw water and drew water for all his camels." The parallel syntax and the barrage of "and's," far from being the reflex of a "primitive" language, are as artfully effective in furthering the ends of the narrative as any device one could find in a sophisticated modern novelist.

Beyond these issues of syntax and local word choice lies a fundamental question that no modern translator I know of has really confronted: what level, or perhaps levels, of style is represented in biblical Hebrew? There is no reason, I believe, to be awestruck by the sheer antiquity of the text. If biblical Hebrew could be shown to reflect a pungent colloquial usage in the ancient setting, or a free commingling of colloquial and formal language, it would be only logical to render it with equivalent levels of diction in modern English. As a matter of fact, all the modern translators— from Speiser to Fox to the sundry ecclesiastical committees in both America and England—have shown a deaf ear to diction, acting as though the only important considerations in rendering a literary text were lexical values and grammatical structures, while the English terms chosen could be promiscuously borrowed from boardroom or bedroom or scholar's word hoard, with little regard to the tonality and connotation the words carried with them from their native linguistic habitat.

Whatever conclusions we may draw about the stylistic level of biblical Hebrew are a little precarious because we of course have no record of the ancient spoken language, and if, as seems likely, there were extracanonical varieties or genres of Hebrew writing in the ancient world, the vestiges have long since crumbled into dust. Did, for example, the citizens of Judea in the time of Jeremiah speak in a parallel syntax, using the *waw* consecutive, and employing roughly the same vocabulary that we find in his prophecies, or in Deuteronomy and Genesis? Although there is no proof, my guess is that vernacular syntax and grammar probably differed in some ways from their literary counterparts. In regard to vocabulary, there is evidence that what we see in the canonical books would not have been identical with everyday usage. First, there is the problem of the relative paucity of vocabulary in biblical literature. As the Spanish Hebrew scholar Angel Sáenz-Badillos has observed in his *History of the Hebrew Language* (1993), the biblical lexicon is so restricted that it is hard to believe it could have served all the purposes of quotidian existence in a highly developed society. The instance of the poetry of Job, with its unusual number of words not found elsewhere in Scripture, is instructive in this regard: the Job-poet in his powerful impulse to forge a poetic imagery that would represent humankind, God, and nature in a new and even startling light, draws on highly specific language from manufacturing processes, food preparation, commercial and legal institutions, which would never be used in biblical narrative. The plausible conclusion is that the Hebrew of the Bible is a conventionally delimited language, roughly analagous in this respect to the French of the neoclassical theater: it was understood by writers and their audiences, at least in the case of narrative, that only certain words were appropriate for the literary rendering of events.

There is evidence, moreover, that people in everyday life may have had different words for many of the basic concepts and entities that are mentioned in the Bible. This argument was persuasively made by the Israeli linguist Abba Ben-David in his still indispensable 1967 study, available only in Hebrew, *The Language of the Bible and the Language of the Sages*. Ben-David offers a fascinating explanation for one of the great mysteries of the Hebrew language—the emergence, toward the end of the pre-Christian era, of a new kind of Hebrew, which became the language of the early rabbis. Now, it is widely recognized that this new Hebrew reflected the influence of the Aramaic vernacular in morphology, in grammar, and in some of its vocabulary, and that, understandably, it also incorporated a vast number of Greek and Latin loanwords. But what is puzzling is that rabbinic Hebrew also uses a good many indigenous Hebrew terms that are absent from the biblical corpus, or reflected only in rare and marginal biblical cognates. The standard terms in rabbinical Hebrew for sun and moon, and some of its frequently used verbs like to look, to take, to enter, to clean, are entirely different from their biblical counterparts, without visible influence from any of the languages impinging on Hebrew. Where did these words come from? Ben-David, observing, as have others before him, that there are incipient signs of an emergent rabbinic Hebrew in late biblical books like Jonah and the Song of Songs, makes the bold and, to my mind, convincing proposal that rabbinic Hebrew was built upon an ancient vernacular that for the most part had been excluded from the literary language used for the canonical texts. This makes particular sense if one keeps in mind that the early rabbis were anxious to draw a line between their own "Oral Torah" and the written Torah they were expounding. For the purposes of legal and homiletic exegesis, they naturally would have used a vernacular Hebrew rather than the literary language, and when their discourse was first given written formulation in the Mishnah in the early third century C.E., that text would have recorded this vernacular, which probably had a long prehistory in the biblical period. It is distinctly possible that when a ninth-century B.C.E. Israelite farmer mopped his brow under the blazing sun, he did not point to it and say *shemesh*, as it is invariably called in biblical prose texts, but rather *ḥamah*, as it is regularly designated in the Mishnah.

There is, of course, no way of plotting a clear chronology of the evolution of rabbinic Hebrew from an older vernacular, no way of determining how far back into the biblical period various elements of rabbinic language may go. It is sufficient for our effort to gauge the level of style of the Bible's literary prose merely to grant the very high likelihood that the language of the canonical texts was not identical with the vernacular, that it reflected a specialized or elevated vocabulary, and perhaps even a distinct grammar and syntax. Let me cite a momentary exception to the rule of biblical usage that may give us a glimpse into this excluded vernacular background of a more formal literary language. It is well known that in biblical dialogue all the characters speak proper literary Hebrew, with no intimations of slang, dialect, or idiolect. The single striking exception is impatient Esau's first speech to Jacob in Genesis 25: "Let me gulp down some of this red red stuff." Inarticulate with hunger, he cannot come up with the ordinary Hebrew term for "stew," and so he makes do with *ha'adom ha'adom*[4] *hazeh*—literally "this red red." But what is more interesting for our purpose is the verb Esau uses for "feeding," *hal'iteini*. This is the sole occurrence of this verb in the biblical corpus, but in the Talmud it is a commonly used term with the specific meaning of stuffing food into the mouth of an animal. One cannot be certain this was its precise meaning in the biblical period because words do, after all, undergo semantic shifts in a period of considerably more than a thousand years. But it seems safe to assume, minimally, that even a millennium before the rabbis *hal'it* would have been a cruder term for feeding than the standard biblical *ha'akhil*. What I think happened at this point in Genesis is that the author, in the writerly zest with which he sought to characterize Esau's crudeness, allowed himself, quite exceptionally, to introduce a vernacular term for coarse eating or animal feeding into the dialogue that would jibe nicely with his phrase, "this red red stuff." After the close of the biblical era, this otherwise excluded term would surface in the legal pronouncements of the rabbis on animal husbandry, together with a host of vernacular words used in the ancient period but never permitted to enter the canonical texts.

All this strongly suggests that the language of biblical narrative in its own time was stylized, decorous, dignified, and readily identified by its audiences as a language of literature, in certain ways distinct from the language of quotidian reality. The tricky complication, however, is that in most respects it also was not a lofty style, and was certainly neither ornate nor euphemistic. If some of its vocabulary may have reflected a specialized literary lexicon, the language of biblical narrative also makes abundant use of ordinary Hebrew words that must have been in everyone's mouth from day to day. Just to mention the few recurrent terms on which I have commented, "hand," "house," "all," and "seed" are primary words in every phase of the history of Hebrew, and they continue to appear as such in the rabbinic language, where so much else is altered. Biblical prose, then, is a formal literary language but also, paradoxically, a plainspoken one, and, moreover, a language that evinces a strong commitment to using a limited set of terms again and again, making an aesthetic virtue out of the repetition. It should be added that the language of the Bible reflects not one level of diction but a certain range of dictions, as I shall explain presently.

What is the implication of this analysis for an appropriate modern English equivalent to ancient Hebrew style? The right direction, I think, was hit on by the King James Version, following the great model of Tyndale a century before it. There is no good reason to render biblical Hebrew as contemporary English, either lexically or syntactically. This is not to suggest that the Bible should be represented as fussily old-fashioned English, but a limited degree of archaizing coloration is entirely appropriate, employed with other strategies for creating a language that is stylized yet simple and direct, free of the overtones of contemporary colloquial usage but with a certain timeless homespun quality. An adequate English version should be able to indicate the small but significant modulations in diction in the biblical language—something the stylistically uniform King James Version however, entirely fails to do. A suitable English version should avoid at all costs the modern abomination of elegant synonymous variation, for the literary prose of the Bible turns everywhere on significant repetition, not variation. Similarly, the translation of terms on the basis of immediate context—except when it becomes grotesque to do otherwise—is to be resisted as another instance of the heresy of explanation. Finally, the mesmerizing effect of these ancient stories will scarcely be conveyed if they are not rendered in cadenced English prose that at least in some ways corresponds to the powerful cadences of the Hebrew.

Notes

1   The symbol ḥ represents the Hebrew consonant *ḥet*, a light fricative that sounds something like j in Spanish.
2   Instead of a clear-cut expression of the temporal frame in which actions occur—past, present, future, past perfect, and so forth—aspects indicate chiefly whether the action has been completed or is to be completed.
3   The modern Hebrew pronunciation is *vav*, with the vowel sounding like the short *a* in a French word like *bave*, with which it would rhyme.
4   The symbol ' designates the Hebrew letter *'aleph*, perhaps once a lightly aspirated sound but now a "silent" letter.

(d) Des Tours de Babel

Jacques Derrida

"Babel": first a proper name, granted. But when we say "Babel" today, do we know what we are naming? Do we know whom? If we consider the sur-vival of a text that is a legacy, the narrative or the myth of the tower of Babel, it does not constitute just one figure among others. Telling at least of the inadequation of one tongue to another, of one place in the encyclopedia to another, of language to itself and to meaning, and so forth, it also tells of the need for figuration, for myth, for tropes, for twists and turns, for translation inadequate to compensate for that which multiplicity denies us. In this sense it would be the myth of the origin of myth, the metaphor of metaphor, the narrative of narrative, the translation of translation, and so on. It would not be the only structure hollowing itself out like that, but it would do so in its own way (itself *almost* untranslatable, like a proper name), and its idiom would have to be saved.

The "tower of Babel" does not merely figure the irreducible multiplicity of tongues; it exhibits an incompletion, the impossibility of finishing, of totalizing, of saturating, of completing something on the order of edification, architectural construction, system and architectonics. What the multiplicity of idioms actually limits is not only a "true" translation, a transparent and adequate interexpression, it is also a structural order, a coherence of construct. There is then (let us translate) something like an internal limit to formalization, an incompleteness of the constructure. It would be easy and up to a certain point justified to see there the translation of a system in deconstruction.

One should never pass over in silence the question of the tongue in which the question of the tongue is raised and into which a discourse on translation is translated.

First: in what tongue was the tower of Babel constructed and deconstructed? In a tongue within which the proper name of Babel could also, by confusion, be translated by "confusion." The proper name Babel, as a proper name, should remain untranslatable, but, by a kind of associative confusion that a unique tongue rendered possible, one thought it translated in that very tongue, by a common noun signifying what *we* translate as confusion. Voltaire showed his astonishment in his *Dictionnaire philosophique*, at the *Babel* article:

> I do not know why it is said in *Genesis* that Babel signifies confusion, for *Ba* signifies father in the Oriental tongues, and *Bel* signifies God; Babel signifies the city of God, the holy city. The Ancients gave this name to all their capitals. But it is incontestable that Babel means confusion, either because the architects were confounded after having raised their work up to eighty-one thousand Jewish feet, or because the tongues were then confounded; and it is obviously from that time on that the Germans no longer understand the Chinese; for it is clear, according to the scholar Bochart, that Chinese is originally the same tongue as High German.

The calm irony of Voltaire means that Babel means: it is not only a proper name, the reference of a pure signifier to a single being—and for this reason untranslatable—but a common noun related to the generality of a meaning. This common noun means, and means not only confusion, even though "confusion" has at least two meanings, as Voltaire is aware, the confusion of tongues, but also the state of confusion in which the architects find themselves with the structure interrupted, so that a certain confusion has already begun to affect the two meanings of the word "confusion." The signification of "confusion" is confused, at least double. But Voltaire suggests something else again: Babel means not only confusion in the double sense of the word, but also the name of the father, more precisely and more commonly, the name of God as name of father. The city would bear the name of God the father and of the father of the city that is called confusion. God, the God, would have marked with his patronym a communal space, that city where understanding is no longer possible. And understanding is no longer possible when there are only proper names, and understanding is no longer possible when there are no longer proper names. In giving his name, a name of his choice, in giving all names, the father would be at the origin of language, and that power would belong by right to God the father. And the name of God the father would be the name of that origin of tongues. But it is also that God who, in the action of his anger (like the God of Böhme or of Hegel, he who leaves himself, determines himself in his finitude and thus produces history), annuls the gift of tongues, or at least embroils it, sows confusion among his sons, and poisons the present (*Gift*-gift). This is also the origin of tongues, of the multiplicity of idioms, of what in other words are usually called mother tongues. For this entire history deploys filiations, generations and genealogies: all Semitic. Before the deconstruction of Babel, the great Semitic family was establishing its empire, which it wanted universal, and its tongue, which it also attempts to impose on the universe. The moment of this project immediately precedes the deconstruction of the tower. I cite two French translations. The first translator stays away from what one would want to call "literality," in other words, from the Hebrew figure of speech for "tongue," where the second, more concerned about literality (metaphoric, or rather metonymic), says "lip," since in Hebrew "lip" designates what we call, in another metonymy, "tongue." One will have to say multiplicity of lips and not of tongues to name the Babelian confusion. The first translator, then, Louis Segond, author of the Segond Bible, published in 1910, writes this:

> Those are the sons of Sem, according to their families, their tongues, their countries, their nations. Such are the families of the sons of Noah, according to their generations, their nations. And it is from them that emerged the nations which spread over the earth after the flood. All the earth had a single tongue and the same words. As they had left the origin they found a plain in the country of Schinear, and they dwelt there. They said to one another: Come! Let us make bricks, and bake them in the fire. And brick served them as stone, and tar served as cement. Again they said: Come! Let us build ourselves a city and a tower whose summit touches the heavens, and let us make ourselves a name, so that we not be scattered over the face of all the earth.

I do not know just how to interpret this allusion to the substitution or the transmutation of materials, brick becoming stone and tar serving as mortar. That already resembles a translation, a translation of translation. But let us leave it and substitute a second translation for the first. It is that of Chouraqui. It is recent and wants to be more literal, almost *verbum pro verbo*, as Cicero said should not be done in one of those first recommendations to the translator which can be read in his *Libellus de Optimo Genera Oratorum*. Here it is:

> Here are the sons of Shem
> for their clans, for their tongues,
> in their lands, for their peoples.
> Here are the clans of the sons of Noah for their exploits,
> in their peoples:
> from the latter divide the peoples on earth, after the flood.
>
> And it is all the earth: a single lip, one speech.
> And it is at their departure from the Orient: they find a canyon,

> in the land of Shine'ar.
> They settle there.
> They say, each to his like:
> "Come, let us brick some bricks.
> Let us fire them in the fire."
> The brick becomes for them stone, the tar, mortar.
> They say:
> "Come, let us build ourselves a city and a tower.
> Its head: in the heavens.
> Let us make ourselves a name,
> that we not be scattered over the face of all the earth."

What happens to them? In other words, for what does God punish them in giving his name, or rather, since he gives it to nothing and to no one, in proclaiming his name, the proper name of "confusion" which will be his mark and his seal? Does he punish them for having wanted to build as high as the heavens? For having wanted to accede to the highest, up to the Most High? Perhaps for that too, no doubt, but incontestably for having wanted thus to make a name for themselves, to give themselves the name, to construct for and by themselves their own name, to gather themselves there ("that we no longer be scattered"), as in the unity of a place which is at once a tongue and a tower, the one as well as the other, the one as the other. He punishes them for having thus wanted to assure themselves, by themselves, a unique and universal genealogy. For the text of Genesis proceeds immediately, as if it were all a matter of the same design: raising a tower, constructing a city, making a name for oneself in a universal tongue which would also be an idiom, and gathering a filiation:

> They say:
> "Come, let us build ourselves a city and a tower.
> Its head: in the heavens.
> Let us make ourselves a name,
> that we not be scattered over the face of all the earth."
> YHWH descends to see the city and the tower
> that the sons of man have built.
> YHWH says:
> "Yes! A single people, a single lip for all:
> that is what they begin to do! . . .
> Come! Let us descend! Let us confound their lips,
> man will no longer understand the lip of his neighbor."

Then he disseminates the Sem, and dissemination is here deconstruction:

> YHWH disperses them from here over the face of all the earth,
> They cease to build the city.
> Over which he proclaims his name: Bavel, Confusion,
> for there, YHWH confounds the lip of all the earth,
> and from there YHWH disperses them over the face of all the earth.

Can we not, then, speak of God's jealousy? Out of resentment against that unique name and lip of men, he imposes his name, his name of father; and with this violent imposition he opens the deconstruction of the tower, as of the universal language; he scatters the genealogical filiation. He breaks the lineage. He *at the same time* imposes and forbids translation. He imposes it and forbids it, constrains, but as if to failure, the children who henceforth *will bear* his name, the name that *he* gives to the city. It is from a proper name of God, come from God, descended from God or from the father (and it is indeed said that YHWH, an unpronounceable name, *descends* toward the tower) and by him that tongues are scattered, confounded or multiplied, according to a descendance that in its very dispersion remains sealed by the only name that will have been the strongest, by the only idiom that will have triumphed. Now, this idiom bears within itself the mark of confusion, it improperly means the improper, to wit: Bavel, confusion. Translation then becomes necessary and impossible, like the effect of a struggle for the appropriation of the name, necessary and forbidden in the interval between two absolutely proper names. And the proper name of God (given by God) is divided enough in the tongue, already, to signify also, confusedly, "confusion." And the war that he declares has first raged within his name: divided, bifid, ambivalent, polysemic: God deconstructing. [. . .]

Babel: today we take it as a proper name. Indeed, but the proper name of what and of whom? At times that of a narrative text recounting a story (mythical, symbolic, allegorical; it matters little for the moment), a story in which the proper name, which is then no longer the title of the narrative, names a tower or a city but a tower or a city that receives its name from an event during which YHWH "proclaims his name." Now, this proper name, which already names at least three times and three different things, also has, this is the whole point, as proper name the function of a common noun. This story recounts, among other things, the origin of the confusion of tongues, the irreducible multiplicity of idioms, the necessary and impossible task of translation, its necessity *as* impossibility. Now, in general one pays little attention to this fact: it is in translation that we most often read this narrative. And in this translation, the proper name retains a singular destiny, since it is not translated in its appearance as proper name. Now, a proper name as such remains forever untranslatable, a fact that may lead one to conclude that it does not strictly belong, for the same reason as the other words, to the language, to the system of the language, be it translated or translating. And yet "Babel," an event in a single tongue, the one in which it appears so as to form a "text," also has a common meaning, a conceptual generality. That it be by way of a pun or a confused association matters little: "Babel" could be understood in one language as meaning "confusion." And from then on, just as Babel is at once proper name and common noun, confusion also becomes proper name and common noun, the one as the homonym of the other, the synonym as well, but not the equivalent, because there could be no question of confusing them in their value. It has for the translator no satisfactory solution. Recourse to apposition and capitalization ("Over which he proclaims his name: Bavel, Confusion") is not translating from one tongue into another. It comments, explains, paraphrases, but does not translate. At best it reproduces approximately and by dividing the equivocation into two words there where confusion gathered in potential, in all its potential, in the internal translation, if one can say that, which works the word in the so-called original tongue. For in the very tongue of the original narrative there is a translation, a sort of transfer, that gives immediately (by some confusion) the semantic equivalent of the proper name which, by itself, as a pure proper name, it would not have. As a matter of fact, this intralinguistic translation operates immediately; it is not even an operation in the strict sense. Nevertheless, someone who speaks the language of Genesis could be attentive to the effect of the proper name in effacing the conceptual equivalent (like *pierre* [rock] in *Pierre* [Peter], and these are two absolutely heterogeneous values or functions); one would then be tempted to say *first* that a proper name, in the proper sense, does not properly belong to the language; it does not belong there, *although and because* its call makes the language possible (what would a language be without the possibility of calling by a proper name?); consequently it can properly inscribe itself in a language only by allowing itself to be translated therein, in other words, *interpreted by* its semantic equivalent: from this moment it can no longer be taken as proper name. The noun *pierre* belongs to the French language, and its translation into a foreign language should in principle transport its meaning. This is not the case with *Pierre*, whose inclusion in the French language is not assured and is in any case not of the same type. "Peter" in this sense is not a *translation* of *Pierre*, any more than *Londres* is a translation of "London," and so forth. And *second*, anyone whose so-called mother tongue was the tongue of *Genesis* could indeed understand Babel as "confusion"; that person then effects a *confused* translation of the proper name by its common equivalent without having need for another word. It is as if there were two words there, two homonyms, one of which has the value of proper name and the other that of common noun: between the two, a translation which one can evaluate quite diversely. [. . .]

Very quickly: at the very moment when pronouncing "Babel" we sense the impossibility of deciding whether this name belongs, properly and simply, to *one* tongue. And it matters that this undecidability is at work in a struggle for the proper name within a scene of genealogical indebtedness. In seeking to "make a name for themselves," to found at the same time a universal tongue and a unique genealogy, the Semites want to bring the world to reason, and this reason can signify simultaneously a colonial violence (since they would thus universalize their idiom) and a peaceful transparency of the human community. Inversely, when God imposes and opposes his name, he ruptures the rational transparency but interrupts also the colonial violence or the linguistic imperialism. He destines them to translation, he subjects them to the law of a translation both necessary and impossible; in a stroke with his translatable-untranslatable name he delivers a universal reason (it will no longer be subject to the rule of a particular nation), but he simultaneously limits its very universality: forbidden transparency, impossible univocity. Translation becomes law, duty and debt, but the debt one can no longer discharge. Such insolvency is found marked in the very name of Babel: which at once translates and does not translate itself, belongs without belonging to a language and indebts itself to itself for an insolvent debt, to itself as if other. Such would be the Babelian performance.

This singular example, at once archetypical and allegorical, could serve as an introduction to all the so-called theoretical problems of translation. But no theorization, inasmuch as it is produced in a language, will be able to dominate the Babelian performance. This is one of the reasons why I prefer here, instead of treating it in the theoretical mode, to attempt to translate in my own way the translation of another text on translation. [. . .] [I] limit myself to "The Task of the Translator".

[. . .]

The allusion to the maturation of a seed could resemble a vitalist or geneticist metaphor; it would come, then, in support of the genealogical and parental code which seems to dominate this text. In fact it seems necessary here to invert this order and recognize what I have elsewhere proposed to call the "metaphoric catastrophe": far from knowing first what "life" or "family" mean whenever we use these familiar values to talk about language and translation; it is rather starting from the notion of a language and its "sur-vival" in translation that we could have access to the notion of what life and family mean. This reversal is operated expressly by Benjamin. His preface (for let us not forget: this essay is a preface) circulates without cease among the values of seed, life, and especially "sur-vival." (*Überleben* has an essential relation with *Übersetzen*). Now, very near the beginning, Benjamin seems to propose a simile or a metaphor—it opens with "just as . . ."—and right away everything moves in and about *Übersetzen, Übertragen, Überleben*:

> Just as the manifestations of life are intimately connected with the living, without signifying anything for it, a translation proceeds from the orig- inal. Indeed not so much from its life as from its survival [*Überleben*]. For a translation comes after the original and, for the important works that never find their predestined translator at the time of their birth, it char- acterizes the stage of their survival [*Fortleben*, this time, sur-vival as continuation of life rather than as life *post mortem*]. Now, it is in this simple reality, without any metaphor ["in völlig unmetaphorischer Sachlichkeit"], that it is necessary to conceive the ideas of life and survival [*Fortleben*] for works of art.

And according to a scheme that appears Hegelian, in a very circumscribed passage, Benjamin calls us to think life, starting from spirit or history and not from "organic corporeality" alone. There is life at the moment when "sur-vival" (spirit, history, works) exceeds biological life and death: "It is rather in recognizing for everything of which there is history and which is not merely the setting for history that one does justice to this concept of life. For it is starting from history, not from nature . . ., that the domain of life must finally be circumscribed. So is born for the philosopher the task [*Aufgabe*] of comprehending all natural life starting from this life, of much vaster extension, that is the life of history."

From the very title—and for the moment I stay with it—Benjamin situates the *problem*, in the sense of that which is precisely *before oneself* as a task, as the problem of the translator and not that of translation (nor, be it said in passing, and the question is not negligible, that of the translatoress). Benjamin does not say the task or the problem of translation. He names the subject of translation, as an indebted subject, obligated by a duty, already in the position of heir, entered as survivor in a genealogy, as survivor or agent of sur-vival. The sur-vival of works, not authors. Perhaps the sur-vival of authors' names and of signatures, but not of authors.

Such sur-vival gives more of life, more than a surviving. The work does not simply live longer, it lives more and better, beyond the means of its author. Would the translator then be an indebted receiver, subject to the gift and to the given of an original? By no means. For several reasons, including the following: the bond or obligation of the debt does not pass between a donor and a donee but between two texts (two "productions" or two "creations"). This is understood from the opening of the preface, and if one wanted to isolate theses, here are a few, as brutally as in any sampling:

1. The task of the translator does not announce itself or follow from a *reception*. The theory of translation does not depend for the essential on any theory of reception, even though it can inversely contribute to the elaboration and explanation of such a theory.

2. Translation does not have as essential mission any *communication*. No more than the original, and Benjamin maintains, secure from all danger of dispute, the strict duality between the original and the version, the translated and the translating, even though he shifts their relation. And he is interested in the translation of poetic or sacred texts, which would here yield the essence of translation. The entire essay extends between the poetic and the sacred, returning from the first to the second, the one that indicates the ideal of all translation, the purely transferable: the intralinear version of the sacred text, the model or ideal (*Urbild*) of any translation at all possible. Now, this is the second thesis; for a poetic text or a sacred text, communication is not the essential. This putting into question does not directly concern the communicative structure of language but rather the hypothesis of a communicable content that could be strictly distinguished from the linguistic act of communication. In 1916, the critique of semiotism and of the "bourgeois conception" of language was already directed against that distribution: means, object, addressee. "There is no content of language." What language first communicates is its "communicability" ("On Language as Such," trans. M. de Gandillac, 85). Will it be said that an opening is thus made toward the performative dimension of utterances? In any case this warns us against precipitation: isolating the contents and theses in "The Task of the Translator" and translating it otherwise than as the signature of a kind of proper name destined to ensure its sur-vival as a work.

3. If there is indeed between the translated text and the translating text a relation of "original" to version, it could not be *representative* or *reproductive*. Translation is neither an image nor a copy.

These three precautions now taken (neither reception, nor communication, nor representation), how are constituted the debt and the genealogy of the translator? Or first, how those of that which is *to-be-translated*, of the to-be-translated?

Let us follow the thread of life or sur-vival wherever it communicates with the movement of kinship. When Benjamin challenges the viewpoint of reception, it is not to deny it all pertinence, and he will undoubtedly have done much to prepare for a theory of reception in literature. But he wants first to return to the authority of what he still calls "the original," not insofar as it produces its receiver or its translators, but insofar as it requires, mandates, demands or commands them in establishing the law. And it is the structure of this demand that here appears most unusual. Through what does it pass? In a literary—more strictly speaking in this case, "poetic"—text it does not pass through the said, the uttered, the communicated, the content or the theme. And when, in this context, Benjamin still says "communication" or "enunciation" (*Mitteilung, Aussage*), it is not about the act but about the content that he visibly speaks: "But what does a literary work [*Dichtung*] 'say'? What does it communicate? Very little to those who understand it. What it has that is essential is not communication, not enunciation."

The demand seems thus to pass, indeed to be formulated, through the *form*. "Translation is a form," and the law of this form has its first place in the original. This law first establishes itself, let us repeat, as a demand in the strong sense, a requirement that delegates, mandates, prescribes, assigns. And as for this law as demand, two questions can arise; they are different in essence. First question: in the sum total of its readers, can the work always find the translator who is, as it were, capable? Second question and, says Benjamin, "more properly" (as if this question made the preceding more appropriate, whereas, we shall see, it does something quite different): "by its essence does it [the work] bear translation and if so—in line with the signification of this form—does it require translation?"

The answers to these two questions could not be of the same nature or the same mode. *Problematic* in the first case, not necessary (the translator capable of the work may appear or not appear, but even if he does not appear, that changes nothing in the demand or in the structure of the injunction that comes from the work), the answer is properly *apodictic* in the second case; necessary, a priori, demonstrable, absolute because it comes from the internal law of the original. The original requires translation even if no translator is there, fit to respond to this injunction, which is at the same time demand and desire in the very structure of the original. This structure is the relation of life to sur-vival. This requirement of the other as translator, Benjamin compares it to some unforgettable instant of life: it is lived as unforgettable, it *is* unforgettable even if in fact forgetting finally wins out. It will have been unforgettable—there is its essential significance, its apodictic essence; forgetting happens to this unforgettableness only by accident. The requirement of the unforgettable—which is here constitutive—is not in the least impaired by the finitude of memory. Likewise the requirement of translation in no way suffers from not being satisfied, at least it does not suffer in so far as it is the very structure of the work. In this sense the *surviving* dimension is an a priori—and death would not change it at all. No more than it would change the requirement (*Forderung*) that runs through the original work and to which only "a thought of God" can respond or correspond (*entsprechen*). Translation, the desire for translation, is not thinkable without this *correspondence* with a thought of God. In the text of 1916, which already accorded the task of the translator, his Aufgabe, with the response made to the gift of tongues and the gift of names ("Gabe der Sprache" "Gebung des Namens"), Benjamin named God at this point, that of a correspondence authorizing, making possible or guaranteeing the correspondence between the languages engaged in translation. In this narrow context, there was also the matter of the relations between language of things and language of men, between the silent and the speaking, the anonymous and the nameable, but the axiom held, no doubt, for all translation: "the objectivity of this translation is guaranteed in God" (trans. M. de Gandillac, 91). The debt, in the beginning, is fashioned in the hollow of this "thought of God."

Strange debt, which does not bind anyone to anyone. If the structure of the work is "sur-vival," the debt does not engage in relation to a hypothetical subject-author of the original text—dead or mortal, the dead man, or "dummy," of the text—but to something else that represents the formal law in the immanence of the original text. Then the debt does not involve restitution of a copy or a good image, a faithful representation of the original: the latter, the survivor, is itself in the process of transformation. The original gives itself in modifying itself; this gift is not an object given; it lives and lives on in mutation: "For in its survival, which would not merit the name if it were not mutation and renewal of something living, the original is modified. Even for words that are solidified there is still a postmaturation."

Postmaturation (*Nachreife*) of a living organism or a seed: this is not simply a metaphor, either, for the reasons already indicated. In its very essence, the history of this language is determined as "growth," "holy growth of languages."

4. If the debt of the translator commits him neither with regard to the author (dead insofar as his text has a structure of survival even if he is living) nor with regard to a model which must be reproduced or represented, to what or to whom is he committed? How is this to be named, this what or who? What is the proper name if not that of the author finite, dead or mortal of the text? And who is the translator who is thus committed, who perhaps finds himself *committed* by the other before having committed himself? Since the translator finds himself, as to the survival of the text, in the same situation as its finite and mortal producer (its "author"), it is not he, not he himself as a finite and mortal being, who is committed. Then who? It is he, of course, but in the name of whom or what? The question of proper names is essential here. Where the act of the living mortal seems to count less than the sur-vival of the text in the *translation*—translated and translating—it is quite necessary that the signature of the proper noun be distinguished and not be so easily effaced from the contract or from the debt. Let us not forget that Babel names a struggle for the survival of the name, the tongue or the lips.

From its height Babel at every instant supervises and surprises my reading: I translate, I translate the translation by Maurice de Gandillac of a text by Benjamin who, prefacing a translation, takes it as a pretext to say to what and in what way every translator is committed—and notes in passing, an essential part of his demonstration, that there could be no translation of translation. This will have to be remembered.

Recalling this strange situation, I do not wish only or essentially to reduce my role to that of a passer or passerby. Nothing is more serious than a translation. I rather wished to mark the fact that every translator is in a position to speak *about* translation, in a place which is more than any not second or secondary. For if the structure of the original is marked by the requirement to be translated, it is that in laying down the law the original begins by indebting itself *as well* with regard to the translator. The original is the first debtor, the first petitioner; it begins by lacking and by pleading for translation. This demand is not only on the side of the constructors of the tower who want to make a name for themselves and to found a universal tongue translating itself by itself; it also constrains the deconstructor of the tower: in giving his name, God also appealed to translation, not only between the tongues that had suddenly become multiple and confused, but first *of his name*, of the name he had proclaimed, given, and which should be translated as confusion to be understood, hence to let it be understood that it is difficult to translate and so to understand. At the moment when he imposes and opposes his law to that of the tribe, he is also a petitioner for translation. He is also indebted. He has not finished pleading for the translation of his name even though he forbids it. For Babel is untranslatable. God weeps over his name. His text is the most sacred, the most poetic, the most originary, since he creates a name and gives it to himself, but he is left no less destitute in his force and even in his wealth; he pleads for a translator.

(e) Thou Art Translated: Bible Translating, Heretic Reading and Cultural Transformation

Valentine Cunningham

Cultural transformation comes about by many means, through many agencies. Among the many motors of cultural shift, translation must rate pretty high. And among the most highly transformative kinds of translation Bible translation ranks historically among the most powerful. So I take Bible translation into English – the reception of the Bible in English, the reading of the Bible in English – as a most potent individual case of the generation of cultural metamorphosis, but also (*mutatis mutandis*) as an example and a model of how cultural change might work more largely in the sphere of the transcultural appropriation of writings. I focus on Bible translating into English as a most obvious example of what I want to label heretic reading, i.e. interpretation against some grain (that is, a dissident, dissenting, resistant, oppositional hermeneutics), because I observe that, historically, cultural transformation, certainly cultural metamorphosis travelling under the flag of progress, of change for the better, of improvements in knowledge and understanding, and so forth, has been utterly dependent upon what the enemies of whatever contemporary enlightenment is afoot have always been eager to label as heresy, as the desposition, desire, action, and generally wicked ways of heretics. Nobody has seemed at once so progressive and so heretical in their times as the Bible translators. And nobody has been so effective in bringing about cultural change.

My main case of a Bible reader is Robinson Crusoe – the sailor from Hull, England, who, according to Daniel Defoe's world-shaking novel of 1719, on 30 September 1659 came ashore on a deserted island from a wrecked ship which was, by a merciful Providence, laden not only with many useful goods, tools, clothes, seeds, and the like, but also three Bibles in English. In 1659 there were Bibles in English only because Defoe's Dissenting, or heretic, predecessors, risked life and limb to translate, to metamorphose, the old Biblical text(s) into English. Crusoe reads in one of these English Bibles. His life is transformed through his reading in this translated text, once outlawed as heretic simply because it was translated. He repents of his sins – the translated text promoting and performing the *metanoia*, the change of thinking, change of mind, the repentance which the Biblical text avidly promotes. The man Crusoe is transformed through the translated text, and so in consequence is everything – Crusoe's language, his narrative, his address to things, his micro-society, his world. With the aid of the same English book, Crusoe transforms his man Friday from cannibal and 'savage' to mimic civilised white man. In other words, this translated book brings about the transformation of persons, transforms their understanding, provides them with the metaphors, the words, that sustain this new understanding, transforms their way with things, transforms culture in every sense – linguisticity, hermeneutics, poetics, narrative, imagination, behaviour, all of the personal and the social. And, of course, the book about Crusoe being transformed by a translated book, Defoe's novel *Robinson Crusoe*, transformed prose fiction, instaurating the novel as we know it, the mode through which the world learned to know and construct itself and which dominated writing for the next three centuries.

'Bless thee, Bottom, bless thee. Thou art translated', say the friends of the comically heretic-reading weaver in *A Midsummer Night's Dream* (III. i. 113), when they find him with an ass's head on – a farcical case of personal metamorphosis straight out of Arthur Golding's English translation of Ovid's *Metamorphoses*, and a wry tribute to the wrenching *imitatio* of a translation that Bottom's crew are about to inflict on one of Ovid's main stories of metamorphosis, the story of Pyramus and Thisbe. Clearly translations don't stop with the mere act of textual translation, with mere textual metamorphosis. About what is going on in Shakespeare's transformation of Ovid, we might well join in with Bottom's cronies and say 'thou art translated' – and the *thou* would have the widest valence. Everything thereabouts is involved in translation – Ovid's text, Golding's version of Ovid's text, Shakespeare's adaptation of Ovid/Golding, Bottom's person, the royal audience's vision, Shakespeare's audience, literary history, the culture of renaissance England, English *mentalité* as such. And so it is with Crusoe's Bible. It has been translated, metamorphosed, and so is *Crusoe*, its reader, and his island, and through him and his story the British islands, and the novel, and indeed the whole of the culture of the British islands and beyond.

What unites the Bible and Ovid's *Metamorphoses* in translation (the *Bible des poètes*, as Ovid was called in a popular French prose translation of the fourteenth century[1]) is what seems to characterise all translation, certainly translation of (great) literature, and that is, precisely, this large convergence and collusion of many metamorphosing practices and outcomes.

Translation (certainly at this level) is, of course, always an alteration, a transformation. Translators may dream of close linguistic replication, an absolute faithfulness to original words and original meanings (as does the Eugene A. Nida school of translation, and of Bible translation in particular[2]), but this is an impossible dream. Translation is by its nature a kind of *katachresis* (an act of verbal *abusio*). It's always pleonasmic, a supplement, an extra, a superfluity. It's an act of necessary 'displacement', the displacing of the source text (as the first formal Renaissance treatise on translation, Leonardo Bruni's *De interpretatione recta* (ca. 1426) agrees)[3]. It's inevitably paraphrastic, an act of inevitable paraphrase, however great the desire to do metaphrase (to use Dryden's famous distinction)[4]. Translation always produces a new text whose words have come alongside the old ones, parasitically feeding off them, being fed by them, taking their life from them in the enjoyment of a new life which is never exactly the old life which is its source. Even Barthélemy Aneau, one of the closest translators in French of Ovid's *Metamorphoses*, one of the very rare theoretical literalists in the Renaissance, who talked (in 1556) of replacing Ovid's substantives as exactly and as closely as possible with French ones, had to admit that even his devotedly close approximation was an act of usurpation[5]. *Traduttore traditore*, of course: the translator is always a kind of betrayer.

Arthur Golding, arguing for the moral truths of Ovid in his poetic "Epistle to the Earl of Leicester" prefaced to his complete translation (1567) of the *Metamorphoses*, celebrates Ovid's lesson that 'nothing under heaven' stays constant. Nothing actually dies, but only because each substance takes 'Another shape than that it had'.[6] Another shape. Metamorphosis. And of course Golding's point about what happens to things applies to his translation, and to all translation. The old text lives on but only by shape changing, by assuming, 'Another shape than that it had'. With the ever present idea of a transgressing, a wronging, a rude forcing ('so rudely forced', as T.S. Eliot has it in *The Waste Land*, of his poem's metamorphosing of Ovid's story of the rape and 'change' of Philomel[7]). In other words the transgressivity of translation rather naturally invites the charge of heresy, the suspicion and allegation that translation is inevitably a species of heretic re-reading. And always with a whiff in the air of a sense that some loss of original nobility has gone on, a lowering of the moral and aesthetic tone, a vulgarising, a farcical descent into whatever the vernacular is which is in play. As in the history of liturgies, where farcing is first heard of in a literary sense: the move from Greek, to Latin, to the vernacular. So rudely farced, as one might say.

Most ironically, at the great Renaissance moment, translation is accepted as a worsening, a wronging, which is performed as a way of righting, and bettering – the righting of a mistake, a persisting error, a catastrophe of history, which has kept this text (whatever it is) from readers in the know. Translation is acknowledged as an act of textual abuse, a rude forcing, which is however utterly necessary for the moral betterment of readers, the education of individuals, the improvement of a culture. In other words, for individual and cultural *metanoia* – a necessary change of mind, conversion, salvation. Characteristically in his 1564 prose "Preface" to the first four books of Ovid, Golding talks of 'my maimed and unperfect translation', a set of 'painful exercises'. The work has been attempted, though, 'of a zeal and desire to enrich' the translator's 'native language with things not heretofore published in the same'[8]. The endgame of the textual maiming is personal and national linguistic and cultural enriching. The religious tone in these discussions is apparent. The zeal of the Christian translator for the house of his countrymen has, in English Biblical words, eaten him up. Golding was, of course, a Calvinist, in fact the major translator of Calvin in his time, turning into English a dozen of Calvin's major works, including sermons and Calvin's *Commentaries on the Psalms*, as well as translating the French Huguenot Calvinist Philippe du Plessis Mornay's *The Trueness of the Christian Religion* (1587). And as Golding's modern editor Madeleine Florey points out, Golding's English keeps Biblicizing his Ovid, in fact, making Ovid sound very much like the Geneva Bible. Golding's 1567 Epistle indeed claims a complete agreement between Ovid and Holy Writ. In effect, in Golding's hands, Ovid's *Metamorphoses* are turned into a kind of Calvinist text.[9]

Which is transgressive translating, a heretic hermeneutic, of the strongest kind. But exemplarily so. And just so – or rather more so – the Bible in English was an altered text, was katachrestic in practice and also in principle. The translators of the 1611 Bible (the *King James*, or *Authorised Version*: the *KJV* or *AV*) were serious when they talked about their predecessors, the ancient translators of the *Septuagint* Greek version, dissenting from the original. Their modern version would dissent in turn. All translation, it cannot be repeated enough, involves a kind of dissent. The *KJV/AV* was, they said, like a man with 'warts upon his hand, yea, not only freckles upon his face, but also skarres'. He was still, though, to be reckoned 'a comely man and lovely'.[10]

Pleonasm, the literary activity of supplementing, adding, effecting a superfluity, was the essence. It always is, more or less. Some of the pleonasticcizing, as with the great Tyndale, the key figure in Reformation English translation, was done for the sake of mere liveliness, of readerly attractiveness, in English; some of it was, even more plainly, for the sake of the ongoing theological and ecclesiastical politics, the current polemical hermeneutical drive. In such times, and cases, and in Tyndale's case not least, the hermeneutics and the aesthetics, the 'Poetik' and the 'Hermeneutik' are very hard to keep apart.

I take as exceedingly revealing Tyndales's version of II Thessalonians 1,4. "We are bound to thank God allwayes for you brethren, as itt is mete, because that youre faith groweth exceedyngly, and every one of you swyimmeth in love towarde another betwene youreselves."[11] Swimmeth in love: it's a lovely phrase, a lovely concept: far more fetching than the plainer, and more cumbersome *KJV* version – 'the charity of everyone of you all toward each other aboundeth'. The *KJV* translators have clung to the Latin of Saint Jerome's *Vulgate* version, the standard version of the unreformed Latin-speaking Church, the one which had been so opaque to the average English reader (and to many priests) that it needed translation if any wider access to the Bible was going to be achieved. The *KJV's aboundeth* comes from *Vulgate* 'abundat'. *Charity* echoes the *Vulgate's* 'charitas'. Tyndale, in the high textual mood of the Reformation, has gone back to the Greek. Greek 'agape' becomes his *love*. Where the *Vulgare* deployed the verb 'abundare', to abound, the Greek text had the verb 'pleonadzei', to superabound, to increase, to be augmented. This Greek word is of course where we get the rhetorical term pleonasm from, the term for the provision of something extra. And, arrestingly, Tyndale has augmented this verb of augmentation – with illegitimate reference (or so it seems) to the Greek verb 'pleo', the verb to float, flow, sail, travel by sea. So that the Thessalonians' superabundance of love becomes a watery abundance, a watery abundance, a *swimming* in love. Hence the translation of 'pleonadzei' is mightily pleonastic. The Thessalonians, according to this generous, pleonastic translation of Tyndale's, are in a sea of love. A metaphoric excess indeed. The result is fetching, striking, lovely. But it is a violence to the original, albeit a most sweet violence. Sweet violence is what the disgruntled, apocalyptic Hebraist Hugh Broughton, annoyed to be left off the panels of *AV* translators, called the *KJV/AV*. He wanted it burned because it offended his linguistic expertise; but it won him over, for all its flaws, he said, by 'a sweet violence'.[12] Tyndale's Thessalonian moment is indeed sweet, but still there's a violence being done. A violence, though, which I would insist is inevitable to translation, and inevitable not least in the greatly charged polemical atmosphere of Tyndale's time. What offended Tyndale's opponents at II Thessalonians 1,4 even more than the swimming (though they could have quibbled at that) was the love. To replace the *Vulgate's* 'charitas' by *love* was to signally undermine the whole thrust of Catholic good works, the charity system, as a pathway to salvation. To have them swimming in this heretical medium was adding translation insult to theological injury. As ever, Tyndale's hermeneutic aggression and his eye and ear for metaphoric attractiveness were going hand in hand.

Hermeneutic positioning is, of course, plainly present all over the history of Bible translations, especially on the Protestant side, so keenly dissenting from centuries of Roman Catholic textual control. Translation was warfare; the Protestants' translated words are carefully targeted missiles. They were supported, of course by the declarations of prefaces and marginal glosses – declarations of hermeneutic aggressivity keenly taken up by the Roman translators when they got involved in their own vernacular versions. (Much of the ideological power of the *Geneva Bible* of 1557 was in its very extensive marginal comments. Even Tyndale, potent wielder of the sharp "Preface" but usually quite sparing of his margins, was up for the occasional fighting gloss – as in Numbers 23 where Balaam asks "How shall I curse God?" and the margin tells you: "The Pope can tell how".) But it was the translated words themselves which gave the offence, and were the focus of the anathemas and the charges of heresy.

What Tyndale's English was doing locally with the likes of 'ekklesia', 'presbuter', 'charis', 'agape' was the ground of his offence. Thomas More and his allies wanted 'Church', 'priest', 'grace', 'charity', where Tyndale had 'congregation' (in his 1526 edition of the *New Testament*) and (in 1534) 'elder', 'favour' and 'love'. This was to do translation precisely as challenge and dissent. This translation was indeed hostile to priests and in favour of the organisation of the church into congregations. *Metanoia* was inevitably just such another battleground. For this Biblical word, indicating a change of heart and mind, a transformative turning of the individual person to God in individual sorrow for sin and personal faith in the saving work of Christ (at any rate that's how the Reformers read it), the *Vulgate* had 'penitentia'. 'Metanoiete', change your heart, change your mind, was translated in the Latin as 'penitentiam agite': pursue penitence, or, as Thomas More, Tyndale's great opponent, understood it, in the usual way and spirit of the Medieval church, do penance, engage in penitential actions, and do good deeds to earn salvation from your sins. The penance system, especially the selling of penances, or indulgences, was one of the great scandals of the Roman Church which particularly excited the ire of the Reformers. Simply turning to God in repentance for sin, in mere penitence of spirit, and receiving God's favour, free, gratis, for that alone, without having to do penance, to work for forgiveness, or even pay a church official for an indulgence or pardon, was a large part of the Reformation contention. Tyndale defiantly translates 'metanoia' as repentance, and defends doing so at some length in his "Preface". This was, as Thomas More recognised, the height of Lutheranism, evident Lutheran heresy.

[. . .]

One of the many ordinary readers to whom the Englished text spoke very directly was, of course, Robinson Crusoe. "One morning being very sad", he opens one of his three Bibles at Hebrews 13.5: "I will never, never leave thee, nor forsake thee". And "immediately it occurr'd, that these words were to me. Why else should they be directed in such a Manner, just at the Moment when I was mourning over my Condition, as one forsaken of God and Man".[13] The words . . . to me. This so egotistic narrator in this text so full of *I, me, my, mine*, all about *my self*, meets some words which are felt as especially for him – in his language, and thus absorbable, and indeed soon absorbed, into his very selfhood. Most commentators on Crusoe assume it is the *Authorised Version* of the Bible that Crusoe possesses, though he isn't actually quoting that – the *AV* has 'never leave thee', with only one never. Nor is Crusoe quoting the standard Dissenter *Geneva Bible*. Crusoe's text seems to be a personalised, remembered, altered version of Defoe's own – Defoe's own metamorphosing translation, paraphrase, *imitatio*. It's as if Protestant personalisation of the text has already begun even before Crusoe open his text. And it continues dramatically. Radical *metanoia* comes about through Crusoe reading "seriously", being touched, conscience-smitten, heart-struck, as comprehension gradually dawns, until the moment when he happens on Acts 5,31: "He is exalted a Prince and a Saviour, to give Repentance and to give Remission" (again the not-quite *AV* text). "I threw down the Book, and with my heart as well as my Hands lifted up to Heaven, in a Kind of Ecstacy of Joy, I cry'd aloud, Jesus, thou exalted Prince and Saviour, give me Repentance". *Repentance*, the contentious translation of *metanoia*, in the text, generating repentance in the reader. This is Crusoe's first true prayer, "for now I pray'd with a sense of my Condition, and with a true Scripture View of Hope founded on the encouragement of the Word of God".[14] The Word of God, it goes without saying in the novel, in translation, in English. There's only the occasional bit of Latin in Crusoe. Crusoe's Brazilian partner says some *Ave Marias* in gratitude for his friend's survival; the rescued Spanish sailor says he's *Christianus*. Latin is the province of Roman Catholics. English is the language of the truly righteous. To become really civilised Man Friday has to learn English, the language of Crusoe's Bibles, and to learn to heed that Word without any interpretative help except from Crusoe the metanoicised reader and the Holy Spirit, which, in true Protestant fashion, is held to guide the free reader – 'the Spirit of God teaching and instructing us by his Word, leading us into all truth'.[15]

Protestant, Dissenting, Biblicist Defoe is of course speaking through Crusoe. And Protestant Crusoe's "true Scripture views" come to pervade everything, sanction everything, define everything, legitimate everything. The Englished Bible gives Crusoe his language with which to know the world, gives him his models for action and imagination, for knowing the self as well as the world. Crusoe names himself, and things, Biblically. He is presented as being constantly on the inside of Bible text, Bible story, Bible hermeneutic. Scriptural promises, the Psalms especially, are taken as being all for him. The Scripture is fulfilled in and for him. Its figures become his reality. For Crusoe all action, all his actions, are read and known Biblically. From his early imitation of the Prodigal Son's transgressions, through his shipwreck experience when Biblical waves go over him, and all his enlargeing of the place of his tent, and his devoted planting and thickening of his hedge, the making of his earthen vessels, and being fed as if by ravens, and pulling down his old barns to build greater ones, all the way through to God giving him the increase of his labours and investments, everything is tagged, named, referenced in language from the English Bible. All of Crusoe's selfhood, his extended accounting of the self, is defined Biblically – and out of the most theological parts of Scripture, too, not merely the vivid narratives of the sort which gave Defoe his Christian name (Defoe was never not conscious that he was named for the Bible's apocalyptic visionary truth-teller Daniel). In this strong emphasis on the theological parts of that Bible I am reminded of Tyndale's biographer David Daniell's nice comment on the difference between medieval and post-Reformation Biblicism. "You can't write a mystery play about the Book of Romans". In the medieval church Bible stories circulated in stained-glass windows, wall paintings, mystery plays. But that vivid pictorial, dramatic, as it were comic-book emphasis had its limitations. To hear, understand, know the main theology texts, such as the Book of Romans, that main focus of Puritan, Calvinist reading, you needed a book, the words on the page in front of you, and of course in your own language.

The sailor Crusoe, Defoe's version of Tyndale's ploughboy, is changed utterly by his Bible reading, his Bible knowledge (and of course it's Defoe's own Protestant, Dissenting, Calvinist hermeneutic which is handed over to Crusoe). In which meta-morphosing, metanoiac process, again courtesy of Protestant Defoe, everything on the island is changed. And so also, through this narrative of changed lives, of meta-noiac reading, everything in the future of English narration, narration in English, the English novel, the entire world of English fiction in fact, gets transformed. This is the luck of Protestant Defoe, and Protestant Robinson Crusoe, and the novel of Protestant *metanoia, Robinson Crusoe* (one can't help being reminded of Tyndale's famous description of Old Testament Joseph as a 'lucky fellow'; Exodus 29,33). The novel, prose fiction, is restarted, re-instaurated as we might say, using a bit of vocab-ulary contemporary to Defoe, as Protestant, Puritan, a reformed mode reformed because of the Protestant Biblicism that Robinson Crusoe brings to bear on it – a mode of narration committed to all the Protestant things which characterise Crusoe's life and the life of the Protestant readership he stands for: the moral education of the self, democratic quotidianism, the life of ordinary people and ordinariness, the value of ethical responsibility, the plot of moral and material luck, a form, a genre, committed to narration as moral accountancy (as well as to the drawing up of the merely financial kind of balance-sheet), an affair of serious bookishness, the earnest reading of the book, the book of the self, the book of the world, the book *per se.*

From translated Biblical text; to the fictional text of Biblicised *metanoia,* this story of the wholesale conversion, transformation, metamorphosis of Crusoe and his island and his world, through the reading of the precedent translated book; to the transfor-mation of a whole arm of cultural work, a whole branch of the imagination, a whole people's mode of self-knowledge, through the impact of Robinson: it's an extraordi-nary story of knock-on metamorphosings. Here is translation upon translation, *meta-noia* upon *metanoia* upon *metanoia.* Here's a whole mode, the novel itself, as a kind of *Robinsonade*: the novel as a form sustained by the genetic encodings of a book, *Robinson Crusoe*, which is to say the genetic code of the Big Book, the Bible in English.

Which is another way of putting the common allegation that English and English-speaking culture – language, literature, poetics, politics, economics, as well as theology and ecclesiology – all became an affair 'of the Book', the Bible – a people of the Book, a culture of the Book. Without the Bible translated into English – no English revolu-tion, no American revolution, no apocalyptic strain in English politics and poetics (no State of Israel of course), let alone almost no novel, no poetry, no canon of writing in English as we've known it and them. No Renaissance writing, no Metaphysicals, none of what T.S. Eliot labelled 'The School of Donne'. Certainly no Shakespeare, Milton, Bunyan, Dryden, Blake, Wordsworth, George Eliot, Thomas Hardy, D.H. Lawrence. They are the obvious prisoners, of course, though they stand for so many others. But even more fundamentally, more widely, no modern sense of the self, of the existential self alone, necessarily individual, a person before the cosmos, burdened with the imperative to make sense for oneself, to read the world aright, feeling, thinking, self-making, on one's own. Without the Biblical tribute, the Bible in English, representatively filtered through Defoe's Biblicist, heretic, dissenting model, the English and the English tradition have, simply, fewer words "to say it".[16] Wherever one looks, post-Reformation Englishness speaks in English Biblical words, identifies itself through English Scripturalism. English radicalism comes armed, as Cromwell's soldiers were, and as gun-toting Crusoe and Friday were, with the sword of the Spirit which is the Word of God, as well as with mere swords and guns.[17] The near-universal knowledge' (as it's been called[18]) of the *KJV* in Victorian times infects all Victorian discourse, whether practising Christian or anti-Christian, and not least the large Victorian discourse of the self (think, for a start, of all that Biblicised self-naming in Victorian life and art – all those Adams, Seths, Melchizedechs, Abigails, Josephs, Maries, Joshuas, Davids, Daniels, and so on and on). Where – to take just one example – did T.S. Eliot and W.H. Auden and Co. get that persistent formula of *the noun of the noun* – 'the beautiful loneliness of the banks', 'The End of the Affair', and so forth – if not from the very same Hebrew formula released into English by Tyndale ('the signs of the times', 'the fat of the land', 'the imagination of man's heart', 'the beasts of the field', and so on)? The tongue of 'Christian' England, even nominal Christian England, was Biblicised to an extreme extent.

[. . .]

The simplicity, the plainness, the thinginess, and above all the strongly paratactic base have obviously been learned from a lifetime's habituation in what David Daniell has called "the classic English prose" of Tyndale and the Tyndalised *KJV*. The mode of the reformed Bible; the mode of Crusoe and Defoe: it became the regular linguistic currency, the clichéd ordinary discourse of English narration, the very normality of English, the voice in fact of a nation, a culture, talking for itself. A national voice this way metamorphosed, because metanoicised this way. Our whole island, then, as Shakespeare might have put it, is full of translated Biblical voice – overt, covert, but all pervasive, and full thus, because repentant Bible-reading Crusoe's island was, because Dissenting, heretic, resistant, English Bible-reading, English Bible-absorbing Defoe's repenting, metanoicised mind was.

Notes

1   Valerie Worth-Stylianou. "Translatio and translation in the Renaissance: from Italy to France," *The Cambridge History of Literary Criticism. The Renaissance*, ed. Glyn P. Norton, vol. III (Cambridge: Cambridge University, Press, 1999) 133.

2   See e.g. Eugene A. Nida, "Principles of Translating as Exemplified by Bible Translating," *On Translation*, ed. Reuben A. Brower (London; Oxford University Press, 1966) 11–31. Nida is the guru of *The Good News Bible* translation.

3   Worth-Stylianou. "Translatio and translation in the Renaissance" III, 128.

4   John Dryden, "Preface to Ovid's Epistles," *Of Dramatic Poesy and Other Critical Essays*, ed. George Watson (1680: London: Everyman, J.M. Dent, 1962) l, 268.

5   Worth-Stylianou, "Translatio and translation in the Renaissance" III, 133.

6   *Ovid's Metamorphoses*, transl. Arthur Golding, ed. Madeleine Florey (Harmondsworth: Penguin, 2002) 5.

7   T.S. Eliot, *The Waste Land* (New York: Boni & Liveright, 1922) Part II, 'A Game of Chess', lines 99–100.

8   *Ovid's Metamorphoses* 3.

9   *Ovid's Metamorphoses* xv.

10   A.W. Pollard, ed., *Records of the English Bible* (London: Oxford University Press, 1911) 362–3.

11   *The New Testament*, transl. William Tyndale, the text of the Worms Edition of 1526 in original spelling, ed. for the Tyndale Society by W.R. Cooper, with "Preface" by David Daniell (London: The British Library, 2000) 437.

12   Quoted by Peter Levi, *The English Bible 1514–1859* (London: Constable, 1974) 37.

13   Daniel Defoe, "Robinson Crusoe", ed. Donald J. Crowley (London: Oxford University Press, 1970), in the reissued *Oxford World's Classics paperback edition*, 1998, 113. This text is based on the first edition of *Crusoe* published 25 April 1719.

14   Defoe, "Robinson Crusoe" 92–97.

15   Defoe, "Robinson Crusoe" 221.

16   I refer of course to the momentous narrative of language-questioning by Marie Cardinal, *The Words to Say It*, transl. P. Goodhart (London: Picador/Pan Books, 1984).

17   See David Daniell, *The Bible in English: its History and Influence* (New Haven, London: Yale University Press, 2003) 471 for the "Cromwellian Soldiers' Pocket Bible" (1643), and of course Christopher Hill, *The English Bible and the Seventeenth Century Revolution* (Allen Lane, London: The Penguin Press, 1993) *passim*.

18   By David Daniell, *The Bible in English* 660.

Works cited

The Cambridge History of Literacy Criticism. The Renaissance. Vol. III. Ed. Glyn P. Norton. Cambridge: Cambridge University Press, 1999.

Cardinal, Marie. *The Words to Say It*. Transl. P. Goodhart. London: Picador/Pan Books, 1984.

"Cromwellian Soldiers' Pocket Bible." 1643. *The Bible in English: its History and Influences*. David Daniell. New Haven, London: Yale University Press, 2003.

Daniell, David. *The Bible in English: its History and Influences*. New Haven, London. Yale University Press, 2003.

———. "Introduction" to Tyndale's *New Testament of 1534*, the 'Ploughboy' edition. In modernized spelling. New Haven, London: Yale University Press, 1995.

———. "William Tyndale, The English Bible, and the English Language" *The Bible as Book*. Ed. Orlaith O'Sullivan. London *et al.*: The British Library & Oak Knoll Press, 2000.

———. *William Tyndale: A Biography*. New Haven, London: Yale University Press, 1994.

Defoe, Daniel. "Robinson Crusoe". Ed. J. Donald Crowley. London: Oxford University Press, 1970. In the reissued *Oxford World's Classics* paperback edition, 1998, 113.

Dryden, John. "Preface to Ovid's Epistles." 1680. *Of Dramatic Poesy and Other Critical Essays*. Ed. George Watson. London: Everyman, J.M. Dent, 1962, I, 268.

Eliot, Thomas Stearns. *The Waste Land*. New York: Boni & Liveright, 1922.

Greenblatt, Stephen. *Renaissance Self–Fashioning From More to Shakespeare*. Chicago *et al.*: University of Chicago Press, 1980.

Hammond, Gerald. *The Making of the English Bible*. Manchester Carcanet, 1982.

Hill, Christopher. *The English Bible and the Seventeenth Century Revolution*. London: Allen Lane, 1993.

Jones, Richard Foster. "Science and English Prose Style, 1650–1675." *Literary English Since Shakespeare*. Ed. George Watson. London: Oxford University Press, 1970. 194–230.

Levi, Peter. *The English Bible 1534–1859*. London: Constable, 1974.

More, Thomas, "Confutation of Tyndale's Answer." 1532. Quoted by David Daniell. *William Tyndale: A Biography*. New Haven. London: Yale University Press, 1994.

The New Testament. Transl. William Tyndale. Ed. W.R. Cooper. London: The British Library, 2000.

Nida, Eugene A. "Principles of Translating as Exemplified by Bible Translating." *On Translation*. Ed. Reuben A. Brower. London: Oxford University Press, 1966. 11–31.

Ovid's Metamorphoses. Transl. Arthur Golding, and ed. Madeleine Florey. London: Penguin Books, 2002.

Patridge, A.C. *English Biblical Translation*. London: André Deutsch, 1973.

Pollard, A.W., ed. *Records of the English Bible*. London: Oxford University Press, 1911.

Sprat, Thomas, *History of the Royal Society*, 1667.

Worth-Stylianou, Valerie. "Translatio and translation in the Renaissance: from Italy to France" *The Cambridge History of Literary Criticism. The Renaissance*. Vol. III. Ed. Glyn P. Norton. Cambridge: Cambridge University Press, 1999.

Chapter 5

Multivocality

AS A LIBRARY OF books, the Bible is inherently multiply voiced. Even for those who privilege a divine author, the biblical text is always dual in its human and divine voices. Multivocality as a concept points to the many within the singular: through the presence and echoes of other writers (what is called intertextuality) as well as the expression of the conflicted nature of the self, familiar now through psycho-analysis and deconstruction. In the case of the Bible we have writings from different centuries and written in at least four languages (Hebrew and Greek as well as smatterings of Aramaic and Persian). The Bible is also read through tradition: the choice of the terms 'Hebrew Bible' or 'Old Testament' lends a specific framework through which reading is meaningful. The Bible has multiple voices within and around it: there are few aspects that are not the subject of theological debate. In short, the Bible is no simple text and especially not when encountered within literary rewritings or allusions.

Multivocality – as Mikhail Bakhtin makes clear in his 'Discourse in the Novel' – is an inherent aspect of any text because language is a 'social phenomenon'. Writing in Russia in the 1930s and 1940s, Bakhtin attempts to identify and outline an aesthetics particular to the novel form. For him, the novel is the exemplar of multivocality, an aesthetic quality that demands a poetic approach. As such, he identifies as ludicrous the fact that the novel is 'denied any artistic value at all' – a complaint not infrequently set against the biblical narrative itself. The novel and Bible alike, then, are often considered primarily for theme and content, with literary, artistic elements ignored or relegated. For Bakhtin, the novel demanded a poetic response because its style (as multivocal) was essential to its expression. Similarly, recognition of the Bible's multivocality demands a response that appreciates its multiple layers, voices, and accents.

The presence of biblical text in a novel adds a distinct voice to those voices already within the text. The quotation of or allusion to biblical narrative rubs shoulders, for example, with the narrator's voice and the direct speech of characters. Whilst distinct, the voice of the biblical text is not uniform: it can sometimes be authoritative or sometimes disruptive, depending on the context within which, and from which, the allusion appears. To think of the Bible as a historically concrete utterance, learnt in church, in school, from the lips of ministers, parents or even TV evangelists, means it is and has always been *someone*'s Bible. John Donne and Gerard Manley Hopkins are both devotional writers whose poetry is infused with the Bible.

But, where for Donne the Bible is a revolutionary, radical text, for Hopkins it is the Bible of the establishment, a familiar – too familiar – text that needs exploding. Thomas Hardy, writing later than Donne and Hopkins, challenges biblical and Christian doctrines with his invocations of the Bible, but his is also a Bible learnt in a devotional, evangelical context, and as a result is often somewhat homely, warm and familiar.[1]

For Bakhtin, language is inherently 'tension-filled' yet still a 'unity' in that it is always both borrowed and new, both conventional and innovative in its every usage. All words are taken from elsewhere – from someone else – and are therefore always at least doubly voiced in their previous and current use. When John writes 'In the beginning', he bifurcates his writing to ventriloquize the voice of Genesis and the (knowledgeable) reader keeps both voices at play: this sort of bifurcation is at the heart of multivocality. When Hardy names the protagonist of *Far from the Madding Crowd* (1874) 'Bathsheba', we have a brand new character that we get to know through the novel's pages, as well as the ghost of the biblical Bathsheba, the infamous temptress, shadowing this new Bathsheba's every step. (The 'infamous temptress': also present are the voices of commentators and tradition that paint an enigmatic biblical figure in colourful terms.)

Because of the inherent sociality of language, any object is 'enveloped in an obscuring mist', 'entangled'. The thing referred to is pulled in different directions by its many labels and their varying significances. A word, Bakhtin usefully illustrates, is like a 'ray of light' that passes through 'alien words, value judgments and accents', a positive atmospheric addition that makes 'the facets of the image sparkle'. The name Gabriel Oak, for instance, exists in an atmosphere full of significance: for Jewish readers he is the Gabriel of the Book of Daniel, interpreting dreams and delivering God's perspective. For Christians and many western readers familiar with the Angel Gabriel of the Christmas narrative, he is an awesome, authoritative, other-worldly figure. In Milton's *Paradise Lost*, Gabriel protects the Garden of Eden. The atmosphere of the word Gabriel – authority, awe-inspiring, protecting – must be travelled through by anyone familiar with the name before reaching the specific character of 'Gabriel' in Hardy's novel. Bakhtin insists that the author 'creates artistically calculated nuances on all the fundamental voices and tones of this heteroglossia': the new Gabriel created by Hardy makes deliberate reference to the assumptions about the name 'Gabriel' he thought he could take for granted as present in his readers' awareness, shaping for them a new Gabriel that fits within the larger Gabrielesque landscape.

The second extract by Daniel Boyarin works from the assumption that the biblical text itself is multivocal: with a 'fractured and unsystematic surface', it is characterized by 'dialogue and dialectic'. The Bible itself, he insists, is not straightforward but in dialogue with itself, creating multiple responses. From this starting point of the Bible's inherent multivocality, Boyarin outlines a threefold theory of the Scriptures that is significant for discussions of the literary citation of biblical text. First, he argues, writing is always borrowed, a 'mosaic of conscious and unconscious citation of earlier discourse' (echoing here Julia Kristeva's image of the 'mosaic of quotations').[2] Second, the Bible is 'a pre-eminent example' of a dialogical text that, far from being homogenously coherent, is instead self-contesting. And, third, the text is produced within – is in dialogue with – the historical conceptual frameworks that constrain what it is possible to think or believe. These theories come from Boyarin's attempt to understand and define midrash, a creative, elaborative and sometimes fanciful form of response to the biblical text that are foundational within Jewish interpretive tradition. From here, Boyarin expands identification of midrash as didactic fiction to consider its significance as a form of fiction. Boyarin turns to Friedrich Gundolf, a German-Jewish literature academic who asserted that history is important only in its production of truthful legends: in other words, the truth discernible in hard and straight accounts of history is less important than the truth of imaginative writings. Facts do not make truth: it is fiction that articulates lived everyday existence – its values, priorities and realities – as the compelling fantasies of Yann Martel's *Life of Pi* (2001) demonstrate. Only fiction can express the 'spiritual reality' of an original text. Boyarin's reading of midrash is, therefore, important for understanding literary borrowings from the Bible. Fictitious and imagined, these new writings that are in dialogue with the Bible can thereby express the spiritual reality of its characters and stories. As such they are a privileged form of commentary, and not least a living expression of certain 'truths'. Because of their inherently dialogic nature, the fictitious may, and even must, speak back into the biblical. Hardy's Bathsheba is both flirtatious and suffers at the hands of duplicitous and bullying men: a characterization that is suggestive for the reading of the biblical character about whom we know so little.

Alicia Ostriker's chapter considers the humanity of the Psalms and the ways in which they express everyday, yet fluctuating, emotions. To read the Psalms for coherence – to expect an artistic whole across and within them – is, in linguistic terms, to assume authorial coherency and perfect control over language. It is also to harmonize God's characteristics of mercy and violence in a way that is simply too comfortable and comforting. Ostriker's 'personal view' contains sensitive readings of the Psalms as both 'glorious and terrible', and as inherently conflicting. Their multivocality makes them meaningful. She writes of their inescapable coupling of love and violence: 'if one denies god's violence, is that not a kind of blasphemy?' she asks. Applying Ostriker's ideas to literary appropriations of the Psalms makes an easy, unproblematic allusion to the Psalms impossible. The Psalms, she insists, are importantly, unavoidably and beautifully difficult. She also demonstrates their presence in New Testament writings. Jesus cites the Scriptures when he speaks of the meek inheriting the earth, of spiritual thirst and even in his final death cry. In doing so he is borrowing from familiar Jewish biblical liturgy, drawing on familiar texts, borrowing their connotations as well as, through new usage, adding his own.

Sometimes the fractures discernible within a narrative can turn out to be a potentially desirable characteristic. David Tollerton's chapter demonstrates why incoherence may be welcome and necessary both theologically and ethically. He considers the disruptive effect of the biblical text upon its space of retelling in a theological context that is intriguingly pertinent to readings of Job in literature; his conclusions about monuments are equally applicable to the poetic. He considers the placing of Job's words (from Job 16: 18) at various Holocaust memorial sites and looks specifically at the way in which the narrative of Job, as 'an internally dissonant text', 'pushes against finalization, forgetfulness, and religious "acceptance" of the Holocaust narrative'. As a text containing multiple perspectives, multiple assertions, it insists upon 'continuing discussion'; necessary, Tollerton insists, for appropriate forms of remembering atrocities. Tollerton outlines the fissures within the Job text, pertinent to any reception of the Job story in literature: this is not a simple story of human frailty, but a tale fraught with the condemnation and commendation of human rebellion. Is Job's defiance 'cautionary (i.e., blasphemous) or exemplary (i.e., challenging injustice)?' It is difficult to find in the book 'any comfortingly clear and easily digestible message' that can be applied to suffering that refuses easy conclusions. Job, as a text that can 'by turns reassure, disturb, confound, and intrigue', needs to be left to 'act as a subversive force within Holocaust memory'.

Notes

1   For works on Donne, Hopkins, Hardy and the Bible see the relevant entries in *A Dictionary of Biblical Tradition in English Literature* (Grand Rapids, MI: Eerdmans, 1992): Donne on pp. 943–44, Hopkins pp. 947–48, and Hardy, p. 946. See also Jeanne Shami, 'John Donne' in *The Blackwell Companion to the Bible in English Literature*, eds. Rebecca Lemon et al., (Oxford: Blackwell, 2009), pp. 239–53, and Paul S. Fiddes, 'G. M. Hopkins' in *The Blackwell Companion to the Bible in English Literature*, pp. 563–76; and Mary Rimmer, 'My Scripture Manner: Hardy's Biblical and Liturgical Allusion', in *Thomas Hardy Reappraised: Essays in Honour of Michael Millgate*, ed. by Keith Wilson (Toronto: University of Toronto Press, 2006), pp. 20–37 and Ralph Pite, *The Guarded Life* (London: Pan Macmillan, 2006).
2   Julia Kristeva, *Desire in Language: A Semiotic Approach to Literature and Art* (1977; Oxford: Blackwell, 1992), p. 66.

Further Reading

Boer, Roland, *Bakhtin and Genre Theory in Biblical Studies* (Atlanta, GA: Society of Biblical Literature, 2007)

Green, Barbara, *Mikhail Bakhtin and Biblical Scholarship: An Introduction* (Atlanta: SBL Publications, 2000)

Hirschkop, Ken, *Mikhail Bakhtin: An Aesthetic for Democracy* (New York and Oxford: Oxford University Press, 1999)

Moore, Stephen D., 'Questions of Biblical Ambivalence and Authority under a Tree outside Delhi, or the Postcolonial and the Postmodern', in Stephen D. Moore and Fernando F. Segovia (eds), *Postcolonial Biblical Criticism: Interdisciplinary Intersections* (London: T & T Clark, 2005)

Newsom, Carol A., *A Contest of Moral Imaginations* (Oxford: Oxford University Press, 2003)

Pearce, Lynne, *Reading Dialogics: Interrogating Texts* (London: Hodder Arnold, 1994)

Reed, Walter L., *Dialogues of the Word: The Bible as Literature According to Bakhtin* (Oxford: Oxford University Press, 1993)

Rojtman, Betty, *Black Fire on White Fire: An Essay on Jewish Hermeneutics: From Midrash to Kabbalah*, trans. by Stephen Rendall (Berkeley: University of California Press, 1998)

Stordalen, T., 'Dialogue and Dialogism in the Book of Job', *SJOT* 20 (2006), 18–37

(a) Discourse in the Novel

Mikhail Bakhtin

The principal idea of this essay is that the study of verbal art can and must overcome the divorce between an abstract "formal" approach and an equally abstract "ideological" approach. Form and content in discourse are one, once we understand that verbal discourse is a social phenomenon—social throughout its entire range and in each and every of its factors, from the sound image to the furthest reaches of abstract meaning.

[. . .]

There is a highly characteristic and widespread point of view that sees novelistic discourse as an extra-artistic medium, a discourse that is not worked into any special or unique style. After failure to find in novelistic discourse a purely poetic formulation ("poetic" in the narrow sense) as was expected, prose discourse is denied any artistic value at all; it is the same as practical speech for everyday life, or speech for scientific purposes, an artistically neutral means of communication.[1]

[. . .]

Such a point of view frees one from the necessity of undertaking stylistic analyses of the novel; it in fact gets rid of the very problem of a stylistics of the novel, permitting one to limit oneself to purely thematic analyses of it.

[. . .]

We list below the basic types of compositional-stylistic unities into which the novelistic whole usually breaks down:

(1) Direct authorial literary-artistic narration (in all its diverse variants);
(2) Stylization of the various forms of oral everyday narration (*skaz*);
(3) Stylization of the various forms of semiliterary (written) everyday narration (the letter, the diary, etc.);
(4) Various forms of literary but extra-artistic authorial speech (moral, philosophical or scientific statements, oratory, ethnographic descriptions, memoranda and so forth);
(5) The stylistically individualized speech of characters.

These heterogeneous stylistic unities, upon entering the novel, combine to form a structured artistic system, and are subordinated to the higher stylistic unity of the work as a whole, a unity that cannot be identified with any single one of the unities subordinated to it.

The stylistic uniqueness of the novel as a genre consists precisely in the combination of these subordinated, yet still relatively autonomous, unities (even at times comprised of different languages) into the higher unity of the work as a whole: the style of a novel is to be found in the combination of its styles, the language of a novel is the system of its "languages." Each separate element of a novel's language is determined first of all by one such subordinated stylistic unity into which it enters directly—be it the stylistically individualized speech of a character, the down-to-earth voice of a narrator in *skaz*, a letter or whatever. The linguistic and stylistic profile of a given element (lexical, semantic, syntactic) is shaped by that subordinated unity to which it is most immediately proximate. At the same time this element, together with its most immediate unity, figures into the style of the whole, itself supports the accent of the whole and participates in the process whereby the unified meaning of the whole is structured and revealed.

The novel can be defined as a diversity of social speech types (sometimes even diversity of languages) and a diversity of individual voices, artistically organized. The internal stratification of any single national language into social dialects, characteristic group behavior, professional jargons, generic languages, languages of generations and age groups, tendentious languages, languages of the authorities, of various circles and of passing fashions, languages that serve the specific sociopolitical purposes of the day, even of the hour (each day has its own slogan, its own vocabulary, its own emphases)—this internal stratification present in every language at any given moment of its historical existence is the indispensable prerequisite for the novel as a genre. The novel orchestrates all its themes, the totality of the world of objects and ideas depicted and expressed in it, by means of the social diversity of speech types [*raznorečie*] and by the differing individual voices that flourish under such conditions. Authorial speech, the speeches of narrators, inserted genres, the speech of characters are merely those fundamental compositional unities with whose help heteroglossia [*raznorečie*] can enter the novel; each of them permits a multiplicity of social voices and a wide variety of their links and interrelationships (always more or less dialogized). These distinctive links and interrelationships between utterances and languages, this movement of the theme through different languages and speech types, its dispersion into the rivulets and droplets of social heteroglossia, its dialogization—this is the basic distinguishing feature of the stylistics of the novel.

Such a combining of languages and styles into a higher unity is unknown to traditional stylistics; it has no method for approaching the distinctive social dialogue among languages that is present in the novel. Thus stylistic analysis is not oriented toward the novel as a whole, but only towards one or another of its subordinated stylistic unities. The traditional scholar bypasses the basic distinctive feature of the novel as a genre, he substitutes for it another object of study, and instead of novelistic style he actually analyzes something completely different. He transposes a symphonic (orchestrated) theme on to the piano keyboard.

[. . .]

Thus stylistics and the philosophy of discourse indeed confront a dilemma: either to acknowledge the novel (and consequently all artistic prose tending in that direction) an unartistic or quasi-artistic genre, or to radically reconsider that conception of poetic discourse in which traditional stylistics is grounded and which determines all its categories.

This dilemma, however, is by no means universally recognized. Most scholars are not inclined to undertake a radical revision of the fundamental philosophical conception of poetic discourse. Many do not even see or recognize the philosophical roots of the stylistics (and linguistics) in which they work, and shy away from any fundamental philosophical issues. They utterly fail to see behind their isolated and fragmented stylistic observations and linguistic descriptions any theoretical problems posed by novelistic discourse. Others—more principled—make a case for consistent individualism in their understanding of language and style. First and foremost they seek in the stylistic phenomenon a direct and unmediated expression of authorial individuality, and such an understanding of the problem is least likely of all to encourage a re-consideration of basic stylistic categories in the proper direction.

[. . .]

Philosophy of language, linguistics and stylistics [i.e., such as they have come down to us] have all postulated a simple and unmediated relation of speaker to his unitary and singular "own" language, and have postulated as well a simple realization of this language in the monologic utterance of the individual. Such disciplines actually know only two poles in the life of language, between which are located all the linguistic and stylistic phenomena they know: on the one hand, the system of a *unitary language*, and on the other the *individual* speaking in this language.

Various schools of thought in the philosophy of language, in linguistics and in stylistics have, in different periods (and always in close connection with the diverse concrete poetic and ideological styles of a given epoch), introduced into such concepts as "system of language," "monologic utterance," "the speaking *individuum*," various differing nuances of meaning, but their basic content remains unchanged. This basic content is conditioned by the specific sociohistorical destinies of European languages and by the destinies of ideological discourse, and by those particular historical tasks that ideological discourse has fulfilled in specific social spheres and at specific stages in its own historical development.

These tasks and destinies of discourse conditioned specific verbal-ideological movements, as well as various specific genres of ideological discourse, and ultimately the specific philosophical concept of discourse itself—in particular, the concept of poetic discourse, which had been at the heart of all concepts of style.

The strength and at the same time the limitations of such basic stylistic categories become apparent when such categories are seen as conditioned by specific historical destinies and by the task that an ideological discourse assumes. These categories arose from and were shaped by the historically *aktuell* forces at work in the verbal-ideological evolution of specific social groups, they comprised the theoretical of actualizing forces that were in the process of creating a life for language.

These forces are *the forces that serve to unify and centralize the verbal-ideological world*.

Unitary language constitutes the theoretical expression of the historical processes of linguistic unification and centralization, an expression of the centripetal forces of language. A unitary language is not something given [*dan*] but is always in essence posited [*zadan*]—and at every moment of its linguistic life it is opposed to the realities of heteroglossia. But at the same time it makes its real presence felt as a force for overcoming this heteroglossia, imposing specific limits to it, guaranteeing a certain maximum of mutual understanding and crystalizing into a real, although still relative, unity—the unity of the reigning conversational (everyday) and literary language, "correct language."

A common unitary language is a system of linguistic norms. But these norms do not constitute an abstract imperative; they are rather the generative forces of linguistic life, forces that struggle to overcome the heteroglossia of language, forces that unite and centralize verbal-ideological thought, creating within a heteroglot national language the firm, stable linguistic nucleus of an officially recognized literary language, or else defending an already formed language from the pressure of growing heteroglossia.

What we have in mind here is not an abstract linguistic minimum of a common language, in the sense of a system of elementary forms (linguistic symbols) guaranteeing a *minimum* level of comprehension in practical communication. We are taking language not as a system of abstract grammatical categories, but rather language conceived as ideologically saturated, language as a world view, even as a concrete opinion, insuring a *maximum* of mutual understanding in all spheres of ideological life. Thus a unitary language gives expression to forces working toward concrete verbal and ideological unification and centralization, which develop in vital connection with the processes of sociopolitical and cultural centralization.

Aristotelian poetics, the poetics of Augustine, the poetics of the medieval church, of "the one language of truth," the Cartesian poetics of neoclassicism, the abstract grammatical universalism of Leibniz (the idea of a "universal grammar"), Humboldt's insistence on the concrete—all these, whatever their differences in nuance, give expression to the same centripetal forces in socio-linguistic and ideological life, they serve one and the same project of centralizing and unifying the European languages. The victory of one reigning language (dialect) over the others, the supplanting of languages, their enslavement, the process of illuminating them with the True Word, the incorporation of barbarians and lower social strata into a unitary language of culture and truth, the canonization of ideological systems, philology with its methods of studying and teaching dead languages, languages that were by that very fact "unities," Indo-European linguistics with its focus of attention, directed away from language plurality to a single proto-language—all this determined the content and power of the category of "unitary language" in linguistic and stylistic thought, and determined its creative, style-shaping role in the majority of the poetic genres that coalesced in the channel formed by those same centripetal forces of verbal-ideological life.

But the centripetal forces of the life of language, embodied in a "unitary language," operate in the midst of heteroglossia. At any given moment of its evolution, language is stratified not only into linguistic dialects in the strict sense of the word (according to formal linguistic markers, especially phonetic), but also—and for us this is the essential point—into languages that are socio-ideological: languages of social groups, "professional" and "generic" languages, languages of generations and so forth. From this point of view, literary language itself is only one of these heteroglot languages—and in its turn is also stratified into languages (generic, period-bound and others). And this stratification and heteroglossia, once realized, is not only a static invariant of linguistic life, but also what insures its dynamics: stratification and heteroglossia widen and deepen as long as language is alive and developing. Alongside the centripetal forces, the centrifugal forces of language carry on their uninterrupted work; alongside verbal-ideological centralization and unification, the uninterrupted processes of decentralization and disunification go forward.

Every concrete utterance of a speaking subject serves as a point where centrifugal as well as centripetal forces are brought to bear. The processes of centralization and decentralization, of unification and disunification, intersect in the utterance; the utterance not only answers the requirements of its own language as an individualized embodiment of a speech act, but it answers the requirements of heteroglossia as well; it is in fact an active participant in such speech diversity. And this active participation of every utterance in living heteroglossia determines the linguistic profile and style of the utterance to no less a degree than its inclusion in any normative-centralizing system of a unitary language.

Every utterance participates in the "unitary language" (in its centripetal forces and tendencies) and at the same time partakes of social and historical heteroglossia (the centrifugal, stratifying forces).

Such is the fleeting language of a day, of an epoch, a social group, a genre, a school and so forth. It is possible to give a concrete and detailed analysis of any utterance, once having exposed it as a contradiction-ridden, tension-filled unity of two embattled tendencies in the life of language.

The authentic environment of an utterance, the environment in which it lives and takes shape, is dialogized heteroglossia, anonymous and social as language, but simultaneously concrete, filled with specific content and accented as an individual utterance.

At the time when major divisions of the poetic genres were developing under the influence of the unifying, centralizing, centripetal forces of verbal-ideological life, the novel—and those artistic-prose genres that gravitate toward it—was being historically shaped by the current of decentralizing, centrifugal forces. At the time when poetry was accomplishing the task of cultural, national and political centralization of the verbal-ideological world in the higher official socio-ideological levels, on the lower levels, on the stages of local fairs and at buffoon spectacles, the heteroglossia of the clown sounded forth, ridiculing all "languages" and dialects, there developed the literature of the *fabliaux* and *Schwänke* of street songs, folksayings, anecdotes, where there was no language-center at all, where there was to be found a lively play with the "languages" of poets, scholars, monks, knights and others, where all "languages" were masks and where no language could claim to be an authentic, incontestable face.

Heteroglossia, as organized in these low genres, was not merely heteroglossia vis-à-vis the accepted literary language (in all its various generic expressions), that is, vis-à-vis the linguistic center of the verbal-ideological life of the nation and the epoch, but was a heteroglossia consciously opposed to this literacy language. It was parodic, and aimed sharply and polemically against the official languages of its given time. It was heteroglossia that had been dialogized.

Linguistics, stylistics and the philosophy of language that were born and shaped by the current of centralizing tendencies in the life of language have ignored this dialogized heteroglossia, in which is embodied the centrifugal forces in the life of language. For this very reason they could make no provision for the dialogic nature of language, which was a struggle among socio-linguistic points of view, not an intra-language struggle between individual wills or logical contradictions. Moreover, even intra-language dialogue (dramatic, rhetorical, cognitive or merely casual) has hardly been studied linguistically or stylistically up to the present day. One might even say outright that the dialogic aspect of discourse and all the phenomena connected with it have remained to the present moment beyond the ken of linguistics.

[. . .]

Discourse in Poetry and Discourse in the Novel

For the philosophy of language, for linguistics and for stylistics structured on their base, a whole series of phenomena have therefore remained almost entirely beyond the realm of consideration: these include the specific phenomena that are present in discourse and that are determined by its dialogic orientation, first, amid others' utterance inside a *single* language (the primordial dialogism of discourse), amid other "social language," within a single *national* language and finally amid different national languages within the same *culture*, that is, the same socio-ideological conceptual horizon.[2]

In recent decades, it is true, these phenomena have begun to attract the attention of scholars in language and stylistics, but their fundamental and wide-ranging significance in all spheres of the life of discourse is still far from acknowledged.

The dialogic orientation of a word among other words (of all kinds and degrees of otherness) create new and significant artistic potential in discourse, creates the potential for a distinctive art of prose, which has found its fullest and deepest expression in the novel.

We will focus our attention here on various forms and degree of dialogic orientation in discourse, and on the special potential for a distinctive prose-art.

As treated by traditional stylistic thought, the word acknowledges only itself (that is, only its own context), its own object, its own direct expression and its own unitary and singular language. It acknowledges another word, one lying outside its own context, only as the neutral word of language, as the word of no one in particular, as simply the potential for speech. The direct word, as traditional stylistics understands it, encounters in its orientation toward the object only the resistance of the object itself (the impossibility of its being exhausted by a word, the impossibility of saying it all), but it does not encounter in its path toward the object the fundamental and richly varied opposition of another's word. No one hinders this word, no one argues with it.

But no living word relates to its object in a *singular* way: between the word and its object, between the word and the speaking subject, there exists an elastic environment of other, alien words about the same object, the same theme, and this is an environment that is often difficult to penetrate. It is precisely in the process of living interaction with this specific environment that the word may be individualized and given stylistic shape.

Indeed, any concrete discourse (utterance) finds the object at which it was directed already as it were overlain with qualifications, open to dispute, charged with value, already enveloped in an obscuring mist—or, on the contrary, by the "light" of alien words that have already been spoken about it. It is entangled, shot through with shared thoughts, points of view, alien value judgments and accents. The word, directed toward its object, enters a dialogically agitated and tension-filled environment of alien words, value judgments and accents, weaves in and out of complex interrelationships, merges with some, recoils from others, intersects with yet a third group: and all this may crucially shape discourse, may leave a trace in all its semantic layers, may complicate its expression and influence its entire stylistic profile.

The living utterance, having taken meaning and shape at a particular historical moment in a socially specific environment, cannot fail to brush up against thousands of living dialogic threads, woven by socio-ideological consciousness around the given object of an utterance; it cannot fail to become an active participant in social dialogue. After all, the utterance; arises out of this dialogue as a continuation of it and as a rejoinder to it—it does not approach the object from the sidelines.

The way in which the word conceptualizes its object is a complex act—all objects, open to dispute and overlain as they are with qualifications, are from one side highlighted while from the other side dimmed by heteroglot social opinion, by an alien word about them.[3] And into this complex play of light and shadow the word enters—it becomes saturated with this play, and must determine within it the boundaries of its own semantic and stylistic contours. The way in which the word conceives its object is complicated by a dialogic interaction within the object between various aspects of its socio-verbal intelligibility. And an artistic representation, an "image" of the object, may be penetrated by this dialogic play of verbal intentions that meet and are interwoven in it; such an image need not stifle these forces, but on the contrary may activate and organize them. If we imagine the *intention* of such a word, that is, its *directionality toward the object*, in the form of a ray of light, then the living and unrepeatable play of colors and light on the facets of the image that it constructs can be explained as the spectral dispersion of the ray-word, not within the object itself (as would be the case in the play of an image-as-trope, in poetic speech taken in the narrow sense, in an "autotelic word"), but rather as its spectral dispersion in an atmosphere filled with the alien words, value judgments, and accents through which the ray passes on its way toward the object; the social atmosphere of the word, the atmosphere that surrounds the object, makes the facets of the image sparkle.

The word, breaking through to its own meaning and its own expression across an environment full of alien words and variously evaluating accents, harmonizing with some of the elements in this environment and striking a dissonance with others, is able, in this dialogized process, to shape its own stylistic profile and tone.

Such is the *image in artistic prose* and the image of *novelistic prose* in particular. In the atmosphere of the novel, the direct and unmediated intention of a word presents itself as something impermissably naive, something in fact impossible, for naiveté itself, under authentic novelistic conditions, takes on the nature of an internal polemic and is consequently dialogized (in, for example, the work of the Sentimentalists, in Chateaubriand and in Tolstoy). Such a dialogized image can occur in all the poetic genres as well, even in the lyric (to be sure, without setting the tone).[4] But such an image can fully unfold, achieve full complexity and depth and at the same time artistic closure, only under the conditions present in the genre of the novel.

In the poetic image narrowly conceived (in the image-as-trope), all activity—the dynamics of the image-as-word—is completely exhausted by the play between the word (with all its aspects) and the object (in all its aspects). The word plunges into the inexhaustible wealth and contradictory multiplicity of the object itself, with its "virginal," still "unuttered" nature; therefore it presumes nothing beyond the borders of its own context (except, of course, what can be found in the treasure-house of language itself). The word forgets that its object has its own history of contradictory acts of verbal recognition, as well as that heteroglossia that is always present in such acts of recognition.

For the writer of artistic prose, on the contrary, the object reveals first of all precisely the socially heteroglot multiplicity of its names, definitions and value judgments. Instead of the virginal fullness and inexhaustibility of the object itself, the prose writer confronts a multitude of routes, roads and paths that have been laid down in the object by social consciousness. Along with the internal contradictions inside the object itself, the prose writer witnesses as well the unfolding of social heteroglossia *surrounding* the object, the Tower-of-Babel mixing of language that goes on around any object; the dialectics of the object are interwoven with the social dialogue surrounding it. For the prose writer, the object is a focal point for heteroglot voices among which his own voice must also sound; these voices create the background necessary for his own voice, outside of which his artistic prose nuances cannot be perceived, and without which they "do not sound."

The prose artist elevates the social heteroglossia surrounding objects into an image that has finished contours, an image completely shot through with dialogized overtones; he creates artistically calculated nuances on all the fundamental voices and tones of this heteroglossia. But as we have already said, every extra-artistic prose discourse—in any of its forms, quotidian, rhetorical, scholarly—cannot fail to be oriented toward the "already uttered," the "already known," the "common opinion" and so forth. The dialogic orientation of discourse is a phenomenon that is, of course, a property of *any* discourse. It is the natural orientation of any living discourse. On all its various routes toward the object, in all its directions, the word encounters an alien word and cannot help encountering it in a living, tension-filled interaction. Only the mythical Adam, who approached a virginal and as yet verbally unqualified world with the first word, could really have escaped from start to finish this dialogic inter-orientation with the alien word that occurs in the object. Concrete historical human discourse does not have this privilege: it can deviate from such inter-orientation only on a conditional basis and only to a certain degree.

It is all the more remarkable that linguistics and the philosophy of discourse have been primarily oriented precisely toward this artificial, preconditioned status of the word, a word excised from dialogue and taken for the norm (although the primacy of dialogue over monologue is frequently proclaimed). Dialogue is studied merely as a compositional form in the structuring of speech, but the internal dialogism of the word (which occurs in a monologic utterance as well as in a rejoinder), the dialogism that penetrates its entire structure, all its semantic and expressive layers, is almost entirely ignored. But it is precisely this internal dialogism of the word, which does not assume any external compositional forms of dialogue, that cannot be isolated as an independent act, separate from the word's ability to form a concept [*koncipirovanie*] of its object—it is precisely this internal dialogism that has such enormous power to shape style. The internal dialogism of the word finds expression in a series of peculiar features in semantics, syntax and stylistics that have remained up to the present time completely unstudied by linguistics and stylistics (nor, what is more, have the peculiar semantic features of ordinary dialogue been studied).

The word is born in a dialogue as a living rejoinder within it; the word is shaped in dialogic interaction with an alien word that is already in the object. A word forms a concept of its own object in a dialogic way.

Notes

1   As recently as the 1920s, V. M. Žirmunskij [important fellow-traveler of the Formalists, ed.] was writing: "When lyrical poetry appears to be authentically a work of *verbal art*, due to its choice and combination of words (on semantic as well as sound levels) all of which are completely subordinated to the aesthetic project, Tolstoy's novel, by contrast, which is free in its verbal composition, does not use words as an artistically significant element of interaction but as a neutral medium or as a system of significations subordinated (as happens in practical speech) to the communicative function, directing our attention to thematic aspects quite abstracted from purely verbal considerations. We cannot call such a *literary work* a work of *verbal art* or, in any case, not in the sense that the term is used for lyrical poetry" ["On the Problem of the Formal Method," in an anthology of his articles, *Problems of a Theory Of Literature* (Leningrad, 1928, p. 173); Russian edition "K voprosu o 'formal'nom metode'," in *Voprosy teorii literatury*, (L., 1928)].

2   Linguistics acknowledges only a mechanical reciprocal influencing and intermixing of languages, (that is, one that is unconscious and determined by social conditions) which is reflected in abstract linguistic elements (phonetic and morphological).

3   Highly significant in this respect is the struggle that must be undertaken in such movements as Rousseauism, Naturalism, Impressionism, Acmeism, Dadaism, Surrealism and analogous schools with the "qualified" nature of the object (a struggle occasioned by the idea of a return to primordial consciousness, to original consciousness, to the object itself in itself, to pure perception and so forth).

4   The Horatian lyric, Villon, Heine, Laforgue, Annenskij and others—despite the fact that these are extremely varied instances.

(b) Toward a New Theory of Midrash

Daniel Boyarin

Reading Heinemann's Darkhe ha'aggadah

[. . .]

I wish to discredit the opposition between reading which is value-free and concerned with the difficulties of the biblical text and that which is unconcerned with those difficulties and speaks to the needs of the moment. It is clear, then, that I am not denying the reality of ideological concerns on the part of the rabbis nor that these ideological concerns may have often had an effect on the interpretive choices they made. I am asserting that we will not read midrash well and richly unless we understand it first and foremost as *reading*, as hermeneutic, as generated by the interaction of rabbinic readers with a heterogeneous and difficult text, which was for them both normative and divine in origin. Viewing the aggada through the eyes of a simplistic understanding of Maimonides results in a fatal reduction of its importance in Jewish culture, rendering it a mere decorative clothing for rabbinic thought.

Isaak Heinemann, at any rate, considered that what Maimonides was talking about was "poetic license," which he claims quite misses the point of the seriousness with which the aggada was presented as biblical interpretation. He suggests, therefore, a fourth way. We could perhaps capture it by defining it as a combination of the first and third of the Rambam's classes, that is, a poetry which nevertheless does intend to be an interpretation of the text. Citing favorably Yehiel Michel Sachs's attack on philology which "for all that it understands the demands of methodology, that much less does it understand meanings," Heinemann argues that, "aggada is not a systematic creation; so far, the approach of the Rambam is justified. However, in spite of this—perhaps, because of this—we must see it as a serious and successful effort to discover the depths of Scripture and to clearly determine the truth which is hidden from the eyes of the rationalists".[1] In order to accomplish this rapprochement, he must find a model of interpretation which does not restrict itself to the "objective," to the "plain sense of things." In order to find such a model, he turns to a strain in the literary and historiographical theory of his day (actually, as we will see, the historiographical theory of the day before his day). He argues that the most current theories of history propose a vital *subjective* character for historiography.

[. . .]

The conviction that historical interpretation is by definition a part of historiography and that Rankean objectivity is a "myth" has become part and parcel of contemporary historiographical theory,[2] and its attractiveness for Heinemann in his project to reach a sympathetic understanding of the rabbis is obvious. Not only will the masters of the aggada not seem naive on this view of historical understanding, but those who attack them for being subjective and their midrash for being value-laden are only revealing the poverty of their own spirits and the degeneration of their own historical sense. The rabbis certainly saw in themselves, in the most important sense, the legitimate continuation of history and their writings are the very embodiment of a transhistorical, absolute, and universal system of values.

However, this version of the validation of subjective historiography will not further too much our reading of midrash aggada, for even those historians who acknowledge the importance of aesthetics and values in the choosing of relevant facts by the historian and their arrangement into cause and effect sequences and complete stories, will not countenance the *creation* of facts *ex nihilo* by the historian. And it is this which the masters of the aggada seem to do all the time, when they tell us stories about conversations and actions which are not written in the Torah, the historical document, at all. But Gundolf's views on a proper task for the historian are in fact much more peculiar than what I have presented so far and provide an exact source for Heinemann's understanding of aggada. I am referring to Gundolf's notion, based on his reading of Goethe, of history itself as only being important owing to the legends that it produces, to the poetry to which it gives rise. "Goethe", Gundolf explained, "saw the justification of history in the historical fables to which it gave rise, because the truths which these fables expressed—though often lacking empirical basis—stimulated through their wealth and grandiosity, the imagination of mankind."[3] The only test, then, of the adequacy of historical writing for this school is in the importance of that writing for the life of the present. The method of the historian is to immerse himself in the documents of the past and achieve a oneness of spirit with their heroes, and out of that oneness fashion legends about those heroes which will be true because they are the product of deep spiritual connection between the great creative genius of the past and the great creative genius of the present. Whether or not the facts are right, this is true history because legends are the product of true apprehensions of the human qualities of the great figures which have given them rise. "The sole criterion of the historian's objectivity was whether or not he apprehended the study of history as a series of intense and personal experiences. In short, to write history was, in a very real sense, to make history."[4]

It should now be quite obvious why this historiosophy was so attractive to Heinemann, even though by the time of his writing it had long been replaced in Germany itself. This school not only provides a vindication for a subjective under-standing of the writing of history—that much could have been gotten from Kant; it specifically promotes the value of the historical legend from a kind of primitive protohistory to the very Parnassus of the historical enterprise. As a philosophy of history, it does precisely the work that Heinemann wants it to, namely, to provide a theoretical model with which to understand aggada positively as a writing of biblical history. The apotheosis of Romanticism in the Symbolist aesthetic and philosophy of history characteristic of the George school has provided the very foundation of all of Heinemann's work on the aggada. It provides the source for his crucial terminology, "creative historiography." We have here the romantic theory of literary production as the creation of the individual genius, carried over, via George and Gundolf, into the realm of biblical interpretation,

We should recognize how deeply immersed all of Heinemann's thought is in a specifically German cultural context.[5] Even his formulation that the goal of the highest kind of history writing is "'to make peace between life,' which requires satisfaction through spiritual contact with ancient heroes, 'and science,' which is indifferent to our longings" is an expression of the German ideology at its most typical. This opposition between "science" and "life" so characteristic of the George school is ultimately of Nietzschean origin.[6] It is certainly significant that the example which Heinemann cites for his theory is Dr. Faustus. "There may be no doubt," he avers, "that the play *Faust* is of more philosophical importance than the biography of the magician Johann Faust who lived in the sixteenth century, his travels and his deceptions" (p. 5). The rabbis are the Goethes of Judaism, who with their gigantic creative abilities understand the "reality" of the salvation history and communicate this reality with their legends, the aggada. There is no small measure of irony, it seems to me, in the fact that Heinemann set out to create a theory of aggada in opposition to Maimonides' claim that aggada is poetry and ended defending a version of precisely that claim, relying on a school of thought for which everything—including any worthwhile historiography—was poetry. All of *Darkhe ha'aggadah* will proceed from this fundamentally German opposition between "second-rate, even trivial 'science,'"[7] and the vital, experienced, lived truth of legend. Even Heinemann's description of the didactic goals of the rabbis could not be more at home in the George school's theories of poetry, which imagines it as "emotional direction and liberation of a people through the artistic means of language,"[8] or as Heinemann puts it, "the aggada, and not only the aggada of the Jewish people, fills in the details [of the historical record] in an imaginative way, in order to find an answer to the questions of the listeners and to arrive at a depiction which will act on their feelings" [p. 21].

A significant example of Heinemann's Gundolfian approach to aggada can be found in his chapter, "The Bringing Near of the Distant," which begins with a strong restatement of his theoretical position:

> The popular legend [aggada]—and the aggada of the sages included—often identifies, as we have seen, the different heroes of the story with each other or with their descendants.[9] Even more important is its way of identifying to a certain extent the lives of the heroes with the lives of the narrators. For here is the difference between the aggada and the scientific historiography. The latter emphasizes the *changes* which have taken place in the course of the generations and interprets the events particularly in accordance with one-time conditions. The organic thinking from which the popular aggada has sprung obliterates as much as possible the barrier between the describer and the described. In this sense it "erases all secondariness," in the words of a great expert.[10] But also the art of the civilized peoples and indeed even science have not always preserved, as will be shown below, the difference between times.
>
> [p. 35]

Heinemann's analogies are indeed to Shakespeare with his Julian clock and to Lessing with his theaters in the twelfth century. Just as these great poets did not care about the facts of history but its true meaning, which they perceived through their creative imaginations, so did the rabbis in presenting the biblical history in aggada. A classic example of this program in Heinemann's text is his statement that "the Abraham of the aggada who baked matzot for Passover, while he is different from the one that the Bible testifies to with regard to the details of the description, is essentially closer to the Abraham of the Bible than the one who was described by the Apostle, that Abraham of whom only faith was considered as righteousness, as if there were no value in works" [p. 39].

While it cannot, of course, be established that Abraham actually baked matzot, the fact is unimportant. This is merely the accident of the one-time, the unrepeatable, and therefore the insignificant. What is important is that the rabbis, in touch with the spiritual reality of Abraham, have understood his true essence, while Paul has missed this truth in his reading.

There may be little doubt, therefore, that the reliance on the George school as a grounding for *Darkhe ha'aggadah* has given Heinemann theoretical tools for a very strong reading of aggadic texts. However, since that grounding is so strongly predicated on the ideology and philosophy of that school, it is prey to the same weaknesses and distortions to which Gundolf's work itself is prey.[11] One of the signal consequences of Heinemann's powerful infusion of the Gundolfian model and sensibility into his study of midrash aggada is that it leads to near total disregard for social and historical forces and meanings in the production of the texts. If the rabbis are lonely geniuses in communion with the biblical heroes and reproducing their "real" essences in the aggada, then the aggada is above and beyond time itself, belonging to the supernal world of spirit and losing all of the specificity of historical and social circumstance. Indeed, this is explicit in Heinemann's thought as he repeatedly privileges the universal and eternal over the one-time occurrence. Once more, the German intellectual atmosphere of Heinemann's writing cannot be emphasized too much, for over and over again, we find in the literature characterizations of poetry as that which is not social, indeed that which is opposed to the social. Indeed Gundolf himself depended for his theory on what is to me a bizarre Germanic opposition between the poet and the writer, holding that while the latter was subject to language and its social meanings and determinations, the former resided in a privileged onto-logical and epistemological space all alone and free of any contamination from his time and society. "Literature is part of society but poetry belongs to nature."[12] Aggada is, of course, poetry and not literature in this taxonomy. Considering how very heavily Heinemann's thought is imbued with the spirit of German romanticism and the George school, I find it, therefore, very understandable how he can have completely missed the social and historical factors in his theory of aggada. Any new theory will have to redress this imbalance, retaining what is valuable in Heinemann's thought and filling in its yawning gaps. I turn now to a programmatic outline of such a possibility for a new *Darkhe ha'aggadah*.

Toward a New Theory of Midrash

Repeating Heinemann's rhetoric, I would begin by saying that if the school which I have synecdochically represented by Joseph Heinemann places midrash aggada too firmly in its own historical circumstances and considers it a mere reflection of them, Isaak Heinemann removes aggada too extremely from any historical and social meanings. What is common to these theories is that they both assume the opposition between "objective" and "subjective," one privileging the objective and the other the subjective. The assumption of this distinction forces one view to assume that the rabbis did not intend to interpret at all and the other to suppose a romantic, near mystical understanding of historical interpretation. Thus, particularly in Isaak Heinemann, the binary opposition between science and aggada leads to acute struc-tural tensions in his work. On the one hand he wishes to claim that the rabbinic midrash *is* interpretation of the biblical text, in direct opposition to what he takes to be the Maimonidean position. On the other hand his founding positivistic assumption that there is a true, objective, scientific meaning to the text which the rabbis depart from leads him again and again to compare aggada with fictional texts as such, which are not representations of the past at all, but "mouthpieces for the views of their authors" [p. 42]. In short, by not deconstructing the opposition between objective and subjective in his theory, Isaak Heinemann is led back to the very position of the Rambam which he had set out to replace. Indeed, the very argument which Heinemann mounted against the Cassuto and Jacob approach, namely, that the rabbis distinguished between *peshat* and *drash* in their text, proves to be a Trojan horse, for it tends more strongly to support the Rambam's contention that they did not intend their midrash to be interpretation than to argue against the former view.[13] Thus Isaak Heinemann argues that "the depictions of the sages are not 'interpretations' in the scientific sense, but even in the places where they supported their opinions with Scripture, in truth they were following the ways of artistic creation" [p. 23]. I, for one, am hard-pressed to find any distinction whatever between this claim and the theory of the Rambam's. It is clear from here how Heinemann's acceptance of the fundamental concept "scientific, objective truth," for all that he valued the intuitive, subjective "reality," nevertheless forced him into unthematized contradictions in his text.

In place of these approaches, I will follow much current thought in proposing that all interpretation and historiography is *representation* of the past by the present, that is, that there is no such thing as value-free, true and objective rendering of documents. They are always filtered through the cultural, socio-ideological matrix of their readers. Continuing Isaak Heinemann's own metaphor which projects a dichotomy between the painter who subjectively represents the inner truth of reality and the photographer who objectively records only what is "really" there, I would suggest that today we hold that the photographer, no less than the painter, produces a representation in which the very image is generated by what the culture encourages and constrains her to see. This understanding is an outgrowth of several currents in contemporary theory. On the one hand Mikhail Bakhtin has revealed for us the social, interactional, dialogical nature of all language use (including the romantic lyric and the scientific description—the painting and the photograph). On the other hand, theoreticians of history such as Hayden White have been exploring the ways in which all historiography is constructed by a culture.[14] Finally, in a more specifically literary context, Frank Kermode has explored how culturally and ideologically determined are all notions of "the plain sense of things."[15] These theoreticians and others of their ilk will occupy in my description of midrash the place that Stefan George and Friedrich Gundolf occupied in *Darkhe ha'aggadah*.

The sovereign notion informing the present reading of midrash is "intertextuality." This concept has several different accepted senses, three of which are important in my account of midrash. The first is that the text is always made up of a mosaic of conscious and unconscious citation of earlier discourse. The second is that texts may be dialogical in nature—contesting their own assertions as an essential part of the structure of their discourse—and that the Bible is a preeminent example of such a text. The third is that there are cultural codes, again either conscious or unconscious, which both constrain and allow the production (not creation) of new texts within the culture; these codes may be identified with the ideology of the culture, which is made up of the assumptions that people in the culture automatically make about what may or may not be true and possible, about what is natural in nature and in history.

In the first place, the analysis of literary systems shows the power of Mikhail Bakhtin's insight that the romantic view of literary creation as *creatio ex nihilo* (such as Heinemann's) cannot be sustained. Every author/speaker/human is constituted by all of the discourses which he/she has heard or read. There is, therefore, no such thing as the self-identical subject of the subject-object dichotomy, and this very distinction is revealed as a term in a specific ideological code. While recent writers on rabbinic literature have already discussed it in terms of intertextuality, I believe that a misreading of this concept often shows up in their texts, for they speak of "intertextuality" as if it were a characteristic of some texts as opposed to others.[16]

[. . .]

Now it is precisely on this point that I wish to address the issues. Neusner's entire discussion both in the monograph on the subject and here is founded on an entirely mistaken conception of the notion of intertextuality as it appears in myriad discussions in literary theory.[17] Intertextuality in virtually all discussions is not a characteristic of some texts as opposed to others but part of the structure of the literary text as such. One could certainly argue against the concept of intertextuality on theoretical grounds, but Neusner's attempt to discredit the concept vis-à-vis rabbinic literature on empirical grounds merely shows that he has not the slightest notion of what he is talking about, *when he uses the term "intertextuality."* Now, if the term "intertextuality" has any value at all, it is precisely in the way that it claims that no texts, including the classic single-authored works of Shakespeare or Dostoevsky, for example, are organic, self-contained unities, created out of the spontaneous, freely willed act of a self-identical subject. What this means is that every text is constrained by the literary system of which it is a part and that every text is ultimately dialogical in that it cannot but record the traces of its contentions and doubling of earlier discourses. The scholars that Neusner is attacking are certainly right in the intuition that if such be true for the texts of Wordsworth, it can only be more true of the texts of group production and redaction which comprise the rabbinic classics. Since these conceptions, in their broadest sense,[18] are, I would claim, among the virtually universally maintained positions in literary theory today, Neusner's wish to see each of the documents of rabbinic Judaism as just such organic texts and as the reflection of a worldview of "authorships" is nothing short of primitive from the perspective of precisely the discipline that he is invoking against Kugel and so-called company.[19] Far from leading to a claim that rabbinic literature is a seamless whole of harmonious views, the concept of intertextuality would suggest that not even one document of that literature (or any other) is nor could be a seamless whole that could reflect the *Weltanschauung* of an "authorship."

Not only a claim about the dialogical and social nature of all text production, the notion of intertextuality is also an extension and concretization of the philosophical position that there is no such thing as a true, objective mimesis of reality in language. Reality is always represented through texts that refer to other texts, through language that is a construction of the historical, ideological, and social system of a people. In these terms we can perhaps retrieve Isaak Heinemann's work, removing from it the mystifying encrustations of romantic ideology. In place of the hero of the spirit in communion with the true timeless essence of the heroes of the Bible, I will imagine the rabbis as readers doing the best they could to make sense of the Bible for themselves and their times and in themselves and their times—in short, as readers. The text of the Torah is gapped and dialogical, and into the gaps the reader slips, interpreting and completing the text in accordance with the codes of his or her culture. In this sense too we can retrieve Gundolf's ideas—however, in terms that he would hardly have understood or been sympathetic to. What I wish to suggest is that the legends that history produces can indeed be read as a historiography and an interpretation of the past, and the aggada can indeed then be read as an interpretation of the

Bible. In other words we will return to the idea that the aggada is the most significant kind of historiography, however, not because it represents a true subjective communion with the past on the part of geniuses, but because it manifests the past as it was represented by the culture in which the aggada was produced. Midrash is a portrayal of the reality which the rabbis perceived in the Bible through their ideologically colored eyeglasses, just as Heinemann and Heinemann are reading the rabbis and the Bible through their eyeglasses—and indeed just as I am reading through mine. In place of one Heinemann's reduction of aggada to a mere reflection of the historical reality of its time and the other's ignoring of its time entirely in the name of a supertemporal psychological connection between the rabbis and the Bible, I propose a reading of aggada in which, from the distance of our time, we try to understand how the rabbis read the Torah in their time—taking seriously their claim that what they are doing is reading, and trying to understand how a committed reading of the holy and authoritative text works in the rabbinic culture. The program for a new *Darkhe ha'aggadah* is to explore and justify the view of midrash as a kind of interpretation that continues compositional and interpretive practices found in the biblical canon itself.[20] Rather than seeing midrashic departures from what appears to be the "simple" meaning of the local text as being determined by the needs of rhetoric and propaganda and rooted in the extratextual reality of the rabbinic period, or as being the product of the creative genius of individual rabbis wholly above time and social circumstance, I suggest that the intertextual reading practice of the midrash is a development (sometimes, to be sure, a baroque development) of the intratextual interpretive strategies which the Bible itself manifests. Moreover, the very fractured and unsystematic surface of the biblical text is an encoding of its own intertextuality, and it is precisely this which the midrash interprets. The dialogue and dialectic of the midrashic rabbis will be understood as readings of the dialogue and dialectic of the biblical text.

The intertextuality of midrash is thus an outgrowth of intertextuality within the Bible itself. Gerald Bruns has written that midrash is founded on the

> ancient hermeneutical insight [that] as the Rabbis, Augustine, and Luther knew, the Bible, despite its textual heterogeneity, can be read as a self-glossing book. One learns to study it by following the ways in which one portion of the text illumines another. The generations of scribes who shaped and reshaped the Scriptures appear to have designed them to be studied in just this way. Thus Brevard S. Childs speaks of "the interpretive structure which the biblical text has received from those who formed and used it as sacred scripture." This does not mean that redaction produced a unified text (or what we would think of as unified: a holistic text, free of self-contradiction, a systematic or organic whole: the Bible is everything but *that*); rather it means that the parts are made to relate to one another reflexively, with later texts, for example, throwing light on the earlier, even as they themselves always stand in the light of what precedes and follows them.[21]

Bruns finds a way to achieve that which Isaak Heinemann set out to do, to explain in what sense the midrash is a reading of the Bible. We do not need the romantic ideology of communion and creation to understand this sense; it is a product of the very process by which the Bible was constituted as Scripture. This perspective comprehends how later texts interpret and rewrite the earlier ones to change the meaning of the entire canon, and how recognizing the presence of the earlier texts in the later changes our understanding of these later texts as well. We have here, then, an almost classic intertextuality, defined as, "the transformation of a signifying system." This is what the midrash itself refers to as "stringing [like beads or pearls] the words of Torah together . . . from the Torah to the Prophets and from the Prophets to the Writings."[22]

Were I to attempt to define midrash at this point, it would perhaps be radical intertextual reading of the canon, in which potentially every part refers to and is interpretable by every other part. The Torah, owing to its own intertextuality, is a severely gapped text, and the gaps are there to be filled by strong readers, which in this case does not mean readers fighting for originality, but readers fighting to find what they must in the holy text. Their own intertext—that is, the cultural codes which enable them to make meaning and find meaning, constrain the rabbis to fill in the gaps of the Torah's discourse with narratives which are emplotted in accordance with certain ideological structures. The type of midrashic parable called the mashal[23] is only the most explicit of these structures, but it can be taken as a prototype—a privileged type—of all midrashic narrative interpretation. It is here that Hayden White's work on the theory of historiography becomes so significant, for he is the theoretician who has most clearly articulated the role of the intertext in historiography.

> What the historian must bring to his consideration of the record are general notions of the kinds of stories that might be found there, just as he must bring to consideration of the problem of narrative representation some notion of the "pregeneric plot structure" by which the story he tells is endowed with formal coherency. In other words, the historian must draw upon a fund of culturally provided mythoi in order to constitute the facts as figuring a story of a particular kind, just as he must appeal to that same fund of mythoi in the minds of his readers to endow his account of the past with the odor of meaning or significance.[24]

In White's theory, then, any historian who writes history as a story has perforce emplotted his discourse using the plot structures that carry the ideology of the culture. Otherwise the story will make no sense to people in the culture. These basic plots—the narratives which the culture allows one to tell—form a vital aspect of the intertext. The mashal and its congeners play a role in the present description of midrash analogous to the "eternal truths" of which Isaak Heinemann spoke. They also serve to take the biblical text out of the accidental and uninterpreted chronicle into the interpretive, value-laden structures of a true historiography; however, the eternal, unchanging verities of romanticism are replaced here by culture-bound, historically conditioned, specific ideological patterns of significance.

Combining the import of all of these insights into the role of intertextuality in the production of the interpretive text leads to the following schema. The biblical narrative is gapped and dialogical. The role of the midrash is to fill in the gaps. The materials which provide impetus for the specifics of the gap filling are found in the intertext in two ways: first in the intertext provided by the canon itself, the intertextual and interpretive interrelations which exist and which can be made to exist between different parts of the canon, and second, within the ideological intertextual coda of the rabbinic culture. The midrash is not, then, a reflex of that ideology but a dialogue with the biblical text conditioned and allowed by that ideology—and as such is no different from any other interpretation.

This story of midrash quite reverses the narrative of hermeneutic that is presupposed by the historical school. As we have seen, their assumption is that the text is clear and transparent at the moment of its original creation, because it speaks to a particular historical situation, and it becomes unclear, owing to the passing of time and that situation. In contrast to this, our conception of midrash is one in which the text makes its meaning in history. We find this insight adumbrated in a crucially important text in the midrash on Genesis, *Bereshit Rabbah:*

> Rabbi Yehuda the son of Simon opened: "And He revealed deep and hidden things" [Dan. 2:22]. In the beginning of the creation of the World, "He revealed deep things, etc." For it says, "In the beginning God created the heavens," and He did not interpret. Where did He interpret it? Later on, "He spreads out the heaven like gossamer" [Isa. 40:22]. "And the earth," and He did not interpret. Where did He interpret it? Later on, "To the snow He said, be earth" [Job 37:6]. "And God said, let there be light," and He did not interpret. Where did He interpret it? Later on, "He wraps Himself in light like a cloak." [Psalms 104:2][25]

This is certainly a very rich and paradoxical *theoretical* statement. The Author of the Book (and indeed the Author of the world) has chosen at the time of creation—at the time of writing about creation—to hide the interpretation, but He, through His prophets, has revealed something of this truth later on. This text bears out Bruns's understanding of midrash completely, as we will see it borne out throughout the readings of the Mekilta in this book. We see now that in this midrashic perspective all of the later books of the Bible are in a strong sense readings of the Torah, and so does the midrash continue to use them as interpretation of the Torah and develop their interpretations further. Thus we often find in midrash the phrase, "About them it has been interpreted in the tradition," ['aleyhem meforash baqqabbalah] before quoting a verse of the Prophets or Writings. When the rabbis of the midrash quote verses from these texts, the quoted verses are the generating force behind the midrashic elaboration and filling in of the gaps in the "historical record."

However, Bruns has even more to teach us about midrash. The gaps and dialogue and contestation of meaning which the biblical text presents to the reader act as a block—indeed a stumbling block in Bruns's words—precisely to those ideologies, whether romantic or positivistic, which set as their goal recovery of the original meaning. "The Bible always addresses itself to the time of interpretation; one cannot understand it except by appropriating it anew" [Bruns, p. 627]. Although Bruns quotes with approval precisely the language of Joseph Heinemann in which the latter proposes that the rabbis were not concerned with the meaning of Scripture, he himself proffers an understanding of midrash which is much more rich and powerful. "Midrash is not only responsive to the Scriptures as a way of coping with the text's wide-ranging formal problems; it is also responsive to the situations in which the Scriptures exert their claim upon human life. Think of midrash as the medium in which this scriptural claim exerts itself" [p. 629]. A theory of midrash for our time will have to account for the midrash's responsiveness to the "formal problems" of Scripture, which I have described as Scripture's own intertextuality, as well as for the responsiveness of midrash to the ways in which Scripture laid claim to human life in the past and lays such claim in the present as well.

In a very strong sense, if the Rambam posited two schools of readers of the aggada before him and then himself, the Aristotelian reader of midrash; and Heinemann then posited himself, the Gundolfian and Crocean reader of midrash; I come to propose a reading of midrash which is in keeping with the intellectual, crit-ical, and theoretical movement of our times. I might indeed claim for my model that it incorporates all of the types of midrashic readers which Maimonides presented. On the one hand, I *will* claim that midrash is true reading of the meaning of the biblical text, a reading which is sensitive to literary values, echoes, contradictions, inter-textuality in all of its senses within the Bible. Midrash is a reading of the "plain sense of things," but only if we recognize that the plain sense grows and changes throughout history and that this is the Bible's underlying meaning. However, I will also accept the characterization of midrash as the product of a disturbed exegetical sense, but only if we recognize that all exegetical senses are disturbed, including most certainly our own. All interpretation is filtered through consciousness, tradition, ideology, and the intertext, and the opposition between subject and object, so characteristic of the romantic ideology, must be deconstructed. Finally, midrash is literature, but all serious literature is revision and interpretation of a canon and a tradition and is a dialogue with the past and with authority which determines the shape human lives in the present and future. The rabbis were concerned with the burning issue of their day, but their approach to that concern was through the clarification of difficult passages of Scripture. Ideology affected their reading but their ideology was also affected by their reading. The task of our research is to try to understand how. Perhaps the *nimshal* of my text is that each generation of serious readers of aggada will have to create a *Darkhe ha'aggadah* for itself. Let us begin.

Notes

1   Joseph Heinemann, *Aggadah and Its Development* [Hebrew], (Jerusalem, 1974), p. 41.
2   See Hayden White, *Tropics of Discourse* (Baltimore, 1986), pp. 53–54, for convenient over-view.
3   G. R. Urban, *Kinesis and Stasis: A Study in the Attitude of Stefan George and His Circle to the Musical Acts* ('S-Gravenhage, 1962), p. 35.
4   Ibid., p. 38.
5   Another perspective on Heinemann is that provided by David Stern, who in a recent article says, "A[nother] . . . model for midrashic discourse, framed in Romanticist language and virtually Viconian mythopoeiac terminology was proposed by Isaac Heinemann in his classic *Darkhe ha'aggadah*". David Stern, "Midrash and Indeterminacy," *Critical Inquiry* 1:1 (1988), p. 146, n. 25. Stern correctly points out the Viconian connections in Heinemann's

thought. Heinemann himself cites Croce. A fuller reading of Heinemann than what I am undertaking here would have to take both elements into consideration and attempt to account for them together. I hope to provide such a reading in a version of this text to be published separately. In that text I plan also to deal more fully with the influence of romanticism on the history of research on midrash in the *Wissenschaft des Judentums*. Midrash has been made to play a role in this ideology analogous to that of *Volkspoesie* for the Romantics. Bialik was quite explicit on this point, as are those critical schools dominant in some Israeli universities in which midrash is studied as the ancient folklore of the Jewish people.

6   Wolf Lepenies, "Between Social Science and Poetry in Germany," *Poetics Today* 9:1 (1988), pp. 117–45.

7   Ibid., p. 123.

8   Ibid., p. 140. See also, George Messe, *Nationalism and Sexuality* (Madison, 1985), p. 58: "Stefan George drew into his coterie some of the best minds in Germany. The poet as intuitive seer was not a new concept at the *fin de siècle;* men like Nietzsche, Richard Wagner, and Gabriele D'Annunzio had already looked upon themselves as prophets of a personal renewal that would change the nation as well."

9   He has referred above to the popular identification of Friedrich III and Frierich I in the stories of the German folk.

10   Heinemann is referring to Lévy-Bruhl, and Handelman accuses him of being unaware of theory!

11   Already in 1922, in his essay on Goethe's *Elective Affinities*, Walter Benjamin mounted a scathing attack on Gundolf's book on Goethe. Walter Benjamin, "Goethes Wahlverwandtschaften," *Gesammelte Schriften*, ed. Rolf Tiedemann and Hermann Scweppenhäuser (Frankfun am Main, 1974), Vol. I part 1, pp. 123–203. The attack on Gundolf is on pp. 155ff.

12   Lepenies, p. 131.

13   It is, moreover, a very questionable claim. There are many scholars who have argued that the distinction between *peshat* as plain meaning and *derash* as application is later than the Talmudic period entirely, while others have located it in the period of the late Babylonian Amoraim. Heinemann makes no chronological distinctions whatever, as has been pointed out in an otherwise laudatory review of his book by Eliezer Margoliot in *Behinot* 2 (1952), pp. 77–78. On this issue in general see the excellent article of Raphael Loewe, "The 'Plain' Meaning of Scripture in Early Jewish Exegesis," *Papers of the Institute of Jewish Studies* I (1964), pp. 140–85, and material cited there. According to Loewe's study, the term *peshat* in tannaitic literature means "authoritative interpretation," no more and no less.

14   See White, *Tropics of Discourse*, pp. 58–60 and passim. Also Dominick LaCapra, *History and Criticism* (Ithaca, 1985), especially the chapter, "Rhetoric and History," pp. 15–45.

15   Frank Kermode, "The Plain Sense of Things," in *Midrash and Literature*, eds. Geoffrey H. Hartman and Sanford Budick (New Haven, 1986), pp. 179–94.

16   For some clarification of this notion and its place in midrashic studies see my review essay entitled "Literature and Midrash" in the *Jewish Quarterly Review* (January, 1989).

17   He admits as much when he cites only one text as being the one from which he has learned everything there is to be known about intertextuality in his "The Case of James Kugel's Joking Rabbis and Other Serious Issues," in *Wrong Ways and Right Ways in the Study of Formative Judaism* (Atlanta, 1988), p. 34. And then, from that one text, he chooses only one acceptation of the term "intertextuality"—arguably the clearest but certainly not the most sophisticated. I suspect that Robert Scholes was pulling a naive colleague's leg when he sent him to one article in a field which has spawned by now almost a small library.

18   This formula is meant to leave room for the many contested areas vis-à-vis "intertextuality" in the literature.

19   Neusner, p. 62. This is doubly ironic in the light of Neusner's almost virulent attack on Baron in the same volume for not being aware of the latest theories in economic history. It may indeed have been the case, but then neither, clearly, is Neusner aware of the latest developments in literary theory and the theory of literary history, so a little more charity toward others would seem to be called for.

20   In this sense, speaking of "inner-biblical midrash," which is practically a common-place of modern biblical study, seems to me rather putting the cart before the horse. Rather we should understand midrash as post-biblical Scripture—or as the rabbis called it, "Oral Torah."

21   Gerald Bruns, "Midrash and Allegory," in *The Literary Guide to the Bible*, ed. Frank Kermode and Robert Alter, (Cambridge, Mass. 1986), pp. 626–27.

22   *Song of Songs Rabba*, pp. 42. See ch. 7 for the full context of this citation.

23   See chapter 7.

24   White, p. 60.

25   My translation from *Bereshit Rabbah*, ed. Theodor-Albeck, vol. 1, p. 3. I wish to thank Menahem Kahana for calling this very important passage to my attention.

(c) Psalm and Anti-Psalm: A Personal View

Alicia Ostriker

A few days after the destruction of the World Trade Center in New York City in September 2001, the recently inaugurated Poet Laureate of the United States was interviewed by the journalist Sandra Martin. Asked what role poetry might play at such a moment, he replied that for him poetry was a private art, and needed a private focus. In a public radio interview on September 11 itself, he suggested that almost any page of any book of poetry would be "speaking for life . . . against what happened today." Or, he said, read the Psalms.[1]

The Psalms? Was he joking?

The Psalms are glorious. No, the Psalms are terrible. No, the Psalms are both glorious and terrible, both attractive and repulsive to me emotionally and theologically. I read as a poet and a woman, a literary critic and a left-wing Jew who happens to be obsessed with the Bible. And when I read these poems, I experience a split-screen effect: wildly contradictory responses.

As Catullus says: I love and hate. And it is excruciating.

I

The Psalms are overwhelmingly beautiful as poems. They represent the human spirit, my own spirit, in its intimate yearning for a connection with the divine Being who is the source of all being, the energy that creates and sustains the universe. Unlike the portions of the Bible that lay down rules and regulations (I skip these), and unlike the narratives that tell compelling tales of patriarchs and matriarchs, judges, warriors and kings, but don't tell how they feel, what they think, what it all means to them—the Psalms are love poems to God. Since the course of true love never does run smooth, the Psalms are poems of emotional turbulence.

Sometimes the psalmist expresses a wonderfully serene, almost childlike faith and trust. *The Lord is my shepherd; I shall not want. He maketh me to lie down in green pastures. He leadeth me beside the still waters. He restoreth my soul.* The ineffable sweetness of this pastoral image surely taps a deep human desire to be relieved of responsibility, including the responsibility of being human. Is that why Psalm 23 is the most popular in the whole psalter? In "He restoreth my soul," the Hebrew for "my soul" is *nafshi*, a term humans share with animals. It is wonderful, too, that the psalmist does not declare "I am a sheep" or "I am like a sheep," but speaks directly as from the animal soul, the *nefesh*, itself. In Psalm 37 we are advised not to "fret" over evildoers; they are going to disappear, and "the meek shall inherit the earth." All of us who are meek, who feel powerless on earth, can identify with this fantasy. Sometimes a psalm runs a video in my frontal lobe, and causes my back to straighten and my lungs to pull in air—*I will lift up my eyes unto the hills, whence cometh my help. My help cometh from the Lord, who made heaven and earth* (121). These two sentences are so physical, but then so metaphysical, shaped like a chiasmus (a kind of word sandwich) but also striking a sequence of registers that expand into larger and larger space: body (eyes), natural environment (vista of hills), cosmos (heaven, earth). I catch my breath every time. I feel confident and alive every time. Commercials for recreational vehicles profiled against a mountain sunrise try to press the same button of exhilaration in me, but something is missing. *My help cometh from the Lord, who made heaven and earth. He will not suffer thy foot to be moved. He that keepeth thee will not slumber. . . . The Lord is thy keeper. The Lord is thy shade upon thy right hand. The sun shall not smite thee by day nor the moon by night. The Lord shall preserve thee from all evil.* God is connected to nature, as its maker. God is in the hills, God is in the mountains. God made heaven and earth, so you and I are protected by the entire cosmos, which makes us very safe. God even makes it possible to shift pronouns from me to you without a touch of anxiety. And look at the security blanket of language when the psalmist has *behaved and quieted myself, like a child just weaned from his mother. My soul is like a weaned child* (131). Not a child in the womb or a nursing child, but one who has left those comforts behind, and probably wept for them, but is confident of being loved anyway.

At other moments the psalmist is racked by doubt and self-doubt. *How long wilt thou forget me, O Lord? For ever?* (13). Here is a voice of suffering, complaining, crying out, feeling abandoned, hurt, tormented. *My God, my God, why hast thou forsaken me? Why art thou so far from helping me, and from the mouth of my roaring?* (22). It seems evident that wicked people prosper in this world, that good people suffer, and that God refuses to intervene. *Why standest thou far off, O Lord? Why hidest thou in time of trouble? The wicked persecute the poor. . . .* [the wicked man] *boasts of his heart's desire. As for his enemies, he puffeth at them* (10). Or, as we would say, the bad guy blows off anyone who bothers him. *They are enclosed in their own fat, with their mouths they speak proudly* (17). *And they say, How does God know?* (73). *O God, how long shall the adversary reproach? Shall the enemy blaspheme thy name for ever?* (74), Evildoers get away with murder, they are shameless, and the psalmist passionately begs God's help.

Many psalms evoke experiences of being alone, attacked, persecuted, punished. Some beg forgiveness for sin: *Have mercy upon me, O God. . . . a broken spirit and a contrite heart, O God, thou wilt not despise* (51). Many speak from desperation. *Save me, O God, for the waters have come into my soul. I sink in deep mire. The ones that hate me without a cause are more than the hairs of my head* (69). *My days are consumed like smoke. My heart is withered like grass* (102). I recognize the sense of sinking dread, the feeling that my life is meaningless, that my emotions have dried up. The poetry articulates my dread and dryness in exquisite metaphors and similes, which makes it hurt both less, because of the beauty, and more, because of the accuracy. And then the feeling modulates with incredible subtlety. One of my favorite Psalms is 42: *As the hart pants after the water brooks, so my soul pants after thee, O God.* What a melancholy yet sweet image of the desire for God, the desire of a thirsting animal. The soul, my soul, is *nafshi* again, here. The yearning is as pure as that physical need. But then it turns. *My soul thirsts for God, for the living God. When shall I come and appear before God? My tears have been my meat night and day while they continually say unto me, "where is thy God?"* It is not simply that I fruitlessly long to be close to God, united with God, but that at the same time, and precisely because everyone knows I go around with this spiritual need, people mock me. Those who do not have my faith or my need, and do not want it, and can live their lives nicely without it, mock me. They stand around and ridicule me. And let me remember that men and women for eons have been mocked in worse circumstances than mine: in jail, under interrogation, under torture, at the point of martyrdom. I imagine there was considerable mockery, and self-mockery, in the concentration camps of Europe in the last century.

Then again many Psalms express jubilation, celebration, wonder and awe. *Make a joyful noise unto God, all ye lands* (66) is a tone repeatedly struck. *Sing unto God a new song* (120), with the sense that God is present throughout the cosmos, and everywhere at once awesome and delightful. *Let everything that lives and breathes give praise to the Lord* (150). The Hebrew title for the book of Psalms is *Tehillim*, derived from *hallel*, to praise (compare the word *hallelujah*), and means "Praises." *Whither shall I go from thy spirit, or whither shall I flee from thy presence? If I send up into heaven, thou art there. If I make my bed in hell, behold, thou art there. If I take the wings of the morning and dwell in the uttermost parts of the sea, even there shall thy hand lead me and thy right hand hold me* (139). This begins with an edge of fear, the suggestion of a wish to escape, but turns out to be very close to love-play, love-teasing, especially in its echo of the sensuousness of the Song of Songs: *his right hand is under my head, and his left hand embraces me.* The voice of the psalmist is the voice of one who would like to be experiencing this sublime wonder, this intimacy, this sense of being surrounded by a tenderly loving yet cosmically powerful God, day and night. Of course it doesn't happen that way, just as in our own relationships. The emotions of the Psalms surge and collapse like breaking waves, as they do in our own emotional lives. There is joy and despair and hope and frustration and fear and anger and grief and sorrow and then the desperation breaks like a wave into trust and joy again.

Uncontrollable, unpredictable. Scholars have tried in vain to find an orderly structure in the sequence of Psalms, since there is very little in the way of rhyme or reason to them. They are not rational, they are intense. Anyone who meditates knows how unruly the mind is. You try to still it and make it serene, and it fails to obey. This is what we find in the Psalms too. They are like a magnifying glass that seems to be looking at the presence and withdrawal of God, but in another sense can be said to be looking at the capacity of the mind to secrete its own calm—and then its inability to grasp that calm for more than moments at a time. What does remain constant throughout is faith that God exists, whether present or absent. *The fool says in his heart that there is no God* (14), but in the world of the Psalms, only a fool would think such a thing. In the world of the Psalms, God is ultimately our deliverer, we have only to trust. *They that sow in tears shall reap in joy* (126).

All this makes for magnificent poetry, obviously, and of the kind that survives translation in language, time, and space. The Psalms exist in hundreds of languages, and form an endless source for Jewish, Christian and Muslim culture. The idea of faith, love and devotion in the Psalms saturates the Gospels, whose early readers would of course have known the Psalms well, since they form a central part of Jewish liturgy. When Jesus in the Beatitudes says that the meek shall inherit the earth, he repeats the psalmist's wishful thinking. When he declares, "If any one thirst, let him come to me and drink," he takes the trope of spiritual thirst from Psalm 42. When on the cross he cries "My God, my God, why hast thou forsaken me," he is crying out as a Jew in his death as well as in his life.

The Psalms have inspired mystics through the centuries, and continue to inspire poets beyond the boundaries of conventional religion. Think, for example, of Whitman's insistence on celebrating every jot and tittle of the created world. Or the close of W H. Auden's elegy on W. B. Yeats, with its parallel death-and-rebirth motif: "Follow, poet, follow right / To the bottom of the night . . . With your uncomplaining voice / Still persuade us to rejoice . . . In the prison of his days / Teach the free man how to praise." How to praise is one great lesson of the Psalms. Literature in English is irrigated by these poems not only because of the multitude of memorable phrases in the King James Version that I and other poets steal, but because they are always telling us to celebrate, praise, open ourselves to the universe. That is the task of the poet, or at least I take it to be my task as a poet and a human being, to open myself in praise of an existence that inevitably includes suffering, anguish, pain, despair.

A poem by Sharon Olds typifies the way the Psalms can be used in ways that may seem shocking but are perfectly faithful to their spirit. The poem is called "Sex Without Love," and is an attempt to imagine how they "do it," the people who make love without love. "How do they come to the / come to the God come to the / still waters and not love / the one who came there with them."[2] Lifted directly from Psalm 23, the poem's stumbling incredulity assumes that when we do love the person we make love with, it is like that moment of blissful safety in the Psalms where we know ourselves to be cared for by the Lord who is our shepherd.

II

Magnificent poems. When I read them through the lens of politics, I shudder at their magnificence. It is perhaps a figure and ground problem. Let me point out that although there has been an explosion of scholarly and critical writing about the Bible by women in the last fifteen or twenty years, almost nothing has been written about the Book of Psalms by contemporary women scholars. That is rather curious. Part of the reason, surely, is that unlike books of the Bible like Genesis, Exodus, the Song of Songs, the Book of Ruth, or the Scroll of Esther, or even Proverbs, with its stereotyped portraits of the evil seductress and the good woman whose price is above rubies, no women at all appear in the Psalms. No Eve with her apple, no laughter of Sarah, no Miriam with her timbrels and her song.

But the problem runs deeper. We do not take literally the old idea that the Psalms were composed by King David, yet the psalmist often seems less a generic human than a public man. A politician, a warrior. The sun may rise in the Psalms like a bridegroom running to meet his bride, but nothing like domestic life or domestic imagery enters. What I hear—when I read consciously as a woman with antiwar tendencies—are the personal meditations and intimate feelings of a man who feels himself to be surrounded by enemies. Are his enemies personal rivals? Are they political or military foes? The categories seem virtually interchangeable. An enemy is an enemy. The psalmist's enemies are *evildoers, workers of iniquity*, and *adversaries*. They are *the proud* and *the heathen*. They *blaspheme* and are *violent*. They oppress the poor and the fatherless. And then again they *persecute* and *lay snares for* the psalmist.

How are we to interpret this motif? If the psalmist is David, the enemies might include King Saul who through much of Samuel I is trying to hunt down David and kill him. Or the enemies might be the Philistines, against whom David waged many battles. But what about us, the readers? Insofar as you and I identify with these poems, our most dangerous and hurtful enemy is probably a family member, a neighbor, a coworker, a boss. Perhaps an unspoken reason for the universal appeal of the Psalms is that ordinary people all over the world feel themselves to be at the mercy of enemies large and small. But here is the rub. In our lives, and the life of history, the animus against personal foes is made to accrue to public ones; the purpose of state propaganda is to funnel our frustration and anger against the foes of our rulers. We the people can always be manipulated to hate some demonized Other. At the same time, whatever damage we endure at the hands of those more powerful than ourselves can be taken out on whoever is weaker than ourselves. "Those to whom evil is done / Do evil in return," as Auden points out in "September 1, 1939," the poem most widely circulated in the wake of the World Trade Center attack. The interchangeability of public and private hostilities is finely mirrored by the ambiguities of the Psalms.

Fascinatingly, in this world of mighty rhetoric, the sins are commonly sins of the tongue. *His mouth is full of cursing and deceit and fraud* (10). They *have sharpened their tongues like a serpent* (140). Their *mouth speaketh vanity* (144). They are foes of Israel, foes of God, and the psalmist wants them destroyed. Is it yearning for goodness and justice on earth that drives his fantasies, is it yearning for vengeance, is it mere hatred of Otherness? Can we necessarily tell the difference? An enemy is an enemy. Occasionally the imagery of punishment is less than lethal, but it is always urgently physical. *Thou shalt break them with a rod of iron; thou shalt dash them in pieces like a potter's vessel* (2). *Break thou the arm of the wicked and the evil man* (10). *Upon the wicked shall he rain snares, fire and brimstone* (11). *The enemies of the Lord shall be as the fat of lambs: they shall consume; into smoke they shall consume away* (37). *Break their teeth, O God, in their mouth: break out the great teeth of the young lions, O lord. Let them melt away like water. . . . The righteous shall rejoice when he seeth the vengeance: he shall wash his feet in the blood of the wicked* (58). Magnificent poetry. Sublimated aggression (which, like latent energy, is easily converted to action). State propaganda. Psychological projection. All of the above. All.

Part of what makes the dream of punishing the enemy in the Psalms so forceful is the way punishment blooms like a flower from pathos. Poetically, the "turn" of numerous Psalms is from devastating grief to its redress, which is sometimes an expectation of deliverance in generalized terms and sometimes the more exciting promise that our enemies will be destroyed. Psalm 137, one of the most evocative in the psalter, speaks from the perspective of the Israelites driven into exile and slavery after the Babylonian destruction of Jerusalem in 587 B.C.E. In a way it is a typical psalm, full of unpredictable changes in tone. It begins with a picture of a crowd of people carrying their few belongings sitting by a river that is not their home. *By the waters of Babylon, there we sat down, yea, we wept when we remembered Zion. We hanged our harps upon the willows in the midst thereof. For there they that carried us away captive required of us a song; and they that wasted us required of us mirth, saying. Sing us one of the songs of Zion.* In these extraordinary opening lines, which audiences all over the world today know from Bob Marley's reggae version, we have a scene of conventional beauty—a river with its willows—suffused by a collective sorrow. The sitting down on the ground is extended by tears falling and harps hanging, further images of helplessness. Simultaneously the sitting and the hanging up of harps is also a kind of passive disobedience during a forced march. And is there not a relation between the waters of Babylon and the flowing tears? Then the mood shifts from simple grief to irony. The bitterness of being mocked by those who are stronger, which is such a powerful theme throughout Psalms, is particularly piercing here. *How can we sing the Lord's song in a strange land?* Nothing in poetry so succinctly captures the trauma of exile. Our enemies, who have conquered our land, destroyed our homes and our holy temple and are herding us along, are making fun of us by asking us to sing, in effect, a psalm. The demand is not only cruel but absurd. How can we sing God's song in a foreign land? The Hebrew Bible claims throughout that the children of Israel cannot separate their identity as a people from the land God has given them. This portion of Psalm 137 is like saying not only won't we sing, but we can't. Song cannot come out of us if we are not in our home place.

And then comes the moment of the vow. I may be in exile now, but I will never forget. These next lines at once intensify and reverse the grief at captivity: *If I forget thee, O Jerusalem, may my right hand forget her cunning. May my tongue cleave to the roof of my mouth if I remember not Jerusalem above my chief joy.* Notice the shift from first person plural to the singular "I," and how the hand that acts, the tongue that converses and sings, become subject to the mind that swears not to become assimilated to the alien culture. I do everything with my right hand, so these lines are asking to be paralyzed if I fail to cherish the memory of Jerusalem above every other pleasure in my life. And in fact the passion of the exile for the homeland has remained alive in Judaism for two thousand years since the destruction of the second temple in the year 70 CE. Jews in diaspora ritually promise each other "next year in Jerusalem" at the close of every year's Passover feast.

The poignance of the vow in Psalm 137 is extraordinary. It signals a spiritual triumph over the initial scene of powerlessness, as if declaring that Babylon may capture bodies but not souls. At this point the psalmist turns to God, reminding God of the destruction of His own sacred city: *Remember, O Lord, the children of Edom in the day of Jerusalem; who said, Rase it, rase it, even to the foundation thereof.* And finally comes the poem's prophetic conclusion: *O daughter of Babylon, who art to be destroyed, happy shall he be, that rewardeth thee as thou hast served us. Happy shall he be, that taketh and dasheth thy little ones against the stones.*

And there we have it, human history, the justification of every blood feud, every literal dashing of children's heads against walls by conquering armies, guerilla armies, occupying forces, terrorist suicide bombers, Arab and Jew, Serb and Bosnian, Hutu and Tutsi, Irish Protestants and Irish Catholics, Buddhist and Hindu in Sri Lanka, Hindu and Muslim throughout the Indian subcontinent, The Shining Path in Peru, to name a few current instances. Not to mention the Crusades, the Inquisition, the burning of heretics at the stake, the religious wars of the sixteenth and seventeenth century in England and Europe, the pogroms, the Holocaust. The righteous, with God on their side, joyously washing their feet in the blood of the wicked. Osama bin Laden, shortly after the September 11, 2001 attack that destroyed the World Trade Center, issued a statement broadcast throughout the Islamic world. Is not the rhetoric chillingly familiar?

> Praise be to God and we beseech Him for help and forgiveness.
>
> We seek refuge with the Lord. . . .
> He whom God guides is rightly guided but he whom God leaves
> to stray, for him wilt thou find no protector to lead him to the
> right way.
>
> I witness that there is no God but God and Mohammed is His slave
> and Prophet.
>
> God Almighty hit the United States at its most vulnerable spot.
> He destroyed its greatest buildings.
>
> Praise be to God.
>
> Here is the United States. It was filled with terror from its north to
> its south and from its east to its west.
>
> Praise be to God.
>
> They champion falsehood, support the butcher against the victim,
> the oppressor against the innocent child.
>
> May God mete them the punishment they deserve.

A handwritten document left behind by a leader among the hijackers, Mohammed Atta, urges the prospective hijacker/martyr: "You should pray, you should fast. You should ask God for guidance. . . . Purify your heart and clean it from all earthly matters." Among the prayers: "O God, open all doors for me. O God, who answers prayers and answers those who ask you, I am asking you for your help. . . . God, I trust in you. God, I lay myself in your hands."[3]

The Psalms are the prototype in English of devotional poetry and possibly of lyric poetry in general. Let nobody say that poetry makes nothing happen. Let nobody say that poetry cannot or should not be political. We have this model before us.

Jews, Christians, and Muslims, and pagans before us,[4] have worshiped a God— have created a God to worship—who is both tender and violent. God is father, judge, warrior, mighty arm, rock, redeemer, and (with a little help from his friends) destroyer of the godless, which in practice can mean anyone I take to be my enemy. Is there any way to get around this? A famous sermon by the German theologian Dietrich Bonhoeffer, written in 1937, at the brink of World War II (in which he died a martyr of the resistance to Hitler), tries to rescue Psalm 58, "this frightful psalm of vengeance," by claiming that it is not really we sinners who "are able to pray this psalm," but King David—or, rather, Jesus Christ praying from within David, for "only he who is totally without sin can pray like that" We sinners must entrust vengeance to God, and endure suffering "without a thought of hate, and without protest." Moreover, if we shudder at the image of the righteous splashing about in the blood of the guilty, we must understand that the death sentence has already been enacted on Jesus, "the Savior who died for the godless, struck down by God's revenge," that the "bloodstained Savior" redeems whoever prostrates himself at the Cross. Jesus, then, is both the psalm's author and its victim; the true Christian is not responsible. Still, Bonhoeffer's solution perpetuates a familiar rhetoric of "the godless," as if we could be certain who they are, and supports a vehemently traditional view of God as chief officer of retribution.[5] In effect, Bonhoeffer recommends that as good Christians we avoid guilt and leave the punishing of sinners to God. It sounds, though I hesitate to say so, like Pilate washing his hands.

A beautiful essay by Kathleen Norris, "The Paradox of the Psalms,"[6] takes another approach toward their violence. Norris writes of what she learned during a year-long residence at a Benedictine convent, where the Psalms are the liturgical mainstay, sung or recited at morning, noon and evening prayer. Asking "How in the world can we read . . . these angry and often violent poems from an ancient warrior culture, [that] seem overwhelmingly patriarchal, ill tempered, moralistic?" she answers that they reflect emotional reality—that the pain in them is essential for praise, that the Psalms are full of anger because "anger is one honest reaction to pain," that women who are trained to deny pain and anger—including Benedictine women—may find their expression healthy, and that "as one sister explained, the 'enemies' vilified in the cursing Psalms are best seen as 'my own demons, not enemies out there.'"

Of Psalm 137, Norris points out that it has a special poignance for women who experience the journey from girlhood to an adulthood that demands prettiness and niceness as a journey to exile. It also "expresses the bitterness of colonized people everywhere . . . the speaker could be one of today's refugees or exiles, an illegal alien working for far less than minimum wage, a slave laborer in China." The vision of brutal vengeance at its close, *O Babylon, . . . happy is he who repays you the ills you brought on us, happy is he who shall dash your children on the rock*, should come as no surprise, she observes; it is "the fruit of human cruelty." She goes on to say that psalms such as this ask us to recognize our own capacity for vengeance and to see it as "a potentially deadly vice" that may be "so consuming that not even the innocent are spared." We should, Norris says, pray over it. Good. But do the vengeance fantasies in the Psalms ask to be read this way? Or is it not rather Norris's rather special temperament that chooses so to read them? Aren't the vengeance fantasies in fact endorsed in the poems' theological framework? Endorsed, that is, by God? And, incidentally, is vengeance morally acceptable if it punishes "the guilty," and reprehensible only if it strikes "the innocent"? If so, we return to the sticky question of how guilt and innocence are to be determined, and the likelihood that "the guilty" and "my enemies" will be mysteriously identical.

We may twist on the hook as we will. Once we have bitten the bait of the Psalms we are in the power of a vision that mirrors our minds. The character of God in these splendid poems is also our projection, deny it as we may. We create him in our image and attribute holiness and power to him. Catherine Marsden, in "Notes on God's Violence," advocates facing the possibility that the Biblical God's character "alternates between tender care and ferocious brutality, between limitless creation and wholesale wreckage" not because the Biblical God rewards nice people and punishes bad ones, but because "the violence of the universe [is] at every point congruent with its nurturance" and because "Hebrew monotheism sets up one source for good and evil, one responsible will from which they both derive."[7]

The God who speaks to Job out of the whirlwind, that explosion of magnificent amoral creativity, is the God of the Psalms, but with the veil of righteousness removed. And can one love such a God? And if one refuses, does praise too dry up? On the other hand, if one denies God's violence, is that not a kind of blasphemy? Stephen Mitchell, the brilliant translator of the Book of Job, recognizes the Voice from the whirlwind as embodying "the clarity, the pitilessness, of nature and of all great art."[8] Mitchell rightly points out how closely this vision of Job resembles the magnificent and terrifying play of divine creation and destruction revealed to Arjuna at the climax of the *Bhagavad Gita*. He quotes Blake's *Marriage of Heaven and Hell:* "The roaring of lions, the howling of wolves, the raging of the stormy sea, and the destructive sword, are portions of eternity too great for the eye of man."[9] Yet I recently walked into a bookstore in Berkeley at a moment when Mitchell was reading his versions of Psalms, and was appalled to hear him omit the close of Psalm 137, letting the poem end with the image of Jerusalem as the exile's chief joy, and not the image of the Babylonian child's head being dashed against a rock. I thought: has New Age sentimental niceness claimed another victim? Is he trying to convert the Psalms to Buddhism? Is he trying to castrate God? Who does he think he is fooling?

Why does the Poet Laureate of America, after terrorism has destroyed the World Trade Center and several thousand human lives in New York City, claim that poetry is about personal and not political matters? And why on earth does he cite the Psalms as "against" acts of terror?

III

My poems wrestle with the need of God, the violence of god. I should rather say that I let these matters attack and wrestle with my poems.

In 1999 I was working on a manuscript provisionally entitled "the space of this dialogue," after a sentence of Paul Celan, "Only in the space of this dialogue does that which is addressed take form and gather around the I who is addressing it." The experience was not so much of writing as of receiving. The poems arrived intermittently, and I had undertaken not to tell them what to say. They often addressed God, not expecting a response. Early in the process I wrote down some lines and called them "psalm." They are more like an anti-psalm. They say this:

I am not lyric any more
I will not play the harp
for your pleasure

I will not make a joyful
noise to you, neither
will I lament

for I know you drink
lamentation, too,
like wine

so I dully repeat
you hurt me
I hate you

I pull my eyes away from the hills
I will not kill for you
I will never love you again

unless you ask me

What I recognize in the poem is my resistance to a God who deals cruelly with us and demands our praise. What the final line tells me is that I want to stop resisting. Perhaps I am like one of those abused women who keeps forgiving her abuser. You read about them. They phone the police and then hide their bruises and refuse to press charges. Another poem ventriloquizes a pious voice that could emerge from any of the monotheistic faiths, and concludes with a last line that is, alas, a vast understatement:

One of these days
oh one of these days
will be a festival and a judgment

and our enemies will be thrown
into the pit while we rejoice
and sing hymns

Some people actually think this way

Later in the manuscript, writing during the 1999 bombing of Kosovo in the former Yugoslavia—remembering that this war of Christian against Muslim is typical of religious wars through the ages, in which God is the gun with which we shoot our enemy—I ask God what he is thinking. The question precipitates a dialogue:

the spot of black point
in the gallon of white

makes it whiter

so the evil impulse
is part of you
for a reason

what reason

greater wilder holiness

*****

so perhaps you want us to understand
it throbs also in you
like leavening

you want us to love that about you
even if you pray that your attribute of mercy
may overcome your attribute of wrath

you want us always to love the evil also
the death-wish also
the bread of hate

because we are your image
confess you prize
the cruel theater of it

An ancient rabbinic story describes God praying in the ruins of the destroyed temple. For what, it is asked, does God pray? He prays that his attribute of mercy will overcome his attribute of justice; my poem slightly alters the story. More painfully, the unnamed responding voice makes a declaration I cannot deny. It brings me to my knees. It sickens me. I am very well aware that I, like just about everyone else I know, rubberneck at traffic accidents. Am outraged by—and avidly read about and discuss—the wickedness of Congress, the Administration, oil interests, anyone whose politics or moral principles deviate from my own, etcetera, etcetera. As Elizabeth Bishop says in her poem to Marianne Moore, "we can bravely deplore." And we all enjoy deploring, don't we? Later still, to my surprise, appear poems such as this, which is again entitled "Psalm":

I endure impure periods
when I cannot touch you

or even look at you
you are a storm I would be electrocuted

by your approach then I feel some sort of angelic laughter
like children behind a curtain

come, I think
you are at my fingertips my womb

you are the wild driver of my vehicle
the argument in my poem

nothing between us
only breath

Where did that come from? I cannot imagine. I feel myself to be an aperture through which the words arrive. Like the biblical Psalms, mine seem to be love poems to God. But I cannot justify my love.

Notes

1   National Public Radio, News Special, 3:00 P.M. ET. 11 September 2001.
2   Sharon Olds, *The Dead and the Living* (New York: Knopf, 1984), p. 57.
3   *The International Herald Tribune*, Saturday–Sunday, 29–30 September 2001, pp. 1, 4.
4   Jonas C. Greenfield, "The Holy Bible and Canaanite Literature Assembly of Gods," in *The Literary Guide to the Bible*, ed. Robert Alter and Frank Kermode (Cambridge, Mass.: Harvard University Press, 1987), p. 552, quotes as one example of the kind of poetry from which our psalms sprang:

Now, your enemy, O Ba'al
  now, you smite your enemy
    you strike your adversary;
you will take your eternal kingdom
  your everlasting dominion.

5   Dietrich Bonhoeffer, "Vengeance and Deliverance," in *A Testament to Freedom: The Essential Writings of Dietrich Bonhoeffer*, ed. Geffrey B. Kelly and F. Burton Nelson (New York: HarperCollins, 1990), pp. 293–298.
6   Kathleen Norris, "The Paradox of the Psalms," in *Out of the Garden: Women Writers on the Bible*, ed. Christina Bachmann and Celina Spiegel (New York: Ballantine, 1994), pp. 221–33.
7   Catherine Marsden, "Notes on God's Violence," *Cross-Currents* 51 (Summer 2001): 229–56.
8   *The Book of Job*, trans. Stephen Mitchell (New York: HarperCollins, 1992), p. xxi.
9   Ibid., p. xiv.

(d) Reading Job as Theological Disruption for a Post-Holocaust World

David C. Tollerton

Earth, do not cover my blood;
Let there be no resting place for my outcry![1] (Job 16:18)

This verse from Job's lament is engraved on memorials at numerous sites of Holocaust memory, such as the Belzec death camp, the Bergen-Belsen concentration camp, and the *Umschlagplatz* (collection point) in Warsaw from which Jews were transported to the Treblinka death camp. The reason for the perceived pertinence of Job's words is not difficult to discern. Their citation in this context reflects a desire not to allow the Holocaust's significance to be forgotten. The British theologian Isabel Wollaston notes the pervasiveness of this urge within the event's memorialization: "[o]ne thread that does remain constant is the insistence that the dead must not be forgotten." Yet she notes also that "any answer to the question 'why remember?' is inevitably influenced by perspective."[2] Secularists draw different meanings than do the religiously committed, Christians draw different meanings than do Jews, and Orthodox Jews draw different meanings than do non-Orthodox. Thus, explanations as to why, and how, the mass murder of Europe's Jews should not be forgotten can vary considerably.

The inner tensions that often characterize collective Holocaust memory should not, however, be necessarily viewed as an entirely negative phenomenon from the perspective of the urge to resist forgetfulness that has made Job 16:18 so resonant in this context. As Wollaston suggests, "Perhaps one of the most enriching ways of remembering the Holocaust is currently to be found in the continuing debates over what and how we remember."[3] What continuing memory requires is not its cementing into a fixed narrative but rather continuing discussion. Within Jewish theological responses to this event, this finds its articulation through a repeated refrain that the Holocaust's religious meaning should not be finalized. The death of six million Jews, as several commentators that will be discussed later in this article attest, should not be allowed to fall neatly into an untroubled place within broader theological narratives.

In this article, I will suggest that the book of Job is a text that can act as a useful resource within this process of resisting the petrifaction of both memory and theological response in this context.[4] The following will focus largely upon modern Jewish theology, though it should be noted that its concerns should nonetheless be of interest also to Christians wishing to contemplate how religious response to atrocity and the biblical might interact.

As one of the archetypal figures of innocent suffering in the HB, Job has been appealed to with frequency among commentators on the Holocaust.[5] The following is not meant as a complete survey of this. Rather, this article, through examining the receptions of the book by two Jewish-American theologians, Irving Greenberg and David Blumenthal, will instead make a new suggestion: that it is not only elements of Job's experiences in the biblical story that render this a resonant text for post-Holocaust thought but also the internal dissonances within the text that disrupt and hold in continued suspension the reader's theological certainties. This is a polyphonic text, it is proposed, that can because of the frequency of its reception in Holocaust memory act as a subversive force unsettling the foundations upon which may be constructed redemptive theodicies.

Job as a Disruptive Text

The book of Job is a text that possesses within itself theological fissures that refuse to resolve themselves entirely. This is a point that has been made by several biblical scholars, but is worth now briefly reconsidering before focusing upon how this interlinks with theological response to the Holocaust.

A useful prism through which to understand these fissures in the text's propositions regarding both the nature of suffering and how it should be responded to can be found in 42:7: "After the LORD had spoken these words to Job, the LORD said to Eliphaz the Temanite, 'I am incensed at you and your two friends, for you have not spoken the truth about Me as did My servant Job.'" This commendation of the protagonist causes at least two headaches for interpreters. The first relates to how innocent suffering should be properly responded to. Robert Gordis notes that there are "two radically different Jobs in the biblical masterpiece. One is the hero of the prose tale, whose righteousness is matched by his piety and who retains his faith and patience under the gravest of provocations. The other is the Job of the dialogue, a passionate rebel against the injustice of undeserved suffering, who challenges God Himself."[6] In the two opening prose chapters it is repeatedly emphasized in 1:22 and 2:10 that Job does not speak sinfully. His submissive attitude at this early stage of the story is exemplified by his comment in 1:21 that "the LORD has given, and the LORD has taken away; blessed be the name of the LORD." In the poetic dialogues that follow, Job's attitude radically changes as he wrestles with his friend's denials of his innocence and the seeming injustice of his plight, lamenting in 9:22–23 that God "destroys the blameless and the guilty" and "mocks as the innocent fail." From the whirlwind, God eventually repudiates Job for "[s]peaking without knowledge" (38:2).

His commendation of Job in 42:7 in the prose section (42:7–17) that follows God's poetic speeches from the whirlwind thus causes something of a difficulty for the reader. God's words might be in support of Job's rather ambiguous final response to the speeches in 42:1–6.[7] However, given that Job had according to God "spoken the truth" in 42:7 specifically in relation to his friends ("for you have not spoken the truth about Me as did My servant Job"), there is good justification for viewing this verse as a commendation of the protagonist's views in the earlier poetic dialogues with Eliphaz, Bildad, and Zophar. This is the view taken by Gordis, who cites the verse as evidence that "[t]he final judgement of the book is not that Job is wrong or blasphemous in challenging his Maker."[8] The problem, of course, is that if Job had "spoken well," God's speeches of repudiation of Job's theological rebellion in chs. 38–41 become difficult to draw fully into focus. Are Job's defiant words in the poetic dialogues to be viewed as cautionary (i.e., blasphemous) or exemplary (i.e., challenging injustice)?

The inner tensions of the book can be seen equally by focusing upon its propositions regarding the nature of innocent suffering and the manner in which 42:7 once again creates narrative disruption. Job begins the story described as both immensely pious and wealthy (1:1–3), suggesting a reality, common through much of the HB, in which people suffer or succeed according to merit. This is rapidly undermined, however, in the description of Job's suffering at the hands of a divine wager between God and the Satan (1:6–12), a wager premised upon Job's suffering being undeserved. It is a test of how he will respond in the future, rather than punishment for inequities in the past. Furthermore, as David Clines notes, with the development of the poetic dialogues between Job and his friends, a reality of divine rewards and punishments is again discredited: "[e]very time Job's friends fail to carry us with them in their denunciations of Job, and every time Job excites our admiration for his injured innocence, the poem convinces us that the doctrine of retribution is naïve, dangerous, inhuman, and, above all, false."[9]

If during much of the book of Job a theodicy of rewards/punishments lies discredited, the situation is nonetheless complicated by the final chapter in which Job is both commended by God (42:7) and then restored to a condition even greater than that described at the story's outset (42:10). While some, such as Norman Habel, have attempted to argue that this restoration is not a reward, the proximity between commendation and material restoration lends considerable weight to a reader's perception that the two are intimately connected.[10] The difficulties presented by this development are noted by Clines as he reflects that in ch. 42 Job's piety "has led to his ultimate superlative prosperity. What the book has been doing its best to demolish, the doctrine of retribution, is on its last page triumphantly affirmed."[11]

The commendation and reward of Job at the book's close thus act to upset any comfortingly clear and easily digestible message from the book. Whether, in the face of undeserved suffering, individuals should or should not rebel against God is a question left held in tension. Whether the cosmos is one bound together by a reality ruled by rewards and punishments is a question finally unanswered by the text. The book of Job is ultimately, as Carol Newsom has argued, a polyphonic text that is at times "overtly disjunctive" and contains within itself "different perspectives on the world."[12]

Resisting Theological Finality in Post-Holocaust Thought

In examining specifically the post-Holocaust reception of the book of Job in this article it is worth now turning aside from discussion of this biblical text and considering some broad points regarding theological response to this event of modern history. Only subsequent to this will focus turn to the weaving together of these dual concerns by examining two case studies of Job's utilization in this context.

The influential Holocaust survivor and novelist Elie Wiesel has been at the forefront of those wishing to avoid this atrocity's seamless integration into wider religious thought structures. An answer he makes to a question posed in a 1990 interview with Philippe-Michaël de Saint-Cheron is illustrative:

> [de Saint-Cheron]
> You would not argue that theodicy died in Auschwitz
> or that providence no longer exists?

> [Wiesel]
> I certainly do not agree with those who say: faith alone
> exists, faith stands above all else. That would amount
> to saying: have faith, and that's that. But neither would
> I agree with the claim that theodicy is dead. The moment
> an answer is given, I get suspicious; as a question,
> I accept it.[13]

What Wiesel seeks is not simply silence as such but rather a refusal for the conversation regarding the Holocaust's meaning to be ended and finalized or for its questions to be fully answered.[14] Wiesel's view is significant because, though not without his critics, he is as Alan Berger notes "widely perceived as a *moreh hador* (teacher of the generation)" because of the influence of his writings and public statements.[15] His resistance to answering the Holocaust theologically or placing it into settled continuity with a religious metanarrative is something more widely reflected by several Jewish practitioners of Holocaust Theology. In his 1998 study *(God) After Auschwitz*, Zachary Braiterman suggests that, with the works of Richard Rubenstein, Eliezer Berkovits, and Emil Fackenheim, we find a striving toward what he terms "antitheodicy"—a refusal to justify God.[16] Certainly with Fackenheim, whose writings constitute, according to one commentator, "the richest and most developed" Holocaust Theology, we see such an urge reflected in his comment that "[n]o meaning, redemptive or other, religious or secular, will ever be found in the Holocaust."[17]

A notable qualification to Braiterman's suggestion is, however, found in Josh Cohen's 2003 work, *Interrupting Auschwitz*. This book focuses upon a number of thinkers, such as Emmanuel Levinas, who see in the aftermath of the Holocaust an imperative "to refuse to bring thought to completion," that is, to refuse totalising ideologies or metanarratives to fully envelope the horrors of the event.[18] Yet while this broadly compliments Braiterman's suggestion that a refusal to seek theological resolution characterises three major figures of Holocaust Theology, Cohen is more suspicious of the antitheodic credentials of the theologians Braiterman cites. With Fackenheim, for example, Cohen questions whether his "sacralized narrative of Jewish history" in which the State of Israel "has ultimate ontological status" can be wholly viewed as nonredemptive theology.[19]

Within the present article, there is no intention to enter in detail into these specific debates. For the present, two general issues should be noted: (1) that there is an urge within response to the Holocaust to avoid theological finalizations of the event's significance, but (2) that suspicions have been raised in some quarters regarding the extent to which certain theological respondents are able fully to maintain the tensions entailed.

The following will examine these themes further with consideration of two post-Holocaust receptions of the book of Job. Both theologians, it will be suggested, seek to maintain theological tension in the aftermath of this atrocity within modern history. However, each, through his interpretation of Job, reveals a powerful countercurrent drifting toward more redemptive finalizations of the event's significance. By a more conscious foregrounding of the disruptive qualities of Job noted above, it will be suggested in conclusion that a resource can be found for subverting these foundations of theological resolution.

Job and the Abusing God for David Blumenthal

From the outset of his 1993 work *Facing the Abusing God*, the Conservative rabbi David Blumenthal views the Holocaust as an event that disturbs the foundations of normal theological discourse: "[h]ow *can* one speak of beauty or meaning with six million ghosts hovering in the background? . . . Caesura, brokenness, fragmentation are all we have to express the disjunction of normal discourse with the reality of the holocaust."[20] This sense of fragmentation Blumenthal perceives is reflected in certain structural characteristics of *Facing the Abusing God*. First, a key section of the book consists of commentary on four Psalms (27, 44, 109 and 128) in which, as Tod Linafelt has noted, "Blumenthal has constructed an intertextual field of exegesis reminiscent of the Talmud. . . . On each page the four voices surround the biblical text, vying for space and the reader's attention. Sometimes one voice dominates, at other times another voice does."[21] A similarly unambiguous move toward being multi-voiced is the inclusion of texts composed by other authors in response to Blumenthal. A significant component of this are the sequences of correspondence between Blumenthal and two commentators, one a victim of child abuse named Diane and the other the Christian theologian Wendy Farley.[22] As will be noted below, these voices are uneven, at times disagreeing markedly with Blumenthal. In including them, Isabel Wollaston notes, he is "resisting consistency and homogeneity."[23]

Central to his motivation for wishing to avoid theological finality is his view that the Holocaust raises serious questions about the goodness of God:

> *God is abusive, but not always.* God, as portrayed in our holy sources and as experienced by humans throughout the ages, acts, from time to time, in a manner that is so unjust that it can only be characterised by the term "abusive." In this mode, God allows the innocent to suffer greatly. In this mode, God "caused" the holocaust, or allowed it to happen.[24]

Blumenthal thus finds himself in the position of wishing to resist a theology that wholly justifies or legitimizes God. Out of this develops his call (reflected in the book's subtitle) for *A Theology of Protest*, and, in turn, his appeal to the figure of Job. For in focusing upon the defiant protagonist of the poetic dialogues, he declares that "[t]he theology of protest goes back to the Bible and is present most forcefully in the Book of Job."[25] Following this comment, Blumenthal considers Job's archetypal rebellion in the poetic section and finds a significant ally within Jewish tradition for his call for a "Theology of Protest."

Yet he is aware that this biblical text cannot be appropriated in such a way entirely without caveat. The closing sections of Job, he notes, present several difficulties for his reading. The first relates to the nature of the divine speeches in chs. 38–41:

> Further reflection on the ending of the book of Job . . . is very disquieting. In the ending according to the poetic section of the book of Job . . . God overwhelms and threatens Job. . . . What kind of God reacts in this way to a suffering loyal servant? What kind of personality does such a God have? . . . [T]he ending of the book of Job according to the poetic section reveals a God Who is an abuser.[26]

In this theologian's view, God's words from the whirlwind reconfirm the abusiveness of the divine which had been the original cause of Job's defiance. Yet worryingly in Blumenthal's view, Job's response in 42:1–6 is decidedly ambiguous and certainly not a "Theology of Protest" comparable to his earlier complaints:

> At the end of this tirade [God's speeches], Job responds in the most enigmatic of texts. . . . Does the enigmatic last sentence mean that Job was

so terrified that he repressed his question completely? Or does it mean that Job had a religious, or mystical, experience which transformed his question and his spiritual being to a higher plane?[27]

Commendably, Blumenthal provides no answer to these questions. His view of the rest of ch. 42 is similarly willing to recognise the ambiguities of the text: "The prose ending to the book of Job (42:7–17) is no easier to understand. . . . [D]id Job simply take up his relationship with God again, with no after-effects? Did Job accept his second blessing without question? Did he resume his pious life without reservation?"[28] Again, he does not answer these questions. Given that no answers are indeed provided by the biblical text, this is a sound approach to facing a book that, as a whole, does not resolve itself neatly into a single-voiced answer to the issues of undeserved suffering. In Job, Blumenthal has found a "Theology of Protest" resonant with the one he seeks to employ in a post-Holocaust context, but also a text that because of its polyphonic qualities does not in all its elements resonate wholly and completely.

Blumenthal's questions regarding the book of Job's appropriateness for post-Holocaust thought do not rest here however. Yet with his final queries regarding the text there can be seen a troubling hint toward the suggestion that his own appeals to the need for theological tensions and fragmentation in the aftermath of the mass murder of Europe's Jews are, in actuality, countervoiced by a significant drift toward redemptive foundations.

After noting the ambiguity of the closing sections of the book of Job and the difficulties it causes for viewing it as an exemplary evocation of a "Theology of Protest," Blumenthal focuses more fully on Job's silence after his restoration in the final chapter:

> The book of Job [is] . . . silent on the religious nature of life after suffering. . . . [A]buse has traumatized the text into a deep silence. But what *would* constitute a proper religious response to abuse in a life lived while healing from abuse? What would be an appropriate spiritual response to abuse within a life which is recovering from suffering?[29]

Unlike the earlier questions Blumenthal asked about the ambiguities of the book of Job's closing chapter, these questions are provided with a set of firm answers three pages later:

> *To have faith in God in a post-holocaust, abuse-sensitive world, we must: (1) acknowledge the awful truth of God's abusing behavior; (2) adopt a theology of protest and sustained suspicion; (3) develop the religious affections of distrust and unrelenting challenge; (4) engage the process of re-new-ed spiritual healing with all that entails of confrontation, mourning and empowerment; (5) resist the evil mightily, supporting resistance to abuse wherever it is found; (6) open ourselves to the good side of God, painful though that is; and (7) we must turn to address God, face to Face, presence to Presence.*[30]

Contained in these proposals are the dual movements toward protest and (at least partial) reconciliation. The hopefulness of the latter is rearticulated in the closing words of *Facing the Abusing God*, written in the form of a prayer: "We will believe in

You, we will place our hope in You. We will yearn for You, we will wait for You, and we will anticipate the time when we will see Your Face again. Amen."[31]

The difficulty here is that some will find the idea of hopefulness in a God who "'caused' the holocaust, or allowed it to happen" simply too problematic a notion, and suspect that Blumenthal is sliding hints of redemptive theology into his narrative via the back door.[32] One of the most interesting elements of *Facing the Abusing God* is the extent to which criticism of this sort emerges from its own pages—specifically from Blumenthal's correspondence partners. In both sets of correspondence, his partners are ultimately resistant to his gestures of reconciliation toward those who are the sources of abuse. Diane declares finally, in the last line of her last letter, that these sources "cannot be excused."[33] Wendy Farley reflects, "*I can't imagine worshipping an abusive father. Psychologically, it is neurotic and ethically it is immoral. . . . You are like someone counselling the abused wife to be a good, obedient wife and take her beatings passively.*"[34] In her final letter she declares that "[y]ou do not take seriously your own claims about God, about anger, abuse, etc."[35]

Their objections rest on perceiving Blumenthal's position as a narrative that drifts inexorably toward resolution. This is resolution in which the "You" of one of the book's final sentences—"We will believe in You, we will place our hope in You"—refers to a divine source of horrendous abuse.[36]

Blumenthal's post-Holocaust reception of Job intertwines with two quite distinct theological movements. The first is to identify where in this biblical book there is (and sometimes is not) to be found something akin to the "Theology of Protest" at an abusive God. This divine responsibility for the Holocaust motivates his expressions of anguish at the idea of a unified, unfragmented theological discourse in the aftermath of the event. Yet his final critical comments regarding the failure in Job to present an ongoing relationship between God and the sufferer of abuse attest to a countervoice in Blumenthal's theology. This is the drift toward resolution and hopefulness with a divinity-as-source-of-suffering Wendy Farley describes as "neurotic."[37]

"Job and Renewed Divine Encounter" for Irving Greenberg

In Blumenthal's *Facing the Abusing God*, we find protestations of the need to refuse theological finalizations of the Holocaust alongside an assertive confidence in the possibility of ongoing hope and relationship with God.[38] That holding both these positions is difficult to maintain is reflected by the unease of his respondents. Another post-Holocaust thinker whose reception of the book of Job intersects with such a difficulty is the Orthodox rabbi Irving Greenberg in his essay "Cloud of Smoke, Pillar of Fire," first delivered at a 1973 symposium on the Holocaust. This work is, in Steven Katz's view, the "most important statement" among Greenberg's numerous article-length publications discussing the theological ramifications of the event.[39]

"Cloud of Smoke, Pillar of Fire" covers considerable ground. Greenberg outlines how he considers the Holocaust to be an event that challenges, in different ways, the secularism and humanism of modernity, Christianity and its traditions of anti-Judaism, and Judaism's own view of its covenantal relationship with God. Within the discussion, he appeals to Job as a biblical archetype "that could come to the fore in a post-Holocaust interpretation of the relationship between God and man."[40] Like Blumenthal, however, Greenberg has his partial doubts about the post-Holocaust resonance of this book and, indeed, begins his treatment with a disclaimer related to the protagonist's final restoration in ch. 42. He states that "the ending of the book, in which Job is restored and has a new wife and children, is of course unacceptable by our principle. Six million murdered Jews have not been and cannot be restored."[41] Greenberg is not unique among post-Holocaust thinkers to have asserted the difficulty of such a parallel. Elie Wiesel reflects that the epilogue "is too abrupt. Too obvious. God says: let us forget our misunderstanding, and Job, a true gentleman, is willing to oblige. And, all of a sudden, Job is once again wealthy, respected and fulfilled."[42]

With Greenberg's reception of the book of Job, however, it should be stressed that this difficulty in paralleling the protagonist's restoration with post-Holocaust theology is not the resting point of his reading. He moves beyond this initial disclaimer by placing more positive meaning on God's appearance in the whirlwind in chs. 38–42:

> [Job's] suffering is not justified by God, nor is he consoled by the words about God's majesty and the grandeur of the universe surpassing man's understanding. Rather, what is meaningful in Job's experience is that in the whirlwind the contact with God is restored. That sense of Presence gives the strength to go on living in the contradiction. The theological implications of Job, then, are the rejection of easy pieties or denials and the dialectical response of looking for, expecting, further revelations of the Presence. This is the primary religious dimension of the reborn State of Israel for all religious people. When suffering had all but overwhelmed Jews and all but blocked out God's Presence, a sign out of the whirlwind gave us the strength to go on, and the right to speak authentically of God's Presence still.[43]

Two key issues should be noted in response to this quotation. The first is that, as well as having previously rejected the notion that Job's restoration parallels a post-Holocaust restoration of the Jewish people, Greenberg here also rejects the idea that Job receives any specific information from the whirlwind that might constitute a theological "answer" to innocent suffering, be it Job's or that of the Jewish people in modernity. Greenberg's presence-oriented reading of the speeches allows him to make (or at least appear to make) a subtle distinction in his theology. The foundation of the State of Israel is, in his view, endowed with significant theological import as an event that provides "the right to speak authentically of God's Presence still."[44] Yet in distinguishing between there being a substantive "message" in the speeches from mere "presence," he is able to imply that this does not mean that the state provides anything akin to an "answer" to the Holocaust. The Jewish people, as has been noted, have not for Greenberg been 'restored' in a manner comparable to Job at the close of the book. The State of Israel does not amount to theological solution to the mass murder of Europe's Jews just as God's speeches do not, in his reading, answer all of the theological questions and tensions left unresolved at the end of the book of Job.

The second issue to consider in relation to this quotation concerns its references to "living in contradiction" and "dialectical response"—phrases that touch upon one of the central elements of Greenberg's theological response to the Holocaust: a resistance to theological finality. He declares earlier in this publication that "[t]he Holocaust offers us only dialectical moves and understandings—often moves that stretch our capacity to the limit and torment us with their irresolvable tensions."[45] A key element of this irresolvable tension is Greenberg's notion of "moment faiths": "We now have to speak of 'moment faiths,' moments when the Redeemer and vision of redemption are present, interspersed with times when the flames and smoke of the burning children blot out faith—though it flickers again."[46] As recently as 2006, Greenberg has described the idea of "moment faiths" as being at the core of his response to the Holocaust.[47]

This concept is one that underlies his reading of Job in "Cloud of Smoke, Pillar of Fire." For God's appearance in the whirlwind does not, in Greenberg's view, amount to providing the theological finality of an intellectual "answer" to the problem of innocent suffering but rather is a "moment faith" "when the Redeemer and vision of redemption are present."[48] In terms of modern Jewish history, this moment is specifically the creation of the State of Israel.

Yet it can be suggested that there is also another, more subtle way in which the notion of "moment faiths" influences his post-Holocaust reception of Job. One of the notable characteristics of this reception is that Greenberg makes no reference to Job's more theologically radical responses to his afflictions in the biblical text. He writes, "It is interesting that his wife proposes that Job 'curse God and die'; his friends propose that he is being punished for his sins. Job rejects both propositions."[49] Job's rejections of these proposals are, of course, important for the story's plot and furthermore fit notably with Greenberg's proposal of a theology of tension ("moment faiths") in which suffering is not simply accepted, nor is God wholly rejected. However, the absence, particularly, of explicit reference to Job's at-times defiant attitude toward God (as well as his friends) is nonetheless significant. Given the tension implied at the heart of Greenberg's theology, one might expect Job's theological rebellion to have a resonance for his thought (in a way comparable to Blumenthal)—at least at those times when faith "is blotted out."

It will be suggested here that the reason why Greenberg focuses upon the "Presence" of the divine speeches rather than Job's defiance relates to a difficulty with his notion of "moment faiths." This difficulty is that the tension espoused is not maintained within his theology and is ultimately somewhat artificial. One way of considering this is to focus upon Greenberg's view of the foundation of the State of Israel in "Cloud of Smoke, Pillar of Fire." In this work it is repeatedly underlined that this event is one in which divine presence can be seen:

> [T]he 'secular' State of Israel is revealed for the deeply religious state that it is. . . . The real point is that after Auschwitz, the existence of the Jew is a great affirmation and an act of faith. The re-creation of the body of the people, Israel, is renewed testimony to Exodus as ultimate reality, to God's continuing presence in history proven by the fact that his people, despite the attempt to annihilate them, still exist.[50]

For the notion of "moment faiths" this immediately raises problems. Israel is, for Greenberg, evidence that ultimately God's presence in history is confirmed. This is problematic because "moment faiths" requires that the destruction of faith be taken as seriously as its affirmation. But it is questionable whether his language in this quotation really allows this kind of equality.

In this quotation, he asserts that the foundation of the state "is renewed testimony to Exodus as ultimate reality, to God's continuing presence in history." The word *ultimate* is revealing. For if Exodus—a key example of God's saving providence in Israel's history—is the "ultimate reality," the affirmation and denial inherent in "moment faiths" can be, at most, merely an outward appearance of what is, when perceiving the "ultimate reality," in the final analysis affirmation alone.

From this overview of what is suggested here to be Greenberg's failure to properly maintain the tension inherent in his concept of "moment faiths" comes a greater sense of why Job's rebellion has little resonance for this theologian. Theological defiance is, within his theology, ultimately superfluous. By focusing upon the providential nature of the foundation of the State of Israel as reflecting the "ultimate reality," it is clear that for all the questions raised by the Holocaust, there nonetheless remains a redemptive bedrock to history.[51] The defiant Job of the poetic dialogues is in this instance of little meaning to a view that is ultimately conciliatory toward God. The foundation of Greenberg's thought is a reality in which it is the divine presence during Job 38–42 that is meaningful rather than the protagonist's lament during the poetic dialogues.

[. . .]

There are at least two reasons for supporting the view that "resolving" the Holocaust theologically should be resisted. The first relates to ethics and the second to memory. Regarding the former, it can be suggested that there is good reason for wishing to resist rendering the mass murder of Europe's Jews "acceptable" in religious terms. If it is rendered thus, what might be deemed "acceptable" in the future? The second issue, related to memory, concerns a dynamic noted at the outset of this article—that it is through ongoing debate regarding the Holocaust's significance for contemporary thought, rather than resolution of its meaning, that tangible memory and reflection continues. The alternative is silence that with time becomes increasingly divested of meaningful engagement and contemplation.[52]

How might the book of Job be read and used as a resource of value in this context? The answer, it is suggested here, is to foreground its elements of inner dissonance and allow it to act as a subversive force within Holocaust memory. As has been noted, this is a text referred to with frequency in this context. What is being proposed here is a view of Job as a text that constantly questions its own reception and the theological frameworks into which its interpreters are attempting to integrate it. This is a biblical story that can by turns reassure, disturb, confound, and intrigue. In response to an event of horror in modernity requiring constant reappraisal of its demands upon contemporary thought, Job is a text that can be used as a resource that, specifically in the field of theology, interrupts finality rather than closing off conversation.

Notes

1   This biblical verse, as with all cited in the following (except those contained within quotations), is taken from the 1988 NJPSV.

2   Isabel Wollaston, *A War against Memory: The Future of Holocaust Remembrance* (London: SPCK, 1996), 6.

3   Ibid., 88–89.

4   This is a suggestion made as a personal outsider to inner-Jewish debates and is thus no more or less than what it is described as: a suggestion.

5   The following is only a limited selection of works specifically focused upon Job's post-Holocaust reception: Robert Dedman, "Job as Holocaust Survivor," *Saint Luke's Journal of Theology* 26 (1983): 165–85; Murray J. Haar, "Job after Auschwitz," *Int* 53 (1999): 265–75; Stephen Kepnes, "Job and Post-Holocaust Theodicy," in *Strange Fire: Reading the Bible after the Holocaust* (ed. Tod Linafelt; Sheffield; Sheffield Academic Press, 2000), 252–66; Henry F. Knight "Facing the Whirlwind Anew: Looking over Job's Shoulders from the Shadows of the Storm," in *Remembering for the Future* (ed. John K. Roth and Elisabeth Maxwell; New York: Palgrave, 2001), 745–59; Richard L. Rubenstein, "Job and Auschwitz," *USQR* 25 (1970): 421–37; David C. Tollerton, "Emancipation from the Whirlwind: Piety and Rebellion among Jewish-American Post-Holocaust and Christian Liberation Readings of Job," *Studies in Christian-Jewish Relations* 2/2 (2007): 70–91.

6   Robert Gordis, *The Book of God and Man: A Study of Job* (Chicago: University of Chicago Press, 1965), 219.

7   Though usually interpreted as repentance on Job's part, there are certain ambiguities in the text. See B. Lynne Newell, "Job: Repentant or Rebellious?" in *Sitting with Job: Selected Studies on the Book of Job* (ed. Roy B. Zuck; Grand Rapids: Baker, 1992), 441–56.

8   Robert Gordis, "A Cruel God or None: Is There No Other Choice?" in *Wrestling with God: Jewish Responses during and after the Shoah* (ed. Steven T. Katz; Oxford: Oxford University Press, 2007), 493.

9   David Clines, "Deconstructing the Book of Job," in *The Bible as Rhetoric: Studies in Biblical Persuasion and Credibility* (ed. Martin Warner; London: Routledge, 1990), 69.

10 Norman Habel suggests that "the restoration of Job's family and goods was a gesture of divine goodness, not a reward for Job's integrity or heroic persistence. God freely chooses to bless Job with good, just as he chose to afflict him with evil" (*The Book of Job* [London: SCM, 1985], 67).

11 Clines, "Deconstructing," 71.

12 Carol A. Newsom, *The Book of Job: A Contest of Moral Imaginations* (Oxford: Oxford University Press, 2003), 16. For another exploration of Job as a polyphonic text that usefully queries elements of Newsom's approach, see T. Stordalen, "Dialogue and Dialogism in the Book of Job," *SJOT* 20 (2006): 18–37.

13 Elie Wiesel and Philippe-Michaël de Saint-Cheron, *Evil and Exile* (Notre Dame: University of Notre Dame Press, 1990), 9.

14 Terrence Des Pres has therefore suggested that "the tension between silence and the need of the witness to speak, is the matrix of meaning on which Wiesel's accomplishment stands" ("The Authority of Silence in Elie Wiesel's Art," in *Confronting the Holocaust: The Impact of Elie Wiesel* [ed. Alvin H. Rosenfeld and Irving Greenberg; Bloomington: Indiana University Press, 1978], 50–51).

15 Alan L. Berger, "Elie Wiesel," in *Interpreters of Judaism in the Late Twentieth Century* (ed. Steven T. Katz; Washington, DC: B'nai B'rith, 1993), 383. For a more critical reading of Wiesel's influence, see Michael Goldberg, *Why Should Jews Survive? Looking Past the Holocaust Toward a Jewish Future* (New York: Oxford University Press, 1995), 59.

16 For his introductory comments on this thesis, see Zachary Braiterman, *(God) After Auschwitz: Tradition and Change in Post-Holocaust Thought* (Princeton, NJ: Princeton University Press, 1998), 3–4.

17 Michael Morgan, *Beyond Auschwitz: Post-Holocaust Jewish Thought in America* (Oxford: Oxford University Press, 2001), 155; Emil Fackenheim, *God's Presence in History* (Northvale, NJ: Jason Aronson, 1997 [original, 1970]), x.

18 Josh Cohen, *Interrupting Auschwitz: Art, Religion, Philosophy* (New York: Continuum, 2003), xvii.

19 Ibid., 18.

20   David R. Blumenthal, *Facing the Abusing God: A Theology of Protest* (Louisville: Westminster John Knox, 1993), 8–9 (emphasis original).

21   Tod Linafelt, "Reading the Hebrew Bible after the Holocaust: Toward an Ethics of Interpretation," in *The Holocaust: Lessons for the Third Generation* (ed. Dominick A. Iorio et al.; New York: University Press of America, 1997), 140.

22   Blumenthal, *Facing the Abusing God*, 195–225.

23   Isabel Wollaston, "The Possibility and Plausibility of Divine Abusiveness or Sadism as the Premise for a Religious Response to the Holocaust," *JRS* 2 (2000): 10.

24   Blumenthal, *Facing the Abusing God*, 247 (emphasis original).

25   Ibid., 250–51.

26   Ibid., 254–55.

27   Ibid.

28   Ibid., 255.

29   Ibid., 256 (emphasis original).

30   Ibid., 259 (emphasis original).

31   Ibid., 299.

32   Ibid., 247.

33   Cited in ibid., 209.

34   Cited in ibid., 221.

35   Cited in ibid., 224 (emphasis original).

36   Ibid., 299.

37   Cited in ibid., 209.

38   The phrase "Job and renewed divine encounter" is taken from a subheading within Irving Greenberg's "Cloud of Smoke, Pillar of Fire: Judaism, Christianity, and Modernity after the Holocaust," in *Auschwitz: Beginning of a New Era? Reflections on the Holocaust* (ed. Eva Fleischner; New York: Ktav, 1977), 34.

39   Steven T. Katz, *Historicism, the Holocaust and Zionism: Critical Studies in Modern Jewish Thought and History* (New York: New York University Press, 1992), 225.

40   Greenberg, "Cloud of Smoke," 34.

41   Ibid., 34. Though of only minor relevance to Greenberg's main point, it is worth noting that the text of Job does not suggest that the protagonist has a *new* wife in ch. 42.

42   Elie Wiesel, "Job," in *Peace, In Deed: Essays in Honor of Henry James Cargas* (ed. Zev Garber and Richard Libowitz; Atlanta: Scholars Press, 1998), 132. For a contrasting view, see Jonathan Sacks, *Crisis and Covenant: Jewish Thought after the Holocaust* (Manchester: Manchester University Press, 1992), 46–47.

43   Greenberg, "Cloud of Smoke," 34–35.

44   Ibid., 35.

45   Ibid., 22.

46   Ibid., 27.

47   Irving Greenberg, "Theology after the Shoah: The Transformation of the Core Paradigm," *Modern Judaism* 26 (2006): 213.

48   Greenberg, "Cloud of Smoke," 27.

49   Ibid., 34.

50   Ibid., 48.

51   This redemptive bedrock is also seen in Greenberg's notion of history as articulated in later works: "the world and the life that emerges within it are grounded in the infinite sources of life and energy which we call God. As the continuum of life unfolds, the emerging life becomes more and more God-like—more and more valuable, more and more responsive to others, more and more free" ("Voluntary Covenant," in *Contemporary Jewish Religious Responses to the "Shoah"* [ed. Steven L. Jacobs; Lanham, MD: University Press of America, 1993], 78).

52   Isabel Wollaston makes a point not dissimilar in noting that sites of memorial, unless they engage their visitors and force them to consider the Holocaust's significance, will become simply familiar and unnoticed elements of the landscape (*The War against Memory*, 36).

Chapter 6

Metaphor and Allegory

Metaphor requires that we apprehend likeness and difference simultaneously and instantaneously.

Alicia Ostriker, 'A Holy of Holies: The Song of Songs as Countertext' (2000)[1]

It is hardly surprising that only here in biblical poetry do we encounter such enchanting interfusions between the literal and metaphorical realms, because only here is the exuberant gratification of love through all five senses the subject.

Robert Alter, 'The Garden of Metaphor' (1985)[2]

THE EXTENSIVE USE OF figurative language in the Bible is no surprise given the scope of the story that it tells: literal specificity may be useful when writing a technical manual but it is less appropriate when talking about cosmic matters of creation, exodus, exile, redemption and eschatology. Furthermore, the ability of figurative language to cross multiple worlds and speak of more than one thing at a time offers some assistance to those seeking a way of talking about God through finite language. While apophatic theology (speaking about God in terms of what he is not) offers one response to the philosophical problem of God talk, kataphatic theology (speaking about God through positive terminology) and its extensive use of analogy and image shows the contribution that figurative language can make to describing who God is and what he is like (the rock of our salvation, the sacrificial Lamb, the light of the world, etc.).[3]

The ambiguity of figurative language can be seen as both a hindrance and help. For Northrop Frye, such language gains more than it loses, and his reading of the Bible begins with an attempt to rescue the Bible from a modern presumption that the literal, whether in its historical or scientific guises, is the highest form of truth. In a range of works, including *The Great Code* (1982) and the essay on 'The Double Vision of Language' (1991) included here, Frye reminds us that literal readings of the Bible developed over time (rather than being natural or fundamental) and can be very limited. Although many of the modern (post 1750) debates about the Bible have focussed on questions of historical veracity or literal truth, the majority of the language in Scripture is figurative rather than technical. Figurative language is most apparent in Wisdom

literature such as the Psalms, the Book of Job and the Song of Songs, but it also dominant in prophetic and apocalyptic writings (e.g. Hosea, Isaiah, Ezekiel, Daniel and
Revelation), pervasive in the Gospels, and common in the Pentateuch, the history
books, and the letters of the New Testament. Frye's own literary reading of Scripture
is rooted in myth, which he describes as 'story or narrative', and metaphor, which he
thinks of as 'figured language'. The advantage of such literary reading, he claims, is the
freedom it offers. Although Frye recognizes the historical dimension of the Gospels, he
argues that myth and metaphor enable the biblical narrative to offer a counter-history
that exposes the limitation of our human grasp of reality. Frye's reading draws on a
similar line of argument to that made by Paul Ricoeur in *The Rule of Metaphor* (1975,
translated 1977), which insists on the ability of metaphor to re-describe the world
rather than simply provide a secondary substitute for clearer and more precise language.
For Frye, metaphor enables 'imaginative literalism' and is key to his account of the
Bible's 'vision of [a] spiritual life that continues to transform and expand our own'.

Although the potential of figurative language is obvious in Frye's ambitious argument for myth and metaphor, the possible weakness of such talk is also apparent in his
writing and that of others who favour this approach. Figurative language can lead to a
lack of specificity or, conversely, to readings that move too quickly to resolve ambiguity. The multi-dimensional ambiguity of figurative language can lose sight of historical particularity or encourage readings that translate a more obvious meaning into
something quite different. This last danger has often been exemplified in Christian readings of the Song of Songs that replace the language of love in the biblical text with less
erotic talk of Christ's love for his Church. But perhaps thinking that we must choose
between naturalistic and allegorical readings of the love imagery in the Song of Songs
is misguided and a sign of interpreters' struggle to live with the different possibilities
that figurative language endeavours to keep open. The multiple interpretative possibilities of the language used in the Song of Songs is central to Paul Ricoeur's essay on 'The
Nuptial Metaphor', which appears in *Thinking Biblically: Exegetical and Hermeneutical
Studies* (1998). In the extract included here, which is part of a much longer account of
the 'multiple, flowering history of reading' of the Song of Songs, Ricoeur begins by
reflecting on the insights made available through a historical-critical close reading of
this biblical text. Ricoeur shows how attention to history and form are compatible with
allegorical readings rather than in opposition to them. At the heart of his argument is
the idea that a close reading of the poem reveals its indeterminate quality: we are never
entirely sure who the lover is that speaks nor the identity of the beloved to whom their
comments are addressed. Furthermore, the 'literary form of the poem contributes to'
the 'subtle liberation of the nuptial' from the 'erotic within which it is rightly enmeshed',
weaving together a series of metaphors (such as the body and landscape) which speak
of sex without doing so exclusively. In other words, the content of the metaphors is
marked as sexual but its indirect language finds space for other readings too.

Harold Fisch finds a similar level of complexity in this biblical text and shares
Ricoeur's reluctance to set the sexual and the allegorical in opposition. In the extract
here from *Poetry with a Purpose: Biblical Poetics and Interpretation* (1988), which is
part of a longer reading of the 'allegorical imperative' in the Song of Songs, Fisch
describes the inevitability of interpreting the figurative language of this biblical text in
a way that is continuous with all allegorical readings, ancient and modern: 'A text so

obviously symbolical, so rich in imaginative suggestions and reference, also so mysterious, calls out peremptorily for interpretation. Critics will be driven by the text itself to
construct allegorical schemes [. . .]'. On this reading, allegorical readings, whether those
of the Rabbis, the Church, or modern interpreters, should not be seen as an outside imposition on the biblical text but as an unavoidable response to its extensive use of figuration. If this is so, then we might think of figurative language as entirely appropriate for
a biblical narrative that invites others to find their place within it and retell its story.

Notes

1   Alicia Ostriker, 'A Holy of Holies: The Song of Songs as Countertext' in *The
     Feminist Companion to the Song of Songs*, ed. by Athalya Brenner and Carole
     Fontaine (Sheffield: Sheffield Academic Press, 2000), pp. 36–54 (p. 48).
2   Robert Alter, 'The Garden of Metaphor', in *The Art of Biblical Poetry* (New York:
     Basic Books, 1985), pp. 185–203 (p. 199).
3   For further discussion of apophatic talk of God, see Arthur Bradley, *Negative
     Theology and Modern French Philosophy* (London: Routledge, 2004) and William
     Franke, ed., *On What Cannot be Said: Apophatic Discourses in Philosophy,
     Religion, Literature and the Arts. Volume 1: Classic Formulations* (Notre Dame:
     Notre Dame University Press, 2007).

Further reading

Davies, Michael, *Graceful Reading: Theology and Narrative in the Works of John Bunyan*
     (Oxford: Oxford University Press, 2002)
Dillie, Sarah, *Mixing Metaphors: God as Mother and Father in Deutero-Isaiah* (London:
     Continuum, 2004)
Frye, Northrop, *The Great Code: The Bible and Literature* (London: Routledge and
     Kegan Paul, 1982)
Prickett, Stephen, *On the Origins of Narrative: The Romantic Appropriation of the Bible*
     (Cambridge: Cambridge University Press, 1996)
Ricoeur, Paul, *The Rule of Metaphor* (Toronto: University of Toronto Press, 1977)
Sherwood, Yvonne, *The Prostitute and the Prophet: Hosea's Marriage in Literary-
     Theoretical Perspective* (Sheffield: Sheffield Academic Press, 1996)
Soskice, Janet, *Metaphor and Religious Language* (Oxford: Clarendon Press, 1985)
—, *The Kindness of God: Metaphor, Gender and Religious Language* (Oxford: Oxford
     University Press, 2007)
Turner, Denys, *Eros and Allegory: Medieval Exegesis of the Song of Songs* (Kalamazoo,
     MI: Cistercian Publications, 1995)

(a) The Double Vision of Language

Northrop Frye

Michael explains to Adam, in the last book of Milton's *Paradise Lost*, that tyranny exists
in human society because every individual in such a society is a tyrant within himself,

or at least is if he conforms acceptably to his social surroundings. The well-adjusted individual in a primitive society is composed of what Paul calls the *soma psychikon*, or what the King James Bible translates as the "natural man" (1 Corinthians 2:14). He has, or thinks he has, a soul, or mind, or consciousness, sitting on top of certain impulses and desires that are traditionally called "bodily." "Body" is a very muddled metaphor in this context: we should be more inclined today to speak of repressed elements in the psyche. In any case the natural man sets up a hierarchy within himself and uses his waking consciousness to direct and control his operations. We call him the natural man partly because he is, first, a product of nature, and inherits along with genetic code the total devotion to his own interests that one writer has called "the selfish gene."[1]

Second, he is a product of his social and ideological conditioning. He cannot distinguish what he believes from what he believes he believes, because his faith is simply an adherence to the statements of belief provided for him by social authority, whether spiritual or temporal. As with all hierarchies, the lower parts are less well adjusted than the upper ones, and "underneath" in the restless and squirming body, or whatever else we call it, is a rabble of doubts telling him that his intellectual set-up is largely fraudulent. He may shout down his doubts and trample them underfoot as temptations coming from a lower world, but he is still what Hegel calls an unhappy consciousness.[2]

For reassurance, he looks around him at the society which reflects his hierarchy in a larger order. A society composed of natural men is also a hierarchy in which there are superiors and inferiors, and if such a society has any stability, one draws a sense of security from one's social position, even if it is "inferior." Discontented inferiors, of course, are the social counterpart of doubts, and also have to be trampled underfoot. It is easy to see why the two most influential thinkers of the twentieth century are Marx and Freud: they were those who called attention, in the social and the individual spheres respectively, to the exploitation in society, to the latent hysteria in the individual, and to the alienation produced by both.

Inside one's natural and social origin, however, is the embryo of a genuine individual struggling to be born. But this unborn individual is so different from the natural man that Paul has to call it by a different name. The New Testament sees the genuine human being as emerging from an embryonic state within nature and society into the fully human world of the individual, which is symbolized as a rebirth or second birth, in the phrase that Jesus used to Nicodemus [John 3:3]. Naturally this rebirth cannot mean any separation from one's natural and social context, except insofar as a greater maturity includes some knowledge of the conditioning that was formerly accepted uncritically. The genuine human being thus born is the *soma pneumatikon*, the spiritual body (1 Corinthians 15:44). This phrase means that spiritual man is a body; the natural man or *soma psychikon* merely has one. The resurrection of the spiritual body is the completion of the kind of life the New Testament is talking about, and to the extent that any society contains spiritual people, to that extent it is a mature rather than a primitive society.

The Crisis in Language

What concerns me in this situation is a linguistic fallacy, the fallacy that relates to the phrase "literally true." Ordinarily, we mean by "literally true" what is descriptively accurate. We read many books for the purpose of acquiring information about the world outside the books we are reading, and we call what we read "true" if it seems to be a satisfactory verbal replica of the information we seek. This conception of literal meaning as descriptive works only on the basis of sense experience and the logic that connects its data. That is, it works in scientific and historical writing. But it took a long time before such descriptive meaning could be fully matured and developed, because it depends on technological aids. We cannot describe phenomena accurately in science before we have the apparatus to do so; there cannot be a progressive historical knowledge until we have a genuine historiography, with access to documents and, for the earlier periods at least, some help from archaeology. Literalism of this kind in the area of the spiritual instantly becomes what Paul calls the letter that kills [2 Corinthians 3:6]. It sets up an imitation of descriptive language, a pseudo-objectivity related to something that isn't there.

In the early Christian centuries it was widely assumed that the basis of Christian faith was the descriptive accuracy of the historical events recorded in the New Testament and the infallibility of the logical arguments that interconnected them. This pseudo-literalism was presented as assertion without the evidence of sense experience, and belief became a self-hypnotizing process designed to eke out the insufficiency of evidence. The rational arguments used were assumed to have a compulsive power: if we accept this, then that must follow, and so on. A compelling dialectic based on the excluding of opposites is a militant use of words; but where there is no genuine basis in sense experience, it is only verbally rational: it is really rhetoric, seeking not proof but conviction and conversion. It is seldom, however, that anyone is convinced by an argument unless there are psychological sympathies within that open the gates to it. So when words failed, as they usually did, recourse was had to anathematizing those who held divergent views, and from there it was an easy step to the psychosis of heresy-hunting, of regarding all deviation from approved doctrine as a malignant disease that had to be ruthlessly stamped out.

I am, of course, isolating only one element in Christianity, but cruelty, terror, intolerance, and hatred within any religion always mean that God has been replaced by the devil and such things are always accompanied by a false kind of literalism. At present some other religions, notably Islam, are even less reassuring than our own. As Marxist and American imperialisms decline, the Moslem world is emerging as the chief threat to world peace, and the spark-plug of its intransigence, so to speak, is its fundamentalism or false literalism of belief. The same principle of demonic perversion applies here: when Khomeini gave the order to have Salman Rushdie murdered, he was turning the whole of the Koran into Satanic verses. In our own culture, Margaret Atwood's *The Handmaid's Tale* depicts a future New England in which a reactionary religious movement has brought back the hysteria, bigotry, and sexual sadism of seventeenth-century Puritanism. Such a development may seem unlikely just now, but the potential is all there.

For the last fifty years I have been studying literature, where the organizing principles are myth, that is, story or narrative, and metaphor, that is, figured language. Here we are in a completely liberal world, the world of the free movement of the spirit. If we read a story there is no pressure to believe in it or act upon it; if we encounter metaphors in poetry, we need not worry about their factual absurdity.

Literature incorporates our ideological concerns, but it devotes itself mainly to the primary ones, in both physical and spiritual forms: its fictions show human beings in the primary throes of surviving, loving, prospering, and fighting with the frustrations that block these things. It is at once a world of relaxation, where even the most terrible tragedies are still called plays, and a world of far greater intensity than ordinary life affords. It does, in short, everything that can be done for people except transform them. It creates a world that the spirit can live in, but it does not make us spiritual beings.

It would be absurd to see the New Testament as only a work of literature: it is all the more important, therefore, to realize that it is written in the language of literature, the language of myth and metaphor. The Gospels give us the life of Jesus in the form of myth: what they say is, "This is what happens when the Messiah comes to the world." One thing that happens when the Messiah comes to the world is that he is despised and rejected, and searching in the nooks and crannies of the Gospel text for a credibly historical Jesus is merely one more excuse for despising and rejecting him. Myth is neither historical nor antihistorical: it is counterhistorical, Jesus is not presented as a historical figure, but as a figure who drops into history from another dimension of reality, and thereby shows what the limitations of the historical perspective are.

The Gospel confronts us with all kinds of marvels and mysteries, so that one's initial reaction may very well be that what we are reading is fantastic and incredible. Biblical scholars have a distinction here ready to hand, the distinction between world history and sacred history, *Weltgeschichte* and *Heilsgeschichte*. Unfortunately, there is as yet almost no understanding of what sacred history is, so the usual procedure is to try to squeeze everything possible into ordinary history, the bulges of the incredible that still stick out being smoothed away by a process called demythologizing. However, the Gospels are all myth and all bulge, and the operation does not work.

As the New Testament begins with the myth of the Messiah, so it ends, in the Book of Revelation, with the metaphor of the Messiah, the vision of all things in their infinite variety united in the body of Christ. And just as myth is not antihistorical but counterhistorical, so the metaphor, the statement or implication that two things are identical though different, is neither logical nor illogical, but counterlogical. It presents the continuous paradox of experience, in which whatever one meets both is and is not oneself. "I am a part of all that I have met," says Tennyson's Ulysses; "I am what is around me," says Wallace Stevens.[3] Metaphors are paradoxical, and again we suspect that perhaps only in paradox are words doing the best they can for us. The genuine Christianity that has survived its appalling historical record was founded on charity, and charity is invariably linked to an imaginative conception of language, whether consciously or unconsciously. Paul makes it clear that the language of charity is spiritual language, and that spiritual language is metaphorical, founded on the metaphorical paradox that we live in Christ and that Christ lives in us.

I am not trying to deny or belittle the validity of a credal, even a dogmatic, approach to Christianity: I am saying that the literal basis of faith in Christianity is a mythical and metaphorical basis, not one founded on historical facts or logical propositions. Once we accept an imaginative literalism, everything else falls into place: without that, creeds and dogmas quickly turn malignant. The literary language of the New Testament is not intended, like literature itself, simply to suspend judgment, but to convey a vision of spiritual life that continues to transform and expand our own. That is, its myths become, as purely literary myths cannot, myths to live by; its metaphors become, as purely literary metaphors cannot, metaphors to live in. This transforming power is sometimes called kerygma or proclamation. Kerygma in this sense is again a rhetoric, but a rhetoric coming the other way and coming from the other side of mythical and metaphorical language.

In the Book of Job we have the rhetorical speech of Elihu, defending and justifying the ways of God; then we have the proclamation of God himself, couched in very similar language, but reversed in direction. The proclamation of the Gospel is closely associated with the myths that we call parables, because teaching by myth and metaphor is the only way of educating a free person in spiritual concerns. If we try to eliminate the literal basis of kerygma in myth and metaphor, everything goes wrong again, and we are back where we started, in the rhetoric of an all-too-human effort to demonstrate the essence of revelation. The reason for basing kerygma on mythical and metaphorical language is that such a language is the only one with the power to detach us from the world of facts and demonstrations and reasonings, which are excellent things as tools, but are merely idols as objects of trust and reverence.

Demonic literalism seeks conquest by paralysing argument; imaginative literalism seeks what might be called interpenetration, the free flowing of spiritual life into and out of one another that communicates but never violates. As Coleridge said (unless Schelling said it first), "The medium by which spirits understand each other is not the surrounding air, but the *freedom* which they possess in common."[4] As the myths and metaphors of Scripture gradually become, for us, myths and metaphors that we can live by and in, that not only work for us but constantly expand our horizons, we may enter the world of proclamation and pass on to others what we have found to be true for ourselves. When we encounter a quite different vision in, say, a Buddhist, a Jew, a Confucian, an atheist, or whatever, there can still be what is called dialogue, and mutual understanding, based on a sense that there is plenty of room in the mind of God for us both. All faith is founded on good faith, and where there is good faith on both sides there is also the presence of God.

The same thing is true of variations of belief among Christians. Some prominent cleric may announce, after much heart-searching and self-harrowing, that he can no longer "believe in" the Virgin Birth. What he thinks he is saying is that he can no longer honestly accept the historicity of the Nativity stories in Matthew and Luke. But those stories do not belong to ordinary history at all: they form part of *Heilsgeschichte*, a mythical narrative containing many features that cannot be assimilated to the historian's history. What he is really saying is that some elements in the Gospel myth have less transforming power for him than others. His version of Christianity could never have built a cathedral to Notre Dame de Chartres or written the hymn to the Virgin at the end of Dante's *Paradiso*, but his version is his, and that is his business only. However, if he had been a better educated cleric he would not have raised the point in the wrong context and created false issues.

The Epistle to the Hebrews says that faith is the *hypostasis* of the hoped for and the *elenchos* or proof of the unseen [11:1]. That is, faith is the reality of hope and of illusion. In this sense faith starts with a vision of reality that is something other than history or logic, which accepts the world as it is, and on the basis of that vision it can begin to remake the world. A nineteenth-century disciple of Kant, Hans Vaihinger, founded a philosophy on the phrase "as if," and the literal basis of faith from which we should start, the imaginative and poetic basis, is a fiction we enter into "as if" it were true. There is no certainty in faith to begin with: we are free to deny the reality of the spiritual challenge of the New Testament, and if we accept it we accept it tentatively, taking a risk. The certainty comes later, and very gradually, with the growing sense in our own experience that the vision really does have the power that it claims to have.

I use the word "risk" advisedly: I am not minimizing the difficulties and dangers of an imaginative literalism. All through history there has run a distrust and contempt for imaginative language, and the words for story or literary narrative—myth, fable, and fiction—have all acquired a secondary sense of falsehood or something made up out of nothing. Overcoming this perversion of language takes time and thought, and besides, there are as many evil myths and vicious metaphors as there are evil doctrines and vicious arguments. But the author of Hebrews goes on to talk, in the examples he gives after his definition of faith, about the risks taken by vision, and he suggests that such risks are guided by more effective powers than merely subjective ones. Besides, we are not alone: we live not only in God's world but in a community with a tradition behind it. Preserving the inner vitality of that community and that tradition is what the churches are for.

I have been trying to suggest a basis for the openness of belief that is characteristic of the United Church. Many of you will still recall an article in a Canadian journal that emphasized this openness, and drew the conclusion that the United Church was now an "agnostic" church.[5] I think the writer was trying to be fair-minded, but his conclusion was nonsense: the United Church is agnostic only in the sense that it does not pretend to know what nobody actually "knows" anyway. The article quoted a church member as asking, "If a passage in Scripture fails to transform me, is it still true?" The question was a central one, but it reminded me of a story told me by a late colleague who many years ago was lecturing on Milton's view of the Trinity. He explained the difference between Athanasian and Arian positions, and how Milton, failing to find enough scriptural evidence for the Athanasian position, adopted a qualified or semi-Arian one. He was interrupted by a student who said impatiently, "But I want to know the truth about the Trinity." One may sympathize with the student, but trying to satisfy him is futile. What "the" truth is is not available to human beings in spiritual matters: the goal of our spiritual life is God, who is a spiritual Other, not a spiritual object, much less a conceptual object. That is why the Gospels keep reminding us how many listen and how few hear: truths of the Gospel kind cannot be demonstrated except through personal example. As the seventeenth-century Quaker Isaac Penington said, every truth is substantial in its own place, but all truths are shadows except the last. The language that lifts us clear of the merely plausible and the merely credible is the language of the spirit; the language of the spirit is, Paul tells us, the language of love, and the language of love is the only language that we can be sure is spoken and understood by God.

Notes

1   Richard Dawkins, *The Selfish Gene* (1976). [NF]
2   See *Phenomenology of Spirit*, by G. W. F. Hegel.
3   [Alfred, Lord Tennyson, *Ulysses*, I. 18; Wallace Stevens,] *Theory*, in *Collected Poems* ([New York: Knopf,] 1954), 86, [NF]
4   See particularly I.A. Richards, *Coleridge on Imagination* [Bloomington: Indiana University Press, 1960]; (rpt. 1960 with comments by Kathleen Coburn), 98. [NF]
5   Ivor Shapiro, "The Benefit of the Doubt," *Saturday Night*, 105, no. 3 (April 1990): 32–40.

(b) The Nuptial Metaphor

Paul Ricoeur

To retrace the trajectory of the Song of Songs is an all the more legitimate undertaking in that it is inevitable. As has often been said, few texts in the history of interpretation have had as exuberant or as encumbering a fortune. For a superficial glance, this fortune may be confused with the rise and fall of allegorical explications of the Song. Today, however, the situation seems to be as follows. Once contemporary exegesis almost unanimously had adopted the explication, which, in contrast to allegorical, has been called "naturalistic," and that I would prefer to call (and shall henceforth speak of as) the erotic interpretation—according to which the Song is nothing more than an epithalamium, a carnal love song in dialogue form—then the allegorical explications, which endured for so long within both the Jewish and Christian traditions, found themselves divested of their ancient credibility and relegated to the prehistory of this erotic explication. Indeed, for many commentators, these allegorical interpretations are only referred to in their introductions as examples of the prescientific antecedents of an investigation of the text that owes everything to the historical-critical method, which was unknown to the initiators of allegorical interpretation and even resisted by the last advocates of this approach.

For my part, I would like to oppose a multiple flowering history of reading, set within the framework of a theory of reception of the text, to this unilinear conception of the "trajectory" of explication of the Song of Songs. This is a history where not just ancient allegorical exegesis finds a place, but also modern scientific exegesis, and—why not?—even new theological interpretations, whether related or not to the older allegorical exegesis.

The Obvious Sense of the Text

Before characterizing this history for itself, I want first to render justice to the exegetical method that is opposed to it, at least as a first approximation, as its polar opposite, before revealing their complementarity, which I shall attempt to justify with great care. The historical-critical method, with its three faces—the history of sources, the history of composition, and the history of redaction—can be assimilated overall to a history of the writing of the texts we now read. It is noteworthy, in fact, that in the interpretation proposed here by André LaCocque, as in most contemporary commentaries on the Song of Songs, the dominant focus is that of the origin of the text, if we include under this heading the questions of author, date, and cultural setting, along with the question, which is inseparable from this dominant question, of the nature of the original audience. Thus André LaCocque, who does not venture any conclusions regarding date and place, does give a great importance to the hypothesis that the author was a woman, a hypothesis accredited by numerous indications within the text. The poem, he says, is "a woman's song from beginning to end" (p. 243). This hypothesis is solidary with the thesis toward which all his detailed explications point, namely that this beautiful erotic poem would be equivalent to a plea in favor of a free, socially unacceptable, and uninstitutionalized love—a plea, moreover, based on a subversive intention directed against accepted thinking, sometimes called "bourgeois" or the "establishment." If André LaCocque tempers his radical thesis somewhat with the admission that the freedom of this free woman "consists in remaining indefectibly faithful to the one she loves," it is no less true that the principal accent of his interpretation is placed not on the fidelity of this love so much as on its expression "outside the bonds of marriage and outside social strictures." This interpretation could enter into a fruitful discussion with other interpretations arising from what I have called the history of the reception of the text if it could be detached from the postulate—which, by the way, it shares with the modern upholders of an allegorical reading—that there exists one true meaning of the text, namely, the one that was intended by its author, authors, or the last redactor, who are held to have somehow inscribed this meaning in the text, from which exegesis has subsequently to extract it, and, if possible, restore it to its originary meaning. Hence the true meaning, the meaning intended by the author, and the original meaning are taken as equivalent terms. And commentary thus consists in identifying this overall true, intended, and original meaning. To identify it, the text has to be explicated in a detailed manner; that is, one has to demonstrate that the solution brought to local difficulties fits with the general meaning assigned the text, coherence becoming the principal epistemological criterion indicating the adequacy of any commentary.

It is striking that contemporary allegorizing commentators base themselves on the same postulates. (This was not the case, for ancient typological and allegorical interpretations, as I shall show in the second section of my remarks.) Thus modern allegorists compete with the explications they call "naturalistic," with the same ambition to identify, to explicate in detail, the true, intended, and original meaning. And hence today's readers find themselves confronted with an alternative that in fact stems from the quasi unanimity among commentators, even those who favor what their opponents call "naturalistic" explication. I would like to show in the second part of my study that another outcome, built on ancient allegorical interpretation on the basis of a history of the reading and the reception of our text, is possible other than the one most modern commentators reserve for our text, an outcome that relocates these interpretations into another epistemological category than the one that is implied by the notion of true, intended, and original meaning, along with the postulates of identification and explication that go with it on the methodological plane.

However, before doing so, I would like to bring to light a few features of the text of the Song of Songs that, I believe, hold it open to a plurality of interpretations, among which allegorical readings, which are themselves multiple and even contrary to one another, would find a place. These features, let me say straightaway, do justify one part of André LaCocque's reading, namely that the Song of Songs can be read as an erotic poem, perhaps one written by a woman (after all, why not?), a poem with several voices that celebrates the love of a man and woman, apart from any reference to the institution of marriage or to the rules of kinship that ordinarily assign to the father and brother of the fiancée a determined social role, in this way imposing a perspective of fertility and descendants on conjugal love. On the other hand, these features fit less well with the hypothesis of a subversive intention indicated by the ironic, nonreverential connotation of those expressions that many commentators have seen as opaque. My hesitation in this regard does not result from my mistrust of too much concern for a recourse to the intention of the presumed author, but from the fact that these connotations seem to me to be compatible with an interpretation that would place the principal accent instead on the metaphorical dimension of a poem dedicated to erotic love, which is raised by its literary structure beyond any exclusive social-cultural context. These features, which I am now going to consider, seem to me to have as their effect—I do not say, intention—precisely to decontexualize erotic love and to render it in this way accessible to a plurality of readings compatible with the obvious sense of the text as an erotic poem.

I propose reserving the phrase "nuptial bond" to designate this love that is rightly called free and faithful, it being understood that nuptial does not signify "matrimonial." And I shall take as indications of the nuptial as such all those metaphorical features that have to do with the erotic, even at the level of the obvious sense of the text. Note that I say "obvious sense" in order to remain on the textual plane, without having to refer in any way to the intention of the presumed author, hence without having to say anything about the "true" or original meaning. Perhaps the metaphorics constitutive of such expressions of erotic love is such that it blocks any inquiry into such an intentional, original, univocal meaning.

I would like to begin by bringing together those quite striking features of indetermination that have to do with the identification of the characters, places, times, and even the emotions and actions, then next to put the accent on those features that characterize what we can call the "movements of love" and that remain relatively indifferent to their individual attribution to the people in question. Finally, remaining strictly on the literary plane, I want to underline the tendency of the whole metaphorical interplay unfolded by the poem to free itself from its proper referential, that is, sexual, function. All these features taken together constitute the indication of the nuptial in the erotic and, by implication, make possible and plausible a disentangling of the nuptial from the erotic and its new reinvestment in other variations of the amorous relation.

Concerning the phenomenon of indetermination, I shall base what I have to say on a remark made by many commentators concerning the difficulty of identifying the lover and the beloved of this poem.[1] Besides the fact that they never identify themselves nor are they called by a proper name, the term Shulamite in book 7 is not a proper name (cf. what André LaCocque has to say, p. 261). We have to admit that we never know with certitude who is speaking, to whom, or where. We can even, without being ridiculed, imagine that there are three personages involved: a shepherd, a shepherdess, and the king, Solomon.[2] Is it a question, for example, in 1:6–8 of a shepherd and a shepherdess, or in 1:4 and 3:2 and 11 of a king and a woman who might be a townswoman, or of a peasant in 1:12–14 and 7:6 and 13? What is more, the dialogue is rendered even more complex by internal explicit and implicit quotations. Nor is it sure that certain scenes are not dreamed or that they might consist of recounted dreams. After all, the appearance of Solomon in 3:7–11 seems to fit quite well with this indecisiveness concerning the boundary between dreaming and wakefulness. Does not the lover say in 5:2: "I am sleeping but my heart is awake. I hear my beloved who is knocking"? Is not the shepherd a king in his dreams, and why not in terms of the figure of Solomon? These features of indetermination are incontestably favorable to the freeing of the nuptial held in reserve within the erotic.

But should we not simply speak of overdetermination rather than of indetermination? Paul Beauchamp, for example, emphasizes the overlapping of generations in the shifting evocation of the characters.[3] If we consider the succession 1:6, 3:4, 3:11, 6:9, 8:1, 8:4, the figure of the mother returns again and again: the mother of the woman, on the one hand, referred to by the young woman in 1:6 and 3:4 (along with the "chamber of the one that conceived me"); that of the young man in 8:5 ("Under the apple tree, I awaken you, there where your mother conceived you, there where she conceived you, the one who engendered you"). Beauchamp observes, "there is no marriage, royal or otherwise, without the marriage of memories and without the couple being marked by the line of generations."[4] How can we not be struck by this coincidence between wakefulness and this access to embodied memory where innovations and rememoration overlap? (Note, too, that this insistent evocation of the mother makes all the more remarkable the absence of the father, so forcefully underscored by André LaCocque, contrary to the presence of the brothers who try to hold back the crazed lovers.)

All these indeterminations and overdeterminations would be incomprehensible if we did not strongly emphasize, as does Paul Beauchamp, the distance opened between the poem and narration. It is within a narrative perspective, not a poetic one, that the question "who?" would be pertinent, or that we would be authorized to speak of individualized characters. In truth, the lover and the beloved are not identifiable characters; by this, I mean the bearers of a narrative identity. In this respect, it is not out of bounds to suggest that the question "who," ordinarily linked to narrative identity, comes into the poem only to accentuate, in what is undoubtedly a rhetorical fashion, but one that is poetically significant, what Beauchamp calls the appearance of the origin: "who is coming up from the desert?" (3:6); "who arises like the dawn?" (6:10); "who is coming up from the desert leaning on her beloved?" (8:5). Is it not from the end of the world and the depth of time that love arises? But then no name corresponds to or answers the question "who?"[5]

The poetic and non-narrative character of the song is further confirmed by another kind of indetermination that affects the division into scenes. Is it a question of seven poems, as Buzy suggests, where the action in each case progresses from the admiring description of one of the lovers to their mutual possession of each other?[6] Or is it really a question of action in a narrative sense?[7] The reader will have a difficult time in situating exactly the alleged moment of consummation of the union in question, which, I repeat, is not recounted but rather sung. And is it not rightly said that a poem places its climax at the middle, not at the end, which authorizes its imminence or recent accomplishment within the void of a narrative present, occupied by the song alone?[8] In this respect, what we can continue to call a denouement—"Set me like a seal on your heart / Like a seal on your arm. / For love is strong as death, / Jealousy is unyielding like Sheol . . ." (8:6)—must not be treated like some sapiential epilogue added to a narrative conclusion: "Under the apple tree, I awakened you, there where your mother conceived you, there where the one conceived you who gave birth to you" (8:5). It is rather the sapiential crown given to what is from one end to another a song and not in any way a narration, the covenant language ("set me like a seal on your heart, like a seal on your arm") serving to tie together the spontaneity of the song and the meditative point of the organlike sententious declaration.[9]

These reflections concerning completion, which the poem places in the center, lead us to a series of comments concerning the primacy of the "movements" of love over the individual identities of the lover and the beloved. I borrow this expression, "movements of love," from Origen, one of the initiators of allegorical interpretation.[10] This phrase from the most important of the witnesses to the allegorism of the Fathers of the Church should make us attentive to what in the Song of Songs has to do with love as a kind of "movement." For one thing, there are movements in space. Hardly has the beloved exclaimed in the Prologue: "Let him kiss me with the kisses of his mouth," then she adds, "draw me in your steps, let us run." Next there is an evocation of wandering like a vagabond "among the herds and their guardians." And a bit further on, she says, "He led me to the storeroom and the banner he placed upon me is love." Then she hears the beloved arrive, "leaping over the mountains, bounding over the hills." And the lover says to her, "Come then, my beloved, my lovely one, come." In a dream, the beloved "seeks the one that [my] heart loves." As the poem unfolds, we come to understand that this mobility, which is sometimes disconcerting to follow with its changes of tone, is the indication of a game, which is the play of desire itself, or rather of two desires intermingled. The texture of this desire is made up of movements away from each other, then back toward each other, and once again away. In this regard, the scene set at the gate, in chapter 5, is particularly troubling. The beloved knocks and asks to enter. He reaches through the opening of the gate and then, "I opened to my Beloved, but, turning his back, he had disappeared." And the chorus, a bit further on, mocks: "Where has your love gone, oh most beautiful of women? Where did your beloved turn away, should we look for him with you?" (6:1). And the chorus adds: "Return, return, Shulamite, return that we may look upon you!" (6:13). Then once again there is a departure: "Come, my beloved, let us go to the fields!" (7:12). This playing with distance sets off the moments of mutual possession, which the poem, let me repeat, does not describe, or show, but only evokes, in the strongest sense of this word; "His left arm is under my head and his right embraces me" (2:6 and 8:2). Or again: "My beloved is mine, and I am his. He pastures his flock among the lilies" (2:16; 6:3). Carnal love is perhaps consummated in 5:1 or 6:3, but this is not said in a descriptive mode. Rather it is sung. Hence we can ask whether the veritable consummation is not in the song itself. And if, as I suggested above, the true denouement is to be found in 8:6 ("set me like a seal on your heart, like a seal on your arm"), then what is important is not the carnal consummation, which is never described, never recounted, but the covenant vow, signified by the "seal," which is the soul of the nuptial, a soul that would have as its flesh the physical consummation that is merely sung. But when the nuptial is invested in the erotic, the flesh is soul and the soul is flesh.

If we follow this path, we discover other indications, both closer and farther from movement in space, that are close to the movements of love itself. This is the case with the oscillations between waking and sleep. And the movement from one pole to another is never linear or narrative. Four times, we read: "I adjure you, daughters of Jerusalem, by the gazelles, by the does of the fields, do not stir up, do not awaken my love, before he is ready" (2:7, 3:5, 5:8, 8:4). And the awakening in 8:5 ("Under the apple tree, I awaken you, there where your mother conceived you, there where the one conceived you who gave birth to you") is not properly speaking a narrative conclusion, inasmuch as, as has been said, the awakening in 8:5 and the seal in 8:6 belong to the same economy of desires mutually accepted and acknowledged and, in this sense, fulfilled. Similarly, the stages of wakefulness—"My beloved is mine and I am his. He pastures his flock among the lilies" (2:16)—easily fails into a kind of dreaming: "On my bed, at night, I sought him whom my heart loves" (3:1), if it does not turn frankly into a dream between 3:1 and 5:1, as some commentators, such as Daniel Lys, have suggested.[11] But these alternations between sleep and being awake, between dreaming and awakening, belong to the same dynamic of intersecting desires and to the interplay of distance that opens and closes.

Someone may object that not everything in the poem is "movement." Apart from the moments of repose, of possession, which we have said belong to the "movements" of love, to love as movement, the poem makes room for admiring descriptions of the body of the beloved and for that of the lover. This is true. And it does not suffice to reply that these pauses can be assimilated, on the linguistic level of the poem, to a stasis of desire. What we need to add to such a response is that the metaphors through which the marvels of the lovers' bodies are sung are themselves metaphors of movement borrowed from the extraordinary bestiary that the poem draws upon, along with the luxuriant flora of an almost Edenlike countryside.[12] This takes nothing away from the stasis of admiration: "You are beautiful, my beloved, and without flaw!" (4:7). However the poetic pause is all the more striking in that the poem leads without transition from the questing movement to the repose of admiration: "Come from Lebanon, my fiancée, come from Lebanon, make your entry" (4:8). In this way, the poem weaves the stasis of admiring description into the very movements of love, so as to heighten, so to speak, the energy, the power of embracing.

I would like to indicate finally in what way the literary form of the poem contributes to this subtle liberation of the nuptial with regard to the erotic within which it is rightly enmeshed. Above I indicated the importance of the metaphors in the admiring descriptions of the bodies but limited myself to pointing to their origin in the marvelous flora and fauna of Creation. We need to return to them now from the point of view of the effect of sublimation that interests us here. Robert Alter had the genial idea of placing his reflections on the Song of Songs under the title the "Garden of

Metaphor," producing in this way his own second-degree metaphor.[13] After having pointed to the unusual frequency of comparisons and the abundance of grammatical expressions that convey these comparisons ("is like," "resembles a," etc.), he takes up the kind of liberation that occurs through the verbal play that consists in the weaving together of these metaphors in relation to their ultimate corporeal referent. The body is not just sowed with vegetal and animal allegories, to the point of becoming a body/landscape; the verbal play itself tends to dissociate the metaphorical network from its support in the body. Even if, as good Freudians, we can indeed give a sexual meaning to the "fountain that makes the gardens fertile" in 4:15, or the garden itself in 4:16 and 5:1, or to the "hole in the gate" in 5:4, or even to the lilies among which the beloved "pastures his flock" in 6:3, or even, why not, to the navel in 7:2 or the "mountain of myrrh" in 4:6—the all-knowing naiveté of the psychoanalyst is always joyful when it is applied to poetry!—what is important is not the euphemism that preserves the sexual referent without directly naming it, but rather the inclusion of the body itself within the overall metaphorical play of the poem, thanks to the phenomenon that Alter rightly calls "double entendre," I do not mean to suggest, out of some hidden some apologetic purpose, that the sexual referent is thereby abolished, as sexual, but rather that it is placed on hold, precisely as a referent. The verbal play thereby becomes an autonomous source of pleasure.

This poetic sublimation at the very heart of the erotic removes the need for contortions meant to desexualize the referent. That it should be poetically displaced is sufficient. And it is in this way that the same metaphorical network, once freed of every realist attachment through the unique virtue of the song, is made available for other investments and disinvestments.

At the end of this series of comments, we can say that through these purely literary procedures of calculated indetermination and metaphorization, a certain distance of meaning is introduced between the nuptial as such and the sexual, without thereby setting the nuptial within the matrimonial orbit. It is even this equidistance preserved between sexual realism and matrimonial moralism that will allow what I am calling the nuptial as such to serve as the analogon for other configurations of love than that of erotic love.

Notes

1   Daniel Lys, *Le plus beau chant de la création. Commentaire du Cantique des Cantiques* (Paris: Cerf, 1968), p. 16.

2   G. Pouget and J, Guitton, *Le Cantique des Cantiques* (Paris: Gabalda, 1934). "We can assume that it was Jacobi who, in 1771, really inaugurated the strict interpretation of the Song of Songs as a drama" (Lys, *Le plus beau chant*, p. 35).

3   Paul Beauchamp, *L'un et l'autre Testament*, vol. 2, *Accomplir les Ecritures* (Paris: Seuil, 1991), p. 177.

4   Ibid.

5   Ibid., pp. 184–91.

6   Cf., for example, the division into seven poems proposed by Denis Buzy, *Le Cantique des Cantiques* (Paris: Letouzey et Ané, 1949), or that into eight segments by Daniel Lys, or the division into two developments and ten sections distributed around a center ("eat, friends, drink" 5:1) of Paul Beauchamp, *L'un et l'autre Testament*, pp. 161ff.

7   Ibid., pp. 173–80.

8   As Beauchamp says, "In a way, love is in the song itself" (ibid., p. 164).

9   Ibid., pp. 180–84.

10   His second *Homily on the Song of Songs* begins as follows: "All the movements of the soul (*motiones animae*), God, the author of all things, created for the good, but in practice it often happens that good objects lead us to sin because we use them badly. Now one of the movements of the soul is love. We use it rightly to love when we love wisdom and truth, but when our love lowers itself toward things less good, it is flesh and blood that we love. . . . You, therefore, who are spiritual, spiritually listen to the song of these words and learn to raise yourself to what is better as regards the movement of your soul as much as the embrace (*incendium*) of your natural love."

11   Lys, *Le plus beau chant*, p. 79.

12   The beloved is said to be like a gazelle, a young stag (2:8). The hair of the female is beautiful like a troop of goats (4:2); her teeth, a troop of shorn ewes coming up from being washed; her breasts, "two fawns, twins of a gazelle, that feed among the lilies" (4:5); etc.

13   Robert Alter, *The Art of Biblical Poetry* (New York: Basic Books, 1986), chap. 8, "The Garden of Metaphor," pp. 185–203.

(c) Song of Solomon: The Allegorical Imperative

Harold Fisch

IV

It seems that there is no way to avoid interpretation and that interpretation—especially in a poem so dreamlike in its symbolism—will tend to partake of the nature of allegory. This is true of all poetry and of all interpretations of poems.[1] It is more compellingly true of the Song of Solomon. If the ancients had not already taken this path, modern literary critics would certainly have felt obliged to do so. The typologists have turned the more straightforward earthy narratives of Chaucer's *Canterbury Tales* into typological renderings of such Christian mysteries as the nature of the Trinity. The same has been done for Shakespeare's comedies; *Twelfth Night*, we are told, has its hidden key: the twins, Viola and Sebastian, represent the dual nature of Christ as divine love, and Sebastian's timely appearance at the end of the play has something of the character of an epiphany or a Second Coming—all this without prejudice to the concretely human, indeed comic character of the plot.[2] It is a possible notion. The Song of Solomon, linked by so many phrases to other parts of the Old Testament Scripture where the "theological" sense is not in doubt and exhibiting a mode of imagery far more enigmatic than Shakespeare's comedies or Chaucer's *Tales*, is an obvious candidate for figural or allegorical interpretation.

As a matter of fact, many modern critics who would impatiently dismiss the Targum, the rabbis, and the church fathers as naïve allegorists have adopted allegorical readings more improbable than that which sees the poem as the story of the covenant drama between God and Israel. A substantial number of modern students, for instance, following the lead of T. J. Meek, have seen the poem as a cult liturgy connected with the rituals of Tammuz and Adonis. *Dôd* or *dôdî* is taken as the Palestinian equivalent of Tammuz, and the Shulammite is no other than his consort

Shala or Shulmanitu, another name for Ishtar, the Palestinian goddess of vegetation who brings the life-giving rains. In 1:6, says Meek, "we have a clear reference to the drying-up of the vegetation under the scorching rays of the sun"—as the lady languishes from sunburn! Then there is the descent of the god into the underworld—the anguished search of the ra'yâ for the dôd is part of this fertility motif. The concluding chapter, in which we are told that "love is strong as death, / jealousy is cruel as Sheol," was "in its original context manifestly a reference to the power of the love of the goddess to win the god back from the netherworld."[3] Nearly all the different spices mentioned in the Song as well as the various flora and fauna are, we are told, related to the Ishtar cult.[4] Now all this is high fantastical, especially as the list of cultic *realia* is so exhaustive that one wonders which plants and animals the poet could have mentioned had he wanted to exclude the slightest suggestion of Ishtarism. But such a reading nevertheless is a tribute to what may be termed the allegorical imperative. A text so obviously symbolical, so rich in imaginative suggestions and reference, also so mysterious, calls out peremptorily for interpretation. Critics will be driven by the text itself to construct allegorical schemes of greater or lesser validity that will account for the hold that its strange and compelling language has upon us, to account also for the ineffable longing that this love song of a shepherd and a shepherdess calls forth. When so much metaphorical energy is expended on a shepherd and a shepherdess, they themselves become metaphor.[5]

It is often claimed that the allegorical reading of the Song was devised by the rabbis in order to justify its inclusion in the canon of holy writ, for otherwise, as a mere secular love song, it would have been in danger of being suppressed and thus lost.[6] The interpretation of the Song as shadowing forth the covenant love of God and Israel would thus be comparable to the allegorizing of Homer's poetry by the Stoics; that was done to give Homer philosophical legitimacy. Similarly, allegory was a means of giving the Song legitimacy within a scheme of dogmatic theology. The trouble with this notion is that, however far back we go, we cannot discern any traces of an earlier "literal" interpretation of the Song such as we can with Homer. Gerson D. Cohen has indeed argued very plausibly that "allegorizing activity took place not long after the Song itself was compiled."[7] It is the notion of the poem as a simple song of lovers that comes late—with Theodore of Mopsuestia in the fourth Christian century and, among Jews, much later. It may have provided material for songs at "banquets" in the early rabbinic period,[8] but this merely testifies to its popularity; it by no means justifies us in assuming that it was understood only in a secular sense. It may also be that the whole notion of a clear-cut canon of Scripture as existing in the pre-Christian period is something of an anachronism. Certainly, there were authoritative texts, chiefly the Torah and the Prophets. But the status of many of the "Writings" remained fluid down to the period of the Mishnah and beyond. In his day, Josephus knew of only twenty-two official books of Scripture. At the Council of Jamniah in the year 90, i.e., after the fall of Jerusalem, the status of both the Song of Solomon and Ecclesiastes was a matter of discussion.[9] And elsewhere in the Talmud, a third-century teacher, Samuel, expressed doubts about the status of the Book of Esther.[10] But this does not mean that such books were not known, treasured, and above all interpreted. Indeed Samuel himself devoted his exegetical efforts to the midrashic interpretation of Esther even though he was of the opinion that it did not "defile the hands," i.e., that the Esther scroll should not be kept in the same bookcase with indubitably sacred writings.

It does not seem that the felt need to *interpret* a text, even to interpret it allegorically, is bound up with any formal decision to "canonize" it. It is the text itself, even, we may suppose, its popularity, that calls attention to the possibility of further meanings. The compulsion exercised by the poem on its readers is what leads to the overdetermining of its meaning in the form of allegory. In the long run this may well lead to the work being regarded as sacred. But it was evidently not to justify such sanctity that the Song of Solomon was allegorized from the earliest period known to us, but because of the need to explain the extraordinary hold that it exercised on the imagination of its readers. Allegory was a way of accounting for the resonance of such a phrase as "I sought him but I found him not," for the intensity of such a phrase as "the one is she, my dove, my unadorned, the one is she . . .," or for the unconditional, absolute devotion intimated by "set me as a seal upon thy heart, as a seal upon thy arm." The power of such images propels us beyond the limits of a marriage song, however exalted.

We are, in short, speaking of the pressure of the text itself, not of some imaginary canon, and of the vibrations that it sets up in the minds of its readers. Nor was the need to interpret by way of allegory, or something very like it, only felt by readers of the poem in the Middle Ages and earlier. It is evidently felt as an undiminished need by many modern readers and commentators. They find themselves as powerfully compelled to "allegorize"—witness the cultic theories of Meek, Schoff, and others. If it is a marriage that is being celebrated, then it must be a marriage between a god and a goddess! As a matter of fact, many modern readers have paid their tribute, sometimes unconsciously, to the traditional Jewish reading. The translation of 8:6 adopted by Robert Graves is: "Wear me like a charm on your breast, / or like a phylactery on your arm. . . ." The phylacteries are of course bound on head and arm in token of the covenant between God and Israel (Deut. 6:8, 11:18)! The same reading is mooted by Robert Gordis and Marvin Pope.[11]

There can be overspill also in the other direction. Rashi, who adheres to the allegorical reading, nevertheless pays his tribute frequently to the human level of meaning. On 8:5—"I roused thee under the apple tree"—he comments: "Thus she [Israel] declares: Remember that beneath Mount Sinai which formed itself over my head like an apple, there I stirred your love. The language is that of the love of a wife for the husband of her youth; she stirs her beloved in the night as they slumber, holds him in her embrace and kisses him." This is the short-circuit effect once again. Robert Graves would say that his mention of phylacteries is merely figure—the poem is not about phylacteries. Rashi would say that his mention of the intimate embrace of the wife and husband in their slumbers is again "merely" figure; the poem is about something different. The truth is that in this poem there is no mere figure, for metaphor and matter-in-hand have a way of moving into each other's territory. Vineyard stands for land, people, and loved one, but equally, loved one stands for vineyard and land. The "flowing streams from Lebanon" flow into the bounteous "garden," which is the maiden's love, but equally, her love makes real the bounty and grace of the land, gives force to those very streams.

As already noted, the only way to account for the amazing richness of the poem's imagery and also for the effect of this imaginative overspill is to see it as composed in the manner of a dream. This does not mean that the author had dreamed it or that it is susceptible to psychoanalytic testing, as one modern reader has suggested,[12] but that in its free-floating movement, its imaginative autonomy, it belongs to the literary genre of dream vision like *Finnegans Wake* or like Coleridge's "Kubla Khan." But here some care is needed. *Finnegans Wake* ends where it begins—it is a circular composition, its closing words completing the sentence with which the book begins. It is dreamy in the sense that it circles around certain unchanging nodes of consciousness. There is, strictly speaking, no advance, no purpose to be fulfilled. The same may be said of "Kubla Khan." The sunny pleasure dome and the caves of ice, the poem's two major symbols, reappear toward the poem's close; the shadow of the dome of pleasure still floats on the waves. The movement, if there is any, is toward a greater interiorization of that same vision. The symbols are self-fulfilling; the yearning expressed at the poem's close is for a more complete possession of those same symbols.

The dream work of the Song of Solomon is of a more active kind; it is, we may almost say, an anti-dream. The images of the garden and of the streams suggest still, tranquil nodes of vision, like Coleridge's dome and caves of ice, but working against these is the sense of what may be termed historical constraint. "I sought him but found him not." That search continues through the poem, underlined as we have seen by the forward movement of the incremental repetition. There are moments of seemingly gratified longing when the lovers seem to be united, eating the choice fruits of their garden, but these moments are overlaid by the struggle and the search, by the tension of a historical program, by memories that weigh us down with responsibility.

> Who is that, coming up from the wilderness,
> leaning upon her beloved?
> I roused thee under the apple tree:
> there thy mother was in travail with thee:
> there she who bore thee was in travail.
>
> (8:5)

The wilderness is not only a great expanse of rock and sand stretching out to the south and east; it is the land from which the loved one—interpreted to mean the collectivity of Israel—emerged at the beginning of its history, following her beloved as in Jer. 2:2. If allegory relates these verses of the Song too precisely to the birth of the Israelite nation, its wanderings in the wilderness and the great covenantal assembly at Mount Sinai, the overtones that lead to such a reading are surely there—they are almost required by the brooding sense in the poem of purposes announced in the past, frustrated often in the present, but weighing on us to the end. According to this reading, the Song takes us back to ancient beginnings; it takes us back also to nearer memories, to the dark night of the exile, when the Shulammite seeks her lover and finds him not and the watchmen wound and beat her. But the triumphant close is not the close of history, it is rather the reaffirmation of a faith that makes history endurable:

> Set me as a seal upon thy heart,
> as a seal upon thy arm;
> for love is strong as death,
> jealousy is cruel as Sheol.

If Job is an aborted tragedy because it gives way to a sense of historical purpose, and if *Ha'ăzînû* is likewise an aborted pastoral, then the Song of Solomon is, by the same token, an aborted dream poem. It is a dream poem invaded by the sense of historical time. The best analogy from this point of view is with some of the tales of the Israeli novelist S. Y. Agnon, and these are particularly relevant for many of them were inspired by a reading of the Song of Solomon. In one short novel, from a collection entitled *On the Handles of the Bolt*, the lovers enact the drama of estrangement and reunion, of bewildered search and longing. It is, as its title insists, "A Simple Tale"; it tells a realistic story of tragic misalliance and of the long struggle, through madness and grief, to repair it and achieve happiness. But there is a symbolic level to the story. We are told of a ruined synagogue, one wall of which is bent over in grief; according to local belief, on the ninth of the month of Ab, the date of the destruction of the Temple, it sheds tears. On Synagogue Street is the window of a house through which Herschel, the lover of the story, nightly seeks his beloved, but seeks her in vain. Both at its literal and symbolic levels, "A Simple Tale" is a story of the exile. It tells of the age-old, sad, and hopeless love of Israel for that divine presence which once dwelt in the Temple. If it tells of dream and delirium, it is thus a dream of history. Elsewhere in Agnon's writings, notably in his *Sepher HaMaasim*, we have an emphatically dream-like mode of fiction, remarkable for its seeming incoherence and seeming confusion of times and places, but brooding over all these tales is a sense of responsibility, of tasks needing to be fulfilled and the difficulty of fulfilling them in the time available.[13] All this is surely not unlike the Song of Solomon, which, in spite of its dreamlike circling movement, also has a more determined incremental progression as well. At the beginning of the poem the maiden complains of not having tended her own vineyard; by the time we reach the close of the poem, she seems to have regained possession of it: "My vineyard is my own." History is not in vain. If there is separation and longing, there is also the sense of a promised reunion at the end of the long day of search and struggle. It is no wonder that this poem has been understood as an account of the troth plighted between a divine bridegroom and his chosen people. The wonder would have been if it had not been so understood. But one can go further than that; the fact is that the poem has had a role in maintaining and actively strengthening that bond. Its reading week by week has served as a confirmation of age-old vows and loyalties. Such an ongoing response of readers is also a dimension of literary understanding.

V

The Bible seeks through numerous systems of imagery to apprehend the mystery of the relation between God and man that is at the center of its meaning. There is the image of the vineyard and its keeper, of king and subject, father and child, mother and child (as in Isa. 66:12–13), master and servant, man and beast, the potter and his clay. Each of these has its richness and power, its mode of apprehending creatureliness and obligation. But none of these images proves ultimately satisfactory. The relations between the covenanting partners as signified by those images tend to be too fixed, too static, and also, too unequal. Dialogue is inhibited. There can be no true dialogue between man and beast, between an owner and a vineyard (or, as we nowadays might say, an automobile), close and even loving though such relationships may be. There are echoes of all these image systems in the Song of Solomon. We have the song of the vineyard (directly echoing, it seems, Isa. 5:1–7), images of royalty, of family authority, of animals—the maiden compared to a dove, the bridegroom to a gazelle, and of course there are the shepherd and his flock. Through all these we seek a language for defining the indefinable. We seek it but we find it not. The unappeased search of the *ra'yâ* in the poem is perhaps at bottom this search for an image that works. And the frustrations and difficulties are bound up with the knowledge that such a language is ultimately unattainable. The profusion of metaphor and simile in psalm and prophecy is a sign of the intensity of this search, but ultimately we reach the point where poetic language fails. "To whom then will you compare me, that I should be like him?—says the Holy One" (Isa. 40:25). If the Bible points to poetic imagery as in a way the only path of knowledge, it also points just as surely to the limits of art, the impotence of poetry. That has been the argument of this book. There is, however, one image that seems to have a better chance than the others. It is the image of bride and bridegroom, man and wife. It is easy to see why. In this relation we have the possibility of true dialogue between the covenanting parties and also something nearer to a genuine equality. It is the bride who in the Song actively seeks out her beloved, stirs him under the apple tree, bids him make haste to come to her, just as in Jer. 2:2 it is the bride, Israel, who, at great hazard, follows her lover into the wilderness. It is this capacity for independent action on the part of both partners which gives to that image a genuinely reciprocal character that is absent from that of master and slave or even parent and child. It also affords it an intensely dramatic quality. A vineyard can disappoint its owner by growing wild grapes, but it cannot really rebel. When it disappoints, the dialogue will be not between the owner and the vineyard but between the owner and the men of Judah who are asked to "judge between me and my vineyard" (Isa. 5:3). By contrast, a wife and husband can enact a true and agonizing drama of estrangement and the renewal of ties. This is the story of the prophet Hosea and his wife Gomer. There is always the potential for dramatic change in a relationship that is never static, a balance that is always shifting.

It has been well said that the conjugal trope is indispensable for expressing the reality of the covenant because it is invincibly historical.[14] It is weighted with a sense of responsibility, with the urgency of historical time. Tasks have to be undertaken in common, a house has to be built, a future has to be forged. Memory and responsibility are its mark, the memory of vows undertaken in one's youth, to be fulfilled and carried out to the end of the day—"before the day cools and the shadows flee away" (2:17, 4:6). Above all, in contrast to the other tropes that the Bible makes use of, the love of man and woman provides us with a means of understanding chosenness. Or perhaps it would be more correct to say that other tropes might give us the notion of choosing—after all, a man might choose an attractive automobile, or vineyard, or animal—but the corresponding awareness by the chosen one of his or her uniqueness and the discovery in that relation of the fullness of one's humanity—these belong to the symbol of espousal, it would seem, and to that alone. We have here an indispensable ground for the covenant relation as known in the Old Testament scripture. It is more than allegory. "I am my beloved's, and my beloved is mine" gives us access to the mystery of divine love because it is itself an incarnate mystery, a testimony to a transforming encounter, a means of transcending the merely natural.

But even that trope in the end declares itself to be merely trope, and, in the exhaustion of images, the divine love remains without words and without similitudes. The last two verses of the "Song of Songs" speak of the importunate need of poetry; there is, it seems, no substitute for poetry; it is man's highest reach. And so the Shulammite is bidden to raise her voice in song:

> Thou that dwellest in the gardens,
> The companions hearken for thy voice:
> cause me to hear it.
> (8:13)

But when the song is heard, it will be a mere similitude, for we strive to encompass that which cannot in the end be encompassed:

> Make haste, my beloved,
> and be thou like a gazelle
> or a young hart
> upon the mountains of spices.
> (8:14)

Again we have the urgency, the sense of a compelling need, as of a task still to be fulfilled, a race still to be run. And again we have the foregrounding of the terms for poetic imagining. "Make haste," says the verse, and *děmēh-lěkā*, "be a similitude." Be the similitude of a gazelle, of a hart. Indeed be the similitude of a lover, a *dôd*, for that too is a similitude, the greatest and the truest of them all. But even that is but a trope. Of God himself, of his choice of a people and of the mystery of that choosing, even this poem of poems will not directly speak. It will offer us instead a riot of images, but it will take care to tell us that these are but images and it will implicitly ask us to weigh the question that Isaiah three times propounds: "To what will you compare me and liken me and make of me a metaphor, that we may be comparable?" (Isa. 46:5).[15] In the end we are left with comparisons, with the beauty of poetic metaphor, but of God himself, whom all metaphors merely conceal, we shall only say what the prophet says of him in the verse preceding, *'anî hû'*, "I am he" (46:4), or again, later, "I am he, I am the first, / and I am the last" (48:12). Before all images are heard and after all images have worked their magic, we are left with just those two pronouns. According to the midrash, all that the people of Israel actually heard at Sinai were the first words of the great pronouncement: "I am the Lord thy God." The rest, we may say, is poetry.

Notes

1   See Morton W. Bloomfield, "Allegory as Interpretation," *NLH* 3 (1971–72): 302f.

2   See Barbara K. Lewalski, "Thematic Patterns in *Twelfth Night*," *Shakespeare Studies* 1 (1965): 176–78.

3   See T. J. Meek, "The Song of Songs and the Fertility Cult," in Margolis, *The Song of Songs: A Symposium*, pp. 54–57, 62. Marvin Pope in the somewhat eccentric introduction to his edition of the Song (especially pp. 210–29) leans toward a cultic reading of the images. He includes also some dozen plates, mainly bas-reliefs of gods and goddesses in various poses, often indecent, to each of which he attaches a verse from the Song that the picture is supposed to illustrate. All rather like reading Lady Macbeth's "out, damned spot" as clear evidence that she worked in a laundry.

4   See W. H. Schoff, "The Offering Lists in the Song of Songs and their Political Significance," in *The Songs of Songs: A Symposium*, pp. 114–20.

5   I am here echoing a remark of Jonathan Culler on G. M. Hopkins's poem "The Windhover." "The reader of poetry knows," he says, "that when such metaphorical energy is expended on a bird the creature itself is exalted and becomes metaphor" (*Structuralist Poetics* [London: Routledge and Kegan Paul, 1975], p. 90).

6   Cf., for instance, H. H. Rowley, *The Servant of the Lord and Other Essays on the Old Testament* (London: Lutterworth, 1952), pp. 189–91. Seeming evidence for this notion is a third-century source (*Abot Derabbi Natan*, 1:4) that speaks of the "Men of the Great Synagogue" "interpreting" Proverbs, Ecclesiastes, and the Song of Solomon so as to make them acceptable.

7   Gerson D. Cohen, "The Song of Songs and the Jewish Religious Mentality," in *The Samuel Friedland Lectures 1960–1966* (New York: The Jewish Theological Seminary, 1966), p. 16.

8   Cf. BT *Sanhedrin*, 101a. See also *Tosefta, Sanhedrin*, 12:10, in the name of R. Akiba.

9   *Mishnah, Yadayim*, 3:5, *Tosefta, Yadayim*, 2:14, etc. Modern discussion of this topic has not yielded a consensus. S. Z. Leiman has argued that there was a fixed canon already in the Maccabean period (*The Canonization of Hebrew Scripture, Transactions of the Connecticut Academy of Arts and Sciences*, vol. 47, February 1976, p. 135). S. Zeitlin and others have argued for a much later date (see Zeitlin, "An Historical Study of the Canonization of the Hebrew Scriptures," *Proceedings of the American Academy for Jewish Research* 3 [1931–32]: 121–58). George Foot Moore argued that the question of a canon proper, i.e., a dogmatically fixed boundary of exclusiveness, only arose among Jews as a result of the rise of Christianity and the need to exclude the Christian Scriptures. (See "The Definition of the Jewish Canon and the Repudiation of Christian Scriptures," in *C.A. Briggs Testimonial Essays in Modern Theology* [New York, 1911], pp. 101, 125.)

10   He said it was inspired by the holy spirit, but it did not "defile the hands" (BT *Megillah*, 7a). The curious regulation about sacred books defiling the hands was introduced it seems to prevent the scrolls' being damaged by mice. Cereal foods set aside for the priests (*tĕrûmâ*) would often be kept in the same cupboard as the sacred books and these attracted mice, which were then liable to attack the scrolls as well. Determining a low-grade defilement for sacred books meant that *tĕrûmâ* could not be brought near to them, and they would consequently be safe from mice! This is as near as the ancient Jewish rabbis seemed to get to a concept of "canonicity."

11   Robert Gordis, *The Song of Songs and Lamentations* (New York: Ktav, 1974), p. 99; Pope, *Song of Songs*, p. 667.

12   Dr. Max N. Pusin, quoted by Pope, *Song of Songs*, pp. 133–34.

13   Cf., by the present author, "The Dreaming Narrator in S. Y. Agnon," *Novel* 4 (Fall 1970): 49–68; *S. Y. Agnon* (New York: Ungar, 1975), pp. 40, 68–83, 93–94.

14   See André Neher, "Le Symbolisme conjugal: Expression de l'histoire dans l'A.T.," *Revue d'Histoire et de Philosophie Religieuses* I (1954): 33–49.

15   Trans. H.F.

PART III

Theological Interpretation

Theological Interpretation

Chapter 7

Parables

> Reading is just as creative an activity as writing and most intellectual development depends upon new readings of old texts. I am all for putting new wine in old bottles, especially if the pressure of the new wine makes the old bottles explode.
>
> Angela Carter, 'Notes from the Front Line' (1983)[1]

WHEN ANGELA CARTER LOOKS for a metaphor to illustrate her embracing of the radically new, she turns to the biblical parable of the wine-skins. Like the parable form itself, Carter's allusion is deceptively simple. She is drawing on Jesus' story of the danger of putting new wine into old wineskins that cannot stretch to accommodate the fermentation process, a parable that advocates the need for new forms for new realities, supporting sustainability for form and content. When put in new wineskins, the new wine will mature to be enjoyed. Carter's reworking of this parable of sustainability goes beyond a call for merely the new, but advocates a deliberate misuse of old forms that will destroy them. In her rejection of stasis, she happily sacrifices the new wine in order to obliterate old forms as well as the notion of formation itself. There are to be no consumables in her regime. Jesus' parable of innovation becomes innovated in her hands against culturally stultified assumptions, an act of radical metamorphosis that she suggests is true of all reading. The reading process is creative precisely because it explodes old forms. Carter's allusion to this specific parable demonstrates both the pervasiveness of the parable form in literature and the potential complexity of drawing on the strange and yet familiar form of the parable.

Parables are the quintessential form of the New Testament writings, and work is done by each of the writers in this section to defamiliarize our approach to them. For those familiar with them, parables have become understood as straightforward illustration stories, simple allegories for moral teachings. Carter contests this understanding by recognizing, in her use of the wineskin parable, something that Frank Kermode underlines: that parables are often about interpretation itself. They draw attention to the interpretive process, to the desire of the listener or reader to understand, to purchase meaning, to get inside. Carter's answer is that reading is creative – there is no need to get inside because the inside is for exploding and spilling. But for

Kermode the parable form works through reflecting back to the reader their desire to glean meaning. The term 'parable' itself – meaning in its various etymological possibilities in the Greek and Hebrew 'comparison', 'riddle', or 'dark saying' – throws the striving for meaning back at the reader, turning her into a riddler and code breaker. Like many others, Kermode turns to Kafka's parables (to the parable of the leopards and *The Trial*'s doorkeeper) to suggest that these are stories that illustrate the existential truth of the outsider-interpreter – that the 'would-be interpreter cannot get inside' and that 'stories can always be enigmatic, and can sometimes be terrible'. For Kermode, readers are not creative, as the optimistic Carter would contend, but they are instead forever thwarted by the inaccessibility of truth. His work has been most influential in its consideration of the Parable of the Sower and his analysis of the verse: 'That seeing they may see, and not perceive; and hearing they may hear, and not understand; lest at any time they should be converted, and their sins should be forgiven them' (Mark 4: 12). Kermode's argument pivots on the substitution of Mark's *hina* (so that) with Matthew's *hoti* (because), turning the 'intolerable' and 'repellant' suggestion in Mark that Jesus tells parables to deliberately confuse ('*so that* seeing they may see and not perceive') to Matthew's more palatable accusation against the people's failure to understand ('I speak to them in parables *because* they see without perceiving'). The harsh Christ of Mark's gospel, however, becomes the intolerant one of Matthew's in which the people's 'stupidity is extremely tiresome'. The parable illustrates the predicament of the outsider, which for Kermode is ultimately a creative one. Drawing from Martin Heidegger a sense of being 'outside', of distance, as a 'prerequisite of interpretation', Kermode posits reading to be ultimately dynamic, bringing into being the text's hermeneutical potential – what it can or may possibly mean.

J. Hillis Miller takes the distinction between sacred and secular parables as his point of departure. He too turns to etymology to consider the meaning of parable as 'thrown beside', analogous to a parabolic curve as a mode that is an 'indirect indication', a gesture towards something distant that 'cannot be described directly in literal language'. For sacred parables it is the Incarnation – the invisible made visible, or the divine made flesh – that both illustrates and makes possible parabolic logic. The impossibility of speaking directly becomes the bind of the parable form: it can only be spoken of obliquely, from an angle and at a distance, and so any attempt to explain is an attempt to make concrete the essential invisibility of the invisible. As such the parable is strangely superfluous. For it to make any sense you must already have a sense of what it is talking about. As Kermode states so starkly: 'If you need them you cannot hope to understand them.' The problems of the parables are like those of translation, Miller claims. Christ the God-man translates the divine into the human: Christ enables and guarantees the translation, but all we ever have is translation, not direct access to the divine. The secular parable, on the contrary, points towards the existential being of humanity as one of the outsider, and like Kermode's interpretation of Kafka, creates the existence of the 'beyond', of the unspeakable, in a speech act that brings into being, like the 'I do' of the wedding ceremony. The secular paradox is that any parable writer must position himself or herself as a Christ figure: translating for others the 'truth' of that which is beyond and otherwise inaccessible. Whilst declaiming divine knowledge, even the secular writer, through the act of being parabolic and pointing beyond, cannot avoid quasi-divine claims.

For Sallie McFague TeSelle, the parable is also something 'not translatable or reducible', a form that cannot be explained in any simpler form, like a metaphor. Like Miller, TeSelle sees the parable as 'the only legitimate way of speaking of the incursion of the divine into history' and for her Jesus is the 'metaphor par excellence'. The parable pushes us towards more refined practices of attention – a greater engagement with the world to 'intensify one's reality'. It does not whirlwind us away to a numinous 'never-never land'. The parable does not offer an escape from the world but instead 'drives us more deeply into it', creating new realizations and perspectives. Like Miller, TeSelle sees parables as incarnational in their everydayness, in their focus on 'doing', not 'knowing'. Whilst Jesus is the parable of God, the parable is the 'linguistic incarnation' (using the term of the theologian of the New Hermeneutic, Gerhard Ebeling). This is an intricate word play, but points towards stories of action and reaction, of listeners and disciples being confronted and responding. The parable is, then, something that does something to its listeners. We do not interpret it, TeSelle insists, but we are interpreted by it.

Susan Colón follows many others in seeing Dickens as a parable-teller – as Janet Larson recounts, at Dickens' funeral service at Westminster Abbey, Dean Stanley lauded 'the sacredness of fictitious narrative' and Dickens own special 'gift of "speaking in parables" '.[2] The final extract in this section underlines the importance of understanding the full complexity of the parabolic form for its workings within a specific literary work – here, that of Dickens' *Our Mutual Friend* (1864–65). His attraction to the parable as a framing narrative for his novel, Colón suggests, is that it is a form in which exists the ability to express, simultaneously, hope and despair, idealism and realism, the coexistence of 'devastated reality and a sublime ideal'. For Colón the parable is 'thrown alongside' in the sense of stories that are 'laid alongside other stories', a narrative form made use of in *Our Mutual Friend* when the character Boffin 'makes himself a parable'. This extract looks to the stewardship parables in particular – in which a master hands over his estate to the care of a steward – an act that, Colón explains, solves the potential corrupting power of ownership and capitalist gain. Parables are intimately linked to theologies of the Kingdom of God (16 of Matthew's 18 parables are explicitly about the Kingdom, Colón explains) and as such correspond to the 'both here and not here' logic of the divine Kingdom. Existing in some form in the here and now, the Kingdom of God is nonetheless only fully elsewhere. Colón uses the parable of the wheat and tares to demonstrate the logic of the presence and absence of the Kingdom. As wheat exists alongside the weeds that potentially strangle them, to preserve the wheat until harvest time, so the Kingdom of God has a compromised existence until its full realization at the end times. It is 'both here and not here'. As such, the parable form offers hope for restoration within corruption. Rather than a form refusing comprehension, the parable for Dickens offered tangible hope without eschewing the realities of a corrupt and suffering Victorian Britain.

Notes

1   From *Critical Essays on Angela Carter*, ed. Lindsey Tucker (New York: G. K. Hall & Co., 1998), pp. 24–30 (p. 24).

2   Janet L. Larson, *Dickens and the Broken Scripture* (Athens, GA: University of Georgia Press, 1985), p. 4.

Further reading

Butler, Octavia E., *Parable of the Sower* (London: The Women's Press, 1995)
— *Parable of the Talents* (London: The Women's Press, 2000)
Kafka, Franz, *Parables and Paradoxes*, ed. Nahum N. Glatzer, trans. Ernst Kaiser and Eithne Wilkins (New York: Schocken Books, 1987)
— *The Trial* (1925; London: Penguin, 2000)
Lewis, Linda M., *Dickens, His Parables and His Reader* (Columbia MI: University of Missouri Press, 2012)
Macneice, Louis, *Varieties of Parable* (London: Faber and Faber, 2008)
Mills, Kevin, *The Prodigal Sign: A Parable of Criticism* (Eastbourne: Sussex Academic Press, 2009)
Naveh, Gila Safran, *Biblical Parables and their Modern Re-creations: From 'Apples of Goldin Silver Setting' to 'Imperial Messages'* (Albany: State University of New York Press, 2000)
Thoma, Clemens and Michael Wyschogrod, eds., *Parable and Story in Judaism and Christianity* (New York: Paulist Press, 1989)
Wilder, Amos, *The Bible and the Literary Critic* (Minneapolis, MN: Augsburg Fortress, 1991)

(a) Hoti's Business: Why are Narratives Obscure?

Frank Kermode

> *He did not speak to them without a parable.*
>
> Mark 4:34

> He settled Hoti's business.
>
> Browning, "A Grammarian's Funeral"

IF WE WANT TO think about narratives that mean more and other than they seem to say, and mean different things to different people, with a particularly sharp distinction drawn between those who are outside and those who are inside, we can hardly do better than consider the parables.

A parable is, first, a similitude. "With what can we compare the kingdom of God, or what parable shall we use for it?" (Mark 4:30): here the word for parable – *parabolē* – could as well be translated "comparison," and sometimes is. It means a placing of one thing beside another; in classical Greek it means "comparison" or "illustration" or "analogy." But in the Greek Bible it is equivalent to Hebrew *mashal*, which means "riddle" or "dark saying," but I gather it can extend its range to include "exemplary tale." Sometimes the Greek word is also used to translate *hidah*, meaning "riddle."

Riddle and parable may be much the same: "Put forth a riddle and speak a parable to the house of Israel," says Ezekiel, proposing the enigma or allegory of the eagle of divers colors and the spreading vine (17:2f). The saying of Jesus that nothing that enters a man from outside can defile him is called by Mark a parable; it is not especially dark, but dark enough to call for an explanation.

What is interesting about parables from the present point of view is first this range of senses, which seems to reflect pretty well all the possibilities of narrative at large. At one end of the scale there is a zero point, a strong saying, perhaps, with no narrative content to speak of; and at the other is the well-formed story which, as structuralist exegetes like to demonstrate, exhibits all the marks of narrativity. But there is another scale to consider. Parables are stories, insofar as they *are* stories, which are not to be taken at face value, and bear various indications to make this condition plain to the interpreter; so the other scale is a measure of their darkness. Some are apparently almost entirely transparent; some are obscure.

All require some interpretative action from the auditor; they call for completion; the parable-event isn't over until a satisfactory answer or explanation is given; the interpretation completes it. In this respect it is like a riddle, sometimes a very easy riddle, sometimes one of the comic kind that contain interpretative traps: for example, the riddle that asks how you fit five elephants into a Volkswagen, which can only be answered if you ignore the hint that it has to do with size; it has to do only with number.[1] But it is more usually a tragic riddle, like that proposed by the Sphinx to Oedipus – if you can't answer it, you die, for that is the fate of the outsider who sees without perceiving and hears without understanding. Or we might try another comparison, and say that the interpretation of parable is like the interpretation of dreams, for the dream-text, when understood, disappears, is consumed by its interpretation, and ceases to have affective force (or would do so, if one were able to conceive of a completed dream-analysis).

But this notion, that interpretation completes parable, and there's an end, is much too crude. The parable of the Good Samaritan, to which I'll return, ends with a question: "Which of these three, do you think, proved neighbor to the man who fell among thieves?" There is only one possible answer: "The Samaritan." Or so it would appear to common sense; though common sense is not our business. The answer may leave an interpreter unsatisfied, because a narrative of some length, like the Good Samaritan, works hard to make the answer obvious and in so doing provides a lot of information which seems too important to be discarded, once the easy act of completion is performed.

[. . .]

FOR THE LAST century or so there has been something of a consensus among experts that parables of the kind found in the New Testament were always essentially simple, and always had the same kind of point, which would have been instantly taken by all listeners, outsiders included. Appearances to the contrary are explained as consequences of a process of meddling with the originals that began at the earliest possible moment. The opinion that the parables must originally have been thus, and only thus, is maintained with an expense of learning I can't begin to emulate, against what seems obvious, that "parable" does and did mean much more than that. When

God says he will speak to Moses openly and not in "dark speeches," the Greek for "dark speeches" means "parables." John uses a different word for parable, but uses it in just the same sense: "speak in parables" is the opposite of "openly proclaim." If a word can cover so many things, from proverbial wisdom to dark sayings requiring recondite rabbinical explanation, and even to secret apocalyptic signs, it seems likely that people who used the word in this way must have interpreted all narrative with a comparable variety and range.

In our own time we cannot easily use the word "parable" in such a way as to exclude the notion of "enigma." Who would deny Kafka the right to call his anecdote of the leopards a parable (*Gleichnis*)?[2] "Leopards break into the temple and drink to the dregs what is in the sacrificial pitchers; this is repeated over and over again; finally it can be calculated in advance, and it becomes part of the ceremony." Webster (third edition, 1961) says that a parable is "a short fictitious story from which a moral or spiritual truth can be drawn." Do we draw any such truth from Kafka's parable? What, to mention first a rather minor difficulty, are we to make of those definite articles: *the* temple, *the* sacrificial pitchers? They imply that the cultus is one with which we ought to be familiar; we ought to know the god whom the temple serves, and what liquid is contained in the pitchers. Of course we don't. All we can suppose is that some familiar rite is being intruded upon, and that the intrusion is assimilated, the cultus altered to accommodate it, in a manner often discussed by sociologists of religion. The alternative procedure, to their way of thinking, would be to shoot ("nihilate") the leopards.

Beyond that, we are left to consider the peculiar nature of the rite. There are ceremonies which claim to enact an historical sequence of events that occurred at a particularly significant moment in the past, and to do so in such a way as to translate them into the dimension of liturgy. The Passover is such a ceremony, and so is the Eucharist; both include expositions of the recurring symbolic senses of the original events. But here the repetitiveness belongs in the first place to the original events ("this is repeated over and over again") and only later becomes liturgical; though it might be argued that the presence of the leopards is all the more a Real Presence. At this point, it must be admitted, we are very close to what might be called "wild interpretation."

Here I will interpolate a reading of the parable by another hand, my wife's. "The letter of the parable," she writes, "masters our freedom to interpret it. The words, we know, must mean more and other than they say; we would appropriate their other sense. But the parable serenely incorporates our spiritual designs upon it. The interpreter may be compared to the greedy leopards. As their carnal intrusion is made spiritual, confirming the original design of the ceremony, so is this figurative reading pre-figured; only complying with the sense, it adds nothing of its own and takes nothing away. In comparing himself to the leopards, the reader finds himself, unlike the leopards, free – but free only to stay outside. Thus dispossessed by his own metaphor, excluded by his very desire for access, he repeatedly reads and fails to read the words that continue to say exactly what they mean."

This reading, which firmly excludes speculation about liturgy or ritual, has, I think, much to be said for it. Thurber, peering into a microscope, saw his own eye, which was wrong; interpreters, often quite rightly, tend to see the Problem of

Interpretation. The sense of the parable, on the view just stated, must be this: being an insider is only a more elaborate way of being kept outside. This interpretation maintains that interpretation, though a proper and interesting activity, is bound to fail; it is an intrusion always, and always unsuccessful. This is bewildering, for we fear damnation and think it unfair, considering how hard we tried. The opinion of Mark is quite similar: he says that the parables are about everybody's incapacity to penetrate their sense. Of course both the interpreters in question go some way toward exempting themselves from this general inhibition.

There is a famous parable in Kafka's *The Trial*. It is recounted to K by a priest, and is said to come from the scriptures. A man comes and begs for admittance to the Law, but is kept out by a doorkeeper, the first of a long succession of doorkeepers, of aspect ever more terrible, who will keep the man out should the first one fail to do so. The man, who had assumed that the Law was open to all, is surprised to discover the existence of this arrangement. But he waits outside the door, sitting year after year on his stool, and conversing with the doorkeeper, whom he bribes, though without success. Eventually, when he is old and near death, the man observes an immortal radiance streaming from the door. As he dies, he asks the doorkeeper how it is that he alone has come to this entrance to seek admittance to the Law. The answer is, "this door was intended only for you. Now I am going to shut it." The outsider, though someone had "intended" to let him in, or anyway provided a door for him, remained outside.

K engages the priest in a discussion concerning the interpretation of this parable. He is continually reproved for his departures from the literal sense, and is offered a number of priestly glosses, all of which seem somehow trivial or absurd, unsatisfying or unfair, as when the doorkeeper is said to be more deserving of pity than the suppliant, since the suppliant was there of his own free will, as the porter was not. Nevertheless it is claimed that the doorkeeper belongs to the Law, and the man does not. K points out that to assume the integrity of the doorkeeper, or indeed that of the Law, as the priest does, involves contradictions. No, replies the priest: "it is not necessary to accept everything as true, one must only accept it as necessary." "A melancholy conclusion," says K. "It turns lying into a universal principle."[3]

"Before the Law" is a good deal longer than any biblical parable, and reminds us that in principle parable may escape restrictions of length, and be, say, as long as *Party Going*. And like Mark's Parable of the Sower, it incorporates very dubious interpretations, which help to make the point that the would-be interpreter cannot get inside, cannot even properly dispose of authoritative interpretations that are more or less obviously wrong. The outsider has what appears to be a reasonable, normal, and just expectation of ready admittance, for the Law, like the Gospel, is meant for everybody, or everybody who wants it. But what he gets is a series of frivolous and mendacious interpretations. The outsider remains outside, dismayed and frustrated. To perceive the radiance of the shrine is not to gain access to it; the Law, or the Kingdom, may, to those within, be powerful and beautiful, but to those outside they are merely terrible; absolutely inexplicable, they torment the inquirer with legalisms. This is a mystery; Mark, and Kafka's doorkeeper, protect it without understanding it, and those outside, like K and like us, see an uninterpretable radiance and die.

Let me now return to Mark's formula of exclusion, which I quoted near the beginning of the book. Jesus is preaching to a crowd, teaching them "many things in parables." The first is the Parable of the Sower. He went out to sow; some of his seed fell by the wayside and was eaten by birds; some fell on stony ground, where it grew without rooting and was scorched by the sun; some fell among thorns, which choked it; and some fell on good ground, yielding at harvest thirty, sixty, and a hundredfold. "He that hath ears to hear, let him hear": this is the formula that tells you the enigmatic part of the text is concluded, and you need to start interpreting. Later, the Twelve, baffled, ask Jesus what the parable means. He replies that they, his elect, know the mystery of the kingdom and do not need to be addressed in parables, but those outside are addressed only thus, "*so that* seeing they may see and not perceive, and hearing they may hear but not understand, *lest* at any time they should turn, and their sins be forgiven them" (Mark 4:11–12). He adds, a little crossly, that if the Twelve can't make out this parable they will not make out any of them, but nevertheless goes on to give them an interpretation. What the Sower sows is the Word. People by the wayside hear it, but Satan (the birds) comes and takes it from their hearts. The stony ground signifies those who receive the Word with gladness, but are unable to retain it under stress and persecution; the thorns stand for those who hear it but allow it to be choked by worldly lust and ambition. The last group are those who hear and receive the Word and bear much fruit (4:14–20).

All this is very odd; the authorized allegory seems inept, a distortion *après coup*,[4] as bad as the priest's exegeses in Kafka. It gives rise to suggestions that Mark did not understand the parable, that its original sense was already lost, and its place taken by an inferior homiletic substitute. But let us put that question aside and look at the general theory of parable pronounced on this occasion: To you has been given the secret of the kingdom of God, but for those outside everything is in parables, so that they may indeed see but not perceive, and may hear but not understand; lest they should turn again and be forgiven. Some argue that Mark's *so that* or *in order that*, the Greek *hina*, is a mistranslation of a word that in the lost Aramaic original meant *in that* or *in such a manner as*, so that Mark's Greek distorts the true sense, which is something like: I have to speak to them in parables, seeing that they are the kind of people who can take stories but not straight doctrine. This is an attempt to make *hina* mean "because," a very desirable state of affairs. In this altered form the theory no longer conflicts with the prefatory remark that Jesus was *teaching* the crowd, which seems inconsistent with his telling stories in order to ensure that they would miss the point. It also fits the run of the sentence better: the Twelve don't need parables, but the crowd does. Apparently Mark misunderstood, or used *hina* carelessly or in an unusual way; and it is a fairly complex word. But the best authorities do not accept these evasive explanations, a refusal all the more impressive because they would really like to. They admit that Mark's *hina* has to mean *in order that*; and we are left with a doctrine described by one standard modern commentator as "intolerable,"[5] by Albert Schweitzer as "repellent," and also, since the meaning of the parables is "as clear as day," unintelligible.[6]

Now it happens that Mark's first interpreter was Matthew (I assume throughout that Mark has priority and is Matthew's principal source, though this long-established position is now under challenge). And Matthew also seems to have found Mark's *hina* intolerable. For though he does not omit the general theory of parable from his big parable chapter (13), he substitutes for *hina* the word *hoti*, "because." This is a substantial change, involving a different grammar; Matthew replaces Mark's subjunctive with an indicative. Later he had to deal with Mark's *mēpote*, "*lest* they should turn," which obviously supports the uncompromising mood of *hina*;[7] here he went to work in a different way. The whole passage about hearing and seeing comes from Isaiah (6: 9–10), though Mark, in paraphrasing it, does not say so. What Matthew does is to quote Isaiah directly and with acknowledgment, so that the lines retain a trace of their original tone of slightly disgusted irony at the failure of the people to perceive and understand. The sense is now something like: As Isaiah remarked, their stupidity is extremely tiresome; this seems the best way to get through to them. The *mēpote* clause is thus bracketed off from the rest; instead of Mark's uncompromising exclusions – outsiders must stay outside and be damned – Matthew proposes something much milder: "I speak to them in parables *because* they see without perceiving . . ." He was, it appears, unhappy with the gloomy ferocity of Mark's Jesus, who is also, in this place, very hard on the Twelve: "if you don't understand this you won't understand anything." Matthew leaves this out, and substitutes a benediction: "Blessed are your eyes, for they see . . ."

It has been argued that Matthew's *hoti* has a causal force, that he is saying something like: It is only because the people lack understanding that the parables will have the effect of keeping them from the secrets of the kingdom.[8] The implication is that the exclusion arises not from the speaker's intention, but from the stupidity of his hearers, so that the blame is theirs. This gives the parables the same effect as they have in Mark's theory, while avoiding his candid avowal that the telling of them was designed to have that effect. I must leave *hoti's* business to the grammarians, but it seems safe to say that Matthew's principle of secret and inaccessible senses, if he had one, is a good deal softer than Mark's.

[. . .]

The attempts of the learned to explain away Mark's *hina* are worthy of Kafka's priest. But there it stands, and has stood for nineteen hundred years, a silent proclamation that stories can always be enigmatic, and can sometimes be terrible. And Mark's gospel as a whole – to put the matter too simply – is either enigmatic and terrible, or as muddled as the commentators say this passage is. Why, to ask a famous question, does Mark so stress the keeping of the secret of the messiahship of Jesus? One answer is that since this was an idea that developed only after the death of Jesus, Mark was forced to include it in his narrative *only* as a secret deliberately kept, concealed from all save the Twelve, and not understood by them until the end of the story. This leaves a good deal unexplained; nor is the theme of secrecy the only mystery in Mark. My present point is simple enough: Mark is a strong witness to the enigmatic and exclusive character of narrative, to its property of banishing interpreters from its secret places. He could say *hina*, even though his ostensible purpose, as declared in the opening words of his book, was the proclamation of good news to all.

[. . .]

[T]here is a fashion still more recent, which revives, in its own way, the notion that the sense of the text is inexhaustibly occult, and accessible in a different form to each and every interpreter. The object of this kind of interpretation is no longer "scientific"; one does not try, like Jeremias, to state what the narrative meant in its original, or in any later setting; one does not try to "re-cognize" it, as the more conservative hermeneutical theorists say one should. Rather one assumes, to quote an opponent of this school, that "the meaning of a text goes beyond its author not sometimes but always" and that "one understands differently when one understands at all."[9] The object of interpretation is now sometimes said to be to retrieve, if necessary by benign violence, what is called the original event of disclosure. This is the language of Heidegger; he takes the Greek word for "truth," *alētheia*, in its etymological sense, "that which is revealed or disclosed, does not remain concealed." Every hermeneutic encounter with a text is an encounter with Being as disclosed in it. For Heidegger indeed, it is the very fact that one is *outside* that makes possible the revelation of truth or meaning; being *inside* is like being in Plato's cave.[10]

Every such hermeneutic encounter is still, in a measure, historically conditioned, though now that limitation is no longer thought of just as a limitation – it is the prerequisite of interpretation, each act of which is unique, one man on one stool, so to speak, seeing what no power can withhold from him, his glimpse of the radiance, his share of what is sometimes called the "hermeneutic potential" of a text. Interpreters in this tradition sometimes think of earlier interpretations, transmitted by institutions, as having attached themselves to the original, and as having tended to close it off, lowering its potential rather as mineral deposits clog a pipe and reduce its flow. Since by their own interpretative act they discover what the parable *originally means*, they are not constricted by the conventional demand that interpretation should say what the parable *originally meant*, to its author and its first audience. What it meant and what it means are both actualizations of its hermeneutic potential, which, though never fully available, is inexhaustible.

Now that which requires to be disclosed must first have been covered, and this view of interpretation certainly implies that the sense of the parable is an occult sense. Its defenders like to say not that the interpreter illumines the text, but that the text illumines the interpreter, like a radiance. For this, as I said, is an outsider's theory. It stems ultimately from a Protestant tradition, that of the devout dissenter animated only by the action of the spirit, abhorring the claim of the institution to an historically validated traditional interpretation. It may be the end of that tradition; for I do not see how, finally, it can distinguish between sacred and secular texts, those works of the worldly canon that also appear to possess inexhaustible hermeneutic potential. (Heidegger's own exegeses of Hölderlin treat the text exactly as if it were sacred.) The tradition is that of a productive encounter between the text and the reader, illuminated by a peculiar grace or, in more secular terms, a divinatory genius, as far as possible independent of institutional or historical control. That encounter is the main concern not only of modern German hermeneutics but also, though their ways are different, of its French rivals. The method has, of course, been applied to the parables.

An interpreter working in this tradition cannot altogether free himself from historical and institutional constraints. He will try to avoid them, insofar as they are avoidable; but he cannot escape his own historicality, and he was trained in an institution. Nor can he acquire divinatory genius for the asking. The book that first made

American readers familiar with the idea of hermeneutic potential was Robert Funk's *Language, Hermeneutic, and the Word of God*.[11] It is an admirable piece of exposition. Yet Funk agrees with Jeremias that the effect of the Good Samaritan story depends on the narrative shock of the discovery that the merciful traveler is a stranger, an enemy. He departs from known paths only when he conjectures that the wounded man might have preferred not to have the assistance of this unclean outcast; but this is a conjecture that owes nothing to the new hermeneutics. Although he denies the Good Shepherd interpretation, he agrees that Jesus is the Samaritan, and we the wounded man; so the Good Shepherd is there somewhere, in a sort of penumbra. There seems to be a traditional quality about this reading that is rather remote from the libertarian possibilities suggested by the speculative parts of Funk's book, and very remote from the unique and somber meditations of Heidegger on Hölderlin.

This is perhaps to say no more than that the interpreter is likely to have a touch of the dyer's hand. Thus structuralist exegesis of this parable will pass from a demonstration of its narrativity to a demonstration that Luke, as many have said before, mistook a parable of the Kingdom for a homiletic example story. And Paul Ricoeur is surely right to assume that interpretation begins where structuralist analysis ends,[12] that such analysis should be thought of as a way of facilitating divination.

[. . .]

So inveterate, so unalterable is this exclusion that it is easy to pass from saying that the outsiders are told stories because they are dull and imperceptive to saying that stories are told in order to keep the dull and imperceptive outside. And suppose that we somehow discovered that all stories were, after all, *hoti* stories. The interpreters *de métier* would, to protect their profession, to continue their privileged conversations with texts, at once strive to discredit the discovery; finally all stories are *hina* stories, even the story that they are all *hoti*.

That all narratives are essentially dark, despite the momentary radiance that attends divination, is a doctrine that would not have surprised pre-scientific interpreters. They might have offered various reasons for holding it, though usually they would have attributed the darkness of the tale to the intention of a divine author. Calvin and Pascal, close as they were to the epoch in which a presumptuous human reason would attempt to explain the mystery away, nevertheless agreed with Mark that the divine author made his stories obscure in order to prevent the reprobate from understanding them; on a kinder Catholic view, he did so in order to minimize the guilt of the Jews in refusing the gospel.[13] Even now, when so many theories of interpretation dispense in one way or another with the author, or allow him only a part analogous to that of the dummy hand at bridge, the position is not much altered; the narrative inhabits its proper dark, in which the interpreter traces its lineaments as best he can. Kafka, whose interpreter dies outside, is a doorkeeper only; so was Mark.

Mark distresses the commentators by using the word "mystery" as a synonym for "parable" and assuming that stories put questions which even the most privileged interpreters cannot answer. For example, he tells two stories about miraculous feedings. Any creative writing instructor would have cut one of them; but Mark's awkwardness can hardly be dismissed as accidental. Later the disciples are on board a boat and discover that they have forgotten to bring bread – there is only one loaf. At this point Jesus gives them an obscure warning: "beware of the leaven of the Pharisees and the leaven of Herod." Puzzled, they say among themselves, "it is because we have no bread" or "this is why we have no bread," or, maybe, "is this why we have no bread?" – the sense of the Greek is uncertain. Whatever they intend, Jesus gets angry. "Do you not yet perceive or understand? Are your hearts hardened? Having eyes do you not see, and having ears do you not hear?" They are behaving exactly like the outsiders in the theory of parable. The sign given them by the Feedings is lost on them, and unless something is done about it they will find themselves in the same position as the Pharisees, to whom Jesus has just refused any sign at all. So he takes them once more, slowly, through the story of the Feedings. Five thousand were fed with five loaves: how many baskets of fragments were left over? Twelve, they correctly reply. Four thousand, at the second Feeding, were served with seven loaves: how many baskets of fragments were left over? Seven. Well then, don't you see the point? Silence. Perhaps the disciples mistook the riddle as we do the one about the elephants: there is a strong suggestion that the answer has to do with number, but it probably doesn't.[14] Anyway, they do not find the answer. Here again Matthew does not want to leave the matter so obscure; his Jesus is much less reproachful, and also explains: "How did you fail to see that I was not talking about bread? Beware of the leaven of the Pharisees and Sadducees." ("Leaven," used figuratively, ordinarily meant something infectiously evil.) "Then they understood that he was not telling them to beware of the leaven of bread, but of the teaching of the Pharisees and Sadducees" (16:11–12). This is not perhaps very satisfactory; but the point is that Mark, with his usual severity, makes Jesus angry and disappointed, and also turns the insiders into outsiders. They cannot answer this riddle, any more than they could read the Parable of the Sower. And although this passage has been subjected to the intense scrutiny of the commentators, no one, so far as I know, has improved on the disciples' performance. The riddle remains dark; so does the gospel.

Parable, it seems, may proclaim a truth as a herald does and at the same time conceal truth like an oracle.

Notes

1   The answer is: two in the front, three in the back.
2   Franz Kafka, *Parables and Paradoxes* (bilingual ed.), New York, 1961, pp. 92–93.
3   *Parables and Paradoxes*, pp. 60–79.
4   "The seed is the Word: yet the crop which comes up is composed of various classes of people." (C. H. Dodd, *The Parables of the Kingdom*, rev. ed., New York, 1961, p. 3.) Dodd of course believes that the allegorical reading came in later and belongs to a different *Sitz im Leben*. "The probability is that the parables could have been taken for allegorical mystifications only in a non-Jewish environment. Among Jewish teachers the parable was a common and well-understood method of illustration, and the parables of Jesus are similar in form to Rabbinic parables. The question therefore, why He taught in parables, would not be likely to arise, still less to receive such a perplexing answer. In the Hellenistic world, on the other hand, the use of myths, allegorically interpreted, as vehicles of esoteric doctrine was widespread, and something of the kind would be looked for from Christian teachers. It was this, as much as anything, which set interpretation going on wrong lines"

(pp. 4–5). The attitude of J. Jeremias, *The Parables of Jesus*, rev. ed., London, 1963, is not very different. These opinions continue to prevail in various modified forms, but they have been cogently questioned; and recently John Drury has shown pretty conclusively that they cannot be right – *Journal of Theological Studies*, new series 24 (1973): 367–79. The Jewish parable could certainly be allegorical and deliberately obscure (cf. Ezekiel), and there is no historical reason to believe that the parables of Jesus could not have been riddling or enigmatic from the beginning. Moreover it was common rabbinical practice to offer private interpretations to favored insiders, and Dodd was wrong to suppose that the privileged explanations of the Sower Parable and of the saying about "things that come out of a man" (Mark, 7) are necessarily later accretions (D. Daube, "Public Retort and Private Explanation," in *The New Testament and Rabbinical Judaism*, London, 1956, pp. 141–50). Finally, it is possible to argue that although the outsiders could not have access to the mystery, the parables were intended to provide them with the best possible substitute; far from being intended to baffle, the parables had senses that yielded themselves to reflection. Only if one saw and heard, but failed to go beyond that, could it be said that one had avoided turning to be forgiven. See J. Bowker, *Journal of Theological Studies*, new series 25 (1974): 300–317.

5   V. Taylor, *The Gospel According to St. Mark: The Greek Text with Introduction, Notes and Indexes*, 2nd ed., New York, 1966, p. 257. C. E. B. Cranfield, *The Gospel According to St. Mark* (*The Cambridge Greek Testament Commentary*), ed. of 1972, pp. 155f, also accepts *hina* as "in order that," pointing out that the philological evidence for other senses is trifling in comparison to the contextual evidence in favor of the harder interpretation; "in order that" he says, "reflects the teleological thinking which is characteristic of the whole of the Bible, including the Synoptic Gospels" Jeremias, pp. 13f, accepts *hina* in the same sense, but thinks the free quotation from Isaiah should be given in quotation marks, with this effect: "in order that (as it is written) they 'may see and not see, etc." ' Jeremias thinks *mēpote* means "unless" (p. 17). Dodd (p. 3n) argues that the crucial passage contains so many words not found elsewhere in the synoptics, but usual in Paul, that it must be apostolic rather than primitive. Jeremias (pp. 77f) makes a similar point.

6   Albert Schweitzer, *The Quest of the Historical Jesus*, translated by W. Montgomery, New York, ed. of 1968, p. 263.

7   It is neither desirable nor possible to report all the arguments about this passage, which are very learned and complex. But I should add that Mark's version of Isaiah 6:9f corresponds to neither the Hebrew nor the Septuagint text; yet it agrees with the Targum (Aramaic version) and this may be thought, since the Targum was used in the synagogue, to support the argument for its historical authenticity (Jeremias, p. 15). Jeremias, however, believes (and he is not alone) that although authentic the logion has got into the wrong place, and probably belongs to the second half of the gospel; Mark, perhaps misled by a catchword (*parabolē*) put it in this sequence of parables, though originally it was an expression, of a not unfamiliar kind, of a general disillusionment, and had nothing to do with the interpretation of parables or the reason for teaching in parables. Matthew's version of the Isaiah quotation exactly reproduces the Septuagint, and gives the whole thing in its original second-person form; it is as if Matthew, as he worried over Mark's text, checked the quotation in his Greek Bible and found that version more congenial. But I am told that the Hebrew of Isaiah supports the purposive sense of *hina*.

8   See Dan O. Via, *The Parables: Their Literary and Existential Dimensions*, Philadelphia, 1967.

9   H.-G. Gadamer, *Truth and Method*, London, 1975, p. 264.

10   "The Origin of the Work of Art," in *Poetry, Language and Thought*, translated and edited by Albert Hofstadter, New York, 1960, pp. 15–87.

11   New York, 1966.

12   Paul Ricoeur, "What is a Text?", in David M. Rasmussen, ed., *Mythic-Symbolic Language and Philosophical Anthropology*, The Hague, 1971.

13   See D. P. Walker, "Esoteric Symbolism," in *Poetry and Poetics from Ancient Greece to the Renaissance*, Ithaca, 1975, pp. 218–31.

14   For an elaborate interpretation of this passage in the context of the gospel as a whole, see Q. Quesnell, *The Mind of Mark: Interpretation and Method through the Exegesis of Mark: 6.52*, Analecta Biblica 38, Rome, 1969.

(b) Parable and Performative in the Gospels and in Modern Literature

J. Hillis Miller

A large contradictory modern secondary literature now exists on the parables of Jesus in the New Testament and on their relation to the tradition of secular parable in modern writers like Kleist and Kafka.[1] Since I am not a biblical scholar, I cannot hope to add much to this discussion except possibly from the point of view of secular literature; but I can begin here with several axioms or presuppositions to guide my investigation, if only as grounds to be ungrounded by what is discovered later on.

The first presupposition is the assumption that it ought to be possible to identify specific differences, in the language, between the parables of Jesus and any secular parables whatsoever. Much is at stake here. The distinction between sacred scripture and secular literature would seem to depend on being able to identify the difference. The authority not only of the Bible as in some sense or other the word of God but more specifically of the words of Jesus as speech of God would seem to hang in the balance here. If the Middle Ages needed a distinction between "allegory of the poets" and "allegory of the theologians," we moderns would seem to need a firm distinction between "parable of the poets" and "parable of the theologians."

The second presupposition is no more than a definition of parable. Etymologically the word means "thrown beside," as a parabolic curve is thrown beside the imaginary line going down from the apex of the imaginary cone on the other side of whose surface the parabola traces its graceful loop from infinity and out to infinity again. Comets on a parabolic trajectory come once, sweep round the sun, and disappear forever, unlike those on a large elliptical orbit which return periodically, Halley's Comet for instance. When this is taken as a parable of the working of parable in literature or in scripture, it suggests that parable is a mode of figurative language which is the indirect indication, at a distance, of something that cannot be described directly, in literal language, like that imaginary invisible cone or like the sun, single controlling focus of the comet's parabola, which cannot be looked in the eye, although it is the condition of all seeing, or like that inaccessible place from which the comet comes and to which it returns. A parabolic narrative is, my parable of the comet would suggest, in some way governed, at its origin and at its end, by the infinitely distant and invisible, by something that transcends altogether direct presentation. The correspondence between what is given in parable – the "realistic" story represented in a literal language – and its meaning is more indirect than is the case, for example, in "symbolic" expression, in the usual meaning of the latter, where, as the name suggests, one expects more of interpretation, of participation, and of similarity. One German name for parable is *Gleichnis*, "likeness." This is what Luther calls a parable of Jesus. The paradox of parable is that it is a likeness that rests on a manifest unlikeness between what is given and what cannot by any means be given directly. A parabolic "likeness" is so "unlike" that without interpretation or commentary the meaning may slip by the reader or listener altogether.

Hegel's discussion of what he called "conscious symbolism" provides a definition of parable that corresponds to the one I have been making. The sublime (*das Erhabene*) is, strangely enough, included by Hegel with fable, parable, apalogue, proverb, and metamorphosis as a mode of "conscious symbolism."

> What has emerged from sublimity as distinct from strictly unconscious symbolizing consists on the one hand in the *separation* [*in dem Trennen*] between the meaning, explicitly known in its inwardness, and the concrete appearance divided therefrom; on the other hand in the directly or indirectly emphasized non-correspondence of the two [*Sichnichtentsprechen beider*] wherein the meaning, as the universal, towers above individual reality and its particularity.[2]

If "separation" and "non-correspondence" characterize all such forms of symbolism, including parable, then the meaning of the parable can hardly be expected to be perspicuous to eyes that cannot see the tenor of which such symbols are the vehicle. For example, says Hegel when he comes to discuss parable in particular:

> The parable of the sower [in all the Synoptics] is a story in itself trivial in content [*für sich von geringfügigem Gehalt*] and it is important only because of the comparison with the doctrine of the Kingdom of Heaven. In these parables the meaning throughout is a religious doctrine to which the human occurrences in which it is represented [*vorgestellt*] are related in much the same way as man and animal are related in Aesop's Fables, where the former constitutes the meaning of the latter.[3]

In parable, human is to religious doctrine as animal is to human. The latter constitutes the meaning of the former across the gap of their separation and non-correspondence.

On the basis of this definition, a distinction, in principle at least, between sacred parable and secular parable may be made. The parables of Jesus are spoken by the Word, the Logos, in person. Even if this terminology is fully present only in the Gospel of John, it is already implicit in the characterization in the first three Gospels of Jesus as the Messiah. The fact that the Messiah speaks the parables guarantees the correspondence between the homely stories he tells of farming, fishing, and domestic economy on the one hand, and the spiritual or transcendent meaning on the other, the meaning that tells of things beyond the threshold of the domestic and visible, the meaning that nevertheless can be spoken only in parable, that is, indirectly. Christ as the Logos is not only the basis of the analogies, echoes, and resemblances among things of the world created in his name and between things created in his name and things hidden since the creation of the world. Christ as Logos is also the basis of the correspondence within the realm of language, for example the correspondence between visible vehicle and invisible and unnamed tenor in a parable. When Jesus speaks the parables, Christ the Word stands visibly before his auditors, for those who have eyes to see and ears to hear, as support of the correspondence between his realistic narrative of sowing, fishing, or household care and those unseeable things of which the parable "really" speaks. This guarantee is, I take it, one of the fundamental meanings of the Incarnation. Believing in the validity of the parables of the New Testament and believing that Jesus is the Son of God are the same thing.

The speakers or writers of secular parables stand in a different place, even though their parables too may deal with religious or metaphysical matters. They are down here with us, and their words about things visible can only be thrown beside things invisible in the hope that their narratives of what can be spoken about, the fencing bear in Kleist's "Über das Marionettentheater," for example, will magically make appear the other invisible, perhaps imaginary, line to which their realistic stories, they hope, correspond. The editor of the Greek New Testament I have consulted, Henry Alford, a nineteenth-century Anglican biblical scholar, put this clearly in his preliminary note on Matthew 13. A parable, he says,

> is *a serious narration within the limits of probability, of a course of action pointing to some moral or spiritual Truth* ("Collatio per narratiunculam fictam, sed veri similem, serio illustrans rem sublimiorem." Unger, de Parabolis Jesu [Meyer]) ["some moral or spiritual truth," it might be noted, is a loose translation of "rem sublimiorem"]; and derives its force from real analogies impressed by the Creator of all things on His creatures. The great Teacher by parables therefore is He who needed not that any should testify of man; for He knew what was in man, John ii.25: moreover, He *made* man, and orders the course and character of human events. And this is the reason why no one can, or dare, teach by parables, except Christ. We do not, as He did, see the inner springs out of which flow those laws of spiritual truth and justice, which the Parable is framed to elucidate. *Our* parables would be in danger of perverting, instead of guiding aright.[4]

The fact that Alford a page later commits the crime he warns against is an amusing example of the *odium theologicum* but also an example of a problem with Christ's parables. Any interpretation of these parables is itself parabolic. In one way or another it must do what Henry Alford warns against, that is, claim to understand "the inner springs out of which flow those laws of spiritual truth and justice, which the Parable is framed to elucidate." Which of us, reading Matthew 13, would admit to being one of those who seeing see not, and hearing hear not, neither understand? So Alford, speaking of that terrifying law of parable Jesus enunciates whereby "For to him who has will more be given, and he will have abundance; but from him who has not, even what he has will be taken away" (Matthew 13:12), applies it to the biblical commentators of his own day, doing in the process what he has said a page before no mere human being should dare do, namely, teach by parable: "No practical comment," says Alford, "on the latter part of this saying can be more striking, than that which is furnished to our day by the study of German rationalistic (and, I may add, some of our English harmonistic) Commentators; while at the same time we may rejoice to see the approximate fulfilment of the former in such commentaries as those of Olshausen, Neander, Stier, and Trench."[5] No doubt Olshausen, Neander, Stier, and Trench were worthy scholars, but there is also no doubt a grotesque incongruity or bathos in using the parable of the sower as a means of dividing the sheep from the goats in the parochial warfare of biblical scholarship. In any case, there is great temerity in doing so, just that merely human preaching by parables against which Alford has warned on the page before. Yet it is obvious that whoever speaks of the parables at all runs the risk, perhaps must endure the necessity, of doing this. The language of parables contaminates, or perhaps it might be better to say inseminates, impregnates, its commentators. Such language forces them to speak parabolically, since it is by definition impossible to speak of what the parables name except parabolically. Commentary on the parables is, or ought to be, an example of the dissemination of the Word, its multiplication thirty-, sixty-, or a hundredfold.

This need to distinguish secular from sacred parable and yet difficulty in doing so leads to my third presupposition. This is that the two kinds of parable may be distinguished by recognizing that both are performative rather than constative utterances but that two radically different kinds of performative would appear to be involved. A parable does not so much passively name something as make something happen. A parable is a way to do things with words. It is a speech act. In the case of the parables of Jesus, however, the performative word makes something happen in the minds and hearts of the hearers, but this happening is a knowledge of a state of affairs already existing, the kingdom of heaven and the way to get there. In that sense, a biblical parable is constative, not performative at all. A true performative brings something into existence that has no basis except in the words, as when I sign a check and turn an almost worthless piece of paper into whatever value I have inscribed on the check, assuming the various contexts for this act are in correct order – even though as the phenomenon of counterfeit money or the passing of bad checks indicates, the performative may make something happen even when some aspect of the contexts is amiss. Secular parable is a genuine performative. It creates something, a "meaning", that has no basis except in the words or something about which it is impossible to describe whether or not there is an extralinguistic basis. A secular parable is like a piece of money about which it is impossible in principle to know whether or not it is true or counterfeit. Secular parable is language thrown out that creates a meaning hovering there in thin air, a meaning based only on the language itself and on our confidence in it. The categories of truth and falsehood, knowledge and ignorance, do not properly apply to it.

My final presupposition is that both kinds of parable tend to be parables about parable. They are about their own efficacy. Jesus' parable of the sower in Matthew 13:1–23, with its parallels in Mark and Luke, is a well-known example of this.[6] Its topic is the efficacy of the word. The distinction is between those who have eyes and ears for the Word and those who do not, or rather the parable distinguishes four possibilities, that the seed will fall by the wayside, in stony places, among thorns, and in good ground, with an appropriate psychological interpretation for each of the different predispositions to receive the Word, as the thorns stand for "the care of this world, and the deceitfulness of riches," which "choke the word" (Matthew 13:22). What in fact is the "word"? It is the good news, the gospel of salvation, the "secrets of the kingdom of heaven" (Matthew 13:11), "what has been hidden since the foundation of the world" (Matthew 13:35). A whole series of paradoxes operates at once in this parable about parable.

First paradox: The presupposition is that the mysteries of the kingdom of heaven cannot be spoken of directly. The things that have been kept secret from the foundation of the world can only be spoken of in parable. Christ as the Logos is in the awkward position of not being able to speak the Logos directly but of being forced to translate it into a form suitable for profane ears. The Word cannot speak the Word as such.

Second paradox: Unless you understand the Word already as such, unless you are already fertile ground for the Word, which means somehow already grounded in it, sown by it, you will not understand it when it is expressed in parable. When the disciples ask, "Why do you speak to them in parables?" Christ's answer is: "To you it has been given to know the secrets of the kingdom of heaven, but to them it has not been given. For to him who has will more be given, and he will have abundance; but from him who has not, even what he has will be taken away. This is why I speak to them in parables, because seeing they do not see, and hearing they do not hear, nor do they understand" (Matthew 13:10–13). The parables are posited on their own inefficacy. If you have knowledge of the kingdom of heaven already, you do not need them. The parables are superfluous, a superabundance, a surplus, a gift beyond gift. If you do not have that knowledge, you will not understand the parables anyhow. They will be a way of covering your eyes and ears further, not a breaking of the seals or a form of unveiling, of revelation. The things that have been kept secret from the foundation of the world will remain secret for most people even after they are spoken in parable. Such things are perhaps made secret by that foundation, veiled by the creation itself rather than revealed by it, and so kept secret by parables that name those secret things with names drawn from familiar created things. The parables translate the Word, so to speak, into the language of familiar things, sowing, fishing, household work. Even so, those for whom the parables are intended are like those to whom one speaks in a foreign language or like someone who does not know Greek presented with the Gospel of Matthew in Greek. The parable, as they say, is all Greek to that person. Such persons lack the gift of tongues or the gift of translating the parable back into the original word. "Hearing they do not hear, nor do they understand." Such people are like Belshazzar confronted by the handwriting on the wall, or they are like those auditors who are not going to understand the prophecy of Isaiah, a failure in understanding that Jesus says the failure of his parables will fulfill. Here is the great text in Isaiah on which Jesus' parable of the sower is a commentary:

> Then flew one of the seraphims to me, having in his hand a burning coal which he had taken with tongs from the altar. And he touched my mouth, and said: "Behold, this has touched your lips; your guilt is taken away, and your sin forgiven." And I heard the voice of the Lord saying, "Whom shall I send, and who will go for us?" Then I said, "Here am I! Send me." And he said, "Go, and say to this people: 'Hear and hear, but do not understand; see and see, but do not perceive.' Make the heart of this people fat, and their ears heavy, and shut their eyes; lest they see with their eyes, and

hear with their ears, and understand with their hearts, and turn and be
healed."

(Isaiah 6: 6–10)

The parables, however, are intended for just such people, and so they are posited on
their own inevitable misreading or nonreading. The problem, once more, is how to
cross over from one kind of language to the other, from the word of God, "Whom
shall I send?" to the word of the human: "Here am I! Send me." If you can understand
the parables, you do not need them. If you need them, you cannot hope to understand them. The parables are not a way of giving the Word but a way of taking away,
a way of adding further deprivation to a deprivation that is already total: "From him
who has not, even what he has will be taken away."

Third paradox: The disciples are said by Jesus to be those to whom it is given to
know the mysteries of the kingdom of heaven. It would seem that this means they
already have the Word and therefore have open eyes and ears, are able to understand
the parables spontaneously, translate their displaced language back to the original
tongue, and at the same time do not need the parables. The parables give them more
when they already have and so do not need. For them the parables are superfluous.
"For to him who has will more be given, and he will have abundance." The paradox
is that, having said that, Jesus proceeds to explain to the disciples the parable of the
sower, spelling it out, translating it back into the language of the kingdom of heaven,
as if they could not understand it without his interpretation. He has said they understand, but he goes on to speak as if they could not possibly understand: "Truly, I say
to you, many prophets and righteous men have longed to see what you see, and did
not see it, and to hear what you hear, and did not hear it. Hear then the parable of the
sower. When any one hears the word of the kingdom and does not understand it, the
evil one comes and snatches away what is sown in his heart; this is what was sown
along the path . . ." and so on through the explicit application of each of the clauses
of the parable to each of the four kinds of people in relation to the proffered insemi-
nation or dissemination of the Word, down to: "As for what was sown on good soil,
this is he who hears the word and understands it; he indeed bears fruit, and yields, in
one case a hundredfold, in another sixty, and in another thirty" (Matthew 13:17–23).

Fourth paradox: The economy of equivalence, of giving and receiving, of equable
translation and measure, of the circulation of signs governed by the Logos as source
of proportion and guarantee of substitution or analogy, is upset by the parables.
Although the parables of Jesus are spoken by the Word, they are not logical. They are
not governed, as, say, medieval allegory is said to be, whatever Henry Alford affirms,
by the "real analogies impressed by the Creator of all things on his creatures." Or, if
they are so governed, they function by a choice of alogical moments in systems of
circulation and exchange in the familiar domestic world to indicate the failure of
analogy between anything human, including human languages – Aramaic, Greek,
Latin, English, or whatever – and the divine Logos, the Word of the kingdom of
heaven. If allegory and symbolism in one way or another work by analogy or by
correspondence, resonance, or participation between one thing and another thing on
a different level, or between one word and another word, as in the proportionalities
of metaphor, the parables of Jesus are ana-analogical, or rather, since "ana" is already

a double antithetical prefix, which may mean either "according to" or "against," it may simply be said that the parables are "analogical" in the sense of "against logic," "counter to logic." "Paradox": the word means etymologically, "against teaching," or against the received opinion of those in authority. The words or parables of Jesus are a stumbling block to the Greeks because they go against the habits of logical thinking. The Logos in the sense of Jesus as the Word contradicts *logos* in the sense of Greek reason, or reasoned thinking, which is reason as such in the West.

The "literal" language of the parables of Jesus and of his actions themselves as described by the gospel makers is drawn from various realms of domestic economy, production, consumption, and exchange in the family or in the immediate social group such as a household with servants or a farm with hired workers. These various realms include eating, sowing and reaping, fishing, sexual reproduction, the donation and receiving of gifts, the exchange of words, translation from one language to another, counting, and the exchange of money, its use and its usury. In all cases the example chosen breaks down the pattern of a closed circuit of exchange of the same for the same or its equivalent. The fisherman draws fish abundantly from the salt and inhospitable sea. A single seed cast in fertile ground reproduces a hundred-, sixty-, or thirtyfold, and a tiny mustard seed produces an enormous tree. He who saves his life will lose it. To save it, it must be thrown away, and the same thing may be said of virginity, which is of value or use only if it is given up, just as money has the power of reproducing itself magically but not if it is hoarded, only if it is invested, put out at risk, used. The distinction between male potency and female passive receptivity is broken down in sexual reproduction, since the female must be fertile ground for the seed and thus in a sense already contain its potentiality, as only fertile ground will multiply the seed cast on it and as only those who already have the Word can receive it and multiply it. Although the image Jesus uses in his exegesis of the parable of the sower is that of sexual reproduction, the sexes are strangely reversed, as they are in the image of the soul as the bride of Christ. Jesus speaks of the different persons who receive the seed of the Word as "he": "But he that received the seed into stony places . . ." and so on, but that fertile ground must in some sense be a feminine matrix, an egg ready to receive the seed. A genuine gift, like the other elements upsetting any domestic economy of equivalence and exchange, is, as Marcel Mauss and Jacques Derrida have in different ways argued, always something incommensurate with any recompense, something suspending the circuit of obligation, of payment and repayment.[7] A true gift can never be returned. It creates an infinite obligation and is not restitution for any claim I have on another. The gift leads to such absurdities as the Northwest American Indian potlatch, in which one man vies with another in destroying great heaps of valuable property.

The power of the gift to break down logical equivalences in social exchange is shown in reverse in what might be called the living parable of the story of the loaves and fishes in Matthew 14. Jesus blesses the bread, breaks it, and gives the five loaves and the two fishes to the disciples. The disciples give them to the multitude. In that double process of giving, the loaves and fishes become multiplied beyond any rational calculation so that there is always enough and some over – twelve baskets of fragments – though about five thousand have been fed. In this case, as in the parables generally, for example the parable of the sower, several different realms, of the ones

I have listed, come together: gift giving and receiving, agriculture and fishing in the bread and fishes, and the illogic of an arithmetical sum in which five loaves and two fishes become a countless number with twelve basketsfull left over. In the case of the parable of the sower, sowing and reaping, on the one hand, and sexual reproduction on the other, are used each as a figure for the paradoxes of the other. There is a contamination of the "literal" language of each of the realms, in any vernacular, with figures drawn from others of the realms, as when we speak of "seed money," or of the "dissemination" of the seed in sowing, as well as of the dissemination of doctrine, or of sexual reproduction in terms of "getting" and "spending," and so on, in a perpetual round in which no one set of these terms is the purely literal language that provides figures for the others. Another way to put this is to say that ordinary language, the language Jesus must use to speak to the multitude or to the disciples, is already irremediably parabolic.

The final realm in which rational equivalence and exchange breaks down is then that of language itself, that dissemination of the Word for which all these other realms are not so much figures as living and material hieroglyphs, that is, places where the paradoxes of sign-making and sign-using enter into the actual process of the living together of men and women in family and community, to be incorporated inextricably into that process.

[. . .]

Is it possible to speak of parables literally, or is the language of the commentators on parables always contaminated by what they talk about, subdued to what they work in, so that their language becomes in its turn inevitably parabolic? Would that necessarily be a bad thing? These are the questions raised by the little alternating dialogue that ends Kafka's "On Parables." In this dialogue two more voices are heard, and the voice of "Kafka" himself, which spoke at first, as well as the voice of the "man" who said we only need to "follow" the parables, vanishes entirely. The little dialogue has to do with the linguistic status of the exhortation to follow the parables and has to do with winning and losing not in the parables themselves but in the interpreter's stance in relation to them and in his language about them:

> Another said: I bet that is also a parable.
> The first said: You have won.
> The second said: But unfortunately only in parable.
> The first said: No, in reality: in parable you have lost.[8]

The reader (I hope) will be able to follow this somewhat bewildering alternation to the point of blinding clarity it reaches. To say something is a parable can only be done from the point of view of reality and of literal language, since the realm of parable and the language of parable are defined by their difference from the real and the literal. They are a transfer from it, a "going over." To say that by following the parables one becomes a parable is a parable all right, but it is a saying that remains immovably still in the realm of everyday life, which, after all, as "On Parables" says at the beginning, "is the only life we have." One wins the bet ("I bet that is also a parable") but only in reality, which means that one loses in parable. The parables ask to be

taken literally. The only way they can become efficacious is for them to become literally true, so that one does literally "go over." As long as they are seen as figures of
speech, as merely parabolic, one loses in parable, one has failed to enter into the
realm of parable. But they cannot be seen otherwise. They produce neither action
nor knowledge. To know that fabulous realm over there is to cross over into it, but
the parables merely throw out incomprehensible figures in the direction of the
incomprehensible. They are like parables proffered by one of the multitude who hear
Jesus speak or at best like a parable given out by one of the disciples. "All these parables really set out to say merely that the incomprehensible is incomprehensible
(*unfassbar*), and we know that already."[9]

[. . .]

I shall now attempt to draw such conclusions as I can from my brief side-by-side
discussion of sacred parable and secular parable. My primary motivation, it will be
remembered, has been to identify distinguishing marks that would allow a firm division between one and the other. I claim to have done this in identifying a different
nature and standing place in each case for the speaker or writer of the parable and in
identifying a different relation in each case to the distinction between performative
and constative language. The latter difference may be phrased by saying that both
kinds of parables are catachreses, the throwing out of language toward an "unknown
X" which cannot be named in proper or literal language. In the case of secular parable
it cannot be known for certain, even by the one who invents the parable, whether or
not there is something out there, across the frontier, which pre-exists the language
for it. Such language may be a true performative, bringing something into being that
exists only in the words or by means of the words. Sacred parable is in principle
spoken by someone who has that knowledge to start with by someone who *is* that
knowledge, by someone who is the Logos itself in all the sense of that word: mind,
reason, knowledge, speech, measure, ratio, ground of all things.

The distinction seems clear but the distinction itself involves a double paradox,
one on each side of the line separating secular from sacred parable. On the one hand,
Christ the Word must in the parables translate the Word into humanly comprehensible language. He is in himself both sides of the dialogue between Jehovah and Isaiah
that he says his parables are meant to fulfill. Christ is both the Word of God, "the
voice of the Lord" called in vocation or in invocation to Isaiah, "Whom shall I send?"
and Isaiah's answering voice in acceptance of vocation, "Here am I! Send me." Christ's
words are therefore subject necessarily to the limitations of human language in whatever language they are spoken or into which they might be translated, in spite of the
suprahuman standing place from which he speaks. Christ's dissemination of the
Word is therefore performed over its logical impossibility, as he says in the parable
of the sower. This impossibility may be expressed by saying that the parables of Jesus
are not properly performative. They do not in themselves make anything happen,
since their auditors must already know the Word to be fertile ground for the Word
the parables speak. The parables of Jesus are constative, but they provide knowledge
that for many is spoken in a foreign tongue, a tongue that is not going to be understood. The paradox of the parables of the Gospels as at once Word of God and at the
same time humanly comprehensible words is "the same as," analogical to in one or

the other meaning of the word analogy, the mystery of the Incarnation, in which God and humanity become one across the barrier of the impossibility of their union.

Of another "analogous" problem with the parables in the Gospels I have not even spoken here, and can only indicate a line to be followed. Do the citations of the parables by the authors of the Gospels have the same efficacy as the parables had when they were originally spoken by Jesus to his auditors, or are they only the report of a form of language that has its efficacy elsewhere? Are they still the Word of the kingdom of heaven, the good news itself, or are they only the translation of that Word so it may be disseminated in another tongue? To employ the terminology of the speech-act theorists, are they "use" or only "mention" of Christ's language? These questions, it will be seen, are analogous to, although not quite the same as, the problem of translation on the one hand and the problem of distinguishing sacred from secular parable on the other.[10]

On the other side of the line separating secular and sacred parable, the paradox is that no purely human parable-maker, even though that person may be someone who, like Kafka, fully accepts the limitations of humanity, can avoid the temerity of at least tentatively, implicitly, or hypothetically putting himself in Christ's place and claiming to serve as an intermediary between this everyday world and the kingdom of heaven on the other side of the frontier of which all parables bring word. Secular parable may be, strictly speaking, a true performative, the creation of something that exists, for humanity at least, only in the words, but this purely performative function is always contaminated by an implicit claim to be based on knowledge and to bring knowledge, even if that knowledge is the negative knowing of the apparent impossibility of "going over." Kafka was fully aware of this danger. It is in fact the fundamental burden of *Von den Gleichnissen*.

Any commentator on parables, secular or sacred, is in the situation of Kafka, or indeed of such a commentator as Henry Alford. One should be anxious to avoid the danger of being parabolic oneself and yet one is unable certainly to do so. The question of the relation between secular and sacred parable is a tiny seed that generates a long line of thought, multiplying itself thirty-, sixty-, or a hundredfold, of which this paper is only a preliminary segment. Such a line of thought is like a parabolic trajectory, sweeping in from an infinite distance and back out again. That my discourse on parable is itself parabolic there can be no doubt, although whether I have been able to keep safely on this side of the line separating secular from sacred parable is not so certain. The uncertainty derives from the difficulty – perhaps the impossibility – in spite of all efforts and in spite of the high stakes involved, of keeping the two kinds of parable absolutely distinct.

Notes

1   See, for example, William Beardslee, *Literary Criticism of the New Testament* (Philadelphia, 1970); Charles Carlston, *The Parables of the Triple Tradition* (Philadelphia, 1975); Dominic Crossan, *In Parables* (New York, 1973); idem, *Raid on the Articulate* (New York, 1976); C. H. Dodd, *The Parables of the Kingdom* (New York, 1961); Robert W. Funk, *Language, Hermeneutic, and the Word of God* (New York, 1966); J. Jeremias, *The Parables of Jesus* (New York, 1972); Norman Perrin, *Jesus and the Language of the Kingdom* (Philadelphia, 1976);

Norman Petersen, *Literary Criticism for New Testament Critics* (Philadelphia, 1978); Jean Starobinski, "Le Combat avec Légion," *Trois fureurs* (Paris, 1974) pp. 73–126; Mary Ann Tolbert, *Perspectives on the Parables: An Approach to Multiple Interpretations* (Philadelphia, 1979); Dan O. Via, *The Parables* (Philadelphia, 1967); Andrzej Warminski, " 'Patmos': The Senses of Interpretation," *MLN*, 91 (1976) pp. 478–500; Amos Wilder, "The Parable," *Early Christian Rhetoric: The Language of the Gospel* (Cambridge, 1971) pp. 71–88. A collection may also be mentioned, *Analyse structurale et exégèse biblique* (François Bovon, ed.; Neuchâtel, 1971), which also contains the essay by Jean Starobinski listed above. In addition, two journals, *Semeia* and *Linguistica Biblica*, have contained many essays on the parables of Jesus. I owe most of this brief bibliography of recent work on the parables to Amos Wilder, who has kindly assisted in educating me in this area, as he has educated me in other ways over the years. I am glad to be able to thank him here for manifold kindnesses.

2   G. W. F. von Hegel, *Aesthetics: Lectures on Fine Art* (tr. T. M. Knox; 2 vols; New York, 1975) 1, 378; *Vorlesungen über die Ästhetik, Werkausgabe* (Frankfurt am Main, 1970) 1, 486.

3   *ibid.*, English, p. 391; German, pp. 502–3.

4   *The Greek Testament* H. Alford, ed. (4 vols; Boston; New York, 1874) 1, 136–37.

5   *ibid.*, p. 138.

6   As Jean Starobinski observes, "Le Combat," 111ff.

7   See Marcel Mauss, *The Gift* (tr. Ian Cunnison; New York, 1967); the seminars by Jacques Derrida at Yale University in the fall of 1980 focused on Mauss' book.

8   Franz Kafka, *Parables and Paradoxes*, in German and English (New York, 1971), pp. 10–11.

9   *ibid.*, p. 258.

10   Werner H. Kelber has completed a study of the parables of the Synoptic Gospels which makes the distinction between citation and original oral utterance suggested in this paragraph.

(c) The Parable: The Primary Form

Sallie McFague TeSelle

It was very early in the morning, the streets clean and deserted. I was on my way to the railroad station. As I compared the tower clock with my watch I realized it was already much later than I had thought, I had to hurry, the shock of this discovery made me feel uncertain of my way, I was not very well acquainted with the town as yet, fortunately there was a policeman nearby, I ran to him and breathlessly asked him the way. He smiled and said: "From me you want to learn the way?" "Yes," I said, "since I cannot find it myself." "Give it up, give it up," said he and turned away with a great sweep, like someone who wants to be alone with his laughter.[1]

This parable by Franz Kafka seems, on a first reading, to invite interpretation—in fact, to insist on it. One can immediately think of autobiographical, psychological, and theological interpretations which might "make sense" out of it. But to attempt such interpretations would be to allegorize it, to treat it as an illustration or embellishment of what we "already know." And all the interpretations do, in fact, fall flat; they are far less interesting than the story itself, and even though they may comfort us for a while with the supposition that we now understand the parable, we find ourselves returning again and again to the story, unsatisfied with *any* interpretation. The parable appears to be more and other than any interpretation.

This is so, I believe, because Kafka's parable is a genuine one—it is not translatable or reducible. It is also an excellent parable to ponder because, if anything, it is even less "translatable" than biblical parables while manifesting many of the same central qualities.

The setting is ostensibly very ordinary: someone, up early in the morning, is rushing through the streets to the railroad station. The sense of haste is heightened by the run-on phrases, punctuated mainly by commas and by the gradual build-up of the person's awareness that "it was already much later than I had thought." A surrealistic note is introduced when the comparison of his watch with the tower clock so shocks him that he is "uncertain of the way." We pause—is that comparison sufficient to make him lose his way? Our credulity is stretched, but not broken. Troubles seem to mount—the person is late, the streets deserted, he is uncertain of the way, and he is apparently new in town—but with "fortunately" we breathe more easily and feel the story will take a turn for the better. Policemen always know their way about town and our credulity is restored completely when the stranger asks the officer "the way" (though we note in passing that he does not add "to the railroad station"). We are, however, unprepared for the answer and even more disturbed—even dumbfounded—by the final reply, "Give it up." The realism of the story has been cracked and through it we glimpse *something*—but what?

This parable is an extended metaphor, and, as a genuine metaphor, it is not translatable into concepts. To be sure, it is shot through with open-endedness, with pregnant silences, with cracks opening into mystery. But it remains profoundly impenetrable. It is, as we shall see, far more impenetrable than biblical parables because what Kafka's parables are all "about" is simply the incomprehensibility of the incomprehensible. Kafka's parables, like all genuine parables, are themselves actuality—the parables are a figurative representation of an actual, total meaning, so they do not "stand for" anything but *are* life. This means we must make a very careful analysis of all the parts of the parable for they *are* the *meaning* of it. The meaning is not a separate realm, something that can be pointed to; the totality of all the processes of life and thought in the parable *is* its meaning. What this totality of all the processes of life and thought amounted to in Kafka's parables was the incomprehensibility of the incomprehensible; but this is not an extrinsic meaning—it is *what the story says*.

> And again Jesus spoke to them in parables saying, "The kingdom of heaven may be compared to a king who gave a marriage feast for his son, and sent his servants to call those who were invited to the marriage feast; but they would not come. Again he sent other servants, saying, 'Tell those who are invited, Behold, I have made ready my dinner, my oxen and my fat calves are killed, and everything is ready; come to the marriage feast.' But they made light of it and went off, one to his farm, another to his business, while the rest seized his servants, treated them shamefully, and killed them. The king was angry, and sent his troops and destroyed those murderers and burned their city. Then he said to his servants, 'The wedding is ready, but those invited were not worthy. Go therefore to the thoroughfares, and invite to the marriage feast as many as you find.' And those servants went out into the streets and gathered all whom they found, both bad and good; so the wedding hall was filled with guests.
>
> (Matt. 22:1–10; cf. Luke 14:16–24)

Initially we may feel on much more solid ground in this parable of the Wedding Feast than with Kafka's parable.[*] The parable starts off as a simile rather than a metaphor and this is a relief: "The kingdom of heaven may be compared to . . ." But while the grammar may suggest a simile—an image that illustrates what we already know—it is obvious that we do have a genuine metaphor here, not only because we do not "already know" what the kingdom of heaven is but also because the image put forth—the ensuing story—is not a discrete comparison but a whole nexus of images, a total situation, an extended metaphor. So we are not much better off than we were when faced with Kafka's parable, though, from an analysis of the parable *itself*, I think we will discover that what the story says is other than the incomprehensibility of the incomprehensible.

The first thing to do with a parable is to read it, several times, work out the relations of those involved, highlight the subtleties of the story—in other words, let the story penetrate *us*, rather than look around for possible interpretations of it. The host is the king, an important, if not *the* important man around, and he gives a marriage feast for his son—the setting is one of high import. The guest list presumably includes the "best" people (the ones with farms, businesses, well-spread tables). The setting is realistic, and in keeping with this realism the king is inviting those on the social register to his son's wedding. The first awkward and unexpected note is introduced with "but they would not come." What possible excuses could *anyone* give for refusing to come to such a dinner, and why should *those* people especially want to refuse the invitation? The king, with unusual generosity and patience, we feel, persists; not only that, he describes in luscious detail the dinner—appealing not to their respect for their king or even to their common courtesy, but to their stomachs! The list of delights to be had at the feast ends with a sweeping assertion, "everything is ready," and with a supplication, "come to the marriage feast." The realism is strained and we are surprised at their responses: one group is indifferent, the other violent. The molestation and murder of the servants strikes the reader with a shock not unlike the "Give it up" of the smiling policeman in Kafka's parable. In both instances a deep crack breaks the surface realism and we glimpse something through it; the context or frame of the story is something out of the ordinary. The king's anger, on the other hand, seems justified, and it is total—the guests are wiped out. At this point a second movement begins in the story: the invitation to others, and the invitation is as total as was the liquidation of the first guests. Once again the frame of the story is not the ordinary one. The servants go "into the streets" and invite indiscriminately "both bad and good" until the hall is filled.

This story is by no means incomprehensible, but neither is it a story with a "moral" or with "one point," two ways of interpreting parables which many New Testament scholars have until late embraced and which many preachers still embrace. It is, first of all, as Robert Funk says, "a paradigm of reality." It is, however, a paradigm of reality as seen in a novel context—one in which "everydayness" is no longer the accepted criterion. Funk speaks of two "logics" of viewing reality in the parable with which the structure of the story and the relations of characters present us.[2] These are, of course, the logics of merit and of grace, or to put it less theologically, the logic of those who view reality in everyday terms and those who view it in a surprising, new context, the perspective of receiving what one does not deserve. The first invitations are offered to the worthy; the second invitations are proffered with no regard to worth.

This comment leads to a second point, for the insight that comes—the new "logic"—is dependent on the deformation of the old "logic." We recall Owen Barfield's comment that the aesthetic moment, the moment of new insight, always involves "a felt change of consciousness," which occurs when everyday language is used in an unfamiliar context. Metaphorical language, parabolic language, does not take us out of everyday reality but drives us more deeply into it, de-forming our usual apprehensions in such a way that we see that reality in a new way. The second "logic" like all new meaning is a deepening of reality, not an escape from it into a never-never land. What we see, then, in the parable of the Wedding Feast is not a new reality but the same reality in a new perspective.[†] The mundane world is transmuted; no new world is created. In both "logics," the "world" is the story of the wedding feast; what changes is the guest list—those who will accept the invitation to the feast. This is an important point, for it means that there is no two-world thinking here—a "secular" and a "religious" perspective; rather the question is a secular and a mundane one, the question of two specific ways of comporting oneself with reality. As genuine metaphors, parables could not do other than turn us toward reality, for, as Wallace Stevens says, the purpose of "the symbolic language of metamorphosis" is to intensify one's sense of reality. Or, as Philip Wheelwright puts it: "What really matters in a metaphor is the psychic depth at which the things of the world, whether actual or fancied, are transmuted by the cool heat of the imagination."[3] If there were a "turn" in the parable of the Wedding Feast away from the everyday, if the gracious closing invitation of the king took our attention away from the concrete story, the parable would be neither a good metaphor nor, as Gerhard Ebeling claims it to be, "the linguistic incarnation," the form of language most appropriate to the incarnation.[4]

This is not to say, of course, that the dimension of grace is passed over in silence in the story. The world of the parable includes *both* the secular and the religious, but with a primary focus on the secular.[§] In Max Black's terminology, the story is the screen or "smoked glass" through which we perceive the new logic of grace; or as Philip Wheelwright says, assertions about this dimension are made "lightly" or in "soft focus"; or as Michael Polanyi would claim, our focal awareness is on the story, our subsidiary awareness on its transcendent dimensions. A New Testament parable is a "linguistic incarnation" and, like its teller, who himself was the parable of God, works by indirection, by, as Leander Keck says, framing "familiar elements in unfamiliar plots."[5] The spectators must participate imaginatively, must so live in the story that insight into its strangeness and novelty come home to them. They are not *told* about the graciousness of God in a parable but are *shown* a situation of ordinary life which has been revolutionized by grace. In other words, parables, and Jesus as a parable, operate in the way metaphor does.

Finally we are brought to a third point: we do not interpret the parable, but the parable interprets us. This watchword of the new hermeneutic is neither a slogan nor a conundrum: it is simply the consequence of taking the parable as metaphor seriously. Metaphors cannot be "interpreted"—a metaphor does not *have* a message, it is a message. If we have really focused on the parable, if we have let it work on us (rather than working on it to abstract out its "meaning"), we find that we are interpreted.¶ That is, we find ourselves identifying with one of the two guest lists—our own logic toward reality is illuminated. In this parable, as in the Prodigal Son and many others (though by no means all) some hear and understand and accept the unmerited invitation and some do not.

Parables as Metaphors

Parables have not always, or usually, been viewed as metaphors.** Historical criticism tended to focus on "what a parable meant" in its historical context (C. H. Dodd and Joachim Jeremias). This approach is perhaps an advance over Jülicher, whose "one-point" interpretation tended to reduce the parables to their ideational possibilities, evidencing little if any appreciation for them as metaphors, in other words, as non-reducible entities. A metaphor is neither reducible to one point nor is its "meaning" foreclosed in some historical moment: it is rather generative of *new* meanings in the plural. C. H. Dodd's definition of Jesus' parables does point to other possibilities.

> At its simplest the parable is a metaphor or simile drawn from nature or common life, arresting the hearer by its vividness or strangeness, and leaving the mind in sufficient doubt about its precise application to tease it into active thought.[6]

The emphasis on strangeness, doubt, and teasing into active thought preclude the reduction of the parabolic form to one point or to a purely historical interpretation. Amos Wilder indicates the same direction when he conceives of the parable as a metaphor in which "we have an image with a certain shock to the imagination which directly conveys vision of what is signified."[7]

But before we can speak directly of the "certain shock to the imagination" which the parable form effects, we must look at its setting—not its historical setting (a question for the New Testament scholars to debate) but its setting as an aesthetic object. As an extended metaphor, the parable is an aesthetic object—and we shall have more to say about this—but, it seems to me, an aesthetic object of a special sort. For to a greater degree than other aesthetic objects, such as an Eliot poem or a Tolstoy novel, the setting of the parable is triangular. The components of the triangle are source or author (Jesus as narrator), the aesthetic object (the parable narrated), and the effect (the listeners to whom the parable is narrated). This triangle pattern points to the original situation of the parables: *Jesus* told *stories* to *people*. All three factors should operate in any analysis of the parables, for they cannot be abstracted from their source or from their listeners. As Norman Perrin points out, there are three kinds of interpretation involved in *any* textual criticism: historical, literary, and hermeneutical; that is, criticism of *who* tells or writes, *what* is told or written, and to *whom* the text is directed.[8]

The parables present a special case, however, for the point of Jesus' parables is not mere illumination, aesthetic insight, or secret wisdom. There is a stress in the parables on confrontation and decision, an emphasis not evident in most other aesthetic objects. "The parables of Jesus were directed to a specific situation, the situation of men and women confronted by the imminence of the irruption of God into their world."[9] Hence, while the three components of the interpretative triangle are crucial, there is an emphasis on the third, on the listeners, though, as we shall see, the power of the confrontation occurs only because of *who* told the parables and *what* is being told to them.

The first component of the triangle, Jesus as narrator, is perhaps the most difficult. We are all well aware of the pitfalls of the Intentional Fallacy, the deleterious effects on the integrity of the aesthetic object through interpretation by means of the "intentions" of the *artist*. And we have no desire to fall into that trap, not because it is unfashionable but because if we take the parable as metaphor seriously, attention must be focused on the parable itself and not on its authority or source. Two qualifications can be made, however. First, it does matter, in the instance of the biblical parables, that Jesus and not someone else told them. They are, as Perrin points out, "highly personal texts" which express "the vision of reality of their author," and that vision "cannot be contemplated except in dialogue with their creator."[10] The "voice" which calls us (as Walter Ong would put it) in the parables is the voice of Jesus.[11] The best way to his vision is through the parables, for, as New Testament scholars agree, the parables not only are Jesus' most characteristic form of teaching but are among the most authentic strata in the New Testament. Hence our attention should not be diverted from the parables to the intentions of their author, for it is only by giving extraordinary attention to the parables themselves that we hear that voice and understand that vision.

Second, Jesus is related to the parables obliquely, not directly. As we noted in the parable of the Wedding Feast, the attention of the listeners is directed not toward the speaker nor toward "religious" questions, but toward two "logics" of comporting oneself with reality. As Robert Funk points out, Jesus, as the speaker of the parable, brings the new "logic" near and in this sense the parable can be considered as "the self-attestation of Jesus, i.e., as the inverbalization of Jesus as the word," but the self-attestation is hidden and indirect—"the parable is an oblique invitation on the part of Jesus to follow him. Since Jesus belongs to the situation figured in the parable, it is he who has embarked upon this way, who lives out of the new 'logic'."[12] In summary, then, it is necessary to attend in a New Testament parable to Jesus as the speaker of the parables, but this can and ought to be done in a way that not only retains their integrity as aesthetic objects but in fact pushes us to focus on the parables themselves.

A second component of the triangle, the listeners, is as essential for a just appreciation of the situation of the parables as is Jesus as narrator. In fact, extraordinary attention is being paid to the listeners by current biblical scholarship: the heart of the new hermeneutic project is as we have seen, not the interpretation of the parables, but the interpretation of the listeners *by* the parables. To return again to the parable of the Wedding Feast, the way in which the hearers "hear" the parable, whether they align themselves with the old "logic" of everydayness or with the new "logic" of grace, interprets them. They are interpreted, understood, defined by their response. And this emphasis by current scholarship on the hearers is not merely an attempt to make the parables "relevant" to today's people; the parables in the New Testament are set in deeply controversial contexts—they are told in response to questions, accusations, demands, and are meant to involve the listeners directly as participants. Implied in parable after parable is the question, "And what do *you* say? What will *you* do?" In fact, as we saw in the parable of the Wedding Feast, the structure of the story—its two "logics"—is predicated on the basis of bringing the listeners, indirectly, to a decision. But again, as with Jesus the speaker, the importance of the role of the listeners does not turn our attention away from the parable but toward it. For we need not and ought not commit the Affective Fallacy at this point—interpreting the parable by means of its effect on the listeners. Rather, concern with the effect forces us back to the parable itself, for if we are to gain *new* insight, if the parable is to work its effect, there is no way to accomplish this but through maximum attention to its own givens, to the parable as metaphor.

We are brought, then, to the parable itself as the way to hear the voice it embodies and the challenge it presents to us. The two central features of the parable as aesthetic object are its realism and its strangeness. In Jesus' parable of the Wedding Feast the realistic story is primary, and this is true of all of Jesus' parables. They are about people getting married, wayward sons, widows on limited incomes, migrant workers, doctors and patients, fools and wise men, and so on. The commonness of the parables, their secularity and mundanity, has been acknowledged and appreciated by all, and it is such an obvious trait that we might be inclined to overlook its importance. But it is special when compared with other bodies of religious literature where gods and their doings (the Greeks), hierarchies of aeons and quasi-deities (the Gnostics), wise sayings and admonitions (the Buddhists) predominate. The Sermon on the Mount, a collection of Jesus' sayings and teachings, is throughout metaphorical—the teaching is evoked in terms of salt losing its savor, lamps under bushels, temple gifts versus brotherly reconciliation, plucked-out eyes and dismembered bodies, an eye for an eye, coats and cloaks, treasures eaten by moth and rust, lilies of the field, birds of the air, pearls before swine, loaves and stones, fishes and serpents. The list of New Testament metaphors seems endless and little needs to be said about the extensiveness and commonness of biblical imagery. But it does need to be stressed that it is *there* and is the *dominant* language of the New Testament.

This realism is not the same as Homeric realism—it is not mere surface detail, all in the "foreground." Rather it is realism "fraught with background," as Erich Auerbach puts it, and this "background," in both the Old Testament and the New, is the "way" the Judaic-Christian tradition has handled the matter of speaking of the divine. *The only legitimate way of speaking of the incursion of the divine into history, or so it appears to this tradition, is metaphorically.* Metaphor is proper to the subject-matter because God remains hidden.[13] The belief that Jesus is the word of God—that God is manifest somehow in a human life—does not dissipate metaphor but in fact intensifies its centrality, for what is more indirect—a more complete union of the realistic and the strange—than a human life as the abode of the divine? Jesus as the word is metaphor par excellence; he is the parable of God.

It is entirely natural or inevitable, then, that the realism of the parables is of a special sort, that it provides again and again "that certain shock to the imagination" which Amos Wilder mentions. The way this shock is conveyed initially is the assumption of the parables that important things happen and are decided at the everyday level. The parables again and again indicate that it is in the seemingly insignificant events of being invited to a party and refusing to go, being jealous of a younger brother who seems to have it all his way, resenting other workers who get the same pay for less work, that the ultimate questions of life are decided.

The "field" which the parable thus conjures up is not merely this or that isolated piece of earthiness, but the very tissue of reality, the nexus of relations, which constitutes the arena of human existence where life is won or lost.[14]

[. . .]

The impact of the parables is directly tied to their qualities as aesthetic objects, their insistence that insight be embodied, incarnated; but the uncanny and unnerving aspect of the New Testament parables is that the peculiar insight they are concerned with, believing in a loving God who upsets the logic of the familiar, must be embodied, incarnated in human *lives*, not in the head alone but in and through the full scope and breadth of a human life. If this is the parabolic way it is necessarily metaphoric, necessarily indirect, because it is concerned not with what we believe, know, or are, but what we are in the process of believing, knowing, and becoming *in our lives*. Parables are not, then, riddles which give privileged knowledge to those who solve them. They are not *primarily* concerned with knowing but with doing (understood as deciding on a way of life based on new insight). Thus, to emphasize the parable as aesthetic object does not mean resting in whatever insight it may give us, but rather, while recognizing that its *power* to bring to decision derives from its aesthetic qualities, we must not forget that the goal of a parable is finally in the realm of willing, not of knowing.[††]

Footnotes

*　　In the comments on this parable and to a lesser extent in the general discussion of parables that follows, I am indebted to Robert W. Funk, particularly his book *Language, Hermeneutic and Word of God*. I do not go into historical critical questions about the parables but as a layperson in the field of New Testament scholarship have relied heavily on the crucial work done on the parables by Joachim Jeremias, C. H. Dodd, A. J. Cadoux, Amos Wilder, Dan Via, and Norman Perrin. My remarks are meant not to add to that body of work but to relate their findings to my central thesis of the importance of parable to theology.

†　　"The parable cannot be accommodated in the 'logic' of everydayness, but neither can it dispence with language attuned to the mundane world; the metaphorical language brings the familiar into the unfamiliar context and distorts it, in order to call attention to it anew, i.e., to bring it into a new frame of reference, a new referential totality" (Funk, *Language*, p. 195).

§　　A parallel point in regard to the focus of the parables is made by Norman Perrin: "It is a remarkable and little noted fact that . . . there is only a very limited number of parables which are concerned to proclaim the Kingdom of God *per se*. The vast majority of them are concerned with the experience and/or subsequent activity of men confronted by the reality of God at work" (*Rediscovering the Teaching of Jesus* [New York: Harper and Row, 1967]. p. 83). It is not primarily knowing about the kingdom that appears to be crucial in the parables, but rather deciding when confronted by it. The emphasis is secular, human, and individual.

¶　　". . . the word of God, like a great work of art, is not on trial. The work of art exists in its own right, to be viewed and contemplated, received or dismissed, but not reconstructed. The text, too, although shaped by human hands, stands there to be read and pondered, but not manipulated . . ." (Funk, *Language*, pp. 11–12).

**　　Of recent Biblical scholars, only A. T. Cadoux. Amos Wilder, Norman Perrin, Dan Via, Robert Funk, and John Dominic Crossan so view them consistently.

†† "The analogies developed in parables are not just any analogies. They are those which help us to develop our policies for living and decide on their adoption. The central analogies are ones which suggest roles and rules in life, such as the role of sonship and the rule of neighbourly love. They are rarely analogies to impersonal features of the universe, designed to aid in speculating about anything as abstruse as 'being as such'" (Peter Slater, "Parables Analogues and Symbols," *Religious Studies*, 4 [1968], 27).

Notes

1 Heinz Politzer, *Franz Kafka: Parable and Paradox* (Ithaca: Cornell University Press, 1962), p. 1.
2 Robert W. Funk, *Language, Hermeneutic and Word of God: The Problem of Language in the New Testament and Contemporary Theology* (New York: Harper and Row, 1960), pp. 193–6.
3 Philip Wheelwright, *Metaphor and Reality* (Bloomington: Indiana University Press, 1962), p. 71.
4 Funk, *Language*, p. 130.
5 Leander Keck, *A Future for the Historical Jesus: The Place of Jesus in Preaching and Theology* (Nashville: Abingdon Press, 1971), p. 246.
6 C. H. Dodd, *The Parables of the Kingdom* (New York: Scribners, 1961), p. 16.
7 Wilder, *Language of the Gospel*, p. 80.
8 Norman Perrin, "Historical Criticism, Literary Criticism, and Hermeneutics: The Interpretation of the Parables of Jesus and the Gospel of Mark Today," *Journal of Religion*, 52 (1972), 361–575.
9 Ibid., p. 365.
10 Ibid., pp. 370–71.
11 Walter J. Ong, "Voice as Summons for Belief: Literature, Faith, and the Divided Self," *Literature and Religion*, ed. Giles B. Gunn (New York Harper and Row, 1971), pp. 68–86.
12 Funk, *Language*, p. 197.
13 Ibid., p. 154.
14 Ibid., pp. 155–56.

(d) "The Agent of a Superior": Stewardship Parables in *Our Mutual Friend*

Susan E. Colón

[. . .]

[N]o nineteenth-century British author has been more often described as a parabolist than Charles Dickens. Dickens's blend of realism with the romantic, sentimental, fantastic, and grotesque – and the moral urgency with which it is all imbued – has long fascinated his readers. Critics have characterized this blend in a wide variety of ways, parable prominent among them. While these critics do capture something important about Dickens's narrative project, they generally fail to provide a taut theory of parable on which to hang their analyses. One result of this failure is that, while they often contribute important insights into the texts under examination, those insights regularly get misdirected to the question of whether or not the hopeful, idealistic, and fantastic elements of the novels are somehow sufficient to offset or recuperate the gritty realism of Dickens's portrayals of society's problems. I suggest instead that when we take account of the role of the biblical parables in heralding the kingdom of God, a kingdom paradoxically described in Christian theology as being both a present reality and a future hope, we can see parable as an answer to the otherwise irreconcilable tension of the realist social critic's pessimism at the condition of the world and the believer's transcendent hope in ultimate redemption. This conceptualization makes intelligible the very dynamic we find in Dickens, namely that "Dickens the social critic, and Dickens the myth-maker . . . are one" (Hornbeck 1). As G. K. Chesterton has it, Dickens "was delighted at the same moment that he was desperate. The two opposite things existed in him simultaneously, and each in its full strength. . . . His soul was like a shot silk . . . of misery and joy" (37). This tension operates in *Our Mutual Friend* (1865) through the novel's complex engagement with the stewardship parables, found largely in Luke 12.

[. . .]

Critics interested in the ethical and religious aspects of Dickens's work are frequently concerned with the balance of the positive, idealist, or life-affirming aspects of a text in comparison with the grim realism with which Dickens portrays social conditions in need of reform. They typically trace a progression from the early novels, in which the ideal is triumphant, to the late novels, in which the realistic portrayal of failures in the social body overpowers the idealistic affirmation of the survival of the good. Whether the pivot is located at *Bleak House*, as Barry Quails has it, or at *Little Dorrit*, as Janet Larson has it, most critics agree that by the time of *Our Mutual Friend* Dickens's buoyant hopefulness is defeated by the social conditions he anatomizes. Consequently, one of the critical remarks most frequently made about *Our Mutual Friend* is that Dickens's negative portrayal of the city's wretchedness and Society's hollowness quells the hopeful glimmers of the plots relating to the Boffins, the Harmons, Eugene Wrayburn, and Twemlow. The Wrayburn-Headstone plot, with its steady look at variations on human depravity, seems to overpower the novel's closing gestures towards a localized redemption in the Boffin-Harmon family circle. Many readers have found the attempted recuperation of all this filth to be unconvincing, and have doubted Dickens's credence in his own fabulous resolutions.

Such conclusions seem to me unsatisfactory. First, there is the difficulty of quantifying degrees of such things as hope and despair, or optimism and pessimism, or coherence and fragmentation. Even more problematic is the inescapable subjectivity by which one decides how much of one it takes to outweigh the other, or at what point the balance tips from, say, coherence ascendant, to equilibrium between coherence and fragmentation, to fragmentation ascendant. The alternative view I will be proposing does not rely on intuitive judgments like these, because it sees the coexistence of both dispositions as precisely the point. I am less interested in proving that either hope or despair, idealism or realism, prevails over the other, and more interested in seeing the survival of the tension between them – the intensity of the pull in both directions at the same time – as the principal achievement. [. . .]

The framework of parable thus gives us another way of looking at the tension between a devastated reality and a sublime ideal that does not depend on a preponderance of empirical evidence for either. Such a framework is especially instructive for a reading of *Our Mutual Friend*, which has been called the "most iconographically Christian of all Dickens's novels" (Nord 36).

*****

The appropriateness of regarding *Our Mutual Friend* in light of the genre of parable can be established with reference to Dickens's overt and covert allusions as well as to his use of the narrative strategy of a reversal leading to moral confrontation. On the latter point, we should note that in *Our Mutual Friend*, characters persistently understand their own stories with reference to other stories. The etymological meaning of *parabole*, throwing alongside, suggests that parables are stories that are laid alongside other stories in order to make visible aspects of those stories, or to intervene in them in some way. Bella recreates the meal of the Three Hobgoblins, Rogue Riderhood turns into a Wolf, Jenny Wren as Cinderella requests transformations by her fairy godmother Riah, and Mr. Boffin pretends to emulate the illustrious misers. Fantastic stories are invoked to illuminate, recall, challenge, and reconfigure the stories the characters are living. This parabolic function, as some critics have noticed, is extended to the reader, who is asked implicitly to lay the story of *Our Mutual Friend* in some way alongside her own.

As we have seen in other parables and retellings of parables, in *Our Mutual Friend* moral growth occurs as a result of self-knowledge, and self-knowledge comes from seeing one's own actions externally dramatized in the form of a story. The most direct biblical model is Nathan's parable of the ewe lamb in 2 Samuel. Likewise, the major moral developments of characters in *Our Mutual Friend* occur in relation to such external dramatization of characters' actions and attitudes. Most obviously, Bella's reformation is effected by Mr. Boffin's apparent celebration of unvarnished greed. As Bella later expresses it (referring to herself in the third person), "[Y]ou showed her, in yourself, the most detestable sides of wealth, saying in your own mind, 'This shallow creature would never work the truth out of her own weak soul, if she had a hundred years to do it in; but a glaring instance kept before her may open even her eyes and set her thinking'" (754). Boffin makes himself a parable, reflecting Bella's attitudes back to herself, so that she can see her own "weak soul" and remedy it. As we have seen throughout this study, the signature achievement of parables is to open one's eyes and set one thinking. Bella's story is not the only such instance in the novel, though it is the most obvious. A number of characters, including Riah, Sophronia Lammle, and Mr. Venus, come to understand the stakes of their ethical dilemmas from the self-knowledge that results from, as Riah puts it, "seeing the whole thing visibly presented as upon a theatre" (708).

This pattern of moral transformation arising from seeing one's own actions in the light of a story about someone else is extended to the reader. Rosemary Mundhenk shows that Dickens's withholding of information from the reader, specifically regarding the "pious fraud" by which Boffin accomplishes the reform of Bella, challenges the reader's confidence in his or her judgments of characters. Though Mundhenk does not use the word parable to name the narrative strategy she uncovers, her account of Dickens's use of this reversal aptly describes parabolic effect. Dickens takes in the reader just as Boffin takes in Bella, and with a similar effect of facilitating self-knowledge. Arguing against those readers who have accused Dickens of changing his mind mid-stream about Boffin's character, Mundhenk demonstrates that the surprise reversal was key to Dickens's conception of this subplot. As John Reed observes, "The narrator withholds information that tests the reader's assessments of characters, therefore implying a warning against rash judgment" (*Dickens and Thackeray* 301). This strategy, moreover, tricks the reader into making excessively severe moral judgments of the characters, thus "promoting a self-correcting impulse in the reader that reinforces the novel's message of restraint" (*Dickens and Thackeray* 301). This withholding of information to mislead the reader's sympathy is much like what we saw in Yonge's *The Heir of Redclyffe*, which similarly induces skepticism about one's ability to judge one's own or another's moral state.

Similarly, Audrey Jaffe writes that "it is precisely at the moment of surprise, when we become aware of how misled we have been, that we glimpse the potential depth of our insecurity. . . . Revelation, then, comes with a double force, the force not just of a solution but of one's own epistemological limitations" (162).

[. . .]

The parable that is most frequently associated with *Our Mutual Friend* is that of the prodigal son, and for good reason. Variations on the prodigal son appear in no fewer than four of the novel's configurations of characters: Jenny Wren and her father Mr. Cleaver, Charley and Gaffer Wexam, Old Harmon and John Harmon, and Eugene and his "M.R.F." In all cases but the last, the parable is inverted in wrenching ways. Instead of the satisfying tale of the beloved lost son returned to the loving father, which the Victorians saw as emblematic of the whole gospel message, Dickens gives us families sundered unto death by greed, pride, and addiction.

[. . .]

As with the prodigal son parable, in which Dickens confounds the roles of parents and children, wrong-doers and well-doers, so in his rendering of the parables of stewardship Dickens turns owners into stewards and stewards into owners. In fact, this interchanging of roles is the thematic crux of the novel's plots about money. The stewardship parables, used unobtrusively but pervasively throughout the novel, supply a conceptual model that enables the transformation of "illth" into wealth (Ruskin's terms). Properties in the hands of stewards make wealth; they are the dust that is really gold, that conduces to life. Conversely, properties in the grip of owners or would-be owners tend to make illth; they are the gold that is really dust that conduces to death.[1]

[. . .]

*****

The stewardship parables conceptually solve the problem that, according to George Levine, lies at the heart of the realist novel, namely, how to reconcile the protagonist's capitalistic success with his moral virtue. Levine writes, "Novelists need the success of their protagonists to bring off their comic endings, but they are hard pressed to imagine ways, within the textured representation of middle class life and economy, to represent it without radically compromising the protagonists' moral integrity" (*Realism, Ethics and Secularism* 228). The usual symptom of this problem is indecisive, colorless male protagonists, and the usual solution is the device of inheritance. Levine claims that this problem "is exacerbated in *Our Mutual Friend*" and finds its fullest instance in "Harmon's status as 'dead'" (*Dying to Know* 153). However, I suggest that Dickens's use of the parabolic trope of stewardship represents a serious and at least partially successful effort to apply a Christian solution to this basic problem. The twin antidotes to greed, for Dickens as for the gospels, are stewardship and gratitude. With the model of grateful stewardship Dickens is able to imagine capitalistic activity without accompanying corruption.

[. . .] The Boffins serve a long apprenticeship in stewardship of the Harmon property, proving their fitness to be the executors of Mr. Harmon's will and indeed the heirs of his fortune. Even while waiting for John Harmon's return from abroad, "The room was kept like this, Rokesmith, against the son's return," Mr. Boffin tells his secretary. "In short, everything in the house was kept exactly as it came to us, for him to see and approve" (185). The teasing irony of Mr. Boffin's saying this while escorting that son, in the persona of the secretary Rokesmith, to see the house should not distract us from the revelation that the Boffins continue, as possessors of the house, to hold their ownership at arm's length.

The Boffins, of course, never crave possession of the fortune. The gold that corrupts Harmon in his possession of it never corrupts Noddy and his "old lady" in their humble management of it. He tells Rokesmith that the single Mound "would have been enough for us . . . in case it had pleased God to spare the last of those two young lives and sorrowful deaths. We didn't want the rest" (185). This declaration is not pious cant: it is corroborated by the revelation at the end of the book that the Boffins had in their possession Old Harmon's last will, disinheriting his son absolutely and leaving the whole property to them. The couple's literally extravagant decision to suppress this will amounts to their choosing to remain as stewards of the son's property rather than claiming the ownership to which the will entitles them.

Even when John Harmon's death is established and the Boffins are legal owners of the property, they retain the habit of regarding themselves in the light of stewards, in part because that role is more conducive to their peace of mind. Boffin declares himself happier in the role of manager than of owner: "When I was foreman at the Bower . . . I considered the business very satisfactory," whereas ownership troubles his mind: "It's a great lot to take care of," he laments to Mortimer Lightwood (94). Lightwood's cynical reminder that others would be happy to take the management of the money upon themselves is no relief to Mr. Boffin, who knows that he would be morally responsible for the actions of his steward as well as for his own. Having a steward would not diminish his responsibility in the way that being a steward does. Mrs. Boffin's plan to adopt a child, give him John's name (not their own), and endow him with the property Mrs. Boffin still refers to as "John's own money," is another way in which the couple maintains a posture of stewardship towards their possessions (330).

The stewardship plot gets more complicated as John Harmon, under the name Rokesmith, becomes secretary (or "Steward," as he says) to Boffin. John, who is thought by both the reader and himself to be the rightful owner of the property, acts as steward to the Boffins, who earlier acted as stewards on behalf of John while awaiting his return. Now John echoes Riah's refrain, telling Headstone on one occasion, "You should know that I am not the principal here" (379). In this role, John "was discerning, discreet, and silent, though as zealous as if the affairs had been his own. He showed no love of patronage or the command of money, but distinctly preferred resigning both to Mr. Boffin. If, in his limited sphere, he sought power, it was the power of knowledge; the power derivable from a perfect comprehension of his business" (193). Most readers will by this point perceive that "Rokesmith" is John Harmon, so the line "as if the affairs had been his own" has ironic resonance. However, we also see that John is using his position as a sort of apprenticeship to learn his affairs thoroughly, all the while conscientiously keeping himself in the position of a steward.

As the plot plays out, further reversals and abdications occur. John considers "coming to life" and asserting (what he believes to be) his rightful ownership, but believing that that action would dispossess his benefactors and would be unwelcome to Bella, he decides against it. Like the unprofitable servant in the parable of the pounds, John is tempted to "bury" himself and his claim to the Harmon property. This apparently safe and altruistic action must not be allowed, for the same reason that the servant is punished for his diffident reluctance to make use of his master's property. As Stirling writes with special relevance for *Our Mutual Friend*, "The [buried] talent is in the wrong place. Dust is an indifferent bank" (92). Harmon's becoming known to the Boffins, though it is not related until much later in the novel, occurs soon after his resolution to bury himself precisely in order to spare him from culpability for such a mistake.

At last, Boffin presents the third and final will, which leaves all the property to himself, in order to deprive Wegg of his power to blackmail Boffin with the second will. However, as a condition of establishing this will Boffin requires John to accept his father's fortune as a gift from himself and his wife. As in the parable, the faithful steward is rewarded by being placed over all his master's possessions. The original faithful steward, Boffin, is given ownership of the property while John is believed dead; then the second faithful steward, John, is given ownership when he comes "back to life." However, even when accepting the title of master de jure, neither considers himself master de facto, but rather each holds himself in the posture of stewardship to the other. So while Harmon is believed dead, Boffin continues to behave like a steward, and when Harmon is fully instated as master, he never forgets that "I owe everything I possess, solely to the disinterestedness, uprightness, tenderness, goodness (there are no words to satisfy me) of Mr. and Mrs. Boffin" (768).

In short, John and the Boffins trade off ownership and stewardship of the property throughout the book, each refusing to appropriate the property as his or their own. These complicated transactions at last bring the long-delayed "satisfactoriness" that, as Boffin mourns, had always been lacking to the Harmon fortune. The fortune is wealth to Mr. and Mrs. Boffin and to John and Bella Harmon because they all steadfastly refuse to own it. Since someone must own it to prevent it from going to sharks like Wegg, Dickens arranges for Harmon, the son and rightful heir, to own it finally, but it comes to him only after his having refused it twice (when he decided to be dead, and then to remain so) and even then only "through the munificence of Mr. Boffin," the legal owner (768).

[. . .]

*****

As noted above, much of the criticism of *Our Mutual Friend* reverts to the question of whether the book's hopeful and restorative elements are sufficient to dispel its disturbing realist elements.[2] Is the Boffin-Harmon plot (generally disliked for its melodramatic absurdities of character and plot) an adequate answer to the Wrayburn-Headstone plot (generally liked for its complex characters and realist plot)?

[. . .]

I have already indicated why I find this dispute unprofitable. A better approach can be found by recognizing that Dickens's use of parables enables precisely the coexistence of persistent hope in the face of pervasive corruption. That coexistence is a function of the theology of the kingdom of God, a topic inseparable from the parables. (Of the eighteen parables in the gospel of Matthew, sixteen of them are explicitly identified as being about the kingdom of God.) The jarring juxtaposition of reasons for despair with reasons for hope is a significant part of what is captured by New Testament parables about the kingdom of God. These parables reinforce the overall gospel message that the kingdom of God is paradoxically both a present reality and a future hope. Jesus's earliest recorded public message was, "The kingdom of God is at hand" (Mark 1:15). Similarly, Jesus told his followers, "The kingdom of God is within you," and he cited his miracles as evidence that "The kingdom of God is come upon you" (Luke 17:21, 11:20). Yet when he taught his disciples to pray, his model prayer included a plea for the kingdom of God to come on earth (Matt. 6:10). This apparent contradiction, it seems, could be best rendered by means of parables. Many of these parables, including those of the sower, the mustard seed, and the leaven, reflect that the growth of the kingdom of God is a mysterious and invisible process, with effects that become visible only after a considerable time. Others, including the wheat and the tares and the dragnet, emphasize that only at the final judgment are the faithful adherents of the kingdom definitively separated from pretenders. Still others, like the ten virgins and the ten talents, suggest that those belonging to the kingdom are in a sense tested according to their faithfulness to that kingdom during a long period of waiting for the kingdom to fully come. According to these parables, the kingdom of God is both here and not here, and that paradox has implications for every aspect of life.

These remarks are the merest sketch of an enormous topic within Christian theology and specifically within discussions of the parables.[3] My basic point – that Jesus's parables of the kingdom of God juxtapose what we may call realist reasons for skepticism or despair with idealist convictions that sustain hope – is more limited and can be sufficiently illustrated by a single example. In the parable of the wheat and the tares, Jesus compares the kingdom of God to a farmer who plants wheat in a field,

> But while men slept, his enemy came and sowed tares among the wheat, and went his way. But when the blade was sprung up, and brought forth fruit, then appeared the tares also. So the servants of the householder came and said unto him, Sir, didst not thou sow good seed in thy field? from whence then hath it tares? He said unto them, An enemy hath done this. The servants said unto him, Wilt thou then that we go and gather them up? But he said, Nay; lest while ye gather up the tares, ye root up

also the wheat with them. Let both grow together until the harvest: and in the time of harvest I will say to the reapers, Gather ye together first the tares, and bind them in bundles to burn them: but gather the wheat into my barn.

(Matt. 13:25–30)

The surprise, discouragement, and misdirected zeal of the servants in this parable signal various inappropriate responses to the fact that the kingdom of God presently coexists with alien and hostile elements. The farmer, for his part, is neither surprised at his enemy's sabotage nor at a loss as to what to do about it. Confident in the eventual sorting out of the good and bad, he is content to leave both in the field to grow. The farmer's response is of course the privileged one: the disciples are asked to realize that throughout the time in between the planting and the harvest, or between the arrival and the fulfillment of God's kingdom, the good and the bad will be mingled.

The stewardship parables we have already examined share this eschatological import. The parable of the pounds is told specifically to correct the error of those followers of Christ who "thought that the kingdom of God should immediately appear" (Luke 19:11). The closely-related parable of the stewards also speaks directly to the conduct of leaders during the time of Jesus's absence, between the resurrection and the second coming. Victorian cleric Robert Govett's explication of the parable of the stewards, for example, primarily addresses its apocalyptic meaning, noting that the sin of the foolish steward begins with his skepticism about the master's return (38). These parables, then, reflect the paradox of the kingdom of God as both a present reality and a future hope. God's gifts sustain the community in the present, and at Jesus's return the fullness of the kingdom will be given to those who have been faithful (the master will "make him ruler over all he hath") or denied to those who have been unfaithful (the master will "appoint him a portion with the unbelievers"). In other words, the parables place temporal stewardship in the context of cosmic time and ultimate reckoning.

The view of reality suggested here is one that enables the simultaneous apprehension of the world's corruption and the preservation of hope for ultimate redemption. To put it another way, a Christian worldview does not deny the evidence that the world is thoroughly and painfully awry. The perseveration of hope does not require that the good in the world outweigh the bad at any particular moment; in fact, the Christian doctrine of original sin predicts that the bad will, on balance, outweigh the good more often than not. Christian hope can be described as having one's eyes fully open to all that can be seen, while still affirming the reality of that which cannot be seen. As Chesterton says in his discussion of Dickens, "If we are idealists about the other world we can be realists about this world" (194).[4]

From this standpoint, then, discussions about whether the good or bad elements finally prevail in the world of a Dickens novel are beside the point. To read Dickens in this way we need not maintain that Dickens subscribed to the theology of the kingdom of God that I have just outlined, but only that elements of Dickens's narrative patterns – including his cheery resolutions that, however limited they may be, he seems unable to do without – owe something to the pattern and paradoxes of what he famously called "the best book that ever was or will be known in the world."[5]

[. . .]

The expectation shown by the (mostly American) critics that Dickens, if he still had any real hope for his society, would have written a triumphalistic book in which the good news somehow shouted down the bad news within the text, may arise from the same distorted understanding of hope and faith that Terry Eagleton attributes to American intellectuals generally. In his recent reflection on *Reason, Faith, and Revolution*, Eagleton insists that the American tendency to "pathological upbeatness . . . is by no means to be confused with the virtue of hope" (138). On the contrary, a realism that he describes as Christian – insisting centrally on the inhumanity and evil expressed in Jesus's crucifixion and therefore rejecting what he calls "superstitious" faith in inevitable human progress – makes it possible to live in a socially transformative way even in a blighted world. Eagleton therefore describes Christian faith in terms that could equally well describe Dickens's implied attitude in *Our Mutual Friend*: authentic Christian faith is "the kind of commitment made manifest in a human being at the end of his tether, foundering in darkness, pain, and bewilderment, who nevertheless remains faithful to the promise of a transformative love" (37). In this view, Dickens's work partakes most strongly of a Christian flavor precisely where he gives up on Whiggish "progress," despairing of the potential of programmatic reform to make his society just and merciful, as long as "faithful[ness] to the promise of transformative love" survives. Such faithfulness indeed survives in *Our Mutual Friend* in extravagant acts of self-effacing stewardship in which ordinary capitalistic conduct is startlingly juxtaposed to extraordinary choices to act out of love rather than self-interest. Those choices redescribe human experience, to use Ricoeur's phrase, and they make visible alternatives to the norms of greed and injustice.

Those like Barry Quails who emphasize the lack of an "apocalyptic pattern" (134) in *Our Mutual Friend* would do well to remember that the gospels, to which Dickens repeatedly affirmed his allegiance until the end of his life, also do not end in an apocalypse. They climax in a resurrection, as does *Our Mutual Friend*. Eugene Wrayburn's and John Harmon's respective symbolic restorations to life, ingeniously contrived within the realist plot, serve to keep alive the hope for the survival and extension of human goodness in the meantime *until* the apocalypse. In particular, Eugene's more unexpected resurrection, combined with his surprising enactment of the rightly-ordered outcomes of both the prodigal son and the stewardship parables, signals his witness to a present though unfulfilled kingdom of harmony and justice. These resurrections, like the faithful stewardship practiced by the Boffins and Harmon, do no more and no less than to *"suggest"* the longed-for restoration of the social body "until fulfillment comes."

Notes

1   My reading here complements rather than argues with Gallagher's and George Levine's discussions of the role of suspended animation or apparent or symbolic death in the right

disposition of wealth. Those critics emphasize that it is only through death that money (Gallagher) or knowledge (Levine) can become life-giving in *Our Mutual Friend*. Yet both of them seem uninterested in the fact that the notion of "life" that is privileged by Dickens is ineluctably rooted in the Christian story and the values that derive from it. Recovering that religious investment will help us explain, to return to Gallagher's and Levine's terms, how and why it is that the liminal state of suspended animation protects one from perverted values. The self-effacement that Levine notices in the novel's life-giving characters has a name familiar to Dickens's New Testament moral framework, and that name is stewardship.

2   As Efraim Sicher phrases the question, "[W]hich is truer – that Dickens's novels aimed to reform a corrupt society or that they represented society as irredeemably wicked?" (330). Though Sicher seems to want to get beyond this question, he does not do so, deciding that "Dickens was attacking abuse more than he was proposing change" (331). My reading escapes this short-sighted binary, which seems to say that Dickens was either without hope or hoped in pragmatic, institutional reform, and therefore mistakenly requires Dickens to eschew the metaphysical realm.

3   C. H. Dodd argued very influentially for reading the parables as expressions of the kingdom of God. Ricoeur similarly sees the kingdom of God as the referent of the parables, albeit a metaphorical referent (126–27). More recently, see Hedrick, "Parable and Kingdom."

4   Dickens is for Chesterton an instance of the "optimistic reformer," who focuses not on the souls being lost, but "on the fact that they are worth saving" (194). This type of reformer is more successful, Chesterton says, because "he keeps alive in the human soul an invincible sense of the thing being worth doing, of the war being worth winning, of the people being worth their deliverance" (195). George Levine similarly writes, *"Our Mutual Friend* depends on Dickens's feeling for the supreme value of life itself" (*Dying to Know* 158).

5   *Letters of Charles Dickens*, vol. 12, 187–88. To Edward Dickens, Sept. 1868.

Works cited

Chesterton, G. K., *Charles Dickens* (1906; London: Methuen & Co., Ltd., 1925).

Dickens, Charles, *Our Mutual Friend*, ed. by Adrian Poole (1865; London: Penguin, 1997).

Eagleton, Terry, *Reason, Faith, and Revolution: Reflections on the God Debate* (New Haven: Yale UP, 2009).

Govett, Robert, 'The Parable of the Talents Explained', in *The Prophesy on Olivet, or Matthew XXIV and XXV Expounded* (Norwich: Fletcher and son, n.d.).

Hornbeck, Bert, *'Noah's Arkitecture': A Study of Dickens's Mythology* (Athens, OH: Ohio University Press, 1972).

Jaffe, Audrey, *Vanishing Points: Dickens, Narrative, and the Subject of Omniscience* (Berkeley: University of California Press, 1991).

Larson, Janet, *Dickens and the Broken Scripture* (Athens, GA: University of George Press, 1985).

Levine, George, *Dying to Know: Scientific Epistemology and Narrative in Victorian England* (Chicago: University of Chicago Press, 2002).

———— *Realism, Ethics, and Secularism: Essays on Victorian Literature and Science* (Cambridge: Cambridge University Press, 2008).

Nord, Deborah Epstein, 'Dickens's "Jewish Question": Pariah Capitalism and the Way Out', *Victorian Literature and Culture* 39 (2011): 27–45.

Qualls, Barry V., *The Secular Pilgrims of Victorian Fiction: The Novel as Book of Life* (Cambridge: Cambridge University Press, 1982).

Reed, John R., *Dickens and Thackeray: Punishment and Forgiveness* (Athens, OH: Ohio University Press, 1995).

———— *Victorian Conventions* (Athens, OH: Ohio University Press, 1975).

Chapter 8

Genesis

'WHERE DO YOU GET your ideas from?' This popular line of journalistic enquiry elicits fear, loathing and occasionally perplexed sarcasm from creative writers. Queries about the provenance of inspiration might be clichéd but, like many truisms, the question speaks to a set of cosmic puzzles. Do human beings 'create', borrow or steal stories? 'I must Create a System, or be enslav'd by another Man's' proclaims the poet-artist William Blake in *Jerusalem*.[1] Creation, according to Blake's Romantic view, is a process toward which all individuals must actively strive rather than an object, generated by others, to be passively observed. In a post-Darwinian world, however, does the term 'creation' make any sense, even in relation to the arts?

Artists, theologians and scientists are all fascinated by concepts of origin. One reason for the enduring appeal of the work of unfashionably conservative, theological writers such as C. S. Lewis and J.R.R. Tolkien might be that readers invest in vividly imagined worlds that have their own creation stories. Yet as distinctive as Narnia or Middle-Earth are, they take their origins not simply from two individual imaginations; these worlds are also shaped by a plethora of rival mythologies, novels, languages and theological sources. For Michael Edwards, the human proclivity for narrative is rooted in a search for order and, in particular, for a harmony between past, present and future. 'Story', in Edwards' view, generates not only 'purposive sequence,' but 'also [. . .] in particular, beginnings and ends. The search for beginnings is, naturally, a fundamental enterprise, in cosmogonies, genealogies, histories. The specific of story is that it appeals to the desire for a new beginning'.[2] Alternative worlds might allow readers to seek out such 'new' beginnings.

Why is there something rather than nothing? This question has been vital in interpreting the purpose of the Jewish-Christian Scriptures. The sequence of divine creation in the first two chapters of Genesis is swiftly followed in the book's third chapter with the fall of humanity and the exile from Eden. Adam and Eve, after disobeying God, have a second beginning in which they are banished from paradise and made responsible for working on a harsh earth and creating new life (Genesis 3: 16–19). This narrative of foundation and catastrophe is also one of the most divisive stories in the canon. It not only separates theists from rationalist non-believers, it also splits the faithful into a vast array of interpretative camps, from biblical literalists, who believe that the creation and fall story is a near verbatim historical record of the origins of the world, to those who read the story in symbolic terms. The tale might engender simultaneous awe for the creator and sorrow regarding human frailty; for other more sceptical readers, Genesis is a pernicious fairy-tale designed to inculcate a guilty conscience and subservience to authority.

The creation and fall story in Genesis is not the only biblical text to address questions of origins. 'In the beginning was the Word,' claims St John, in perhaps the most celebrated and poetic line from the four canonical gospels. In John's narrative, the *logos* is coterminous with the creation of all things. In some senses, all texts – whether explicitly theological or not – are concerned with the question of their own origin. Detective stories, for example, constitute a consummately rational genre but they rely on a hidden origin – a misdemeanour – without which there would be no subsequent story. In a short introduction to the book of Genesis, the American novelist E. L. Doctorow reflects on the connection between the Eden narrative and 'all mystery stories' which demand a kind of 'backward' knowledge on the part of the author. The story of Adam and Eve's fall and the suffering that it generates, suggests Doctorow, 'has turned the human condition into a sequential narrative of how it came to be; it has used conflict and suspense to create a moral framework for *being*'.[3]

The fall narrative is not just part of a book of beginnings; it has inspired a vast number of writers to re-create the story of the start. The most famous of these is John Milton's epic poem, *Paradise Lost* (1667; 1674), which self-identifies as a work designed to 'justify the ways of God to men'. The twelve-book narrative re-imagines both the 'war in heaven' – the rebellion of Satan against God – and the fall of humanity. Milton's theodicy, however, is also grounded in defining questions about points of origin, temporality and creativity. Twenty-first-century culture is replete with allusions to the biblical account of creation and humanity's first rebellion. The most Miltonic of these is Philip Pullman's *His Dark Materials* sequence (1995–2000). This rationalist-mystic epic includes a re-writing of elements of Genesis that draws on William Blake's Romantic re-interpretation of *Paradise Lost*. Stephanie Meyer's bestselling Gothic romance *Twilight* (2005) is prefaced by a quotation from Genesis 2: 17 (and its UK cover features two hands cupping a blood red apple). The creation story offered by Ridley Scott's science fiction movie *Prometheus* (2012) may allude to Greek myth but its narrative still implicitly depends on Jewish-Christian ideas of a fall into knowledge. David Maine's *Fallen* (2005) is more openly engaged with Genesis in its intriguing reverse narration of the first biblical family, beginning with the death of an elderly Cain and ending moments after Adam and Eve have rebelled against God.

All four extracts that feature in this section address stories from Genesis, and three of this quartet – those by Regina Schwartz, Stanley Fish and Terry R. Wright – explore aspects of the creation and fall narrative from Genesis 1–3. In his detailed preface to the second edition of *Surprised by Sin: The Reader in Paradise Lost* (1967; 1998), Fish emphasizes the originating connection between the disobedience of Adam and Eve and the possibility of narrative itself. The absence of a 'first fall' would also mean 'no story, no plot, since plot and story depend on agents who are either not where they should be or not where they want to be'.

Fish's study mediates between two clashing ways of reading Milton's epic. One tradition, represented by Lewis, maintained that the poem presents an orthodox critique of the consequences of disobedience to God. The rival interpretation, embodied by William Blake and William Empson, defends Satanic and human rebellion and views the God of the poem as an oppressive tyrant. Fish, reflecting on his work, claims to have been able to 'reconcile the two camps' by proposing a new thesis. For Fish, *Paradise Lost* is 'about how its readers came to be the way they are; its method [. . .] is to provoke in its readers wayward, fallen responses which are then corrected by one of several authoritative voices (the narrator, God, Raphael, Michael, the Son)'. This mode of interpretation suggests that the poem dramatizes, in a manner of speaking, the creation of the reader. Fish is also interested in other kinds of creation. 'When Satan decides in his freedom to break union,' argues Fish, 'he alters more than his relationship to the sustaining power of the universe; he alters the universe and creates a new one'.

In the extract from chapter one of *Remembering and Repeating* (1988), Schwartz addresses Milton's wrestling with the problem of evil and its relationship with creation. Is the universe flawed from the very inception? Not so for the 'monist' author of *Paradise Lost*. 'In Milton's cosmos,' notes Schwartz, 'all proceeds from God, a good God; hence, all – including first matter – must be good'. This is vital, Schwartz argues, for the kind of theological worldview to which Milton subscribed: to suggest that the universe was created out of an 'evil chaos' would, she notes, 'indict rather than justify a God from whom all proceeds, accusing him of fashioning a universe rotten at its very core'. Although this view is consistent with Milton's non-dualist theology, Schwartz also detects what she calls 'a dark side' to his beliefs about good and evil. Iniquity is represented as a passive rather than active phenomenon. Yet how and when might such 'corruption' have occurred in a 'perfect creation'? For Schwartz, this is a key question that Milton's 'epic both invites and silences'.

Comic ambiguity is the defining mood of Mark Twain's responses to the Jewish and Christian scriptures. The creator of Tom Sawyer and Huckleberry Finn turned to Adam and Eve, the two 'original' human creations, in a variety of parodic diaries and philosophical digressions. In *The Genesis of Fiction* (2007), Wright suggests that Twain's satirical iterations of the story are, at least tacitly, 'critical of orthodoxy'. Elements of the work considered blasphemous were suppressed during Twain's lifetime and, indeed, some of this material did not appear until the end of the twentieth century with the publication of *The Bible According to Mark Twain* (1995). In one of Twain's versions of the first rebellion, Adam abandons his principles and eats the apple because he is hungry. This 'materialist' explanation, argues Wright, is a way in which Twain 'subverts the high-minded tragedy conventionally associated with the Fall'. Twain's interpretations are sympathetic to human frailties and seem hostile to an orthodox theology that insists on both God's goodness and all-powerfulness.

Mieke Bal's *Loving Yusuf: Conceptual Travels from Past to Present* (2008) is an exception in the quartet of extracts in that the text does not focus on Adam and Eve. It is, however, another story of beginnings with a particular focus on the things that shape shared practices of reading and interpretation. In the opening chapter, 'First Memories, Second Thoughts', Bal recalls her earliest encounter with the story of Joseph and Potifar's wife (Genesis 39) as re-told by a primary school teacher. She 'tells this tale of getting to know the story not to make this essay unnecessarily personal but' in order 'to understand how books and lives hang together'.

Bal makes a key distinction between what she calls *literalism* (of which she claims to be 'a strong advocate') and *fundamentalism* (a mode that 'makes a devastating appeal to an immutably referential, prescriptive meaning, an appeal that is based on a radical denial or negligence of how signs work'). 'Reading,' argues Bal, 'is establishing a meaningful connection between [. . .] relatively stable texts and the varying, historically shifting meanings they generate'. Bal fuses a mode of scriptural exegesis with what she calls 'cultural memory'. The piece addresses the way in which an early aural encounter with a text shaped her understanding of gender (specifically the idea that women represent a danger to men and that love was associated with lies). Bal is also clear that one of the crucial questions asked by any interpreter ('Why?') is contained not by the original text but by the reader and the reader's world. This reflection on the nature of reading is something that implicitly binds the quartet of extracts included in this section. Each critic displays an interest in the relationship between transgression, interpretation and creativity. 'Why?' is the kind of question that can push a reader across thresholds and into new, unmapped territories.

Notes

1   William Blake, *Jerusalem: The Emanation of the Giant Albion*, ed. by Morton D. Paley (Princeton: Princeton University Press, 1998), p. 144.

2   Michael Edwards, *Towards a Christian Poetics* (London: Macmillan, 1984), p. 73.

3   E. L. Doctorow, 'The First Book of Moses, Called *Genesis*', in *Revelations: Personal Responses to the Books of the Bible* (Edinburgh: Canongate, 1998), pp. 17–23 (pp. 18–19).

Further reading

Alter, Robert, *Genesis* (New York: Norton, 1996)

Armstrong, Karen, *In the Beginning: A New Interpretation of Genesis* (London: Vintage, 2011)

Clark, Timothy, *The Theory of Inspiration: Composition as a Crisis of Subjectivity in Romantic and Post-Romantic Writing* (Manchester: Manchester University Press, 1997)

Edwards, L. Clifton, 'Artful Creation and Aesthetic Rationality: Toward a Creational Theology of Revelatory Beauty', *Theology Today*, 61.1 (2012), 56–72

Empson, William, *Milton's God* (London: Chatto and Windus, 1965)

Fiddes, Paul S., ed., *The Novel, Spirituality and Modern Culture* (Cardiff: University of Wales Press, 2000)

Hart, Trevor and Ivan Khovacs, eds., *Tree of Tales: Tolkien, Literature and Theology* (Waco: Baylor University Press, 2007)

Jacobs, Alan, *Original Sin: A Cultural History* (London: SPCK, 2008)

Jasper, David, *Coleridge as Poet and Religious Thinker: Inspiration and Revelation* (London: Macmillan, 1985)

Kermode, Frank, *The Genesis of Secrecy: On the Interpretation of Narrative* (Cambridge, Mass.: Harvard University Press, 1979)

Sanders, Theresa, *Approaching Eden: Adam and Eve in Popular Culture* (Lanham: Rowman & Littlefield, 2009)

Twain, Mark, *The Bible According to Mark Twain*, ed. by Howard G. Baetzhold and Joseph B. McCullough (New York: Touchstone, 1996)

(a) Preface to the Second Edition of *Surprised by Sin: The Reader in* Paradise Lost

Stanley Fish

Paradise Lost, as everyone knows, opens *in medias res*, and it is only in Book V that we get the beginning of the story; in fact we get the beginning of story itself, for if there had been no first fall, no first breaking of union, there would have been no story, no plot, since plot and story depend on agents who are either not where they should be or not where they want to be. In Heaven, and for a while in Paradise, everyone is in his or her proper place (the place ordained by God), doing the right thing (exemplifying and attesting to God's goodness and glory), and perfectly happy (since happiness is defined as union with the highest and worthiest). Another (negative) way to put this is that in Heaven and in pre-lapsarian Paradise nothing happens, if we think of a 'happening' as something that alters basic conditions and sets in motion energies that either lead to the establishment of a new order or become reabsorbed into an old one. So the question, 'where did evil come from?' might be rephrased as 'how did anything ever happen?'

It is (literally) tempting to equate that question with the question posed by the epic voice at I. 28, 'what cause?' In that form the question assumes a psychology in which motives (causes) come from the outside: the agent's understanding of the world and his or her place in it is challenged by something (a new phenomenon, an anomalous outcome) and as a result he or she begins to act differently. But this view of causality and of change from a previous state of equilibrium turns out to be the wrong one, although for reasons I hope to make clear it is a view that remains powerfully attractive. We find out that it is wrong when Satan's story provides no answer to the question of cause, and instead piles mystery upon mystery. The first mystery is the identity of the agent who somehow changes and in changing brings evil into the world. We never see him, but see only what he has become, '*Satan*, so call him now, his former name/ Is heard no more in Heav'n' (V. 658–59). His former name is heard no more not because it is anathema to pronounce it (as might be the case in some blood feud when the patriarch says, 'never mention his name again in this house') but because *he* no longer exists. (As Regina Schwartz observes, this is true of all the fallen angels: 'Having lost their positive identity, they have lost their names.'[1]) At the very beginning of what promises to be an explanation of how the whole thing got started the agent whose act we hope to understand disappears. To be sure, we know something about him, but what we know only deepens the puzzle. Along with the other angels he has heard the Father's pronouncement – 'This day I have begot whom I declare/ My only Son' (V. 603–4) – and it is clear that before this moment he was in a particularly favoured position:

> . . . he of the first,
> If not the first Arch-Angel, great in Power,
> In favor and preëminence, yet fraught
> With envy against the Son of God.
>
> (659–62)

'yet' is the hinge word here, and what it means is 'nevertheless' or 'despite' or 'who would have thought it?' It works exactly like 'Favor'd of Heav'n so highly' (describing Adam and Eve) works in Book I.I.30, to emphasize the *absence* of an intelligible connection between the agent's situation and his or her response to it: it's the last thing you would have expected from the last person. One moment there is the now obliterated (his-name-is-heard-no-more) angel, and the next there is Satan, a new being who is fraught with envy. That is to say, he is *full of* envy; envy, the desire to be somewhere and/or someone else, is what constitutes and animates him, and it is also what determines his perception: 'fraught/ With envy against the Son of God . . ./. . . could not bear/ Through pride that sight, and thought himself impair'd./ Deep malice thence conceiving and disdain' (661–62, 664–66).

The awkwardness of the syntax in these lines is significant. Had Milton written 'could not bear/ That sight through pride' the verse would have given 'that sight' an independent status as something with its own perspicuous features which are then – that is, subsequently – distorted by Satan's prideful lens. But in the sequence as we have it the 'sight' quite literally comes into view 'through' – under the aegis of – Satan's pride, and the point is (again quite literally) brought home to us when the verse insists that before reaching 'that sight' we must go through the words 'through pride'. The effect is to alert us to the nature of Satan's 'mistake' which is not one he could have avoided by getting closer to the object (in the manner of an experimental scientist) or by acquiring more information about it; rather he could have seen 'that sight' (the exaltation of the Son) more clearly only if the lens through which he was looking was not made of envy or pride, but of something else, say, for example, faith and obedience. These alternative perspectives are not produced by events; it is the other way around: pride and obedience name the positions perceiving agents already occupy, and it is within those positions that the shape of events emerges, and it will emerge differently depending on the point of perspectival origin. The fact that Satan sees 'through pride' does not mean that he should have seen directly or without mediation, but that he should have seen through something else. 'Seeing through' is not a condition to be shunned; it is the condition of all agents who are partial and situated, and that includes angels as well as men. You have to see through something, just as you have to be fraught with (informed by) something, and the only questions are, through what shall you see and with what shall you be fraught?

But how do you make the choice if the facts do not precede that choice but are its results? How are you to know what is good and right? This is also Catherine

Belsey's question – 'What . . . are the grounds of true knowledge?'[2] – which she answers by implying that in this poem there are none. (In a sense, but not her sense, this is true.) If Satan makes a wrong choice, she reasons, we only know it because the narrative turns out badly for him. In the scene where he debates with Abdiel the wisdom and rightness of rebellion neither he nor his opponent makes a point the other cannot dispute and each argues from what seems to be the relevant, but different, features of his experience. In the end, Belsey observes, the difference between the two parties and their respective positions is political and rhetorical, a matter of who seems the more plausible to the larger number of hearers: 'Satan succeeds in persuading one group: God retains the allegiance of the rest.' But given the equal plausibility of the cases they put, why should we be persuaded by one rather than the other? 'How are we to be sure that we recognize the truth?' (78).

The answer is (1) we (readers and/or characters) can't be sure; that's not the kind of world this is; and (2) the fact that we can't be sure is not a flaw in the poem's epistemology but a necessary condition of the drama of choice. If recognizing the truth meant simply attending to evidence that was self-declaring, the choosing intelligence would have nothing to do except assent to the undeniable. In the world Milton creates, however, such evidence (for which Satan searches endlessly in *Paradise Regained*) is unavailable to limited agents who make their choices not on the basis of indisputable facts but on the basis of prior dispositions – prior convictions as to how the universe is disposed – in relation to which the facts, now experienced as indisputable, emerge. When God 'retains the allegiance' of Abdiel and his fellow loyalists, it is not because events and actions unambiguously attest to his goodness (as Empson and others remind us, he sends his servants on unnecessary errands, commands them to actions they cannot perform, and stage manages situations in order to provide a showcase for his only begotten Son), but because they begin with the assumption of his goodness and then reason about events in the light of that prior assumption. And the same holds on the other side: when Satan decides to 'dislodge' his legions (V. 669) and take them to the North, it is not because the sight he sees compels that response, but because 'that sight' is itself seen through a lens, a conviction, that configures and precedes it. In both cases the sequence reverses the order of empirical investigation: first the conclusion (God is good or God is a tyrant) and then the proof which is presented as validating it, but is in fact produced by it. The anointing of the Son by God does not cause Satan's envy and pride; they are what is inside him and they determine for him what 'that sight' obviously signifies.

But this is only to push our original question (where does evil come from?) back further. How, given that he like the rest of the angels was created good, did pride and envy get inside him? The answer is given (by not being given) in V. 1. 665:

> . . . could not bear
> Through pride that sight, and thought himself impair'd.
> (664.b–665)

The second half of the line – 'and thought himself impair'd' – reads first as what it surely is, an account of Satan's psychology. He saw the Son's exaltation and took it as a slight, as an affront to his honour, as a diminishing of his own status: he thought himself impaired, made less. But the phrase will bear another reading in which impairment is not simply what he thinks about but what he suffers as the result of so thinking. That is, by thinking of the honour done to the Son as something that made him less (as opposed to Abdiel who later in the book thinks of the same honour as returning to him and his fellows) he becomes less, becomes the diminished creature whom we know as Satan. In short he thought in a certain way when other ways were available and by so thinking he thought himself into a state of impairment ('thought himself impair'd'); he made himself less – a being made of envy and pride rather than of trust and faith – by his thoughts.

But the puzzle returns in another (really the same) form. Why does he think *that* way? The question arises naturally, but it cannot be answered without pointing to some cause or prompting external to Satan's mental and moral processes. In the psychology Milton imagines for his characters, however, promptings always well up from *within*, whether they be good ('those free and unimposed expressions which from a sincere heart unbidden come into the outward gesture'[3]) or bad ('Though ye take from a covetous man all his treasurs, he has yet one jewell left, ye cannot bereave him of his covetousnesse'[4]). The only appropriate answer to the question 'why does Satan think himself into a state of impairment?' is tautological and unhelpful. Satan thinks that way (in a manner that impairs him even as he worries about being impaired) because he is capable of doing so, although the fact that he *can* think that way doesn't mean that he *must* think that way; it is a possible not a determined direction of thought. That is what free will means: a will poised between alternative conceptions (and therefore between alternative programmes for action) the choice of which is entirely within its power as opposed to being dictated by the pressures of external circumstance. As Adam puts it, the free agent is 'Secure from outward force; within himself/ The danger lies, yet lies within his power:/ Against his will he can receive no harm' (IX. 348–50). The formulation is precise and is designed to ward off two mistakes; the mistake of enthralling the will to forces outside it, and the mistake of turning the internal vulnerability of the will into a form of determinism, as Christopher Ricks does when he asks 'if they could fall, were they not already in some sense fallen?'[5] The danger within is also a danger within the agent's control, and the space of control (or of its loss) is precisely the space of free will.

If there can be no answer to the question, 'why does Satan think as he does?', then there can be no answer to the question, 'why does Satan fall?' for any answer will compromise the freedom of will he here exercises. In Dennis Danielson's words, 'a free choice is not, independently of the choice itself, sufficiently caused one way or the other. Therefore . . . there is finally no answer to the question *why*.'[6] At the point where we most want an explanation, we find only a mystery whose (non)shape is perfectly (un)represented in the spontaneous and unmotivated ('*yet* fraught with envy') emergence of a new being who has literally conceived himself without any outside aid: 'Deep malice thence conceiving and disdain.' (The fact that this conceiving occurs at line 666 speaks for itself and for the extraordinary care with which Milton structures almost every detail of the epic.) There is then a truth to Satan's claim to have been 'self-begot,' although not in the sense he makes it. What he means is that his first creation (out of primordial material or out of nothing) was self engineered by his 'own quick'ning power' (v. 861), a conclusion he draws (absurdly) from the fact that he doesn't remember being created by anybody else. But the second creation from the 'his-name-is-heard-no-more' angel to the present apostate is indeed his responsibility; it is a feat entirely self-accomplished by a will with the capacity either to maintain the state of original creation or to alter it for no other reason than that it is free to.

John Rogers in *The Matter of Revolution*[7] ties this moment to Milton's praise in *Defensio Populi* of the Puritan leaders as 'their own ancestors', '*ex se natos*' (128). But I would remark the difference rather than the similarity. Whereas Satan is claiming to be the origin of himself in an (impossible) absolute way, the Puritan leaders are nurturing the seed of virtue planted in them by God. (Like Adam and Eve as described by Marshall Grossman, they seek to 'author a life history conformable to that which God desires.'[8]) They are their own ancestors only in the sense that they look inward to that seed (which they cultivate) rather than outward to the accidental marks of courtly or class honour. (Milton makes the same point in *An Apology* when the members of Parliament are found to be virtuous *despite* the advantages of birth, education, and family.) The self-fashioning of which Milton approves and of which he considers himself an example, is rooted in a recognition of dependence of exactly the kind Satan here flatly rejects in a moment of bad self-fashioning. The only thing that links the two kinds of self-fashioning is a will that is free in the sense that it cannot be forced by circumstances external to it.

But if the exercise of a free will is an internal event undetermined by circumstances, its effects are not so narrowly confined. Even though the operation of the will is independent of the world ('Vertue could see to do what vertue would/ By her own radiant light, though Sun and Moon/ Were in the flat Sea sunk' [*Comus*, 372–74]), the world is not independent of it and will change – at least for the willing agent – depending on the direction freely, but momentously, taken. When Satan decides in his freedom to break union he alters more than his relationship to the sustaining power of the universe; he alters the universe and creates a new one populated by persons, events, possibilities, aspirations and facts that come into being (for him) simultaneously with his self-transformation. At the moment he thinks himself impaired he also, necessarily and at a stroke, thinks into existence a cast of supporting characters: a Father who would play favourites with his children and elevate an undeserving youth over a loyal and long serving elder son; a younger son who would accept this undeserved honour and assume powers he hasn't earned; and an army of servile foot soldiers who continue to warble hallelujahs before a corrupt throne even as a gross injustice is done. And to think these is also to think the world in which they move and have their being, a world where merit can always be trumped by dynastic politics, where earned privileges and responsibilities can be lost in an instant, where you never know who's going to be created or ruined next and you had better grab what you can while there is still time.

This, then, is the world – fully elaborated and equipped with an ontology (things create themselves), an epistemology (seeing is believing), an ethics (when you don't get what you want, take it by force), a politics (might makes right), an aesthetics ('what can Heav'n show more?') – that springs full blown from Satan's brain (the moment is replayed in the allegory of the birth of Sin) in the instant when he thinks himself impaired. Moreover, once he generates this world, he has no choice (he has already made it) but to live in it, to see what it allows him to see, to draw conclusions based on its assumed outlines, to read the present and project possible futures by its lights. He has made his bed and now he must lie in it. What you freely will is what you get, and what he gets by choosing to read his situation (and the situation of everyone and everything else) in a certain way is a succession of experiences structured by that first choice. If he begins by conceiving of God as a paternal tyrant whose reign is an accident of time and power, that conception will structure his understanding of everything that happens subsequently.

Notes

1   Regina Schwartz, *Remembering and Repeating* (Cambridge: Cambridge University Press, 1988), p. 19.
2   Catherine Belsey, *John Milton: Language, Gender, Power* (Oxford: Oxford University Press, 1988), p. 79.
3   Milton, *Apology* in *Complete Prose Works*, I, ed. Don M. Wolfe, p. 941.
4   Milton, *Areopagitica* in *Complete Prose Works*, II, p. 527.
5   Christopher Ricks, *Milton's Grand Style* (Oxford: Oxford University Press, 1964), p. 99.
6   Dennis Danielson, *Milton's Good God* (Cambridge: Cambridge University Press, 1982), p. 146. Steven Knapp offers a powerful objection to this account of free will when he asks 'if the agent, in the moment of decision, is causally disconnected from his/her prior mental states, then what exactly makes the self that performs the act identical to the self that already existed before the decision occurred' (*Literary Interest*, Cambridge, Mass.: Harvard University Press, 1993, pp. 19–20). That is, in what sense can a discontinuous self – one unaffected by past experiences – be said to *be* a self? George Herbert worries over the same problem from the other direction. It is his project to *unweave* or *unbuild* his life so that its fragmentary condition will offer no resistance to God's will. What blocks him is the inescapably temporal nature of his self-understanding. Both Herbert and Milton wish to escape from continuity for opposite reasons. One wants to be wholly taken over, the other to be wholly free. Knapp's analysis suggests that both states are impossible (something Herbert at least knows) and that Milton's libertarian account of the fall is rationally incoherent. As he observes, the only way out of this dilemma is to declare that the thesis of a will disconnected from its own history is in the poem a point of doctrine not to be inquired into, a position he correctly attributes to me.
7   John Rogers, *The Matter of Revolution* (Ithaca: Cornell University Press, 1996).
8   Marshall Grossman, *Authors to Themselves* (Cambridge: Cambridge University Press, 1987), p. 8.

(b) "And the sea was no more": Chaos vs. Creation

Regina M. Schwartz

> The angels fell; man's soul fell; and their fall shows us what a deep chasm of darkness would still have engulfed the whole spiritual creation if you had not said at the beginning *"Let there be light"*; and the light began.
>
> Augustine, *Confessions*

Milton the theologian is as emphatic and unambiguous as he could be on the subject of a good chaos.

> This original matter was not an evil thing, nor to be thought of as worthless: it was good, and it contained the seeds of all subsequent good. It was a substance, and could only have been derived from the source of all substance. It was in a confused and disordered state at first, but afterwards God made it ordered and beautiful.
>
> (*CP*, 6, 308)

He goes on to anticipate the objection that, lacking form, such a first matter must have been imperfect: "But in fact, matter was not, by nature, imperfect. The addition of forms (which, incidentally, are themselves material) did not make it more perfect but only more beautiful." In Milton's cosmos, all proceeds from God, a good God; hence, all – including first matter – must be good.

> O *Adam*, one Almighty is, from whom
> All things proceed, and up to him return,
> If not deprav'd from good, created all
> Such to perfection, one first matter all . . .
>
> (V. 469–72)

Milton argues for a good chaos with good reason. Not only is it consistent with his materialistic cosmos, it is vital to the success of his theodicy. An evil chaos would indict, rather than justify a God from whom all proceeds, accusing him of fashioning a universe rotten at its very core. Then, too, any intimation of an evil creative act would soon plunge Milton into the mire of Gnostic thinking so antithetical to his own cosmology that it suggests Blake's radical revision instead. Milton's creation is no "fall" into base materialism; it is an emanation of divine goodness. He even substitutes the theory of creation *de Deo* for the orthodox doctrine of creation *ex nihilo* to safeguard its goodness.[1]

If the author of an evil chaos were not God, the implications would be equally heretical: an evil principle coeternal with God suggests dualism at worst; at best, some hedge upon divine omnipotence. But we know Milton to be an avowed and consistent monist. Meric Casaubon (1599–1671) thought that the devil introduced to men the common mistakes concerning the origin of evil, prominent among them "that God is not omnipotent, and wanted not will, but power to amend what they conceived to be amiss in the world: or, that there were two Authors and Creators of all things, the one good, and the other evill . . . For, said they, were God as omnipotent, as he is good, why hath he not made all things as goodnesse would have prompted?"[2] With no less than the justice, oneness, and omnipotence of God at stake, Milton's position on the nature of chaos is no arcane piece of cosmological speculation. Rather, it is with the greatest care that he must deliberately and explicitly assert the goodness of first matter.

There is, nonetheless, a dark side to even his most confident assertions. Raphael's definitive-sounding discourse on cosmic perfection finesses the problem of evil, relegating it unobtrusively to the passive voice. All is perfect if not "deprav'd from good." This must be among the most troubling uses of the passive in the poem: "deprav'd" by whom, given that all proceeds from God; and how and why is such a corruption of a perfect creation even possible? Here, in the most explicit doctrine of a perfect world, the possibility of its corruption still lurks. We are offered a creation that cannot be evil but can become evil, as mysteriously as that agentless passive. Just how far back to seek the source of that corruption – whether in the fall of man, of Satan, in a flawed creation, or in the Creator himself – is the hard question the epic both invites and silences.

A cosmological explanation for the problem of evil has not been the primary approach of Christianity. Instead, it has focused on man's fall and on the redemption from the fall made possible by divine mercy. Seeking the origin of evil in the universe itself invites the kinds of questions Casaubon attributes to the devil, with dualism prominent among them. Augustine, the theologian who does inquire into the cosmological dimension, offers a solution that preserves both God's goodness and his omnipotence: evil is privation. But Milton's uncompromising monism leads him to suspect latent dualism even here, to wonder if Augustine has not merely substituted "nothing" for evil as a second principle. A.S.P. Woodhouse tells us that Milton's doctrine of a good first matter turns him away from the "avowed dualism of the Platonic tradition, and the concealed dualism of the Augustinian, to a form of monism." With that insistence upon a single good substrate of all things, Woodhouse claims, Milton "cuts away the cosmological groundwork of . . . evil, . . . sacrific[ing] the Christian solution of the problem of evil on the cosmological level."[3] I would suggest that, on the contrary, it is precisely to this level that Milton's inquiry leads him. In his quest for beginnings – "Say first," he implores the Muse of Creation, "say first what cause / Mov'd our Grand Parents in that happy state, / Favor'd of Heaven so highly, to fall off" (I. 28–30)–Milton is thrust back again and again to *the* beginning. And for all its disturbing implications, the chaos he finds there is far more hostile than he would ever acknowledge in prose. Despite his doctrine of a good chaos, his poem depicts a very different one: a region that is "waste and wild" and an allegorical figure who claims that "havoc and spoil and ruin are my gain."

Impressive scholarly excavation has been done on the subject of Milton's chaos, searching out its rightful place in tradition. A.B. Chambers has explored Milton's debt to classical antiquity and A.S.P. Woodhouse has located it in its Neoplatonic context, but surprisingly little has been written about the imaginative place of chaos in Milton's poem itself.[4] By and large, scholars have taken their cue from *De Doctrina Christiana*, accepting Milton's word on the goodness of first matter. When they have peered into the chaos of the epic, they have found it, at worst, neutral. Robert M. Adams tells us that "Chaos is neutral as between good and evil; all he likes is disorder. That inclines him to evil, of course, but not all the way, for evil is itself a principle of order; and Chaos is, so to speak, beyond good and evil."[5] Even so, Adams is apparently drawn toward another conclusion, one he rejects only on the grounds that evil must be "organized." But far from being ordered, evil is the very violation of order in *Paradise Lost*, with Satan himself the harbinger of disorder. He promises to turn the new world over to chaos and his "designs" of imperialism degenerate into the upheaval of mountains in heaven. Satan's protean nature – clouded angel, good cherub, toad, cormorant, serpent – is reminiscent of the "unstable visage" of the Anarch, Chaos, and the Adversary's countenance (or one of them) is distorted by chaotic passions on Mt. Niphates. Michael Lieb also finds chaos itself neutral: "The Abyss is not inherently evil, although it can be put to evil use. Nor is it inherently good, although it can be put to fruitful use." God finds in it "the womb of nature" while for Satan it is "a grave."[6] Even this depiction of chaos, as a pliable realm definable only by interpretation, is not true to the destructive, threatening region described in the poem. Chambers shows a greater awareness of the hostility of chaos, especially in his conclusion: "Chaos is as true an exemplar as hell of that state which everywhere prevails when the laws of providence are set aside, when the ways of God to man are opposed and overturned."[7] Nonetheless, his essentially scientific approach to the composition of first matter reduces a would-be active threat into the safety of a remote principle. Woodhouse tentatively concedes the possibility that chaos may be evil, consigning the observation to a footnote – a remarkable footnote to be sure, one which runs against the grain of his (and Milton's) entire argument in favor of a good first matter:

> It must, for example, be plain to every reader of *Paradise Lost* that the description of the Chaos there throws a very much heavier emphasis on its formlessness and disorder than does the account of the original matter in the *De Doctrina*, so that it is difficult to escape the inference, denied in the treatise, that this disorder is, or at all events has some affinity with, evil.[8]

I find the inference of an evil chaos so difficult to escape that it is not worth trying. Instead, I plan to plunge into this dark abyss and search, amid its very confusion, for some resolution of the conflict between Milton's doctrine and depiction, for the place allotted chaos in Milton's theodicy.

The Unclean Realm

In *Paradise Lost*, Milton depicts the creation as the act of delimiting, of setting bounds.

> ride forth, and bid the Deep
> Within appointed bounds be Heav'n and Earth.
> (VII. 166–67)

> He took the golden Compasses, prepar'd
> In God's Eternal store, to circumscribe
> This Universe, and all created things:
> One foot he centred, and the other turn'd
> Round through the vast profundity obscure,
> And said, Thus far extend, thus far thy bounds,
> This be thy just Circumference, O World.
> (VII. 225–31)

In this, Milton adheres to the Bible, where the Priestly account of Genesis I describes creation as a series of separations. God divides the light from the darkness, he separates the waters above the firmament from the waters below, and he divides the dry land from the sea. One rabbinic commentator insists that the Hebrew verb for "to create," *bara*, stems from "to cut."[9] Others add the image of the compass to Proverbs 8:27, underscoring the sense of delimiting: "When he established the heavens, I was there, when he drew a circle on the face of the deep." Rashi describes the circle on the deep as "a great limit that could not be over-run."[10]

The divisions of creation are only the beginning of distinction-making in the Bible. "Hallowing begins," according to Ernst Cassirer, "when a specific zone is detached from space as a whole, when it is distinguished from other zones and one might say religiously hedged around."[11] What is sacred is what is set apart; Milton's garden with its high walls, the holy ground Moses stands on, Jerusalem, the Temple, and heaven itself are all marked off by thresholds. Israel is hallowed, for it is drawn from among the nations, a people set apart. As God says to Moses, "And you shall be holy unto me for I the Lord am holy, and have separated you from the peoples, that you should be mine" (Lev. 20:26). The Hebrew root for "holy" also means separated, cut off, whereas "profane" means open for common use.[12] One scrupulous translator has even rendered the commandment, "Be Holy for I am Holy":

> I am the Lord your God, who rescued you from the land of Egypt;
> I am set apart and you must be set apart like me.[13]

The creation is sanctified by its divisions. As the Bible repeatedly tells us, they are "very good."

In contrast, Milton's chaos is virtually "defined" by its lack of definition, its limitlessness. In that "immeasurable" abyss – not yet measured by the golden compasses – all of the categories of time, place, and dimension established at creation are missing. Chaos is an

> Illimitable Ocean without bound,
> Without dimension, where length, breadth, and highth,
> And time and place are lost.
>
> (II. 891–93)

As the divisions that mark creation are "good," their absence suggests the opposite. The classical tradition seconds this Biblical verdict on the unbounded. For the Pythagoreans and Plato "limit and the unlimited . . . are set off against each other as the determinant and the indeterminant, form and formlessness, good and evil."[14] Plotinus tells us to think of evil "by thinking of measurelessness as opposed to measure, of the unbounded against the bound, the unshaped against the principle of shape." His expanded definition of evil is strikingly applicable to Milton's chaos:

> [T]hink of the ever-undefined, the never at rest, the all-accepting but never suited, utter dearth; . . . whatsoever fragment of it be taken, that part is all lawless void, 'while whatever participates in it and resembles it

> becomes evil. . . . Evil is that kind whose place is below all the patterns,
> forms, shapes, measurements, and limits, that which has no trace of good
> by any title of its own but (at best) takes order and grace from some prin-
> ciple outside itself.[15]

Certainly Milton's chaos cannot claim any title to good of its own; it is only when God "puts forth his goodness" that chaos becomes the material of creation. Milton's ever-warring "lawless void" is also never at rest, and the evil that "participates in and resembles" chaos most is Satan, the breaker of all bounds.

To classical and Biblical precedent, we can add Milton's own depiction of the perils of boundlessness, a judgment made on his own grounds. In his material universe, where "from the root / Springs lighter the green stalk, from thence the leaves / More aery, last the bright consummate flow'r / Spirits odorous breathes" (V. 479–82), moral categories tend to assume physical shape. Boundaries take on far more than physical significance. The sacred space of Paradise is delimited by no less than four natural walls (IV. 131–47); nonetheless, Satan "At one slight bound high overleap'd all bound" (IV. 181) – a rich adumbration of his every action in the poem. When Gabriel apprehends Satan, he rebukes him:

> Why hast thou, Satan, broke the bounds prescrib'd
> To thy transgressions, and disturb'd the charge
> Of others, who approve not to transgress
> By thy example, but have power and right
> To question thy bold entrance on this place;
>
> (IV. 878–82)

Dense with allusion to bound-breaking, this passage includes references to each of Satan's transgressions: the first, when he "broke peace in Heav'n and Faith, till then / Unbrok'n" (II. 690–91); the second, when he breaks through hell's gates of "burning Adamant" which "Barr'd over us prohibit all egress" (II. 436–37); his latest violation of Paradise and a fourth that Gabriel piously refuses, to transgress the command to stay Satan. Throughout these and its many other uses in the poem, "transgress" carries its literal meaning, "to step over," and, in turn, "unbounded" carries its moral signif-icance, to transgress. So the "boundless continent" of the Paradise of Fools will be inhabited by transgressors of various kinds. With the fall, the world is "fenceless," Death "stuffs" a "vast unhide-bound Corpse," and hell can no longer hold Sin and Death "in her bounds." Most striking is Satan's own confession that his ambition to reign in heaven is an "unbounded hope." Literally unbounded, we might add, for that ambition seeks to break the bounds of hierarchy. In Milton's world, to violate bounds is to fall.

With this emphasis on boundaries, Milton subscribes to that rich category of thinking on the sacred and profane, pollution and purity, that informs Biblical thought. As the creation is first hallowed by separations, so it is remembered and sanctified by observing those original distinctions. Leviticus tells us that it is written to "put difference between holy and unholy, and between unclean and clean" (Lev. 10:10, AV). In parallel structural studies, Mary Douglas and Jean Soler have demonstrated that the force of Israel's dietary laws with their seemingly recondite distinctions (why should the frog be clean and the hare unclean?) is just that: to preserve the distinctions made at the Beginning, to keep holiness inviolate.[16] "Every time a Jew eats," according to Soler, "he remembers the Creation." A fish that crawls (shellfish), a bird that walks (the stork), an animal that flies (insects) – any creature that violates its category is unclean, for such creatures violate no less than world order. "They are unclean because they are unthinkable." Because God made each thing "according to its kind," man must not mix what God has separated.

> You shall not sow your field with two kinds of seed;
> Nor shall there come upon you a garment of cloth made of two kinds of stuff.
> (Lev. 19:19)

All hybrids and confusions are abominated. Furthermore, the sanctity of life – God blesses life at creation – makes death unclean. Neither high priest nor Nazirite can go near a dead body (Lev. 21:11, Num. 6:6–7), one of the vows Samson violates when he eats honey from the carcass of the dead lion. Deriving sustenance from the dead is a macabre confusion of life and death. Separating them pays homage to life, to creation, to the Creator.

A poet committed to distinction-making, who repeatedly dramatizes that most difficult separation of good from evil, "culling and sorting asunder" truth from falsehood, is clearly drawn to the Bible's own emphasis on distinctions. Mary Douglas' observation is as applicable to Milton as it is to the Bible:

> Defilement is never an isolated event. It cannot occur except in view of a systematic ordering of ideas . . . the only way in which pollution ideas make sense is in reference to a total structure of thought whose key-stone boundaries, margins and internal lines are held in relation by rituals of separation.[17]

Virtually all of the significant action of *Paradise Lost* is conceived with reference to these categories. The poem centers on the distinction between forbidden and permitted food. An ur-dietary law governs Paradise.[18] Like the later injunctions of Leviticus, the force of that first law is not simply to forbid, to exact obedience, but to commemorate and sanctify the creation. In that law, Paradise is given a constant reminder of the Maker. Its violation is accompanied by a lapse of memory: Eve addresses the serpent as her author. Adam's first words to his faded flower are a lamenting reminder – too late – of the gift of life she has forgotten and thereby forsaken: "O fairest of Creation, last and best / Of all God's Works . . ." (IX. 896–97). Furthermore, obedience to the law is tacit assent to the very notion of lawgiver and receiver, an acknowledgment of the most fundamental of Biblical distinctions – between the Creator and his creation, between the Maker and his work. To transgress the law is not only to forget, but to effect the most heinous of confusions, aspiring, as Eve does, to become "as the Gods." Such ambition is "unclean," and it is expressed, appropriately enough, in terms of Biblical pollution. When Eve eats the forbidden fruit, she commits the most abhorred of abominations:

"eating Death," that "mortal taste." The grim image recurs in the Thyestian banquet simile at the fall. Satan's scorn of his easy seduction of man —

> Him by fraud I have seduc'd
> From his Creator, and the more to increase
> Your wonder, with an Apple
>
> (X. 485–87)

stems from one who has long ago denied that all-important distinction between Creator and creation, one who is "sustained" by the doubly unclean diet of apples turned to ashes.

Creaturely categories are violated by a talking snake and Leviticus even singles out the serpent for special censure: "Every swarming thing that swarms upon the earth is an abomination. . . . You shall not make yourselves abominable with any swarming thing that swarms; and you shall not defile yourselves with them, lest you become unclean" (11:41–43). Swarming things are particularly unclean because their mode of locomotion is unclear; they neither swim, walk, nor fly and so they fail to belong in either sea, land, or air. As serpent alone, Satan is unfit for creation. He understands his own descent into a serpent as a fall from pure to mixed, from holy to unclean.

> O foul descent! that I who erst contended
> With Gods to sit the highest, am now constrain'd
> Into a Beast, and mixt with bestial slime,
> This essence to incarnate and imbrute,
> That to the highth of Deity aspir'd;
> But what will not Ambition and Revenge
> Descend to?
>
> (IX. 163–69)

To the irony of his ascent leading to a descent, Satan adds the self-awareness that his unclean ambition to violate "his kind" and sit with the highest results in this unclean mixture with a beast. As his ambition issues in revenge, so one mixture gives rise to another. His anti-creative goal is to "mingle and involve" earth with hell, and the bridge Sin and Death build between them does literally break their bounds. Appropriately, the providential design frustrates that effort in like terms. Those sent by Satan to pollute are ultimately employed in the divine service to clean. Sin and Death will "lick up the draff and filth / Which man's polluting Sin with taint hath shed / On what was pure" and heaven will be restored forever "To sanctity that shall receive no stain" (X. 629–31; 39). The fall of the unclean angels only results in the purification of heaven.

> Then shall thy Saints unmixt, and from th' impure
> Far separate . . . sing.
>
> (VI. 743–44)

In the banquet scene of *Paradise Regained*, Satan offers Jesus unclean food, asserting that he has the right to all created things (*PR*, II. 320–28). Jesus refuses on the grounds that this giver is unacceptable. In his study of the scene, Michael Fixler concludes that Milton is thereby rejecting the dietary prohibitions of Leviticus:

> such detailed ritualistic prohibitions as are enjoined *in Leviticus* xi would have for him no positive force as expressing the everlasting will of God. Moreover, there is an indication here that any assumption restricting Man's free will and faith by chaining piety or virtue to such injunctions would act as an instrument of temptation. The danger latent in these laws, when considered as absolute commandments, becomes apparent when Satan deliberately assumes that their prohibitive force is still binding upon Jesus.[19]

When he considers these laws as "absolute commandments," Fixler fails to distinguish – as Milton invites us to – between the two contrary senses of the term "bounds." Those that shackle the will, that mark legalism, are anathema to this spokesman for freedom. But when the will is perceived not as the passive recipient of binding, but as the active force that binds, it replicates the divine creative act of separating, distinguishing – Miltonic choosing. Jesus' criterion of purity – its dependence upon the nature of the giver – is true to the spirit informing the dietary laws: to remember the Giver.

Notes

1   See J.H. Adamson, "Milton and the Creation," *Journal of English and Germanic Philology*, 61 (1962), 756–78.

2   Casaubon, *The Originall Cause of Temporall Evils* (London, 1645), the fifth page of the preface (n.p.) cited in Dennis Danielson, *Milton's Good God; A Study in Literary Theodicy* (Cambridge: Cambridge Univ. Press, 1982), 32–33.

3   A.S.P. Woodhouse, "Notes on Milton's Views on the Creation: The Initial Phase," *Philological Quarterly*, 28 (1949), 233.

4   Studies of the tradition include, along with Woodhouse's: A. B. Chambers, Jr., "Chaos in *Paradise Lost*," *Journal of the History of Ideas*, 24 (1963), 55–84; Walter Clyde Curry, "The Genesis of Milton's World," *Anglia*, 70 (1951), 129–49; Curry, *Milton's Ontology, Cosmogony, and Physics* (Lexington: Univ. of Kentucky Press, 1957); Michael Lieb, "Further Thoughts on Satan's Journey Through Chaos," *Milton Quarterly*, 12 (1978), 126–33; Lieb, *The Dialectics of Creation: Patterns of Birth and Regeneration in "Paradise Lost"* (Amherst: Univ. of Massachusetts Press, 1970); and Danielson, 32–57. In a provocative paper, Robert M. Adams does focus on the chaos of Milton's epic; his interest is "not in where Milton got his Chaos but in what he did when he got it." "A Little Look into Chaos," in *Illustrious Evidence: Approaches to English Literature of the Early Seventeenth Century*, ed. Earl Miner (Berkeley: Univ. of California Press, 1975). He opens his paper lamenting the lack of critical interest in that subject: "It would have been nice to find other people's definitions, descriptions, and doctrines of Milton's Chaos, for guidance and support, as well as the always welcome occasions of polemic. But I was unable to find more than passing remarks on the subject, and will welcome suggestions as to where else I should look" (71). With gratitude for his contribution, I second the sentiment.

5   Adams, 76.

6   Lieb, *The Dialectics of Creation*, 16–17.

7   Chambers, 84.

8   Woodhouse, 229, n.30.

9   Ibn Ezra, whose commentary, according to Fletcher, was written in the margin of Milton's Buxtorf rabbinic Bible. Harris Francis Fletcher, *Milton's Rabbinical Readings* (Urbana: Univ. of Illinois Press, 1930), 83.

10   Fletcher, 99.

11   Ernst Cassirer, *The Philosophy of Symbolic Forms*, trans. Ralph Manheim, vol. 2 of 3 vols., *Mythical Thought* (New Haven: Yale Univ. Press, 1955), 99.

12   Michael Lieb, *Poetics of the Holy: A Reading of "Paradise Lost"* (Chapel Hill: Univ. of North Carolina Press, 1981), 15. See also Lieb's helpful discussion of holiness in ancient Israel, 6–22.

13   Lev. 11:45 in Ronald Knox's version of the Old Testament, cited in Mary Douglas, *Purity and Danger: An Analysis of Concepts of Pollution and Taboo* (London: Routledge and Kegan Paul, 1966), 8.

14   Cassirer, 101.

15   Plotinus, *The Enneads*, trans. Stephen MacKenna, 3rd edn., rev. by B.S. Page (London: Faber and Faber, 1962), 68.

16   In her seminal analysis of the concept of pollution, *Purity and Danger*, Mary Douglas demonstrates that the Biblical notion of holiness suggests not just separation, but wholeness, completeness, "keeping distinct the categories of creation." See also Jean Soler, "The Dietary Prohibitions of the Hebrews," trans. E. Forster, *The New York Review of Books*, June 14, 1979, 24–30; and Julia Kristeva, *The Powers of Horror: An Essay on Abjection* (New York: Columbia Univ. Press, 1982).

17   Douglas, 41.

18   Michael Lieb comments that Adam and Eve become unclean upon violating God's command, noting that seventeenth-century commentators also made the connection between the forbidden fruit and the unclean food of Leviticus. In *The Forbidden Fruit: Or a Treatise of the Tree of Knowledge* (1640), Sebastian Frank writes that the fall was an "offense" to God, causing man to become "unclean": we shall become clean again only when we "doe vomitt up the Fruit of the Tree of Knowledge of Good and Evill" (14–16). Lieb's interest is in the prohibition as "extralegal and dispensational" – not in any of its commemorative impulses (Lieb, *Poetics of the Holy*, 114–18).

19   Michael Fixler, "The Unclean Meats of the Mosaic Law and the Banquet Scene in *Paradise Regained*," *Modern Language Notes*, 70 (1955), 573–77, 575.

(c) Adam, Eve and the Serpent: Mark Twain

Terry R. Wright

The Diaries of Adam and Eve and Letters from the Earth

Adapted as they are to a readership expecting 'vintage, funny "Mark Twain" ', *The Diaries of Adam and Eve* have been seen to lack both the 'complexity and pathos' of Twain's later writing on the topic, and the pointed satire of *Letters from the Earth* and *The Mysterious Stranger*.[1] Stanley Brodwin calls them 'sophisticated folktales':

> They serve not only as seemingly naïve (or radically innocent) commentaries on one of the most influential stories in Western literature and religion, but also supply an imaginatively instructive alternative . . . to the Sunday school Bible images that Twain had rejected.[2]

There is an appropriateness, in other words, in Twain's choice of genre here, matching the original folktales of the early chapters of Genesis with his own.

'Extracts from Adam's Diary' first appeared as part of *The Niagara Book*, a souvenir of the Buffalo World Fair of 1893. Unsuccessful in placing his original text elsewhere, Twain deliberately added material relating to Niagara Falls (which, of course, contains a fortuitous pun on the central theme of the diary). The 'Extracts' have a complex textual history, reappearing as a separate work (complete with Strothman's illustrations) in 1904 and together with 'Eve's Diary' as *The Private Lives of Adam and Eve* in 1931. Neither of these editions, however, incorporated the revisions Twain had made in 1893 so it was not until 1995, in *The Bible According to Mark Twain*, that 'Adam's Diary' appeared in the form Twain wanted.[3] Even the Oxford edition of *The Diaries of Adam and Eve* of 1996 and the Hesperus Press *Diary of Adam and Eve* of 2002 reprint the Niagara version.

This version of Adam's Diary, as well as having frequent references to the Falls,[4] attributes the Fall not to the eating of an apple but the making of an 'old chestnut', a 'mouldy joke' in which Adam says the Falls would be even more wonderful if the water fell upwards.[5] This has been variously construed as an act of pride (mocking the Creator's work)[6] or even a confession on Twain's part that humour was the 'sin' which prevented him from being a 'great' writer.[7] 'To attribute man's fallen condition and the source of his suffering to a bad joke', as Joseph McCullough argues, certainly 'undermines the tragic consequences of the event'.[8] But it does not work particularly well either as a theological strategy or as a joke.

Removing these elements in the Niagara version, as Twain wanted, increases the pathos of 'the first couple as innocent victims of an incomprehensible prohibition' but leaves the 'Extracts' primarily as a comedy.[9] There are plenty of gender jokes: Eve is the first to use the word 'we' (thus inventing relationships), the first to cry (in Adam's defamiliarising words, to 'shed water out of the holes it looks with') and also, as Adam complains, she 'is always talking'.[10] He is later relieved to report that she 'has taken up with a snake' (even though this illustrates her over-trusting nature) because the snake talks back 'and this enables me to get a rest'.[11] The jokes are not merely misogynistic, however: Eve is shown to have more initiative than Adam (he finds her 'trying to clod apples out of that forbidden tree'[12]) and more intellectual curiosity. According to Adam,

> She engages herself in many foolish things—among others to study out why the animals called lions and tigers live on grass and flowers, when as she says, the sort of teeth they wear would indicate that they were intended to eat each other.

'That is foolish', Adam insists, 'because to do that would be to kill each other' and introduce 'death' into the Park.[13] Twain apparently told a friend that he had been reading commentaries on Genesis, one of which claimed that 'the meat-eating animals on the ark became vegetarians during the voyage', conjuring up the image in his mind of a Barbary lion calling on Noah to bring him a bale of hay.[14] There is a serious point, however, behind the carnivorous teeth of the lions, which clearly suggest that the Fall was predetermined. Later, when Adam hears 'a tempest of frightful noises' and sees that 'every beast was destroying its neighbour', he realises that Eve's observations were well founded, that death has indeed 'come into the world'.[15] He has no qualms about eating the apple himself, not out of any great Miltonic magnanimity but because he was 'so hungry. It was against my principles, but I find that principles have no real force except when one is well fed'.[16] Twain again subverts the high-minded tragedy conventionally associated with the Fall, making Adam the unwitting advocate of a materialist position. It is also apparent that Adam finds it hard to attach so much importance to the eating of a piece of fruit.

The gender differences continue after the Fall with the stuffy and rather pompous Adam objecting to the way in which the postlapsarian Eve 'tittered and blushed', which he finds 'unbecoming and idiotic'.[17] He proceeds to express complete bafflement over Cain, whom he first sees as a kind of fish, then as 'some kind of a bug', then as a kangaroo or possibly even a bear. He continues for ten years to puzzle over 'this unclassifiable zoological freak' but does eventually come to recognise the merits of his partner, acknowledging that 'it is better to live outside the Garden with her than inside without her'.[18] Human companionship is made to outweigh theological correctness. This 'message' having been acknowledged, it must also be admitted that what satire there is in this first diary is very mild, executed in what Twain called 'a kind of friendly and respectful way that will commend him [Adam] to the Sunday schools'.[19] Most of the key action takes place off stage (the command, the temptation, even the Fall itself) while God remains respectfully invisible, Reading between the lines, it is possible to see that Adam at least (if not Eve) has improved as a result of his Fall. But Twain's contemporaries could hardly take offence at what was written in so unprovocative a manner.

The same could be said of 'Eve's Diary', written for the Christmas issue of *Harper's Magazine* in 1905, the year Twain's wife Olivia died. It was reprinted the following year with line-drawings by Ralph Lester. At least one library however, withdrew the book from its shelves because of the nudity depicted, which may have been 'a trap for the committees of decency', since 'to denounce nudity in *Eve's Diary* was to contradict the Bible'.[20] In the text Eve tells the story of her encounters with Adam both before and after the Fall. The gender jokes of the first diary continue with Eve wanting to tidy everything up, including the landscape. She also makes a somewhat garrulous and gushing narrator, insisting that 'the core and centre of my nature is love of the beautiful'.[21] This is partly to excuse her hankering after stars to put in her hair, tiger-skins to wear, and butterflies for 'wreaths and garlands'.[22] To begin with, she is quite critical of Adam, 'the other Experiment', who likes resting, 'has low tastes and is not kind'.[23] When he admires her, however, she finds it 'very agreeable' and when he tries to avoid her, she feels her 'first sorrow'. She also notices that 'He talks very little. Perhaps it is because he is not bright, and is sensitive about it'.[24] Eve spends her time admiring her reflection in the water while Adam fishes. It is Eve who invents religion, coming to the conclusion that she was made 'to search out the secrets of this wonderful world and be happy and thank the Giver of it all for devising it'. Even after the Fall she does not seem to suffer much, consoling herself for the loss of her garden with an increased closeness to Adam: 'I have found *him*, and am content. He loves me as well as he can; I love him with all the strength of my passionate nature'.[25] The final line, supposedly written by Adam beside Eve's grave, underlines the fact that he too has learned to love: 'Wherever she was, *there* was Eden'.[26] The theological point, softened by sentiment as it is, appears, as in some of the fragments of *What is Man?*, to be that Adam and Eve have risen, have matured morally and emotionally, as a result of the supposed Fall.

'Eve Speaks', written in the early 1900s but not published until 1923, adopts an entirely different tone, displaying more of the private, less acceptable side of Twain's thinking. It opens three months after the Fall with Eve still burning with indignation at her treatment:

> They drove us from the Garden with their swords of flame, the fierce cherubim. And what had we done? We meant no harm. We were ignorant and did as other children might do. We could not know it was wrong to disobey the command, for the words were strange to us and we did not understand them.

Eve repeats the arguments to be found elsewhere in Twain that without the Moral Sense it was impossible for them to know right from wrong and therefore unfair for God to punish them. She is also scathing about the 'knowledge' the fruit of the tree has gained for them:

> We were ignorant then; we are rich in learning, now—ah, how rich! We know hunger, thirst, and cold; we know pain, disease, and grief; we know hate, rebellion, and deceit; we know remorse, the conscience that prosecutes guilt and innocence alike, making no distinction; we know weariness of body and spirit, the unrefreshing sleep, the rest which rests not, the dreams which restore Eden and banish it again with the waking; we know misery; we know torture. . . .

This ironic list of benefits reaches an apparent climax in 'the rich product of the Moral Sense', with which she wishes 'we could degrade the animals'.[27] The remainder of 'Eve Speaks' dramatises her discovery of the meaning of death. At first she thinks Abel is merely sleeping but finally grasps the fact that she will never be able to wake him, that this is the 'death' which is their punishment for eating the forbidden fruit. The final irony, however, is left to Satan, who observes sardonically, 'The Family think ill of death' but 'will change their minds'.[28]

The longest of the Adamic papers is 'Eve's Autobiography', which Twain began writing in 1901 or 1902. The manuscript originally numbered some 98 pages with Eve as narrator throughout but Twain then decided to recast the material, assigning some of it to different narrators.[29] Some of this material was included by DeVoto in 'Papers of the Adam Family' in *Letters from the Earth* when that was published in 1962 but the fullest version can be found in *The Bible According to Mark Twain*. It is supposedly written by Eve around the year 900 AC (After Creation) as she rereads her old diaries and worries about the approaching Flood. Quite how carefully Twain studied the biblical text while writing it is apparent from the extensive planning notes which he wrote on the back of page 41 of the manuscript. These are reprinted in the notes to *The Bible According to Mark Twain* (although the fact that the editors refer to 'items

9 and 16' serves almost to conceal the allusion here to the verse numbers of Chapter 2 of the Book of Genesis).[30]

Twain's notes begin with 'a line squeezed in above the original first line': 'II 10 Before Eve's birth—forenoon, Jan.l', which shows him working hard on the chronology of the story. He notes from verse 15 that 'Adam is to "dress the garden & keep it"—but he doesn't fatigue himself'. Then come a series of notes from other verses in Genesis chapter 2:

> 9. Tree of life & knowledge
> 16. The Prohibition.
> 17. Shalt die
> 19. Naming the things.—Before Eve's birth
> 'But for Adam (the others had mates)

This last quotation is not closed in the manuscript presumably because what begins as a quotation from verse 20 ('but for Adam there was not found an help meet for him') becomes a summary in Twain's own words. Twain then moves on to chapter 3, 'in the Garden', where he has Eve say 'What is die?', presumably adding his own dialogue to verse 3, in which she summarises for the serpent's benefit God's command that they must not eat of 'the fruit of the tree which is in the midst of the garden . . . lest ye die'. Twain then turns his attention to the command 'Be fruitful' (Gen. 1:28) and to the phrase 'as the gods', which is part of the serpent's argument that 'God doth know that in the day ye eat thereof . . . ye shall be as gods' (3:5). The rest of the notes develop Twain's own ideas, for instance that Adam kept a diary but it was 'not reliable' and he 'couldn't spell'.[31] Twain's development of the story, it is worth noticing, like that of the rabbis, begins with close analysis of the original text before proceeding to supplement its narrative with his own.

'Eve's Autobiography', the final product of all this planning, begins with an older, sadder Eve re-reading the diary entries she wrote immediately after creation. The first entry shows her asking urgent questions both about her identity and about her strange predicament: 'Who am I? What am I? Where am I?' A week later these 'questions remain unanswered' while after a fortnight, not yet having encountered Adam, she starts to register just how 'lonely' and 'tedious' her life is. She gazes longingly at her own reflection in a pool, admiring her Miltonic 'slender white body' and long 'yellow hair',[32] all of which makes her jealous of the other animals, which have mates (Twain here transferring to Eve the feelings he had attributed to Adam in his note on Genesis 2:19 cited above). She derives some pleasure from playing with the animals, whose sheer exuberance and sense of fun make her 'laugh till the tears come'. She also occupies herself classifying the observable flora and fauna and continuing to ask questions about who she is and why she was created.[33]

These original diary entries are interrupted at this point by the older, sadder and wiser Eve recalling 'the splendid enthusiasm of youth' with some nostalgia.[34] The pattern for the whole autobiography is now established, with details of the young Eve's early adventures in the 'enchanted valley' of Eden interspersed with the older Eve's mournful reflections, for instance after the Fall. She recalls the day she managed to enter that valley but found no one there:

> This faded manuscript is blurred by the tears which fell upon it then, and
> after ten centuries I am crying over it again. Crying over it for pity of that
> poor child; and from this far distance it seems to be not me, but a child
> that I have lost—*my* child.[35]

The diaries continue into Eve's second year, when she encounters an Adam who is
not only beautiful ('Curly brown hair, tumbling negligently about his shoulders—
oh, *so* handsome') but unattached ('Such a bewitching boy—and all mine!').[36] Her
passionate kisses, however, succeed only in frightening him away, leaving her as
lonely as before. Adam meanwhile occupies himself by making 'a lot of fossils'. Eve
appears to think these will help to reconcile Science and the Scriptures (a satirical
sideswipe by Twain at some of the more implausible creationist arguments, including
the idea that the fossil record was designed by God at the moment of creation to
make it appear that the world had been in existence for a long time).[37]

The young Eve continues in her diary to recount her oscillating but eventually
successful endeavours to re-unite herself with Adam while the older postlapsarian
Eve looks back with nostalgia at her idyllic life in the days before pain, disease or
sorrow. There was instead the pleasure of constantly learning about the world: the
older Eve recalls the scientific pride with which the young Adam formulated his Law
of Fluidic Precipitation (that all water flows downhill) and her younger self discovered that lions were not designed to be vegetarians. In another extract from the
young Eve's diary, however, Twain introduces the figure of God, or at least of a
disembodied 'Voice' heard by Adam, who attributes it to 'the Lord of the Garden'
and reports its command not to eat the fruit of the tree of the knowledge of good and
evil lest we should die. The couple engage in an extended debate over the meaning
of these new words: good, evil and death, concluding that the only way to discover
their meaning is to eat of the fruit. Ironically, Adam is just 'reaching for the apple
when a most curious creature came floundering by', distracting him and consequently
postponing the Fall as the two natural scientists pursue it.[38] In Twain's version of
Genesis, in other words, the Fall is at least temporarily 'postponed *because* of intellectual curiosity rather than brought about because of it'.[39]

This particular rewriting of Genesis has the children arriving before rather than
after the Fall. Adam again has some difficulty in working out what they are but by year
10 Eve can report that they have nine of them, including the incongruously named
Gladys and Edwina. Since the Fall has not yet occurred, they can wander around
eating poisonous berries without any ill effects. Cain is particularly bright, 'really
expert at making the simpler kinds of fossils'.[40] Here the manuscript 'breaks off
abruptly in mid-sentence',[41] as if Twain could not bring himself to write directly
about the unspoken event which looms large throughout the autobiography, the Fall
itself. An attempted continuation of the narrative, much of it deleted and reassigned
to other 'Diaries Antedating the Flood', appears as an appendix to *The Bible According
to Mark Twain*. In this we learn that Gladys dies, victim of 'a famine reinforced by
pestilence', and that Adam too 'is gone from us' as a result of scenes over which Eve
wishes to draw a veil: 'they were not becoming to him'.[42] A mad prophet called
Reginald Selkirk tells Eve about the catastrophes in store for the human race, including
the Flood, foreknowledge of which succeeds only in sending her into despair:

> For a while my mind was thronged and oppressed with pathetic images of
> that coming calamity—appealing faces, imploring faces, despairing
> faces—multitudes upon multitudes, the rocks and crags and mountain
> ranges dense with them, and all bone of my bone, flesh of my flesh . . . I
> could not bear it![43]

This manuscript ends with Reginald the Mad Prophet reading an extract from a first
edition of Eve's diary, which again breaks off abruptly.[44] The memories of happier
past times seem too painful to continue, both for Eve herself and for Twain.

   The final perspective from which Twain rewrites the early chapters of Genesis is
that of Satan. As early as 1856, according to Brodwin, Twain had read and admired
Milton, finding 'the greatest thing in *Paradise Lost*—the Arch-Fiend's terrible
energy'.[45] His own Satan, the narrator of 'That Day in Eden', written in the early
1900s but not published until 1923, is characterised rather by his sympathy for Adam
and Eve than by the ferocity of his opposition to God. His account of events
surrounding the Fall begins with a lyrical description of the first couple:

> Long ago I was in the bushes near the Tree of Knowledge when the Man
> and Woman came there and had a conversation. I was present, now,
> when they came again after all these years. They were as before – mere
> boy and girl – trim, rounded, slender, flexible, snow images lightly
> flushed with the pink of the skies, innocently unconscious of their naked-
> ness, lovely to look upon, beautiful beyond words.[46]

They are still puzzling over the words 'good', 'evil', and 'death' so Satan tries to
explain these concepts along with related ideas such as 'fear' and 'pain'. 'It is impossible for you to do wrong', he explains to Eve, 'for you have no more notion of right
and wrong than the other animals have'. He also cautions her against acquiring the
dreaded Moral Sense: because 'it is a degradation, a disaster', having 'but one office,
only one—to teach how to do wrong'. He cannot prevent Eve reaching for the apple,
however, lamenting its consequences in Miltonic vein:

> Oh farewell, Eden and your sinless joys! Come poverty and pain, hunger
> and cold and heartbreak, bereavement, tears and shame, envy, strife,
> malice and dishonour, age, weariness, remorse, then desperation and the
> prayer for the release of death, indifferent that the gates of hell yawn
> beyond it.

Satan watches in horror as Adam observes the immediately visible changes in Eve
(her skin loses its 'satin lustre', her hair turns grey, and wrinkles form around her
eyes and mouth) but 'loyally and bravely' chooses to join her in exile.[47]

   Satan becomes even more outspoken in his attack on God's injustice in *Letters
from the Earth*, which was written in 1909, actually prepared for publication in 1939
(when Twain's daughter Clara refused permission), but not finally published until
1962. 'This book will never be published', Twain wrote sarcastically to a friend, 'for
it has much Holy Scripture in it of the kind that . . . can't properly be read aloud,

except from the pulpit and in family worship'.[48] As with many of these late works, it is primarily concerned to draw attention to absurd or unjust elements in the biblical text, obscured for many readers by their familiarity with it. *Letters from the Earth* begins with the creation of the universe, observed by the archangels Satan, Michael and Gabriel, who are all suitably impressed. A hundred million years pass and they observe the creation of the animals, all with their own laws, including 'the masterpiece—*Man!*' Banished from heaven 'on account of his too flexible tongue', Satan travels to the earth to 'see how the Human-Race experiment was coming along',[49] sending letters back to his fellow-archangels.

Satan's initial reports emphasise what a 'strange place' earth is, especially its inhabitants, who 'are all insane', imagining that the Creator cares for each of them and listens to their prayers, beliefs in which they are encouraged by 'salaried teachers' who tell them that God is loving, kind and merciful.[50] Satan has much fun at the expense of conventional Christianity and of the Bible, a book he describes as 'full of interest. It has noble poetry in it; and some clever fables'. Its history, however, is somewhat 'blood-drenched' and some of its morality 'execrable'. It also contains 'a wealth of obscenity; and upwards of a thousand lies'. Constructed 'mainly out of the fragments of older Bibles that had their day and crumbled to ruin', it 'noticeably lacks in originality'.[51] Satan finds the early chapters of Genesis particularly entertaining, with their absurdly anthropocentric account of God spending five days creating the Earth and 'only *one* day to make *twenty million suns and eighty million planets!*'[52]

Notes

1   William Macnaughton, *Mark Twain's Last Years as a Writer* (Columbia: University of Missouri Press, 1979), p.219.

2   Stanley Brodwin, 'Extracts from Adam's Diary', *Mark Twain Encyclopedia*, p.274.

3   Howard G. Baetzhold and Joseph B. McCullough, eds, *The Bible According to Mark Twain: Writings on Heaven, Eden, and the Flood* (Athens, GA: University of Georgia Press, 1995), pp. 4–7.

4   Mark Twain, *The Diary of Adam and Eve* (London: Hesperus Press, 2002), pp. 3–4.

5   *Ibid.*, p.12.

6   Joseph B.McCullough, 'Mark Twain's First Chestnut: Revisions in "Extracts from Adam's Diary" ', *Essays in Arts and Sciences* 23 (1994) pp.49–58 (p.54).

7   Laura E.Skandera-Trombley, 'Afterword', in Mark Twain, *The Diaries of Adam and Eve*, ed. Shelley Fisher Fishkin (Oxford: Oxford University Press, 1996), p.5.

8   McCullough, 'Mark Twain's First Chestnut', p.56.

9   *Ibid.*, p.55.

10   Twain, *Diary of Adam and Eve*, p.5.

11   *Ibid.*, p.10.

12   *Ibid.*, p.7.

13   *Ibid.*, p.8.

14   Alison Ensor, *Mark Twain and the Bible* (Lexington: University of Kentucky Press, 1969), p. 115, n. 48.

15   Twain, *Diary of Adam and Eve*, p.10.

16   *Ibid.*, p.11.

17   *Ibid.*, p.11.

18   *Ibid.*, p.15–18.

19   Edgar M. Branch, Michael B. Frank and Kenneth M. Sanderson, eds., *Mark Twain's Letters* (Berkeley: University of California Press, 1988–2002), 6 vols., II. 591–92.

20   Skandera-Trombley, 'Afterword', pp.6 and 24.

21   Twain, *Diary of Adam and Eve*, p.22.

22   *Ibid.*, pp.22–23 and 29.

23   *Ibid.*, pp.23–24.

24   *Ibid.*, pp.26–27.

25   *Ibid.*, pp.37–38.

26   *Ibid.*, pp.39–40.

27   *Ibid.*, pp.73–74.

28   *Ibid.*, pp.75–76.

29   Howard G.Baetzhold, Joseph B.McCullough and Donald Malcolm, 'Mark Twain's Eden/ Flood Parable: "The Autobiography of Eve" ', *American Literary Realism* 24 (1991), pp.23–38 (p.24).

30   Baetzhold and McCullough, *Bible According to Mark Twain*, p.337.

31   *Ibid.*

32   *Ibid.*, p.42. See the note on p.335 for the description of Eve's 'golden tresses' and 'slender waist' in *Paradise Lost* IV 304–5 and 458–59.

33   *Ibid.*, pp.44–46,

34   *Ibid.*, p.47.

35   *Ibid.*, p.49.

36   *Ibid*, p.50. See the note on p.336 for the description of Adam's 'hyacinth locks' in *Paradise Lost* IV 301–3.

37   *Ibid.*, pp.50–51. The note on p.336 explains that Twain would have encountered these arguments in Andrew Dickson White's *History of the Warfare of Science with Theology*.

38   *Ibid.*, p.58.

39   *Ibid.*, p.338.

40   *Ibid.*, p.62.

41   *Ibid.*, p.339.

42   *Ibid.*, pp.264–65.

43   *Ibid.*, p.272.

44   *Ibid.*, p.274.

45   Stanley Brodwin, 'The Humour of the Absurd: Mark Twain's Adamic Diaries', *Criticism* 14 (1972), pp. 49–64 (p. 58).

46   Twain, *Diary of Adam and Eve*, p.65.

47   *Ibid.*, pp.66–70.

48   Paula Garrett, 'Letters from the Earth', in J. R. LeMaster and James D. Wilson, eds., *The Mark Twain Encyclopedia* (New York: Garland, 1993), pp. 461–63 (p. 461).

49   Baetzhold and McCullough, *Bible According to Mark Twain*, pp.218–21.

50   *Ibid.*, pp.221–22.

51   *Ibid.*, p.227.

52   *Ibid.*, p.228.

(d) First Memories and Second Thoughts

Mieke Bal

It was a winter afternoon in primary school, perhaps third or fourth grade. I attended a Catholic girls-only school in a predominantly Protestant village near Haarlem in the Netherlands. In the afternoon, when concentration is hard to muster, the classroom was hot, and many girls had trouble keeping their eyes open. Not me. Given my lifelong obsession with narrative, it comes as no surprise to me to recall, decades later, that I was such an eager listener to the stories the schoolmistress used to tell. I think she told at least one story every few hours, often after the break or at the end of the day. At such sleep-inducing times of the day she dished up an incredible number of stories, the sole common feature of which was their baggage of moral lessons. We never read the Bible, ever. Nevertheless, I think it was a form of religious education, as usual with religion and ideology not very clearly distinguished. With my rather vivid imagination, I tended to bring the stories to bear on my own life all the time.

With the story of Potiphar's wife's wicked attempt at Joseph's virtue this proved to be a bit difficult. Neither I nor, I expect, my classmates had any education on matters sexual at the age of eight or nine. I even remember wondering what it was exactly that the woman wanted Joseph to do. But whatever it was, he didn't want to do it. And I understood that she insisted and he fled. I never doubted that she was evil. The heart of the story, of course, was her lie. This was what the teacher was trying to convey. Potiphar's wife lied, and as a result, Joseph went to prison. The horror was obvious, translated into absolute silence while the teacher lowered her voice to a near-whisper, and somehow I went home with the notion that women can be dangerous to men.

This was a point worth making. More often than not, stories about danger targeted men. These cautionary tales of terror concerned strangers offering candy only in order to abduct children; bad men hidden in dark corners, so that I tended to walk close to the edge of the sidewalk; men grabbing children who were alone in the street against their parents' admonitions; men hiding under my bed. Now, I learned, women could be dangerous as well. But strangely, in ways I did not understand, they were dangerous especially or exclusively to men.

These are my first memories of the story of Joseph and Potiphar's wife. I don't recall the precise story, but I do know it was about a woman in whose house Joseph was working. He was in good standing; his master appreciated him a lot, and so did, in fact, his mistress. She wanted something from him that he didn't want to give her, and he was right in his refusal. I don't remember what I thought it was she wanted. She then trapped him and deceived her husband, and Joseph went to jail. Luckily, and as a reward for his steadfastness, he went up from there like a comet because he was so good at explaining dreams.

I tell this tale of getting to know the story not to make this essay unnecessarily personal but because I want to understand how books and lives hang together. I am a literary scholar by training, and I love texts. Later I also learned to love images, to which I relate as other kinds of texts: as objects or artifacts that solicit me to make sense out of them. With images, I was also sensitive to their materiality. Whenever I worked on art, I yearned to touch, to hold the actual object, and did not rest until I had seen the real thing, wherever on earth it might be. Later in this book this contact with the material object will prove to be as crucial as the textual "letter" of the written stories. In this chapter, I will propose the concept of *cultural memory* as the first in a small series of concepts I wish to put forward as relevant for the interpretation of such well-known—as well as ill-known—stories as the one of Joseph's mishaps at the hands of a woman. These stories circulate and shape minds and lives.

Perhaps because of my training, I am in sympathy with scholars who are as dissatisfied with the reliance on oral transmission as I am and who therefore seek to trace the "original" version of any given tale that goes around and around in as many versions as the world has cultures. I take this to be a standard scientific attitude. The disciplines of philology are all based on this intellectual posture. Hence, on a gut level, I tend to a qualified adherence to the tale's firm *anchoring* in the Hebrew Bible, as suggested by James Kugel in his study on biblical exegesis for which he uses this tale (1990). Kugel is a well-known, highly respected biblical scholar, and for this reason alone his book will stand for that academic field and be a constant companion for me throughout my current exploration. But as I will argue throughout this essay, living with stories requires also a constant questioning not only of their oral retellings but of written versions as well. My vague childhood memory, his expert textual study—what kind of combination is this?

Introducing the discursive genre of biblical exegesis Kugel calls "narrative expansion," the subject of his book *In Potiphar's House*, he insists that "such narrative expansions are, by definition, *exegetical* because they are ultimately based on something that is in the text" (1990, 4, emphasis Kugel's). How can such an affirmative assertion of positive anchoring match memories of a humid classroom so long ago yet so recent? The question is crucial for what I do with my life. The utterly subjective, fleeting memory does not come out of a cultural blue. But how can I believe that a text thousands of years old can affect my life, my flesh? I intend to make the textual approach of Kugel and others cohere—theoretically and semantically—with my childhood memory. *Cultural memory*, then, is the subject of this chapter. It is the first concept I propose for an intertextual and intercultural study of this love story and others like it.

Kugel applies the term *exegesis* to all narrative expansions that answer implicit questions raised by "an unusual word, an apparently unnecessary repetition, an unusual grammatical form" that arouses the need to "bring . . . out all possible nuances implied in the *precise* wording of each and every sentence" (1990, 3–4, emphasis added). He talks the talk of one who will not have the text abducted by ideological abuse. I wish to heed this injunction, if only as a remedy to the kinds of ideological appropriation and political misuse to which canonical religious literature is subjected more frequently than are any other texts. But these abductions happen all the time. They cannot be wished away, because they are the result of texts; they are how texts *act*. I cannot believe in those textual roots of truths that suit some purpose while damaging others. So even if a text is an artifact and if it contains words that have meaning, each of them and in their arrangement, I take issue with the notion that they also *contain* the questions we ask of them.

The leap from words to questions is significant. In the course of this book I will argue that interest in the precise wording is a reading attitude I call *literalism*, of which I am a strong advocate. On the other hand, the idea that the texts *contain* the questions we ask of them is, I will argue, akin to *fundamentalism*. My argument in this book seeks to carefully delineate the distinction between these two understandings of textuality and reading. The one treasures the cultural inheritance and opens it up for the contemporary world. The other makes a devastating appeal to an immutably referential, prescriptive meaning, an appeal that is based on a radical denial or negligence of how signs work.

However, it is not enough to align ourselves with reception theory and to simply assume the reader is in charge. I contend it is in the questions, not in the texts as hard core, that we must understand the texts that traditions have managed to save for us. Yet our questions are, in turn, culturally framed, embedded in ways of thinking and common conceptions of social life. Reading is establishing a meaningful connection between these relatively stable texts and the varying, historically shifting meanings they generate.

The practice of interpretation is not quite in step with this conception of reading. Instead, I contend, the standard question of interpretation of which Kugel's study is a prime example is, simply, "why?" We ask questions of the order of "why?" to understand things whose meanings have shifted and slid from underneath the relatively stable blanket of the text. "Why did X do what he did" (Kugel 1990, 2). These questions of "why"—why does a figure do or say something, why doesn't the husband understand, why is the interlocutor refusing to comply, and the like—emerge not from the text but from the cultural frameworks of the interpreter, who feels the text does not fully flesh out the concerns of those who read it. In other words, it is from within our own conceptions that we wonder and ask why characters do or say what they do. These frames and conceptions change all the time, whereas the texts as artifacts retain more—although by no means total—stability. This stability is due, in large part, to the process of canonization, which is by definition conservative. The readings change faster. What I resist, therefore, is the reasoning that a "why" question is anchored in the *text* whenever there is something considered enigmatic "in" a text, something the reader has to contend with: a seeming contradiction, a missing detail, an unexpected form. "Seeming" begs more specific questions. Who is the person or group of persons for whom there is a seeming contradiction? For whom and from which expectation would the detail be lacking? From which horizon of expectation would the form appear unexpected? These are questions of readership, the group identities and mythologies that inform a text's readers. Given this, I take these questions very seriously but will deny them their self-evident universality. With these qualifications and specifications in mind, I will refer to such questions of readership and expectations with the shorthand phrase "why questions."

This asking of "why questions" of the text is never finished, because readers move on with the times and hence meanings keep sliding along. Moreover, they have personal baggage to bring to the text as well as the cultural framings of this baggage. This is where my personal childhood memory joins the cultural memory in which I was and am steeped. Indeed, if we take seriously the cultural situation from which the text came to us, we must assume that the "why?" comes from the reader—who is, in turn, framed by her culture—not from the text. There are two paces at work— the long-term continuity of the artifact's existence and availability on the one hand and the faster pace of changing communities of readers on the other. Between these two paces the inevitable discrepancies define what has been called "cultural memory." To put it simply, cultural memory is the gap—sometimes abyss—between the words on the page and the meanings such as the one I took home that winter day in the 1950s. The question "Why?" is the most tangible site of that cultural memory. As such, it is neither "in" the text nor outside of it, but "into" it, toward it; it is the reader's relationship to the text.

I take Kugel's authoritative study to stand for the discrepancy between belief in the text's "precise wording"—literalism—and the belief that the questions are located in the text—a potentially fundamentalist attitude. I will flesh out what I understand fundamentalism to be in the context of readings of tradition-transmitted texts such as the Joseph story. Kugel's formulation does not address the issue of whether "why questions" can be considered based on something other than his own frame of reference, something stable that *is* (ontologically) *in* (locally) the text, although he does acknowledge from the start that the texts "exercised a central role in everyday life" (1990,1). I will return to this issue throughout this book. For now, however, I qualify this alleged anchoring by means of my memory of primary school. School, as Louis Althusser argued long ago, is one of those "Ideological State Apparatuses" where memories are shaped to fit the cultural frame (1971). It is the site where children learn to think, and to think in certain ways. This is both necessary and unavoidable, and I am not going to argue that this kind of education shouldn't happen. But how it takes place—and what interests it serves—is worth considering if we wish to understand the intertwining of individual and social identities, as well as that between past and present. In order to understand this intertwining I will draw on three areas of study: semiotics, or the theory of sign and sign use; aesthetics, or the theory of humans' relationship to the material world; and religion, or the relationships among people and with deities.

Like so many others, I was raised to despise, hate, and at the very least blame Potiphar's wife for Joseph's mishaps. His stint in prison, which cannot have been pleasant to say the least, was brought about by her lie. And lying, I was taught, is bad. The emotion we were compelled to feel for Joseph was pity. He did not deserve his unfortunate downfall. With this firm and emotionally sustained hatred of the guilty woman I entered adulthood—becoming a woman myself. The story was safely stored away in my memory for later use. When, much later, I was led to *read* the story for the first time, I had this affective tie to the characters already set in place. I could not read the story without it. And only because I had not been raised reading the biblical stories firsthand was I able to be surprised by it. Something did not match the sources; something remained stubbornly alien to me. This book is an account of that surprise. I seek to understand and unravel that mismatch between memory and text.

Between memory and text lies a gap, or a stumbling block, and stumbling over it is the cause of my surprise. That surprise emerged from a clash between a memory and a text. Several times during my encounters with biblical literature, with retellings of biblical stories in modern Western literature, and with what, for the sake of fairness, I consider "versions" of such stories—among which the Qur'an text of 12:23–31—I have felt such a clash. These were often productive, indeed exciting moments of learning. It was always to the extent I did not recognize what I saw before me that I found the text or image *interesting*. This rather flat word, a word of politeness and often of polite dismissal, receives new meaning when we take it in the German sense awoken by such writers as Jürgen Habermas. His seminal book *Knowledge and Human Interest* (1972 [orig. 1968]) remains an inspiring source for reflection on how knowledge thrives on interestedness—the opposite of Kant's ideal of aesthetic contemplation, defined as *dis*interestedness.

I am interested in exploring the interestedness of interpretation on the level of self-evidence. The kind of self-evidence I was carrying along concerning Potiphar's wife I can now recognize as a moral, indeed moralistic lesson against love or sexual attraction. A lesson in innocence defined as abstinence. Against women, protecting men.

How, then, can I articulate the imbrications of personal memory with cultural memory—in other words, how can my memory from schooldays become relevant in a discussion of a scholarly nature? The connection lies in the self-evidence, the unspoken implications of that warm schoolroom with the story told in it. These self-evident ideas, a culture's stock of wisdom, include what we call stereotypes. This notion points to fixed ideas that articulate the self's opinion about "others," construed as a group. Mireille Rosello's book *Declining the Stereotype* (1998) discusses the mechanism of stereotyping within a culture in terms congenial to what I set out to do in this book. She constructs the notion of the "reluctant witness," which I find a very useful, productive counterpart to the stereotype as itself an artifact. This reluctant witness is someone recruited to listen to a stereotyping discourse, a listening that entails the appearance of at least partly acquiescing to that discourse. When the listener herself belongs to the group being stereotypically constructed, she may be infuriated and feel offended, but often it is easiest to just go along for the ride. And then, after a time, to forget to get off. I think this happens to girls, to women-in-the-making, in misogynistic cultures such as my own. In my memory of it, I was a witness, only slightly reluctant, to my own stereotyping through the story of the wicked woman.

Rosello introduces the concept of the reluctant witness with the following examples, which are easy to recognize:

> An overtly gay person may be invited to agree with the supposedly legitimate disapproval of a straight interlocutor. A Jewish guest may be asked to swallow his or her host's anti-Semitic stereotypes with dinner, the French relative of Arab origin may be entrusted with more or less carefully worded revelations about anti-Arab feelings in his or her immediate surroundings, he or she, of course, constructed as the exception to the rule.
>
> (1998, 1)

The exceptional status of the witness is at the heart of my story. Readers are witnesses, and as we will see, their act of witnessing is embedded in the story in one of its versions. Women are dangerous, the story intimated to me as a child, but if you do your best to be good, you can belong to the good guys. The invitation offers hospitality within the group in recompense for acceptance of the insult. The insult is mitigated. The morality that suggests the possibility of avoidance of the condemned behavior is the lesson—to stay with school parlance—that helps overcome the unease that would otherwise lead to its rejection or, as Rosello's pun has it, "declining."

In the case of our tale, this lesson, clearly, was gender specific. Told to an audience of gullible girls, unknowing about sex and inexperienced in that event referred to as "falling in love," the tale of Joseph's downfall was meant to instill in its listeners, specifically, a repulsion against lying as well as against what only later was named "love." It worked. As far as I can remember, I have tended to associate falling in love with guilt and being in love with the need to lie. Lying to the loved person, who would, without any doubt, run away if told about my thrill; lying to parents, who, without giving me the necessary information to judge for myself, told me repeatedly how bad, dirty, and dangerous all this unnamed stuff was; lying to myself, thinking something was wrong with me and I had better rid myself of that emotion that kept me awake at night.

Not that I came ever close to the specific kind of lie the woman in the Genesis story had performed. The situation was never quite like that. But associations flow in the direction in which they can go, like a river; and like rivers, they carve out an ever-deeper channel that tames the water. Speaking in very general terms, the tale was one of several stories—a corpus later supplemented by other stories, novels, paintings, and films—that prepared me to grow up into a "decent" female, ready to organize my life accordingly. Whether or not this worked is not important. It never works to perfection; it never fails to work altogether. For the cultural critic I ended up being, the point is that any reading I was later able to perform on any "version" of the story of Joseph and Potiphar's wife was always already framed by the earliest memories of a story half-understood and rapidly abducted. Where and who was I in that process, and what is this "me" to begin with, if I can be so framed?

"Me" is an individual shaped by many frames, but inescapably strongly shaped by school. In my case it was a Catholic school, in which the church participated, directly and indirectly. I remember the priests who came to teach religion, because they were the only men in the school and for a time I thought they wore robes to dress like women. Even within the relatively small village of my childhood, other children grew up in other environments, just as specific but also just as collective. *Cultural memory* is the term that has been used to theorize this togetherness of memories through which individuals are shaped as part of communities. The storytelling of my teacher and my processing of the story told would be "acts of memory" in this cultural sense (Bal, Crewe, and Spitzer 1999).

Works cited

Althusser, Louis, "Ideology and Ideological State Apparatuses (Notes towards an Investigation)," in *Lenin and Philosophy and Other Essays*, trans. Ben Brewster (London: New Left Books, 1971)

Bal, Mieke, Jonathan Crewe, and Leo Spitzer, eds., *Acts of Memory: Cultural Recall in the Present* (Hanover, NH: University Press of New England, 1999)

Kugel, James L., *In Potiphar's House: The Interpretive Life of Biblical Texts* (San Francisco: Harper San Francisco, 1990)

Rosello, Mireille, *Declining the Stereotype: Ethnicity and Representation in French Cultures* (Hanover, NH: University Press of New England, 1998)

Chapter 9

Salvation, Transformation and Apocalypse

CONTEMPORARY WESTERN CULTURE THRIVES on visions of its own downfall: on page and screen, the world regularly succumbs to environmental disaster, pestilence and alien invasion. On one occasion in the 1990s the world was saved from collision with an asteroid by the heroic self-sacrifice of Bruce Willis (or, at least, by the wise-cracking astronaut he played in the 1998 movie *Armageddon*). And though stories of catastrophe are clearly very big business, near-extinction-level events are not always so spectacular. Cormac McCarthy's austere, elemental novel *The Road* (2006), for example, imagines a world *after* the end, in which a father and son walk across a denatured, ruined American landscape, encountering violence, decay and (for that extra feel-good touch) cannibals.

How do such disturbing and violent narratives connect with biblical ideas of what Paul Fiddes has called 'the promised end'? In Christian theology, Fiddes notes, the end is associated with four specific 'last things': 'the final advent of the Lord of the cosmos, the last judgement, heaven and hell'. This understanding of the world's end, rooted in readings of the last book of the Bible, the Revelation of St John, has often provided inspiration for artists and writers: for example, the final words of Charlotte Brontë's *Jane Eyre* (1847) (' "Amen; even so come, Lord Jesus!" ') echo the penultimate line of the Authorized Version of the Bible (Revelation 22: 20). In the early 1850s, the painter John Martin produced an enormously popular triptych of paintings depicting the end of the world, the last judgement and heaven. The first of these vast, arresting landscapes – commonly known as *The Great Day of His Wrath* (1851–53) – is often seen as anticipating the scale and spectacle of twentieth-century disaster movies.

Much contemporary narrative excels at staging cataclysmic, photo-real images of the end and of hell-on-earth but it also often lacks the messianic hope that is central to eschatology. The instrument of 'judgement' is often a material rather than supernatural threat: comets, asteroids or mysterious planets hurtle towards earth in *Deep Impact* (1998), *Armageddon* (1998) and *Melancholia* (2011); a new ice age is the result of ecological folly in *The Day After Tomorrow* (2004). *The Day the Earth Stood Still* (1951; remake 2008) witnesses an alien visiting earth as a kind of avenging angel, ready to pronounce a guilty verdict on humanity. These films play out like secular (or, at least, non-sectarian) versions of 'end-times' narratives prevalent amongst certain strands of millennialist Christianity that remain highly influential in the United States. The status of 'dispensationalist' beliefs regarding the second coming of Christ, the rapture and the tribulation is displayed, for example, in the commercial success of Tim LaHaye and Jerry Jenkins' *Left Behind* series of novels (1995–2007).

The popularity of stories that see the earth face imminent destruction suggests that the term 'apocalypse' is now widely understood exclusively in relation to one of its more recent meanings: the end of life as we now know it. Yet the primary sense of the Greek term from which apocalypse is derived – *apocálypsis* – is 'uncovering', the disclosure of things once hidden. Revelation, in this sense, is not necessarily accompanied by disaster, violence and damnation. In *The Sense of Ending* (1967) Frank Kermode offers an alternative reading of 'end-determined fictions' and addresses, in particular, the ways in which certain kinds of narrative mediate a complex consciousness of different kinds of temporality.

Tom Wright suggests that there is an enormous disparity between popular understandings of the world-to-come and Christian eschatology.[1] Yet a number of contemporary novelists display a more nuanced sense of the apocalyptic than we have come to expect from much popular culture. Douglas Coupland's fiction frequently features moments of epiphany that suggest revelation might be part of everyday experience rather than an exclusive 'religious' category. His fifth novel, *Girlfriend in a Coma* (1998), a blend of science fiction and miraculous realism, parodies populist pre-millennial tension but also represents an intriguing turn towards the sacred. Coupland's core characters – mysteriously chosen as a kind of elect to survive a sleep plague that destroys humanity – start to ask the kinds of religious questions that their suburban, comfortable lives of Thoreauvian 'quiet desperation' have taught them to avoid. In this iteration of the apocalypse, replete with allusions to *It's a Wonderful Life* and 1980s music, the world ends not with a bang, nor even a whimper, but a series of gentle snores. More recently, another Canadian novelist with an acute eye for the dystopian has narrated a defamiliarizing set of end-of-the-world fables in *Oryx and Crake* (2003) and *The Year of the Flood* (2009). Although neither Coupland nor Margaret Atwood self-identify as orthodox believers, both ask serious questions about salvation, the possibility of transformation and the nature of apocalypse.

For some critics, the originating textual source of Christian apocalyptic is horrifying. Will Self, iconoclastic novelist and essayist, describes the Revelation of St John as 'a sick text' and the King James Version, in particular, as 'a guignol of tedium, a portentous horror film'.[2] Kathleen Norris, by contrast, believes that the book of Revelation 'has suffered from bad interpretation' and that the narrative itself, far from 'cruel', 'boldly asserts that our cruelties and injustices will not have the last word'.[3] The quartet of extracts included in this section all meditate on different kinds of injustice and address sometimes overlapping, sometimes competing understandings of revelation and salvation.

Few contemporary theologians have done more than Graham Ward to place biblical thought in conversation with contemporary critical theory. He was editor of the interdisciplinary journal *Literature and Theology* for a decade and his many monographs offer a combative but fruitful exploration of the contours of postmodern culture in the light of theology and vice versa. In 'Suffering and Incarnation' (2001), Ward continues this project. The essay is typically replete with reference to the work of Jacques Derrida, Sigmund Freud and Slavoj Žižek. However, this exploration of phenomenological accounts of pain is supplemented by orthodox theological figures such as the apostle Paul, St Augustine and Hans Urs von Balthasar.

'What role does suffering play in the economy of Christian redemption?' The theologian considers issues of salvation history and the apocalyptic with a specific focus on the suffering human body or, in Ward's terms, 'with what it means to be a soul enfleshed'. And, far from denying the reality of bodily or emotional affliction, Ward suggests that 'there is a suffering which is intrinsically meaningful because it is a continuation, a fleshing out, and a completing of the suffering of Christ'. He counters both the 'mind–body dualism' and the tacit merging of 'suffering and bliss' tendencies evident in much western thinking with reference to the different kind of suffering represented in Jesus Christ. This analysis is rooted in a theology of *kenosis*, the self-emptying act of Christ as outlined in chapter two of Paul's epistle to the Philippians. This sacrificial act, in Ward's reading, is not the same as a contemporary nihilism that would empty all words, gestures and deeds of meaning. Indeed, the suffering embodied in Christ's passion 'undoes the economics of sin through a therapy of desire'. Such a claim, Ward acknowledges, is only available within a theological framework that is 'maintained by faith and established by eschatological judgement'. These ideas, particularly a recuperation of suffering, are likely to seem radical to an atheist reader. Yet Ward's defence of what he terms 'a transcendental hope' provides a bracing counterpoint to contemporary narratives that often make an empty spectacle of suffering, destruction and death without eschatological expectation.

Eve Kosofsky Sedgwick, like Ward, is alert to unforeseen relations between desire, embodiment and the dynamics of disclosure. Sedgwick's pioneering work on sexuality and literature is celebrated (and, occasionally, disparaged) for identifying surprising – and frequently covert – associations between public declaration and private longing, particularly in the realm of a male-focused literary canon. If her writing is less obviously concerned with the apocalyptic in a specifically theological sense than is the case for Ward, it is emphatically oriented towards revelation of that which has been hidden. Where Ward prioritizes theological readings of cultural activity, Sedgwick makes a reverse movement: in the section from *Epistemology of the Closet* (1990), Sedgwick travels from contemporary debates regarding homophobic discourse, 'coming out' and gay identity to the book of Esther, one of the most controversial narratives in the Jewish-Christian scriptures.

Sedgwick's characteristically witty reading of Esther is mediated by two French authors: Jean Racine who rewrote the story of Queen Esther for the stage in 1689 and Marcel Proust who cites Racine's rewriting in *A La Recherche du Temps Perdu* (1913–27). This palimpsest provides the context for a playful analysis of Esther's secret identity in the court of King Ahasuerus. In the biblical narrative, Esther is effectively forced into marriage with the ruler – a man who has already violently disposed of a previous wife for insubordination – and, for reasons of self-preservation, must keep her Jewish identity a secret. She is prompted by Mordecai, Esther's mentor, that 'the time for her revelation has come' in order to prevent the annihilation of the Jewish people. Esther decides to speak out, uttering a defiant *cri de coeur*: ' "And if I perish, I perish" ' (Esther 4. 16). For Sedgwick this act – one that saves Esther's people – might be read as analogous to coming out as gay in a homophobic culture.

Political re-readings of Esther are not new: the festival of *Purim* – the holiday that celebrates the deliverance of the Jewish people following Esther's brave deed – has interpreted the event in the context of continuing forms of oppression throughout the centuries.[4] Yet Sedgwick's reading is distinctive for the ways in which it openly critiques its own appropriation of the narrative to explore another kind of oppression. Sedgwick imagines a story that echoes the basic plot of Esther playing out in a contemporary US court, with 'a hypothetical closeted gay clerk' outing themselves to 'a hypothetical Justice of the same gender' who is on the verge of supporting a law that will discriminate against gay people. This appropriation is skilfully narrated but Sedgwick acknowledges that there are a 'whole family of reasons why too long a lingering on moments of *Esther*-style avowal must misrepresent the truths of homophobic oppression'.

Sedgwick's audacious reinterpretation of Esther is sensitive both to the problems of cultural translation and unpredictable operations of power. She is clear that '[i]n the theatrical display of an *already institutionalized* ignorance no transformative potential is to be looked for'. Yet the piece is also charged with a sense of the transformative potential of reading and revelation. Esther's self-declaration disrupts the oppressive logic of her world and brings about salvation, for her people at least.

The power of revelation (such as 'coming out') has, as Sedgwick suggests, consequences that cannot necessarily be 'circumscribed within *predetermined* boundaries'. The question of boundaries or limits – and specifically the postmodern aversion to such confines or borders – is central to Paul Fiddes' exploration of 'the last things'. In the opening chapter of *The Promised End*, Fiddes focuses on the 'difficulties of "closure" ' that seems to preoccupy much late twentieth-century fiction. 'Many modern novelists seem to find it difficult to bring their books to an end,' notes Fiddes. How does this much deferred and sometimes open-ended '*eschata*' of postmodern narrative connect with the biblical 'sense of an ending'? The extract included glosses the exemplary postmodern 'endings' of John Fowles' *The French Lieutenant's Woman* (1969) and Julian Barnes' *Flaubert's Parrot* (1984). Fiddes argues that 'eschatology [is] the basic mood' not just of theology but also of 'literary creation'.

Yet Fiddes does not simply conflate all such deferred endings and damp squib, never-endings. *The Promised End* wrestles with contemporary narrative and 'the Christian understanding of the last things' and draws on the alternative versions of apocalypse represented by Frank Kermode, Northrop Frye, Jacques Derrida and Paul Ricoeur. Fiddes concurs with Ricoeur, the great author of *Time and Narrative*, that 'anti-closure must have a limit'. Such limits appear to be demanded by narrative, even when the same narrative and its readers resist the 'promised' end.

In his exploration of 'Wordsworth's Apocalypse', Jonathan Roberts counters the view that apocalyptic endings need always be belligerent. The critical field of Romanticism – and Wordsworth studies more specifically – has produced much scholarship on millenarianism, visionary states and epiphany. Yet Roberts presents a different kind of revelatory mode in his reading of Wordsworth who, he suggests, offers a 'non-violent, non-eschatological approach to apocalypse'. His exploration of Wordsworth's specific apocalyptic style emphasizes a retrospective rather than anticipatory understanding of revelation and he makes an engaging parallel between chapter 25 of Matthew's gospel – in which, to quote Roberts, 'the encounter with God turns out to have been anticipated in the most everyday events' such as 'caring for the sick' – and elements of *The Prelude*. For Roberts, Wordsworth 'offers a hermeneutical alternative to the 1790s millennial interpretations of apocalypse'. Alongside the other writers in this section, Roberts and, indeed, Wordsworth suggest that far from a singular, simple phenomenon, there are competing versions of apocalypse and the possibility of salvation – by what and from what, for example – is a question that proliferates a variety of intriguing answers.

Notes

1   Tom Wright, *Surprised by Hope* (London: SPCK, 2007), p. 6.
2   Will Self, introduction to The Revelation of St John the Divine, in *Revelations: Personal Responses to the Books of the Bible*, Intro. by Richard Holloway (Edinburgh: Canongate, 2005), pp. 375–83 (p. 381).
3   Kathleen Norris, introduction to The Revelation of St John the Divine, in *Revelations*, pp. 367–73 (p. 370).
4   For more detailed discussion of iterations of the Esther narrative see the work of Jo Carruthers including *Esther Through the Centuries* (Oxford and New York: Blackwell, 2008).

Further Reading

Agamben, Giorgio, *The Time that Remains: A Commentary on the Letter to the Romans*, trans. by Patricia Dailey (Stanford: Stanford University Press, 2005)
Bull, Malcolm, ed., *Apocalypse Theory and the Ends of the World* (Oxford: Blackwell, 1995)
Ermath, Elizabeth Deeds, *Sequel to History: Postmodernism and the Crisis of Representational Time* (Princeton: Princeton University Press, 1992)
Falconer, Rachel, *Hell in Contemporary Literature: Western Descent Narratives Since 1945* (Edinburgh: Edinburgh University Press, 2007)
Hughes, Robert, *Heaven and Hell in Western Art* (London: Weidenfeld and Nicolson, 1968)
Kermode, Frank, *The Sense of an Ending: Studies in the Theory of Fiction* (Oxford: Oxford University Press, 1967)
Kovacs, J. L., Christopher Rowland, and Rebekah Callow, *Revelation: The Apocalypse of Jesus Christ* (Oxford: Blackwell, 2004)
Lawrence, D. H., *Apocalypse and the Writings on Revelation*, edited by Mara Kalnins (Cambridge: Cambridge University Press, 1980)
McDannell, Colleen, and Bernhard Lang, *Heaven: A History* (New Haven: Yale University Press, 1988)
Mills, Kevin, *Approaching Apocalypse: Unveiling Revelation in Victorian Writing* (Lewisburg: Bucknell University Press, 2007)

Nichols, Ashton, *The Poetics of Epiphany: Nineteenth-Century Origins of the Modern Literary Moment* (Tuscaloosa: University of Alabama Press, 1987)

(a) Suffering and Incarnation

Graham Ward

The concern of this essay lies with a comparison and, ultimately, a confrontation between two cultures: the secular and the Christian with respect to the character and economies of pain and pleasure, suffering, sacrifice, and ultimate satisfaction.[1]

We need to begin with the corporeal, since it is the body which registers suffering and it is the theological nature of embodiment itself which is the concern of incarnation. Suffering is a mode of embodied experience: a theological account then of suffering must concern itself with what it means to be a soul enfleshed. The character of bodily experience is registered according to a pain-pleasure calculus. Those of us who are academics spend much of our time, I suggest, experiencing the extremes of neither. Perhaps most people, indeed, only take account of their embodiment when the body demands account to be taken because its experiences register the intensity of suffering or the delights of bliss. But in beginning with the corporeal let me emphasize what I am *not* doing.

First, I am not suggesting a mind–body dualism – there are intellectual pleasures (as Kantian aesthetics and the joy of reading evidence) and there is intellectual pain (as existentialism emphasized and psychiatry treats). To draw upon a distinction St Paul makes, and which we will return to later, perhaps most of us inhabit the body (*soma*) rather than the flesh (*sarx*) or the symbolics of embodiment rather than its sensate materiality. The reason for this lies in the difficulty of registering sensation as such. That is, most of the time we experience our body's sensations through cultural prisms and personal expectations. The raw givenness of the body and its experiences are already encoded, Judith Butler neatly sums this up in her book *Bodies That Matter* through a play on the word "matter" as it refers to both materiality and something of significance. That which is matter already matters, is already caught up in the exchanges of signification.[2] The soul enfleshed (where soul has much wider connotations than just the mind's cognition), the only "body" we know, sublates any mind–body dualism.

Second, I do not wish to suggest that there is a spectrum with pain at one extreme and pleasure at the other. Since early modernity the Protestant awareness of the transcendence of the divine beyond human reasoning, accounts of peering into the infinite reaches of the heavens, and aesthetic descriptions of the sublime, have each appealed to experiences which are simultaneously both painful and consummately beatific.[3] The mystic's cry of ecstasy,[4] the mathematician's speechless awe at the dark spaces between the stars,[5] the exquisite intellectual confusion as the experience of what is beautiful sheers towards the edge of the *tremendum*[6] – each testify to experiences that exceed the neat categorization, the spectrum extremities, of pain and pleasure. Though it does seem to me that to conflate suffering and bliss can also be a sign of decadence announcing a sadomasochistic culture.

Contemporary Pain and Pleasure

For some time now, at least since the 1960s and 1970s (though its roots lie in Hegel's *Phenomenology of Spirit*), intellectual debates concerned with the economies of desire – whether in Deleuze, Lacan, Lyotard, Barthes, Foucault, or Žižek – have been oriented around the notion of *jouissance*. Suffering constitutes itself as the lack or absence of *jouissance*. Bliss, as one translation, is the ultimate human goal. With Lacan and Žižek the lack itself is pleasurable. They would argue that what we desire is not the fulfillment of our desire, but the desiring itself, the prolongation of desire. To attain our desire would collapse the distinction between the imaginary and the symbolic. The extended game of hunt the slipper would come to an end. Desire only operates if there remains an *objet petit a*, a hole, a gap, a void, a loss that can never (and must never) be fully negotiated or filled. And so we fetishize – turn the hole itself into what we desire: "in fetishism we simply make the cause of desire directly into our object of desire."[7] But since the hole itself cannot be negotiated then objects substitute for and veil this ultimate void. Bliss then is endlessly deferred, yet remains the *telos* and organizing point for any local and ephemeral construction of the meaning of embodiment. Lacan (and Žižek) develop into a sacrificial logic the system of compensations and substitutions which Freud increasingly recognized as symptomatic of the way the libidinal drive operated alongside the death drive in the economy of desire. Civilization, for Freud, is founded upon its profound and ineliminable discontent. In this sacrificial logic we are caught up in a denial of what we most want and produce substitutionary forms, objects, laws, empty symbols for that which is unsubstitutional. And so we deny, sometimes even murder, what we most value, in order to maintain our fantasies about it.[8] There takes place here a renunciation in the form of a negation of negation. It is this sacrificial logic that I wish to examine. It has the structure of sado-masochism.

It finds similar forms in other poststructuralist discourses. Derrida's accounts of the economy of the sign, the economy of *différance* and the logic of the supplement, is also a sacrificial economy. In his essay "How to Avoid Speaking" (*Comment ne pas parler*), he coins the word "denegation" (*dénégation*) or the negation of negation, to describe the effects of *différance* in discourses of negative theology. Writing in the interstices between the story of Abraham and Isaac in the Old Testament and Kierkegaard's reading of the story in *Fear and Trembling*, Derrida emphasizes,

> The trembling of *Fear and Trembling*, is, or so it seems, the very experience of sacrifice . . . in the sense that sacrifice supposes the putting to death of the unique in terms of its being unique, irreplaceable, and most precious. It also therefore refers to the impossibility of substitution, the unsubstitutional; and then also to the substitution of an animal for man; and finally, especially this, it refers to what links the sacred to sacrifice and sacrifice to secrecy . . . Abraham . . . speaks and doesn't speak. . . . He speaks in order not to say anything about the essential thing he must keep secret. Speaking in order not to say anything is always the best technique for keeping a secret.[9]

Speaking in order not to say is the work of *différance* such that deconstruction produces a specific kind of syntax: in *The Gift of Death* it is "religion without religion"; in *The Politics of Friendship* it is "community without community" and "friendship without friendship"; elsewhere it is "justice without justice." The syntagma of this sacrificial economy, that keeps concealed what it most wishes to say, is "X without X."[10] It conceals a continual wounding presented as a perpetual *kenosis*, the *kenosis* of discourse.[11] The sign is always involved in a diremption of meaning as it differs and defers in its logic of sacrificial substitution and supplementation. It is this which brings *différance* into a relation with negative theology (a saying which cannot say). The sign yields up its significance in what Derrida terms a serierasure. But what governs the yielding is the logocentric promise, the call to come, an eschatology which can never arrive, can never be allowed to arrive. Suffering, sacrifice, and satisfaction are intrinsic to the economy of the sign. "Every time there is '*jouissance*' (but the 'there is' of this event is in itself extremely enigmatic), there is 'deconstruction'. Effective deconstruction. Deconstruction perhaps has the effect, if not the mission, of liberating forbidden *jouissance*. That's what has to be taken on board. It is perhaps this *jouissance* which most irritates the all-out adversaries of 'deconstruction'."[12] But this is "*jouissance* without *jouissance*" for deconstruction cannot deliver the delay it describes. Thus, a culture is produced which is fundamentally sadomasochistic: it cannot allow itself to enjoy what it most profoundly wants. Derrida composes a scenario:

> What I thus engage in the double constraint of a *double bind* is not only myself, nor my own desire, but the other, the Messiah or the god himself. As if I were calling someone – for example, on the telephone – saying to him or her, in sum: I don't want you to wait for my call and become forever dependent upon it; go out on the town, be free not to answer. And to prove it, the next time I call you, don't answer, or I won't see you again. If you answer my call, it's all over.[13]

Michel de Certeau and Emmanuel Levinas, in their different models of selfhood with respect to the other, portray the sacrificial logic in terms of an endless journeying into exile (Certeau)[14] or the position of always being accused by the other (Levinas).[15] For both, the self can never be at rest. It must always suffer displacement by the other, always undergo a passion. The displacement and suffering is given, in both their accounts, an ethical coloring, for it is constituted in and by a Good beyond being (Levinas) or the utopic horizon of union with the One (Certeau's "white ecstasy").[16] The suffering is inseparable from accounts of desire, *jouissance*, and substitution.[17]

With various modulations each of these discourses operates a sacrificial logic in which love is not-having (Cixous's formulation).[18] The suffering, the sacrifice, the *kenosis*, is both necessary and unavoidable, for it is intrinsic to the economy itself. But unlike Hegel's dialectic, the negative moment is not appropriated and welded firmly both into the providential chain of time and the constitution of the subject. The negative moment remains unappropriated, unsublated, impossible to redeem because forever endlessly repeated. Furthermore, because bound to a construal of time as a series of discrete units, each negative moment is utterly singular and utterly arbitrary insofar as the moment is infinitely reiterated to the point where difference between moments becomes a matter of indifference (rendering the utterly singular moment identical and identically repeated). All suffering is both the same and yet singular; renunciation and sacrifice are both universal (in form) and particular. The relation of this operative negativity to the utopic horizon that governs it (*jouissance* in its various guises) is contradictory rather than paradoxical. It governs the suffering as its antithesis, not its *telos*. An infinite distance, a distance without analogy or participation, is opened constituting the other as absolutely other. In Derrida's words, "*tout autre est tout autre*"[19] As such the dreams of the bliss of union intensify the suffering in the way that Sisyphus is tormented by seeing the goal for which he strives while also knowing it can never be attained. Or, to employ another Greek myth, *jouissance* is the grapes held out to the thirsting Tantalus. And so one is led to ask what the sacrifice achieves in this infinite postponement of pleasure. As an operation, which is no longer governed by a single or a simple agency (for the poststructural subject is profoundly aporetic), it is required by and maintains the possibility of the economy. It is immanent to the economy but not assimilable to it. It resolves nothing with respect to that economy, only fissures it with the aneconomic trauma which allows the economy to proceed. What it produces, and continually reproduces then, is the economy itself: the endless production of pseudo-objects. This economy of sacrifice is fundamental to capitalism itself. For it sustains growth, limitless productivity, which is capitalism's profoundly secular fantasy. It repeats, in a sociopsychological, semiotic, and ethical keys our various monetary projects in which we deny present delights by investing for greater delights in the future (wherein the pleasures we deny ourselves are only utilized by investment banks to further develop market operations). Sacrifice as enjoying one's own suffering, in this immanent economy of desire, sustains current developments in globalism (and current illusions that such globalism is liberal and democratic).

Christian Pain and Pleasure

What role does suffering play in the economy of Christian redemption? What of its own sacrificial logic? I suggest we need to make a distinction between sacrificial suffering (as *kenosis* and passion), which undoes the economics of sin through a therapy of desire, and the suffering which is a consequence and a perpetuation of sin, which undoes the orders of grace that sustain creation in its being. Of course, this distinction is a theological one, maintained by faith and established by eschatological judgment. Living *in media res*, as Augustine reminds us, "ignorance is unavoidable – and yet the exigencies of human society make judgment also unavoidable."[20] Nevertheless, the distinction is important for it marks out a place for suffering as a passion written into creation (the first incarnation of the divine). That cryptic verse from the Book of Revelation announces that Christ was the Lamb "slain from the foundation of the world" (13.8). Creation, then, issues from a certain kenotic giving, a logic of sacrifice that always made possible the passion of Jesus Christ on the Cross, the slaying of the Lamb. The Cross becomes the place where the two forms of suffering – the sacrificial and that which is a consequence of sin – meet. Jesus is both the obedient lamb given on behalf of sinful human beings and the suffering victim of the disrupted orders of creation brought about by the lust to dominate. The kenotic abandonment assuages and reorientates the powers of disintegration, establishing grace as the principle of nature. But prior to the fall, to sin, and the judgment that installed suffering (and death) as a consequence of disobedience, prior to the judgment on Eve ("I will increase your labour and your groaning," Genesis 3.16) and the judgment on Adam ("You shall gain your food by the sweat of your brow," Genesis 3.19), there was a foundational giving that cost.

We will return to the nature of this primordial suffering later. Evidently it concerns the divine economy with respect both to its internal relations and creation. For the moment I wish to point out how this logic of sacrifice operates in respect of divine history or *Heilsgeschichte*. For it is that which reveals itself as flesh and history, recorded in the scriptures, which, for Christians, stakes out the limits and possibilities for theological speculation. And it is in that revelation of God made flesh that the relationship between suffering and incarnation, the mystery of that relationship, can be apprehended.

The suffering that marks the incarnation is figured early in the gospel narrative of Luke in scenes and tropes of wounding and scarification. John the Baptist's circumcision is reiterated in the circumcision of Christ (1.59 and 2.21) and the prophesied rejection of Christ by the world is followed by an oracle to Mary that "a sword shall pierce your heart also" (2.35). The circumcision was interpreted by the early Church Fathers as an early blood-letting foreshadowing the sacrifice on the Cross. Suffering was also a glorification, for the detail that it took place on the eighth day was traditionally interpreted as a reference to the eschatological day of judgment; the day following the final and consummating Sabbath when the dead rise with new bodies to dwell eternally in the kingdom of light. This paradoxical nature of suffering and glorification is echoed throughout the New Testament. We will meet it in the Pauline epistles, and in the Gospel of John Christ on the Cross is portrayed as both the ultimate victim and the exalted ensign for the healing of the nations. In the Book of Revelation the Lamb worshipped and adored, the disseminator of light throughout the Eternal City, remains a Lamb that was slain.

The scenes and tropes of scarification in those opening chapters of Luke's Gospel focus other acts of violence with which the Incarnation is announced and brought about: the sacrificial offering made by Zechariah the Priest (1.10), the offering of doves or pigeons at the Presentation of Christ (2.24), the terror struck in Zechariah, Mary, and the shepherds at the visitation of the angel(s), the striking dumb of Zechariah "because you have not believed me" (1.20). The suffering of incarnation is registered somatically and psychologically in the flesh of those called to play a part in its human manifestation. The Incarnation of Christ intensifies the experience of embodiment through the sufferings it engenders, just as – in an unfolding of the same logic – it is the experience of suffering which most deeply draws the believer to prayer (in the garden of Gethsemane, in the upper room following the death, resurrection, and ascension of Christ, in Paul's imprisonment). In suffering the soul is recognized at the surface of the body, the ensoulment of the body is most exposed.[21] With the darkest nights of the soul, in which is evident the inseparability of consciousness, subconsciousness, and the sensitivities of the flesh, come the profoundest awareness of participation in the divine.

There is no deliverance from suffering promised in the New Testament before the messianic return: "He will dwell among them and they shall be his people, and God himself will be with them. He will wipe every tear from their eyes; there shall be an end to death, and to mourning and crying and pain; for the old order has passed away" (Revelation 21.3–4). In fact, in his Epistle to the Colossians, Paul cryptically remarks that he rejoices to suffer for the church at Colossi because "This is my way of helping to complete, in my poor human flesh, the full tale of Christ's afflictions still to he endured, for the sake of his body which is the church" (1.24). This is a well-wrought translation, but it filters out some of the syntactic and semantic complexity of Paul's Greek. A close, more literal translation would read:

> Now I rejoice in suffering [*en tois pathemasin*] on your behalf and fill up in turn [*antanaplero*] things lacking of the afflictions [*thlipseon*] of Christ in my flesh [*sarxi*] on behalf of his body [*somatos*] which is the church.

The Greek gives emphasis to three interrelated themes. First, it builds upon and develops spatial figurations which preoccupy Paul through this letter and (possibly) his letter to the Ephesians. Throughout the letter Paul draws attention to Christ as a cosmic space filled with all the riches and treasures of wisdom and knowledge (2.3), speaking repeatedly of Christians as living *en Christo* or *en auto* employing a locative use of the dative. All things upon earth and in heaven are reconciled "in the body of his flesh [*en to somati tes sarxos autou*]" (1.22). Second, the Greek emphasizes the inter-dependency of bodies and flesh such that there is a series of coactivities between the individual believer and the body of Christ as *both* the church and the person of Christ. Later in the letter Paul will talk about being co-buried [*suntaphentes*], co-raised [*sunegerthete*], and co-quickened [*sune-zoopoiesen*] in Christ (2.12–13), such that there is an economy for growth and expansion through "the operation of him operating in me in power [*ten energian autou ten energoumenen en emoi en dunamei*]." The prose borders on poetry, as alliterative and assonantal effects resonate within an iterative litany. Paul's flesh (*sarx*) participates in an unfolding and outworking of Christ's body (*soma*), just as Jesus Christ's own flesh opens up to enfold all things in earth and heaven in one body. Third, the verse picks up a rich and profound play on the verb *pleroo* and the noun *pleroma*. The verb *pleroo* stands as the opposite to the important word for Christ's descent from God in Paul's Letter to the Philippians, *kenoo* – to empty, to pour out.[22] There Paul exhorts believers to "Have this mind among yourselves, which is yours in Christ Jesus, who, though he was in the form of God, did not count equality with God a thing to be grasped, but emptied himself, taking the form of a servant, being born like other human beings" (2.5). The economics of emptying that governed the Incarnation are now reversed. The lack that *kenosis* brought about is now being satisfied. There is a filling and a fulfilling, not only of Christ but of each believer with respect to Christ. Paul works and prays for the Colossians that "you may be filled [*plerothete*] with the full knowledge of the will of him in all wisdom and spiritual understanding [*en pase sophia kai sunesei pneumatike*]" (1.9). The *pleroma* is presented as the glory or the wisdom of God filling a space, defining a certain sacred spatiality like the *Shekinah* in the tabernacle in the wilderness. Earlier in the letter Paul writes that in Christ "all the fullness [*pan to pleroma*]" dwells (1.19). Later in the letter he writes that "in him dwells all the fullness of the Godhead bodily [*to pleroma tes theotetos somatikos*] and you are in him having been filled [*pepleromenoi*]" (2.9–10). In the verse following 1.24 he presents himself as the minister according to God's economic handling [*oikonomian*] "to fulfil the word of God [*plerosa ton logon tou theou*]" (1.25) for the Colossians.

Here in 1.24 *antanaplero* is utterly distinctive. Found only at this point in the New Testament, it combines *ana-plero* (to fill up to the brim, to make up, supply, satisfy, and fulfill) with the prefix of *anti*. As J. B. Lightfoot pointed out back in 1876, if Paul's meaning was simply to fill up then the prefix is redundant.[23] With the prefix a self-reflexivity is announced. Twice in the verse the word "on behalf of [*uper*]" is employed: Paul suffers on behalf of the Colossians and on behalf of the body of Christ as the church. His suffering in the flesh is filling what remains of the afflictions of Christ *as* Christ suffered on behalf of him in his own flesh. Jesus Christ as flesh (*sarx*) is no longer: "even though we once knew Christ from the human point of view, we know him no longer in that way" Paul tells the church at Corinth (2 Corinthians 5.16). There remains the body of Christ as the church composed of the flesh (*sarx*) of believers like Paul. Paul's suffering is, then, an extension of and a participation in the suffering of Christ. Now, on one level this is living *imitatio Christi* – the church suffers persecution as Christ suffered persecution. But, considered in the light of the three emphases we have been outlining – Christ as a cosmic and spiritual space in which the operation of a divine economy of "filling" engages and makes itself manifest through the embodiment of those believers composing the body of Christ – then we have to ask what the relationship is between suffering and glorification, affliction and fulfillment. For the filling is an activity described both in terms of suffering and full knowledge, wisdom and spiritual understanding. And it is an activity that not only builds up, but defines the operation of the divine with respect to, the body of Christ. A suffering inseparable from the Incarnation of Christ is experienced in believers as a suffering inseparable from coming to the fullness of the stature of Christ or "being renewed in the full knowledge according to the image of the creator" (3.10).

Paul's writing is a theological reflection on the economics of divine power with respect to embodiment in Christ. It is a reflection upon divinity as it manifests itself in the concrete historicity of the death, burial, and resurrection of Jesus the Christ. It is not speculative in the sense of conceiving operations in the Godhead on the basis of which earthly events might be explained. Rather he develops and unfolds the logic of Christ's incarnation and crucifixion, examining the space that has been opened up "in the body of his flesh through his death" (1.22). This is not, then, an example of *deipassionism* in the sense of God suffering with humankind – the suffering of God described by Moltmann, for example. One recalls how Moltmann reads Elie Wiesel's account of the hanging of a child in the German concentration camp. Wiesel observes how the question of where God is is raised by Jewish onlookers. Moltmann examines this question and Wiesel's own response, in terms of God being in the very suffering of the child.

To speak here of a God who could not suffer would make God a demon. To speak here of an absolute God would make God an annihilating nothingness. To speak here of an indifferent God would condemn men to indifference. . . . Does the Shekinah, which wanders with Israel through the dust of the streets and hangs on the gallows in Auschwitz, suffer in the God who holds the ends of the earth in his hand? In that case not only would suffering affect God's *pathos* externally, so that it might be said that God himself suffers at the human history of injustice and force, but suffering would be the history in the midst of God himself.[24]

God suffers with us such that the negative moment is taken up into God in the eschatological coming of the kingdom. Moltmann's theology, endorsing a certain interpretation of Hegel's, radicalizes God being with us, compromising God's transcendence.

Balthasar's account of Christ's descent into hell and into solidarity with the most profound alienation from God the father, retains the transcendent and impassable source, opening wide the difference between the father and the son, the trinitarian processions. In the silence of Holy Saturday God is extended to the point where even that which is most remote from the Godhead is incorporated. The depths of abjection are plumbed and God is found there. "The Redeemer showed himself therefore as the only one who, going beyond the general experience of death, was able to measure the depths of that abyss."[25] Through Christ's suffering there is redemption, but once redemption has been achieved – the extreme boundaries of hell encompassed – then all is reconciled. "Hell is the *product* of redemption," Balthasar informs us.[26] Subsequent suffering is not really suffering at all, objectively speaking. For the victory has been won in Christ through the events of those three days (Good Friday, Holy Saturday, and Easter Sunday): "Inasmuch as the Son travels across the chaos in virtue of the mission received from the Father, he is, objectively speaking, whilst in the midst of the darkness of what is contrary to God, in 'paradise', and the image of triumph may well express this."[27]

But Paul's account views things differently: subsequent suffering is not epiphenomenal (which Balthasar's account may seem to render it). It participates in a true and ongoing suffering; a true and ongoing passion located in the very Godhead itself. Following this interpretation of Paul we can conclude that there is a suffering which is rendered meaningless because it has no part in redemption. This is a suffering which rejects and fights against redemption. It has no truth, no existence in Augustine's ontology of goodness, because it is privative – it deprives and strips creation of its orders of being, its treasures of wisdom. Suffering which is a consequence and promulgation of sin can find no place in the *pleroma* unless as a therapy for the orientation of desire towards sin. Only *pleroma* gives space, provides a dwelling. But there is a suffering which is intrinsically meaningful because it is a continuation, a fleshing out, and a completing of the suffering of Christ.

In several places Gregory of Nyssa will speak of this suffering as the wounding of love (a double genitive). The suffering issues from the experience of the agony of distance which is installed by difference (between the Bride of Christ and the Christ himself) and discerned by love. The agony is the very laboring of love whereby "the soul grows by its constant participation in that which transcends it."[28] Nyssa takes up a theological account of circumcision to describe this movement: "Here, too, man is circumcised, and yet he remains whole and entire and suffers no mutilation in his material nature."[29] The question raised here, with respect to the sado-masochistic economy of desire informing postmodern secularity, is how does it differ since the internalization of a pleasurable pain is common to both. For the moment let us allow that question to hang and draw, whilst I emphasize, again, that only God can discern and distinguish what is true suffering, and therefore what is being outlined here is not a theodicy, nor the grounds for providing theological rationales for human tragedies. Enlightenment theodicies preempt (and therefore in an act of hubris usurp) eschatological judgment. There is a "filling up" and therefore an end, when "Christ is all and in all [panta kai en pasin Christos]," but that "filling up" is not yet concluded and we remain caught between contingent knowledges and truth; intuition, ignorance, and hope.

If kenosis and completion, emptying and filling, are not two opposites, but two complementary operations of the divine, like breathing out in order to breathe in, then there is no lack, absence, or vacuum as such. Both movements are associated with a suffering that simultaneously glorifies. The self-emptying of Christ reaches its nadir in death only to be reversed in a final coronation: "Therefore God raised him to the heights and bestowed upon him the name above all names, that at the name of Jesus every knee should bow" (Philippians 2.9–10). The "filling up in turn [antana-plero]" also involves "being empowered [dunamoumenoi] according to the might of His glory for all endurance and long-suffering with joy [eis pasan hupomonm kai makrothu-mian meta charas]" (Colossians 1.11). This leads us to the heart of a theological mystery: what it is that constitutes the intradivine passion? That the passion is the basis for the economy of kenoo and, plero and that this economy opens up a space for divine redemptive activity with respect to creation is evident. It is also evident that this passion is grounded in trinitarian relations. Paul, in his Letter to the Colossians, mainly treats of the relationship between Christ and the Godhead, but the content and dynamic of that relationship he expresses in terms of wisdom, knowledge, glory, and energia. There is much debate between and among New Testament scholars and dogmatic theologians over how developed trinitarian thinking is within the New Testament. Nevertheless it would appear to be true that the passion that is the basis for the economy of kenoo and plero – with respect to the glorification of all things created – is an intradivine passion that Christians have understood in terms of the differences-in-relation, the differences-in-identity between the Father, the Son, and the Holy Spirit.

The suffering comes by, through, and with the infinite capacity for divine self-exposition. Taking up the double nature of the genitive in "the wounding of love," another way of putting this would be to say that the wounding is intrinsic to the operation of love not only between the Bride and the Bridegroom, the church and Christ, but between the persons of the Trinity. This is not an account of the self divided from itself – God is one in substance – nor is this an account of the sovereignty of the Father splitting to constitute the Son. The suffering does not issue from any subordination. Father, Son, and Spirit are co-constituted; the self-exposition is eternal. But the very equality-in-difference-of-one-substance expresses the creative tensions of loving communion. The primordial suffering, then, is within the Godhead itself and is given expression in the very act of creation, so that a certain suffering is endemic to incarnate living, a suffering that always made possible the sacrifice on the Cross.

Notes

1   I also need to clarify here that the relationship between these cultures is complex, not oppositional or even dialectical. The character of Christianity today cannot be extracted from its cultural context. Christianity, though rooted in all its various previous forms and traditions, is conceived in the cultural terms available, the cultural terms which maintain its current relevance and render it comprehensible (and believable) in contemporary society.

2   *Bodies That Matter: On the Discursive Limits of "Sex"* (London: Routledge, 1993).

3   See my essay "Language and Silence" in Oliver Davis and Denys Turner (eds.), *Silence and the Word: Negative Theology and Incarnation* (Cambridge: Cambridge University Press, 2001): John Milbank, "Sublimity: The Modern Transcendent," in Paul Heelas (ed.), *Religion, Modernity and Postmodernity* (London: Routledge, 1998), pp. 258–84.

4   See Michel de Certeau, *The Mystic Fable*. Vol. 1: *The Sixteenth and the Seventeenth Centuries*, trans. Michael B. Smith (Chicago: University of Chicago Press, 1992).

5   See J. V. Field, *The Invention of Infinity: Mathematics and Art in the Renaissance* (Oxford: Oxford University Press, 1997).

6   See Immanuel Kant, *Critique of Judgement*, trans. James Creed Meredith (Oxford: Clarendon Press, 1952).

7   Slavoj Žižek, *The Fragile Absolute – or Why is the Christian Legacy Worth Fighting For?* (London: Verso, 2000), p. 21.

8   See Žižek on the relationship between Clara and Robert Schumann in *Plague of Fantasies* (London: Verso, 1997), pp. 66–67, 192–212.

9   Jacques Derrida, *The Gift of Death*, trans. David Wills (Chicago: University of Chicago Press, 1995), pp. 58–59.

10   Jacques Derrida, *The Politics of Friendship*, trans. George Collins (London: Verso, 1997), p. 47.

11   See Jacques Derrida, *On the Name*, trans. Thomas Dutoit (Stanford, CA: Stanford University Press, 1995), pp. 50–60.

12   "An Interview with Jacques Derrida," in Derek Attridge, *Jacques Derrida: Acts of Literature* (London; Routledge, 1992), p. 56.

13   Derrida, *The Politics of Friendship*, p. 174.

14   See Michel de Certeau, *The Mystic Fable*, trans. Michael B. Smith (Chicago: University of Chicago Press, 1992), pp. 273–96.

15   See Emmanuel Levinas, *Autrement qu'être ou au-dela de essence* (The Hague: Martinus Nijoff, 1974), pp. 206–19.

16   See Michel de Certeau, "White Ecstasy," trans. Frederick Christian Bauerschmidt and Catriona Hanley in Graham Ward (ed.), *The Postmodern God* (Oxford: Blackwell Publishers, 1998), pp. 155–58.

17   For Levinas see *Autrement qu'être*, pp. 116–20, 156–205.

18   See Hélène Cixous, " 'The Egg and the Chicken': Love as Not Having" in *Reading Clarice Lispector*, trans. Verena Andermatt Conley (Hemel Hempstead: Harvester Wheatsheaf, 1990), pp. 98–122. Cixous describes two types of love as not-having: a masculine economy of renunciation and a feminine economy of enjoying that which is always excessive to possession. Lacan himself drew attention to two economies of desire in his later work, notably *Seminar XX: Encore;* see Žižek, *The Fragile Absolute*, pp. 144–48 for an important reading of this shift in Lacan for Christian construals of "charity."

19   Derrida, *Gift of Death*, pp. 82–115.

20   Augustine, *De Civitate Dei*, XIX.6.

21 This should alert us to other possible readings of Christian asceticism: the putting to death of the fleshly desires in order to focus on the soul's perfection need not entail a body–soul dualism. This would be gnostic. Christian ascetic practices intensify the experience of the body and it is in that intensification that the soul is rendered most visible, most engaged.

22 In a highly insightful and technical article on the great kenotic hymn or *Carmen Christi* in Paul's Letter to the Philippians (2.5–11) by the New Testament scholar C. F. D. Moule, the point is made that "what is *styled* kenosis is, itself, the height of plerosis: the most divine thing to give rather than to get" ("Further Reflections on Philippians 2: 5–11," in W. W. Groque and R. P. Martin (eds.), *Apostolic History and the Gospels* (Grand Rapids, MI: Eerdmans, 1970), p. 273. I am attempting to develop this insight theologically, whilst avoiding some of the neater ethical pronouncements "to give rather than to get" that Moule makes upon its basis.

23 J. B. Lightfoot, *Epistle to the Colossians* (London: Macmillan, 1876), pp. 164–65.

24 Jürgen Moltmann, *The Crucified God: The Cross of Christ as the Foundation and Criticism of Christian Theology* (London: SCM, 1974), pp. 273–74.

25 Hans Urs von Balthasar, *Mysterium Paschale*, trans. A. Nichols (Edinburgh: T. & T. Clark, 1990), p. 168.

26 Ibid, p. 174.

27 Ibid, p. 176.

28 Nyssa's *Commentary on the Canticle of Canticles* in Herbert Musurillo, SJ (ed.), *From Glory to Glory: Texts from Gregory of Nyssa's Mystical Writings* (Crestwood: St Vladimir's Seminary Press, 1995), p. 190.

29 Ibid, p. 193.

(b) *Epistemology of the Closet*

Eve Kosofsky Sedgwick

Proust, in fact, insistently suggests as a sort of limit-case of one kind of coming out precisely the drama of Jewish self-identification, embodied in the Book of Esther and in Racine's recasting of it that is quoted throughout the "Sodom and Gomorrah" books of *A la recherche*. The story of Esther seems a model for a certain simplified but highly potent imagining of coming out and its transformative potential. In concealing her Judaism from her husband, King Assuérus (Ahasuerus), Esther the Queen feels she is concealing, simply, her identity: "The King is to this day unaware who I am."[1] Esther's deception is made necessary by the powerful ideology that makes Assuérus categorize her people as unclean ("cette source impure" [1039]) and an abomination against nature ("Il nous croit en horreur à toute la nature" [174]). The sincere, relatively abstract Jew-hatred of this fuddled but omnipotent king undergoes constant stimulation from the grandiose cynicism of his advisor Aman (Haman), who dreams of an entire planet exemplarily cleansed of the perverse element.

> I want it said one day in awestruck centuries:
> "There once used to be Jews, there was an insolent race;
> widespread, they used to cover, the whole face of the earth;
> a single one dared draw on himself the wrath of Aman,
> at once they disappeared; every one, from the earth."
>
> (476–80)

The king acquiesces in Aman's genocidal plot, and Esther is told by her cousin, guardian, and Jewish conscience Mardochée (Mordecai) that the time for her revelation has come; at this moment the particular operation of suspense around her would be recognizable to any gay person who has inched toward coming out to homophobic parents. "And if I perish, I perish," she says in the Bible (Esther 4:16). That the avowal of her secret identity will have an immense potency is clear, is the premise of the story. All that remains to be seen is whether under its explosive pressure the king's "political" animus against her kind will demolish his "personal" love for her, or vice versa: will he declare her as good as, or better, dead? Or will he soon be found at a neighborhood bookstore, hoping not to be recognized by the salesperson, who is ringing up his copy of *Loving Someone Jewish*?

The biblical story and Racinian play, bearable to read in their balance of the holo-caustal with the intimate only because one knows how the story will end,[2] are enact-ments of a particular dream or fantasy of coming out. Esther's eloquence, in the event, is resisted by only five lines of her husband's demurral or shock: essentially at the instant she names herself, both her ruler and Aman see that the anti-Semites are lost ("*AMAN, tout bas:* Je tremble" [1033]). Revelation of identity in the space of inti-mate love effortlessly overturns an entire public systematics of the natural and the unnatural, the pure and the impure. The peculiar strike that the story makes to the heart is that Esther's small, individual ability to risk losing the love and countenance of her master has the power to save not only her own space in life but her people.

It would not be hard to imagine a version of *Esther* set in the Supreme Court in the days immediately before the decision in *Bowers v. Hardwick*. Cast as the ingenue in the title role a hypothetical closeted gay clerk, as Assuérus a hypothetical Justice of the same gender who is about to make a majority of five in support of the Georgia law. The Justice has grown fond of the clerk, oddly fonder than s/he is used to being of clerks, and . . . In our compulsive recursions to the question of the sexualities of court personnel, such a scenario was close to the minds of my friends and me in many forms. In the passionate dissenting opinions, were there not the traces of others' comings-out already performed; could even the dissents themselves represent such performances, Justice coming out to Justice? With the blood-let tatters of what risky comings-out achieved and then overridden—friends', clerks', employees', children's—was the imperious prose of the majority opinions lined? More painful and frequent were thoughts of all the coming out that had not happened, of the women and men who had not in some more modern idiom said, with Esther,

> I dare to beg you, both for my own life
> and the sad days of an ill-fated people
> that you have condemned to perish with me.
> (1029–31)

What was lost in the absence of such scenes was not, either, the opportunity to evoke with eloquence a perhaps demeaning pathos like Esther's. It was something much more precious: evocation, articulation, of the dumb Assuérus in all his imperial inel-oquent bathos of unknowing: "A périr? Vous? Quel peuple?" ("To perish? You? What people?" [1032]). "What people?" indeed—why, as it oddly happens, the very people whose eradication he personally is just on the point of effecting. But only with the utterance of these blank syllables, making the weight of Assuérus's powerful igno- rance suddenly audible—not least to him—in the same register as the weight of Esther's and Mardochée's private knowledge, can any open flow of power become possible. It is here that Aman begins to tremble.

Just so with coming out: it can bring about the revelation of a powerful unknowing *as* unknowing, not as a vacuum or as the blank it can pretend to be but as a weighty and occupied and consequential epistemological space. Esther's avowal allows Assuérus to make visible two such spaces at once: "You?" "What people?" He has been blindly presuming about herself,[3] and simply blind to the race to whose extinction he has pledged himself. What? you're one of *those*? Huh? *you're* a *what*? This frightening thunder can also, however, be the sound of manna falling.

*   *   *

There is no question that to fixate, as I have done, on the scenario sketched here more than flirts with sentimentality. This is true for quite explicable reasons. First, we have too much cause to know how limited a leverage any individual revelation can exercise over collectively scaled and institutionally embodied oppressions. Acknowledgment of this disproportion does not mean that the consequences of such acts as coming out can be circumscribed within *predetermined* boundaries, as if between "personal" and "political" realms, nor does it require us to deny how disproportion- ately powerful and disruptive such acts can be. But the brute incommensurability has nonetheless to be acknowledged. In the theatrical display of an *already institutionalized* ignorance no transformative potential is to be looked for.

There is another whole family of reasons why too long a lingering on moments of *Esther*-style avowal must misrepresent the truths of homophobic oppression; these go back to the important differences between Jewish (here I mean Racinian-Jewish) and gay identity and oppression. Even in the "Sodom and Gomorrah" books of Proust, after all, and especially in *La Prisonnière*, where *Esther* is so insistently invoked, the play does not offer an efficacious model of transformative revelation. To the contrary: *La Prisonnière* is, notably, the book whose Racine-quoting hero has the most disastrous incapacity either to come out or to *be come out to*.

The suggested closeted Supreme Court clerk who struggled with the possibility of a self-revelation that *might* perceptibly strengthen gay sisters and brothers, but *would* radically endanger at least the foreseen course of her or his own life, would have an imagination filled with possibilities beyond those foreseen by Esther in her moment of risk. It is these possibilities that mark the distinctive structures of the epistemology of the closet. The clerk's authority to describe her or his own sexuality might well be impeached; the avowal might well only further perturb an already stirred-up current of the open secret; the avowal might well represent an aggression against someone with whom, the clerk felt, after all, a real bond; the nongay- identified Justice might well feel too shaken in her or his own self-perception, or in the perception of the bond with the clerk, to respond with anything but an increased rigor; the clerk might well, through the avowal, be getting dangerously into the vicinity of the explosive-mined closet of a covertly gay Justice; the clerk might well fear being too isolated or self-doubting to be able to sustain the consequences of the avowal; the intersection of gay revelation with underlying gender expectations might well be too confusing or disorienting, for one or the other, to provide an intelligible basis for change.

To spell these risks and circumscriptions out more fully in the comparison with *Esther*:

1. Although neither the Bible nor Racine indicates in what, if any, religious behaviors or beliefs Esther's Jewish identity may be manifested, *there is no suggestion that that identity might be a debatable, a parous, a mutable fact about her.* "Esther, my lord, had a Jew for her father" (1033)—ergo, Esther is a Jew. Taken aback though he is by this announcement, Assuérus does not suggest that Esther is going through a phase, or is just angry at Gentiles, or could change if she only loved him enough to get counseling. Nor do such undermining possibilities occur to Esther. The Jewish identity in this play—whatever it may consist of in real life in a given historical context—has a solidity whose very unequivocalness grounds the story of Esther's equivocation and her subsequent self-disclosure. In the processes of gay self-disclosure, by contrast, in a twentieth-century context, questions of authority and evidence can be the first to arise. "How do you know you're really gay? Why be in such a hurry to jump to conclusions? After all, what you're saying is only based on a few feelings, not real, actions [or *alternatively:* on a few actions, not necessarily your real feelings]; hadn't you better talk to a therapist and find out?" Such responses—and their occurrence in the people come out to can seem a belated echo of their occurrence in the person coming out—reveal how problematical at present is the very concept of gay identity, as well as how intensely it is resisted and how far authority over its definition has been distanced from the gay subject her- or himself.

2. *Esther expects Assuérus to be altogether surprised by her self-disclosure; and he is.* Her confident sense of control over other people's knowledge about her is in contrast to the radical uncertainty closeted gay people are likely to feel about who is in control of information about their sexual identity. This has something to do with a realism about secrets that is greater in most people's lives than it is in Bible stories; but it has much more to do with complications in the notion of gay identity, so that no one person can take control over all the multiple, often contradictory codes by which information about sexual identity and activity can seem to be conveyed. In many, if not most, relationships, coming out is a matter of crystallizing intuitions or convictions that had been in the air for a while already and had already established their own power-circuits of silent contempt, silent blackmail, silent glamorization, silent complicity. After all, the position of those who think they *know something about one that one may not know oneself* is an excited and empowered one—whether what they think one doesn't know is that one somehow *is* homosexual, or merely that one's supposed secret is known to them. The glass closet can license insult ("I'd never have said those things if I'd *known* you were gay!"—yeah, sure); it can also license far warmer relations, but (and) relations whose potential for exploitiveness is built into the optics of the asymmetrical, the specularized, and the inexplicit.[4] There are sunny and apparently simplifying versions of coming out under these circumstances: a woman

painfully decides to tell her mother that she's a lesbian, and her mother responds, "Yeah, I sort of thought you might be when you and Joan started sleeping together ten years ago." More often this fact makes the closet and its exits not more but less straightforward, however; not, often, more equable, but more volatile or even violent. Living in and hence coming out of the closet are never matters of the purely hermetic; the personal and political geographies to be surveyed here are instead the more imponderable and convulsive ones of the open secret.

3. *Esther worries that her revelation might destroy her or fail to help her people, but it does not seem to her likely to damage Assuérus, and it does not indeed damage him.* When gay people in a homophobic society come out, on the other hand, perhaps especially to parents or spouses, it is with the consciousness of a potential for serious injury that is likely to go in both directions. The pathogenic secret itself, even, can circulate contagiously *as* a secret: a mother says that her adult child's coming out of the closet with her has plunged her, in turn, into the closet in her conservative community. In fantasy, though not in fantasy only, against the fear of being killed or wished dead by (say) one's parents in such a revelation there is apt to recoil the often more intensely imagined possibility of its killing *them*. There is no guarantee that being under threat from a double-edged weapon is a more powerful position than getting the ordinary axe, but it is certain to be more destabilizing.

4. The inert substance of *Assuérus seems to have no definitional involvement with the religious/ethnic identity of Esther.* He sees neither himself nor their relationship differently when he sees that she is different from what he had thought her. The double-edged potential for injury in the scene of gay coming out, by contrast, results partly from the fact that the erotic identity of the person who receives the disclosure is apt also to be implicated in, hence perturbed by it. This is true first and generally "because erotic identity, of all things, is never to be circumscribed simply as itself, can never not be relational, is never to be perceived or known by anyone outside of a structure of transference and countertransference. Second and specifically it is true because the incoherences and contradictions of homosexual identity in twentieth-century culture are responsive to and hence evocative of the incoherences and contradictions of compulsory heterosexuality.

5. *There is no suggestion that Assuérus might himself be a Jew in disguise.* But it is entirely within the experience of gay people to find that a homophobic figure in power has, if anything, a disproportionate likelihood of being gay and closeted. Some examples and implications of this are discussed toward the end of Chapter 5; there is more to this story. Let it stand here merely to demonstrate again that gay identity is a convoluted and off-centering possession if it is a possession at all; even to come out does not end anyone's relation to the closet, including turbulently the closet of the other.

6. *Esther knows who her people are and has an immediate answerability to them.* Unlike gay people, who seldom grow up in gay families; who are exposed to their culture's, if not their parents', high ambient homophobia long before either they or those who care for them know that they are among those who most urgently need to define themselves against it; who have with difficulty and always belatedly to patch together from fragments a community, a usable heritage, a politics of survival or resistance; unlike these, Esther has intact and to hand the identity and

history and commitments she was brought up in, personified and legitimated in a visible figure of authority, her guardian Mardochée.

7. Correspondingly, *Esther's avowal occurs within and perpetuates a coherent system of gender subordination*. Nothing is more explicit, in the Bible, about Esther's marriage than its origin in a crisis of patriarchy and its value as a preservative of female discipline. When the Gentile Vashti, her predecessor as Ahasuerus's queen, had refused to be put on exhibition to his drunk men friends, "the wise men, which knew the times," saw that

> Vashti the queen hath not done wrong to the king only, but also to all the princes, and to all the people that are in all the provinces of the king Ahasuerus. For this deed of the queen shall come abroad unto all women, so that they shall despise their husbands in their eyes, when it shall be reported.
>
> (Esther 1:13–17)

Esther the Jew is introduced onto this scene as a salvific ideal of female submissiveness, her single moment of risk with the king given point by her customary pliancy. (Even today, Jewish little girls are educated in gender roles—fondness for being looked at, fearlessness in defense of "their people," nonsolidarity with their sex—through masquerading as Queen Esther at Purim; I have a snapshot of myself at about five, barefoot in the pretty "Queen Esther" dress my grandmother made [white satin, gold spangles], making a careful eyes-down toe-pointed curtsey at [presumably] my father, who is manifest in the picture only as the flashgun that hurls my shadow, pillaring up tall and black, over the dwarfed sofa onto the wall behind me.) Moreover, the literal patriarchism that makes coming out to *parents* the best emotional analogy to Esther's self-disclosure to her *husband* is shown with unusual clarity to function through the male traffic in women: Esther's real mission, as a wife, is to get her guardian Mardochée installed in place of Aman as the king's favorite and advisor. And the instability and danger that by contrast lurk in the Gentile Aman's relation to the king seem, Iago-like, to attach to the inadequate heterosexual buffering of the inexplicit intensities between them. If the story of Esther reflects a firm Jewish choice of a minority politics based on a conservative reinscription of gender roles, however, such a choice has never been able to be made intelligibly by gay people in a modern culture (although there have been repeated attempts at making it, especially by men). Instead, both within and outside of homosexual-rights movements, the contradictory understandings of same-sex bonding and desire and of male and female gay identity have crossed and recrossed the definitional lines of gender identity with such disruptive frequency that the concepts "minority" and "gender" themselves have lost a good deal of their categorizing (though certainly not of their performative) force.

Notes

1   Jean Racine, *Esther*, ed. H. R. Roach (London: George G. Harrap, 1949), line 89; my translation. Further citations of this play will be noted by line number in the text.

2   It is worth remembering, of course, that the biblical story still ends with mass slaughter: while Racine's king *revokes* his order (1197), the biblical king *reverses* his (Esther 8:5), licensing the Jews' killing of "seventy and five thousand" (9:16) of their enemies, including children and women (8:11).

3   In Voltaire's words, "un roi insensé qui a passé six mois avec sa femme sans savoir, sans s'informer même qui elle est" (in Racine, *Esther*, pp. 83–84).

4   On this, see Eve Kosofsky Sedgwick, "Privilege of Unknowing," *Genders* 1 (1988): 102–124 (esp. p. 120).

(c) Facing the End

Paul S. Fiddes

Many modern novelists seem to find it difficult to bring their books to an end. I am not only referring here to the increase in the *size* of novels, although this is an alarming phenomenon which some commentators blame on the use of the word processor; it is, after all, so much easier to go on adding material when a page does not have to be retyped as a consequence. Nor is this a trivial observation. The advance of technology may be giving scope for making clear what has been the case all along, that there is an inherent openness of meaning about a text that can never be brought to a final close. This is a truth to which I intend to return often in this book, although the unpleasant fact that the computer may encourage writers to indulge a lack of discipline should also warn us that we need to consider *limits* to openness. At this opening moment, however, I am concerned with the difficulties of 'closure' in a narrower sense than mere size. I am thinking about the problem of an appropriate end to a plot, about the nature of 'the last things' – the *eschata* – of a narrative.

The Problem of Closure

In his novel *The French Lieutenant's Woman*, John Fowles relates the obsession of Charles Smithson with a mysterious young governess, Sarah Woodruff. Charles, a Victorian gentleman and amateur paleontologist, is investigating the fossils around Lyme Regis when he becomes intrigued by the tragic and silent figure of Sarah, who apparently carries with her the sorrow of being deserted by her French lover. He has a one-night affair with her, discovers she has invented the story of her ruin, and painfully breaks his engagement with his fiancée with the intention of marrying the enigmatic Sarah. However, Sarah has now disappeared without trace. After several years of fruitless searching, he finally discovers her living in the bohemian household of Gabriel and Christina Rossetti. After a stormy interview, he comes to understand her need to find her own identity rather than being a mere extension of others' lives; he meets the child of their brief and passionate union, the scene ends with 'the pressure of lips upon auburn hair',[1] and we are left with the clear impression that they will marry. It is a happy, if uneasy, ending.

But there are still half a dozen pages of the novel left, and the novelist chooses at this point to appear in the narrative *in persona*, as 'the sort of man who cannot bear to be left out of the limelight . . . for whom the first is the only pronoun' and who has now 'got himself in *as he really is*'.[2] This impressario-like figure stares at the Rossettis' house 'with an almost proprietary air', takes out his watch, and turns back the hands by a quarter of an hour. "We find ourselves back in the middle of the meeting between Charles and Sarah, but this time there is no mutual understanding; he bitterly accuses her of cruelty, refuses her implicit offer of a liaison without marriage as making him into 'the secret butt of this corrupt house . . . the pet donkey', misses seeing the child, and storms off to a lonely exile in America. The narrator bids us not to think that 'this is a less plausible ending to their story'. After all, Charles has found 'an atom of faith in himself, a true uniqueness, on which to build'. He has learnt that life cannot be reduced to one riddle and one solution, however well Sarah fits the role of the Sphinx; though with agony in his heart, he can venture onto the 'unplumb'd, salt, estranging sea'.[3]

These are the alternative endings provided, though we immediately become aware that the options are not exhausted. There could have been others as well; as Fowles himself points out, life is not to be shrunk to one riddle. The film of *The French Lieutenant's Woman*, written by Harold Pinter and directed by Karel Reisz, presents the two alternatives in an ingenious way, though in doing so it does perhaps reduce the options to two only. The movie is a film within a film, relating the story of the actors who play Charles and Sarah and the affair on which they embark, as well as the Fowles' story itself; at the end, Charles and Sarah are reunited, but the actor who plays Sarah breaks the relationship with her fellow actor and leaves him deserted. The 'film within the film' opts for the first ending, and the 'film outside the film' for the second.

Another modern novelist, Julian Barnes, has the narrator of his novel *Flaubert's Parrot* protest against this kind of multiple ending. He mocks at the idea that a hesitant and ambiguous ending somehow reflects reality:

> When the writer provides two different endings to his novel (why two? why not a hundred?), does the reader seriously imagine that he is being 'offered a choice' and the work is reflecting life's variable outcomes? Such a 'choice' is never real, because the reader is obliged to consume both endings. In life, we make a decision – or a decision makes us – and we go one way; had we made a different decision (as I once told my wife, though I don't think she was in a condition to appreciate my wisdom), we would have been elsewhere. The novel with two endings doesn't repro-duce this reality; it merely takes us down two diverging paths.[4]

The narrator therefore suggests that if novelists really wanted to simulate the spec-trum of possibilities in life, they would supply a set of sealed envelopes at the back of the book, in various colours. Each would carry clear labels such as 'Traditional Happy Ending', 'Traditional Unhappy Ending', 'Modernist Arbitrary Ending', 'End of the World Ending', 'Dream Ending' and so on. Readers would be allowed only one, and would be obliged to destroy the envelopes they did not select.

Of course, Barnes is giving us here a satire on the belief that novels *should* be realistic, that they *should* mirror life. The narrator, Geoffrey Braithwaite, is an amateur Flaubert enthusiast, who is trying to find the stuffed parrot that served as a model for the parrot Loulou in Flaubert's short story, *Un Coeur Simple*. He is a realist critic, who thinks that he will find the author's true voice and intention if he can only establish various hard facts about Flaubert's life, including the train timetable by which he travelled to meet his mistress, and above all if he can find the parrot. Finding the creator's voice will, he believes, in some way also throw light on his own life story, and in particular enable him to come to terms with his wife's suicide.

But the parrot of Flaubert's story is a mystical beast, an inspiration for the poor maid Felicité's religious feelings, sheltering her with its wings like the Holy Ghost. We realize that no factual information will ever bring us to this parrot. Geoffrey sets out in a scholarly way to resolve the dispute between two rival Flaubert museums, each claiming to preserve the original parrot, which Flaubert borrowed from the Museum of National History and returned there. The book ends with his discovery that the museum had owned fifty similar parrots, and the curators of the two museums, confronted with this largesse, had 'read to themselves Flaubert's description of Loulou . . . And then they chose the parrot which looked most like his description.'[5] It seems that the text had created the referent, rather than the other way round. As Alison Lee wittily suggests, it is the readers and critics of the novels who are all Flaubert's parrots.[6] Arguing that neither museum might have chosen rightly, Geoffrey persists in viewing the remains of the collection in a dusty attic. Three remain, their once-bright colours dimmed by a covering of pesticide, and the novel ends with Geoffrey staring at them and thinking, 'Perhaps it was one of them.'

The end of the book, like its fantastic text which is a ragbag of historical research, literary criticism and story, subverts the realism it pretends to support. The narrator constantly undermines his own obsessions with finding the reality behind the text, as in the little piece about realistic endings quoted above, where his logical case is blown apart by the passing ironic comment, 'as I once told my wife, though I don't think she was in a position to appreciate my wisdom'. Though the book purports to have one, semi-realistic ending, it implies several ways of closure; we are left in uncertainty about whether the narrator is pleased or disappointed by the failed quest for the parrot ('. . . it was an ending and not an ending . . . Well, perhaps that's as it should be', he reflects at one point),[7] and we do not know whether or not the quest has helped him to rationalize his wife's suicide, or in what way.

The reluctance to close a novel has been magnified in recent writing, and shortly we shall be investigating some movements of thought in our contemporary culture to which critics refer when they dub Fowles and Barnes as 'postmodern' novelists.[8] Yet it cannot be denied that the reader demands some kind of closure to a narrative. Frank Kermode judges that we are predisposed to seek what he calls '*pleroma*, fullness, the fullness that results from completion'.[9] Paul Ricoeur notes that in our age the traditional paradigms of narrative are under threat, and particularly the dictum of Aristotle that a myth is 'an imitation of an action that is whole and complete in itself';[10] but however ambiguous, unexpected or inconclusive the ending might be, Ricoeur rightly maintains that anti-closure must have a limit; beyond a certain boundary we no longer have a work of art or any confidence in language to arrange what happens in life into a meaningful form.[11] Our samples from Fowles and Barnes thus leave us with two questions. Why do we demand some kind of ending to a story, and why does an end seem more difficult to achieve today than before? But by now you may be asking a different question altogether; is this a book about theology at all?

Theology and Literature – A Dialogue

In fact, there is a remarkable convergence going on between theologians and literary critics in their focus upon eschatology. Among the theologians, Jürgen Moltmann has been influential in claiming that eschatology is not just an appendix to Christian doctrine, to be abandoned to the enthusiasms of fanatical sects and revolutionary groups; since eschatology is the doctrine of Christian hope and witnesses to the God of hope, it is 'the medium of Christian faith as such, the key in which everything is set, the glow that suffuses everything here in the dawn of an expected new day.'[12] In the same tones, literary critics declare that the basic nature of texts is eschatological, and that this dimension is too important to be left to the minority interests of science fiction and disaster novels.[13] Indeed, Jacques Derrida claims that the apocalyptic mood of the nuclear age 'has been dealt with more "seriously" in texts by Mallarmé, or Kafka, or Joyce, for example, than in present-day novels that would offer direct and realistic descriptions of a "real" nuclear catastrophe.'[14] All texts are eschatological, both in being open to the new meaning which is to come to them in the future, and also in being 'seriously' open to the horizon which death gives to life, though the relation between this openness and the interior 'eschaton' of the closure of narrative is debated as vigorously as theologians debate realized and future eschatology.

Nor is the appeal to eschatology as the basic mood of theology and literary creation just an accidental convergence. On the one hand the Christian understanding of the last things – the final advent of the Lord of the cosmos, the last judgement, heaven and hell – is located in a story, the death and resurrection of Jesus Christ, and is dependent on certain basic texts. On the other hand, literary critics are generally concerned not only about the text but about human existence, human society, human hope and especially (as we shall see) the threat of death. We may regard our agenda as being set by Prospero in Shakespeare's *Tempest*, contemplating in one apocalyptic sweep the end of the magical play he has produced on his island, the end of life and the end of the cosmos:

> . . . be cheerful, sir.
> Our revels now are ended. These our actors,
> As I foretold you, were all spirits, and
> Are melted into air, into thin air:
> And, like the baseless fabric of this vision,
> The cloud-capp'd towers, the gorgeous palaces,
> The solemn temples, the great globe itself,
> Yea, all which it inherit, shall dissolve,
> And, like this insubstantial pageant faded,
> Leave not a rack behind. We are such stuff
> As dreams are made on; and our little life
> Is rounded with a sleep.[15]

In a previous study, *Freedom and Limit*, I have set out in some detail what I believe to be a fruitful method of 'dialogue' between creative literature and the work of the doctrinal theologian.[16] There I propose a relationship of mutual influence without confusion, where the images and narratives of literature can help the theologian to make doctrinal statements, while at the same time doctrinal thinking can provide a perspective for the critical reading of literary texts. There is, admittedly, a fundamental difference between the nature of literature and doctrine. Poetic metaphor and narrative rejoices in ambiguity and the opening up of multiple meaning; doctrine will always seek to reduce to concepts the images and stories upon which it draws – including those within its own scripture. Literature emphasizes the playful freedom of imagination, while doctrine aims to create a consistent and coherent system of thought, putting into concepts the wholeness of reality that imagination is feeling after. Of course, doctrinal statements are bound to go on using symbol and metaphor since it is not possible to do without analogies in speaking of God as infinite and transcendent Reality. I certainly do not mean to suggest that doctrine is 'literal' speech about God in contrast to the images of poetry. But doctrine uses metaphor in an attempt to *fix* meaning, to define and limit a spectrum of possible interpretations. In short, literature tends to openness and doctrine to closure.

However, because no doctrine can be absolute or final, it needs to be constantly broken open by the impact of image and story in changing times and situations. Creative literature can also help the theologian in deciding between various options of interpretation; there are alternative ways in which the multiple meanings of the metaphors and stories of faith might be fenced around by concepts, and imaginative writing can enable the theologian to make judgements. For instance, with regard to eschatology we might ask whether there is any reason to prefer a doctrine of resurrection to the immortality of the soul. The questions of identity and personal life involved have been well argued from the viewpoint of philosophy of religion, but the study of a novelist such as Doris Lessing will show that there are aspects that can be overlooked within such a narrow discussion (see chapter 4). On the other hand, Christian belief and doctrine can provide a reader with a perspective for the interpretation of literary texts. As E. H. Gombrich aptly puts it, 'the innocent eye sees nothing.'[17] Without imputing religious intentions to the author where they do not exist, the attempt of theologians to achieve a coherent grasp of patterns of human experience can make readers sensitive to aspects of experience within and beyond the text that they might otherwise miss. In particular we shall find that theological reflection on the nature of an 'end' to personal and cosmic existence will make us more aware of the way that texts are orientated towards an end, and the effect this has upon the consciousness of the reader.

Such a dialogue is not to be entered upon in a purely pragmatic manner, just to see if it might happen to work. There is a theological justification for embarking upon it in the first place, which again I have worked out in detail in my earlier study. I suggest that images and stories on the one hand, and concepts on the other, are all to be understood as *responses* to revelation. None are *identical* with revelation, for in revelation we are concerned with the self-disclosure of God's own being, not with the transmission of a message or even a picture. Nor is this revelation to be limited to the Bible, though the Hebrew and Christian scriptures are witness to revelation in an exceptional way. Wherever God opens God's own self to draw human persons into relationship with the divine life, there will be response of varying kinds, including that of the imagination. Only this universal self-opening of God can justify the making of connections between theology and other 'writings' in our culture, of whatever kind.

Notes

1   John Fowles, *The French Lieutenant's Woman* (London: Pan Books, 1987 [1969]), p. 393.
2   Ibid., p. 394.
3   Ibid., pp. 398–99.
4   Julian Barnes, *Flaubert's Parrot* (London: Picador, 1985 [1984]), p. 89.
5   Ibid., p. 187.
6   Alison Lee, *Realism and Power: Postmodern British Fiction* (London: Routledge, 1990), p. 39.
7   Barnes, *Flaubert's Parrot*, p. 189.
8   See e.g. Linda Hutcheon, *A Poetics of Postmodernism: History, Theory, Fiction* (London and New York: Routledge, 1990), pp. 44–48, 77–78, who classifies such novels as 'metafiction.'
9   Frank Kermode, 'Waiting for the End' in Malcolm Bull (ed.), *Apocalypse Theory and the Ends of the World* (Oxford: Blackwell, 1995), p. 251.
10   Aristotle, *Poetics* 50b.23–25; see Paul Ricoeur, *Time and Narrative*, vol. 2, transl. K. McLaughlin and D. Pellauer (Chicago and London: University of Chicago Press, 1985), p. 20.
11   Ibid., p. 22.
12   Jürgen Moltmann, *Theology of Hope. On the Ground and Implications of a Christian Eschatology*, transl. J. Leitch (London: SCM Press, 1967), pp. 15–16.
13   See, e.g. Frank Kermode, *The Sense of an Ending: Studies in the Theory of Fiction* (Oxford: Oxford University Press, 1968), pp. 5–17, and 'Lawrence and the Apocalyptic Types' in C. B. Cox and A. E. Dyson (eds), *Word in the Desert* (London: Oxford University Press, 1968), pp. 14–38; Brian McHale, *Postmodernist Fiction* (London and New York: Routledge, 1989), pp. 65–68; Patricia Waugh, *Practising Postmodernism: Reading Modernism* (London; Edward Arnold, 1992), pp. 7–16; Fredric Jameson, 'Progress Versus Utopia' in Brian Wallis (ed.), *Art After Modernism: Rethinking Representation* (Boston: David Godine, 1984), pp. 239–52. On science fiction and eschatology, see David Ketterer, *New Worlds for Old: The Apocalyptic Imagination, Science Fiction and American Literature* (New York; Anchor, 1974).
14   Jacques Derrida, 'No Apocalypse, Not Now (full speed ahead, seven missiles seven missives)', *Diacritics* 14/2 (1984), pp. 27–28.
15   Shakespeare, *The Tempest*, IV.l.147–58.
16   Paul S. Fiddes, *Freedom and Limit: A Dialogue between Literature and Christian Doctrine* (Basingstoke: Macmillan Press, 1991), pp. 15, 33–35.
17   E. H. Gombrich, *Art and Illusion: Studies in the Psychology of Pictorial Representation* (Oxford: Oxford University Press, 5th edn. 1983), p.271.

(d) Wordsworth's Apocalypse

Jonathan Roberts

I. Introduction

In 1790, during his summer vacation from Cambridge, the 20-year old Wordsworth and his friend Robert Jones went on a walking tour through revolutionary France towards the Alps in search of the sublime. The anticlimactic account of what actually happened there was written almost 15 years later in Book VI of *The Prelude*, a story presaged by the first sight of Mont Blanc which proved not merely to disappoint, but actually to destroy the hoped-for vision:

> That day we first
> Beheld the summit of Mont Blanc, and grieved
> To have a soulless image on the eye
> Which had usurped upon a living thought
> That never more could be.
>
> (VI, 453–56)[1]

Worse was to follow, as the long-anticipated moment of actually crossing the Alps was missed by the travellers completely, a fact they were to discover only through questioning a local peasant when the path ran out and the only way was down. In recounting this story, Wordsworth interrupts his own narrative at the point of this discovery with a much-discussed apostrophe to the Imagination:

> Imagination!—lifting up itself
> Before the eye and progress of my song
> Like an unfathered vapour, here that power,
> In all the might of its endowments, came
> Athwart me. I was lost as in a cloud,
> Halted without a struggle to break through,
> And now, recovering, to my soul I say
> 'I recognise thy glory:' in such strength
> Of usurpation, in such visitings
> Of awful promise, when the light of sense
> Goes out in flashes that have shewn to us
> The invisible world, doth greatness make abode,
> There harbours whether we be young or old,
> Our destiny, our nature, and our home,
> Is with infinitude—and only there[.]
>
> (VI, 525–39)

This apostrophe provides a sort of compensation narrative for Wordsworth as Imagination turns out to be better than reality anyway. He then resumes his story with an account of the descent into the Gondo Ravine on the far side of the pass. Now with 'the brook and the road' as 'fellow-travellers in this gloomy strait', Wordsworth describes how Nature begins to mutter and speak to him, its words unclear until the dissonance of his feelings and surroundings is resolved in a tentative vision of the 'characters of the great apocalypse':

> The immeasurable height
> Of woods decaying, never to be decayed,
> The stationary blasts of waterfalls,

And everywhere along the hollow rent
Winds thwarting winds, bewildered and forlorn,
The torrents shooting from the clear blue sky,
The rocks that muttered close upon our ears—
Black drizzling crags that spake by the wayside
As if a voice were in them—the sick sight
And giddy prospect of the raving stream,
The unfettered clouds and region of the heavens,
Tumult and peace, the darkness and the light–
Were all like workings of one mind, the features
Of the same face, blossoms upon one tree,
Characters of the great apocalypse,
The types and symbols of eternity,
Of first, and last, and midst, and without end.

(VI, 556–72)

The Simplon Pass narrative has become a test ground of Wordsworth criticism. As Alan Liu writes at the very outset of *Wordsworth: The Sense of History* (1989):

> The readings we now have of the Simplon Pass episode, among which Geoffrey Hartman's is in the vanguard, are so powerful that the episode has become one of a handful of paradigms capable by itself of representing the poet's work.[2]

Indeed, Liu's own discussion of the Simplon Pass episode that follows this comment has itself become the paradigmatic New Historicist reading of this paradigmatic work of Romanticism.

The Simplon Pass episode is important for another reason too: it is the only time that Wordsworth ever uses the word 'apocalypse' in his poetry (hence my title). Yet the word 'apocalypse' has been widely discussed in Wordsworth studies for almost a century, attracting detailed discussion from critics including A. C. Bradley, Geoffrey Hartman and M. H. Abrams. Despite this, these critical works provide very little consensus as to what kind of apocalypse this is—a question I will explore in this article by suggesting that Wordsworth offers a fundamentally different understanding of apocalypse, not only from his millenarian contemporaries of the 1790s, but also from his critical interpreters of the last hundred years. This article, then, is in four parts. The first part provides an overview of key uses of the term 'apocalypse' in Wordsworth criticism, with particular reference to the Simplon Pass episode. The second part discusses New Historicist (and other) critical perspectives on the narrative that have foregrounded the concept of 'displacement' in this passage. In the third part, I discuss the possibility that 'displacement' is a formal strategy of the text itself signalling Wordsworth's wider concerns about language and violence, rather than a furtive attempt to bury history. In the final part, I suggest that the Simplon Pass episode offers a hermeneutical alternative to the allegorical interpretation of apocalypse found in poems such as Coleridge's 'Religious Musings'. I end by briefly discussing the similarities and differences between the apocalypses of *The Prelude*, the Book of Revelation and chapter 25 of the gospel of Matthew.

II. Part One: A Brief Critical History of 'Apocalypse' in Wordsworth Studies

In a lecture of almost a century ago (1909), A. C. Bradley discussed the account of Book XI of *The Prelude* in which the young Wordsworth waits near 'The single sheep, and the one blasted tree' (1850, XI, 319) 'for the ponies that were coming to take him home for the holidays'.[3] Bradley says of this scene:

> Everything here is natural, but everything is apocalyptic. And we happen to know why. Wordsworth is describing the scene in the light of memory. In that eagerly expected holiday his father died; and the scene, as he recalled it, was charged with the sense of contrast between the narrow world of common pleasures and bland and easy hopes, and the vast unseen world which encloses it in beneficent yet dark and inexorable arms.[4]

Bradley's use of the term 'apocalyptic' implies an account of the everyday that carries a surplus freight of meaning, the nature of which is not apparent at the actual moment of experience. But in poetic memory, the event itself and the feelings that follow cannot be separated. Here Bradley puts his finger on the centrality of prolepsis—'the representation of a thing as existing before it actually does or did so'[5]—to Wordsworth's writing.

Fifty years later Geoffrey Hartman, noting that despite Bradley's essay, the ' "apocalyptic" Wordsworth [had] been neglected for the poet of natural blendings and healing interchanges',[6] proceeded to write perhaps the most influential discussion of the topic in Wordsworth criticism, in *Wordsworth's Poetry: 1787–1814* (1961). Hartman uses the term 'apocalypse' to mean a number of things, including (i) the Book of Revelation; (ii) eschatological thinking; (iii) 'a mind which actively desires the inauguration of a totally new epoch'; and (iv) 'any strong desire to cast out nature and to achieve an unmediated contact with the principle of things'.[7] This last definition is important in relation to the larger thesis of his book, as at key moments in the poet's writing, Hartman argues, consciousness of nature leads into a 'consciousness of consciousness',[8] a moment at which nature itself vanishes, and the poetry becomes all mind. Hartman calls this moment 'apocalyptic' and sees the apostrophe to Imagination following the Simplon Pass anticlimax as 'the purest instance of apocalypse and usurpation'.[9] For Hartman, this passage is not only a paradigm of Wordsworth's poetry, but it also shows that Wordsworth 'was haunted [. . .] by the fear that coming-to-consciousness was connected with the sense of violation or trespass'.[10] Hartman suggests that Wordsworth's response to this fear is to attempt to bind consciousness to nature again (Hartman here offers the parallel figure of 'akedah': Abraham binding his son (Genesis, 22:9)). He writes, 'A true though rather simple view of the structure of *The Prelude* would be gained by showing how the poet continually displaces or interprets apocalypse as akedah'.[11]

A decade later, in *Natural Supernaturalism* (1971) M. H. Abrams criticised the 'vogue in recent literary criticism' to apply the term apocalypse 'loosely to signify any sudden and visionary revelation, or any event of violent and large-scale destruction—or even anything which is very drastic', and proposed to 'restrict "apocalypse" to the sense used in Biblical commentary, where it signifies a vision in which the old world is replaced by a new and better world'.[12] Like Hartman, Abrams finds in apocalypse a Wordsworthian paradigm, but for Abrams the paradigm is that of the marriage of mind and nature, which is modelled on the marriage of the Lamb and the New Jerusalem (Revelation 19–21). Thus apocalypse, for Abrams, is 'an act of unaided vision, in which the Lamb and the New Jerusalem are replaced by man's mind as the bridegroom and nature as the bride'.[13] The significance of the Simplon Pass episode for Abrams lies in its emphasis on the reconciliation of opposites:

> [T]his *coincidentia oppositorum* suddenly expresses a revelation which Wordsworth equates with the showing forth of the contraries of God in the Apocalypse, the Book of Revelation itself. There the Lamb of the gospel of love had manifested Himself as the terrifying deity of the *dies irae*[.][14]

In 1984, Andrzej Warminski's 'Mixed Crossing: Wordsworth's Apocalypses' provided a reading that bypassed the biblical figures of Hartman and Abrams, and offered something closer to Bradley's discussion of prolepsis. Warminski's deconstructionist reading suggests that Wordsworth's writing gains its distinct tone by demanding a double reading through which the audience understands his poetry to be simultaneously 'natural' (as they read it literally) and 'apocalyptic' (as they read it figuratively).[15]

Stimulated by the end of the millennium, the most recent wave of work on Wordsworthian apocalypse—including Morton Paley's *Apocalypse and Millennium in English Romantic Poetry* (1999) and Tim Fulford's *Romanticism and Millenarianism* (2002)—have not developed the linguistic emphasis of Warminski's work, but have instead sought to give a more clearly historically contextualised understanding of apocalypse and millennium during the Romantic period, and to distinguish the relationship between these topics in the work of different Romantic authors.

Paley, like Abrams, questions modern uses of the term 'apocalypse', although his chief concern is not with the nature of apocalypse itself, but with its relationship to millennium. He writes:

> The poets of the Romantic period drew with great familiarity upon the situations, figures, and language of the Book of Revelation. However, far more important that any accumulation of details is their adaptations of the model underlying them, a model in which there is a transition from apocalypse to millennium.[16]

Like others, Paley uses the Simplon Pass episode as an explicatory example, although in actual application his chronology of this transition from apocalypse to millennium is unclear.[17] Drawing on Abrams's model of an internalised apocalypse, Paley writes of the Simplon Pass episode:

[T]he 'flashes that have shewn to us / The invisible world' (535–36) are liminal. The glimpse of forces beyond the veil is for the moment presented as a triumph, at which point apocalypse is succeeded by an internalized millennium, with the mind 'Strong itself, and in the access of joy / Which hides it like the overflowing Nile' (547–48).[18,19]

III. Part Two: The Simplon Pass, New Historicism and 'Displacement'

With the advent of New Historicism,[20] the viability of some of the readings discussed above (particularly those of Abrams and Hartman) have been questioned on the grounds that they accept and reiterate the poetry's own ideological separation of mind and world.[21] In a struggle to anchor the discussion back in the material again, there has been a critical attempt to unmask the metaphysical self-representations of such poetry, and to reveal the displaced history that lies beneath this 'poetic of denial'.[22] In *Wordsworth: The Sense of History*, Alan Liu shows the Simplon Pass account to be a paradigm of historical repression, as the post-revolutionary Wordsworth displaces his historical knowledge of Napoleon crossing the Alps when narrating his own autobiographical journey through that same region. In the light of this type of reading, Hartman's model of imaginative emancipation looks like a freedom that can only come at the cost of a historical lie. Liu writes:

> Where we have come in our tour, then, is to the annunciation of the argument of this book. The true apocalypse for Wordsworth is refer-ence. [. . .] [R]eference to history, I assert, is the only "power" of Wordsworth's Imagination [. . .]; this power is as unstable, surprising, and full of hidden lights as any figure Mind can conceive; and its hold over Mind in not less but *more* persistent when, as in *The Prelude*, it is manifest only in a poetics of denial, of reference lost.[23]

Liu is not alone, however, in thinking the Simplon Pass episode to be a narrative of displacement. Robert A. Brinkley locates a shift between the 1805 and 1850 versions whereby:

> The Apostrophe to Imagination, describing an event during the composi-tion of the 1805 text, no longer refers to the experience which it initially described; through *displacement*, it now describes an event which occurred on a walking tour of the Alps[.][24]

In a similar fashion, David Miall has argued that the apocalyptic vision of the Gondo Ravine is part of Wordsworth '*displacing* one construal of his Alpine experience by another [. . .] dismissing the picturesque for an ecological, participatory account of Nature'.[25]

For Liu, however, this 'displacement' is specifically connected to apocalyptic, and he goes so far as to suggest that displacement is a general characteristic of apoca-lyptic writings. For Liu, 'a Book of Daniel or a Revelation', have 'suffered firsthand the most brutal facts of history'.[26] They, therefore, represent a type of writing in which disbelief slips into denial. Liu states that apocalypse is:

> [T]he writing that says, "No, this should not be," by means of fantastic figurations saying, in essence, "No, this *is* not." That such figuration denies history is indisputable. But surely such denial is also the strongest kind of engagement with history.[27]

Liu does not develop his discussion of the relationship between apocalypse and historical displacement in this work, but the topic has been taken up and examined in detail by Steven Goldsmith in *Unbuilding Jerusalem* (1993). Goldsmith's argument is detailed and complex, but Deanne Westbrook[28] gives the following helpful summary:

> Examining the history of representations and emphasizing the notion of the end of both history and book, Goldsmith finds in texts a tendency to represent that end in spatial terms, terms in which stasis and eternity supersede process, diversity, strife, and the polyglot babble of earthly tongues, and, rid of those whose names are not written in the book of life, permits a conservative and monoglot harmony of voices and a uniformity of attitude and behaviour in eternal worship.[29]

Goldsmith thinks that apocalypse is a deeply problematic genre that specifically tries to end history, and he reads this as a formal strategy from a new historicist perspective. This argument embodies a certain way of understanding apocalypse that Judith Kovacs and Christopher Rowland have recently described as 'decoding':

> Decoding involves presenting the meaning of the text in another, less allusive form, showing what the text *really* means, with great attention to the details [. . .] Meaning is confined as the details of images and actions are fixed on some historical passage or event.[30]

This method of reading apocalyptic texts effectively allegorises them. By 'allegory' in this context, I mean, simply, 'a story, poem or picture which can be interpreted to reveal a hidden meaning'.[31] In readings that 'decode' the Book of Revelation, the text is treated as an allegory that is interpreted in order to reveal its hidden historical referent. Historically, this has been a common mode of understanding the book, as William Kinsley explains:

> Various individuals and groups have attempted to read their own immediate future in the visions of Revelation and other biblical apocalypses. In 17th-cent. England the Fifth Monarchists expected the imminent establishment of the "kingdom which shall never be destroyed" (Dan. 2:44), the successor to the kingdoms of Babylon, Persia, Greece and Rome. Sir Isaac Newton labored tirelessly to correlate the prophecies of Daniel and Revelation with ancient and modern history. The American and French Revolutions revived a variety of apocalyptic speculations. In 19th-cent.

America the Millerites and other groups fixed precise dates for the end of the world and made elaborate preparations for it. After World War II the establishment of a Jewish state in Israel provided a new point of departure for apocalyptisists, and prompted a spate of popular works of prophetic speculation (e.g. H. Lindsey, *The Late Great Planet Earth* [1970], a national best-seller in the United States).[32]

In each of these cases, a particular (usually imminent) historical moment is understood to be the hidden referent of the apocalyptic text, and in this way, signifier and signified, text and historical situation, are placed in a closed semiotic circuit: for history to be conclusively ended, there cannot be multiple apocalypses, there can be only one possible historical referent for the apocalyptic text. It is because of this one-to-one correlation (between text and the end of history) that I use the term 'allegorical' to describe this type of reading rather than, say, 'symbolic' or 'analogical'.

This is the form of apocalyptic interpretation that New Historicist writers such as Liu and Goldsmith have battened onto, but it is, as Kovacs and Rowland point out, only one of a number of possible forms of interpretation of apocalypse.[33] This New Historicist definition and reading of apocalypse is not, therefore, a transparent or objective one. It actually brings a mode of apocalyptic interpretation to the text, critiques it as a characteristic of that text, then (paradoxically) re-enacts it by declaring that the hidden meaning of the poetry *is* history.[34] It thereby inadvertently effects closure through what is ostensibly a critique of closure. This manoeuvre is not, however, restricted to new historicist readings: allegorical readings of apocalypse are also evident in Hartman, Abrams and Paley. Each of these analogous cases is predicated on a two-term apocalyptic structure, whether apocalypse is being interpreted as the movement from nature to consciousness, from an external to an internal apocalypse, or from apocalypse to millennium.

IV. Part Three: Book VI of The Prelude as a Critique of Allegorical Reading

In this section, I will suggest that in Book VI of *The Prelude* Wordsworth offers a critique of allegory, and that this critique takes the form of enacting the limitations of allegorical understanding. I will also suggest that Wordsworth delivers a form of apocalypse that subverts hermeneutical attempts to close down history. In making this argument, I link allegorical readings of apocalypse to what I understand to be a wider struggle in Wordsworth's writing with the alienating nature of allegorical language. In order to explain this connection, I will first offer a brief discussion of Wordsworth's anxieties about language.

Throughout his career, Wordsworth is concerned with the idea of 'natural' language, which he discusses at length in both the Preface to *Lyrical Ballads* (1800) and in the *Essays upon Epitaphs* (1809–10). In these works, he puts forward an argument that splits language into a benevolent form and a malevolent form, these forms corresponding variously to the distinction between the natural and the artificial, between the body and clothing and between incarnation and impersonation. The issue goes deep in Wordsworth's thinking and poetry, yet the difference between these two types of language is, paradoxically, *not* linguistic. There is not, for example, a good vocabulary and a bad vocabulary in his work, nor is he concerned with the difference between urban and rural dialects. He is not even occupied here with the difference between poetic and non-poetic language. I offer two examples to illustrate this disjuncture between poetry and language: first, Wordsworth calls his brother John, a number of times, a 'silent Poet'.[35] He does so not because of his brother's use of words (John writes no poetry), but because of the latter's affections and sensitivity to nature. Second, in the *Essays upon Epitaphs*, Wordsworth presents the epitaph as a paradigm of the best poetry: it is open, honest, sincere, democratic, socially cohesive and in sympathy with nature; it 'is not a proud writing shut up for the studious: it is exposed to all—to the wise and the most ignorant; it is condescending, perspicuous, and lovingly solicits regard' (I, 399–402). When, in one of the later essays, Wordsworth describes the most affecting epitaph he has ever seen, it is a very small stone that bears 'nothing more than the name of the Deceased with the date of birth and death, importing that it was an infant which had been born one day and died the following'. Wordsworth goes on:

> I know not how far the Reader may be in sympathy with me, but more awful thoughts of rights conferred, of hopes awakened, of remembrances stealing away or vanishing were imparted to my mind by that Inscription there before my eyes than by any other that it has ever been my lot to meet with upon a Tomb-stone.
>
> (III, 473–80)

In short, this superlative example of writing—the most powerful instance of what is for Wordsworth a paradigmatic form of poetry—is simply two dates, nothing but numbers. Writing is at its best here for the poet because its meanings are sustained by the non-linguistic: the grave, the churchyard, the community within which that inscription makes sense. Such meanings cannot be transcribed, no dictionary could contain those numbers and fix them to the emotions that they evoke for Wordsworth; such meanings can only be established and maintained through community, shared experience, shared affections, a shared world.

Wordsworth's fear is that when these material and interpersonal grounds of meaning are lost, words may become their substitutes. At this moment, language begins to take on an abstract power of its own: meaning becomes grounded in language (rather than the world), and words and meanings thereby enter the same allegorical (and transcendent) relationship as that of text and history discussed above. For Wordsworth, such language is dangerous because it becomes the ghost of lost reality, transfixing individuals with a world of abstractions: the vitiating process that Wordsworth narrates in 'Michael'. Wordsworth contrasts these two types of language in the *Essays:*

> Words are too awful an instrument for good and evil to be trifled with: they hold above all other external powers a dominion over thoughts. If words be not [. . .] an incarnation of the thought but only a clothing for it, then surely they will prove an ill gift; such a one as those poisoned

vestments, read of in the stories of superstitious times, which had power to consume and to alienate from his right mind the victim who put them on. Language, if it do not uphold, and feed, and leave in quiet, like the power of gravitation or the air we breathe, is a counter-spirit, unremittingly and noiselessly at work to derange, to subvert, to lay waste, to vitiate, and to dissolve.

(III, 178–88)

Wordsworth expresses a similar response, I would suggest, to apocalypse. The form of apocalypse that Wordsworth fears is one in which the relationship between biblical prophecy and historical fulfilment becomes fixed and omnipotent. This type of fixed relationship can be seen, for example, in Coleridge's 1794 poem 'Religious Musings', in which, as M. H. Abrams puts it, '[i]n both text and lengthy footnotes the details of the Revolution are represented as fulfilling the violent prophecies of the apocalypse of St John'.[36]

By 1805, Wordsworth had seen where this type of thinking led. In writing about revolutionary France in Book VI of *The Prelude* he has the advantage of hindsight that Coleridge lacked, and was highly aware of the ideological function and real world effects of this sort of discourse. Something of the public nature of this discourse can be gleaned from Tim Fulford's discussion of Burke's response to Coleridge's hermeneutical role models:

> Horrified at [the] optimistic interpretation of revolutionary violence, Edmund Burke depicted Price, Priestley, and their fellow millenarians as dangerous subversives, comparing them with the regicide sectarians of Britain's revolution of the 1640s. From then on, millenarianism, real and accused, became a crucial factor in the vituperative war of words that polarized British politics and precipitated the imprisonment of many opponents of the government.[37]

Wordsworth's retrospective position, together with his antipathy to allegory lead me to argue that he is doing something quite in his treatment of apocalypse. Just as Wordsworth is deeply suspicious of allegorical language, so he is also deeply suspicious of allegorical apocalypse as a deterministic embrace of purificatory violence. The means by which Wordsworth expresses this is by attempting to forestall the possibility of his apocalypse being read allegorically, and he achieves this, I think, by creating a discussion of the troubling nature of language that runs throughout his description of revolutionary France, and is framed by the symmetrical meditations on the nature of language at the end of Book V and the apocalypse late in Book VI.

The end of Book V of *The Prelude* provides a meditation on the dark nature of language, which is one of the most strikingly abstract passages to be found anywhere in Wordsworth:

> Visionary power
> Attends the motions of the winds
> Embodied in the mystery of words;

> There darkness makes abode, and all the host
> Of shadowy things do work their changes there
> As in a mansion like their proper home.
> Even forms and substances are circumfused
> By that transparent veil with light divine,
> And through the turnings intricate of verse
> Present themselves as objects recognized
> In flashes, and with a glory scarce their own.
>
>   (V, 619–29)

Here, 600 lines before Book VI's account of the 'apocalypse' itself, the specifics of that later passage are already being anticipated. Here the presence of words such as 'visionary', 'mystery' and 'darkness' is made substantially more threatening by talk of 'the host / Of shadowy things'. The phrase brings to mind the 'heavenly host', but here those associations are subverted because that host is 'shadowy'. Nothing is made explicit here, but the passage prompts many questions: what is a shadowy host?, is the dark work of language being implicitly likened to that of Milton's fallen angels?, is the mansion that is their 'proper home' Pandemonium?, what are the endless 'changes' being wrought through the dark materials of language here? This passage begins to sound like the section described earlier in the *Essays* in which language takes up life as a 'counter-spirit' (III, 186).

Language here is menacing, but it is also clearly full of beauty and wonder, and these dark images are interwoven with light counterparts that invoke 'apocalypse' etymologically as an 'uncovering' or 'unveiling': Wordsworth writes, for example, of the 'transparent veil with light divine', that presents objects 'with a glory scarce their own'. The passage also suggests that divine language cannot be fixed or stabilised: Wordsworth notes that these moments of revelation are just that, moments. They come, Damascus-style, in 'flashes', a word takes us forward to the 'flashes that have shewn to us / The invisible world' in the apostrophe to Imagination quoted earlier (VI, 535–36). That later passage exhibits much the same ambiguity insofar as the poet is inspired by a muse—'an unfathered vapour'—that could be the Holy Spirit, or that could be something much more duplicitous.

This same ambiguity is evident in the revelation—the apocalypse of Book VI—that all of this builds towards, which is, as Abrams and Beer suggest, a singularly dialectical conclusion in which nature speaks in words that cannot be understood:

> The rocks that muttered close upon our ears—
> Black drizzling crags that spake by the wayside
> As if a voice were in them
>
>   (VI, 562–64)

The landscape is speaking here, but it is speaking indecipherably, and this moment of revelation is simultaneously a moment of obscurity. In this manner, Book VI partakes in the Book of Revelation without becoming its allegorical completion, by sharing with its biblical original an unveiling that is shrouded in mystery. These passages resist allegorisation because their meaning will not settle.

Set within these framing visions of Books V and VI are a series of discussions and exemplifications of fixed or 'allegorical' language within Book VI itself. This begins in Wordsworth's account of Cambridge as the poet describes how nature gave him a standard by which to judge new experiences. He contrasts this with what he has learnt from books:

> I was a better judge of thoughts than words,
> Misled as to these latter not alone
> By common inexperience of youth,
> But by the trade in classic niceties,
> Delusion to young scholars incident—
> And old ones also—by that overprized
> And dangerous craft of picking phrases out
> From languages that want the living voice
> To make of them a nature to the heart,
> To tell us what is passion, what is truth,
> What reason, what simplicity and sense.
>
> (VI, 124–34)

Classical literature, Wordsworth argues, is dangerous because it is a dead language, only comprehensible by the type of allegorical translation I discussed earlier. Dead languages are fixed languages that can only communicate through decoding, they lack the 'living voice' that can 'make of them a nature to the heart'.

This meditation on allegorical language continues in the succeeding narrative of the journey through revolutionary France, a narrative containing writing that critics since Coleridge have found awkward and unsatisfying. Paley writes:

> [T]he descriptions of revolutionary celebration are self-undermining. 'Gaudy with reliques of that Festival' appropriates diction typical of English Protestant denunciations of Papist idolatry, and the 'Flowers left to wither on triumphal Arcs' (362–63) testify to a failure to appropriate nature to a political cause.[38]

The stiffness of the writing in this section is typified by the lines that Coleridge, as Paley notes (168), particularly objected to:

> There doth the reaper bind the yellow sheaf,
> The maiden spread the haycock in the sun,
> While Winter like a tamèd lion walks,
> Descending from the mountain to make sport
> Among the cottages by beds of flowers.
>
> (464–69)

Paley comments:

> There appears something willed about these lines [. . .] [O]ne senses a desire to furnish materials for a view of humankind and the natural world

in harmony that will justify the variant on the traditional idea of the Book
of Nature that follows[.][39]

Wordsworth holds reality at arm's length throughout the account of revolutionary
France. We are never told people's names: everyone—from the peasant to
Wordsworth's travelling companion—remains anonymous, undifferentiated and
emblematic. But this is just the allegorical manner in which revolutionary France and
the French were being read at the time by contemporary millenarians. Wordsworth
knows this, and writes in a formal, alienated manner not because of a failure of poetic
verve or nerve, but because he has seen what an uncritical and non-dialectical
commitment to an allegorical revolution and apocalypse can lead to. Wordsworth
critiques this allegorical understanding by embodying it (as he does in his slightly
later medieval poems[40]) through an alienated formality. It feels wrong for a reason.

Earlier in this piece, I highlighted the critical emphasis on displacement in the
Simplon Pass episode. Displacement is common to all the critical narratives in which
apocalypse is understood as a shift between two domains, whether those domains
equate to 'nature', composition of the self, revolutionary hope, Imagination, the
sublime or whatever else. In each case, I would suggest, Wordsworth's text encourages these diverse allegorical readings of displacement as a means to exposing its own
claims and fictions, and that the reason it does so is in order to prevent itself from
becoming the type of fixed tyrannical (that is allegorical) language or narrative that I
have discussed throughout this section. In these ways, Book VI provokes its reader to
allegorise its meaning, and in doing so it shows the shortfall of allegorical reading.
This is why, I would suggest, the book has provoked so many readings predicated on
'displacement'. Allegory is closure, but Book VI subverts violent millennial apocalyptic by repeatedly exposing its own devices and locality: wherever meaning might
be battened down, the text betrays itself and the allegory is shaken loose.

The apocalypse that Wordsworth writes, then, is one of a type that Kovacs and
Rowland describe as 'actualized interpretation'. In this form:

> [T]he imagery of the Apocalypse is juxtaposed with the interpreter's own
> circumstances, whether personal or social, so as to allow the images to
> inform understanding of contemporary persons and events and to serve
> as a guide for action. Such interpretation has deep roots in the Christian
> tradition, going back at least to the time of Tyconius and Augustine[.]
> [. . .] In contrast with 'decoding', it preserves the integrity of the textual
> pole and does not allow the image or passage from the Apocalypse to be
> identified solely with one particular historical personage or circumstance.
> The text is not prevented from being actualized in different ways over
> and over again.[41]

The apocalypse that Wordsworth experiences (or creates) at the Simplon Pass is
temporal and individual. It might still be said to be allegorical (as he reads biblical
apocalypse coming to pass in his own textual or historical moment), but it is a type
of allegorical reading that is used and then discarded, never reified as a transcendent
truth that locks down the meaning and ends of history.

In summary, Book VI of *The Prelude* is a text in which poetry is used to express the darkness and duplicity of language itself; it is a text that shows its consciousness of a history that it simultaneously refuses to narrate; a text that visibly unknits the notions of identity that it works so hard to create; and a text that dissolves the very 'nature' it posits as its touchstone of truth. However, these negations do not dissolve meaning. Rather, they indicate that the text is doing two separate but related things. It is inviting us to commit to its narrative as readers, to share in the poem's joys and sorrows, but it is also constantly—and simultaneously—suggesting that those narratives may be false. Thus the relationship of Wordsworth's text to its apocalyptic originals is necessarily fractured and incomplete. His work does not seek the closure of history, identity or biblical meaning. Wordsworth had at this time come to recognise that only partial, fractured representation can offer an image of truth. We see but through a glass darkly, and any greater claim than that is naïve idealism: this is the chastened wisdom of 1806's 'Elegiac Stanzas, Suggested by a Picture of Peele Castle, in a Storm'. John Beer writes 'one could not easily write an ode to a non-apocalypse'[42] though in some senses that is exactly what Book VI is.

V. *Part Four: Similarities Between Apocalypse in* **The Prelude** *and the Bible*

Does, then, the Simplon apocalypse bear any relation to biblical apocalypse? Can biblical apocalypse help us to read Wordsworthian apocalypse and vice versa? If so, Wordsworth may provide a hermeneutical method of reading apocalypses such as the Book of Revelation that forestalls locking their interpretation into prophecies of modern-day social or global destruction.

New Testament apocalypse is usually associated with dramatic symbolism, shifting time perspectives, and scenes of wrath and punishment. This is true of the Book of Revelation in particular. However, the apocalyptic signs that typify the genre come to an end (or at least pause) when humanity finally encounters God. As the Christian hymn puts it, 'Types and shadows have their ending' (Thomas Aquinas, tr. E. Caswall, 1861). Revelation 21:4 offers the gentle image of God wiping away human tears, and the inhabitants of the New Jerusalem needing no longer to see 'in a glass darkly' but face to face (22:4). There is something similar in another eschatological scene when the face-to-face moment at the Last Judgment is shown to righteous and unrighteous alike through prolepsis: in Matthew 25, the encounter with God turns out to have been anticipated in the most everyday events: caring for the sick, welcoming a stranger, visiting those in prison, feeding the hungry (25:34–45). It is at the final moment of 'unveiling' (apocalypsis), when that which is covered up will be uncovered (Matt 10:26, where the cognate verb 'apokalupto' is used). Then those who have acted in these ways are given the knowledge that their action is proleptic of service to the Eschatological Judge: 'whatever you did for one of the least of these brothers of mine, you did for me' (25:40).[43]

In each of these cases, when the veil is removed, humanity comes face to face with the divine: in Revelation 22:4 it is God, in Matthew 25 it is the discovery that the Eschatological Judge has been encountered in the poor, and in Book VI of *The Prelude*, it is woods, crags, the 'unfettered clouds and region of the heavens' (566) that open a vision of the 'types and symbols of eternity' (571). Like Matthew, Wordsworth's apocalypse provides a revelation of the divine as—or in—the everyday, and in both texts, although the language may be violent (or at least extreme), the earthly contents of the revelation are not: a brook and a road; something to eat, something to drink. Hence Book VI, which initially offers a divine revelation under 'banners militant' in historical events, goes on to subvert this militarism through a non-violent natural encounter that discloses the historically self-centred nature of closed allegorical understanding.[44]

Despite these similarities, there are of course many differences between Book VI and New Testament apocalypse. Wordsworth's book resembles Matthew 25 in being immanentist, but unlike that text it is not incarnational, for God is not revealed (as in Matthew 25) in human form. So, unlike both the Book of Revelation and Matthew, Wordsworth's apocalypse is not Christocentric. Finally, unlike the Matthean apocalypse, the Simplon apocalypse has no obvious moral content, it is not tied up with acts of charity (such as feeding the hungry), and in this respect although it is hermeneutically similar to New Testament apocalypse, it differs in content.

To summarise, in this article, I have argued that Wordsworth offers a hermeneutical alternative to the 1790s millennial interpretations of apocalypse. I have also argued that his engagement of apocalypse is not one in which it means a revelation of the transformation of the mind, nor one in which it means the anticipation of revolutionary bloodshed, but it is one in which apocalyptic language is fulfilled in the everyday. Like Matthew 25, there is no sudden transformation of history, everything is revealed to be what it always was: everyday and divine. In the apocalypse of Simplon Pass, every thing is shown, but no thing is revealed. It is a humanised (though not anthropocentric) understanding of apocalypse that has much in common with Matthew 25. As ever, Wordsworth is reticent, singular, and endlessly provocative: his account of a highly personal revelation crossing the Alps offers a critique of the sort of allegorical readings of apocalypse which—both in Wordsworth's day and our own—are too easily connected to the actuality of earthly violence.[45]

Notes

1   All quotations from *The Prelude* taken from the 1805 text in William Wordsworth, *The Prelude, 1799, 1805, 1850*, J. Wordsworth, M. H. Abrams, and S. Gill (eds), 1st ed. (New York: Norton, 1979).

2   A. Liu, *Wordsworth, the Sense of History* (Stanford, California: Stanford University Press, 1989), p. 4.

3   A.C. Bradley, *Oxford Lectures on Poetry*, 2nd ed. (London: Macmillan, 1941), p. 134.

4   Bradley, pp. 134–35.

5   "prolepsis n." in *The Concise Oxford English Dictionary* (Oxford University Press, 2004 [cited 20 December 2005]); available from http://www.oxfordreference.com.

6   G.H. Hartman, *Wordsworth's Poetry, 1787–1814*, Rev. ed. (New Haven: Yale University Press, 1971), p. 349.

7   *Ibid.*, p. xxii.

8   *Ibid.*, p. xii.

9   *Ibid.*, p. 228.

10   *Ibid.*, p. xii.

11   *Ibid.*, p. 225.

12   M.H. Abrams, *Natural Supernaturalism: Tradition and Revolution in Romantic Literatim:* (New York, London: Norton, 1973), p. 41.

13   *Ibid.*, p. 56.

14   *Ibid.*, p. 106.

15   A. *Warminski*, 'Missed Crossing: Wordsworth's Apocalypses', *MLN 99*, (1984) 983–1006, p. 987.

16   M.D. Paley, *Apocalypse and Millennium in English Romantic Poetry* (Oxford: Clarendon Press, 1999), p. 5.

17   Paley initially mentions an 'apocalypse in nature, as Wordsworth recollects the Gondo gorge' (169), but also suggests that both apocalypse and millennium take place in the earlier apostrophe to the imagination.

18   Paley, pp. 170–71.

19   In a similar vein, John Beer has argued that Blake, Coleridge and Wordsworth all realised at a certain point that the apocalypse which they had anticipated had passed by, and they therefore sought to internalise it. This is also indebted to Abrams, but Beer develops the discussion by suggesting that this manoeuvre is parallel to Albert Schweitzer's idea of the 'realized eschatology' of the early church. In his discussion of the Simplon Pass, Beer also picks up on what Abrams calls the 'coincidentia oppositorum' arguing that in the Gondo Ravine, Wordsworth found 'a strong sense of unity and harmony [which] was the moment when apocalypse became truly revelation' (63–64). See J. Beer, 'Romantic Apocalypses', in Tim Fulford (ed.) *Romanticism and Millenarianism*, (Basingstoke: Palgrave, 2002).

20   I do not mean to suggest that 'New Historicism' is a simple or homogenous entity. Nonetheless, the term can be used, in this context, to indicate the shared methodological and hermeneutical strategies of, for example, Alan Liu, Stephen Goldsmith, Jerome McGann and Marjorie Levinson.

21   See for example, pp. 32–33 (on Abrams) and pp. 72–73 (on Hartman) of J.J. McGann, *The Romantic Ideology: A Critical Investigation* (Chicago; London: University of Chicago Press, 1983).

22   Liu, p. 35.

23   *Ibid.*

24   R.A. Brinkley, 'The Incident in the Simplon Pass: A Note on Wordsworth's Revisions', *The Wordsworth Circle 12*, (1981) 122–25, p. 123 (my emphasis).

25   D.S. Miall, 'The Alps Deferred: Wordsworth as the Simplon Pass', *European Romantic Review 9*, (1998) 87–102, p. 87 (my emphasis).

26   Liu, p. 35.

27   *Ibid.*

28   Westbrook draws on Goldsmith in her own work on 'Wordsworthian Apocalyptics' in *Wordsworth's Biblical Ghosts* (Basingstoke: Palgrave, 2001). In that work she brings the discussion of apocalypse closer again to Bradley and Warminski. She is committed to the idea that everything in Wordsworth is simultaneously apocalyptic and natural, and thinks her own 'interpreter's task' is to trace how this happens (186). Westbrook's emphasis is on how Wordsworth's poetry is able to reveal the unspoken, and she summarises her own argument as follows:

    [I]n articulating the visionary or apocalyptic experience, the poet depends upon what I have identified as the interwoven linguistics of negative theology and para-praxical writing, in this case with a particular dependence on the manipulation of the negative combined with a certain syntactic legerdemain. (179).

29   D. Westbrook, *Wordsworth's Biblical Ghosts* (Basingstoke: Palgrave, 2001), p. 149.

30   J.L. Kovacs, Christopher Rowland, and Rebekah Callow, *Revelation: The Apocalypse of Jesus Christ, Blackwell Bible Commentaries* (Oxford: Blackwell, 2004), p. 9.

31   'allegory n.' in *The Concise Oxford English Dictionary*.

32   W. Kinsley, 'Apocalypse', in David Lyle Jeffrey (ed.) *A Dictionary of Biblical Tradition in English Literature*, (Grand Rapids, Michigan: W.B. Eerdmans, 1992), p. 46.

33   Goldsmith and Liu also assume that apocalypse is necessarily concerned with heralding the end of the world, a view that has been widely challenged in recent decades. See, for example, C. *Rowland*, ' "Open Thy Mouth for the Dumb": A Task for the Exegete of Holy Scripture', *Biblical Interpretation* 1 (1993) 228–41.

34   Kevis Bea Goodman's critique of New Historicism and the 'Apocalyptic Fallacy' provides a focus on the importance of time and prolepsis in Wordsworth. She argues that the temporal and aesthetic dimensions of his writing (which relate to Freud's ideas about the work of mourning) cannot be shoved aside in the scramble for historical meaning. However, her reading of 'apocalypse' as trauma has little in common with the biblical and eschatological focus of this paper. See K.B. Goodman, 'Making Time for History: Wordsworth, the New Historicism', *Studies in Romanticism 35*, (1996).

35   See the 1800 poem, *When first I jorney'd hither, to a home*, 1. 88, and W to SGB, 11 Feb. 1805, *EY*, p. 541 in which he calls John 'a Poet in every thing but words.'.

36   Abrams, pp. 338–39.

37   T. Fulford, (ed.) *Romanticism and Millenarianism* (New York; Basingstoke: Palgrave, 2002), p. 3.

38   Paley, p. 167.

39   *Ibid.*, 168.

40   See S. Allen and J. Roberts, 'Wordsworth and the Thought of Affection: "Michael," "The Force of Prayer," "Song at the Feast of Brougham Castle",' *European Romantic Review 16* (2005) 455–70.

41   Kovacs and Rowland, p. 9.

42   Beer, 'Romantic Apocalypses', p. 61.

43   All biblical quotations taken from *The NIV Study Bible: New International Version*, K.L. Barker (ed.) (London: Hodder & Stoughton, 1998).

44   Why, then, do these writers use apocalyptic language at all? Perhaps because it is such a powerful means of drawing attention to the 'ordinary', and showing the divine presence there. This certainly seems to be the case with Book VI and Matthew 25. It is also the case that in both of these texts, the understanding of the divine significance of events is only given in retrospect.

45   See, for example, K.G.C. Newport, *The Branch Davidians of Waco: The History and Beliefs of an Apocalyptic Sect* (Oxford: OUP, 2006).

Bibliography

In his late, strange meditation on revelation, *Apocalypse* (1929–30), D. H. Lawrence claims that a 'fathomed' book is dead. The Bible – a teeming, dizzying library of texts – has not yet been fathomed, although, to borrow the diving metaphor, many continue to plumb its depths. As the diverse range of this Reader illustrates, the Scriptures have been much read, debated and re-presented by creative writers, theorists and scholars who have sought to understand their work. And, in spite (or perhaps as a consequence) of narratives of secularization and the apparent decline of mainline Western Christianity, these collected works of creation narrative, family saga, law, poetry, wisdom, epistle and messianic expectation continue to fascinate, enthuse, frustrate, infuriate and confound contemporary authors on both sides of the critical and creative divide. Atheists and agnostic writers are as likely to turn to a biblical story as their believing counterparts in the search for stimulating source material. In their introduction to *Sixty-Six Books* (2011), Christopher Haydon, Rachel Holmes and Josie Rourke reflect on the curious status of the sacred volume in twenty-first-century art and literature:

> As anyone knows who has properly read the Bible, it's full of really dirty and offensive stuff. Not to mention contradictions and paradoxes. There is something in the Bible that every Christian should find offensive and there is something that every atheist should find inspirational.[1]

This extended bibliography is designed as a way into the vast array of scholarship that thrives on the 'contradictions and paradoxes' of Scripture and its continuing relationship with the diverse forms of writing that we know as 'literature'. The list is arranged under subheadings for the sake of accessibility but many of the titles might easily fit under other headings. You might detect a privileging of work published in the last 30 years or so. This by no means exclusive emphasis on scholarship after 1980 is designed to signify the rich quality of current biblical-literary work rather than to disregard the excellent work of previous generations. It should also be clear that this bibliography, though extensive, is far from exhaustive.

Note

1   Foreword, Christopher Haydon, Rachel Holmes and Josie Rourke, *Sixty-Six Books: 21st Century Writers Speak to the King James Bible* (London: Oberon, 2011) [Kindle Edition, 2012], 320 of 15833

The Bible and the Canon

Alter, Robert, *The World of Biblical Literature* (London: S.P.C.K., 1992)

Alter, Robert and Frank Kermode, *The Literary Guide to the Bible* (Cambridge, MA: Harvard University Press, 1987)

Frye, Northrop, *The Great Code: The Bible and Literature* (London: Routledge & Kegan Paul, 1982)

Hamlin, Hannibal, and Norman W. Jones, eds., *The King James Bible after Four Hundred Years: Literary, Linguistic, and Cultural Influences* (Cambridge: Cambridge University Press, 2010)

Hass, Andrew, David Jasper and Elisabeth Jay, eds., *The Oxford Handbook of English Literature and Theology* (Oxford: Oxford University Press, 2007)

Jasper, David, *The Study of Literature and Religion: An Introduction* (Basingstoke: Macmillan, 1989)

Jasper, David and Stephen Prickett, eds., *The Bible and Literature: A Reader* (Oxford: Blackwell, 1999)

Jeffrey, David Lyle, ed., *Dictionary of Biblical Tradition in English Literature* (Grand Rapids, MI: Eerdmans, 1992)

Knight, Mark, *An Introduction to Religion and Literature* (London: Continuum, 2009)

Knight, Mark and Thomas Woodman, eds., *Biblical Religion and the Novel, 1700–2000* (Aldershot: Ashgate, 2006)

Lemon, Rebecca, et al., eds., *The Blackwell Companion to the Bible in English Literature* (Oxford: Wiley-Blackwell, 2009)

Lieb, Michael, Emma Mason and Jonathan Roberts, eds., *The Oxford Handbook of the Reception History of the Bible* (Oxford: Oxford University Press, 2010)

Norton, David, *A History of the English Bible as Literature* (Cambridge: Cambridge University Press, 2000)

Prickett, Stephen, *Words and The Word: Language, Poetics and Biblical Interpretation* (Cambridge: Cambridge University Press, 1986)

Sawyer, John F. A., ed., *The Blackwell Companion to the Bible and Culture* (Oxford: Blackwell, 2006)

Wood, James, *The Broken Estate: Essays on Literature and Belief* (London: Jonathan Cape, 1999)

Wright, T.R., *Theology and Literature* (Oxford: Blackwell, 1988)

Aesthetics

Alter, Robert, *The Art of Biblical Narrative* (New York: Basic Books, 1981)

————, *The Art of Biblical Poetry* (New York: Basic Books, 1985)

Baker, Naomi, *Plain Ugly: The Unattractive Body in Early Modern Culture* (Manchester and New York: Manchester University Press, 2010)

Begbie, Jeremy S., *Voicing Creation's Praise: Towards a Theology of the Arts* (Edinburgh: T&T Clark, 1991)

Carruthers, Jo, *England's Secular Scripture: Islamophobia and the Protestant Aesthetic* (London: Continuum, 2011)

Eagleton, Terry, *Sweet Violence: The Idea of the Tragic* (Oxford: Blackwell, 2003)

Franke, William, *Poetry and Apocalypse: Theological Disclosures of Poetic Language* (Stanford: Stanford University Press, 2009)

Harries, Richard, *Art and the Beauty of God: A Christian Understanding* (London: Mowbray, 1993)

Hart, Trevor, Gavin Hopps and Jeremy Begbie, eds., *Art, Imagination and Christian Hope* (Aldershot: Ashgate, 2012)

Kort, Wesley A., 'Narrative and Theology', *Literature and Theology*, 1.1 (1987), 27–38

————, *Story, Text, and Scripture: Literary Interests in Biblical Narrative* (London: Pennsylvania State University Press, 1988)

Quash, Ben, *Theology and the Drama of History* (Cambridge: Cambridge University Press, 2005)

Sheldrake, Philip, *Spaces for the Sacred: Place, Memory and Identity* (London: SCM, 2001)

Sherry, Patrick, *Images of Redemption: Art, Literature and Salvation* (London: T&T Clark, 2003)

Williams, Rowan, *Lost Icons: Reflections on Cultural Bereavement* (Edinburgh: T&T Clark, 2000)

Wolterstorff, Nicholas, *Art in Action: Toward a Christian Aesthetic* (Grand Rapids: Eerdmans, 1980)

Wood, Ralph C., *The Comedy of Redemption: Christian Faith and Comic Vision in Four American Novelists* (Notre Dame: University of Notre Dame Press, 1988)

Yandell, Keith E., ed., *Faith and Narrative* (Oxford: Oxford University Press, 2001)

Hermeneutics and Critical Theory

Agamben, Giorgio, *The Time That Remains: A Commentary on the Letter to the Romans*, translated by Patricia Daley (Stanford: Stanford University Press, 2005)

Blanton, Ward, *Displacing Christian Origins: Philosophy, Secularity, and the New Testament* (Chicago: University of Chicago Press, 2007)

Bradley, Arthur, *Negative Theology and Modern French Philosophy* (London: Routledge, 2004)

Caputo, John D. and Michael J. Scanlon, eds., *God, the Gift and Postmodernism* (Bloomington: Indiana University Press, 1999)

Caputo, John D., *On Religion* (London: Routledge, 2001)

Contino, Paul and Susan D. Felch, eds., *Bakhtin and Religion: A Feeling for Faith* (Evanston: Northwestern University Press, 2001)

Cunningham, Valentine, 'It is No Sin To Limp', *Literature and Theology*, 6.4 (1992), 303–9

——, *In the Reading Gaol: Postmodernity, Texts, and History* (Oxford: Blackwell, 1994)

——, *Reading After Theory* (Oxford: Blackwell, 2002)

Derrida, Jacques, *Acts of Religion*, ed. by Gil Anidjar (London: Routledge, 2002)

de Vries, Hent, *Philosophy and the Turn to Religion* (Baltimore: Johns Hopkins University Press, 1999)

Edwards, Michael, *Towards a Christian Poetics* (London: Macmillan, 1984)

——, *Of Making Many Books: Essays on the Endlessness of Writing* (Basingstoke: Macmillan, 1990)

Ferretter, Luke, *Towards a Christian Literary Theory* (Houndmills: Palgrave, 2003)

Hart, Kevin, *The Trespass of the Sign: Deconstruction, Theology and Philosophy* (New York: Cambridge University Press, 1989)

Ingraffia, Brian D., *Postmodern Theory and Biblical Theology: Vanquishing God's Shadow* (Cambridge: Cambridge University Press, 1995)

Jacobs, Alan, *A Theology of Reading: The Hermeneutics of Love* (Boulder and New York: Westview Press, 2001)

Loades, Ann, and Michael McLain, eds., *Hermeneutics, the Bible and Literary Criticism* (London: Macmillan, 1992)

Loughlin, Gerard, *Telling God's Story: Bible, Church and Narrative Theology* (Cambridge: Cambridge University Press, 1999)

Mills, Kevin, *Justifying Language: Paul and Contemporary Literary Theory* (Basingstoke: Macmillan, 1995)

——, *The Prodigal Sign: A Parable of Criticism* (Brighton: Sussex Academic Press, 2009)

Moore, Stephen D., *Poststructuralism and the New Testament: Derrida and Foucault at the Foot of the Cross* (Minneapolis: Fortress Press, 1994)

——, *Empire and Apocalypse: Postcolonialism and the New Testament* (Sheffield: Sheffield Phoenix Press, 2006)

Prickett, Stephen, ed., *Reading the Text: Biblical Criticism and Literary Theory* (Oxford: Blackwell, 1991)

Schwartz, Regina M., ed., *The Book and the Text: The Bible and Literary Theory* (Oxford: Basil Blackwell, 1990)

Sherwood, Yvonne, ed., *Derrida's Bible* (Basingstoke: Palgrave, 2004)

Sherwood, Yvonne M., and Stephen D. Moore, *The Invention of the Biblical Scholar: A Critical Manifesto* (Minneapolis: Fortress Press, 2011)

Sherwood, Yvonne and Kevin Hart, eds., *Derrida and Religion: Other Testaments* (New York: Routledge, 2005)

Sugirtharajah, R. S., *Postcolonial Criticism and Biblical Interpretation* (New York: Oxford University Press, 2002)

Vanhoozer, Kevin J., ed., *The Cambridge Companion to Postmodern Theology* (Cambridge: Cambridge University Press, 2003)

Ward, Graham, *Theology and Contemporary Critical Theory*, second edition (Basingstoke: Macmillan, 2000)

Žižek, Slavoj, *The Fragile Absolute – or Why is the Christian Legacy Worth Fighting For?* (London: Verso, 2001)

Historical Studies

(i) Medieval and Early Modern Literature

Baker, Naomi, *Scripture Women* (Nottingham: Trent Editions, 2005)

———, "Grace and Favour: Deconstructing Hospitality in 'The Pilgrim's Progress'." *The Seventeenth Century* 27.2(2012): 183–211

Beadle, Richard and Alan J. Fletcher, eds., *The Cambridge Companion to Medieval English Theatre* (Cambridge: Cambridge University Press, 2008)

Besserman, Lawrence L., *Chaucer and the Bible: A Critical Review of Research, Indexes and Bibliography* (New York: Garland, 1988)

Clarke, Elizabeth, *Theory and Theology in George Herbert's Poetry: 'Divinitie, and Poesie, met'* (Oxford: Clarendon Press, 1997)

———, *Politics, Religion and the Song of Songs in Seventeenth-Century England* (Basingstoke: Palgrave, 2011)

Davies, Michael, *Graceful Reading: Theology and Narrative in the Works of John Bunyan* (Oxford: Oxford University Press, 2002)

Edwards, Karen, *Milton and the Natural World: Science and Poetry in 'Paradise Lost'* (Cambridge, Cambridge University Press, 1999)

Fisch, Harold, *Hamlet and the Word: The Covenant Pattern in Shakespeare* (New York: Ungar, 1971)

———, *The Biblical Presence in Shakespeare, Milton and Blake: A Comparative Study* (Oxford: Clarendon Press, 1999)

Forshaw, Peter J. and Kevin Killeen, eds., *The Word and the World: Biblical Exegesis and Early Modern Science* (Basingstoke: Palgrave, 2007)

Fowler, David C., *The Bible in Early English Literature* (Seattle: University of Washington Press, 1976)

———, *The Bible in Middle English Literature* (Seattle: University of Washington Press, 1984)

Gilman Richey, Esther, *The Politics of Revelation in the English Renaissance* (Columbia: University of Missouri Press, 1998)

Groves, Beatrice, *Texts and Traditions: Religion in Shakespeare, 1592–1604* (Oxford: Clarendon Press, 2007)

Hamlin, Hannibal, *Psalm Culture and Early Modern English Literature* (Cambridge: Cambridge University Press, 2004)

Harris, Johanna and Elizabeth Scott-Baumann, eds., *The Intellectual Culture of Puritan Women, 1558–1680* (Basingstoke: Palgrave Macmillan, 2011)

Hawkins, Peter, *Dante's Testaments: Essays in Scriptural Imagination* (Stanford: Stanford University Press, 1999)

Hessayon, Ariel and Nicholas Keene, eds., *Scripture and Scholarship in Early Modern England* (Aldershot: Ashgate, 2006)

Hinds, Hilary, *God's Englishwomen: Seventeenth-Century Radical Sectarian Writing and Feminist Criticism* (Manchester: Manchester University Press, 1996)

———, *George Fox and Early Quaker Culture* (Manchester: Manchester University Press, 2011)

Jeffrey, David Lyle, ed., *Chaucer and Scriptural Tradition* (Ottawa: Ottawa University Press, 1984)

Killeen, Kevin, *Biblical Scholarship, Science and Politics in Early Modern England: Thomas Browne and the Thorny Place of Knowledge* (Aldershot: Ashgate, 2009)

Lieb, Michael, *Theological Milton: Deity, Discourse And Heresy in the Miltonic Canon* (Pittsburgh: Duquesne University Press, 2006)

Marx, Steven, *Shakespeare and the Bible* (New York: Oxford University Press, 2000)

Monta, Susannah, *Martyrdom and Literature in Early Modern England* (Cambridge: Cambridge University Press, 2005)

Newman, Barbara, *God and the Goddesses: Vision, Poetry, and Belief in the Middle Ages* (Philadelphia: University of Pennsylvania Press, 2003)

Nuttall, A. D., *Overheard by God: Fiction and Prayer in Herbert, Milton, Dante and St. John* (London: Methuen, 1980)

Sims, James H. and Leyland Ryken, eds., *Milton and Scriptural Tradition: The Bible into Poetry* (Columbia: University of Columbia Press, 1984)

Turner, Denys, *Eros and Allegory: Medieval Exegesis of the Song of Songs* (Kalamazoo, MI: Cistercian Publications, 1995)

(ii) The Eighteenth Century and Romanticism

Abrams, M. H., *Natural Supernaturalism: Tradition and Revolution in Romantic Literature* (New York: Norton, 1971)

Acosta, Ana, *Reading Genesis in the Long Eighteenth Century: From Milton to Mary Shelley* (Aldershot: Ashgate, 2006)

Altizer, Thomas J.J., *The New Apocalypse: The Radical Christian Vision of William Blake* (East Lansing: Michigan State University Press, 1967)

Barbeau, Jeffrey W., *Coleridge, the Bible and Religion* (New York: Palgrave, 2008)

Branch, Lori, *Rituals of Spontaneity: Sentiment and Secularism from Free Prayer to Wordsworth* (Waco: Baylor University Press, 2006)

Fulford, Tim, ed., *Romanticism and Millenarianism* (New York; Basingstoke: Palgrave, 2002)

Hopps, Gavin and Jane Stabler, eds., *Romanticism and Religion from William Cowper to Wallace Stevens* (Aldershot: Ashgate, 2006)

Jager, Colin, *The Book of God: Secularization and Design in the Romantic Era* (Philadelphia: University of Pennsylvania Press, 2007)

Jasper, David, *The Sacred and Secular Canon in Romanticism: Preserving the Sacred Truths* (Basingstoke: Macmillan, 1999)

Prickett, Stephen, *Romanticism and Religion: The Tradition of Coleridge and Wordsworth in the Victorian Church* (Cambridge: Cambridge University Press, 1976)

——, *Origins of Narrative: The Romantic Appropriation of the Bible* (Cambridge: Cambridge University Press, 1996)

Roberts, Jonathan, *Blake. Wordsworth. Religion.* (London: Continuum, 2010)

Rowland, Christopher, *Blake and the Bible* (New Haven: Yale University Press, 2011)

Shaffer, E. S., *'Kubla Khan' and the Fall of Jerusalem: The Mythological School in Biblical Criticism and Secular Literature, 1770–1880* (Cambridge: Cambridge University Press, 1975)

Sheehan, Jonathan, *The Enlightenment Bible: Translation, Scholarship, Culture* (New Jersey: Princeton University Press, 2005)

Tannenbaum, Leslie, *Biblical Tradition in Blake's Early Prophecies* (Princeton: Princeton University Press, 1982)

Westbrook, Deeanne, *Wordsworth's Biblical Ghosts* (New York: Palgrave, 2001)

(iii) The Long Nineteenth Century

Blair, Kirstie, *Form and Faith in Victorian Poetry and Religion* (Oxford: Oxford University Press, 2012)

Bradley, Ian, *The Call to Seriousness: The Evangelical Impact on the Victorians* (London: Cape, 1976)

Bush, Harold K., *Mark Twain and the Spiritual Crisis of His Age* (Tuscaloosa, AL: University of Alabama Press, 2007)

Cunningham, Valentine, *Everywhere Spoken Against: Dissent in the Victorian Novel* (Oxford: Clarendon Press, 1975)

Dieleman, Karen, *Religious Imaginaries: The Liturgical and Poetic Practices of Elizabeth Barrett Browning, Christina Rossetti, and Adelaide Proctor* (Athens, Ohio: Ohio University Press, 2012)

Fraser, Hilary, *Beauty and Belief: Aesthetics and Religion in Victorian Literature* (Cambridge: Cambridge University Press, 1986)

Hall, Donald E., ed., *Muscular Christianity: Embodying the Victorian Age* (Cambridge: Cambridge University Press, 1994)

Hanson, Ellis, *Decadence and Catholicism* (Cambridge, Mass: Harvard University Press, 1997)

Henderson, Heather, *The Victorian Self: Autobiography and Biblical Narrative* (Ithaca: Cornell University Press, 1989)

Jackson, Gregory, *The Word and Its Witness: The Spiritualization of American Realism* (Chicago: University of Chicago Press, 2009)

Jay, Elisabeth, *The Religion of the Heart: Anglican Evangelicalism and the Nineteenth-Century Novel* (Oxford: Clarendon, 1979)

Knight, Mark and Emma Mason, *Nineteenth-Century Religion and Literature: An Introduction* (Oxford: Oxford University Press, 2006)

Landow, George, *Victorian Types, Victorian Shadows: Biblical Typology in Victorian Literature, Art and Thought* (Boston: Routledge, Paul, 1980)

Larson, Janet L., *Dickens and The Broken Scripture* (Athens: University of Georgia Press, 1985)

Mason, Emma, *Women Poets of the Nineteenth-Century* (Tavistock: Northcote House, 2006)

Milbank, Alison, *Dante and the Victorians* (New York: Manchester University Press, 1998)

Miller, J. Hillis, *The Disappearance of God: Five Nineteenth-Century Writers* (London: Oxford University Press, 1963)

Mills, Kevin, *Approaching Apocalypse: Unveiling Revelation in Victorian Writing* (Lewisburg: Bucknell University Press, 2007)

Schramm, Jan-Melissa, *Testimony and Advocacy in Victorian Law, Literature and Theology* (Cambridge: Cambridge University Press, 2000)

Styler, Rebecca, *Literary Theology by Women Writers of the Nineteenth Century* (Aldershot: Ashgate, 2010)

Tennyson, G. B., *Victorian Devotional Poetry: The Tractarian Mode* (Cambridge, Mass.: Harvard University Press, 1981)

Wheeler, Michael, *Death and the Future Life in Victorian Literature and Theology* (Cambridge: Cambridge University Press, 1990)

——, *Ruskin's God* (Cambridge: Cambridge University Press, 1999)

——, *The Old Enemies: Catholic and Protestant in Nineteenth-Century English Culture* (Cambridge: Cambridge University Press, 2006)

——, *St John and the Victorians* (Cambridge: Cambridge University Press, 2012)

Zemka, Sue, *Victorian Testaments: The Bible, Christology, and Literary Authority in Early-Nineteenth-Century British Culture* (Stanford: Stanford University Press, 1997)

(iv) The Twentieth Century

Brennan, Michael G., *Graham Greene: Fictions, Faith and Authorship* (London: Continuum, 2011)

Ferretter, Luke, *The Glyph and the Gramophone: D. H. Lawrence's Religion* (London: Continuum, 2013)

Ketterer, David, *New Worlds for Old: The Apocalyptic Imagination, Science Fiction and American Literature* (New York: Anchor, 1974)

Kojecky, Roger, *T. S. Eliot's Social Criticism* (London: Faber and Faber, 1971)

Lewis, Pericles, *Religious Experience and the Modernist Novel* (Cambridge: Cambridge University Press, 2010)

Moseley, Virginia, *Joyce and the Bible* (DeKalb: Northwestern University Press, 1967)

Purdy, Dwight, *Biblical Echo and Allusion in the Poetry of W. B. Yeats: Poetics and the Art of God* (Lewisburg: Bucknell University Press, 1994)

Schad, John, ed., *Writing the Bodies of Christ: The Church from Carlyle to Derrida* (Aldershot: Ashgate, 2001)

——, *Queer Fish: Christian Unreason from Darwin to Derrida* (Brighton: Sussex Academic Press, 2004)

Woodman, Thomas, *Faithful Fictions: The Catholic Novel in British Literature* (Milton Keynes: Open University Press, 1991)

Wright, T. R., *D. H. Lawrence and the Bible* (Cambridge: Cambridge University Press, 2000)

(v) Debates in Contemporary Literature and Culture

Bloom, Harold, *Omens of Millennium: The Gnosis of Angels, Dreams, and Resurrection* (London: Fourth Estate, 1996)

Bradley, Arthur and Andrew Tate, *The New Atheist Novel: Fiction, Philosophy and Polemic After 9/11* (London: Continuum, 2010)

Detweiler, Robert, 'Theological Trends of Postmodern Fiction', *Journal of the American Academy of Religion*, 44.2 (1976), pp. 225–37

——, *Breaking the Fall: Religious Readings of Contemporary Fiction* (Basingstoke: Macmillan, 1989)

Dix, Andrew and Jonathan Taylor, eds., *Figures of Heresy: Radical Theology in English and American Writing* (Brighton: Sussex Academic Press, 2006)

Fiddes, Paul S., *Freedom and Limit: A Dialogue between Literature and Christian Doctrine* (Basingstoke: Macmillan Press, 1991)

——, ed., *The Novel, Spirituality and Modern Culture* (Cardiff: University of Wales Press, 2000)

Fisch, Harold, *New Stories for Old: Biblical Patterns in the Novel* (Basingstoke: Macmillan, 1998)

Hartman, Geoffrey, *The Third Pillar: Essays in Judaic Studies* (Philadelphia: University of Pennsylvania Press, 2011)

Holderness, Graham, ' "The Undiscovered Country": Philip Pullman and the "Land of the Dead" ', *Literature and Theology*, 21.3 (2007), 276–92

Hungerford, Amy, *Postmodern Belief: American Literature and Religion Since 1980* (Princeton: Princeton University Press, 2010)

Jacobs, Alan, *Shaming the Devil: Essays in Truthtelling* (Grand Rapids: Eerdmans, 2004)

——, *Original Sin: A Cultural History* (London: SPCK, 2008)

Jansen, Henry, *Laughter Among the Ruins: Postmodern Comic Approaches to Suffering* (Frankfurt: Peter Lang, 2001)

Jasper, David, *The Sacred Desert: Religion, Literature, Art and Culture* (Oxford: Blackwell, 2004)

King, Jeanette, *Women and the Word: Contemporary Women Novelists and the Bible* (Houndmills: Palgrave, 2000)

McClure, John A., *Partial Faiths: Postsecular Fiction in the Age of Pynchon and Morrison* (Athens: University of Georgia Press, 2007)

Mazur, Eric Michael, and Kate McCarthy, eds., *God in the Details: American Religion in Popular Culture* (London: Routledge, 2001)

Prickett, Stephen, *Narrative, Religion and Science: Fundamentalism Versus Irony, 1700–1999* (Cambridge: Cambridge University Press, 2002)

Robinson, Marilynne, *The Death of Adam: Essays on Modern Thought* (Boston: Houghton Mifflin, 1998)

Saunders, Ben, *Do The Gods Wear Capes?: Spirituality, Fantasy, and Superheroes* (London: Continuum, 2011)

Tate, Andrew, *Contemporary Fiction and Christianity* (London: Continuum, 2008)

Walton, Heather and Andrew W. Hass, eds., *Self/Same/Other: Re-visioning the Subject in Literature and Theology* (Sheffield: Sheffield Academic Press, 2000)

Walton, Heather, *Imagining Theology: Women, Writing and God* (London: Continuum, 2007)

——, *Literature, Theology and Feminism* (Manchester: Manchester University Press, 2007)

Ward, Graham, *True Religion* (Oxford: Blackwell, 2003)

Index